October 7–12, 2012
Tampere, Finland

Association for Computing Machinery

Advancing Computing as a Science & Profession

I0038233

EMSOFT'12

Proceedings of the Tenth ACM International Conference on

Embedded Software 2012 (co-located with ESWEEK)

Sponsored by:

ACM SIGMICRO, ACM SIGBED, and ACM SIGDA

Technical Supporters:

IEEE Computer Society, IEEE Circuits and Systems Society, and IEEE Council on Electronic Design Automation

Supporters:

IFIP, IEEE Finland Section, and Federation of Finnish Learned Societies

Association for Computing Machinery

Advancing Computing as a Science & Profession

The Association for Computing Machinery
2 Penn Plaza, Suite 701
New York, New York 10121-0701

Notice to Past Authors of ACM-Published Articles

ACM intends to create a complete electronic archive of all articles and/or other material previously published by ACM. If you have written a work that has been previously published by ACM in any journal or conference proceedings prior to 1978, or any SIG Newsletter at any time, and you do NOT want this work to appear in the ACM Digital Library, please inform permissions@acm.org, stating the title of the work, the author(s), and where and when published.

ISBN: 978-1-4503-1423-7 (Digital)

ISBN: 978-1-4503-1425-1 (Print)

Additional copies may be ordered prepaid from:

ACM Order Department
PO Box 30777
New York, NY 10087-0777, USA

Phone: 1-800-342-6626 (USA and Canada)
+1-212-626-0500 (Global)
Fax: +1-212-944-1318
E-mail: acmhelp@acm.org
Hours of Operation: 8:30 am – 4:30 pm ET

ACM Order Number: 618122

Printed in the USA

Welcome Message

On behalf of the Organizing Committee and the committees of our participating conferences - CASES, CODES+ISSS, and EMSOFT - we would like to welcome you to Embedded Systems Week - ESWEEK 2012 - in Tampere, Finland. 2012 marks the 8th edition of ESWEEK. Earlier meetings were held in Jersey City, Seoul, Salzburg, Atlanta, Grenoble, Scottsdale and Taipei. This meeting has grown from two conferences and a handful of workshops to three conferences and ten workshops and symposia. ESWEEK is now widely recognized as the premier technical event in embedded computing.

The combined programme of the three conferences will offer three plenary keynotes, an industry day, and over 100 technical paper presentations. ESWEEK will also offer a number of half-day tutorials that cover hot topics of general interest to the embedded systems community. Additionally, this year, the International Symposium on System-on-Chip (SoC) will be co-located with ESWEEK. First of all, special thanks go to the technical programme chairs of the three conferences: Vincent Mooney, Rodric Rabbah, Franco Fummi, Naehyuck Chang, Florence Maraninchi, and John Regehr. This year, Embedded Systems Week includes ten workshops featuring outstanding contributions on specific topics. We especially wish to thank the workshop organisers: Aviral Shrivastava, Wolfgang Ecker, Wolfgang Mueller, Shahrokh Daijavad, Sumedh Sathaye, Seraphin Calo, Dimitrios Serpanos, Jian-Jia Chen, Maurizio Palesi, Nikil Dutt, Jason Xue, Jeff Jackson, Peter Marwedel, Kenneth Ricks, Fabiano Hessel, Jérôme Hugues, Frédéric Rousseau, Rolf Ernst and Alberto Sangiovanni-Vincentelli.

A complex event such as ESWEEK is a team effort that requires a dedicated group of volunteers to manage the success of the conference's growth in scale and offerings. We wish to thank every member of the organizing committee for their dedicated efforts in making the event a success. In particular, special thanks go to the following people for managing critical aspects of the conference organization: Jari Nurmi and Irmeli Lehto for local organization; David Atienza for finances; Suzanne Lesecq for publications; Francescantonio Della Rosa and Aviral Shrivastava for the conference website; Edward Chu and Frédéric Pétrot for electronic media and the paper submission system; Sungjoo Yoo, Tapani Ahonen and Yuan Xie for industry liaison; Gabriela Nicolescu, Jian-Jia Chen and Roberto Airoldi for workshops; Saddek Bensalem for tutorials; Henri-Pierre Charles, Xiaobo Sharon Hu and Hamaguchi Kiyoharu for publicity; Enrico Macii for coordinating the best paper award selections; Rolf Ernst for panels and special sessions; Hiroto Yasuura and Hiroyuki Tomiyama for handling the Asia liaison; Luigi Carro and Fabiano Hessel for handling Latin America liaison; Rajesh Gupta, Alex Orailoglu, Marilyn Wolf, Naehyuck Chang and Donald Thomas for professional society liaisons.

We also thank the Steering Committee members and the Technical Programme Committee members of each conference and workshop for selecting papers of the highest quality. Finally, we thank our sponsoring societies: ACM (SIGBED, SIGDA, SIGMICRO), IEEE (CAS, Computer, CEDA), and the cooperation with IFIP.

Tampere – the SoC city – is situated in the heart of beautiful Finnish Lakeland. The banks of the Tammerkoski rapids still feature old traditional industrial buildings which have now been converted to house pleasant restaurants, pubs or high-tech companies. Tampere is also a city of theatres, arts, sciences, sport and modern industrial culture. We therefore invite you to attend ESWEEK 2012 to learn about the latest in embedded system technologies, and also discover the beauty, culture and technological miracles of Finland.

Ahmed Jerraya
ESWeek 2012 General Chair
CEA, France

Luca Carloni
ESWeek 2012 General co-Chair
Columbia University, USA

Message from the EMSOFT Program Chairs

Embedded systems play a critically important role in the modern world; the complexity of such systems is increasing at a breathtaking pace. EMSOFT, the International Conference on Embedded Software, is the flagship conference sponsored by ACM SIGBED, the Special Interest Group on Embedded Systems. In this role, EMSOFT seeks to bring together, on an annual basis, researchers and developers from academia, industry, and government to advance the science and the practice of embedded software development.

We believe that the papers published in these proceedings are representative of our research domain, ranging from hardware support and operating systems to theoretical models, programming languages and control theory, and from engineering practice to foundations of the discipline. This edition of EMSOFT will, once again, illustrate the efforts made by our research community to improve the analysis, design, implementation and validation of embedded software and systems.

This year 95 submissions were received and reviewed by the program committee. After a very rigorous review process, a total of 23 papers were selected for presentation at EMSOFT and inclusion in the proceedings. We would like to thank all the members of the EMSOFT 2012 Program Committee and the additional reviewers for their hard work which made this conference possible. We also thank all authors for choosing EMSOFT as a forum to publish their research.

In addition to the peer-reviewed papers, EMSOFT this year includes two invited sessions, one focused on timing analysis of embedded software, and the other intended to give an overview of the career of Paul Caspi. We would indeed like to dedicate this year edition of EMSOFT to Paul, who died last April. Paul was an outstanding scientist, working in the interface between control systems and their software/hardware realization. Paul was a very modest person and an original thinker, bringing fruitful ideas to various domains such as dependability analysis, formal verification, programming languages and embedded systems. The special session will review some of his work.

We hope that you will find this program interesting and that the symposium will provide you with a valuable opportunity to share ideas with other researchers and practitioners from institutions around the world.

Florence Maraninchi   **John Regehr**
Grenoble INP & VERIMAG   *University of Utah*

Table of Contents

Session 2A: Operating Systems

Session 2B: Control Theory

Session 3: Hardware Support

Session 4: Invited Session – Code-Level Timing Analysis

Session 5: Timing Analysis
Session Chair: Heiko Falk *(Ulm University)*

Session 6: Special Session: An Overview of the Career of Paul Caspi

Session Chair: Florence Maraninchi *(Grenoble INP)*

Session 7: Languages, Formal Models and Algorithms (1)

Session 8: Languages, Formal Models and Algorithms (2)

Tutorials

Author Index

ESWEEK 2012 Organizing Committee

General Chairs:	Ahmed Jerraya *(CEA-Leti, France)*
	Luca Carloni *(Columbia University, USA)*
Conference Programme Chairs:	CASES
	Vincent Mooney *(Georgia Institute of Technology, USA)*
	Rodric Rabbah *(IBM, USA)*
	CODES+ISSS
	Franco Fummi *(University of Verona, Italy)*
	Naehyuck Chang *(Seoul National University, Korea)*
	EMSOFT
	Florence Maraninchi *(Grenoble INP, France)*
	John Regehr *(School of Computing, University of Utah, USA)*
Finance Chair:	David Atienza *(EPFL, Switzerland)*
Local Arrangements Chairs:	Jari Nurmi *(Tampere University of Technology, Finland)*
	Irmeli Lehto *(Tampere University of Technology, Finland)*
Workshop Chairs:	Gabriela Nicolescu *(Polytechnique Montréal, Canada)*
	Jian-Jia Chen *(Karlsruhe Institute of Technology, Germany)*
	Roberto Airoldi *(Tampere University of Technology, Finland)*
Publication Chair:	Suzanne Lesecq *(CEA-Leti, France)*
Awards Chair:	Enrico Macii *(Politecnico di Torino, Italy)*
Tutorials Chair:	Saddek Bensalem *(Université Joseph Fourier, France)*
Panels & Special Sessions Chair:	Rolf Ernst *(TU Braunschweig, Germany)*
Web Chairs:	Aviral Shrivastava *(Arizona State University, USA)*
	Francescantonio Della Rosa *(Tampere University of Technology, Finland)*
Electronic Media Chairs:	Edward Chu *(National Yunlin University of Science and Technology, Taiwan)*
	Frederic Pétrot *(Grenoble INP, France)*
Publicity Chair Europe:	Henri-Pierre Charles *(CEA-List, France)*
Publicity Chair North America:	Xiaobo Sharon Hu *(University of Notre Dame, USA)*

Publicity Chair Asia Pacific:	Hamaguchi Kiyoharu *(Osaka University, Japan)*
Industry Liaison Asia Pacific:	Sungjoo Yoo *(Postech, Korea)*
Industry Liaison Europe:	Tapani Ahonen *(Tampere University of Technology)*
Industry Liaison North America:	Yuan Xie *(Pennsylvania State University, USA)*
Latin America Liaison Chairs:	Luigi Carro *(Federal University of Rio Grande do Sul, Brasil)* Fabiano Hessel *(PUCRS, Brasil)*
Asia Liaison:	Hiroto Yasuura *(Kyushu University, Japan)* Hiroyuki Tomiyama *(Ritsumeikan University, Japan)*
IEEE CEDA/CAS Liaison:	Rajesh Gupta *(University of California, San Diego, USA)*
IEEE CS Liaison:	Alex Orailoglu *(University of California, San Diego, USA)*
IFIP Liaison:	Marilyn Wolf *(Georgia Tech, USA)*
ACM SIGDA Liaison:	Naehyuck Chang *(Seoul National University, Korea)*
ACM SIGBED Liaison:	Donald Thomas *(Carnegie Mellon University, USA)*
Steering Committee:	CASES Joerg Henkel *(Karlsruhe Institute of Technology, Germany)* Vinod Kathail *(Xilinx, Synfora, USA)* CODES+ISSS Reinaldo Bergamaschi *(Odysci, USA)* Don Thomas *(Carnegie Mellon University, USA)* EMSOFT Insup Lee *(University of Pennsylvania, USA)* Lothar Thiele *(ETH Zurich, Switzerland)*

EMSOFT 2012 Organization

General Chairs: Ahmed Jerraya *(CEA)*
Luca Carloni *(Columbia University)*

Program Chairs: Florence Maraninchi *(Grenoble INP & VERIMAG)*
John Regehr *(University of Utah)*

Advisory Committee: Gerard Berry *(INRIA)*
Tom Henzinger *(ISTA)*
Edward Lee *(University of California)*
Ragunathan Rajkumar *(Carnegie Mellon University)*
Alberto Sangiovanni-Vincentelli *(University of California)*
Joseph Sifakis *(EPFL)*
Janos Sztipanovits *(Vanderbilt University)*
Stewart Tansley *(Microsoft)*
Reinhard Wilhelm *(Saarland University)*
Marilyn Wolf *(Georgia Institute of Technology)*

Executive Committee Chairs: Lothar Thiele (chair) *(ETHZ)*
Insup Lee (vice-chair) *(University of Pennsylvania)*

Executive Committee: Luca Carloni *(Columbia University)*
Samarjit Chakraborty *(TU Munich)*
Nicolas Halbwachs *(Verimag/CNRS)*
Christoph Kirsch *(University of Salzburg)*
Sang Lyul Min *(Seoul National University)*
Stavros Tripakis *(UC Berkeley)*
Reinhard Wilhelm *(Saarland University)*
Wang Yi *(Uppsala University)*

Program Committee: James Anderson *(University of North Carolina at Chapel Hill)*
Purandar Bhaduri *(Indian Institute of Technology Guwahati)*
Geoff Challen *(State University of New York, Buffalo)*
Pascal Cuoq *(CEA LIST)*
Stephen A. Edwards *(Columbia University)*
Petru Eles *(Linkoping University)*
Heiko Falk *(Ulm University)*
Gerhard Fohler *(TU Kaiserslautern)*
Martin Fränzle *(Oldenburg University)*
Abdoulaye Gamatié *(LIFL/CNRS)*
Chris Gill *(Washington University in St. Louis)*
Edward Lee *(UC Berkeley)*
Guiseppe Lipari *(Scuola Superiore Sant'Anna)*
Rahul Mangharam *(University of Pennsylvania)*
Michael Norrish *(NICTA)*

Additional reviewers (continued):

Liu Cong	Reineke Jan
Liu Isaac	Rigo Sandro
Lobachev Oleg	Robert Frederic
Lochbihler Andreas	Saha Indranil
Lohstroh Marten	Salvadori Claudio
Lublinerman Roberto	Sampath Prahladavaradan
Luong Anh	Schneider Beck Antonio Carlos
Lv Mingsong	Schneider Christian
Mallon Christoph	Schorr Stefan
Matsikoudis Eleftherios	Schulze Christoph Daniel
Metzner Alexander	Seo Jaebaek
Min Kyeong	Shaver Chris
Mohalik Swarup	Shukla Sandeep
Mohan M. Raj	Spoenemann Miro
Mollison Mac	Stergiou Christos
Mollner Nils	Stierand Ingo
Motika Christian	Stigge Martin
Moy Matthieu	Swaminathan Mani
Nghiem Truong X.	Teige Tino
Nicácio Daniel	Torngren Martin
Pajic Miroslav	Travassos Guilherme Horta
Perrone Gian	Wachter Björn
Petters Stefan	Wang Qi
Phan Linh T.X.	Wang Shaohui
Puaut Isabelle	Ward Bryan
Quesel Jan-David	Wehrmeister Marco
Raty Tomi	Zimmer Michael
Raymond Pascal	

ESWEEK 2012 Sponsors & Supporters

Sponsors:

Technical Supporters:

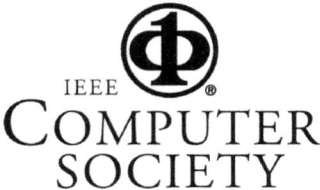 

Supporters:

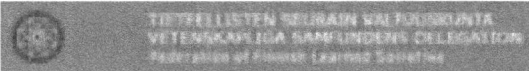

Wireless Innovations for Smartphones

Hannu Kauppinen
Nokia Research Center,
Helsinki, Finland
hannu.kauppinen@nokia.com

ABSTRACT

The ever increasing demand for fast mobile internet connectivity continues to set challenges for research in radio communications. On one hand the capacity demand can be served by offloading data traffic to local networks. On the other hand using more bandwidth, and possibly dynamically allocating spectrum in a flexible way, will improve the usage of the available spectrum. The future of wireless access continues to be defined by the 3GPP and IEEE standards setting bodies. Radios can also provide innovative features that offer new functionalities for consumers, such as ultra-fast local connectivity, sensing and positioning. This talk will present examples of various radio, sensing and multimedia innovations for smartphones.

Categories and Subject Descriptors

H.4.3 [**Information Systems Applications**]: Communications Applications

General Terms

Design.

Keywords

Radio connectivity, mobile internet connectivity, dynamic spectrum allocation.

BIOGRAPHY

Dr. Hannu Kauppinen is currently holding the position of Vice President, Head of Nokia Research Center. In this capacity he is responsible for the long term research of mobile technologies that will secure product differentiation and long-term profitable growth for Nokia. Hannu Kauppinen has a strong track record in bringing research innovations to products.

Hannu Kauppinen joined Nokia Research Center in 1997 has since then held key leadership positions in Nokia's wireless research. He has contributed to and overseen research in cognitive radio systems, cellular systems, wireless local connectivity, networking technologies, software defined radios, RF and antenna design, as well as sensing and positioning radios. During 2007-2008 and 2010-2011 Hannu Kauppinen was the Director of the Radio Systems Laboratory in Nokia Research Center. He was responsible for the research for 3GPP and IEEE radio standards as well as the research for cognitive and sensor radios to ensure innovativeness and competitiveness of wireless communication solutions in Nokia's products.

Hannu Kauppinen holds a PhD degree in Physics from the Helsinki University of Technology (1997) and an Executive MBA from the Helsinki School of Economics (2007).

Computing Without Processors

Satnam Singh
Technical Infrastructure division,
Google
1600 Amphitheatre Parkway
Mountain View, CA 94043
s.singh@acm.org

ABSTRACT

The duopoly of computing has up until now been delimited by drawing a line in the sand that defines the instruction set architecture as the hard division between software and hardware. On one side of this contract Intel improved the design of processors and on the other side of this line Microsoft developed ever more sophisticated software. This cozy relationship is now over as the distinction between hardware and software is blurred due to relentless pressure for performance and reduction in latency and energy consumption. Increasingly we will be forced to compute with architectures and machines which do not resemble regular processors with a fixed memory hierarchy based on heuristic caching schemes. Other ways to bake all that sand will include the evolution of GPUs and FPGAs to form heterogeneous computing resources which are much better suited to meeting our computing needs than racks of multicore processors. This presentation will highlight some of the programming challenges we face when trying to develop for heterogeneous architectures and a few promising lines of attack are identified.

Categories and Subject Descriptors

D.1.0 [**Programming Techniques**]: General

General Terms

Algorithms, Design.

Keywords

HW/SW frontier, programming, heterogeneous architecture.

BIOGRAPHY

Prof. Singh works in the Technical Infrastructure division of Google in Mountain View, California and focuses on the configuration management of Google's data-center services. Previously Prof. Singh worked on the design of heterogeneous systems at Microsoft Research in Cambridge UK and on parallel programming techniques at Microsoft's Developer Division in Redmond USA. He has also worked on re-configurable computing and formal verification at Xilinx in San Jose, California and as an academic at the University of Glasgow. He also currently holds a part-time position as the Chair of Reconfigurable Systems at the University of Birmingham.

A Standards-Based, Fully-Open Software Platform for Smart Embedded Systems

Jong-Deok Choi
Samsung Electronics
Suwon, Gyeonggi-Do, Korea
jd11.choi@samsung.com

ABSTRACT

There has been an explosion of smart mobile devices over the last few years. These smart devices, such as smartphones and tablets, have changed many aspects of modern life. They have also enabled whole new industries to grow up that develop and manufacture "companion products" of the smart devices. These companion products, however, are mostly built around the smart devices, instead of being tightly integrated into them, and fail to utilize the full capabilities of the smart devices. The main cause for their failure is that the software platforms these smart devices are built on are not fully open. This hinders efforts by device manufacturers or software developers to create innovative new products or product categories based on those software platforms.

In this talk, we present Tizen (www.tizen.org), which is a "fully open" software platform for embedded systems. Tizen allows for everyone involved in building and using devices built on it to freely define, invent, add new features or business models, or create new device categories. Tizen offers an industry leading HTML5-based application APIs, the preferred development environment for apps and services for the future. The HTML5-based APIs make it easy for developers to create applications that run across various categories of devices such as mobile, in-vehicle infotainment (IVI), Digital TV, netbooks, health and medical devices, etc. In this talk we also present Tizen's optimization technologies that enable HTML5-based applications to enjoy performance comparable to that of native applications. We also describe how Tizen balances the trade-offs between performance and power consumption, which is of extreme importance for mobile devices.

Categories and Subject Descriptors

D.3.3 [**Programming Languages**]: Language Constructs and Features – *frameworks.*

General Terms

Languages.

Keywords

Tizen, HTML5, smart device, software platform.

BIOGRAPHY

Dr. Jong-Deok Choi is an Executive Vice President at Samsung Electronics in Korea, and is currently in charge of the Software Platform Team within Samsung's Software Research Center. Before joining Samsung Electronics, he worked at IBM T. J. Watson Research Center as a Research Staff Member and Manager.

While working at IBM Research, he contributed to optimizing Java Webservices applications, the JikesRVM open-source Java virtual machine (JVM), the PTRAN parallelizing-compiler project, and others.

Dr. Choi has published over 50 technical papers in top journals and conferences on various fields in computer science, and holds over 20 US patents. He has served as a program (co-)chair, conference steering-committee member, and program-committee member for numerous technical conferences.

Dr. Choi received his Ph.D. and M.S. in Computer Sciences from University of Wisconsin - Madison, USA, in 1989 and 1985, respectively; M.S. in Electrical Engineering from KAIST, Korea, in 1981; and B.S. in Electronic Engineering from Seoul National University (SNU), Korea, in 1979.

Internet-of-Energy: Combining Embedded Computing and Communication for the Smart Grid

Randolf Mock
Siemens AG
Munich, Germany

Moritz Neukirchner, Rolf Ernst
TU Braunschweig
Braunschweig, Germany

Ruud Wijtvliet
Centrosolar Group
Hamburg, Germany

Michael Huetwohl
Lantiq GmbH
Munich, Germany

Pascal Urard
ST Microelectronics
Crolles, France

Ovidiu Vermesan (organizer)
Sintef ICT
Oslo, Norway
Ovidiu.Vermesan@sintef.no

ABSTRACT

Driven by increasing cost of energy and by the inclusion of renewable but time variant sources of energy on the production side, and by new requirements from electromobility, building and home automation on the consumption side, the energy grid has moved in the focus of research, industry and infrastructure development. One of the key challenges is the interaction of the numerous em-bedded systems controlling energy producing and consuming devices using an "internet of energy."

This session will provide different views on this development towards a smart energy grid. The first talk given by a leading provider of energy grid equipment will give an overview on the new developments and challenges in modeling and simulating local grid behavior. The second talk discusses building energy management at the interface between home automation and the smart grid, both from the application and the embedded platform perspective. The third talk addresses home automation which serves many objectives, besides being a terminal network of the smart grind. Last not least, the fourth talk presents new development in wireless sensor devices as an important component of future home and energy networks.

Categories and Subject Descriptors

J.7 [**Computer Applications**]: COMPUTERS IN OTHER SYSTEMS – *Command and control; Process control; Real time.*

Keywords

Design, Measurement, Performance, Reliability, Verification, Smart Energy, Smart Grid.

1. Interactions of Large Scale EV Mobility and Smart Grids - Chances and Challenges of Grid Infrastructure Simulations

Randolf Mock, Siemens, Germany

The complex interactions between electric mobility on a large scale with the electric distribution grid constitute a considerable challenge regarding the feasibility, the efficiency and the stability

of smart electric distribution grids. Grid infrastructure simulations which take into account the details of these interactions and which are backed by comprehensive demonstrators may help to shed light on crucial aspects of both energy and information exchange between the traffic and the electric energy infrastructure regime. This will be highlighted by selected topics which intend to shed light on the scope and the challenges inherent in this area of simulation.

2. Reliable Building Energy Management in the Smart Grid

Moritz Neukirchner, Rolf Ernst, TU Braunschweig; Ruud Wijtvliet, Centrosolar, Germany

Reliable building energy management must guarantee a variety of services, support of local network control for grid stability and optimization, access for remote device maintenance and diagnosis, tamperfree metering, security against attacks targeting the building or network operations. The talk discusses applications, derives embedded platform requirements, and shows first solutions based on virtualization and self-protection.

3. Home Networks for the Smart Grid and Other Future Applications

Michael Huetwohl, Lantiq, Germany

The number of connected devices in our daily live has significantly increased. And it will continue to further increase x-fold in the near future. IPv6 is the key enabler. The huge social-economic challenges like the transition to renewable energy sources or the aging society are the drivers for this development. The devices and related applications will have a wide spread of different requirements: data rates from kbit/s to Gbit/s, Qualtity of Service, security and reliability will be of significant importance. In order to support these requirements a powerful Home Network and smart, easy-to-use, interoperable communication devices will be needed. The current status of Home Networks is not adequate and needs improvement.

4. Wireless Sensor Components (Draft title)

Pascal Urard, ST Microelectronics, France

Abstract not available at time of publication.

Trends in Automotive Embedded Systems

Dan Gunnarsson
BMW Group
Munich, Germany

Stefan Kuntz
Continental Corp.
Regensburg, Germany

Glenn Farrall
Infineon
Bristol, UK

Akihiko Iwai
Denso Corp.
Kariya-shi, Japan

Rolf Ernst (organizer)
Technische Universität Braunschweig
Braunschweig, Germany
r.ernst@tu-bs.de

ABSTRACT

Automotive embedded systems have developed from single controllers to networked embedded systems integrating an ever growing variety of distributed applications. New features for driving assistance, improved safety, motor and energy management, and infotainment lead to shorter innovation cycles for software architectures, network technologies, and hardware architectures. While, e.g., the new FlexRay bus standard has just been introduced, next generation Ethernet is already at the edge of introduction. The 4 talks in this session present OEM, 1st tier supplier and semiconductor vendor views from leading automotive companies and suppliers.

Categories and Subject Descriptors

C.3 [**Computer Systems Organization**]: Real-time and embedded systems.

Keywordss

Design, Economics, Performance, Reliability, Security, Verification, Automotive electronics.

1. Trends and new Challenges in Automotive E/E Architectures

Dan Gunnarsson, BMW, Germany

Over the last decades integrated systems, where functions are partitioned on several ECUs, connected with data communication networks has evolved. During this development new communication methods and principal have been introduced, starting with system with low to moderate complexity moving to highly complex systems. Current requirements on the E/E Architecture are increasingly complex e.g. through the introduction of new and more advanced driver assistance systems where new use-cases like transmission of video streams with real-time requirements are becoming more common. To meet these requirements Ethernet is currently being introduced as an automotive network. This means that new challenges with regard to gateways and the transition between different protocols and networks have to be mastered. To cope with these increasingly complex tasks new modeling and analysis capabilities are needed.

2. New Challenges in HW and SW Integration

Stefan Kuntz, Continental, Germany

The continuing increase in/of functionality and density of functions in embedded distributed real-time systems within the automotive industry, as well as the importance of satisfying safety and security requirements in such systems require new approaches in managing the resulting complexities. Namely the integration of hardware and software is a concern and faces new challenges with the advent of multicore and manycore systems in the automotive domain. This presentation identifies the main challenges and sketches out some directions to tackle those challenges utilizing model based development and methodologies.

3. Virtualisation Support for an Embedded Automotive Environment

Glenn Farrall, Infineon, UK

Virtualisation is now a well established and relied upon technology for many environments - servers, cloud computing and even some environments that can be considered embedded. There is a difference however between soft-real time or multimedia embedded environments and systems in the safety and the hard-real time application space. This presentation covers some of the differences in the Automotive arena making the problem both easier and harder in various aspects and some of the features and solutions provided in the AURIX(r) multicore devices to address these issues.

4. Software Engineering for the next-generation automotive systems

Akihiko Iwai, Denso, Japan

Nowadays automotive E/E systems are getting large and complex due to its growing needs for new functionalities. The source of such new functionalities include active safety applications using vehicle to infrastructure communication, telematics services cooperating with services on cloud, vehicle to grid/home energy management applications. In this talk, while introducing some cooperative works in Japanese embedded systems industries, we will talk about current works and some technical issues of automotive software development.

ESWEEK 2012 Special Presentation
CASES'12, CODES+ISSS'12, EMSOFT'12,
Oct. 7–12, 2012, Tampere, Finland.
ACM 978-1-4503-1424-4 & 978-1-4503-1426-8
   & 978-1-4503-1425-1/12/09.

Research Issues in Smart Phones, Notepads and Related Services

Petri Liuha
Nokia
Finland

Kari Pehkonen
Renesas Mobile
Finland

Juhani Rummukainen
ST-Ericsson
Finland

Veli-Pekka Vatula
Intel
Finland

Tatu Koljonen *(organizer)*
VTT
Finland
Tatu.Koljonen@vtt.fi

ABSTRACT

Networked embedded systems are building intelligence to every-place. There are more and more incentives to open proprietary data and interfaces for free to third party service developers. This development called "ubiquitous communication" or "internet of things" requires new dominant design for user interfaces, interoperability and contextuality. In the user interface design, for example, we have witnessed the growth of the smartphone display, which today is at about 5 inches. Developing the new dominant designs is part of the "ecosystem war", where the most attractive platforms are getting the most developer, users and profits. The four speakers of today represent companies that have entered the competition with different platforms, assets and strategies and hence have different research challenges to be solved..

Categories and Subject Descriptors

C.3 [**Computer Systems Organization**]: Real-time and embedded systems.

General Terms

Design, Economics, Performance, Reliability, Security, Verification.

1. Challenges in Building Smart Spaces (Draft title)

Petri Liuha, Nokia, Finland

2. Role of Wireless in Networked Embedded Systems (Draft title)

Kari Pehkonen, Renesas Mobile, Finland

3. Enable Coolest, Richest, Affordable Devices (Draft title)

Juhani Rummukainen, ST-Ericsson, Finland

4. Expanding from Chips to Handset (Draft title)

Veli-Pekka Vatula, Intel, Finland

Debugging Embedded Multimedia Application Traces through Periodic Pattern Mining

Patricia López Cueva*†   Aurélie Bertaux*   Alexandre Termier*

Jean François Méhaut*   Miguel Santana†

†STMicroelectronics
Crolles, France
FirstName.LastName@st.com

*University of Grenoble, LIG
Grenoble, France
FirstName.LastName@imag.fr

ABSTRACT

Increasing complexity in both the software and the underlying hardware, and ever tighter time-to-market pressures are some of the key challenges faced when designing multimedia embedded systems. Optimizing the debugging phase can help to reduce development time significantly. A powerful approach used extensively during this phase is the analysis of execution traces. However, huge trace volumes make manual trace analysis unmanageable. In such situations, Data Mining can help by automatically discovering interesting *patterns* in large amounts of data. In this paper, we are interested in discovering periodic behaviors in multimedia applications. Therefore, we propose a new pattern mining approach for automatically discovering all periodic patterns occurring in a multimedia application execution trace.

Furthermore, gaps in the periodicity are of special interest since they can correspond to cracks or drop-outs in the stream. Existing periodic pattern definitions are too restrictive regarding the size of the gaps in the periodicity. So, in this paper, we specify a new definition of frequent periodic patterns that removes this limitation. Moreover, in order to simplify the analysis of the set of frequent periodic patterns we propose two complementary approaches: (a) a lossless representation that reduces the size of the set and facilitates its analysis, and (b) a tool to identify pairs of "competitors" where a pattern breaks the periodicity of another pattern. Several experiments were carried out on embedded video and audio decoding application traces, demonstrating that using these new patterns it is possible to identify abnormal behaviors.

Categories and Subject Descriptors

D.2.5 [**Software Engineering**]: Testing and Debugging, Tracing; H.2.8 [**Database Management**]: Database Applications, Data Mining

Keywords

Embedded Systems, Multimedia Applications, Periodic Pattern Mining, Debugging

1. INTRODUCTION

The current trend in consumer electronics is to have products that support multimedia applications, such as set-top boxes, tablets, smartphones and MP4 players. All these products are powered by highly integrated System-on-a-Chip (SoC) solutions, that contain, in a single die, several processing units, memory blocks and specialized units for audio and video decoding. Developing efficient and robust applications for systems using these SoCs is a challenging issue. It is thus critical for companies developing embedded software to have comprehensive programming frameworks with advanced features for debugging and optimizing their applications.

Nowadays, the most widely used technique to give insight into the behavior of an embedded application for debugging and optimization purposes is *trace* analysis [19]. That is, to collect events generated by the system and the application in order to perform a post-mortem analysis of the execution. Many recent embedded systems directly integrate tracing hardware support in order to minimize intrusiveness, i.e. the act of tracing has minimal impact on the behavior of the application, allowing complex interactions to be shown in real-time applications such as video decoding.

Over the past decade, the software and hardware of embedded systems have faced an increase in complexity due to the use of techniques such as multi-threading, power and memory optimization, and so on. Consequently, the size of the execution traces of applications running on these systems has also increased, and we can only expect an even bigger increase with the introduction of many-core processors in embedded systems. Therefore, the manual analysis of execution traces is becoming an unmanageable task.

To overcome this issue we intend to use data mining in order to automatically extract pertinent information (called *patterns*) from traces. In this context, we consider a *pattern* as a set of functions and system events that are found together frequently in the trace. Multimedia applications have a periodic execution based on frame decoding, i.e. the same operations are performed on each frame or every n frames. Therefore, in this paper, we use *frequent periodic pattern mining* on execution traces to discover periodic behaviors of multimedia applications.

However, sometimes this periodic behavior is not perfect: cracks in the sound or drop-outs in the video stream are often the consequence of a disruption in the periodicity of a pattern, showing up as a *gap*. Therefore, these *gaps* should be investigated as a priority for debugging and optimizing multimedia applications. The state of the art (see Section 7) considers only regular sized gaps, i.e. a multiple of the period, while in multimedia applications it is not possible to know the size of the gaps in advance. Therefore, we propose a new definition of periodic patterns that allows to have arbitrary sized gaps.

Frequent pattern mining generally generates a large amount of patterns which can make their analysis difficult. Therefore, we propose a reduced representation of the set of frequent periodic patterns, based on ternary relation theory [22] and the minimal generator concept [18], while keeping the same amount of information.

In this paper, we explore the current status of trace debugging on embedded systems as well as explain how to pre-process execution traces to analyze them with our pattern mining algorithm in Section 2. We propose a new definition of frequent periodic pattern in Section 3, and introduce our approach to reduce the set of outputted patterns mentioned above in Section 4. In Section 5, we present a new algorithm to mine the reduced set of frequent periodic patterns, as well as introduce an analysis tool that helps to identify pairs of competitor periodic patterns. By competitors we mean that their executions are in competition, i.e. a pattern breaking the periodicity of another pattern, which helps to identify possible conflicts between different parts of the system. In Section 6, we present the insights given by analyzing application traces. Next, we explore the state-of-the-art regarding pattern mining in system analysis, periodic pattern mining and pattern mining of ternary relations in Section 7. Finally, we present our conclusions and future work in Section 8.

2. MULTIMEDIA APPLICATIONS AND EMBEDDED PLATFORMS

In this section, we introduce the context in which trace debugging is used on embedded systems. We also explain how to pre-process the traces so that they can be analyzed by our pattern mining algorithm.

2.1 Trace Debugging on Embedded Systems

During the development of applications for embedded systems, development and evaluation boards are used by developers to test their applications. An example is the *STi7200-MBoard* platform [21] which contains an *STi7200* SoC, whose architecture is shown in Figure 1. This SoC is used in high-definition set-top boxes produced by *STMicroelectronics*. Apart from all the necessary connectivity, this system-on-chip contains a *ST40* core and two *ST231* cores. The *ST40* core is dedicated to application execution and device control, while the *ST231* cores are in charged of the audio and video decoding.

These development boards offer a way of collecting traces that can vary from a dedicated trace port, to a network connexion that allows the developer to retrieve the traces from the board. Execution traces provide a full view of the

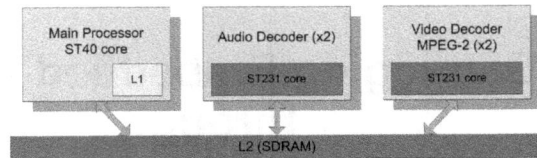

Figure 1: STi7200 SoC architecture

running system (operating system and application) while minimizing the intrusiveness.

In some cases, software tracing solutions are provided by the operating system. For instance, on an *ST40* core, applications run on a Linux distribution for *STMicroelectronics* products. This operating system provides a tracing tool based on KProbes [8], which registers system and application events: interrupts, context switches, function calls, system calls, etc. In this paper, we focus on the analysis of software execution traces. Moreover, the execution traces used for the experiments were produced by the tracing tool mentioned above in this paragraph.

In other cases, hardware tracing solutions provide very accurate information about the execution of the system with no intrusion. The main problem with hardware-based tracing techniques is the extremely large amount of data generated. Moreover, transferring the trace out of the chip requires a large I/O bandwidth with a significant cost increase.

Embedded systems are complex entities composed of several processing units, accelerators, GPUs, DSPs and so on. Moreover, multimedia applications often consist of filter pipelines, in which certain steps are carried out by accelerators or GPUs instead of the main core. Therefore, in order to have an insight into what is really happening in the system, it is necessary to trace every component of the SoC. Companies such as Intel [16] or STMicroelectronics are currently working on system tracing solutions that tackle this necessity. Certainly traces obtained by this new approach will be a lot richer in terms of the amount of information, but also a lot bigger than current traces. In consequence, the need for automatic trace analysis tools will be even more important in the near future. Currently, we focus on the analysis of software execution traces, but our approach is generic and would be easily extended to be able to analyze this new generation of traces.

2.2 Execution Traces in Pattern Mining

An execution trace is a sequence of events and their timestamp, registered during the execution of an application, as shown in Figure 2. However, most pattern mining algorithms search for patterns common to a sequence of sets [1]. This makes it necessary to split the execution trace into sets of events, called *transactions*, in order to apply pattern mining algorithms.

We propose two methods to split the trace:

(a) using a time interval [11], where a transaction contains all events of the trace registered in the same time window, or

(b) using a function name, where a transaction contains all events of the trace that occurred between two occurrences of the given function.

As an example, we can observe the result of splitting a trace using a time interval of 0.1 ms in Figure 2. The timestamp of the events is not included in the transactions, so

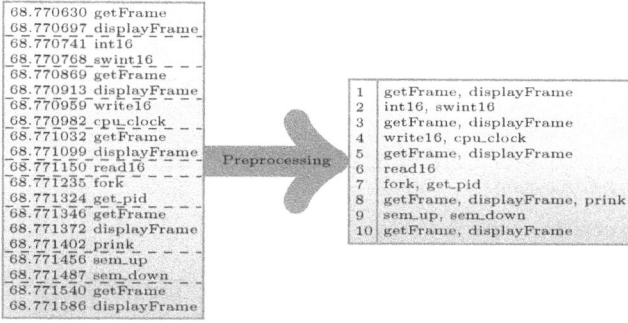

Figure 2: Preprocessing of an execution trace by splitting it into time intervals of 0.1 ms. Timestamp: seconds.microseconds

the information about when exactly an event was executed is not considered in the analysis. In this paper, we are interested in discovering sets of events that occur periodically in the execution trace, but the order in which those events are executed is not taken into account. Considering that the executing environment is multi-threaded, the order of the events might change according to the decision taken by the scheduler. Therefore, even if the order is not taken into account, our approach is able to discover interesting relationships between the events in the execution trace.

For a more exhaustive analysis where the order of event execution is considered important, there exist pattern mining techniques that can discover ordered sets of events, called sequences, that occur frequently in the trace. Nevertheless, these techniques are more complex and computationally expensive. The results obtained by these techniques might be interesting but these techniques are out of the scope of this paper.

Unless stated otherwise, in this paper we use the function that starts the decoding of a frame to split the trace in order to discover events that happen while decoding frames. Being able to identify the events that occur when decoding a frame allows us to more easily identify sets of events that might affect the application's behavior.

3. DEFINITIONS

In this section, we give basic definitions that allow us to present our definition of frequent periodic patterns.

As we have seen in Section 2, an execution trace is split into sets of events which, in data mining, are called *transactions*. We define our dataset $\mathcal{D}$ as the ordered set of transactions $\{t_1, t_2, ..., t_n\}$ obtained by splitting an execution trace, and the set of items $\mathcal{I}$ as the set of all possible events found in the trace. An itemset is a set of events belonging to $\mathcal{I}$, e.g. $\{sem\_up, int16, cpu\_clock\}$. For instance, Table 1 presents the dataset obtained after preprocessing the execution trace shown in Figure 2 by splitting the trace using a time interval of 0.1 ms.

DEFINITION 1. *Given a set of items $\mathcal{I} = \{i_1, i_2, ..., i_r\}$, a **dataset** $\mathcal{D}$ is an ordered set of transactions $\{t_1, t_2, ..., t_n\}$ where each transaction is a subset of $\mathcal{I}$, i.e. $t_k \subseteq \mathcal{I}$ for $1 \leq k \leq n$, and where the order is defined by $t_i < t_j$ if and only if $i < j$. The length of the dataset $\mathcal{D}$ is the number of transactions that form part of the dataset and is denoted by $|\mathcal{D}|$.*

Table 1: A dataset in the context of system trace analysis.

t_k	Itemset
t_1	getFrame, displayFrame
t_2	int16, swint16
t_3	getFrame, displayFrame
t_4	write16, cpu_clock
t_5	getFrame, displayFrame
t_6	read16
t_7	fork, get_pid
t_8	getFrame, displayFrame, printk
t_9	sem_up, sem_down
t_{10}	getFrame, displayFrame

An itemset X is denoted by $\{x_1, x_2, ..., x_j\}$ where x_t is an item, i.e. $x_t \in \mathcal{I}$. Considering $X \subseteq I$, we say that an itemset X *occurs* in the transaction t_k if and only if $X \subseteq t_k$.

Given a transaction t_k, its transaction identifier, denoted as $tid(t_k)$, is its position in the dataset, i.e. k. We also define the distance d between two transactions t_i and t_j as the difference between their transaction identifiers, i.e. $d = j - i$ with $i \leq j$.

When an itemset occurs over a set of transactions and the distance between any two consecutive transactions is constant, this set of transactions forms a *cycle*.

DEFINITION 2. *Given an itemset X and a period p, a cycle of X, denoted **cycle**(o, p, l, X), is a maximal set of l transactions in $\mathcal{D}$ containing X, starting at transaction t_o and separated by equal distance p: $cycle(o, p, l, X) = \{t_k \in \mathcal{D} | X \subseteq t_k, k = o + p * i, 0 \leq i < l, X \nsubseteq t_{o-p}, X \nsubseteq t_{o+p*l}\}$ where $0 \leq o < n$, $2 \leq l \leq n$ and n is the number of transactions in $\mathcal{D}$.*

EXAMPLE 1. *In the dataset in Table 1, the itemset $X = \{getFrame, displayFrame\}$ is found at a period $p = 2$ on transactions from t_1 ($o = 1$) to t_5, therefore it forms a cycle of length $l = 3$, denoted*
$cycle(1, \mathbf{2}, 3, \{getFrame, displayFrame\}) = \{t_1, t_3, t_5\}$[1].

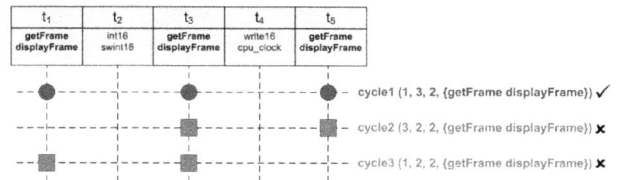

Figure 3: Examples of cycles and non-cycles

Figure 3 offers a graphical representation of a set of transactions where $cycle1(1, \mathbf{2}, 3, \{getFrame, displayFrame\})$ is maximal. $cycle2(3, \mathbf{2}, 2, \{getFrame, displayFrame\})$ and $cycle3(1, \mathbf{2}, 2, \{getFrame, displayFrame\})$ are not maximal since they can be extended with transactions t_1 and t_5 respectively, and therefore they are not valid cycles in our context.

A set of consecutive cycles (the end of a cycle happens before the beginning of the following cycle) over the same itemset and the same period forms a *periodic pattern*.

---

[1] Periods are presented in bold for clarity.

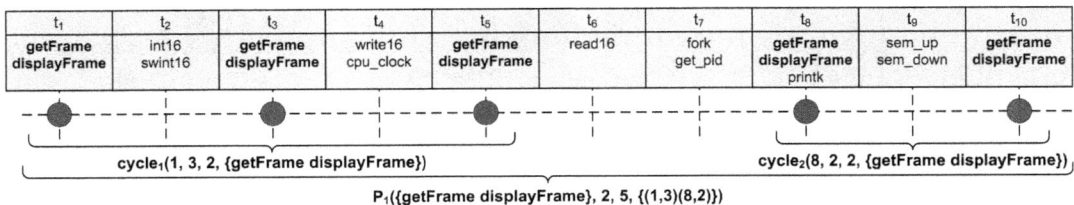

t_1	t_2	t_3	t_4	t_5	t_6	t_7	t_8	t_9	t_{10}
getFrame displayFrame	int16 swint16	getFrame displayFrame	write16 cpu_clock	getFrame displayFrame	read16	fork get_pid	getFrame displayFrame printk	sem_up sem_down	getFrame displayFrame

cycle$_1$(1, 3, 2, {getFrame displayFrame}) cycle$_2$(8, 2, 2, {getFrame displayFrame})

P_1({getFrame displayFrame}, 2, 5, {(1,3)(8,2)})

Figure 4: Periodic pattern formation

DEFINITION 3. *An itemset X together with a set of cycles C and a period p form a **periodic pattern** if the set of cycles $C = \{(o_1, l_1), ..., (o_k, l_k)\}^2$, with $1 \leq k \leq m$ and m being the maximum number of cycles of period p in the dataset $\mathcal{D}$, is a set of cycles of X such that:*

1. *All cycles have the same period p.*

2. *All cycles are consecutive: $\forall (o_i, l_i), (o_j, l_j) \in C$ such that $1 \leq i < j \leq k$, we have $o_i < o_j$.*

3. *Cycles do not overlap: $\forall (o_i, l_i), (o_j, l_j) \in C$ such that $i < j$, we have $o_i + (p * (l_i - 1)) < o_j$.*

We denote this periodic pattern $P(X, p, s, C)$.

The **support** of a periodic pattern, denoted s, is the sum of all cycle lengths in C, i.e. given $C = \{(o_1, l_1), ..., (o_k, l_k)\}$ with $1 \leq k \leq m$ then $s = \sum_{i=1}^{k} l_i$.

EXAMPLE 2. *In Figure 4 we can observe that the cycles $cycle_1(1, \mathbf{2}, 3, \{getFrame, displayFrame\})$ and $cycle_2(8, \mathbf{2}, 2, \{getFrame, displayFrame\})$ form a periodic pattern $P_1 = (\{getFrame, displayFrame\}, \mathbf{2}, 5, \{(1,3)(8,2)\})$ with period 2 and a support of 5 transactions.*

We now introduce the notion of *frequent periodic patterns*.

DEFINITION 4. *Given a minimum support threshold min_sup, a periodic pattern P is **frequent** if its support is greater than min_sup, i.e. $P(X, p, s, C)$ is frequent if and only if $s \geq min\_sup$.*

EXAMPLE 3. *Given the dataset shown in Table 1 and a minimum support of two transactions, the set of frequent periodic patterns is presented in Table 2^3.*

As we can see in Table 2, the set of frequent periodic patterns is highly redundant. On one hand, all combinations of large itemsets are consider as patterns. For example, P_1, P_2 and P_3 are present in exactly the same transactions and the itemset of P_3 contains the itemsets of P_1 and P_2. Therefore P_1 and P_2 do not give any more information than P_3. On the other hand, combinations of small periods by addition or multiplication generate redundant patterns. For example, P_9 is redundant with respect to P_3 since its period is multiple of P_3's period while the transactions in P_9 can be found in P_3. Therefore P_9 does not give any more information than P_3.

In real datasets tens of thousands of frequent periodic patterns might be found, which are impractical to analyze by an application developer. In order to produce a reduced representation of the set of frequent periodic patterns we adopt a triadic approach by introducing the periods into the dataset.

---

^{2}For simplicity of notation, a cycle is represented here by its origin o and its length l since all cycles in the set share the same itemset X and period p.

^{3}Only periods not greater that the length of the dataset divided by min_sup are considered.

Table 2: Set of frequent periodic patterns

Frequent Periodic Patterns
$P_1(\{getFrame\}, \mathbf{2}, 5, \{(1,3)(8,2)\})$
$P_2(\{displayFrame\}, \mathbf{2}, 5, \{(1,3)(8,2)\})$
$P_3(\{getFrame, displayFrame\}, \mathbf{2}, 5, \{(1,3)(8,2)\})$
$P_4(\{getFrame\}, \mathbf{3}, 2, \{(5,2)\})$
$P_5(\{displayFrame\}, \mathbf{3}, 2, \{(5,2)\})$
$P_6(\{getFrame, displayFrame\}, \mathbf{3}, 2, \{(5,2)\})$
$P_7(\{getFrame\}, \mathbf{4}, 2, \{(1,2)\})$
$P_8(\{displayFrame\}, \mathbf{4}, 2, \{(1,2)\})$
$P_9(\{getFrame, displayFrame\}, \mathbf{4}, 2, \{(1,2)\})$
$P_{10}(\{getFrame\}, \mathbf{5}, 2, \{(3,2)\})$
$P_{11}(\{displayFrame\}, \mathbf{5}, 2, \{(3,2)\})$
$P_{12}(\{getFrame, diaplayFrame\}, \mathbf{5}, 2, \{(3,2)\})$
$P_{13}(\{getFrame\}, \mathbf{5}, 2, \{(5,2)\})$
$P_{14}(\{displayFrame\}, \mathbf{5}, 2, \{(5,2)\})$
$P_{15}(\{getFrame, displayFrame\}, \mathbf{5}, 2, \{(5,2)\})$

4. NON-REDUNDANT PATTERNS

In this section, we present the application of ternary relation theory to periodic pattern mining and the definition of minimal periodic generators that will allow us to generate a reduced set of periodic patterns that are easier to analyze by the developer.

As we have seen in Section 3, the set of frequent periodic patterns is highly redundant. This is a common drawback when using pattern mining techniques which complicates the analysis of the results. A major breakthrough has been the study of closed operators applied to patterns such as itemsets [18], gradual patterns [2] and so on. The set of closed patterns, mined by closed operators, is a reduced representation of the set of frequent patterns but contains the same information.

No previous study has been carried out regarding closed periodic patterns. This might be because the theory behind closed patterns, called Galois connection, is based on binary relations, such as the relation *items* $\times$ *transactions* for itemset mining. Analyzing the structure of periodic patterns, we can observe that they are based on ternary relations involving the items, the transactions and the periods. In ternary relations, it is not possible to make use of a Galois connection to generate closed patterns [3], therefore it is not possible to apply the Galois theory to periodic pattern mining.

Instead, we are going to use a triadic approach to Formal Concept Analysis [10] to mine a reduced representation of the set of frequent periodic patterns, which in this context is called the set of **triadic concepts**. Nevertheless, since all possible periods are considered, the set of triadic concepts might contain redundant periods, such as multiples of smaller periods, periods formed by the concatenation of two smaller periods, and so on. So, to reduce this redundancy, we define the concept of minimal periodic generators which allows us to extract the minimal set of periodic patterns

Table 3: Representation of the relation $\mathcal{Y}$

$I/P-T$	2										3									
	t_1	t_2	t_3	t_4	t_5	t_6	t_7	t_8	t_9	t_{10}	t_1	t_2	t_3	t_4	t_5	t_6	t_7	t_8	t_9	t_{10}
getFrame	×		×		×			×		×						×		×		
displayFrame	×		×		×			×		×						×		×		
...																				

$I/P-T$	4										5									
	t_1	t_2	t_3	t_4	t_5	t_6	t_7	t_8	t_9	t_{10}	t_1	t_2	t_3	t_4	t_5	t_6	t_7	t_8	t_9	t_{10}
getFrame	×				×								×		×			×		×
displayFrame	×				×								×		×			×		×
...																				

that explains the behavior of the application, without losing information.

4.1 Triadic Approach to Periodic Pattern Mining

Our dataset, introduced in Definition 1, corresponds to a relation between two attributes, *items × transactions*, i.e. $\mathcal{R} \subseteq \mathcal{I} \times \mathcal{D}$ and each $r \in \mathcal{R}$ can be represented by a couple $r = \{(i,t)|i \in \mathcal{I}, t \in \mathcal{D}\}$, denoting that the item i occurs on transaction t.

In order to mine periodic patterns, the period should be included in the dataset, but in order to do so, the binary relation $\mathcal{R} \subseteq \mathcal{I} \times \mathcal{D}$ has to be transformed into a ternary relation $\mathcal{Y} \subseteq \mathcal{I} \times \mathcal{P} \times \mathcal{D}$, with $\mathcal{P}$ the set of all possible periods that we limit to the range $[1..|\mathcal{D}|/min\_sup]$.

To formalize this ternary relation we are going to introduce a triadic approach to formal concept analysis first introduced by Lehmann et al. [10] in 1995. Specifically, the concepts of triadic context and triadic concepts are presented here including some modifications needed in order to adapt them to periodic pattern mining.

DEFINITION 5. *A **periodic triadic context** is defined as a quadruple $(\mathcal{I}, \mathcal{P}, \mathcal{D}, \mathcal{Y})$ where $\mathcal{I}$ is the set of items, $\mathcal{P}$ is the set of periods, $\mathcal{D}$ is the set of transactions, and $\mathcal{Y}$ is a ternary relation between $\mathcal{I}$, $\mathcal{P}$ and $\mathcal{D}$, i.e. $\mathcal{Y} \subseteq \mathcal{I} \times \mathcal{P} \times \mathcal{D}$.*

An element of the relation $y \subseteq \mathcal{Y}$ is denoted by the triple $y = \{(i,p,t)|i \in \mathcal{I}, p \in \mathcal{P}, t \in \mathcal{D}\}$ and is read: the transaction t forms part of a cycle of period p of the item i.

EXAMPLE 4. *Given the dataset shown in Table 1, the corresponding triadic context is shown in Table 3[4]. Each cross in the table represents an element of the ternary relation $\mathcal{Y}$. For example, $P_1(\{getFrame\}, 2, 5, \{(1,3)(8,2)\}$ in Table 2 is transformed into the triples $(getFrame, 2, t_1)$, $(getFrame, 2, t_3)$, $(getFrame, 2, t_5)$, $(getFrame, 2, t_8)$, $(getFrame, 2, t_{10})$ shown by the corresponding crosses in Table 3.*

DEFINITION 6. *Given a minimum support threshold min_sup, a triple (I, P, T), with $I \subseteq \mathcal{I}$, $P \subseteq \mathcal{P}$, $T \subseteq \mathcal{D}$ and $I \times P \times T \subseteq \mathcal{Y}$, is **frequent** if and only if $I \neq \emptyset$, $P \neq \emptyset$ and $|T| \geq min\_sup$.*

EXAMPLE 5. *In Table 3, given a min_sup of 2, we can observe several frequent triples such as $(\{getFrame\}, \{2,3\}, \{t_5,t_8\})$ or $(\{getFrame, displayFrame\}, \{5\}, \{t_3,t_5,t_8, t_{10}\})$, since the number of transactions forming those triples is greater or equal to 2.*

---

[4] All items, excluding $getFrame$ and $displayFrame$, do not form any cycle of any possible period and, for clarity, they are not included in the table.

The set of frequent triples is highly redundant since it includes all possible combinations between items, periods and transactions included in the ternary relation $\mathcal{Y}$. A *lossless reduced representation* of this set was introduced by Wille [22] and named *triadic concepts*. Saying the representation is lossless means that it is possible to reconstruct the set of frequent triples from the set of triadic concepts without any extra information.

DEFINITION 7. *A **triadic concept** of a triadic context $(\mathcal{I}, \mathcal{P}, \mathcal{D}, \mathcal{Y})$ is a triple (I, P, T) with $I \subseteq \mathcal{I}$, $P \subseteq \mathcal{P}$ and $T \subseteq \mathcal{D}$, such that none of its three components can be enlarged without violating the condition $I \times P \times T \subseteq \mathcal{Y}$.*

EXAMPLE 6. *In Table 4, we can observe the set of triadic concepts extracted from the set of frequent triples obtained from the dataset shown in Table 3. The triples forming this set are triadic concepts since it is not possible to extend any of the attributes of the triple without violating the relation $\mathcal{Y}$.*

Table 4: Set of triadic concepts

Triadic Concepts
$T_1(\{getFrame, displayFrame\}, \{2\}, \{t_1, t_3, t_5, t_8, t_{10}\})$
$T_2(\{getFrame, displayFrame\}, \{2,4\}, \{t_1, t_5\})$
$T_3(\{getFrame, displayFrame\}, \{2,5\}, \{t_3, t_5, t_8, t_{10}\})$
$T_4(\{getFrame, displayFrame\}, \{2,3,5\}, \{t_5, t_8\})$
$T_5(\{getFrame, displayFrame\}, \{2,3,4,5\}, \{t_5\})$

It can be observed that the set of triadic concepts is a lossless representation of the set of frequent periodic patterns even if they are presented using a different notation. Moreover, it is important to note that the set of triadic concepts presented on Table 4 is considerably smaller than the set of frequent periodic patterns presented in Table 2.

This set can be translated into a set of frequent periodic patterns by calculating the cycles included in the set of transactions of each triadic concept. For instance, $T_2(\{getFrame, displayFrame\}, \{2,4\}, \{t_1, t_5\})$ contains only one cycle of period 4 with transactions t_1 and t_5 which would give us the periodic pattern $(\{getFrame, displayFrame\}, 4, 2, \{(1,2)\})$ (period=4, support=2, cycle offset=1 and cycle length=2) which is P_9 from Table 2, being able to deduce as well P_7 and P_8 since their itemsets are subsets of $\{getFrame, displayFrame\}$.

Nevertheless, this set still contains redundant information in terms of redundant periods. For example, if we consider the triadic concepts T_1 and T_2 from the set of triadic concepts shown in Table 4, we can see that T_2 is "included" in T_1, i.e. they have the same itemset and the transactions belonging to T_2 are a subset of the transactions belonging to T_1 and therefore, period 4 of T_2 can be "deduced" from the set of transactions of T_1. As a result, T_2 can be removed without losing information. The same logic can be applied to T_3, T_4 and T_5, reducing the set to pattern T_1.

The way of deducing T_2 from T_1 is by calculating the possible periods between all transactions in T_1, and then generating the cycles belonging to each period, this way, from T_1 we can obtain periods 2 ($\{t_1, t_3, t_5, t_8, t_{10}\}$), 3 ($\{t_5, t_8\}$), 4 ($\{t_1, t_5\}$) and 5 ($\{t_3, t_8, t_{10}\}$). The last step is to calculate the maximal subsets involving several periods on the same set of transactions as is the case with t_1 and t_5 which are found in periods 2 and 4 generating the triadic concept ($\{getFrame, displayFrame\}, \{2, 4\}, \{t_1, t_5\}$).

In order to obtain a reduced representation of the set of triadic concepts we propose removing triadic concepts with redundant periods. For this, we present here the definition of *minimal periodic generator* which allows us to extract the set of triadic concepts that does not contain redundant periods.

4.2 Minimal Periodic Generators

In general terms, a minimal generator is the smallest pattern that will determine a closed pattern using the closure operator [18]. In this context, a minimal periodic generator is the triadic concept with the smallest set of periods and the biggest set of transactions that can determine another triadic concept using the method introduced above. For it to determine another triadic concept they have to share the same itemset, it has to include all transactions of the other triadic concept and have a smaller set of periods than the other triadic concept. Indeed, the set of periods of the minimal periodic generator is a subset of the set of periods of the other triadic concept. This is because the set of transactions of the triadic concept are included in the set of transactions of the minimal periodic generator, and therefore all those transactions have associated the periods of the minimal periodic generator and a few more.

DEFINITION 8. *A triadic concept* (I, P, T) *is a **minimal periodic generator** if there does not exist any other triadic concept* (I', P', T') *such that* $I = I'$, $P' \subset P$ *and* $T' \supset T$.

EXAMPLE 7. *In Table 5, we can observe the set of minimal periodic generators extracted from the set of triadic concepts shown in Table 4. For instance, $T_2(\{getFrame, displayFrame\}, \{2, 4\}, \{t_1, t_5\})$ is not a minimal periodic generator since there exists $T_1(\{getFrame, displayFrame\}, \{2\}, \{t_1, t_3, t_5, t_8, t_{10}\})$ with the same itemset $\{getFrame, displayFrame\}$, a smaller set of periods $\{2\} \subset \{2, 4\}$ and a bigger set of transactions $\{t_1, t_3, t_5, t_8, t_{10}\} \supset \{t_1, t_5\}$.*

Table 5: Set of minimal periodic generator

Minimal Periodic Generators
$M_1(\{getFrame, displayFrame\}, \{2\}, \{t_1, t_3, t_5, t_8, t_{10}\})$

It is important to note that the set of minimal periodic generators shown in Table 5 is considerably smaller than the set of triadic concepts shown in Table 4, and therefore smaller than the set of frequent periodic patterns shown in Table 2, and that it does not contain redundant periods.

In order to fit the periodic pattern notation introduced in Definition 3, the set of minimal periodic generators should be post-processed. For each minimal periodic generator the set of periods is extracted. Then, for each period in the set of periods, the set of cycles corresponding to that period is generated by reading the set of transactions, generating a

new periodic pattern containing the period and the set of cycles.

In the example, from Table 5 which contains only one minimal periodic generator $M_1(\{getFrame, displayFrame\}, \{2\}, \{t_1, t_3, t_5, t_8, t_{10}\})$, we obtain the frequent periodic pattern $P(\{getFrame, displayFrame\}, 2, 5, \{(1, 3)(8, 2)\})$, which corresponds to P_3 from Table 2. This is a reduced representation of the set of frequent periodic patterns containing enough information to deduce all other frequent periodic patterns. As explained in the previous section, the set of triadic concepts can be deduced from the set of minimal periodic generators. Then, the whole set of frequent periodic patterns can be deduced from the set of triadic concepts by generating all triples contained in the set and then grouping them by item and period (taking into account all possible combinations between the items to form the itemsets).

5. MINING PERIODIC PATTERNS

In this section, we introduce an algorithm to mine minimal periodic generators from a dataset, called *PerMiner*. We also present a tool called *Competitors Finder* that helps to identify pairs of "competitors", pairs of periodic patterns where a pattern breaks the periodicity of another pattern. This tool helps to identify possible conflicts between different entities in the system.

Algorithm 1 Periodic Pattern Miner

1: **procedure** $PerMiner(I, D, min\_sup)$
Input: Itemset I, dataset D, minimum support min_sup
Output: All frequent periodic patterns that occur in D
2:   $TS := TripleMiner(I, D, min\_sup)$
3:   $TC := $ DATA-PEELER (TS, min_sup)
4:   $MPG := MPGMiner(TC)$
5:   $FPP := PostProcess(MPG)$
6:   $Print(FPP)$
7: **end procedure**

The *PerMiner* algorithm in Algorithm 1, is divided into three steps:

1. The set of triples TS is generated. All possible periods with their transactions are calculated for individual items and then outputted in the form of triples.

2. The set of triadic concepts TC is generated from the set of triples TS. For this step an existing algorithm called DATA-PEELER [3] has been used.

3. The set of minimal periodic generators MPG is generated from the set of triadic concepts TC.

The set of minimal periodic generators MPG set is then transformed into frequent periodic patterns before being outputted.

The procedure $TripleMiner$ in Algorithm 2 generates all triples (i, p, t), i.e. for each item and for each possible period in the range $[1..|\mathcal{D}|/min\_sup]$ it searches all cycles of the selected period with transactions containing the selected item. The objective of this function is to transform our dataset into a triadic context exploitable by DATA-PEELER.

The function $build\_triples$ in Algorithm 3 is used by *TripleMiner* to generate all triples of a given item and a given period. For this, it scans the support set of the item i, given

Algorithm 2 Triple Miner

1: **procedure** $TripleMiner(I, D, min\_sup)$
Input: Itemset I, dataset D, minimum support min_sup
Output: All triples that occur in D
2: $TS \Leftarrow \emptyset$
3: **for all** $i \in I$ **do**
4:     **for all** $p \in [1, D.size/min\_sup]$ **do**
5:       $TS := TS \cup build\_triples(i, p, D)$
6:     **end for**
7: **end for**
8: **return** TS
9: **end procedure**

by $D[\{i\}]$, which is the set of transactions of D in which i occurs. For each transaction in $D[\{i\}]$, the function tries to build a cycle of the given period starting in that transaction. If a cycle is found, its length being at least two transactions, the cycle is transformed in triples and added to the output list. Visited transactions are marked to avoid generating redundant cycles.

Algorithm 3 Build triples

1: **function** $build\_triples(i, p, D)$
Input: Item i, period p, dataset D
Output: Set of triples of item i and period p
2: $L_T \leftarrow \emptyset$
3: **for all** $t \in D[\{i\}]$ **do**
4:     **if** t not visited yet **then**
5:       $t \leftarrow visited$; $len \leftarrow 0$; $next \leftarrow tid(t)$
6:       **while** $t_{next} \in D[\{i\}]$ **do**
7:         $t_{next} \leftarrow visited$; $len := len + 1$; $next := next + p$
8:       **end while**
9:       **if** $len > 2$ **then**
10:         **while** $len > 0$ **do**
11:           $L_T := L_T \cup (i, p, tid(t) + ((len - 1) * p))$
12:         **end while**
13:       **end if**
14:     **end if**
15: **end for**
16: **return** L_T
17: **end function**

DATA-PEELER generates all triadic concepts, containing at least min_sup transactions, contained in the set of triples generated by $TripleMiner$. Then, the procedure MPG-$Miner$ in Algorithm 4 is in charge of generating the set of minimal periodic generators from the set of triadic concepts generated in the previous step. Following Definition 8, the function compares the set of triadic concepts two by two, and if it finds a triadic concept that is "included" in another triadic concept in the set, the former is deleted from the list. As explained in section 4.2, by "included" we mean that they have the same itemset, the set of periods of the latter is included in the set of periods of the former, and the set of transactions of the former is included in the set of periods of the latter.

The procedure $PostProcessMPG$ in Algorithm 5 generates a set of frequent periodic patterns from the set of minimal periodic generators MPG. For each period p in the set of periods P of each minimal periodic generator (I, P, T), $build\_cycles$ generates all possible cycles of period p that

Algorithm 4 Minimal Periodic Generators Miner

1: **procedure** $MPGMiner(CTS)$
Input: Set of triadic concepts TC
Output: Set of minimal periodic generators MPG
2: $MPG \Leftarrow TC$
3: **for all** $(I, P, T) \in MPG$ **do**
4:     **for all** $(I', P', T') \in MPG$
                with $(I, P, T) \neq (I', P', T')$ **do**
5:       **if** $I == I'$ AND $P \subset P'$ AND $T \supset T'$ **then**
6:         $MPG := MPG \setminus (I', P', T')$
7:       **end if**
8:     **end for**
9: **end for**
10: **return** MPG
11: **end function**

can be formed using the set of transactions T of the minimal periodic generator.

Algorithm 5 Post processing of the set of Minimal Periodic Generators

1: **procedure** $PostProcessMPG(MPG)$
Input: Set of minimal periodic generators MPG
Output: Set of frequent periodic patterns FPP
2: $FPP \Rightarrow \emptyset$
3: **for all** $(I, P, T) \in MPG$ **do**
4:     **for all** $p \in P$ **do**
5:       $FPP.add(I, p, build\_cycles(p, T))$
6:     **end for**
7: **end for**
8: **return** FPP
9: **end function**

The function add includes the itemset I, with the period p and the associated cycles to the list of frequent periodic patterns in the form of frequent periodic pattern. If there exists a frequent periodic pattern in the set with the same itemset and the same period, the sets of cycles are joined, checking if there exist overlap between any two cycles of the set. If an overlap between two cycles is found, the frequent periodic pattern is split in as many patterns as needed in order not to have overlaps between the cycles of the same set. Functions $build\_cycles$ and add are not detailed here due to lack of space, but their implementation is straightforward.

5.1 Competitors Finder

Here we introduce a new analysis tool called *Competitors Finder* that helps to identify pairs of competitor periodic patterns from the set of frequent periodic patterns deduced from the set of minimal periodic generators. This tool allows the developer to easily identify possible conflicts between different parts of the system, i.e. between the application and the operating system, between different modules or drivers of the operating system, and so on, saving a significant amount of time to the developer. In this sense, we consider that a conflict or competition between two patterns is simply the inverse of the overlap between the two patterns. This is, if one pattern P_1 disrupts another pattern P_2, then during the disruption P_1 will be active but not P_2. So, our objective is to automatically identify these situations.

The procedure $CompetitorsFinder$ in Algorithm 6 receives the set of frequent periodic patterns deduced from

Algorithm 6 Competitors Finder

1: **procedure** $CompetitorsFinder(MPG', min\_ratio)$
Input: Set of frequent periodic patterns MPG', minimum rate of competition min_ratio
Output: Set of pairs of competitors $MaxComp$
2:    $MaxComp \Leftarrow \emptyset$
3:    **for all** $p \in MPG'$ **do**
4:      $max\_ratio := 0$
5:      **for all** $p' \in MPG'$ with $p \neq p'$ **do**
6:        $comp\_ratio := competition\_ratio(p, p')$
7:        **if** $comp\_ratio > max\_ratio$ **then**
8:          $max\_ratio \Leftarrow comp\_ratio; max\_pat \Leftarrow p'$
9:        **end if**
10:     **end for**
11:     **if** $(max\_pat, p, *) \notin MaxComp$ AND $max\_ratio \geq min\_ratio$ **then**
12:       $MaxComp.add(p, max\_pat, max\_ratio)$
13:     **end if**
14:    **end for**
15:    **return** $MaxComp$
16: **end procedure**

the set of minimal periodic generators, and for each frequent periodic pattern it searches the pattern that is the most in competition with it. For each pattern, this procedure compares it with all other patterns and calculates the competition ratio by invoking $competition\_ratio$ function. In max_ratio and max_pat, the procedure stores the maximum ratio found and the pattern linked to that ratio.

When the pattern has been compared to all other patterns, the procedure checks if the competition ratio is bigger than the competition ratio threshold given as an input, and as well, whether the two patterns were already stated as competitors, in which case they are not outputted to avoid repetitions. Finally the list of competitors with their competition ratio is returned by this procedure.

Algorithm 7 Competition Ratio Calculator

1: **function** $competition\_ratio(P, P')$
Input: Two periodic patterns
Output: The ratio of competition between P and P'
2:    **for all** $c_i, c_{i+1} \in P.cycles$ **do**
3:      **for all** $c' \in P'.cycles$ **do**
4:        $match\ += calculate\_coexecution(c, c')$
5:        $match\ += calculate\_cogap(c_i, c_{i+1}, c')$
6:      **end for**
7:    **end for**
8:    **return** $(1 - ((num\_trans - match)/num\_trans)) * 100;$
9: **end function**

The function $competition\_ratio$ in Algorithm 7 calculates the competition ratio between two frequent periodic patterns. By comparing the cycles between them, it uses the function $calculate\_coexecution$ to calculate the area of coexecution of two cycles, and the function $calculate\_cogap$ to calculate the area between two cycles of the first periodic patterns (gap) not occupied by a cycle of the second periodic pattern. The sum of all the output values of these two functions is called matching ratio, and the competition ratio is the result of calculating just the opposite, i.e. 100% - matching ratio.

6. EXPERIMENTAL RESULTS

In this section, we present several experiments carried out on embedded multimedia application traces. The experiments show that periodic pattern mining can help to debug applications by automatically extracting representative information from their execution traces. These experiments could have been carried out by analyzing exclusively the set of frequent periodic patterns but it would have taken a lot longer since the difference in size between the set of frequent periodic patterns and the set of minimal periodic generators is considerable as stated below.

Figures 5 and 6 correspond to two visualization tools developed to facilitate the analysis of the periodic patterns. In Figure 6 the list of periodic patterns can be explored by navigating the list of itemsets. When the user selects an itemset from the list, the periodic patterns associated with that itemset, one for each period, are shown on the bottom part of the tool. Each line corresponds to a periodic pattern with the period value on the left part of the figure and the occurrences on the right. The occurrences are visualized by a sequence of vertical lines representing all possible transactions on the dataset (from left to right). A line is colored when the corresponding transaction forms part of the selected periodic pattern. Similarly, Figure 5 shows the list of pairs of competitors. When a pair of competitors is selected, the occurrences of both patterns are shown, pattern 1 on top and pattern 2 at the bottom.

6.1 HNDTest Application

In this example, we retrieved a trace from an execution of a video and audio decoding test application called *HNDTest*, test application for *STMicroelectronics* development boards, on an *ST40* processor, introduced in Section 2.1. Then, we preprocessed it, as explained in Section 2.2, in order to split the trace into frames. The execution trace occupied 7.2 MB of memory. After preprocessing, the dataset contained 240 frames, and with a support threshold of 10% our algorithm mined 859 minimal periodic generators, faster to analyze than 7.2 MB of execution trace. This trace would produce 109,668 triadic concepts and 38,459 frequent periodic patterns. Therefore, we can observe that mining minimal periodic generators considerably reduces the number of patterns to analyze.

The bigger number of triadic concepts with respect to the number of frequent periodic patterns can be explained by the fact that the number of periods in frequent periodic patterns is limited to one per pattern while in the triadic concepts is not limited. Consequently, all possible combinations of all lengths of the set of possible periods are generated as triadic concepts. All these extra patterns are then removed by the minimal periodic generator miner. Also, the transactions of the dataset used in this example have an average of 8 items per transaction which produces patterns with relatively short itemsets that consequently do not produce many combinations in terms of frequent periodic patterns.

As part of the analysis of the set of frequent periodic patterns mined, we used the tool *Competitors Finder* (see Section 5.1) to identify possible conflicts between different entities of the system. We highlight here a pair of competitors found by the tool involving on one hand, *Interrupt 16*, which is the clock of the processor, and *Interrupt 168*, which is a USB port interrupt, and on the other hand, a context

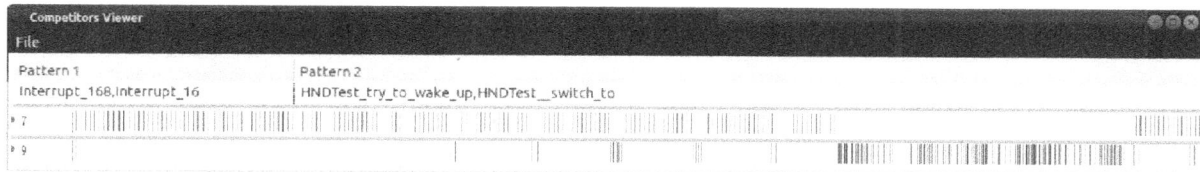

Figure 5: Conflict between application and operating system

switch and a system call (`try_to_wake_up`) involving thread *HNDTest*.

In Figure 5 we can observe that these two patterns are in competition: the top pattern (interrupts) stops executing when the bottom pattern (*HNDTest*) increases its frequency. In this context, the processor periodically polls the device connected to the USB port to check whether it has data to transfer. This is achieved using interrupt 168. When *HNDTest* increases its activity, it masks the interrupts and therefore prevents the processor from transferring any incoming data from the USB port, which causes a delay in transmission. This might have further repercussions if the USB reception buffer becomes full while waiting to transfer the data, causing the data to be overwritten.

6.2 Gstreamer Application

GStreamer is a pipeline-based multimedia framework that has been adopted by many different corporations such as Nokia, Texas Instruments and so on. In this experiment, we used a trace that registered an audio decoding applications, using GStreamer, while playing back an audio file. The application was executed on a platform that contained an ARM processor over an Orly SoC [20]. Our algorithm, with a support threshold of 10%, mined 1,467 minimal periodic generators. This trace would have produced 21,588 triadic concepts and 3,086,321 frequent periodic patterns.

In this example, the number of frequent periodic patterns is much bigger than the number of triadic concepts. This is because the transactions in the dataset of this example are very long, 35 items per transaction in average, and therefore generate patterns with a long itemset. For this reason, the number of frequent periodic patterns per itemset and per period is large since there is a frequent periodic pattern for each combination (of any length) of the items in the itemset.

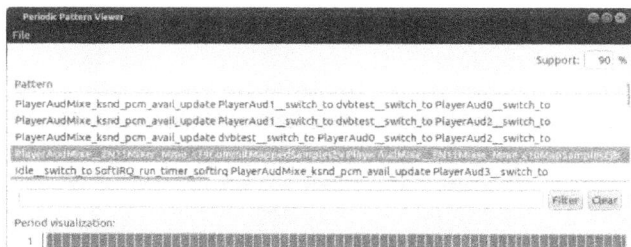

Figure 6: Trace visualization

In this context, the mixer maps audio samples every 32ms, so we decided to split the trace using a time interval of 32ms to see whether the expected period was preserved or not. In the minimal periodic generators mined, we expected to find some patterns with a period of 1 (32ms) over all the data. Surprisingly, the patterns found exhibit *gaps* in the periodicity (vertical white lines in period visualization in Figure 6) showing that the application is unable to keep up the expected mixing rate.

The application developers investigated these *gaps* and found that there was a bug in the calculation of an interrupt period. This interrupt was in charge of flushing a buffer of samples read from memory but it was being generated too late causing buffer overflows and higher level drivers to underflow when operating double buffered.

Discussion. In these experiments, we have shown that our approach allows developers to quickly discover certain problems in the execution of their applications by automatically analyzing their execution traces, that otherwise would have taken a long time to be discovered by manually analyzing execution traces.

7. RELATED WORK

Pattern mining is starting to play an important role in system analysis, even more in embedded systems, where tracing is widely used in order to analyze the system while avoiding high intrusiveness.

First uses of pattern mining in system analysis focused on detecting bugs, e.g. introduced by copying-and-pasting kernel source code [12] or caused by the violation of programing rules [13], or more generally detecting systemic problems [9]. Lo et al. [14] studied how to classify software behaviors, obtained by pattern mining of known normal and failing execution traces, in order to detect failures in future executions of the system.

Recently, Chang et al. [4] worked on system verification using pattern mining in order to extract assertions from simulated traces of the system being validated. In terms of performance analysis, Zou et al. [23] used pattern mining to reduce vast amounts of hardware sample data into a set of easier-to-analyze frequent instruction sequences, in order to help to analyze the performance of the system.

Nevertheless, none of the previous studies have applied periodic pattern mining to system analysis.

The first studies carried out on periodicity focused on association rules. As an example Ozden et al. [17] looked for cyclic association rules in transactional databases. Their objective was to find association rules that hold in all segments of the database over a given period. This kind of periodicity, called perfect periodicity, is very useful for certain contexts but is too restrictive in our case.

Han et al. [6, 5] introduced a certain confidence in the periodicity which means that the pattern does not need to be found in all instances, but allows certain misses. Nevertheless, when there is a gap in the periodicity of the pattern, this gap is always regular, i.e. multiple of the period.

The first study to include irregularity in the periodicity was carried out by Ma et al. [15]. In their study, the authors extended the concept of partial periodicity introduced by Han et al. considering that periodic behavior might be found in part of the dataset and it is not necessarily expected to be persistent. The authors allowed gaps in the periodicity but they restricted their sizes to a certain time window.

None of the previous studies regarding periodic pattern mining have allowed for irregular gaps without any restriction on the length of the gap. It is important for us to allow irregularities in the gaps in order to discover different types of periodic patterns, e.g. patterns that are periodic during certain segments of the trace with big gaps between those segments, or patterns with a regular periodicity but that every time there is a gap the pattern gets shifted by n positions.

Triadic Concept Analysis was first introduced by Rudolf Wille in 1995 [22, 10]. Since then, several algorithms that mine triadic concepts have been proposed, among them we can find CubeMiner proposed by Ji et al. [12], Trias proposed by Jaschke et al. [7] and Data-Peeler proposed by Cerf et al. [3]. The latter was chosen in this paper since the authors showed through an experimental comparison that their algorithm was more efficient than CubeMiner or Trias. Moreover, the authors generalized the computation of triples previously studied by [12] and [7] to a constraint-based approach for mining closed sets from n-ary relations. But none of the previous studies have applied ternary relation theory to mining periodic patterns.

8. CONCLUSIONS AND FUTURE WORK

In the context of analyzing traces of multimedia embedded applications, we have presented a new definition of periodic patterns that allows unrestricted-sized gaps in the periodicity. Moreover, we have presented a lossless representation of the set of frequent periodic patterns, called minimal periodic generators, that simplifies the analysis. Also, we have introduced an algorithm for mining such minimal periodic generators and a tool that identifies pairs of competitors from the set of minimal periodic generators.

Through experiments on execution traces, we have demonstrated how pattern mining can help to discover problems more quickly than manually analyzing raw execution traces. We have applied our mining method and our *Competitors Finder* tool to an execution trace and identified a conflict between the application and the operating system, demonstrating the interest of our approach.

We have also shown how discovering the periodic behavior of multimedia applications can help to pinpoint when this periodicity is lost and therefore what affects the expected execution of the application.

The scope of this paper is to present our approach, its applicability and its interest. We intent to study the use of other patterns such as sequences (ordered itemsets) which would help to discover other behaviors of the application, and therefore complete the analysis. Moreover, we are planning to design an algorithm to mine minimal periodic generators directly, without having to generate the set of triadic concepts, in order to increase efficiency.

9. REFERENCES

[1] R. Agrawal and R. Srikant. Fast algorithms for mining association rules in large databases. In *VLDB*, pages 487–499, San Francisco, CA, USA, 1994.

[2] S. Ayouni, A. Laurent, S. B. Yahia, and P. Poncelet. Mining closed gradual patterns. In *ICAISC*, pages 267–274, 2010.

[3] L. Cerf, J. Besson, C. Robardet, and J.-F. Boulicaut. Closed patterns meet n-ary relations. *TKDD*, 2009.

[4] P.-H. Chang and L.-C. Wang. Automatic assertion extraction via sequential data mining of simulation traces. In *ASPDAC*, pages 607–612, 2010.

[5] J. Han. Efficient mining of partial periodic patterns in time series database. In *ICDE*, pages 106–115, 1999.

[6] J. Han, W. Gong, and Y. Yin. Mining segment-wise periodic patterns in time-related databases. In *KDD*, pages 214–218, 1998.

[7] R. Jaschke, A. Hotho, C. Schmitz, B. Ganter, and G. Stumme. TRIAS An algorithm for mining iceberg tri-lattices. In *ICDM*, pages 907–911, 2006.

[8] R. Krishnakumar. Kernel korner: KProbes-A kernel debugger. *Linux J.*, 2005.

[9] C. LaRosa, L. Xiong, and K. Mandelberg. Frequent pattern mining for kernel trace data. In *SAC*, pages 880–885, 2008.

[10] F. Lehmann and R. Wille. A triadic approach to formal concept analysis. In *Conceptual Structures: Applications, Implementation and Theory*, volume 954 of *Lecture Notes in Computer Science*, pages 32–43. Springer Berlin / Heidelberg, 1995.

[11] Z. Li, Z. Chen, S. M. Srinivasan, and Y. Zhou. C-Miner: Mining block correlations in storage systems. In *FAST*, pages 173–186, 2004.

[12] Z. Li, S. Lu, S. Myagmar, and Y. Zhou. CP-Miner: Finding copy-paste and related bugs in large-scale software code. *TSE*, pages 176–192, 2006.

[13] Z. Li and Y. Zhou. PR-Miner: Automatically extracting implicit programming rules and detecting violations in large software code. In *ESEC/FSE*, 2005.

[14] D. Lo, H. Cheng, J. Han, S.-C. Khoo, and C. Sun. Classification of software behaviors for failure detection: a discriminative pattern mining approach. In *KDD*, pages 557–566, 2009.

[15] S. Ma and J. Hellerstein. Mining partially periodic event patterns with unknown periods. In *ICDE*, pages 205 –214, 2001.

[16] R. Mijat. Better trace for better software. White paper, ARM, 2010. http://www.arm.com/products/system-ip/debug-trace/index.php.

[17] B. Ozden, S. Ramaswamy, and A. Silberschatz. Cyclic association rules. In *ICDE*, pages 412 –421, Feb 1998.

[18] N. Pasquier, Y. Bastide, R. Taouil, and L. Lakhal. Efficient mining of association rules using closed itemset lattices. *Inf. Syst.*, 24(1):25–46, Mar. 1999.

[19] C. Prada-Rojas, V. Marangozova-Martin, K. Georgiev, J.-F. Mehaut, and M. Santana. Towards a Component-Based Observation of MPSoC. In *ICPPW*, pages 542–549, 2009.

[20] STMicroelectronics. Orly SoC. http://bit.ly/wUmu5Y.

[21] STMicroelectronics. STi7200-MBoard platform. http://bit.ly/z81nho.

[22] R. Wille. The basic theorem of triadic concept analysis. *Order*, 12:149–158, 1995.

[23] J. Zou, J. Xiao, R. Hou, and Y. Wang. Frequent instruction sequential pattern mining in hardware sample data. In *ICDM*, pages 1205–1210, 2010.

Smart Layers and Dumb Result: IO Characterization of an Android-Based Smartphone

Kisung Lee and Youjip Won

Dept. of Electronics and Computer Engineering
Hanyang University, Republic of Korea
{kisunglee|yjwon}@hanyang.ac.kr

ABSTRACT

In this paper, we offer an in-depth IO characterization of the Android-based smartphone. We analyze the IO behaviors of a total of 14 Android applications from six different categories. We examine the correlations among seven IO attributes: originating application, file type, IO size, IO type (read/write), random/sequential, block semantics (*Data/Metadata/Journal*), and session type (buffered vs. synchronous IO). For the purposes of our study, we develop Mobile Storage Analyzer (MOST), a framework for collecting IO attributes across layers. Let us summarize our findings briefly. SQLite, which is the most popular tool for maintaining persistent data in Android, puts too much burden on the storage. For example, a single SQLite operation (update or insert) results in at least 11 write operations being sent to the storage. These are for creating short-lived files, updating database tables, and accessing EXT4 *Journal*. From the storage point of view, more than 50% of writes are for EXT4 *Journal* updating. Excluding *Metadata* and *Journal* accesses, 60-80% of the writes are random. More than 50% of the writes are synchronous. 4KB IO accounts for 70% of all writes. In the Android platform, each SQLite and EXT4 filesystem requires a great amount of effort to ensure reliability in supporting transactions and journaling, respectively. When they are combined, the results are rather dumb. The operations of SQLite and EXT4, when combined, generate unnecessarily excessive write operations to the NAND-based storage. This not only degrades IO performance but also significantly reduces the lifetime of the underlying NAND flash storage. The results of this study clearly suggest that SQLite, EXT4, and the underlying NAND-based storage need to be completely overhauled and vertically integrated so as to properly and effectively incorporate their respective characteristics.

Categories and Subject Descriptors

C.3 [**Special-Purpose and Application-Based Systems**]: Real-time and embedded systems; D.4.3 [**OPERATING SYSTEMS**]: File Systems Management—*Access methods*; D.4.8 [**OPERATING SYSTEMS**]: Performance—*Measurements*

General Terms

Measurement, Performance

Keywords

Android, Smartphone, IO Characterization, NAND flash

1. INTRODUCTION

The smartphone is growing ever more popular. It is expected that over 800,000,000 smartphones will be sold in 2016 [8]. The smartphone has changed and continues to change the way people live. It provides a variety of extremely accessible functionalities, for example, social networking, picture management, music, and movies, to list only a few. Application programs in the smartphone have made all of these possible. While we are well familiar with the functions and features that these applications provide, little is known about how they interact with the underlying Operating System and underlying storage. IO access characteristics in enterprise servers [22], OLTP servers [17], Web servers [10], and desktop PCs [26, 13] are relatively well understood, but not in smartphones.

In this work, we aim to obtain a comprehensive understanding of how smartphone applications utilize and stress underlying storage. To that end, we analyze the interaction across software layers: applications, smartphone platform (Android OS), filesystem, and underlying storage device. For this purpose, we study the behaviors of the 14 representative smartphone applications. We categorize these into six groups: Web, legacy phone applications, SNS, Multimedia, System, and Game; further, we select one or more representative commodity applications from each of the categories. In our cross-layer IO characterization, we carefully select seven IO attributes to investigate the correlations among the IOs; The attributes are originating application, file type (.apk, .db), block type (*Metadata*, *Data*, and *Journal*), IO type (read/write), session type (buffered vs. synchronous), randomness, and IO size.

The well-defined layered structure of the modern Operating System makes it impossible to collect these IO attributes at a single point of observation. For example, at the block device layer, neither the file type nor the session type of a given IO operation is available. Thus, in this work, we develop Mobile Storage Analyzer (MOST), a framework for collecting and analyzing block IO operations of the Android smartphone. MOST, significantly, enables collection of all seven attributes at a block device level. It addresses three major issues: LBA-to-file mapping, LBA-to-process mapping, and retrospective mapping. First, MOST obtains file type information from the LBA. Second, MOST obtains the process information that *originally* triggered a given IO. The Android system delegates all IO requests to the dedicated kernel process. The kernel daemon, when observed at the block device level where the trace is captured, looks like the original process that generated the given IO request. Therefore, we modify the Linux kernel of Android to keep the process ID for a given IO. The third issue, which is the most intricate of the three, is the retrospective LBA-to-file mapping. The Android platform creates a large number of ephemeral files due to the SQLite operation. In MOST, LBA-to-file mapping is performed posthumously, so that it does not interfere with ongoing system behavior. However, posthumous analysis, if the owner file of the respective blocks has been deleted, inevitably yields orphan blocks. We modify the Linux kernel to capture IO operations to these short-lived files. MOST can perform LBA-to-file mapping retrospectively: this way, it can find the owner file even though that file had been deleted. MOST uses `blktrace` [11] and `debugfs` [24] to collect block level IO traces and to map LBA to files in the EXT4 filesystem, respectively. MOST is available at [1]. Let us summarize our findings as follows.

Smart layers and dumb result: Android OS exports the SQLite database to allow applications to manage their own persistent data in a structured manner. Most Android platforms use the EXT4 filesystem to manage underlying NAND flash-based storage devices. Both SQLite and EXT4 adopt sophisticated techniques for reliable maintenance of data. SQLite creates temporary files (logs) for each database operation to support transactions [5], and EXT4 adopts journaling [23]. But when they work in combination, the result is rather dumb. SQLite calls *fsync()* three times in every database operation. In EXT4, each *fsync()* entails two to three IOs for *Journal* writes. Combining all of these, we observe that a single SQLite operation (update/insert) results in at least 11 block IOs to the storage device! This excessive IO behavior not only negatively affects IO performance, but also significantly shortens the endurance of NAND storage devices, which is of the utmost concern in adopting NAND flash for computing devices.

Most write operations are 4KB: In all applications, more than 70% of write operations are 4KB. They consist mostly of database updates from SQLite, file creation and deletion by SQLite, and *Journal* writes. NAND storage for mobile devices (e.g. eMMC [9] and UFS [6]), therefore, should focus on efficient handling of 4KB random write operations.

Buffered IO is rare: We observe that in smartphone applications, for example Contact, SMS, Browser and SNS applications, buffered IO represents less than 30% of write. This is an IO characteristic unique to the smartphone. This phenomenon, in fact, has not been observed in the desktop or server environment, because smartphone applications use SQLite to manage persistent data, exploiting *fsync()* to preserve the atomicity of database operations. This phenomenon dictates that the filesystem and NAND flash storage for mobile devices should devote greater efforts to opti-

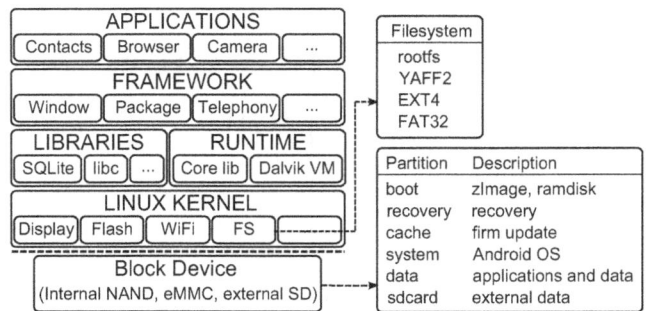

Figure 1: Android Architecture and Storage Partition

Table 1: Storage Partition of typical Android smartphones: Nexus One, Nexus S, and Galaxy S2.

	Internal Flash		eMMC		External SD	
Nexus One	boot	rootfs	None		sdcard	FAT32
	recovery	rootfs			-	-
	cache	yaffs2			-	-
	system	yaffs2			-	-
	data	yaffs2			-	-
Nexus S	boot	rootfs	system	EXT4	None	
	recovery	rootfs	data	EXT4		
	cache	yaffs2	sdcard	FAT32		
Galaxy S2	None		boot	rootfs	sdcard	FAT32
			recovery	rootfs	-	-
			cache	EXT4	-	-
			system	EXT4	-	-
			data	EXT4	-	-
			sdcard	FAT32	-	-

mizing themselves for delivery of more synchronous IO performance.

Each Storage Partition has unique access characteristics: Android OS devotes great care to harboring files with similar characteristics at the same partition. Because IO requests to individual partitions exhibit unique IO characteristics, this approach makes partition management easier and simpler. However, since the physical and logical addresses of a block do not coincide in NAND flash, the blocks in each partition are not likely to be clustered together in the storage device. Therefore, efforts to maintain files with similar characteristics in the same partition should be exploited in the NAND flash.

The results of this study provide insights into and directions for designing future smartphone filesystems and storage subsystems.

The remainder of this paper is organized as follows. In Section 2, we briefly describe the architecture of Android OS along with the storage configurations of Android smartphones. Section 3 discusses the measurement environment, and Section 4 introduces Mobile Storage Analyzer (MOST), a framework for tracing IO operations in Android smartphones. Sections 5 and 6 provide the results of an analysis of the IO characteristics of applications and daily usage. Section 7 discusses the future of smartphone filesystem design. Section 8 acknowledges prior efforts, and Section 9 concludes the paper.

Table 2: Applications and their use. [ ] denotes short names in figures. * denotes pre-installed in Nexus S. Others are installed from the market. All applications are executed for one minute and repeated ten times.

Category	Application	Scenarios
Web	Dolphin Browser [Br]	1. Execute browser and open "www.google.com." 2. Web search by any keyword. 3. View results and repeat web searching two more times.
Basic	Contact* [Con]	1. Execute Contact and scroll lists. 2. Search a person by name. 3. Delete the item. 4. Create a new item. [Precondition: Contact is filled with 200 addresses.]
	SMS* [Sms]	1. Execute SMS. 2. Write a message. 3. Send a message. 4. Receive a message.
SNS	Twitter [Twi]	1. Execute Twitter and view new tweets. 2. Write a status.
	Facebook [Fb]	1. Execute Facebook and view new messages. 2. Write a status.
	Kakao-Talk [Kt]	1. Execute Kakao-Talk and choose a counterpart. 2. Start to exchange messages.
Multimedia	Camera* [C]	1. Execute Camera and take a picture. 2. Take four more pictures.
	Camcorder* [Cc]	1. Execute Camcorder and start to record. 2. After 50 seconds, stop recording.
	Media player* [Me]	1. Execute Media player and select a movie file. 2. Play the movie and change volume.
	Music player* [Mu]	1. Execute Music player and select a music file. 2. Play the music and change volume.
	Gallery* [Gal]	1. Execute Gallery and scroll thumbnails. 2. Select a picture and view. 3. Repeat this five times. [Precondition: Gallery is filled with 500 pictures.]
	Youtube [You]	1. Execute Youtube and search a video by any keyword. 2. View the video.
System	Install* [Ins]	1. Execute Android market and select one application. 2. Install the application. (We select 3-5MB applications that can be completely installed in 1 minute.)
Game	Angry birds [Gam]	1. Execute Angry birds. 2. Select a level and play the game.

2. BACKGROUND

2.1 Brief note on Android OS

Android [7] is an open-source software stack for mobile devices. It consists of the Operating System (Linux kernel), Java Virtual Machine (Dalvik) and various libraries. Figure 1 shows the Android architecture. Android applications are written in Java and packaged to the Android application package file (.apk). Android includes a set of libraries used by various components: SQLite, libc, Media libraries, and others. The Android application runs on its own process, with its own instance of the Dalvik virtual machine. The Dalvik VM executes files in the Dalvik Executable (.dex) format, which is optimized for a minimal memory footprint.

2.2 Storage Configuration for Smartphones

Android manages several filesystem partitions: /boot, /recovery, /cache, /system, and /data. Table 1 summarizes the storage configuration and partition information for three smartphones recently deployed to the market: Nexus One [2] (Jan. 2010), Nexus S [3] (Dec. 2010), and Galaxy S2 [4] (May 2011). The storage configuration of the smartphone evolves with time. Nexus One, the first-generation Android reference phone, has a 512MB internal raw NAND flash and an external SD slot. It uses the YAFFS2 filesystem to manage the storage partitions (/cache, /system, and /data) in the internal NAND flash. Beginning from Android 2.3 (Nexus S), EXT4 filesystem is used to manage /system, and /data on an eMMC block device (16GB). Galaxy S2, the most recent among the three phones, does not have any internal flash storage. It uses eMMC to harbor all storage partitions. The EXT4 filesystem is used to manage storage partitions on eMMC; YAFFS2 filesystem is no longer used. In this paper, we focus on the /system, /data, and /sdcard partitions because Android applications only access these partitions. The rest of the partitions are only used for firmware updates (/cache) and boot image maintenance (/boot, /recovery).

3. MEASUREMENT ENVIRONMENT

3.1 Device: Nexus S

We select an Android smartphone, Nexus S [3] which runs Android OS 2.3 (Gingerbread) based on Linux Kernel 2.6.35.9. This phone is a reference model that represents the standard architecture of Android OS. As most Android-based smartphones have a similar storage configuration, the results of this study should be sufficiently representative. Table 1 shows the partition information of Nexus S. The /system partition (512MB) is mounted with READ-ONLY. It contains Android-executable files and pre-installed applications. The /data partition (1GB) is mounted with READ-WRITE and contains the user's data. These data can include contacts, messages, settings, and applications. Both /system and /data are formatted with EXT4. The /sdcard partition (13.3GB) is formatted with FAT32, and can be used to store external data such as media files, documents, and other types.

3.2 Applications

Smartphone is a literally multipurpose device. It is used, additionally to its phone functionality, as a Camera, MP3 player, Web browser, and SNS. For any comprehensive study, selection of a sufficiently representative set of applications is mandatory. We define six application categories (Basic, Web, SNS, Multimedia, System, and Game) and select 14 applications from among them.

Basic: Contact is an address book that stores people's names, phone numbers, and other identifying information. Contact operations such as search are frequently shared by many basic applications, for example SMS, VOICE CALL, and others. SMS is a means of communicating with others in traditional mobile phones, but its usage is gradually decreasing with the popularity of SNS applications.

Web: Web browser is an extremely popular application on the Internet, and is included in the smartphone as well. We select the Dolphin browser for our test, which is very popular in the Android OS.

SNS: Social Networking Service (SNS) is another very popular application for the smartphone. We select Facebook, Twitter, and Kakao-Talk, which latter is one of the most rapidly growing IP-based multi-party chatting services.

Multimedia: We select six applications in this category: Camera, Camcorder, Media player, Music player, Gallery, and Youtube. These applications are enabling the smartphone to replace traditional handheld multimedia devices such as portable media players (PMP), MP3 players, and digital cameras. Youtube provides an interactive means of sharing videos; users can easily upload and play videos through this website. This represents a very different mode of access from that of traditional Media players, which store and play video files locally in the device.

System: The installing application is another new feature of the smartphone. It enables the user to install new applications in the Application market, and greatly expands the usability of smartphones.

Game: Advanced computing ability makes the smartphone a powerful video game console. We select Angry birds, which is a very popular puzzle game in Android and also in Apple's iOS.

3.3 Collecting Data

Table 2 summarizes the application scenarios. All of the applications were executed for one minute and repeated ten times. To verify the generality of the application-specific IO traces, we also collected IO traces from daily usage. We installed the Mobile Storage Analyzer to the smartphone being tested, and collected IO traces for seven different 24 hour periods from Dec. 1 to Dec. 14, 2011. The purpose was to examine the aggregate storage access pattern of the smartphone. We used the smartphone in the normal ways, without any specific scenarios. Web surfing, exchanging messages, listening to music, and playing games are among the typical functionalities tested. As the smartphone is a personal and private device that users are reluctant to share with others, installing a modified Android kernel on the smartphones tested, and collecting traces in the regular manner, is neither an easy task nor a major part of this work. Collecting IO traces from just one user served our purpose adequately well in verifying the results of our analysis.

4. MOST: MOBILE STORAGE ANALYZER

For the purposes of the present study, we develop Mobile Storage Analyzer (MOST). It consists of (i) a modified Linux kernel that maintains processes and file-related information for IOs; (ii) a block analyzer that enables identification of a file for a given block, and (iii) `blktrace` utility. Figure 2 provides a schematic illustration of MOST. We make MOST publicly available at [1].

Due to the layered structure of a modern IO subsystem, it is not possible to identify session-related information at the block device level. When an IO request is passed across layers, for example, from the filesystem to the block device layer, the session-related information (i.e., file id and process id), are lost. In order to be able to analyze the relationships among blocks, respective files, and processes, the information needs to be collected from the different layers. MOST collects the IO trace at the block device driver level and deduces the file information and the process information for each respective block. MOST addresses three reverse-

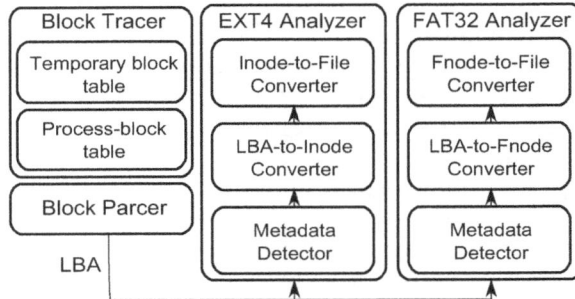

Figure 2: Mobile Storage Analyzer

Table 3: Output of Mobile Storage Analyzer

1	IO completion time
2	Flags for read and write
3	Sector address and IO size
4	Process id and process name
5	Block type: *Metadata*, *Journal*, and *Data* block
6	File name in case of the *Data* block

mapping issues: LBA-to-file mapping, LBA-to-process mapping, and retrospective LBA mapping.

For LBA-to-file mapping, MOST can reverse-map the disk block to the respective file where it belongs. It accepts a logical block number as an input, and generates a file name. MOST uses `debugfs` [24] to reverse-map the block in the EXT4 filesystem, and an in-house module for the FAT32 filesystem.

MOST identifies the original process that issued a given IO. In Android, *mmcqd* daemon manages the mmc card device driver and is responsible for issuing all block IOs. Without any modification, `blktrace` reports that all block IOs are initiated by the *mmcqd* daemon, which is not the information we are interested in. We create the process-block table in the Android Kernel. The entry of the table is <LBA, process id>. When the IO scheduler inserts the IO request into the queue, MOST inserts the <LBA, process id> information into process-block table. MOST references the process-block table later in order to retrieve the process id with a given LBA.

MOST allows retrospective LBA mapping. In Android, we find that many files are short-lived and are created and rapidly deleted by SQLite. Proper understanding how these files are utilized is very significant. Although they are short-lived, these files are all *fsync()*ed to NAND storage, which greatly affects system performance. We need the file information for a given LBA when the trace is recorded, not when posthumously analyzed. When MOST initiates the analysis procedure for a given LBA, the temporary file where the block belonged might have been deleted and therefore cannot be found. To address this issue, MOST creates a file-block table in the Android kernel. A file-block table is an array of <LBA, file>. When the IO scheduler plugs in the LBA to the scheduler queue, MOST inserts <LBA, file> entry to file-block table. Later, MOST references this table to obtain the file information for a given LBA. To reduce the table size, MOST inserts an <LBA, file> entry only for temporary files, that is, when the file extension is `.db-journal`, `.db-mjxxxx`, `.bak`, or `tmp`. When `blktrace` creates a log for

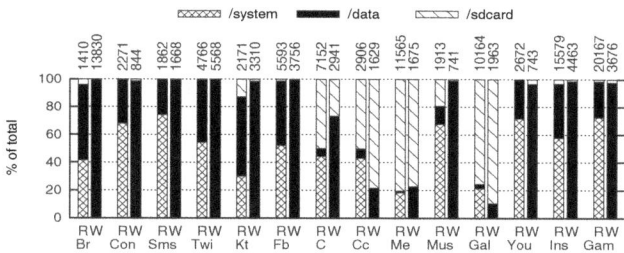

Figure 3: IO distribution on each partition. The number at the end of each bar indicates the number of IO for R (Read) and W (Write), respectively.

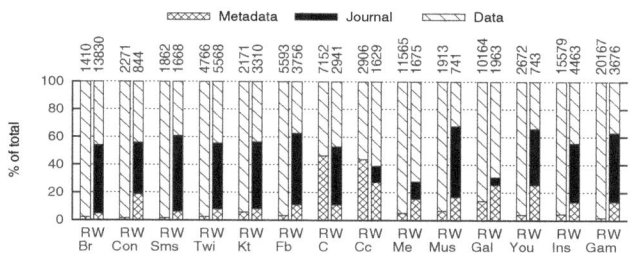

Figure 4: IO distribution on block type. The number at the end of each bar indicates the number of IO for R (Read) and W (Write), respectively.

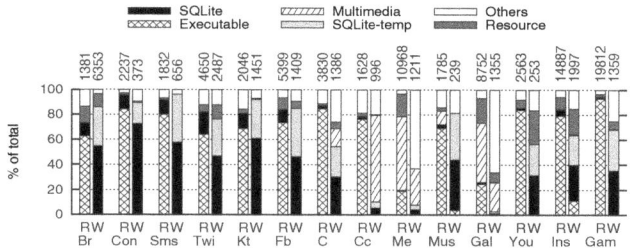

Figure 5: IO distribution of each file type. The number at the end of each bar indicates the number of *Data* block IO for R (Read) and W (Write), respectively.

the trace file, it consults the temporary block table to determine if the given block belongs to the temporary files that triggered the respective IO.

One of the important objectives of this study is to find IO characteristics based on the block type. MOST categorize logical blocks into three types: *Metadata*, *Journal*, and *Data*. In the EXT4 filesystem, *Metadata* blocks are blocks harboring a superblock, group descriptor, data block bitmap, inode bitmap, and inode table. In the FAT32 filesystem, *Metadata* blocks correspond to blocks harboring a boot record and File Allocation Table (FAT). *Journal* is a journal block of the EXT4 filesystem. *Data* blocks are those harboring file data and directory entries. Table 3 illustrates the entry format of MOST output.

5. ANALYSIS OF APPLICATION USAGE

5.1 Accesses on Filesystem Partition

We first examine how the individual applications access each of the partitions. Figure 3 illustrates the results. The labels on the X-axis denote the short names of the 14 applications. The label RW denotes Read and Write. The number on the top of each bar denotes the number of the respective operations. We find that multimedia applications and the rest exhibit very different partition usage patterns. In non-multimedia applications, accesses on the /data partition are mostly write, and /sdcard is rarely accessed. Multimedia applications, for example Camera, Camcorder, Gallery, and Media player, access the /sdcard partition much more frequently. These access characteristics reflect the Android OS partition management strategy, which aims to effectively exploiting the very limited storage capacity.

The /sdcard partition is used mostly by multimedia applications that read and write very large files such as MP3, pictures and movies. The underlying filesystem should be optimized to effectively accommodate this workload. FAT32, which maintains file blocks as a linked list, leaves much to be desired in its handling of large files.

5.2 Access Characteristics of Block Type

We define the three block types in NAND storage devices: *Metadata*, *Journal*, and *Data*. We examine how the individual applications utilize each type. This is critical information for both the filesystem and the storage controller. It can be used in devising a hot/cold identification algorithm for the NAND storage controller. The filesystem also can

use this to design an efficient layout and caching strategy. Figure 4 illustrates the results.

In legacy text-based applications such as Browser, Contact, and SMS, most read operations are for *Data* blocks. Read operations for *Metadata* constitute less than 5% of the total. Interestingly, in Camera and Camcorder, 50% of read operations are for *Metadata*. We find that these applications aggressively allocate *Data* blocks to accommodate incoming data (jpeg images or video recordings). This aggressive allocation behavior results in heavy accesses of the File Allocation Table of FAT32 for location or allocation of such *Data* blocks.

One notable point in Figure 4 is the IO operation on EXT4 *Journal*. In most applications, *Journal* block accesses represent 40-50% of write operations. Given that write is approximately ten times slower than read in NAND flash, and given also the limited cell duration of NAND flash, such excessive journaling activity not only can seriously aggravate system performance but also can seriously curtail NAND device lifetimes. We herein dedicate a separate section (section 5.4) to an in-depth discussion of EXT4 journaling activity in Android OS.

5.3 Access Characteristics of File Type

We examine the correlation between each file type and the ways in which individual applications utilize them. We categorize the files into six groups: executable, SQLite (database tables), SQLite-temp (ephemeral database files), multimedia (image, video, and music), resources (application properties), and others. The file type is determined based on the file extension: executable files (.apk, .dex, .odex, .so), SQLite (.db), SQLite-temp (.db-journal, .db-mjxxxx), multimedia (.3gp, .jpg, .mp3, etc), resources (.dat, .xml, .cache, etc), and others (including directory entry).

Figure 5 illustrates the results. In most cases, executable files are accessed in READ-ONLY mode. Installation is an exception to this rule. Among all of the 14 applications tested, more than 60% of read operations are for accessing executable files. A number of studies have proposed prefetching of executable files to reduce application launch latency [15]. These techniques manifest themselves further in the smartphone environment, since most read operations are on executable files.

Excepting some multimedia applications, the dominant fractions of the write operations relate to SQLite database tables. Android OS provides several options for managing persistent data, but SQLite is the most popular storage method because application developers can easily make structured and private databases for individual applications. We find that even multimedia applications use SQLite to store information. Media player and Music player use *AudioService* to adjust the audio volume level with respect to the user's volume control, and *AudioService* records the volume level to setting.db. In Camera and Camcorder, external.db is used to manage media files.

We also find that there are many ephemeral files, most of which, surprisingly, are created by SQLite. SQLite, in order to implement atomic commit and rollback capabilities, does make use of many temporary files in the course of database processing. These temporary files have .db-journal and .db-mjxxxx extensions. Severe performance degradation occurs due to *fsync()* calls for each creation and update in these files.

Our analysis shows that each file type exhibits very unique access characteristics. In most applications, 80% of write operations are on SQLite database, SQLite-temp, and resource files. Seventy percent (70%) of read operations are for executable files. Significantly, the strong correlation between the file type and its access characteristics can be effectively exploited by the NAND storage controller. For example, FTL can exploit file type information in making hot/cold decisions on a given logical block. This makes the hot/cold identification algorithm more accurate, and, subsequently, the performance of garbage collection for page-mapping FTL, and of log block merge operations for hybrid FTL, can improve significantly.

5.4 Analysis of Excessive Journaling

In section 5.2, we observe that the number of *Journal* writes accounts for 40-50% of all write operations. Given that EXT4 is mounted with *Metadata only* journaling (Ordered mode), the number of *Journal* writes should constitute a much smaller fraction of the entire write operation, which phenomenon we regard as not only excessive but also anomalous. This phenomenon is observed in all applications that use SQLite. We perform an in-depth analysis of this issue using the Facebook application to find a root cause. Specifically, we examine the IO patterns generated when SQLite performs write operations on a Facebook database table: fb.db. Figure 6 illustrates the LBA write accesses over a 60 msec period. The accesses are clustered in two distinct LBA regions: 100,000 and 300,000, the former being the location of the EXT4 *Journal* and latter, the locations of the SQLite database tables and the temporary files, respectively. In the Figure, there are five dashed rectangles, each denoting the

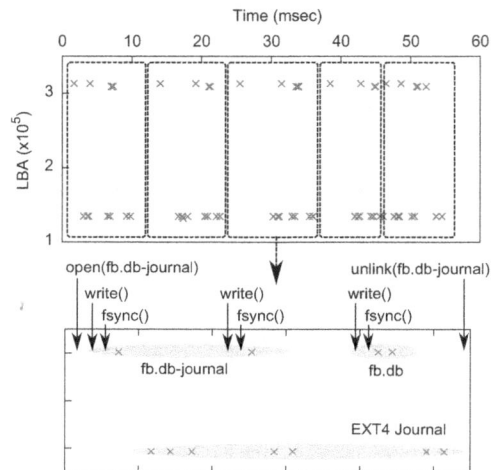

Figure 6: Block IO accesses of Facebook database table (fb.db) for 60 msec.

IOs generated by a single database operation (insert or update). The bottom graph of the Figure is a magnified image of the IOs involved in this single operation.

Let us explain the details of the operations in one of the single dashed rectangles in Figure 6. The first IO (in the $3x10^5$ LBA region) is for creating and updating a fb.db-journal file. The second IO (in the $3x10^5$ LBA region) is a commit log write to this journal file. The third IO (in the $3x10^5$ LBA region) consists of actually two IOs, which are visible in the magnified image. In each of these steps, SQLite forces the results to storage via *fsync()*. The IO overhead compounds according to the EXT4 filesystem. The IOs at the bottom are for EXT4 *Journal* writes. In EXT4, a *fsync()* call accompanies two or three *Journal* writes, each of which accounts for a writing journal descriptor and a metadata. There are a total of 7 IOs in the EXT4 *Journal*. In summary, a single SQLite operation triggers at least 11 writes to the storage device when used with the EXT4 filesystem. In this example, the database update to fb.db consists of two of the 11 IOs. Eighty percent (80%) of the write operations are for purely managerial purposes!

Here, we suggest an improvement. *fsync()* forces both the *Metadata* and *Data* of a file to storage. However, if write does not cause any removal from or addition to the *Data* block, storing *Metadata* might be unnecessary. In this case, *fdatasync()*, instead of *fsync()*, is a good alternative for mitigation of the burden of excessive journaling. *fdatasync()* forces only *Data* block. In the magnified bottom graph of Figure 6, the second write operation to fb.db-journal updates the header portion of a file of 12Bytes. It does not cause any removal from or addition to the *Data* block. In this case, *fdatasync()* can be a better choice, as it can significantly improve the excessive journaling phenomenon.

5.5 IO Size Distribution

We examine the IO size distribution. We group the IOs into five categories according to size: $\leq$ 4KB, $\leq$ 16KB, $\leq$ 64KB, $\leq$ 256KB, and > 256KB. We perform analyses on the IO and Byte counts, respectively.

Let us first examine the IO count. In all applications, the 4KB IO is dominant (top graph in Figure 7), accounting

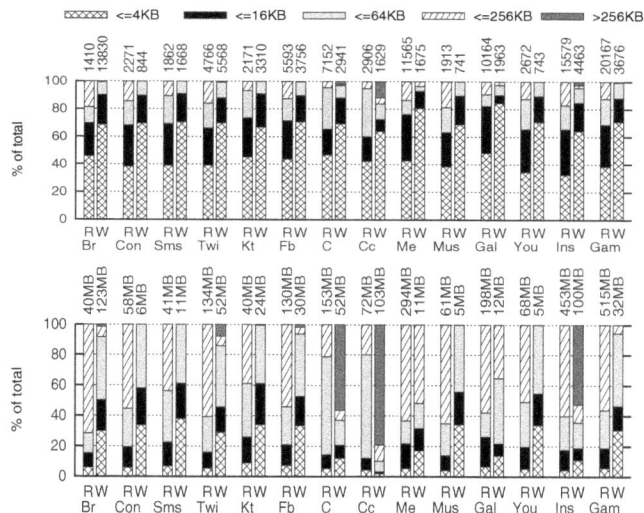

Figure 7: IO size distribution. At the top is the distribution by IO count, and at the bottom, the distribution by Byte count.

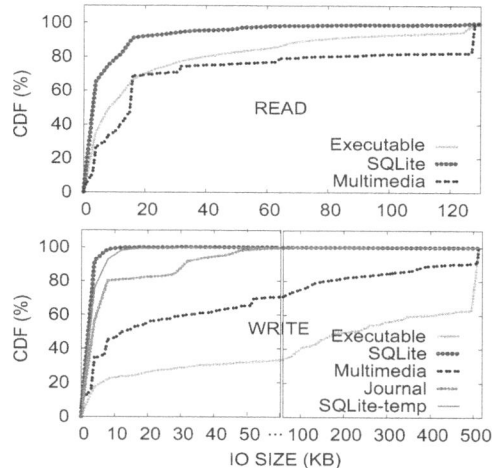

Figure 8: Cumulative IO size distribution

for 40% and at least 65% of read and write operations, respectively. Even in Camera and Camcorder, which handle large data files such as video clips and pictures, 4KB constitutes more than 60% of writes. We find two reasons for this phenomenon. The first is excessive journaling, explained above. The second, which is very interesting and important, is the updates on the File Allocation Table (FAT) of the /sdcard partition. While multimedia applications normally deal with large IO (e.g. copying images, mp3 files, video files), the FAT32 filesystem updates its FAT object very frequently when a new block is allocated. Therefore, via a reduction of the number of FAT synchronization operations (e.g. delayed write or periodic synchronization), we can greatly prolong the cell lifetime. This approach is even more useful in dealing with the sdcard, since sdcard normally uses an inexpensive MLC (or TLC, Tri-Level Cell) flash device, due to its strict cost requirements. These devices have a very limited Erase/Write cycle. The success of the storage and filesystem of Android-based smartphones critically relies on efficient handling of small random writes.

The bottom graph in Figure 7 shows the Byte count statistics. For read, whereas 4KB IO constitutes the dominant fraction of all IO requests (40%), the resultant IO volume is not significant (less than 5%). For write, 4KB IOs account for 35% and 17% of text-based applications (Browser, SMS, and SNS) and multimedia applications (Camera, Media player, Gallery), respectively. Contrary to our expectation, 4-64KB IOs constitute a significant fraction of entire IO volumes. The reason for this is the EXT4 *Journal* IO size (Figure 8). Half of *Journal* writes are accessed in 4KB units, but the rest are accessed in much larger sizes (8-50KB). In Camera and Camcorder, IOs larger than 256KB constitute 60% and 80% of the entire writes, respectively. These applications create new video (or image) files; the maximum write IO is as large as 512KB.

We examine the IO size distribution as subject to individual file types and EXT4 *Journal*. Figure 8 illustrates the cumulative IO size distribution, which we determine by

aggregating IO traces from the 14 Android applications. Resources and other files show a pattern similar to SQLite, and so are not shown in the Figure. In read, the 4KB IOs are dominant in SQLite. There are no read accesses to SQLite temporary files, because those files are accessed only to recover from a crash. Executable and multimedia files are accessed in much larger units. One interesting phenomenon is that among all of the file types, the maximum read IO is 128KB; the eMMC interface has a maximum IO size of 512KB, which is four times larger than that of the SAT interface. Few applications exploit this larger IO size in reading files.

In write, half of *Journal* writes are accessed in 4KB units, but the rest are accessed in much larger sizes (8-50KB). SQLite and its temporary files are accessed in 4KB units. The actual updated data in SQLite and its temporary files are much smaller than 4KB (not shown in the graph). Most SQLite files request data updates of 1KB size. Half of the IOs from SQLite temporary files are for updating about 3KB of data, but the rest are only for updating 12Bytes commit logs. This throws light on an important design guideline for future mobile storage design: the FTL mapping unit should be smaller than a page. This mapping technique generally is called sub-page mapping.

5.6 Access Characteristics: Spatial Aspect

We examine IO randomness for individual smartphone applications. Random writes are considered to be very harmful to NAND flash storage in the performance and reliability aspects, and thus in-depth investigation is required. The top half of Figure 9 illustrates the sequential and random IO volume of read operations for all types of blocks (A) and for only *Data* blocks (D). For all of the applications, reads are mostly sequential, which is to say that 80% of read operations are sequential. We find that most read operations are for executable files or multimedia files, and that the read operations for these files are mostly fully loaded (128KB).

The bottom half of Figure 9 shows the spatial characteristics of write operations. In the 14 applications excepting Multimedia applications (Camera, Camcorder, Media player, and Gallery), most of the *Data* block writes (60-80%) are random. These accesses are for SQLite database tables

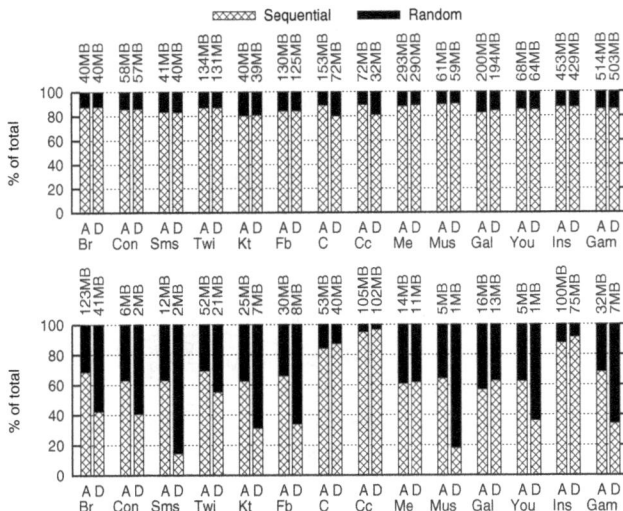

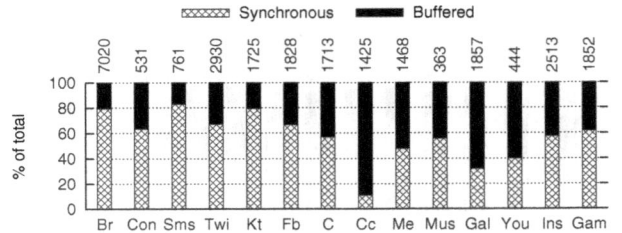

Figure 9: Randomness of IO traffic: Read (top) and Write (bottom). A denotes all blocks; D denotes *Data* blocks.

Figure 10: Buffered write IO distribution. The number at the end of each bar indicates the number of *Data* block IOs.

and their temporary files. If we consider all of the block types, sequential write constitutes rather a significant portion. This is because more than half of all *Journal* writes in the EXT4 filesystem fall in the 10-50KB range. This analysis provides us with important guidelines for performing IO characterization studies. If the spatial pattern of write is examined without consideration of the block type, the dominant fraction of writes will be sequential, which result can be misleading. When we focus our analysis on *Data* block accesses, writes are mostly (more than 60% in terms of `volume`) random. These *Data* block IOs are not only random, but also are frequently accessed and forced to storage.

5.7 Buffered write vs. Synchronous write

Buffered IO and synchronous IO stress the system in different ways, and thus their optimization should be approached from different perspectives. We examine the fraction of writes that are buffered and synchronous IO from applications, respectively. *Journal* and *Metadata* IOs are not included in this case study. We find that a buffered IO is *rare*. Most smartphone applications are found to update data in a synchronous manner, due to the fact that they use SQLite to manage information. However, multimedia applications such as Media player, Music player, and Gallery exploit buffered IO to download contents.

Synchronous write is no longer a supplemental option for updating data. In Android-based smartphones, synchronous write constitutes a significant portion of all write IO, and thus efficient handling of it is critical. IO subsystems of the modern Operating System adopt interrupt-driven IO to effectively share CPU cycles among multiple threads and, thereby, cope with the large IO latency (longer than a few msec) of a storage device. Polling-based IO is being revisited for IO subsystems for high-end SSD and storage class memory [25]. We argue that polling-based IO subsystems should be carefully studied as an alternative IO subsystem for future smartphone storage.

6. ANALYSIS OF NORMAL DAILY USAGE

It is important to verify that the IO characteristics we have observed in the individual applications properly incorporate the IO characteristics of the normal daily use of Android-based devices. Accordingly, we installed a Mobile Storage Analyzer in a volunteer's smartphone (Nexus S) and collected IO traces for seven periods of 24 hours each. The objective of this user study is not to perform any extensive user survey on smartphone usage; rather, the purpose is to verify that the IO characteristics we have observed from individual applications are not groundless but have practical implications.

Figure 11 plots the results. We examine both IO count and Byte count characteristics. In summary, the IO characteristics observed from daily usage are very similar (if not identical) to what we observed in an IO characteristics study for individual applications.

- **Partition Accesses**: From the IO count point of view, 90% of the writes are for `/data` and 60% of the reads are for `/system`. The IOs for each partition exhibits very different characteristics. This phenomenon suggests that the FTL of NAND-based storage should be able to effectively handle IOs for both write-dominant partitions and read-dominant partitions, which requires precise hot/cold detection and support for multiple-address-mapping granularity.
- **Block types**: The EXT4 *Journal* IO accounts for more than 60% of all writes. In contrast, *Metadata* write constitutes only 10% of all writes. The overhead of *Journal* IOs, significantly, are very expensive.
- **File types**: SQLite and its temporary files constitute 70% of write IOs. Most applications maintain their persistent data using SQLite. Accesses to the executable files are mostly read.
- **IO SIZE**: 4KB IO is dominant in both read and write. It accounts for 40% and 50% of the IO counts for read and write, respectively. The 4KB IO does not constitute a significant fraction of IO volume. However, overall system performance will critically rely on the performance of 4KB IO, since 4KB is mostly synchronous IO, which blocks the application until it completes.
- **Randomness**: Sequential IO constitutes 80% of all writes. This is because IOs from multimedia files and half of EXT4 *Journal* are of very large IO size.
- **Buffered write**: Synchronous IOs from applications account for 70% of all writes. However, buffered IOs are much larger, because these usually are IO accesses of large multimedia files.

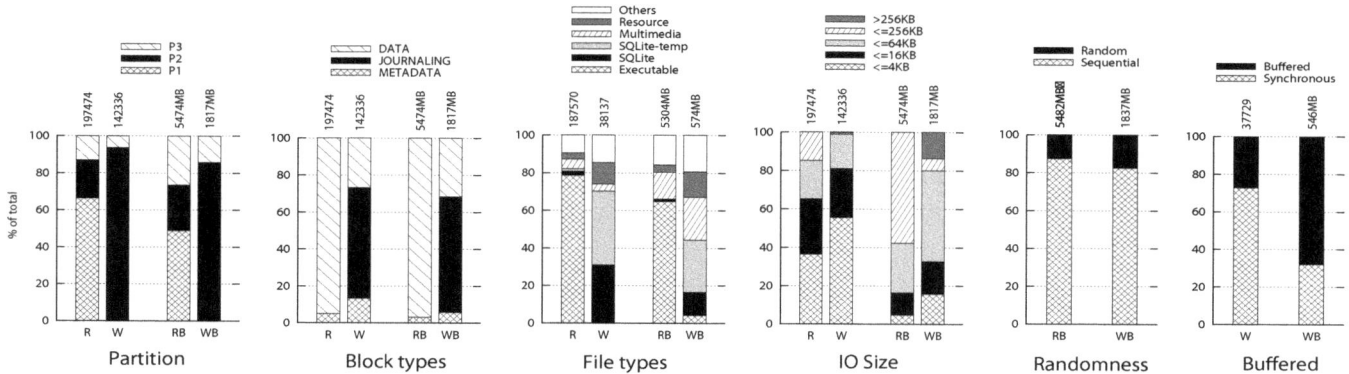

Figure 11: Daily block IO characteristics. The numbers at the R and W bars indicate the number of IOs, and the numbers at the RB and WB bars indicate the total bytes accessed for R (Read) and W (Write), respectively.

7. DISCUSSION

We summarize the technical issues relevant to the current IO subsystems and possible directions for improvement of future Android-platform filesystem and storage design.

Smart layers and Dumb result: SQLite adopts journaling to preserve the integrity of information. It creates a temporary journal file for each transaction. The EXT4 filesystem adopts journaling to maintain filesystem consistency and to achieve fast crash recovery. Each of these techniques is sophisticated and mature. However, as we observed, when these two are combined, they interact in unexpected ways, generating excessive EXT4 *Journal* block accesses. SQLite and EXT4 should be integrated in a rational manner so that duplicate operations can be eliminated.

Efficient handling of Synchronous write is critical: To improve IO performance, a number of cache-replacement algorithms have been developed for NAND flash storage devices [18, 14]. These algorithms work via exploitation of the temporal locality and asynchronous nature of IO operations. In the Android platform, however, neither of these hold: Reads are mostly for cold blocks, and writes are mostly synchronous. Further, write is at least ten times slower than read. In the Android platform, efficient handling of synchronous write operation, certainly, demands more attention. The recent proposal for a polling-driven IO [25] represents a good alternative for improvement of synchronous IO performance.

IO access pattern in smartphone is potpourri: The smartphone is a multi-purpose device. In addition to legacy phone functions, which include management of contacts, schedules and text messaging, it is used as a camera, music player, web browser and game console, among others. Accordingly, the IO access pattern in smartphones is a mixture of a wide variety of different access characteristics. IO accesses to the /system are mostly read, while IO accesses to the /data are mostly write. Accesses to the /sdcard entails large IOs, which accompany significant numbers of random writes caused by FAT updates.

File type information should be exploited by underlying storage and filesystem: Different types of files have unique characteristic accesses. Accesses to executable files are mostly large reads. Accesses to SQLite are mostly 4KB random. SQLite temporary files are only *written* with 4KB IO, and are short-lived. By examining the file type, that is, the extension, we can easily predict the characteristics of incoming IO. This information can be effectively exploited by prefetch strategies [15]. Interestingly, the recently proposed eMMC interface standard [9] allows the host to inform the eMMC of details on data blocks being transferred.

8. RELATED WORK

IO characterization studies in desktop and enterprise server environments have been conducted for several decades and have attained sufficient maturity. Despite the fact that some papers are now decades old, they still provide important guidelines to the understanding the intrinsic behavior of IO workloads. Riska et al. [20] studied the characteristics of disk-drive workloads in three different computing environments: enterprise, desktop, and consumer electronics. They showed that the access pattern for an enterprise server is more random than for a desktop one. Zhou et al. [26] found that the read/write ratio in the filesystem is 80%/20%, and that the majority of IO operations are random. Ruemmler et al. [22] analyzed disk IO in three different HP-UX systems. Their research showed that a majority of IO operations are writes and that the majority of writes (67-78%) are to *Metadata*, user-data IOs representing only 13-41% of all accesses. Roselli et al. [21] analyzed filesystem traces in a variety of different environments, including both UNIX and NT systems. They found that file access has a bimodal distribution pattern: some files are written repeatedly without being read, whereas other files are almost exclusively read.

The recent and rapid proliferation of NAND flash-based storage devices necessitates thorough understanding of the block level access characteristics of SSD [19, 12]. The following studies examined the temporal, spatial, and frequency aspects of the block-access trace, and exploited findings for devising various FTL algorithms (e.g. hot/cold identification, wear-leveling, a hybrid FTL log block management scheme, etc.).

Harter et al. [13] studied the IO behavior of the Mac OS filesystem. They showed that due to the complex XML-based document format, sequential IO on a file rarely results in sequential IO on a block device. Whereas it has generally been believed that in smartphones, the speed of the air link interface is a bottleneck to overall performance, it was recently found that the performance of smartphone applications are governed not by the communication speed of the air link but rather by storage performance [16]. It is of the utmost importance that a firm understanding of the ways in which newly emerging applications in smartphones use storage devices, which is to say, application-specific block-access characteristics. The result of our study provide explanations for the phenomenon observed in Kim et al. [16] and an important direction for the future filesystem development for smartphones.

9. CONCLUSIONS

We studied the Android smartphone's storage IO characteristics using Mobile Storage Analyzer (MOST). Our analysis revealed unique smartphone IO characteristics. These include the partition management strategy, the dominance of SQLite files, the excessiveness of *Journal* block accesses, the limited number of file types incurring block IO, and the low usage of buffered IO. We discovered that the IO subsystem and filesystem designs of the current state-of-the-art smartphone leave much to be desired in terms of fully exploiting the potential of the underlying NAND storage. Guaranteeing integrity from SQLite and EXT4 is a very complex undertaking. However, they need to be optimized in an integrated manner, so that redundant efforts are eliminated. The filesystem affords in-depth knowledge on the access characteristics of individual block IOs, which can be effectively exploited by the NAND storage controller. It is important that any modern NAND storage controller interface adopts a rich set of interfaces for sharing of valuable information between host and storage devices.

10. ACKNOWLEDGEMENTS

This work was supported by IT R&D program MKE/KEIT [No. 10035202, Large Scale hyper-MLC SSD Technology Development] and [No. 10041608, Embedded System Software for New-memory based Smart Device].

11. REFERENCES

[1] Mobile storage analyzer (most). http://dmclab.hanyang.ac.kr/sub/main_most.htm.

[2] Nexus one (google/htc). http://en.wikipedia.org/wiki/Nexus_One.

[3] Nexus s (google/samsung). http://www.google.com/phone/detail/nexus-s.

[4] Samsung galaxy s2. http://www.samsung.com/global/microsite/galaxys2/html/.

[5] Sqlite's use of temporary disk files. http://www.sqlite.org/tempfiles.html.

[6] Universal flash storage (ufs). http://www.jedec.org/standards-documents/focus/flash/universal-flash-storage-ufs.

[7] What is android? http://developer.android.com/guide/basics/what-is-android.html.

[8] World mobile phone market 2010 to 2011. http://www.yanoresearch.com/press/pdf/709.pdf.

[9] Embedded multi-media card(e-mmc), electrical standard (4.5 device), June 2011.

[10] M. Arlitt and C. Williamson. Internet web servers: Workload characterization and performance implications. *IEEE/ACM Trans. on Networking (ToN)*, 5(5):631–645, 1997.

[11] J. Axboe and A. D. Brunelle. Blktrace user guide, 2007.

[12] F. Chen, D. Koufaty, and X. Zhang. Understanding intrinsic characteristics and system implications of flash memory based solid state drives. In *Proc. of the eleventh international joint conference on Measurement and modeling of computer systems*, pages 181–192. ACM, 2009.

[13] T. Harter, C. Dragga, M. Vaughn, A. C. Arpaci-Dusseau, and R. H. Arpaci-Dusseau. A file is not a file: understanding the I/O behavior of apple desktop applications. In T. Wobber and P. Druschel, editors, *SOSP*, pages 71–83. ACM, 2011.

[14] H. Jo, J. Kang, S. Park, J. Kim, and J. Lee. Fab: Flash-aware buffer management policy for portable media players. *Consumer Electronics, IEEE Trans. on*, 52(2):485–493, 2006.

[15] Y. Joo, J. Ryu, S. Park, and K. G. Shin. FAST: Quick application launch on solid-state drives. In *Proc. of the 9th USENIX Conference on File and Storage Technologies, San Jose, CA, USA, February, 2011*.

[16] H. Kim, N. Agrawal, and C. Ungureanu. Revisiting storage for smartphones. In *Proc. of the 10th USENIX Conference on File and Storage Technologies, San Jose, CA, USA, February, 2012*.

[17] S. Lee, B. Moon, and C. Park. Advances in flash memory ssd technology for enterprise database applications. In *Proc. of the 35th SIGMOD international conference on Management of data*, pages 863–870. ACM, 2009.

[18] S. Park, D. Jung, J. Kang, J. Kim, and J. Lee. Cflru: a replacement algorithm for flash memory. In *Proc. of the 2006 international conference on Compilers, architecture and synthesis for embedded systems*, pages 234–241. ACM, 2006.

[19] M. Polte, J. Simsa, and G. Gibson. Comparing performance of solid state devices and mechanical disks. In *Petascale Data Storage Workshop, 2008. PDSW '08. 3rd*, pages 1 –7, 17-17 2008.

[20] A. Riska and E. Riedel. Disk drive level workload characterization. In *Proc. of the USENIX Annual Technical Conference, General Track*, pages 97–102. USENIX, 2006.

[21] D. Roselli, J. R. Lorch, and T. E. Anderson. A comparison of file system workloads. In *Proc. of the 2000 USENIX Annual Technical Conference*, pages 41–54, Berkeley, CA, June 18–23 2000.

[22] C. Ruemmler and J. Wilkes. Unix disk access patterns. In *Proc. of Winter USENIX*, pages 405–20, 1993.

[23] K. Sovani. Linux: The journaling block device. http://kerneltrap.org/node/6741, June 20, 2006.

[24] T. Ts'o. Debugfs. http://linux.die.net/man/8/debugfs.

[25] J. Yang, D. Minturn, and F. Hady. When poll is better than interrupt. In *Proc. of the 10th USENIX Conference on File and Storage Technologies, San Jose, CA, USA, February, 2012*.

[26] M. Zhou and A. Smith. Analysis of personal computer workloads. In *Proc. of the 7th International Symposium on Modeling, Analysis and Simulation of Computer and Telecommunication Systems, MASCOTS*, pages 208 –217, 1999.

XEMU: An Efficient QEMU Based Binary Mutation Testing Framework for Embedded Software

Markus Becker[1]   Daniel Baldin[2]   Christoph Kuznik[1]

Mabel Mary Joy[1]   Tao Xie[1]   Wolfgang Mueller[1]

[1]C-LAB, University of Paderborn, Fürstenallee 11, 33102 Paderborn, Germany
{beckerm, kuznik, mabeljoy, tao, wolfgang}@c-lab.de

[2]Heinz Nixdorf Institute, University of Paderborn, Fürstenallee 11, 33102 Paderborn, Germany
dbaldin@hni.upb.de

ABSTRACT

This paper presents the XEMU framework for mutation based testing of embedded software binaries. We apply an extension of the QEMU software emulator, which injects mutations at run-time by dynamic code translation without affecting the binary software under test. The injection is based on a mutation table, which is generated by control flow graph (CFG) analysis of the disassembled code prior to its execution without presuming access to source code. We introduce our approach by the example of the ARM instruction set architecture for which a mutation taxonomy is presented. In addition to extending the testing scope to target specific low level faults, XEMU addresses the reduction of the mutants creation, execution, and detection overheads. Moreover, we reduce testing efforts by applying binary CFG analysis and constraint-based test generation for improved test quality. The experimental results of a car motor management software show significant improvements over conventional source code based approaches while providing 100% accuracy in terms of the computed test quality metrics.

Categories and Subject Descriptors

D.2.5 [**Software Engineering**]: Testing and Debugging—*Testing tools (e.g., data generators, coverage testing)*; D.2.8 [**Software Engineering**]: Metrics—*performance measures*; D.2.4 [**Software Engineering**]: Software/Program Verification—*Formal methods, Reliability*; D.3.4 [**Programming Languages**]: Processors—*Compilers, Optimization, Run-time environments*

Keywords

Embedded systems, Software emulation, Just-in-Time compilation

1. INTRODUCTION

Embedded software development requires profound testing and validation of software artifacts before the final shipping of the product. This especially applies for areas like automotive, avionics, and health care with hard requirements for dependability, robustness and faultlessness are omnipresent in the software development cycle. Therefore, various verification techniques and methodologies, each targeting different aspects of the embedded software, have been introduced. In this context, mutation based testing methods are well established for the functional qualification of complex test benches to enhance embedded software quality. They measure the quality of test cases by means of identifying faults in the hardware model or software, respectively. As such, mutants in form of faulty software modifications are injected into the code of the system under test.

The fault injections are modeled by a set of mutation operators. Each mutation operator represents a type of a syntactic modification reflecting a coding error in the program such as:

$$c = a + b; \; \rightarrow c = a - b;$$
$$if(a < b)...; \rightarrow if(true)...;$$

To assess the test data, each mutant from the data base is separately executed with the tests and its outputs are compared with the executions of the original program. If under any test case the mutant produces a different output compared to the output of the original program, it is considered to be killed by the test data. One of the biggest challenges with mutation testing is its high computation cost in generation, execution, and recognition of individual mutants, which is addressed by our approach.

In general, mutation based testing for software is applied to high-level languages (e.g., Fortran, Java, C/C++) by instrumenting the source code coming with the following drawbacks for practical application: (i) it requires the availability of source code which is sometimes not accessible; (ii) the instrumented source code is different from the final code and thus may give different results. Additionally, mutants are derived either by compilation of the instrumented source code or through a special compiler. Therefore, it either results in additional compilation overhead as each mutant has to be compiled individually or it requires the modification of the compiler.

We introduce a novel approach for *mutation testing* of binary software in conjunction with formal methods to enhance test set quality. The testing is seamlessly integrated at run-time into the binary translation cycle of the software emulation framework. Mutants are derived from the original software binary under test by control flow analysis prior to its execution. Though we introduce mutation operators by the example of the ARM instruction set [1] [20], the basic principles apply to other embedded processors as well.

As such, our approach does neither presume the availability of

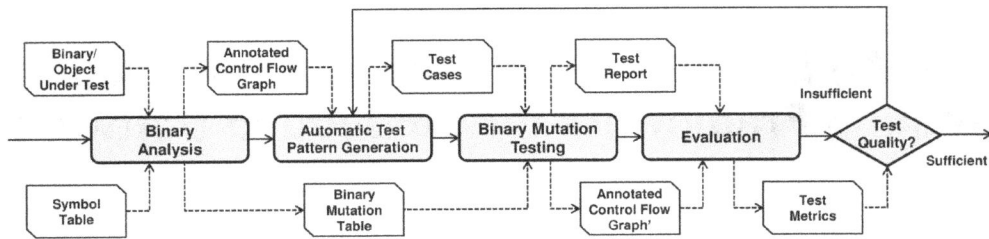

Figure 1: XEMU binary mutation testing flow.

the source code nor does it require modifications of the applied target compiler. By creating mutations at binary code level, we can also capture faults specific to different target instruction set architectures (ISA) and vendor-specific tool chain and cover compiler-specific effects like code optimization.

Though we introduce our approach by the example of QEMU [6][2], our approach applies to the general concepts of dynamic binary translation and Just-in-Time (JIT) compilation which are used by several software emulators for efficient run-time conversion of different ISAs, i.e., from guest to host ISA. In contrast to instruction interpreting instruction set simulators (ISS), dynamic code translation is typically performed on basic block level, i.e., linear code segments closing with a final branch instruction. Unlike static code translation only those blocks encountered at run-time are considered thereby avoiding unnecessary translation overhead. Moreover, basic blocks are translated into translated blocks (TB), which are stored in a translation buffer to avoid redundant translations at run-time and keeping the execution speed close to native execution. In the case of QEMU, the effort of porting to new target and host platforms is reduced by an intermediate code level, i.e., a canonical set of micro operations, which is then translated to native code by the so-called tiny code generator (TCG). For our evaluations, we applied and extended user mode QEMU. The user mode provides user space emulation for a single program on top of the Linux operating system (OS). However, the basic principles also apply to QEMU full system mode, which provides emulation of an entire target system including physical memory and I/O in order to run a complete software stack, i.e., boot firmware, operating system, and kernel space device drivers.

Our results are evaluated by a case study from the automotive industry, a fault tolerant fuel injection control system. Our experiments showed that binary mutation testing can generate and cover identical set of mutants compared to source code instrumentation. Therefore, focusing on control flow mutation we reached 100% accuracy compared to source code instrumentation with a GDB/ARMulator tool chain with a speed up of up to 100-1000x at the same time. Though our framework is based on the execution of non native binary code, we can even outperform the native (i.e., host-compiled) source code based approaches as we avoid significant compilation overhead. Moreover, by efficiently utilizing multicore hosts we further reduce testing efforts proportional to the number of available cores.

The remainder of this paper is organized as follows. Section 2 describes our binary mutation testing approach, its application to the ARM instruction set architecture, and the binary translation based testing framework. Section 3 presents the experimental results. Thereafter, related work is discussed before the final chapter closes with a conclusion.

2. BINARY MUTATION TESTING

Our approach is based on the XEMU binary mutation testing flow. We start with a description of the general flow and its application to the ARM instruction set format followed by a detailed description of our mutation testing framework based on the QEMU user mode emulator.

Our test flow (see Fig. 1) is composed of four major steps: binary analysis followed by automatic test pattern generation (ATPG), binary mutation testing and evaluation. In a first step, a table of mutations is derived from the original binary by static code analysis presuming the provision of relevant symbol information but no availability of source code. For this, the considered symbols of the input binary or object code are disassembled in order to construct an annotated control flow graph (CFG). Based on a further analysis of the annotated CFG, a mutation table is generated describing binary mutations for creating a set of mutants from the original binary. In the next step, advanced ATPG techniques are applied to the annotated CFG in order to provide pertinent test cases for reaching sufficient test quality.

In the mutation testing step binary mutants are created and tested by injecting mutations from the table separately and executing each mutant with all test cases. For each combination of mutant and test case, its output is compared with the output of a golden run, i.e., a first run of the original binary that is carried out in advance. Section 2.3 introduces our QEMU based testing framework that applies mutation testing efficiently at run-time. Finally, the evaluation step extends the annotated CFG with mutation testing report data, i.e., instruction address coverage, mutation coverage, and mutation detection (killed mutants). This is done in order to extract quality metrics for the applied set of test cases, e.g., the number of killed mutants w.r.t. the total number of mutants. In case the computed metrics do not meet the targeted level of test quality, steps two to four have to be repeated until a sufficient level is reached or the computed metrics converge to an upper bound.

2.1 Binary Analysis

For the derivation of a mutation table and the generation of test cases from the binary under test, we apply static analysis techniques. In order to construct an annotated CFG, we first disassemble the binary code to identify the static basic blocks and the control flow between these blocks of the program. In general, every program can be uniquely partitioned into a set of non-overlapping static basic blocks, i.e., blocks with a single entry and exit point. The analysis of binary code is a non-trivial task. Disassembling and interpreting binary files can be challenging due to the Code Discovery Problem as many ISAs allow binary data to be mixed up with executable instructions. Not distinguishing between instructions and data may invalidate the analysis process since control flows may not be discovered and data may be misinterpreted as instructions or vice versa. However, on ARM platforms this issue is addressed by the embedded applications binary interface (EABI) that specifies the provision of position information for data and instruction blocks by special mapping symbols inside the symbol table (see Section 4.6.5 in [5]).

In the next step the constructed CFG is annotated by static data flow analysis. For this, we use the common approach of forward substitution as described by Cifuentes et al. [8, 9] to derive complex

```
1  int check_bounds(int a, int b, int c)  {
2    if (a<=b && b<=c) { /* Is b inside [a,c]? */
3      return 1; /* True */
4    }
5    return 0; /* False */
6  }
```

Listing 1: Example function *check_bounds* **in C language.**

expressions from low level expressions, which are the assembler instructions of the binary in our case. For assembly code, one can express the contents of a register r in terms of a set a_k at instruction i as $r = f_1(\{a_k\}, i)$. If the definition at instruction i is the unique definition of a register r that reaches an instruction j along all paths in the program without any of the registers a_k being redefined, one can forward substitute the register definition at instruction j with $s = f_2(\{r\}, j)$, resulting in:

$$s = f_2(\{f_1(\{a_k\}, i)\}, j)$$

Fig. 2 depicts an annotated CFG generated from the example C code function *check_bounds* (see Listing 1). We use expressions from forward substitution analysis to annotate the edges of the CFG with constraints that need to be fulfilled in order to be taken. With the binary analysis framework [23] we are able to map the high level information from header files such as the function interfaces to the binary CFG. Applying global data flow analysis techniques to the extracted information we can annotate parts of the CFG with high level constraints based on the input parameters of the binary objects. However, detecting access to high level data structures is not trivial as there can be an unlimited amount of access possibilities generated by the compiler. Thus, an expression normalization step is applied to allow a meaningful and usable annotation of the binary CFG.

In order to extract a table of mutants from the CFG, the applicability of instruction set specific mutation operators (mutators) to the individual basic blocks has to be investigated. ARM instructions commonly take two, three, or four operands, e.g., source and destination registers Rs and Rd with optional operand registers Rm and Rn. They are broadly classified into five classes: data processing instructions, branch instructions, load-store instructions, software interrupt instructions, and program status register instructions. Some instruction classes additionally make use of instruction flags.

Almost all ARM instructions can be executed conditionally, i.e., it can be specified that the instruction only executes if the condition code flags pass a given condition or test. By using conditional execution performance and code density can be increased. The conditional code is a two letter mnemonic appended to the instruction mnemonic. The default mnemonic is AL, or always execute. Conditional execution reduces the number of branches, which also reduces the number of pipeline flushes and thus improves the performance of the executed code. Conditional execution depends upon two components: conditional code and condition flags. The condition code is located in the instruction word, and the conditional flags negative (N), zero (Z), carry (C), and overflow (V) are held in the current program status register (CPSR). Condition flags can be updated through instructions by appending the according instruction flag mnemonic (S).

In general, the pattern of an ARM instruction word is as follows *<operator> <condition> <flags> <operands>* where the latter two fields are optional/mandatory due to the individual instruction. According to that pattern we define a set of atomic mutator classes. Table 1 shows the main atomic mutator classes for ARM with their mnemonics and a concrete mutator example for each. The *Operator* mutator class (OPTR) covers all possible mutations of operators sharing the same format, i.e.,

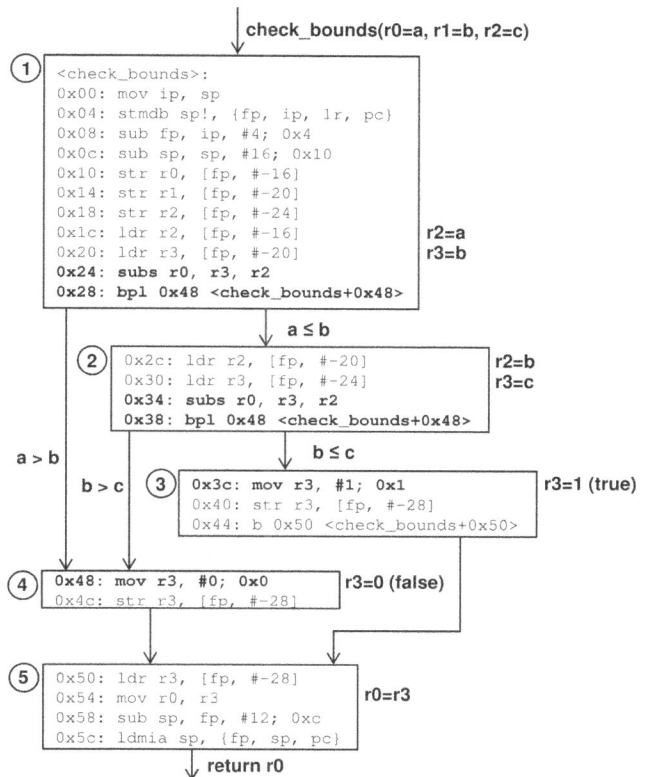

Figure 2: Annotated control flow graph of the disassembled *check_bounds* **function.**

number and type of operands and flags. This can be for instance OPTR(add↔sub) in order to turn an arithmetic addition into a subtraction. The *Condition* mutator class (COND) covers all possible mutations of an instruction's condition, i.e., it applies to almost all ARM instructions. A typical mutator of this class is for instance COND(AL→NV), i.e., changing the condition from always to never in order to prevent instructions from being executed. The *Flag* mutator class (FLAG) covers all possible mutations to operation flags. A useful mutator is for instance FLAG(S↔ ¬S) in order to switch on/off an update of the condition flags in the CPSR register. The *Operand* mutator class (OPRD) covers all possible mutations of operands. Useful mutators of this class are for instance OPRD(Rd↔Rs) for toggling source and destination register.

Additionally, we introduce the general DATA mutator in order to change constant or variable data at a given address and ADDW in order to insert a new instruction word. We chose this set of atomic mutator classes as they are orthogonal in changing different aspects of the instruction word. Moreover, by combining multiple atomic mutations we can efficiently cover any complex mutations such as source level faults or target specific faults, e.g., related to binary interfaces (see Table 2).

Table 3 shows a portion of the corresponding mutation table which is generated from the *check_bounds* CFG . The first column of that table gives the mutation type. Here, A stands for an atomic mutation and C stands for a complex mutation, i.e., the composition of multiple atomic mutations spanning over multiple lines. Columns two to four contain the atomic mutator class, the concrete mutator and the affected instruction word address (given by bold characters in the CFG of Fig. 2). Column five shows the equivalence in the affected source code line according to the binary mutation table entry. Row eight shows that the mapping of a typ-

Atomic mutator class	Mnemonic	Example mutator
Change operator	OPTR	OPTR(add→sub)
Change condition	COND	COND(AL→NV)
Change flag	FLAG	FLAG(S↔ ¬S)
Change operand	OPRD	OPRD(Rd↔ Rs)

Table 1: Atomic binary mutator classes for the ARM instruction set.

Binary interface issues	Coverage through mutation
Symbol table/header	Branch, load and store address
Subroutine arguments passing	Register/stack access
Subroutine return value passing	Register/stack access
Endianness	Byte access order
Data/stack alignment/padding	Load and store offsets

Table 2: Coverage of binary interface related errors.

ical simple source code mutator, e.g., switching off the evaluation of an if statement's expression, may require the application of a complex mutation at the according binary code. Here, the mutation of an expression composed of a conjunct condition to $true$ requires the mutation of two instruction words.

2.2 Automatic Test Pattern Generation

We apply automatic test pattern generation (ATPG) by extracting new test cases from the annotated binary CFG using constraint satisfaction problem (CSP) solving. Our CSP/ATPG approach can be applied to both the generation of test cases from scratch and/or to improve existing test case sets with insufficient test quality such as a low percentage of killed mutants (mutant detection rate). As bad mutant detection is likely to be related to a lack of code and path coverage increasing, the coverage is applied as a heuristic for improving also the mutant detection. For this, we derive CSPs from the annotated CFG according to paths leading to a mutated basic block that has not been reached by the existing test cases. Let us consider basic block four of Fig. 2 to be unreached by the current set of test cases as an example. Thus, the mutant defined at address 0x48 cannot be killed as it does not impact the output. By path backtracking we find all paths and the constraints for each path by combining the edge constraints as logical conjunctions. For basic block four in Fig. 2, this leads to the following set of path constraints:

$$a > b$$
$$(a \leq b) \wedge (b > c)$$

The basic block will be reached if any of the two constraints is fulfilled. Thus, for a reachability analysis the existence of a test case (i.e., a tuple of input values) that fulfills the following expression must be computed:

$$\exists (a, b, c) : ((a > b) \vee (a \leq b) \wedge (b > c))$$

By generating and solving the expressions for all unreached basic blocks, we then automatically create test cases, which fulfill all constraints to ensure that the path will be taken during test execution in order to increase the chance on killing the corresponding mutant. Our developed framework uses the STP Constraint Solver [11] to automatically derive the values of the variables for the test cases. In general, the constraints may contain subexpressions that may not be solvable or variables we may not be able to calibrate by the test environment. In this case we try to solve as many test case relevant subexpressions and use the solutions as the input parameters for the test cases. Although it may not be guaranteed that the path will be taken at run-time, we can show that the chance of it will be significantly increased.

As mutant killing does not just depend on the coverage of the block with the undetected mutant but also on the path to reach it, we need to compute test cases that cover as many paths as possible. As the number of paths to a single block can become very high, we apply a random approach that tries to solve the path constraints for n randomly chosen paths.

2.3 Run-Time Binary Mutation by QEMU

For efficient generation and testing of mutants, we induce mutations online during the execution of the original binary under in-

Type	Class	Mutator	Addr.	Source code equivalence
A	OPRD	Rm↔Rn	0x24	2: if($b \leq a$&&$b \leq c$)
A	OPTR	sub→add	0x24	2: if($-a \leq b$&&$b \leq c$)
A	OPRD	Rm↔Rn	0x34	2: if($a \leq b$&&$c \leq b$)
A	OPTR	sub→add	0x34	2: if($a \leq b$&& $-b \leq c$)
A	FLAG	S→ ¬S	0x34	2: if($a \leq b$)
A	COND	MI→AL	0x28	2: if($b \leq c$)
A	COND	MI→NV	0x28	2: if(false)
C	COND	MI→AL	0x28	2: if(true)
	COND	MI→AL	0x38	
A	OPRD	Op2→0x1	0x48	3: return 1;
A	OPRD	Op2→0x0	0x3c	5: return 0;

Table 3: Binary mutation table.

vestigation. For that we modified the dynamic binary translator of QEMU. Thus, there is no need for instrumenting the original binary itself. The induced mutation during the translation also allows the application of more complex mutations, which cannot be applied through simple patching of the binary file.

For the mutation of the translated code, we follow an instrumentation approach similar to [13] to make it easily portable to other target platforms supported by QEMU. They introduced a generic instrumentation interface for QEMU that is based on event-triggered plug-ins. The plug-in interface consists of a set of callback functions invoked at the occurrence of an event. Such events can be translation related or execution related. A callback function assigned to a translation related event may access the translator's code generator API in order to affect the emulation. Thus, it can suppress, extend, or modify the generation of translated code. Callback functions assigned to execution related events have access to the emulator's run-time environment. Thus, they can trace or modify the state of the emulated CPU and memory. Plug-in code can be compiled into shared objects in order to be linked to the generic interface at run-time.

Fig. 3 shows the QEMU emulation cycle extended by mutation injection. The original fetch-decode-execute cycle performs alternating translation and execution phases. A translation phase is entered when the emulated program counter (PC) encounters an unknown target address, i.e., when looking up of the corresponding translated block from translation buffer failed. The translation loop consists of fetching and decoding single instruction words from memory until the encounter of a branch instruction. Then, the content of the intermediate buffer is rewritten as a native TB into the translation buffer. The TB's entry address is stored with the target code PC entry address in a hash table.

This process can be interrupted by our mutation extensions. For this, the encounter of a mutation affected address triggers the callback of a mutation plug-in. The remainder outlines our approach by the example of an instrumentation plug-in for the emulation of the COND mutator for ARM binaries. However, as it can be easily seen, it can be similarly applied to any of the proposed ARM mutator classes from Table 1.

In order to inject a condition code mutation into the translated code, the translation of the affected instruction address through the original translator function $disas\_arm\_insn()$ is replaced by the slightly different function $disas\_arm\_insn\_cond()$ executed by

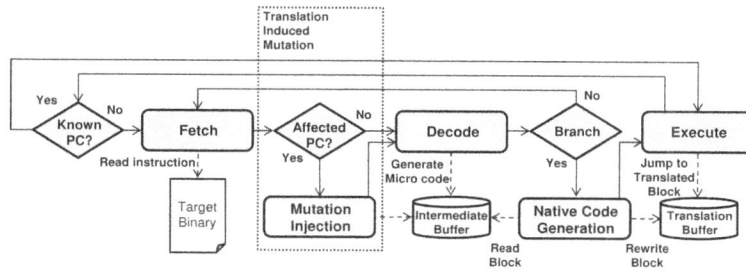

Figure 3: Binary translation induced mutation.

the COND mutator plug-in. In contrast to the original function, it additionally accepts an argument specifying the condition code to be used for translation. In the QEMU ARM translator, conditional execution is supported by instrumenting the translated instruction with a preamble code performing the condition test and – for that case the condition test fails – a conditional branch to a label that is inserted just behind the translated instruction. In order to generate the condition test, the condition code is usually extracted from the four most significant bits of the instruction word. In contrast, the COND mutator plug-in uses the condition code argument provided through the currently selected mutation table entry. The suppression of the original code generation is then indicated by the mutator plug-in through a specific return code. Obviously, condition code mutations could be achieved more easily by patching the four most significant bits of the affected instruction word directly in the emulator's memory. However, our approach is more powerful as it is not limited to mutations relying on patching of instruction words.

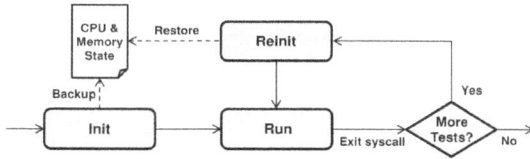

Figure 4: QEMU testing loop extensions.

2.4 Efficient Mutant Execution and Detection

Mutant sets can become very large when applying the full set of mutators to complex software. Therefore, we introduce several extensions to the QEMU user mode emulator in order to speed up binary mutation testing. For this, three major improvements were made: (i) reduction of initialization and binary translation efforts, (ii) reduction of mutant execution and detection efforts, and the (iii) utilization of multicore hosts for parallelization.

For this, we combine the golden run and all the subsequent mutant runs in a single emulator invocation. As such, we avoid restarting the emulator for each mutant, so that we save the translator initialization and avoid redundant code translation as mutants do not largely differ. By performing a mutation coverage analysis already at the golden run we can also reduce the number of runs by skipping mutants that cannot be killed anyway due to a lack of coverage.

Several extensions to the QEMU user mode emulator are required in order to extend the lifetime, which usually ends with the executed program's termination. First, we need to make a backup of the initialized CPU and memory state in order to reset QEMU efficiently. Since the emulator and the binary under test share a single host process we just need to allocate the amount of memory that is big enough to hold a copy of the initialized memory regions. In order to minimize backup efforts, we copy those memory areas that are affected during a test, i.e., the CPU context and the program's

data section. After a mutation run, the QEMU translation buffer contains mutated code. In order to avoid flushing the buffer after each mutation run, a list of affected translated blocks is maintained for deletion. Finally, we need to prevent QEMU from termination, which is usually done by forwarding of the final *exit* syscall to the host OS which then kills the QEMU process. For that, we trap the *exit* syscall in order to perform the reinit. Fig. 4 depicts the extended QEMU lifetime for executing multiple program runs in a loop with fast reinitialization.

The definition of strong mutation analysis states that a mutant is being killed when it is propagated to the design interfaces, i.e., resulting in a deviation of the mutant's output and the golden run's output. Typically, relevant program output is written directly or indirectly (i.e., via standard output) to a dump file using $printf()$ and $fprintf()$ or it is written to a device file using $fwrite()$. Under $POSIX$ based OS like $Linux$ all output related standard library functions end up with a $write()$ syscall to a device handle. The QEMU user mode emulator, for instance, treats system calls by raising an exception for returning QEMU to its main loop after the execution of the current TB. In the main loop, the system call is trapped by forwarding it to the host's OS system call API. We adopt this mechanism in two ways. During the golden run, we copy the data of all $write()$ system calls to an output buffer storing the reference data. As the amount of output data can be really huge and is not known a priori, the size of the allocated buffer grows dynamically.

Then, the same mechanism is used during mutation run to compare a mutant's output with the previously stored golden run data in an online fashion, i.e., instantly when a $write()$ system call occurs. In case of the first deviating output character, the current mutant is marked as being killed and execution stops immediately in order to reset QEMU and proceed with the next mutant. Online mutant detection saves unnecessary execution overhead. By suppressing the actual syscall to be forwarded to the OS, we can also save costly context switching and kernel time.

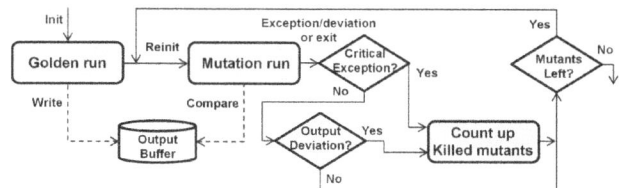

Figure 5: Mutation testing loop with online detection.

Besides output deviation a mutation can also lead to program abortion when the emulator or executed program enters a critical state, e.g., a segmentation fault or an illegal instruction. In that case, we also trap exceptions in order to avoid QEMU abortion and consider the current mutant as being killed. Under certain circumstances, a mutation may lead to an infinite loop. Infinite loop detec-

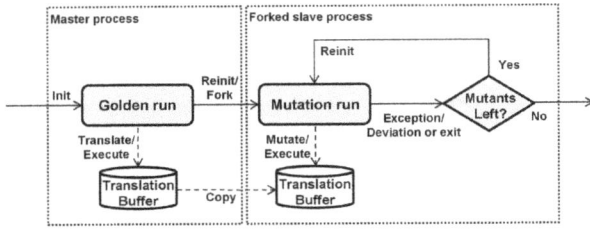

Figure 6: Multicore host utilization by process forking.

tion is hard when there is no output generated in that loop. In that case, we can only set a timeout w.r.t. the golden run. If the timeout expired, the host thread executing the current mutant is killed and the mutant itself is considered as being killed. Fig. 5 depicts the extended QEMU lifetime with mutation testing loop and online detection.

As mutation testing is inherently parallel, our testing framework supports multicore hosts by means of distributing the mutants' execution on top of a set of worker threads. The QEMU translation buffer is a global data structure that is shared among multiple virtual CPUs. Since the translation buffer contains mutated code, we need to be sure that mutants do not get corrupted by executing mutated code from different mutants. In order to avoid additional thread synchronization overhead, we introduce a private translation buffer for each of the worker threads. For this, we make use of the $fork()$ system call to create copies of the original QEMU process, which becomes the master process and acts like a watchdog process that kills and restarts worker threads being timed out due to infinite loops. By forking the master process directly before executing the mutant loop all data structures,e.g., CPU state, reference output buffer and the translation buffer, are in a ready-to-use state. This avoids redundant QEMU initialization and redundant golden run execution. By repeating the $fork()$ system call n times, we create 2^n worker threads. Now, as processing of mutants has no interdependencies the synchronization overhead is negligible. The assignment of mutants to worker threads is achieved by a semaphore initialized to the total number of mutants. The worker threads update the global testing report via shared memory. After all worker threads have completed, the master process finalizes the metrics report. Fig. 6 depicts the forking of the QEMU master process for efficient multicore host utilization.

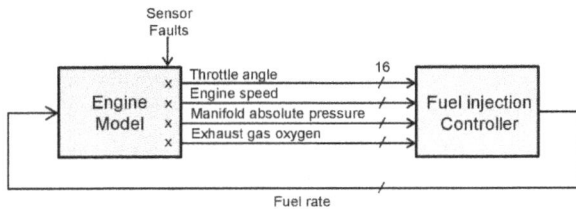

Figure 7: Closed-loop engine model test case generator for the fault tolerant fuel injection controller software.

3. EXPERIMENTAL RESULTS

Our case study is based on the embedded software of a fault-tolerant fuel injection controller, which is a part of the car motor management system. The software is internally composed of two components: *Sensor Correction* and *Fuel Rate Computation*. The software requires four signed 16 bit integer sensor signals such as throttle angle or engine speed. The sensor correction component is able to compensate one signal fault at a time by use of approxi-

mation functions. Based on the corrected sensor data the fuel rate computation component computes the fuel injection rate for the actuator.

The controller was originally modeled in MATLAB/Simulink where thehe software was automatically generated by the *dSPACE TargetLink* production code generator [3]. The generated C code consists of 10 functions with a total complexity of 3397 lines of code. The target binary was compiled with arm-elf-gcc version 4.1.1 using $-O0$, i.e., no code optimization. The case study comes with two test case generators: a generic *delta generator* and an *engine model*. The delta generator is a combinatorial approach that produces test cases by iterating integer input values with a pre-defined *delta* step. The *delta* can be any integer divisor of the signal's range. Thus, for our four 16 bit input signals (each having a range from 0..65535) and a *delta* of 4096 (resulting in 16 steps per signal) a total of $16^4 = 65536$ test cases is generated. The engine model test case generator is more specific to the software as it provides a physical model of the engine. Test cases are generated in a closed-loop with the feedback of the controller's output (see Fig. 7). Moreover, certain error situations are stimulated by injecting sensor faults, e.g., one or more sensor faults at a time. The engine model test case generator is set up by a virtual execution time. As the controller software is designed to run with a 10ms period 15000 test cases correspond to the execution of 150s of virtual time.

We compare our framework with two different mutation testing tool chains: a native source code mutation tool chain based on instrumentation and compilation and another binary tool chain executing patched ARM code for a conventional ISS. The first tool chain is implemented by a *sed* based source code instrumentation script. The script wraps preprocessor macros around C statements. This is done to switch on mutations separately through providing an according flag to the host compiler. The resulting executable runs natively on the host computer just like any other program.

The second tool chain is based on the GDB/ARMulator ISS that comes as a part of the GDB debugger provided with the ARM GCC tool chain. GDB/ARMulator is a pure functional, i.e., no cycle accurate, simulator/emulator of a single ARM CPU running in user mode. In contrast to QEMU, ARMulator relies on a simple instruction interpreter loop. Here, binary mutations are directly applied to the ARM executable prior to its execution. For mutant detection standard outputs are piped to a dump file in order to be compared to a golden run output using *diff*.

3.1 Test Quality

We consider three different metrics in order to assess the test quality of a used set of test cases: instruction coverage, mutation coverage, and mutant detection (killed mutants). Instruction coverage measures the percentage coverage of instruction words reached by the test set's control flow. Mutation coverage measures the rate of mutants reached by control flow. Mutant detection (killed mutants) measures the percentage of mutants that were killed in terms of propagating a program deviation to the outputs. For the comparison of metrics accuracy, we consider two typical C mutation operators that were easily applied to all of the three tool chains: *if(<cond>)→if(true)* and *if(<cond>)→if(false)*. For proving the reasonability of our metrics, we matched mutations using the *addr2line* tool provided with the *GCC binutils* though our approach does not rely on exact mapping of source level to binary level. Therefore, we used the $-O0$ flag as the relationship of source to optimized binary code cannot be easily followed. However, our approach also applies to optimization.

As the case study source code contains 115 if-statements, this leads to a total number of 230 mutants by applying two mutators to each. Fig. 8 shows the testing metrics generated according to the test cases from the two generators. The x-axis denotes the num-

Test case set	Metric	SensorCorrection							FuelrateComputation			TOTAL
		DetectFailures	CorrectSensors	Cc26_Running_ex	FuelingMode_du	SensFailCounter_du	Tab2DIntpI1T1_c	TabIdxS17T1_c	CalculateAirflow	CalculateFuelrate	Tab2DS17I2T4169_c	
Engine Model: 150s sim. time #15000	Instruction coverage*	1720/97%	456/100%	256/83%	792/63%	360/69%	344/56%	272/91%	764/98%	852/98%	688/92%	**6504/85%**
	Mutation coverage	74/97%	6/100%	2/50%	32/80%	26/81%	10/83%	6/100%	12/100%	26/100%	16/100%	**210/91%**
	Killed mutants	52/68%	5/83%	1/25%	24/60%	19/59%	2/17%	6/100%	9/75%	18/69%	11/69%	**147/64%**
Delta Gen.: Step size 2048 #1048576	Instruction coverage*	1780/100%	456/100%	308/100%	656/52%	520/100%	612/100%	300/100%	776/100%	856/98%	704/95%	**6968/91%**
	Mutation coverage	76/100%	6/100%	4/100%	26/65%	32/100%	12/100%	6/100%	12/100%	26/100%	16/100%	**216/94%**
	Killed mutants	55/72%	6/100%	3/75%	19/48%	28/88%	9/75%	6/100%	12/100%	19/73%	14/88%	**171/74%**
Engine Model + CSP/ATPG: #15000+1054	Instruction coverage*	1780/97%	456/100%	308/100%	960/75%	520/100%	612/56%	300/91%	776/99%	856/95%	704/90%	**7272/95%**
	Mutation coverage	74/97%	6/100%	4/100%	40/100%	32/100%	10/83%	6/100%	12/100%	26/100%	16/100%	**226/98%**
	Killed mutants	58/76%	6/100%	3/75%	33/83%	30/94%	2/17%	6/100%	10/83%	20/77%	12/75%	**180/78%**

*Instruction coverage only provided by binary testing

Table 4: Comparison of test quality metrics reached by different test case generator approaches.

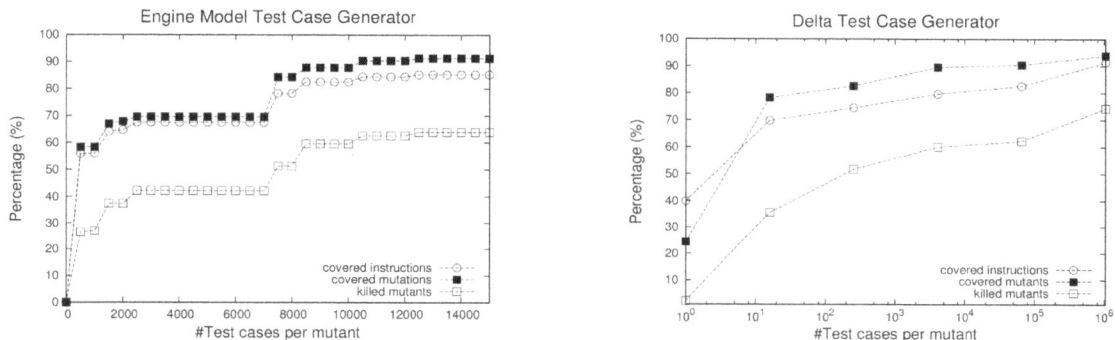

Figure 8: Evaluation of the test quality metrics w.r.t. the number of test cases per mutant.

ber of applied test cases per mutant. The y-axis shows the corresponding metric in percent. Since the generated metrics are identical for all approaches, we proved that binary mutation testing can reach 100% accuracy w.r.t. the considered control flow mutators. It turned out that the significant increase of metrics between test cases #5000 and #10000 with the engine model test case generator corresponds to the stimulation of two sensor faults at a time leading to an increased code coverage. As expected, the engine model performs better in terms of providing sufficient test quality with few test cases as it is more aware of the functionality of the controller software. Table 4 shows a detailed evaluation of the test quality metrics w.r.t. different test case generators. It shows that the engine model kills 64% of the mutants with 15000 test cases. The delta generator reaches a killing rate of 74% at the cost of 1048576 test cases (using a step size of 2048). Though the delta generator is generic and simple it is inefficient as the number of generated test cases exponentially depends on the inputs. Thus, many of the generated test cases turn out to be useless or redundant in terms of killing mutants. We applied our proposed CSP/ATPG approach starting from the 15000 test cases generated by the engine model. For this, we computed 1054 additional test cases by trying to solve 100 random path constraints per uncovered basic block. It took us 347 seconds to generate the additional test cases. With the CSP/ATPG generated test cases, all metrics of the delta generator could be outperformed significantly with applying only 15000+1054 test cases. The mu-

tant killing could be improved to 78%. Manual examination of the residual undetected mutants turned out that many of them can be considered as so-called equivalent mutants as they have no impact on the considered outputs. Fig. 9 impressively demonstrates the superiority of the CSP/ATPG approach over the delta generator by the example of the *FuelingMode_du* function. The annotated CFG in Fig. 9(a) corresponds to the test results of the delta generator (delta step size 2048, 1048576 test cases). The annotated CFG in Fig. 9(b) corresponds to the engine model with CSP/ATPG improved test cases (15000+1054). A filled box denotes a covered basic block. Boxes with diagonal corners contain two control flow mutators each. With the CSP/ATPG approach the mutation coverage could be increased from 65% to 100%. The mutant killing rate could be increased from 48% to 83%.

3.2 Test Performance

Fig. 10(a) shows the performance numbers comparing the different testing approaches. The experiments were carried out on an Intel Xeon Quadcore HT processor running at 3.4 GHz. Here, the y-axis denotes the measured testing time in seconds and the x-axis denotes the number of applied test cases per mutant. As each test case was applied to all 230 mutants, this leads to a total number of $(230+1)*1048576 = 242221155$ tests to be investigated (including the golden run). Basically, we can see that all approaches scale linearly w.r.t. the number of test cases (and mutants).

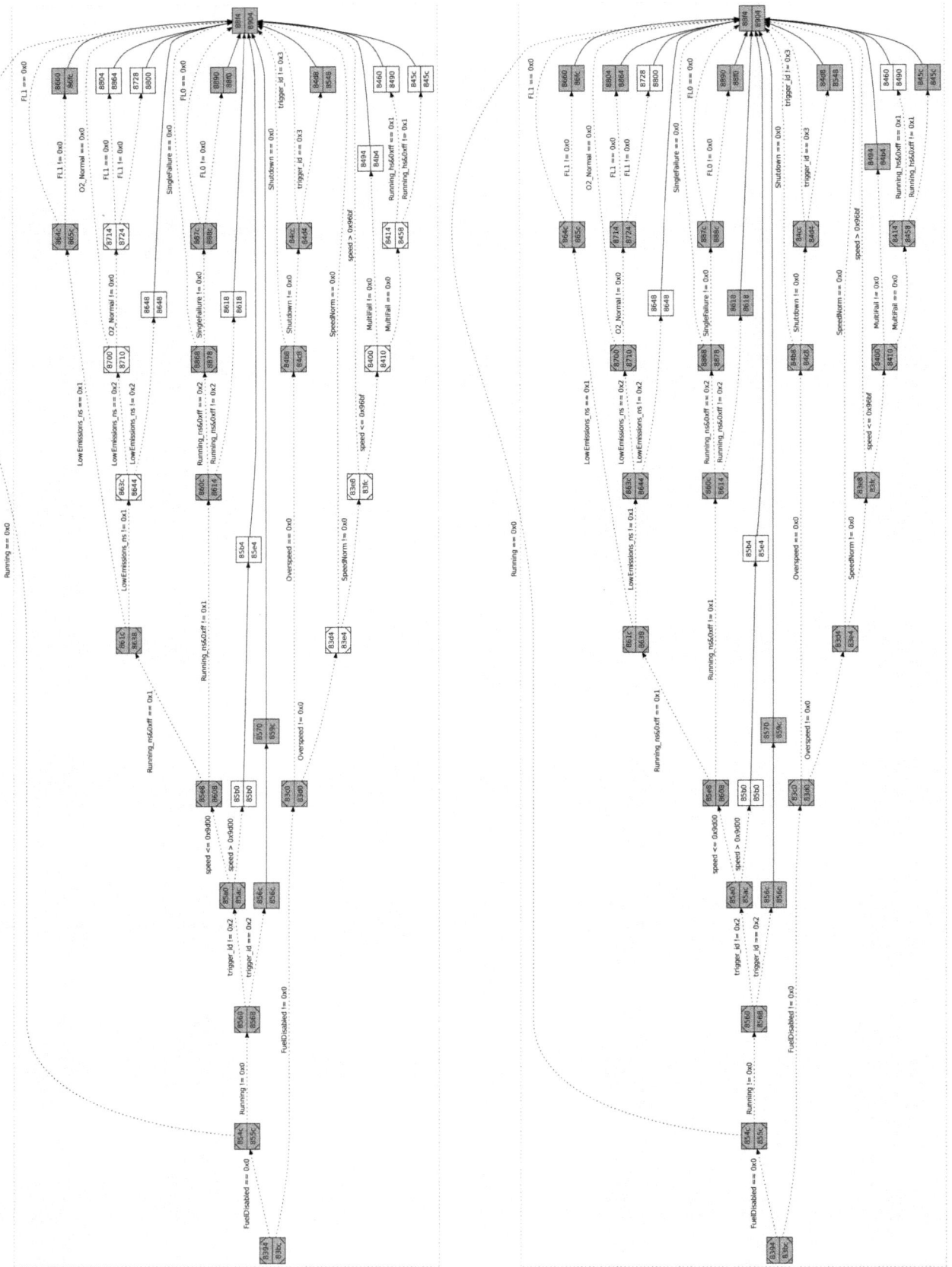

(a) 65% covered mutants and 48% killed mutants applying 1048576 tests by delta test case generator.

(b) 100% covered mutants and 83% killed mutants applying 15000+1054 tests by engine model test case generator with CSP-based ATPG.

Figure 9: Annotated binary level control flow graphs of the FuelingMode_du function demonstrating efficient test quality improvement by constraint solving based automatic test pattern generation.

Typically, with source code mutation testing there is a higher base effort related to the number of mutants as each mutant has to be compiled from sources. Here, the native approach is dominated by compilation efforts, i.e., testing time increases very slightly with the number of test cases. Fig. 10(a) shows the break even for the GDB/ARMulator is only below 10-100 test cases per mutant.

The figures show that the break-even point can be extended to below 100,000-1,000,000 test cases and XEMU performs in average 100-1000x faster than GDB/ARMulator. Fig. 10(b) demonstrates the speed up achieved by online detection and mutant skipping extensions. Finally, Fig. 10(c) depicts the additional speed up that can be achieved by utilizing multicore hosts. The gradient of the curve is nearly halved by doubling the available cores. We utilized four full cores with hyper threading.

4. RELATED WORK

Mutation testing has inherent higher execution costs, hence various mutant reduction and execution cost reduction techniques have been proposed [14]. Most of the existing approaches focus on white-box testing and source code instrumentation, so the source code or intermediate object code of the design-under-verification, such as Java bytecode in [19], has to be available for the generation of mutants. Moreover, most frameworks focus on high-level software programming languages such as C# and Java [7]. For example, a large set of C language mutation operators were introduced in [17]. Later it was shown in [16] that a reduced number of operators still achieves a high mutation score. For hardware design, CERTITUDE by SpringSoft supports functional qualification for C and VHDL/Verilog [21]. In [22] mutation operators for IP-XACT electronic component descriptions were introduced. In contrast the XEMU framework aims to leverage mutation testing in the embedded software domain, which is mainly C and SystemC based. By doing so, it also targets mutation faults at the application binary interface (ABI) for COTS libraries.

DeMillo et al. [10] modified a GNU C compiler chain to generate patches in order to enable compiler-integrated mutant generation. In [18] they also introduced Godzilla an automatic constraint-based test data generation framework which was integrated with the Mothra mutation testing framework.

The authors of [15] propose a SystemC error and mutation injection tool based on compiler injection via a plugin for the GCC compiler based on four mutant operators. Another approach for SystemC and TLM mutation testing [12] allows to selectively activate one mutant at a time through the use of a configuration variable, properly driven by the testbench during the simulation phase. In contrast to the presented compiler-induced and super mutant techniques, our proposed binary translation based approach allows to perform mutation testing for different ISAs and offers much greater mutation flexibility by means of the event-triggered callbacks mechanism during translation. Moreover, targeting COTS libraries (with no source code available) our approach is language and compiler independent. In [4] the authors propose a software fault injection technique for the IA32 platform by means of machine-code level patterns. Mutations are induced directly in the target executable. In contrast to traditional mutation testing, the targeted application is to emulate residual software.

Though we are considering embedded code such as ARM binaries, our approach can be even faster than native approaches by applying an extended QEMU dynamic translation. Additionally, this enables more complex and efficient mutations as it is based on a modified code translation at run-time and not on binary pattern search expression. Moreover, our framework also provides feedback to the verification engineer via graphically rendered CFGs annotated with testing results such as a lack of coverage and non detected faults with the corresponding address to line information.

5. CONCLUSION

In this paper we introduced the XEMU framework for efficient *mutation testing* of binary software. The testing is seamlessly integrated into binary translation cycle of QEMU software emulation cycle at run-time. Mutants and test patterns are derived from the original software binary under test by a CFG analysis prior to testing. Though we introduce our approach by mutation operators for the ARM instruction set, the basic principles are applicable to other embedded processors. Our approach comes with several major advantages: (i) it does not presume the availability of the source code nor does it require modifications of the applied target compiler; (ii) we can capture specific faults of different target ISAs and tool chains, e.g., compiler bugs and anomalies in the code optimization or binary interface issues; (iii) we can considerably reduce the mutant generation, execution, and detection efforts. Our results are evaluated by a case study from the automotive industry, a fault tolerant fuel injection control system. Our experiments reached a 100% accuracy w.r.t. source code mutation testing at the same time providing a speed up of up to 100-1000x compared to the execution with GDB/ARMulator ISS. We can even outperform native execution as we avoid individual mutant compilation. The utilization of multicore hosts through efficient multi-threading further improves testing speed. By employing advanced ATPG techniques based on binary analysis and constraint solving, we improved the test quality significantly at the same time reducing the number of required test cases.

6. AKNOWLEDGEMENTS

This work was partly funded by the German Ministry of Education and Research (BMBF) through the DFG SFB 614, the project SANITAS (01M3088), the ITEA2 projects VERDE (01S09012) and TIMMO-2-USE (01IS10034).

7. REFERENCES

[1] *ARM Architecture Ref. Manuals.* http://infocenter.arm.com.

[2] *QEMU - Open Source Processor Emulator.* http://www.qemu.org.

[3] *TargetLink, dSPACE GmbH.* http://www.dspace.com.

[4] J. ao A. Durães and H. S. Madeira. Emulation of Software Faults: A Field Data Study and a Practical Approach. *IEEE Transactions on Software Engineering*, 32:849–867, 2006.

[5] ARM Ltd. ELF for the ARM Architecture, 2009.

[6] F. Bellard. QEMU, a Fast and Portable Dynamic Translator. In *ATEC '05: Proceedings of the Annual Conference on USENIX Annual Technical Conference*, pages 41–41, Berkeley, CA, USA, 2005. USENIX Association.

[7] B. Bogacki and B. Walter. Aspect-Oriented Response Injection: An Alternative to Classical Mutation Testing. In K. Sacha, editor, *Software Engineering Techniques: Design for Quality*, volume 227, pages 273–282. 2007.

[8] C. Cifuentes. Interprocedural Ddata Flow Decompilation. *Journal of Programming Languages*, 4:77–99, 1996.

[9] C. Cifuentes, D. Simon, and A. Fraboulet. Assembly to High-Level Language Translation. In *In Int. Conf. on Softw. Maint.*, pages 228–237. IEEE-CS Press, 1998.

[10] R. DeMillo, E. Krauser, and A. Mathur. Compiler-Integrated Program Mutation. In *Computer Software and Applications Conference, 1991. COMPSAC '91., Proceedings of the Fifteenth Annual International*, pages 351–356, sep 1991.

[11] V. Ganesh and D. L. Dill. A Decision Procedure for Bit-Vectors and Arrays. In *Computer Aided Verification (CAV '07)*, Berlin, Germany, July 2007. Springer-Verlag.

[12] V. Guarnieri, N. Bombieri, G. Pravadelli, F. Fummi, H. Hantson, J. Raik, M. Jenihhin, and R. Ubar. Mutation

(a) Speed comparison w.r.t. GDB/ARMulator and native execution.

(b) Speed up through online detection and mutant skipping.

(c) Speed up through multicore utilization.

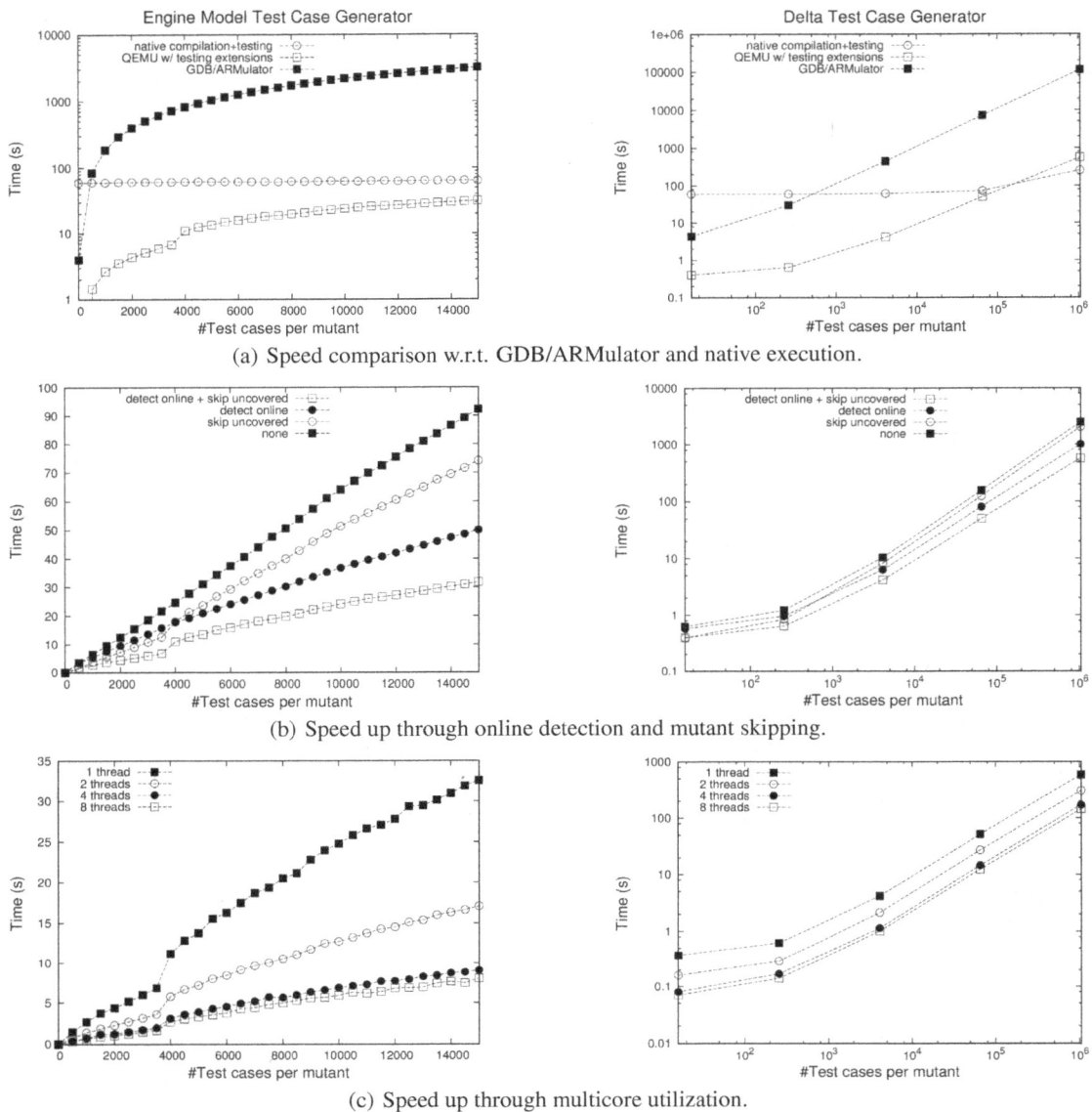

Figure 10: Evaluation of mutation testing performance.

Analysis for Systemc Designs at TLM. In *Test Workshop (LATW), 2011 12th Latin American*, pages 1 –6, march 2011.

[13] C. Guillon. Program Instrumentation with QEMU. In *DATE '11: Proceedings of the Conference on Design, Automation and Test in Europe*, Grenoble, France, 2011.

[14] Y. Jia and M. Harman. An Analysis and Survey of the Development of Mutation Testing. *IEEE Transactions on Software Engineering*, 2010.

[15] P. Lisherness and K.-T. T. Cheng. SCEMIT: A SystemC Error and Mutation Injection Tool. In *Proceedings of the 47th Design Automation Conference*, DAC '10, pages 228–233, New York, NY, USA, 2010. ACM.

[16] A. S. Namin, J. H. Andrews, and D. J. Murdoch. Sufficient Mutation Operators for Measuring Test Effectiveness. In *IN PROC. ICSE*, pages 351–360, 2008.

[17] H. A. Richard, R. A. Demillo, and B. H. et al. Design of Mutant Operators for the C Programming Language. Technical report, 1989.

[18] R. A. DeMillo and J. A. Offut Constraint-Based Automatic Test Data Generation. In *IEEE Trans on Software Eng.*, vol. 17, no. 9, pages 900–910, 1991.

[19] Y. seung Ma, J. Offutt, and Y. R. Kwon. Mujava: An Automated Class Mutation System. *Software Testing, Verification & Reliability*, 15:97–133, 2005.

[20] A. Sloss, D. Symes, and C. Wright. *ARM System Developer's Guide: Designing and Optimizing System Software*. Morgan Kaufmann Publishers Inc., San Francisco, CA, USA, 2004.

[21] SpringSoft Inc. CERTITUDE Functional Qualification System. 2011.

[22] T. Xie, W. Mueller, and F. Letombe. IP-XACT Based System Level Mutation Testing. In *High Level Design Validation and Test Workshop (HLDVT) IEEE International*, 2011.

[23] D. Baldin, S. Groesbrink, and S. Oberthuer. Enabling Constraint-Based Binary Reconfiguration by Binary Analysis. In *International Journal on Computing (JoC), 2011*.

Finite Automata with Time-Delay Blocks *

Krishnendu Chatterjee[1]   Thomas A. Henzinger[1]   Vinayak S. Prabhu[2]
[1]IST Austria (Institute of Science and Technology, Austria)   [2]University of Porto
krishnendu.chatterjee@ist.ac.at   tah@ist.ac.at   vinayak@fe.up.pt

ABSTRACT

The notion of delays arises naturally in many computational models, such as, in the design of circuits, control systems, and dataflow languages. In this work, we introduce *automata with delay blocks* (ADBs), extending finite state automata with variable time delay blocks, for deferring individual transition output symbols, in a discrete-time setting. We show that the ADB languages strictly subsume the regular languages, and are incomparable in expressive power to the context-free languages. We show that ADBs are closed under union, concatenation and Kleene star, and under intersection with regular languages, but not closed under complementation and intersection with other ADB languages. We show that the emptiness and the membership problems are decidable in polynomial time for ADBs, whereas the universality problem is undecidable. Finally we consider the linear-time model checking problem, i.e., whether the language of an ADB is contained in a regular language, and show that the model checking problem is PSPACE-complete.

Categories and Subject Descriptors

F.4 [**Mathematical Logic and Formal Languages**]: Formal Languages—*Classes defined by grammars or automata, Decision problems*

---

*This work has been financially supported in part by the European Commission FP7-ICT Cognitive Systems, Interaction, and Robotics under the contract # 270180 (NOPTILUS); by Fundação para Ciência e Tecnologia under project PTDC/EEA-CRO/104901/2008 (Modeling and control of Networked vehicle systems in persistent autonomous operations); by Austrian Science Fund (FWF) Grant No P 23499-N23 on Modern Graph Algorithmic Techniques in Formal Verification; FWF NFN Grant No S11407-N23 (RiSE); ERC Start grant (279307: Graph Games); Microsoft faculty fellows award; ERC Advanced grant QUAREM; and FWF Grant No S11403-N23 (RiSE).

General Terms

Theory, Verification, Performance

Keywords

Time-delay Systems, Model Checking, Buffers, Queues

1. INTRODUCTION

The class of dynamical systems (or processes) with delays occur frequently in control systems where delays arise due to physical constraints (see *e.g.* [6, 9, 15, 17]). The notion of delays is also common in systems where transmission of information is involved. Delay blocks have been used for modeling such time delays in engineering systems, for example, the unit delay block in Simulink [12] delays the input signal by one sample period, corresponding to the z^{-1} discrete time Z-transform operator. The memory block in Simulink, meant for continuous time signals, delays the input by one integration time step. Mathworks' Control Systems Toolbox [11] can be used for modeling delays in control systems using the $e^{-\Delta s}$ Laplace transform operator (in the transfer functions) for modeling a delay of Δ time units; the coupling between the delay and the system dynamics is tracked in the internal state space model. The notion of delays arises naturally in other computational models, e.g., time delays are used in the design and analysis of circuits (timing analysis and analysis of circuits with latches), and delays are a key component in dataflow languages (*e.g.* in the Ptolemy II framework [7, 14]).

Although delay constructs have been widely used in control systems, design of circuits, and dataflow languages, they have not been considered in the classical automata theoretic settings in computer science. One approach to model delays in the automata theoretic setting has been by the introduction of an automaton model for an intermediate buffer for explicitly modeling the state of the buffer. This approach suffers from three crucial drawbacks: (1) the buffer length has to be fixed in any given model, (2) the buffer contents have to be explicitly modeled leading to unnecessary model complexity, and (3) the state space of the system blows up with increasing buffer size, due to state space modeling of the buffer contents.

In this work, we introduce an extension of the standard finite state automata model by enriching automata with variable discrete-time delay blocks for deferring individual output symbols. We call the resultant structures *automata with delay blocks* (ADBs). Viewing the automata as generators of strings, the string generated by an accepting run of a standard finite state automaton is the same as the sequence of symbols observed as the output of the run. In automata with delay blocks, the output symbols are *generated* by a regular automaton structure, but the *output sequence* of the symbols differs from the symbol generation sequence due to the delay blocks involved. In an ADB, there is an associated discrete-time delay Δ with each transition e labelled by an output symbol; in the output the symbol labeling the edge e appears after a delay of Δ time units. Time passes in the model in discrete time steps, either via an explicit *tick* transition in the ADB, or when the automaton run ends in an accepting state. We present a couple of examples to illustrate the model. Given an ADB $\mathcal{A}$, let $\mathcal{L}(\mathcal{A})$ denote the (discrete-time) output language of the automaton, and let $\mathcal{U}(\mathcal{A})$ denote the untimed output language.

Example 1. Consider a shipwreck scenario where hazardous material containers from a wrecked ship are floating in the ocean, and are being dispersed by ocean currents. A team of autonomous underwater vehicles (AUVs) is monitoring the situation, their goal being to (1) detect the possible locations of the drums using sonar data, and (2) monitor affects on underwater marine life due to leaking materials from the containers. For illustrative purposes, consider a team of two vehicles named AUV-1 and AUV-2. AUV-1 is operating at a depth of 10 meters, and is taking sonar imaging data above it and processing it to detect the floating drum locations. AUV-2 is operating at a depth of 150 meters and monitoring the underwater marine life situation. The search pattern of AUV-2 depends on the possible sightings of containers given by AUV-1 which are conveyed through acoustic communication. AUV-1 periodically, surfaces as it is close to the surface, sends its full detailed imaging data to the base station through GSM communication (high datarate and only works above water, underwater acoustic communication is extremely low datarate and has limited range) where human operators study data and update the earlier sighting inferences of AUV-1, and send the updates back to AUV-1, which must then convey the updates back to AUV-2 through underwater acoustic communication. The human operators may also change the resurfacing frequency of AUV-1 depending on the data received.

We are interested in describing the pattern of messages received by AUV-2. We define one discrete time unit to be the time in between two AUV-1 resurfacings (note that this corresponds to variable physical times, and a variable number of point monitorings). In one such time unit, AUV-1 sends k point locations to AUV-2, each annotated with $\mathtt{y}$ and $\mathtt{m}$ (for possible container sightings, $\mathtt{m}$ denotes "maybe"). The updates from the base station are conveyed to AUV-2 in the next time slot from AUV-1 as simply a k-bit sequence corresponding to the same k locations as in the previous time slot (the locations are not sent again to AUV-2 as underwater communication is extremely expensive). Let us denote the sending of the point coordinates as the event $\mathtt{p}$. Then the (untimed) language describing the pattern of messages from AUV-1 to AUV-2 is

$$\{(w\#w') \mid w \in \{\mathtt{py},\mathtt{pm}\}^* \text{ and } w' \in \{\mathtt{y},\mathtt{n}\}^* \text{ and } 2|w'| = |w|\}^*$$

where $\#$ denotes the demarcation between two adjacent time slots. This language can be described in a natural and intuitive fashion by the ADB in Figure 1. The automaton also makes it clear that the i-th $\mathtt{y},\mathtt{n}$ that appears after the $\#$ corresponds to the i-th $\mathtt{py},\mathtt{pm}$ in the previous time slot; this relationship may be useful for further processing of the

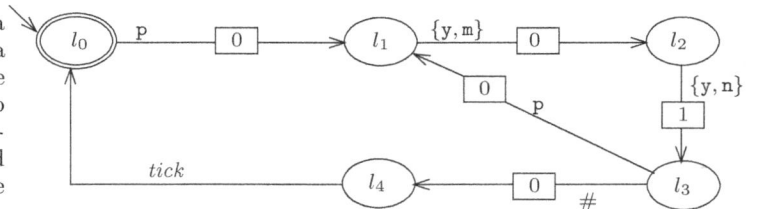

Figure 1: Automaton $\mathcal{A}_0$ with delay blocks.

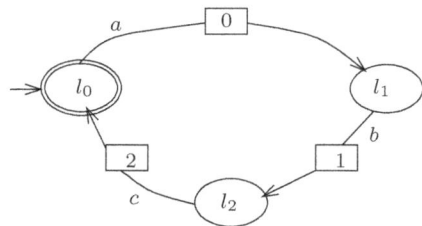

Figure 2: Automaton $\mathcal{A}_1$ with delay blocks.

point coordinates values. We explain the workings of the automaton $\mathcal{A}_0$ in detail below.

The initial location is l_0 which is also the only accepting location. Each edge has a delay block, with the number inside the block denoting the time delay associated with the block. Consider accepting runs of the automaton. The output symbols are *generated* in accepting runs according to the regular expression sequence $(\mathtt{p}\{\mathtt{y},\mathtt{m}\}\{\mathtt{y},\mathtt{n}\})^*$ (the transition labeled *tick* denotes time passing by one time unit and *tick* is not an output symbol). However, because of the associated delays with the transitions, the output symbols (namely $\mathtt{p},\mathtt{y},\mathtt{m},\mathtt{n}$) appear in a different sequence. Consider a particular run sequence $r = \mathtt{pyy}\#\ tick\ \mathtt{pynpmn}\#\ tick$. Recall that time advances in ADBs either via the explicit *tick* transition, or when the run ends in an accepting state. Thus, in the run r, the first four symbols (*i.e.* $\mathtt{pyy}\#$) are generated at time 0. The second $\mathtt{y}$ symbol has an associated delay of 1, the rest have an associated delay of 0. The 0-delay symbols appear immediately in the output (at time 0). Then, we have the first *tick* transition, which results in time advancing to 1. At time 1, first the 1-delay symbol, $\mathtt{y}$ (generated previously) appears at the output. Then, the sequence $\mathtt{pynpmn}\#$ is generated, with the first and the second $\mathtt{n}$ symbols having a delay of 1. Except for these two delayed $\mathtt{n}$ symbols, the rest appear immediately at time 1. Then comes the second *tick* transition which results in time advancing to 2, and at time 2, the two delayed $\mathtt{n}$ symbols appear. Thus, the time stamped output sequence corresponding to the run r after time 2 is $\langle \mathtt{p},0\rangle\langle \mathtt{y},0\rangle\langle \#,0\rangle\langle \mathtt{y},1\rangle\langle \mathtt{p},1\rangle\langle \mathtt{y},1\rangle\langle \mathtt{p},1\rangle\langle \mathtt{m},1\rangle\langle \#,1\rangle\langle \mathtt{n},2\rangle\langle \mathtt{n},2\rangle$ (the second element in the tuples denotes the timestamp when the first element of the tuple appears in the output). $\square$

Example 2. Consider the ADB $\mathcal{A}_1$ in Figure 2. The initial state is l_0, which is also the only accepting state. Consider an accepting run of the automaton. The output symbols are generated in accepting runs according to the regular expression sequence $(abc)^*$. However, the output delay associated with the transition for a is 0, for b is 1, and for c the delay is 2. As there are no explicit time advancing *tick* transi-

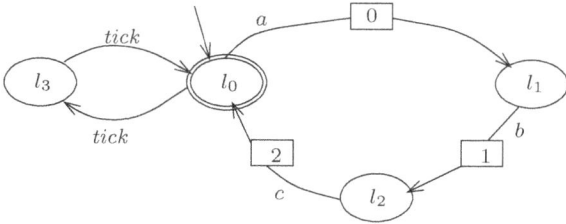

Figure 3: Automaton $\mathcal{A}_2$ with delay blocks.

tions, time advances only when the run ends in the accepting state, and then the symbols with delay 0 are observed (according to their generation sequence), then the symbols at time 1, and so on. It can be seen that the output symbol sequence for the ADB $\mathcal{A}_1$ is $a^n b^n c^n$. Thus, the untimed language $\mathcal{U}(\mathcal{A}_1)$ is $\{a^n b^n c^n \mid n \geq 0\}$. Including the output time stamps in the words, we get the timed language $\mathcal{L}(\mathcal{A}_1)$ as $\{\langle a, 0 \rangle^n \langle b, 1 \rangle^n \langle c, 2 \rangle^n \mid n \geq 0\}$ (no output symbols appear after time 2). $\square$

Example 3. Consider the ADB $\mathcal{A}_2$ in Figure 3. The initial state is l_0, which is also the only accepting state. The accepting runs of the automaton correspond to the regular expression sequence $(abc\,(tick\ tick)^*)^*$. Consider a particular run sequence $r = abc\,abc\ tick\ tick\ abc\ tick\ tick\ tick\ tick\ abc$. Recall that time advances in ADBs either via the explicit *tick* transition, or when the run ends in an accepting state. In the run r, the first two a occurrences are generated at time 0 as no *tick* transitions have been encountered until then; these two a occurrences appear immediately in the output at time 0 (the associated delay is 0 for the delay block). The first two b occurrences are also generated at time 0, but appear in the output at time 1, when the first *tick* transition is taken. The first two c occurrences are generated at time 0, and appear in the output at time 2, when the second *tick* transition is taken. Thus, after the first two *tick* transitions, the time-stamped output string is $\langle a, 0 \rangle^2 \langle b, 1 \rangle^2 \langle c, 2 \rangle^2$. The third a occurrence in r is generated at time 2 (after the first two *tick* transitions), and appears immediately at time 2. The third b occurrence in r is generated at time 2, and appears after a delay of one time unit, when the third *tick* transition is taken. The third c occurrence in r is generated at time 2, and appears at time 4, when the fourth *tick* transition is taken. Continuing in this fashion, we see that the time-stamped output corresponding to the run r is $\langle a, 0 \rangle^2 \langle b, 1 \rangle^2 \langle c, 2 \rangle^2 \langle a, 2 \rangle \langle b, 3 \rangle \langle c, 4 \rangle \langle a, 6 \rangle \langle b, 7 \rangle \langle c, 8 \rangle$.

Letting , $\langle \sigma, i \rangle^0$ denote the empty string, the timed language of the automaton $\mathcal{A}_2$ can be observed to be

$$\mathcal{L}(\mathcal{A}_2) = \left\{ \begin{array}{c} \langle a, 0 \rangle^{n_0} \langle b, 1 \rangle^{n_0} \langle c, 2 \rangle^{n_0} \langle a, 2 \rangle^{n_2} \langle b, 3 \rangle^{n_2} \langle c, 4 \rangle^{n_2} \cdots \\ \langle a, 2k \rangle^{n_{2k}} \langle b, 2k+1 \rangle^{n_{2k}} \langle c, 2k+2 \rangle^{n_{2k}} \\ \text{such that} \\ n_i \geq 0 \text{ for all } i, \text{ and } k \geq 0 \end{array} \right\}$$

The untimed language of the automaton $\mathcal{A}_2$ can be observed to be

$$\mathcal{U}(\mathcal{A}_2) = \left\{ \begin{array}{c} a^{n_0} b^{n_0} c^{n_0} a^{n_1} b^{n_1} c^{n_1} \cdots \\ a^{n_k} b^{n_k} c^{n_k} \end{array} \;\middle|\; n_i \geq 0 \text{ for all } i \text{ and } k \geq 0 \right\}$$

Equivalently, using the untimed language of the automaton $\mathcal{A}_1$ from the previous example, $\mathcal{U}(\mathcal{A}_2) = \{w_0 w_1 \ldots w_n \mid w_i \in \mathcal{U}(\mathcal{A}_1) \text{ for } 0 \leq i \leq n\}$. $\square$

Our contributions. In this work, along with the introduction of ADBs, we study their expressive power, closure properties, and the basic decision and model checking problems. Our main results are as follows:

⋆ *Expressive power:* We show that the untimed languages of ADBs strictly subsume regular languages, and are incomparable in expressive power to context-free languages. ADBs are able to express a simple class of languages not expressible by context-free languages. For example, the automata $\mathcal{A}_1$ of Figure 2 has the untimed language $\{a^n b^n c^n \mid n \geq 0\}$ which is not context free.

⋆ *Closure properties:* We show that untimed ADB languages are closed under union, concatenation, Kleene star, and intersection with regular languages, but not under complementation and intersection with other untimed ADB languages.

⋆ *Decision and model checking problems:* We show that the emptiness and the membership problems are decidable for ADBs in polynomial time, whereas the universality of untimed ADB languages is undecidable. Finally, we consider the model checking problem, where an ADB is considered as the model generating words, and a regular language specifies the desired set of words. The model checking problem is then the containment of the untimed ADB language in the regular language, and we show that the problem is PSPACE-complete.

Thus, ADBs provide a natural and practical extension of finite state automata for modeling discrete time processes involving delays where the output generation is via a regular process. ADBs though incomparable in expressiveness to context-free languages, enjoy several nice properties similar to that of context-free languages, for instance, ADBs admit decidable emptiness, membership and model checking algorithms. We note that the delays used in ADBs are of most use in *modelling* and *analysis* of naturally occurring delays in physical systems, not in directly *building* engineering systems. Thus, non-closure under intersection of ADBs is not a deal-breaker — systems are built compositionally as regular automata; delays are only used in the analysis of the composed system.

For our technical contribution we present illustrative ideas behind two of the key results. (1) We show that the balanced parenthesis language is not expressible as an untimed ADB language. This is a bit surprising because ADBs can express non context-free languages like $a^n b^n c^n$. This inexpressibility (which establishes incomparability to context-free languages) is a result of the fact that the maximum delay present in an ADB limits the "depth" of the nestings in the generated word. Consider a word $a^n \circ w \circ b^n$, where $\circ$ is the concatenation operator, and w is a subword. To match the a^n with the b^n, the ADB needs to use at least one delay block, say of delay k. Then, to express matchings in the word w, it can only use delay blocks of delay *strictly less than* k. (2) We can model check an untimed ADB language against a regular specification (*i.e.* a finite state automaton). To show this, we check for emptiness of an untimed ADB language and a regular language complement of the specification by constructing a non-deterministic finite state automaton which has an accepting path iff the intersection of the languages is non-empty. This automaton maintains a guess of the future executions of the regular specification automaton for M future timepoints, where M is the largest delay of the given ADB. The guesses are verified whenever time advances. The omitted proofs can be found in [5].

Related Work. The model of timed automata [1] is a widely studied formalism for timed systems. Timed automata do not have any construct for delaying generated output symbols, and their untimed languages are regular, unlike for ADBs. In the task scheduling context, a model which is somewhat related has recently been introduced in [16], the digraph real-time task model (DRT). In a DRT instance, jobs are released according to a specified directed weighted graph, where the weights on the edges denote the time that must elapse in between the job releases. The nodes, which correspond to jobs, are annotated with the worst case execution times and the deadlines for the jobs. Thus, the deadline sequence for when the jobs must finish differs from the jobs release sequence due to the deadline and execution time "delays". However, the edge weights in the DRT model are *strictly* positive and integer valued — this implies that the "queue" of currently executing jobs has length at most N where N can be computed from the DRT instance. Thus, the deadline sequences form a regular set. In ADBs, an *unbounded* number of symbols can be generated, before an output symbol is seen, thus the implicit queue is of unbounded length. This additional power of ADBs can be used to model scheduling problems where a bound on the number of job creations per unit time is not known a priori. The work in [13] only delays signals which "hold" for a given time d, where d is a given constant; signals which do not persist for at least d time units are not output. This gives regularity, allowing the system to be modeled as a timed automaton. We do not require a hold time, in our discrete time framework, an unlimited number of letters (actually all) in between two time ticks are delayed if so specified.

The ADB model also has some similarity to computational models of automata augmented with queues. An ADB with M delay blocks can be viewed as writing to M unbounded queues at any given point in time, corresponding to the M delays indexed by the delay blocks. The work in [10] presents decidability results for reader-writer systems augmented with one unbounded queue in between the reader and writer for communication, one pushdown stack for either the reader or writer, and finitely many reversal bounded counters for both. It also shows undecidability for two finite state automata (reader and writer) with two unbounded communication queues in between. The work of [4] shows decidability results for two finite state automata augmented with an unbounded one way communication queue in between them, and mention undecidability if there are more than two communicating finite state automata augmented with just one unbounded queue in the system. The work of [3] presents symbolic semi-algorithms for analyzing communicating finite state automata with queue communication channels. If the queue channels are *lossy*, then decidability can be shown for a variety of problems [2]. Model checking is usually done on systems with *bounded* buffers (see *e.g.* [8]), and suffers from the state explosion problem with increasing buffer size. Our key result shows that the ADB model has the decidable model checking property in spite of containing any number of unbounded *delay* buffers. One key intuition behind the decidable result is the fact that messages corresponding to time Δ are invisible to an observer until all messages corresponding to the previous time-points have been output and consumed.

2. AUTOMATA WITH DELAY BLOCKS

In this section we introduce our model of automata with delay blocks, and illustrate with examples the timed and untimed languages generated by these automata.

Automata with delay blocks (ADB). A finite *automata with delay blocks* (ADB) is a tuple $\mathcal{A} = (L, D, \Sigma, \delta, l_s, L_f)$ where

- L is a finite set of locations.
- $l_s \in L$ is the starting location.
- $L_f \subseteq L$ is the set of accepting locations.
- Σ is the set of output symbols.
- D is a finite set of delay blocks. Each delay block $d \in D$ is indexed by a natural number $t \geq 0$ to indicate the amount of delay for the outputs. We denote a delay block with delay t by $\boxed{t}$.
- δ is the transition relation,

$$\delta : \Big((L \times \Sigma \times D) \ \cup \ (L \times \{\epsilon, tick\}) \Big) \mapsto 2^L$$

where ϵ denotes the empty string, and $tick \notin \Sigma$ denotes a time passage of one time unit.

- A transition $\delta(l, \sigma, \boxed{t}) = L'$ denotes a location change from l to a location in L' non-deterministically, with σ being output t time units into the future.
- A transition $\delta(l, \epsilon) = L'$ denotes an epsilon transition from l to a location in L' non-deterministically, with no new output requirements.
- A transition $\delta(l, tick) = L'$ denotes time advancing by one time unit, and the location changing from l to a location in L' non-deterministically.

A finite string w is a sequence of elements. Given a string w, we let $|w|$ denote the length of the string w, and let $w[i]$ denote the i-th element (starting from index 0) in the string w if $|w| > i$. The empty string is denoted by ϵ. The concatenation of two words w_1 and w_2 is denoted $w_1 w_2$ and also $w_1 \circ w_2$. We also use the standard regular expression constructs. For $i \geq 0$, we denote by $\mathsf{repeat}_i(w)$ the string w repeated i times (letting $\mathsf{repeat}_0(w) = \epsilon$), *i.e.*, $\mathsf{repeat}_i(w)$ is the string $\underbrace{ww \ldots w}_{i \text{ occurences}}$.

Discrete Timed words. A (discrete) timed word w is a finite string belonging to $(\Sigma \times \mathbb{N})^*$ where $\mathbb{N}$ denotes the set of natural numbers. We refer to the first element of the tuple $w[i]$ as the *output symbol* and the second element of the tuple $w[i]$ as the *timestamp*. The timestamps denote the discrete time at which the first element of the tuples appear in the word. We require that for $i < j < |w|$, and for $w[i] = \langle w_i^\sigma, w_i^t \rangle$ and $w[j] = \langle w_j^\sigma, w_j^t \rangle$, we have $w_i^t \leq w_j^t$ (i.e. the timestamps are non-decreasing). Given a timed word $w \in (\Sigma \times \mathbb{N})^*$, let $\mathsf{untime}(w) \in \Sigma^*$ be the untimed word denoting the projection of w onto Σ^*, that is, if $w = \langle \sigma_0, t_0 \rangle \ldots \langle \sigma_m, t_m \rangle$, then $\mathsf{untime}(w) = \sigma_0 \ldots \sigma_m$. Given a timed word $w = \langle \sigma_0, t_0 \rangle \ldots \langle \sigma_n, t_n \rangle$ and a natural number $\Delta \geq 0$, we let $w \oplus \Delta$ be the timed word $\langle \sigma_0, t_0 + \Delta \rangle \ldots \langle \sigma_n, t_n + \Delta \rangle$ (the time stamps are advanced by Δ for all $w[i]$). Given an untimed word $w = \sigma_0 \sigma_1 \ldots \sigma_m$, let $\kappa_t(w)$ denote the timed word $\langle \sigma_0, t \rangle \langle \sigma_1, t \rangle \ldots \langle \sigma_m, t \rangle$, that is, the timed word where each output symbol of w occurs at time t.

Generation of discrete timed words by ADBs. A generating *run* r of the automaton $\mathcal{A}$ is a finite sequence $l_0 \xrightarrow{\alpha_0} l_1 \xrightarrow{\alpha_1} \ldots l_n$ for $\alpha_i \in \{\epsilon, tick\} \cup (\Sigma \times D)$, such that

l_0 is the starting location, l_n is an accepting location and $l_{i+1} \in \delta(l_i, \alpha_i)$ for $0 \leq i \leq n-1$. The automaton $\mathcal{A}$ *outputs* or *generates* the timed word w if there exists a generating run $l_0 \xrightarrow{\alpha_0} l_1 \xrightarrow{\alpha_1} \ldots l_n$ such that $\mathsf{outword}(\alpha_0 \ldots \alpha_n) = w$ where, informally, the $\mathsf{outword}()$ function timestamps the output symbols according to their generation and delay block times, and arranges them in the proper timestamp order. A delay block $\boxed{j}$ delays the output symbol by j time units. At time $t \in \mathbb{N}$ in a run, a delay block $\boxed{j}$ can be considered to be feeding symbols to a queue $\mathcal{Q}_{t+j}$ which will output the stored symbols at time $t+j$ (there is only one queue corresponding to an output time t). A *tick* transition explicitly advances time by one time unit. We also have that once the automaton stops at a final state, time automatically advances with symbols stored in the queues being output at the appropriate times. We note that time advances *only* at *tick* transitions, or when the automaton comes to rest at a final state.

Formally, $\mathsf{outword}(\alpha_0 \ldots \alpha_n)$ is the unique timed word w belonging to $(\Sigma \times \mathbb{N})^*$ defined as follows. For $\overline{\alpha} = \langle \alpha_0 \ldots \alpha_n \rangle$, and $\langle \alpha_i^\sigma, \boxed{\alpha_i^t} \rangle \in \{\alpha_0, \ldots, \alpha_n\}$, let $\mathsf{wtime}(\langle \alpha_i^\sigma, \boxed{\alpha_i^t} \rangle, \overline{\alpha}) = \alpha_i^t + t_i$, where t_i denotes the number of occurrences of *tick* in $\alpha_0, \ldots, \alpha_{i-1}$. Intuitively, the σ-element α_i^σ of each $\langle \alpha_i^\sigma, \boxed{\alpha_i^t} \rangle \in \{\alpha_0, \ldots, \alpha_n\}$, appears exactly once in w, with $\mathsf{wtime}(\langle \alpha_i^\sigma, \boxed{\alpha_i^t} \rangle, \overline{\alpha})$ denoting its timestamp. Formally, $\mathsf{outword}(\alpha_0 \ldots \alpha_n)$ is the unique timed word w such that

- $|w|$ is equal to the number of times symbols from $\Sigma \times \mathbb{N}$ appear in the string $\alpha_0 \alpha_1 \ldots \alpha_n$.

- For all $i < |w|$, we have $w[i] = \langle \alpha_j^\sigma, \mathsf{wtime}(\langle \alpha_j^\sigma, \boxed{\alpha_j^t} \rangle, \overline{\alpha}) \rangle$ where $\langle \alpha_j^\sigma, \boxed{\alpha_j^t} \rangle = \alpha[j]$ is such that for all k and $\alpha[k] = \langle \alpha_k^\sigma, \boxed{\alpha_k^t} \rangle$, the following conditions hold.
  1. If either
     - $k < j$ and $\mathsf{wtime}(\alpha[k], \overline{\alpha}) \leq \mathsf{wtime}(\alpha[j], \overline{\alpha})$; or
     - $k > j$ and $\mathsf{wtime}(\alpha[k], \overline{\alpha}) < \mathsf{wtime}(\alpha[j], \overline{\alpha})$,
     then for some $i' < i$, we have $w[i'] = \langle \alpha_k^\sigma, \mathsf{wtime}(\alpha[k], \overline{\alpha}) \rangle$.
  2. If either
     - $k < j$ and $\mathsf{wtime}(\alpha[k], \overline{\alpha}) > \mathsf{wtime}(\alpha[j], \overline{\alpha})$; or
     - $k > j$ and $\mathsf{wtime}(\alpha[k], \overline{\alpha}) \geq \mathsf{wtime}(\alpha[j], \overline{\alpha})$,
     then for some $i' > i$, we have $w[i'] = \langle \alpha_k^\sigma, \mathsf{wtime}(\alpha[k], \overline{\alpha}) \rangle$.

Thus, the placement of the σ-element of each $\alpha[j]$ is in increasing order of the timestamps $\mathsf{wtime}(\alpha[j], \overline{\alpha})$, and if $\alpha[j]$ and $\alpha[k]$ result in the same timestamp, then the relative ordering is dictated by the relative ordering between j and k.

An equivalent alternative algorithmic definition of the function $\mathsf{outword}()$ is given in Function 1 with $\mathsf{StableSortTime}$ being a stable sorting function which sorts based on the second element of tuples [1].

Output languages of ADBs. The timed output *language* of $\mathcal{A}$ is denoted by $\mathcal{L}(\mathcal{A})$ where $\mathcal{L}(\mathcal{A}) = \{w \mid w$ is a timed word generated by $\mathcal{A}\}$. For a timed language $\mathcal{L}$, we let $\mathsf{untime}(\mathcal{L}) = \{\mathsf{untime}(w) \mid w \in \mathcal{L}\}$. We also let $\mathcal{U}(\mathcal{A})$ denote the untimed language $\mathsf{untime}(\mathcal{L}(\mathcal{A}))$. We have

---
[1] Stable sorting algorithms maintain the original relative ordering of elements with equal key values.

---

input : A string α from $((\Sigma \times D) \cup \{\epsilon, tick\})^*$
output: A timed word w in $(\Sigma \times \mathbb{N})^*$
$w = \epsilon$;
$curr\_time = i = j = 0$;
while $i < |\alpha|$ **do**
    switch $\alpha[i]$ **do**
        case ϵ
            $i := i + 1$;
        case *tick*
            $i := i + 1$;
            $curr\_time := curr\_time + 1$;
        case $\langle \sigma, \boxed{m} \rangle$
            $w[j] = \langle \sigma, curr\_time + m \rangle$;
            $i := i + 1$;
            $j := j + 1$;
    end
end
return $\mathsf{StableSortTime}(w)$;

Function $\mathsf{outword}(\alpha)$

already illustrated languages of ADBs with two examples in the introduction.

ADB Languages obtained from the $\mathsf{outword}$ operation on Regular Languages. Given an ADB $\mathcal{A} = (L, D, \Sigma, \delta, l_s, L_f)$ with the output symbol set Σ and M_d as the largest index for a delay block, there exists a corresponding regular finite automaton $\mathsf{reg}(\mathcal{A}) = (L, \Sigma^\circledcirc, \delta^\circledcirc, l_s, L_f)$ over the delay-stamped symbol set $\Sigma^\circledcirc = \Sigma \times \{0, \ldots, M_d\} \cup \{tick, \epsilon\}$ such that

1. $\delta^\circledcirc(l, \langle \sigma, t \rangle) = \delta(l, \sigma, \boxed{t})$
2. $\delta^\circledcirc(l, \epsilon) = \delta(l, \epsilon)$.
3. $\delta^\circledcirc(l, tick) = \delta(l, tick)$

Intuitively, $\mathsf{reg}(\mathcal{A})$ is just the ADB $\mathcal{A}$ "interpreted" as a regular automaton. The regular language of $\mathsf{reg}(\mathcal{A})$ is denoted by $\mathcal{R}(\mathcal{A})$. We define $\mathsf{outword}(\mathcal{R}(\mathcal{A}))$ to be the timed word language $\{\mathsf{outword}(w) \mid w \in \mathcal{R}(\mathcal{A})\}$.

Proposition 1. *Let $\mathcal{A}$ be an ADB, and let $\mathsf{reg}(\mathcal{A})$ be the corresponding regular finite automaton with the corresponding regular language $\mathcal{R}(\mathcal{A})$. We have $\mathcal{L}(\mathcal{A}) = \mathsf{outword}(\mathcal{R}(\mathcal{A}))$.* $\square$

3. EXPRESSIVENESS OF UNTIMED LANGUAGES OF ADBS

In this section we compare the expressive power untimed languages of ADBs against regular and context free languages. Given a regular or pushdown automaton $\mathcal{A}$ without timed delay blocks, we let $\mathcal{U}(\mathcal{A})$ be the language of $\mathcal{A}$. First we show that ADBs can be considered to be a generalization of regular automata.

Proposition 2 (Generalization of regular automata). *Let $\mathcal{A}$ be a regular automaton without timed delay blocks. Consider the ADB $\mathcal{A}'$ obtained from $\mathcal{A}$ such that (1) $\mathcal{A}'$ has the same set of locations, set of accepting locations and starting location as $\mathcal{A}$; and (2) the transition function $\delta^{\mathcal{A}'}$ is such that $\delta^{\mathcal{A}'}(l, \langle \sigma, 0 \rangle) = \delta^{\mathcal{A}}(l, \sigma)$ and $\delta^{\mathcal{A}'}(l, \epsilon) = \delta^{\mathcal{A}}(l, \epsilon)$. Then, $\mathcal{U}(\mathcal{A}) = \mathcal{U}(\mathcal{A}')$.*

PROOF. The ADB $\mathcal{A}'$ has no tick transitions. Thus since $\mathcal{A}'$ only has delay blocks of duration 0, given a run r of $\mathcal{A}'$, the symbols from Σ are output in the order in which they are encountered in the run r. By construction, there is a one to one correspondence between the runs of $\mathcal{A}'$ and $\mathcal{A}$ such that the output symbol sequence in a run r of $\mathcal{A}'$ is the same as the output symbol sequence in the corresponding run of $\mathcal{A}$. Hence, $\mathcal{U}(\mathcal{A}) = \mathcal{U}(\mathcal{A}')$. $\quad\square$

We next show that the expressive power of untimed languages of ADBs is incomparable to that of context free languages.

Proposition 3. *Let* $\mathcal{U}^{\dagger}$ *be the untimed language*

$$\mathcal{U}^{\dagger} = \left\{ \begin{array}{c} a^{n_1} \# a^{n_2} \# \ldots \# a^{n_m} \# b^{n_m} \# b^{n_{m-1}} \# \ldots \# b^{n_2} \# b^{n_1} \\ such\ that \\ m \geq 0\ and\ n_i \geq 1\ for\ 1 \leq i \leq m \end{array} \right\}.$$

There is no ADB $\mathcal{A}$ such that $\mathcal{U}(\mathcal{A}) = \mathcal{U}^{\dagger}$

PROOF. Intuitively, the proof below shows that the maximum delay present in an ADB limits the "depth" of the nestings in the generated word.

We prove by contradiction. Let $\mathcal{A} = (L, D, \Sigma, \delta, l_s, L_f)$ be any ADB with $\{a, b, \#\}$ as the set of output symbols such that $\mathcal{U}(\mathcal{A}) = \mathcal{U}^{\dagger}$. The automaton $\mathcal{A}$ has a natural graph representation with the nodes in the graph corresponding to locations and the edges corresponding to δ. Let $G = \{S_1, \ldots, S_p\}$ denote the set of strongly connected components (SCCs) of $\mathcal{A}$ which are reachable from l_s, can reach a final location, and which contain at least one a-edge. Observe that every SCC S_i in G:

1. Must have a b-edge, and
2. Cannot have a *tick*-edge (for then an a can be made to appear after a b).
3. Every b-delay in the SCC must be greater than every a-delay (otherwise an a can be made to appear after a b since there are no *tick* edges).

Consider an SCC S from G. Let $p = l_0 l_1 \ldots l_x$ be any path from l_s to an accepting location which passes through S. For $0 \leq i \leq j \leq x$, let $p[i]$ denote the state l_i and $p[i..j]$ the sub-path $l_i \ldots l_j$. Let $p[\alpha..\beta]$ be a (maximal) sub-path which lies entirely within S, *i.e.* such that (1) $\alpha = 0$ or $p[\alpha-1] \notin S$, and (2) $\beta = x$ or $p[\beta+1] \notin S$. Let $C_\alpha^1, \ldots, C_\alpha^q$ be all the non-overlapping cycles (each C_α^k has only one cycle) in $p[\alpha..\beta]$ such that the C_α^j occurs after C_α^i for $j > i$. The sub-path $p[\alpha..\beta]$ can then be written as

$$p[\alpha]\, p[\alpha+1] \ldots p[e_1]\, (C_\alpha^1)^{h_1}\, p[f_1] \ldots p[e_2]\, (C_\alpha^2)^{h_2} \ldots$$
$$(C_\alpha^q)^{h_q}\, p[f_q] \ldots p[\beta]$$

for some $e_1, f_1, h_1 \ldots e_q, f_q, h_q$ such that the following sub-paths of $p[\alpha..\beta]$ are all cycle free: (1) the path $p[\alpha]\, p[\alpha + 1] \ldots p[e_1]$; (2) the paths $p[f_{k-1}] \ldots p[e_k]$ for all $2 \leq k \leq q$; and (3) the path $p[f_q] \ldots p[\beta]$. The structure of the subpath $p[\alpha..\beta]$ is illustrated in Figure 4. Thus, C_α^1 is the first cycle in the $p[\alpha..\beta]$ sub-path, C_α^2 is the next cycle and so on. Observe that we may have $C_\alpha^i = C_\alpha^j$ for $i \neq j$.

Observe that each cycle C_α^i must have an a-transition (otherwise two consecutive $\#$ symbols can be made to appear in the output). Note that for any path $p[\alpha..\beta]$ and any such subcycle of the path, we must have that the number of a-edges in the subcycle equals the number of b-edges (otherwise we can "pump" the cycle to get a's that are unmatched by b's; as the matching must occur inside the the same cycle). Thus, each C_α^i can generate some $a^k..b^k$ pair. Consider any C_α^i. Let the maximum a-delay be Δ_a^i in C_α^i, and let the

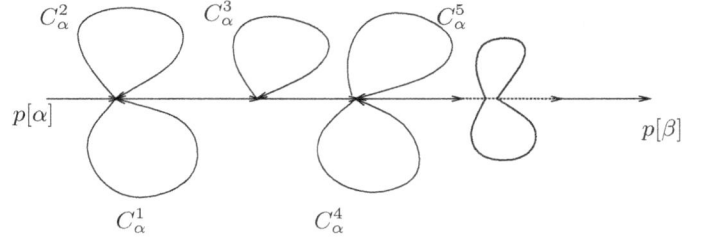

Figure 4: Structure of sub-path $p[\alpha..\beta]$.

minimum b-delay be Δ_b^i. For any $j \neq i$, we must have one of the following to hold:

1. Either $\Delta_a^i = \Delta_a^j$ and $\Delta_b^i \neq \Delta_b^j$;
2. Or $\Delta_b^i = \Delta_b^j$ and $\Delta_a^i \neq \Delta_a^j$; or
3. $\Delta_b^i \neq \Delta_b^j$ and $\Delta_a^i \neq \Delta_a^j$.

For otherwise, if $\Delta_a^i = \Delta_a^j$ and $\Delta_b^i = \Delta_b^j$ the two cycles will generate an untimed subpart $a^{n_{k_1}} \# a^{n_{k_2}} \# b^{n_{k_1}} \# b^{n_{k_2}}$ (with enough pumping), when they should be generating the string with the b's switched (*i.e.* the string $a^{n_{i_1}} \# a^{n_{i_2}} \# b^{n_{i_2}} \# b^{n_{i_1}}$). Thus, in any accepting path $p[\alpha..\beta]$ via the SCC S, we can only have at most M^2 subcycles $C_\alpha^1, \ldots, C_\alpha^q$, *i.e.* $q \leq M^2$ (as there are only at most M^2 distinct values of $\langle \Delta_a, \Delta_b \rangle$ tuples.

Since the maximum delay is finite (say $M - 1$), the cycles in S can generate at most M^2 pairs of unbounded numbers of a's and b's. That is, the SCC S cannot generate the untimed language

$$\left\{ \begin{array}{c} a^{n_1} \# a^{n_2} \# \ldots \# a^{n_{M^2+1}} \# b^{n_{M^2+1}} \# b^{n_{M^2}} \# \ldots \# b^{n_2} \# b^{n_1} \\ such\ that \\ n_i \geq 1\ for\ 1 \leq i \leq M^2 + 1 \end{array} \right\}.$$

Hence, if there are K SCCs in $\mathcal{A}$, then $\mathcal{A}$ cannot generate the untimed language

$$\left\{ \begin{array}{c} a^{n_1} \# a^{n_2} \# \ldots \# a^{n_{M^2+K+1}} \# b^{n_{M^2+K+1}} \# b^{n_{M^2+K}} \# \ldots \# b^{n_2} \# b^{n_1} \\ such\ that \\ n_i \geq 1\ for\ 1 \leq i \leq M^2 + K + 1 \end{array} \right\}.$$

Hence, it follows that there does not exist an ADB $\mathcal{A}$ such that $\mathcal{U}(\mathcal{A}) = \mathcal{U}^{\dagger}$. $\quad\square$

Proposition 4 (Incomparability with Pushdown Automata). *The following assertions hold.*

1. *There exists an ADB $\mathcal{A}$ such that $\mathcal{U}(\mathcal{A})$ is not context free.*
2. *There exists a visibly pushdown automata $\mathcal{A}$ such that there is no ADB $\mathcal{A}'$ with $\mathcal{U}(\mathcal{A}) = \mathcal{U}(\mathcal{A}')$.*

PROOF. For the first part of the proposition, consider the ADB $\mathcal{A}_1$ of Figure 2. The untimed language of $\mathcal{A}_1$ is $\{a^n b^n c^n \mid n \geq 0\}$ which is not context free. The second part of the theorem follows from Proposition 3, noting that there exists a visibly pushdown automaton which generates the language $\mathcal{U}^{\dagger}$. $\quad\square$

Proposition 4 shows that there is a tradeoff between the expressive power of ADBs and pushdown automata. On one hand, ADBs are not restricted to matching only once (i.e., they can generate $a^n b^n c^n$), but on the other they lose the infinite nesting capability of pushdown automata (e.g., in the language $\mathcal{U}^{\dagger}$ of Proposition 3).

Theorem 1 (Expressive power of ADBs). *The following assertions hold: (1) The class of untimed languages of ADBs strictly subsumes the class of regular languages. (2) The class of untimed languages of ADBs is incomparable in expressive power as compared to the class of context-free languages.*

PROOF. The results follow from Propositions 2 and 4. □

4. CLOSURE PROPERTIES

In this section we will study the closure properties of timed and untimed languages of ADBs with respect to operations like union, intersection, complement, concatenation and Kleene star.

Proposition 5 (Closure under union). *Let $\mathcal{A}_1$ and $\mathcal{A}_2$ be ADBs. There exists an ADB $\mathcal{A}$ such that $\mathcal{L}(\mathcal{A}) = \mathcal{L}(\mathcal{A}_1) \cup \mathcal{L}(A_2)$.*

PROOF. The ADB $\mathcal{A}$ has a special initial states, and two ϵ transitions from this initial state to copies of $\mathcal{A}_1$ and $\mathcal{A}_2$. □

Proposition 6 (Closure under intersection with regular languages). *Given an untimed ADB language $\mathcal{U}$ and a regular language $\mathcal{R}$, the language $\mathcal{U} \cap \mathcal{R}$ is an untimed ADB language.*

PROOF. Given an ADB $\mathcal{A}_1$ with $\mathcal{U}$ and a finite-state automata $\mathcal{A}_2$ for a regular language $\mathcal{R}$, we will present an explicit construction of an ADB with untimed language $\mathcal{U} \cap \mathcal{R}$ in Proposition 15. The desired result will follow from the construction. □

Concatenation and Kleene star. We will now consider closure under concatenation and Kleene star. Given untimed languages $\mathcal{U}, \mathcal{U}_1$ and $\mathcal{U}_2$, we define their concatenation $\mathcal{U}_1 \circ \mathcal{U}_2$ and Kleene star $\mathcal{U}^*$ as follows:

$$\mathcal{U}_1 \circ \mathcal{U}_2 \triangleq \{w_1 \circ w_2 \mid w_1 \in \mathcal{U}_1 \text{ and } w_2 \in \mathcal{U}_2\}$$

$$\mathcal{U}^* \triangleq \{\epsilon\} \cup \{w_1 \circ w_2 \circ \ldots \circ w_i \mid i \in \mathbb{N}, 1 \leq j \leq i. w_j \in \mathcal{U}\}$$

Proposition 7 (Closure under concatenation). *Let $\mathcal{U}_1$ and $\mathcal{U}_2$ be untimed ADB languages. Then $\mathcal{U}_1 \circ \mathcal{U}_2$ is an untimed ADB language.* □

Proposition 8 (Closure under Kleene star). *Let $\mathcal{U}$ be an untimed ADB language. Then $\mathcal{U}^*$ is an untimed ADB language.* □

We will now show the ADB languages are not closed under some Boolean operations, and towards this goal we first prove a pumping lemma.

Proposition 9 (Pumping Lemma for ADB runs). *Let $\mathcal{A}$ be an ADB and let L be the set of locations of $\mathcal{A}$. Let $w \in \mathcal{L}(\mathcal{A})$ with $|w| > |L|$ be the output timed word corresponding to an accepting run $r = l_0 \xrightarrow{\alpha_0} l_1 \xrightarrow{\alpha_1} \ldots l_n$. Consider any subrun r_s of r, i.e. $r = r_0 \circ r_s \circ r_1$, such that r_s contains at least $|L|$ transitions. Then, there exists a subrun r_p of r_s, i.e. $r_s = r_{s_0} \circ r_p \circ r_{s_1}$ with r_p containing at most $|L|$ transitions such that for all $i \geq 0$ the runs $r_0 \circ r_{s_0} \circ \mathsf{repeat}_i(r_p) \circ r_{s_1} \circ r_1$ are also accepting runs of $\mathcal{A}$.*

PROOF. The proof follows from the pumping lemma for regular finite state automata, and from Proposition 1. □

Remark 1. There are difficulties in obtaining a pumping lemma for timed words. We give an example. Let $r, r_0, r_{s_0}, r_p, r_{s_1}, r_1$ be as in Proposition 9. Let w be the timed word corresponding to the run r. Let $\langle \sigma_\alpha, t_\alpha \rangle$ and $\langle \sigma_\beta, t_\beta \rangle$ be the timestamped symbols generated by some transition in $r_0 \circ r_{s_0}$, and by some transition in $r_{s_1} \circ r_1$ respectively. Let us denote these two transitions as tr_α and tr_β. We may have $t_\alpha > t_\beta$, *i.e.* $\langle \sigma_\alpha, t_\alpha \rangle$ appears after $\langle \sigma_\beta, t_\beta \rangle$ in the timed word w, even though the transition which generates $\langle \sigma_\alpha, t_\alpha \rangle$ occurs before the transition which generates $\langle \sigma_\beta, t_\beta \rangle$. Let the number of *tick* transitions in r_p be Δ_p. Each "pump" of r_p introduces an additional delay of Δ_p between when the transitions tr_α and tr_β occur. Eventually, after enough pumps, the delay will large enough that the timestamped output symbol corresponding to tr_β will appear after the timestamped output symbol corresponding to tr_α. Thus, when we pump an accepting run, the resulting timed word, with each pump, may undergo a *reordering* of the output symbols corresponding to the unpumped run parts. There is also a reordering corresponding to the pumped run part. □

Proposition 10 (Non-closure under intersection). *There exist ADBs $\mathcal{A}_1$ and $\mathcal{A}_2$ such that (1) $\mathcal{L}(\mathcal{A}_1) \cap \mathcal{L}(\mathcal{A}_2)$ is not an ADB language, and (2) $\mathcal{U}(\mathcal{A}_1) \cap \mathcal{U}(\mathcal{A}_2)$ is not an untimed ADB language.*

PROOF. (Sketch.) Consider the language

$$\mathcal{L}^\dagger = \left\{ \kappa_0(w\#)\kappa_1(w\#)\kappa_2(w\#)\ldots\kappa_n(w\#) \left| \begin{array}{l} w \in \{a,b\}^* \text{ and} \\ n \geq 0 \end{array} \right. \right\}$$

where $\kappa_i()$ is the function defined in Section 2. We show $\mathcal{L}^\dagger$ is not an ADB language, and that there exist ADBs $\mathcal{A}_1$ and $\mathcal{A}_2$ such that $\mathcal{L}^\dagger = \mathcal{L}(\mathcal{A}_1) \cap \mathcal{L}(\mathcal{A}_2)$. To show the first claim, let $\mathcal{L}^\dagger$ be the output language of an ADB $\mathcal{A}^\dagger$ containing K locations. Consider a timed word $w_\dagger = \kappa_0(w\#)\kappa_1(w\#)\kappa_2(w\#)\ldots\kappa_{K+2}(w\#)$ with $|w| > K$. Let $r_\dagger$ be the generating run for $w_\dagger$. Using the pumping lemma, we can show there exists a subrun r_p of $r_\dagger$ such that (1) the subrun r_p contains at least one output symbol transition, and (2) the subrun contains at most K output symbol transitions; and (3) for $r_\dagger = r_0 \circ r_p \circ r_1$, we have that $r_0 \circ r_1$ is also a generating run for $\mathcal{A}^\dagger$ (*i.e.*, we pump down r_p). Let w_{01} be the output word corresponding to the generating run $r_0 \circ r_1$. Because of the constraints on r_p, we have that w_{01} contains at least one, and at most K output symbols less than w. It can be checked that this means that w_{01} is not a member of $\mathcal{L}^\dagger$, a contradiction. To show that $\mathcal{L}^\dagger$ is the intersection of two ADB languages, we consider two ADBs, the first ADB checks that the word with timestamp $2j$ matches the word with time $2j + 1$ for all j; the second ADB checks that the word with timestamp $2j + 1$ matches the word with time $2j + 2$ for all j. It can checked that such ADBs exist and that the intersection of the languages is $\mathcal{L}^\dagger$. □

Proposition 11 (Non-closure under complementation). *Given and ADB $\mathcal{A}$, let $\overline{\mathcal{L}}(\mathcal{A})$ denote the complement language of $\mathcal{L}(\mathcal{A})$. There exists an ADB $\mathcal{A}$ such that for all ADBs $\mathcal{A}'$ we have $\overline{\mathcal{L}}(\mathcal{A}) \neq \mathcal{L}(\mathcal{A}')$, and $\overline{\mathcal{U}}(\mathcal{A}) \neq \mathcal{U}(\mathcal{A}')$.* □

We summarize our results in the following theorem.

Theorem 2 (Closure properties). *The class of untimed languages of ADBs are closed under union, concatenation, Kleene star, and intersection with regular languages, but not closed under intersection and complementation.* □

5. DECISION PROBLEMS AND MODEL CHECKING

In this section we first study the decision problems such as emptiness, universality for ADBs, and then study the model checking problem. In the model checking problem we consider an ADB as the model to generate words, and a specification given as regular language. Our goal is to check the containment of the untimed language of the ADB in the regular language.

5.1 Decision Problems

Proposition 12 (Emptiness checking). *Given an ADB $\mathcal{A}$, it can be checked in linear time whether $\mathcal{L}(\mathcal{A}) = \emptyset$.*

PROOF. The proposition follows from the fact that $\mathcal{L}(\mathcal{A})$ is non-empty iff there is a path from the initial location to an accepting location. $\square$

Proposition 13 (Membership checking of timed words). *Given an ADB $\mathcal{A}$ with $n_{\mathcal{A}}$ locations and $m_{\mathcal{A}}$ edges, and a timed word w, checking whether $w \in \mathcal{L}(\mathcal{A})$ can be checked in time $O\left(M \cdot (n_{\mathcal{A}} + m_{\mathcal{A}} + |w| + \mathsf{T_e})\right)$, where $\mathsf{T_e}$ is the largest timestamp in w, and M is the largest delay of a delay block in $\mathcal{A}$ (thus, if M is a constant and $\mathsf{T_e} = O(n_{\mathcal{A}} + m_{\mathcal{A}} + |w|)$, then we have a linear time algorithm).*

PROOF. (Sketch.) Let $w = \langle w_0^{\sigma}, w_0^t \rangle \langle w_1^{\sigma}, w_1^t \rangle \ldots \langle w_n^{\sigma}, w_n^t \rangle$. Let the end timestamp of w be $\mathsf{T_e}$ (*i.e.* $w_n^t = \mathsf{T_e}$). We first construct a finite state deterministic regular automaton $\mathcal{A}_w$ with just one path (corresponding to w) over the alphabet $\Sigma_w = \{tick, \langle w_0^{\sigma}, w_0^t \rangle, \langle w_1^{\sigma}, w_1^t \rangle \ldots \langle w_n^{\sigma}, w_n^t \rangle\}$. We then construct a (non-deterministic) ADB $\mathcal{A}^{\ddagger}$ based on $\mathcal{A}$ and $\mathcal{A}_w$ such that $\mathcal{A}^{\ddagger}$ has an accepting path iff $\mathcal{A}$ outputs the timed word w. Let M be the largest delay of a delay block in $\mathcal{A}$. The automaton $\mathcal{A}^{\ddagger}$ will simulate the executions of $\mathcal{A}$; and of $\mathcal{A}_w$ simultaneously for the current time, and for time upto M time units in the future. That is, the automaton $\mathcal{A}^{\ddagger}$ is able to verify that $\mathcal{A}_w$ first generates the output symbols corresponding to the current time outputs in $\mathcal{A}$, then generate output symbols corresponding to current time plus one in $\mathcal{A}$, and so on. The details of the construction are omitted for lack of space. $\square$

Proposition 14 (Universality). *Let $\mathcal{A}$ be an ADB. It is undecidable to check whether $\mathcal{U}(\mathcal{A}) = \Sigma^*$.*

PROOF. Let $\mathcal{T}$ be a Turing machine with Σ as the tape alphabet Let a valid computation of $\mathcal{T}$ be denoted by an untimed string $w = w_0 \# w_1 \# \ldots w_n$ such that w_0 represents the initial tape configuration, w_{i+1} is a tape configuration that follows from w_i for $i \geq 0$, and $\#$ is a special delimiter symbol. We first show that there exists an ADB $\mathcal{A}$ such that $\mathcal{U}(\mathcal{A})$ is the set of strings denoting the invalid computations of $\mathcal{T}$.

If a string w represents an invalid computation, then one of the following conditions must hold.

1. The string w is not of the form $w_0 \# w_1 \# \ldots w_n$, where each w_i denotes a tape configuration.
2. w_0 is not an initial tape configuration.
3. w_n is not an accepting tape configuration.
4. w_{i+1} does not follow from w_i for some i.

The set of strings satisfying conditions 1,2 or 3 is regular. There exists an ADB $\mathcal{A}'$ such that $\mathcal{U}(\mathcal{A}')$ is the set of strings satisfying the last condition. The automaton $\mathcal{A}'$ first generates strings from $(\Sigma \cup \{\#\})^*$ at time 0. It then non-deterministically moves to a location from which it generates $w_i \# w_{i+1}$ such that (a) w_i is a configuration (*i.e.*, a string from $\Sigma^* Q \Sigma^*$ where Q is the set of locations of $\mathcal{T}$, (b) the configuration w_i is generated at time 0 and w_{i+1} generated at time 1, and (c) w_{i+1} is not a configuration that follows from w_i (this can be done by "knowing" some future two symbols of w_i at time 0, and accordingly generating a symbol at time 1 for w_{i+1} such that w_{i+1} cannot be a configuration following w_i. Once such $w_i \# w_{i+1}$ is generated, $\mathcal{A}'$ then generates strings from $(\Sigma \cup \{\#\})^*$ at time 2. Since ADBs are closed under union, we can take the union of ADBs generating untimed strings satisfying either of the four conditions. The ADBs for conditions 1,2 and 3 "operate" at times 3, 4 and 5 respectively (*i.e.* they are regular automatons with delay blocks of 3,4 and 5 respectively at every transition). This union ADB $\mathcal{A}$ will then generate all untimed strings denoting invalid computations of $\mathcal{T}$.

Now, if were decidable to check whether $\mathcal{U}(\mathcal{A}) = \Sigma^*$, then it would mean we can check whether the language of $\mathcal{T}$ is non-empty, as the language of $\mathcal{T}$ is non-empty iff the there exists a valid computation of $\mathcal{T}$, and a valid computation of $\mathcal{T}$ exists iff $\mathcal{U}(\mathcal{A}) \neq \Sigma^*$, Thus, if $\mathcal{A}$ is an ADB, it is undecidable in general to check whether $\mathcal{U}(\mathcal{A}) = \Sigma^*$. $\square$

Corollary 1 (Equivalence to a regular language). *Let $\mathcal{A}$ be an ADB and let $\mathcal{R}$ be a regular language. It is undecidable to check whether $\mathcal{U}(\mathcal{A}) = \mathcal{R}$.* $\square$

Corollary 2 (Containment in another delay model). *Let $\mathcal{A}$ and $\mathcal{A}'$ be ADBs. It is undecidable to check whether $\mathcal{U}(\mathcal{A}) \subseteq \mathcal{U}(\mathcal{A}')$.*

PROOF. We reduce universality of untimed languages of ADBs to this problem. Let $\mathcal{A}$ be an ADB such that $\mathcal{U}(\mathcal{A}) = \Sigma^*$. Then, given any ADB $\mathcal{A}'$, we have $\mathcal{U}(\mathcal{A}) \subseteq \mathcal{U}(\mathcal{A}')$ iff $\mathcal{U}(\mathcal{A}') = \Sigma^*$. $\square$

Theorem 3 (Decision problems). *The following assertions hold for timed and untimed ADB languages:*
1. *The emptiness checking can be achieved in linear time, and the membership checking can also be achieved in linear time if the largest delay of the delay blocks is constant, and the largest timestamp in the word is of the order of the length of the word plus the automaton size.*
2. *The universality, containment in other untimed ADB languages, and equivalence to regular languages are undecidable.*

PROOF. The first item follows from Proposition 12 and Proposition 13. The second item follows from Proposition 14, Corollaries 1 and 2. $\square$

5.2 Model Checking

In this section we study the containment of a given untimed language of an ADB within a given regular language.

Proposition 15 (Checking emptiness of intersection with a regular language). *Let $\mathcal{A}$ be an ADB, and let $\mathcal{A}_r$ be a regular finite state automaton. It is decidable to check emptiness of $\mathcal{U}(\mathcal{A}) \cap \mathcal{U}(\mathcal{A}_r)$ in time $O(n_{\mathcal{A}} \cdot n_{\mathcal{A}_r}^{2M+1} + m_{\mathcal{A}} \cdot m_{\mathcal{A}_r}^{M+1} + m_{\mathcal{A}} \cdot n_{\mathcal{A}_r})$ where $n_{\mathcal{A}}, n_{\mathcal{A}_r}$ are the numbers of locations in $\mathcal{A}, \mathcal{A}_r$ and $m_{\mathcal{A}}, m_{\mathcal{A}_r}$ the numbers of edges in $\mathcal{A}, \mathcal{A}_r$ respectively, and M is the largest delay of a delay block in $\mathcal{A}$.*

PROOF. We construct a non-deterministic ADB $\mathcal{A}^\dagger$ such that $\mathcal{U}(\mathcal{A}^\dagger) = \mathcal{U}(\mathcal{A}) \cap \mathcal{U}(\mathcal{A}_r)$ and then apply Proposition 12.

Let M be the largest delay of a delay block in $\mathcal{A}$. The automaton $\mathcal{A}^\dagger$ will simulate the executions of $\mathcal{A}$; and of $\mathcal{A}_r$ simultaneously for the current time, and for time upto M time units in the future. That is, the automaton $\mathcal{A}^\dagger$ is able to verify that some execution of $\mathcal{A}_r$ is such that $\mathcal{A}_r$ first generates the output symbols corresponding to the current time outputs in $\mathcal{A}$, then generates symbols corresponding to current time plus one in $\mathcal{A}$, and so on. To concurrently simulate executions of $\mathcal{A}_r$ corresponding to $M+1$ time points,

the automaton will maintain a tuple of locations. The tuple will have $2M + 2$ components:

1. The first component will correspond to a location of $\mathcal{A}$, and is used to simulate executions of $\mathcal{A}$.
2. The next $M+1$ components will correspond to locations of $\mathcal{A}_r$ used for concurrently simulating $\mathcal{A}_r$ corresponding to the current time point, and the next M time points.
3. The final M components correspond to the "guesses" on the locations of $\mathcal{A}_r$ for the final locations of the initial and following $M-1$ timepoints. Whenever time elapses in $\mathcal{A}$ via an explicit *tick* transition, we verify that our "guesses" for the ending locations of $\mathcal{A}_r$ are correct.

Formally, let $\mathcal{A} = (L^{\mathcal{A}}, D^{\mathcal{A}}, \Sigma, \delta^{\mathcal{A}}, l_s^{\mathcal{A}}, L_f^{\mathcal{A}})$ and $\mathcal{A}_r = (L^{\mathcal{A}_r}, \Sigma, \delta^{\mathcal{A}_r}, l_s^{\mathcal{A}_r}, L_f^{\mathcal{A}_r})$. The ADB $\mathcal{A}^\dagger$ is as follows:

- The location set $L^{\mathcal{A}^\dagger}$ is $L^{\mathcal{A}} \times \left(L^{\mathcal{A}_r}\right)^{2M+1} \cup \{l_s^{\mathcal{A}^\dagger}\}$ where M is the largest delay of a delay block in $\mathcal{A}$, and $l_s^{\mathcal{A}^\dagger}$ is a new location.
- The initial location is $l_s^{\mathcal{A}^\dagger}$.
- The transition function $\delta^{\mathcal{A}^\dagger}$ is as follows:

  - $\delta^{\mathcal{A}^\dagger}(l_s^{\mathcal{A}^\dagger}, \epsilon) = \left\{ \langle l_s^{\mathcal{A}}, l_s^{\mathcal{A}_r}, l_1^{\mathcal{A}_r}, \ldots, l_M^{\mathcal{A}_r}, l_1^{\mathcal{A}_r}, \ldots, l_M^{\mathcal{A}_r} \rangle \;\middle|\; \begin{array}{l} l_s^{\mathcal{A}} \text{ is the initial location of } \mathcal{A}, \\ \mathcal{A}_s^{\mathcal{A}_r} \text{ is the initial location of } \mathcal{A}_r \\ \text{and } l_j^{\mathcal{A}_r} \in L \text{ for } M \geq j \geq 1 \end{array} \right\}$

    The locations $l_s^{\mathcal{A}_r}, l_1^{\mathcal{A}_r}, \ldots, l_M^{\mathcal{A}_r}$ for $\mathcal{A}_r$ correspond the starting location for the current time, and for the following M time points. The guessed locations $l_1^{\mathcal{A}_r}, \ldots, l_M^{\mathcal{A}_r}$ are explicitly stored as the last M components (to be verified later). There is an ϵ-transition from $l_s^{\mathcal{A}^\dagger}$ to various locations corresponding to all the possible guesses for the starting locations for times 1 through M.

  - $\delta^{\mathcal{A}^\dagger}(\langle l_0^{\mathcal{A}}, l_0^{\mathcal{A}_r}, l_1^{\mathcal{A}_r}, \ldots, l_M^{\mathcal{A}_r}, \tilde{l}_1^{\mathcal{A}_r}, \ldots, \tilde{l}_M^{\mathcal{A}_r} \rangle, \sigma, \boxed{t}) =$

    $$\left\{ \langle {l'_0}^{\mathcal{A}}, {l'_0}^{\mathcal{A}_r}, {l'_1}^{\mathcal{A}_r}, \ldots, {l'_M}^{\mathcal{A}_r}, \tilde{l}_1^{\mathcal{A}_r}, \ldots, \tilde{l}_M^{\mathcal{A}_r} \rangle \;\middle|\; \begin{array}{l} {l'_0}^{\mathcal{A}} \in \delta^{\mathcal{A}}(l_0^{\mathcal{A}}, \langle \sigma, \boxed{t} \rangle), \\ {l'_t}^{\mathcal{A}_r} \in \delta^{\mathcal{A}_r}(l_t^{\mathcal{A}_r}, \sigma), \text{ and} \\ {l'_j}^{\mathcal{A}_r} = l_j^{\mathcal{A}_r} \text{ for } j \neq t \end{array} \right\}$$

    This transition corresponds to the case when $\mathcal{A}$ transitions on $\langle \sigma, \boxed{t} \rangle$ from location $l_0^{\mathcal{A}}$. In the location $\langle l_0^{\mathcal{A}}, l_0^{\mathcal{A}_r}, l_1^{\mathcal{A}_r}, \ldots, l_M^{\mathcal{A}_r}, \tilde{l}_1^{\mathcal{A}_r}, \ldots, \tilde{l}_M^{\mathcal{A}_r} \rangle$ of $\mathcal{A}'_r$, the component corresponding to t time units in the future is updated. The location component of $\mathcal{A}$ is also updated. The rest of the components remain the same.

  - $\delta^{\mathcal{A}^\dagger}(\langle l_0^{\mathcal{A}}, l_0^{\mathcal{A}_r}, l_1^{\mathcal{A}_r}, \ldots, l_M^{\mathcal{A}_r}, \tilde{l}_1^{\mathcal{A}_r}, \ldots, \tilde{l}_M^{\mathcal{A}_r} \rangle, \epsilon) =$

    $$\left\{ \langle {l'_0}^{\mathcal{A}}, {l'_0}^{\mathcal{A}_r}, {l'_1}^{\mathcal{A}_r}, \ldots, {l'_M}^{\mathcal{A}_r}, \tilde{l}_1^{\mathcal{A}_r}, \ldots, \tilde{l}_M^{\mathcal{A}_r} \rangle \;\middle|\; \begin{array}{l} {l'_0}^{\mathcal{A}} \in \delta^{\mathcal{A}}(l_0^{\mathcal{A}}, \epsilon) \cup \{l_0^{\mathcal{A}}\} \text{ and} \\ {l'_j}^{\mathcal{A}_r} \in \delta^{\mathcal{A}_r}(l_j^{\mathcal{A}_r}, \epsilon) \cup \{l_j^{\mathcal{A}_r}\} \text{ for } M \geq j \geq 0 \end{array} \right\}$$

    The ϵ-transitions of $\mathcal{A}^\dagger$ correspond to the case when either $\mathcal{A}$ or $\mathcal{A}_r$ make ϵ-transitions. The automaton $\mathcal{A}_r$ can make ϵ-transitions either at the current time, or be supposed to make them in the future.

  - $\delta^{\mathcal{A}^\dagger}(\langle l_0^{\mathcal{A}}, l_0^{\mathcal{A}_r}, l_1^{\mathcal{A}_r}, \ldots, l_M^{\mathcal{A}_r}, \tilde{l}_1^{\mathcal{A}_r}, \ldots, \tilde{l}_M^{\mathcal{A}_r} \rangle, tick) =$

    * If $l_0^{\mathcal{A}_r} = \tilde{l}_1^{\mathcal{A}_r}$ then

      $$\left\{ \langle {l'_0}^{\mathcal{A}}, {l'_0}^{\mathcal{A}_r}, {l'_1}^{\mathcal{A}_r}, \ldots, {l'_M}^{\mathcal{A}_r}, {\tilde{l}'_1}^{\mathcal{A}_r}, \ldots, {\tilde{l}'_M}^{\mathcal{A}_r} \rangle \;\middle|\; \begin{array}{l} {l'_0}^{\mathcal{A}} \in \delta^{\mathcal{A}}(l_0^{\mathcal{A}}, tick), \\ {l'_j}^{\mathcal{A}_r} = l_{j+1}^{\mathcal{A}_r} \text{ and } {\tilde{l}'_j}^{\mathcal{A}_r} = \tilde{l}_{j+1}^{\mathcal{A}_r} \text{ for } 0 \leq j \leq M-1, \\ {l'_M}^{\mathcal{A}_r} \in L^{\mathcal{A}_r} \text{ and } {\tilde{l}'_M}^{\mathcal{A}_r} \in L^{\mathcal{A}_r} \text{ with } {l'_M}^{\mathcal{A}_r} = {\tilde{l}'_M}^{\mathcal{A}_r} \end{array} \right\}$$

    * $\emptyset$ otherwise.

    When time advances from time t to $t+1$ in $\mathcal{A}^\dagger$ (and in $\mathcal{A}$), we need to verify that the initial guess $\tilde{l}_1^{\mathcal{A}_r}$ was correct (recall that $\tilde{l}_1^{\mathcal{A}_r}$ was guessed previously in time t to be the location in $\mathcal{A}_r$ at the beginning of time $t+1$). Also, since one time unit has passed, the guess $\tilde{l}_{j+1}^{\mathcal{A}_r}$ for the earlier $j+1$-th future time unit now becomes the guess corresponding to j-th future time unit. Similarly, the location component $l_{j+1}^{\mathcal{A}_r}$ corresponding to the $j+1$-th future time unit now becomes the location component corresponding to j-th future time unit. A new guess for the starting location for the M-th future time unit is also chosen.

- The set of final locations is

$$\left\{ \langle l_0^{\mathcal{A}}, l_0^{\mathcal{A}_r}, l_1^{\mathcal{A}_r}, \ldots, l_M^{\mathcal{A}_r}, \tilde{l}_1^{\mathcal{A}_r}, \ldots, \tilde{l}_M^{\mathcal{A}_r} \rangle \ \middle| \ \begin{array}{l} l_0^{\mathcal{A}} \in L_f^{\mathcal{A}} \text{ and } l_M^{\mathcal{A}_r} \in L_f^{\mathcal{A}_r} \text{ and} \\ l_j^{\mathcal{A}_r} = \tilde{l}_{j+1}^{\mathcal{A}_r} \text{ for } 0 \le j \le M-1 \end{array} \right\}$$

$\mathcal{A}^{\dagger}$ ensures that the automaton $\mathcal{A}_r$ ends up in an accepting location at the end. Also, $\mathcal{A}^{\dagger}$ checks that the guesses for the starting locations at each of the M future timepoints were correct.

The automaton $\mathcal{A}^{\dagger}$ has an accepting run $\pi^{\dagger}$ only if both of the conditions hold.

1. The run $\pi^{\dagger}$ corresponds to a matching generating run π in $\mathcal{A}$.

2. The untimed word $\mathsf{untime}(w_\pi)$ can be generated from $\mathcal{A}_r$, where w_π denotes the timed word output by $\mathcal{A}$ corresponding to the generating path π. That is, the automaton $\mathcal{A}_r$ generates the output symbols in w_π in the *right order* corresponding to $\mathsf{untime}(w_\pi)$.

Thus, we have that $\mathcal{U}(\mathcal{A}^{\dagger}) = \mathcal{U}(\mathcal{A}) \cap \mathcal{U}(\mathcal{A}_r)$., and that $\mathcal{U}(\mathcal{A}) \cap \mathcal{U}(\mathcal{A}_r)$ is non-empty iff $\mathcal{U}(\mathcal{A}^{\dagger})$ is non-empty. The number of locations in $\mathcal{A}^{\dagger}$ is $1 + n_{\mathcal{A}} \cdot n_{\mathcal{A}_r}^{2M+1}$. The number of edges is $n_{\mathcal{A}_r}^M + m_{\mathcal{A}} \cdot m_{\mathcal{A}_r}^{M+1} + m_{\mathcal{A}} \cdot n_{\mathcal{A}_r}$. Thus, emptiness of $\mathcal{U}(\mathcal{A}) \cap \mathcal{U}(\mathcal{A}_r)$ can be checked in time $O(n_{\mathcal{A}} \cdot n_{\mathcal{A}_r}^{2M+1} + m_{\mathcal{A}} \cdot m_{\mathcal{A}_r}^{M+1} + m_{\mathcal{A}} \cdot n_{\mathcal{A}_r})$. $\square$

Theorem 4 (Model Checking)**.** *Let $\mathcal{A}$ be an ADB and $\mathcal{A}_r$ be a regular non-deterministic finite-state automaton, and let $n_{\mathcal{A}}, n_{\mathcal{A}_r}$ be the numbers of locations in $\mathcal{A}, \mathcal{A}_r$ and $m_{\mathcal{A}}, m_{\mathcal{A}_r}$ be the numbers of edges in $\mathcal{A}, \mathcal{A}_r$ respectively, and M be the largest delay of a delay block in $\mathcal{A}$. The following assertions hold:*

1. *The problem whether $\mathcal{U}(\mathcal{A}) \subseteq \mathcal{U}(\mathcal{A}_r)$ can be checked in time $O(n_{\mathcal{A}} \cdot 2^{n_{\mathcal{A}_r} \cdot (2M+1)} + m_{\mathcal{A}} \cdot 2^{m_{\mathcal{A}_r} \cdot (M+1)} + m_{\mathcal{A}} \cdot 2^{n_{\mathcal{A}_r}})$.*

2. *If M is constant, then the problem of whether $\mathcal{U}(\mathcal{A}) \subseteq \mathcal{U}(\mathcal{A}_r)$ is PSPACE-complete.*

PROOF. The result is obtained as follows: (i) we first obtain an automata for the complement of the language of $\mathcal{A}_r$ (and the automata can be obtained by first determinizing $\mathcal{A}_r$ and then complementing, and thus has at most $2^{n_{\mathcal{A}_r}}$ locations and $2^{m_{\mathcal{A}_r}}$ edges); and (ii) then check emptiness of intersection using Proposition 15. This gives the result for the first item. For the second item we note that if M is constant, then we obtain an exponential size automata and the emptiness check is achieved by checking reachability to a final location (in non-deterministic log-space over an exponential graph). This gives the PSPACE upper bound, and the PSPACE lower bound follows from the fact the containment is PSPACE hard for regular non-deterministic finite-state automata (which are special cases of ADBs). The desired result follows. $\square$

References

[1] R. Alur and D. L. Dill. "A Theory of Timed Automata." In: *Theor. Comput. Sci.* 126.2 (1994), pp. 183–235.

[2] P.A. Abdulla and B. Jonsson. "Undecidable Verification Problems for Programs with Unreliable Channels". In: *Inf. Comput.* 130.1 (1996), pp. 71–90.

[3] A. Bouajjani and P. Habermehl. "Symbolic Reachability Analysis of FIFO-Channel Systems with Nonregular Sets of Configurations". In: *Theoretical Computer Science*. 1998.

[4] D. Brand and Z. Pitro. "On Communicating Finite-State Machines". In: *J. ACM* 30 (2 1983), pp. 323–342. ISSN: 0004-5411.

[5] K. Chatterjee, T. A. Henzinger, and V. S. Prabhu. "Finite Automata with Time-Delay Blocks (Extended Version)". In: *CoRR* arXiv:1207.7019 (2012).

[6] J.N. Chiasson and J.J. Loiseau. *Applications of time delay systems*. Lecture notes in control and information sciences. Springer, 2007. ISBN: 9783540495550.

[7] J. Eker et al. "Taming heterogeneity - the Ptolemy approach". In: *Proceedings of the IEEE* 91.1 (2003), pp. 127–144.

[8] G. Frehse and O. Maler. "Reachability Analysis of a Switched Buffer Network". In: *HSCC*. 2007, pp. 698–701.

[9] K. Gu, V.L. Kharitonov, and J. Chen. *Stability of time-delay systems*. Vol. 41. 12. Birkhauser, 2003, pp. 1458–1463.

[10] O.H. Ibarra. "Reachability and Safety in Queue Systems". In: *CIAA*. LNCS 2088. Springer, 2000, pp. 145–156.

[11] MathWorks. *Control System Toolbox*. 2012. URL: http://www.mathworks.com/products/control/.

[12] MathWorks. *Simulink*. 2012. URL: http://www.mathworks.com/help/toolbox/simulink/slref/unitdelay.html.

[13] O. Maler and A. Pnueli. "Timing analysis of asynchronous circuits using timed automata". In: *CHARME*. LNCS 987. Springer, 1995, pp. 189–205.

[14] *Ptolemy II*. 2012. URL: http://ptolemy.berkeley.edu/ptolemyII/.

[15] R. Sipahi et al. *Time Delay Systems: Methods, Applications and New Trends*. Lecture Notes in Control and Information Sciences. Springer, 2012.

[16] M. Stigge et al. "The Digraph Real-Time Task Model". In: *RTAS*. IEEE Computer Society, 2011, pp. 71–80.

[17] Q.C. Zhong. *Robust control of time-delay systems*. Springer, 2006. ISBN: 9781846282645.

Synthesis from Incompatible Specifications*

Pavol Černý
IST Austria

Sivakanth Gopi
IIT Bombay

Thomas A. Henzinger
IST Austria

Arjun Radhakrishna
IST Austria

Nishant Totla
IIT Bombay

ABSTRACT

Systems are often specified using multiple requirements on their behavior. In practice, these requirements can be contradictory. The classical approach to specification, verification, and synthesis demands more detailed specifications that resolve any contradictions in the requirements. These detailed specifications are usually large, cumbersome, and hard to maintain or modify. In contrast, quantitative frameworks allow the formalization of the intuitive idea that what is desired is an implementation that comes "closest" to satisfying the mutually incompatible requirements, according to a measure of fit that can be defined by the requirements engineer. One flexible framework for quantifying how "well" an implementation satisfies a specification is offered by simulation distances that are parameterized by an error model. We introduce this framework, study its properties, and provide an algorithmic solution for the following quantitative synthesis question: given two (or more) behavioral requirements specified by possibly incompatible finite-state machines, and an error model, find the finite-state implementation that minimizes the maximal simulation distance to the given requirements. Furthermore, we generalize the framework to handle infinite alphabets (for example, real-valued domains). We also demonstrate how quantitative specifications based on simulation distances might lead to smaller and easier to modify specifications. Finally, we illustrate our approach using case studies on error correcting codes and scheduler synthesis.

Categories and Subject Descriptors

D.1.2 [**Programming Techniques**]: Automatic Programming

---

*This research was supported in part by the European Research Council (ERC) Advanced Investigator Grant QUAREM and by the Austrian Science Fund (FWF) project S11402-N23.

General Terms

Theory, Verification

Keywords

synthesis, incompatible specifications

1. INTRODUCTION

A major problem for the wider adoption of techniques for the formal verification and synthesis of systems is the difficulty of writing quality specifications. Quantitative specifications have the potential to simplify the task of the designer, by enabling her to capture her intent better, and more simply. In this paper, we focus on how quantitative specification and reasoning can be useful in cases when specifications are mutually incompatible. In practice, specifications of systems are often not monolithic. They are composed of parts that express different design requirements, possibly coming from different sources. Such high-level requirements can be therefore often contradictory (see, for instance, [16, 2, 14] which provide methods for requirements analysis). Using the classic boolean approach, the solution would be to resolve conflicts by writing more detailed specifications that cover all possible cases of contradictions, and say how to resolve them. However, such specifications may become too large, and more importantly, the different requirements become entangled in the specification. The specifications are then much more difficult to maintain than the original requirements, as it is hard to modify one requirement without rewriting the rest of the specification. In contrast, quantitative frameworks allow the formalization of the intuitive idea that what is desired is an implementation that comes "closest" to satisfying the requirements. More technically, we consider two questions: first, the (rigorously defined) distances from the implementation to (boolean) requirements are within given bounds, and second, the maximal distance to a requirement is minimized.

Furthermore, quantitative reasoning about systems is gaining importance with the spread of embedded systems with strict requirements on resource consumption and timeliness of response. The quantitative approach in this paper is fully compatible with quantitative resource (e.g. memory, energy) consumption requirements: the framework allows us to consider multiple specifications that model resource consumption, and it allows us to express the relative importance of resources. We can then ask the same two questions as above: first, we would like an implementation such that it consumes resources within given bounds; or, second, an implementation such that its maximal total consumption of a resource is minimized.

Synthesis from specifications [18, 17, 9] has been studied extensively as a technique to improve designer and programmer productivity. If designers are forced to write detailed low-level specifications to reconcile contradictory requirements, it decreases the usefulness of synthesis. First, it requires more effort from designers, requiring consideration of *how* a certain task will be performed, as opposed to *what* task should be performed. Second, the space of solutions to the synthesis problem is reduced, with possibly good implementations being ruled out. We therefore propose quantitative synthesis as a solution to the problem of synthesis from incompatible specifications.

Motivating example. Consider a system that grants exclusive access to a resource to two processes which periodically seek access to it. The specification of the system consists of two parts: the first (resp. second) part R_1 (resp. R_2) states that a request for the resource from Process 1 (Process 2) should be satisfied with a grant in the same step. The input alphabet $\mathcal{I}$ consists of symbols r_1, r_2, r_1r_2 and nr representing that requests from either Process 1, Process 2, both, or neither, respectively, coming in the current step. The output alphabet $\mathcal{O}$ consists of symbols g_1 (g_2) representing granting the resource to Process 1 (Process 2), and a special "don't care" symbol $*$. The two parts of the specification are shown in Figures 1a and 1b. The specifications are incompatible, because on input r_1r_2 the specification $\mathcal{S}_1$ allows only g_1, whereas specification $\mathcal{S}_2$ allows only g_2. Classically, the designer would have to manually resolve the conflict by, for example, constructing a specification that grants to Process 1 whenever both processes request in the same step (requirement R_3). However, the designer might not want to resolve the conflict at the specification level, but instead might want to state that she wants an implementation that comes close to satisfying the two mutually incompatible specifications, according to a measure of correctness. We provide a rigorous way for defining such measures.

Measuring correctness of an implementation. We model both systems and specifications as finite-state machines. For defining distances between systems (or between systems and specifications), we build on the simulation distances framework of [6]. Simulation distances generalize the simulation relation, which is a standard correctness condition, to the quantitative setting by measuring how "close" an implementation comes to satisfying a specification. In the classic boolean case, simulation can be seen as a 2-player game between an implementation $\mathcal{I}$ and a specification $\mathcal{S}$, where Player 1 chooses moves (transitions) from the implementation and Player 2 tries to match each move in the specification. In order to generalize this definition to the quantitative setting, we allow the players to make errors (intuitively, choose non-existent transitions), but they pay a certain price for each such choice. The cost of a trace is given by an objective function. We focus on the limit average objective (and thus long-term behavior of systems). The goal of Player 1 (resp., Player 2) is to maximize (resp. minimize) the cost. The best value Player 1 can achieve is then taken as the cost of an implementation with respect to the specification. In this paper, we extend the simulation distances of [6] in two ways: first we consider finite-state machines with both inputs and outputs, and second, we allow specifying simulation distances using error mod-

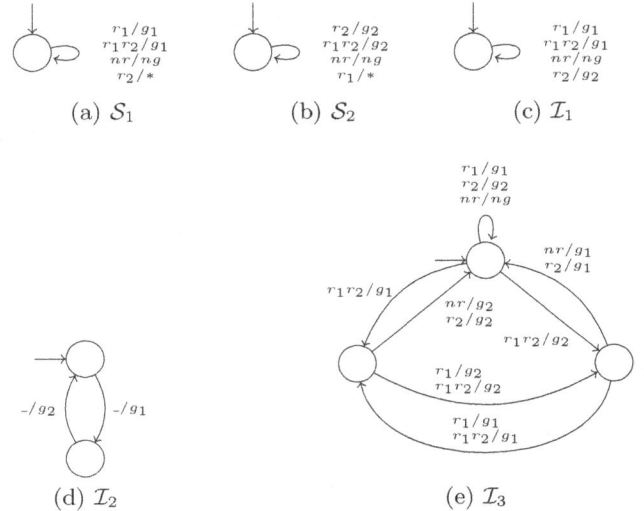

Figure 1: Example 1

els. The error models are finite-state machines that specify what other additional options the simulating player (Player 2) has. Intuitively, the error models allow specifying how the simulating player can "cheat" in the simulation game.

Synthesis from incompatible specifications. The main technical problem we concentrate on in this paper is the problem of synthesis from incompatible specifications. The input to the synthesis problem consists of a set of (two or more) mutually incompatible specifications given by finite-state open reactive systems, and a simulation distance (given by an error model). The output should be an implementation, given by a deterministic open reactive system, that minimizes the maximal simulation distance to the given specifications.

Motivating example (continued). Let us consider an error model that, intuitively, (i) assigns a cost 1 if the implementation does not grant a request that has arrived in the current step, and assigns the same cost for every step before the implementation grants the request, and (ii) assigns a cost 1 if the implementation grants a request that is not required in the current step. Let us now consider the three different implementations in Figures 1c, 1d, and 1e, and their distances to the specifications $\mathcal{S}_1$ and $\mathcal{S}_2$. The implementation $\mathcal{I}_1$ always prefers the request r_1 when the two requests arrive at the same time. The implementation $\mathcal{I}_1$ satisfies the specification $\mathcal{S}_1$, but on the input $(r_1r_2)^\omega$, $\mathcal{I}_1$ makes a mistake at every step w.r.t. $\mathcal{S}_2$. The implementation $\mathcal{I}_1$ thus has distance 0 from $\mathcal{S}_1$, and distance 1 from $\mathcal{S}_2$. The implementation $\mathcal{I}_2$ handles the sequence $(r_1r_2)^\omega$ gracefully by alternation (note that _ in Figure 1d matches any input). However, on the input sequence $(nr)^\omega$, $\mathcal{I}_2$ grants at every step, even though it should not grant at all. It thus has a distance of 1 to both $\mathcal{S}_1$ and $\mathcal{S}_2$. The implementation $\mathcal{I}_3$ also alternates grants in cases when the requests arrive at the same step, but does not grant unnecessarily. Its distance to both specifications would be $\frac{1}{2}$. This is because the worst-case input for this implementation is the sequence $(r_1r_2)^\omega$ and on this input sequence, it makes a mistake in every other step, w.r.t. $\mathcal{S}_1$ as well as $\mathcal{S}_2$.

The quantitative approach can be compared to the classical boolean approach to illustrate how it leads to specifications that are easier to modify:

- Consider an alternate requirement R_1' which says that every request by Process 1 should be granted in the next step (instead of the same step). In the boolean case, replacing requirement R_1 by R_1' also involves changing the requirement R_3 which resolves the conflict between R_1 and R_2. Requirement R_3 needs to be changed to R_3' which says that given that request r_1 happened in the previous step and r_2 happened in the current step, the output must be g_1 in the current step. However, in the quantitative case, no changes need to be done other than replacing R_1 with R_1'.

- Similarly, we can consider other ways of resolving the conflict between requirements R_1 and R_2, instead of using R_3 which prioritizes Process 1 over Process 2. We could have the requirement that we are equally tolerant to missed grants in each process (say requirement R_3') or that we tolerate twice as many missed grants in Process 1 than in Process 2, just by modifying the penalties in the error models. In the boolean case, the requirement R_3 is easily expressible, but the requirement R_3' is very hard to state without adding additional constraints to the specification. In the quantitative case, we can simply switch between R_3 and and R_3' just by changing the relative penalties for not granting r_1 or r_2.

- To illustrate how our framework can model resource consumption, we consider a system that sends messages over a network, as governed by a correctness specification. It costs a certain amount (in dollars) to send a kB of data, so it might be useful to compress data first. However, compression uses energy (in Joules). In our framework, we could add two boolean requirements saying that (a) data should not be sent on the network, and (b) compression should not be used. Then we can relax the requirement, by giving error models that have costs for sending data and using compression. In this way, the framework allows to synthesize a system where e.g. both total energy costs and total network costs are within certain bounds. For further illustration of resource consumption modeling, we refer the reader to our case study on forward error correction codes, where the number of bits sent is the resource tracked.

Overview of results The main result of this paper is an ϵ-optimal construction for the synthesis from incompatible specifications problem. We first consider the decision version of the problem: given k possibly mutually incompatible specifications, and a maximum distance to each specification, the problem is to decide whether there exists an implementation that satisfies these constraints. We show that the decision problem is CONP-complete (for a fixed k). The result is obtained by reduction to 2-player games with multiple limit average objectives [7]. We then present a construction of an ϵ-optimal strategy for the problem of synthesis for incompatible specifications. Furthermore, for the case of two specifications, and for a specific error model (already considered in [6]), we show that the result of our optimal synthesis procedure is always better (in a precise sense) than the result of classical synthesis from just one of the specifications.

Moreover, we extend the framework of simulation distances [6] to open reactive systems (with both inputs and outputs), and introduce parametric stateful error models. We prove that simulation distances define a directed metric (i.e., the distance is reflexive and the triangle inequality holds) in this generalized setting.

We also study an extension of the framework to distances for automata on infinite metric alphabets, to model for example controlling a real-valued output. We present an algorithm (simpler than in the finite-alphabet setting) for solving the problem of synthesis from incompatible specifications in this more flexible setting. We then study the case when the controller can set the output only to a finite number of values from the infinite alphabet, and in this case we give an algorithm as well as a more efficient heuristic based on a projection theorem.

Finally, we demonstrate how our methods can enable simpler specifications, while allowing the synthesis of desirable solutions, using two case studies: on synthesis of custom forward error correction codes and on scheduler synthesis.

Related work. The fact that in practice requirements on systems might be inconsistent was recognized in the literature, and several approaches for requirement analysis [16, 2, 14] and requirement debugging [15] were proposed. The problem of an inconsistent specification was approached in [8] by synthesizing additional requirements on the environment so that unrealizability in the specification is avoided. It was also observed that quantitative measures can lead to simpler specifications [3]. There have been several attempts to give a mathematical semantics to reactive processes based on quantitative metrics rather than boolean preorders [19, 10]. In particular for probabilistic processes, it is natural to generalize bisimulation relations to bisimulation metrics [11], and similar generalizations can be pursued if quantities enter through continuous variables [4]. In contrast, we consider distances between purely discrete (non-probabilistic, untimed) systems.

Synthesis from inconsistent specifications was considered in [13, 12]. Here the conflicts between various components of the specification are resolved by considering priorities for different components, in contrast to our approach of using quantitative measures of correctness. However, it is not possible to express requirement such as R_3' from the motivating example using priorities. Synthesis with respect to quantitative measures was considered in [3, 5], but only for consistent specifications, and not for simulation distances.

2. DISTANCES ON SYSTEMS

Alternating Transition Systems. An *alternating transition system* (ATS) $\langle S, \Sigma, E, s_0, (S_1, S_2) \rangle$ consists of a finite set of states S, a finite alphabet Σ, an initial state s_0, a transition relation $E \subseteq S \times \Sigma \times S$ and a partition (S_1, S_2) of S into Player 1 and Player 2 states. We require that for every state $s \in S$, there exists a transition from s, i.e., $\forall s \in S : \exists \sigma \in \Sigma, s' \in S : (s, \sigma, s') \in E$. A *run* in a transition system is an infinite path $\rho = \rho_0 \sigma_0 \rho_1 \ldots$ where $\rho_0 = s_0$ and $\forall i \geq 0 : (\rho_i, \sigma_i, \rho_{i+1}) \in E$. If the set S_1 is empty in an ATS, we call it a *transition system* and denote it by $\langle S, \Sigma, E, s_0 \rangle$. *Reactive Systems.* An *open reactive system* is a restriction of an ATS where: (i) Alphabet Σ is the disjoint union of inputs $\mathcal{I}$ and outputs $\mathcal{O}$; (ii) Transition relation is strictly alternating on S_1 and S_2, and inputs and outputs, i.e., $E \subseteq (S_1 \times \mathcal{I} \times S_2) \cup (S_2 \times \mathcal{O} \times S_1)$; (iii) Transition relation is deterministic in inputs, i.e., $(s, \sigma, s') \in E \wedge (s, \sigma, s'') \in E \wedge$

$\sigma \in \mathcal{I} \implies s' = s''$; and (iv) Transition relation is input enabled, i.e., $\forall s \in S_1, \sigma \in \mathcal{I} : \exists s' : (s, \sigma, s') \in E$.

In a reactive system, the computation proceeds with the environment (Player 1) choosing an input symbol from every state in S_1 and the system (Player 2) choosing an output symbol from every state in S_2. Each run is called a *behavior* of the system. We say a reactive system is an *implementation* if for all $s \in S_2$, there is exactly one transition leading out of s.

2-player Games. A 2-player game is an ATS (called game graph) along with an objective (defined below). In a game, a token is placed on the initial state; and Player i chooses the successor whenever the token is on a state in S_i. The set of all runs is denoted by Ω.

Strategies. A *strategy* for Player i in a game is a recipe that tells the player how to choose the successors in a game. Formally, a Player i strategy $\pi_i : (S \times \Sigma)^* \cdot S_i \to \Sigma \times S$ is a function such that for each $w \cdot s \in (S \times \Sigma)^* \cdot S_i$ and $\pi_i(w \cdot s) = (\sigma, s')$, we have $(s, \sigma, s') \in E$. Each w is called a history. The sets of all Player 1 and Player 2 strategies are denoted by Π_1 and Π_2, respectively. A play $\rho = \rho_0 \sigma_0 \rho_1 \sigma_1 \ldots$ *conforms* to a Player j strategy if $\forall i \geq 0 : \rho_i \in S_j \implies (\rho_{i+1}, \sigma_i) = \pi_i(\rho_0 \sigma_0 \ldots \rho_i)$. The *outcome* of strategies π_1 and π_2 is the unique path $out(\pi_1, \pi_2)$ that conforms to both π_1 and π_2.

We use two restrictions of strategies. Strategy π_i is:

- *Memoryless* if the output of the strategy function depends only upon the last state in the history. More formally, a strategy is memoryless if $\forall w_1, w_2 \in (S \times \Sigma)^*$ and all $s \in S_i$, we have $\pi_i(w_1 \cdot s) = \pi_i(w_2 \cdot s)$;

- *Finite-memory* if the output depends only upon the current state of a finite memory and the last state in the history. The memory is updated using a memory update function every time a player makes a move. More formally, a strategy is finite-memory, if there exists a finite memory set M, an initial memory state m_0, a memory update function $\pi_i^M : M \times (S \times \Sigma)^* \cdot S \to M$ and a output function $\pi_i^O : S_i \times M \to \Sigma \times S$ such that:
  - $\pi_i(w \cdot s) = \pi_i^O((s, \pi_i^M(m_0, w)))$ for all $w \in (S \times \Sigma)^*$ and $s \in S_i$; and
  - $\pi_i^M(m, \rho_0 \sigma_0 \ldots \rho_i \sigma_i \rho_{i+1}) = \pi_i^M(\pi_i^M(m, \rho_0 \sigma_0 \ldots \rho_i), \rho_i \sigma_i \rho_{i+1})$.

The set of Player i finite-memory and memoryless strategies is denoted by Π_i^{FM} and Π_i^{ML} respectively.

Objectives. A *boolean objective* is a function $\Phi : \Omega \to \{0, 1\}$ and *quantitative objective* is a function $\Psi : \Omega \to \mathbb{R}$ and the goal of Player 1 in each case is to choose a strategy such that no matter what strategy Player 2 chooses, the value of the outcome is maximized.

Optimal strategies and Values. For a boolean objective Φ, a strategy π_1 (π_2) is *winning* for Player 1 (2) if all plays conforming to it map to 1 (0). For a quantitative objective Ψ, the *value* of a Player 1 strategy π_1 is $Val(\pi_1) = \inf_{\pi_2 \in \Pi_2} \Psi(out(\pi_1, \pi_2))$, and a Player 2 strategy π_2 is $Val(\pi_2) = \sup_{\pi_1 \in \Pi_1} \Psi(out(\pi_1, \pi_2))$. The *value of the game* is $Val(\Psi) = \sup_{\pi_1 \in \Pi_1} Val(\pi_1)$. A strategy π_i is optimal if $Val(\pi_i)$ is equal to value of the game.

If the above definitions are restricted to finite-memory strategies instead of arbitrary strategies, we get the notions of finite-memory values of strategies and games. In this paper, by default, value is taken to mean finite-memory value.

Reachability and LimAvg objectives. A boolean *reachability objective* $Reach(T)$ for $T \subseteq S$ has

$Reach(T)(\rho_0 \sigma_0 \rho_1 \sigma_1 \ldots) = 1$ if and only if $\exists i : \rho_i \in T$, i.e., Player 1 tries to reach the target states T while Player 2 tries to avoid them.

For any ATS, a *weight function* ν maps the transition set E to $\mathbb{N}^k$. Given ν:

- *Limit-average objective* $LimAvg^\nu : \Omega \to \mathbb{R}$ for $k = 1$ has $LimAvg(\rho_0 \sigma_0 \rho_1 \ldots) = \liminf_{n \to \infty} \frac{1}{n} \cdot \sum_{i=0}^n \nu((\rho_i, \sigma_i, \rho_{i+1}))$.
- *Multi-limit-average objective* $MLimAvg^\nu : \Omega \to \mathbb{R}$ maps plays to the maximum $LimAvg$ value of projections of ν to each component of the tuple.
- *Multi-limit-average threshold* objective $MLimAvg_{\mathbf{v}}$ ($\mathbf{v} \in \mathbb{R}^k$) is a boolean objective where a path is mapped to 1 if and only if there is an i, the $LimAvg$ of the ith component of ν is more than the ith component of $\mathbf{v}$.

Note that we use the dual of the standard definition of $MLimAvg_{\mathbf{v}}$ used in [7], i.e., we use existential quantification over i rather than universal. However, all results from [7] can be transferred by switching Player 1 and Player 2.

2.1 Quantitative Simulation Games

The simulation preorder is a widely used relation to compare two transition systems and was extended in [1] to alternating transition systems. The simulation preorder can be computed by solving a 2-player game.

Simulation and Simulation Games. Let $\mathcal{A} = \langle S, \Sigma, E, s_0, (S_1, S_2) \rangle$ and $\mathcal{A}' = \langle S', \Sigma, E', s_0', (S_1', S_2') \rangle$ be two reactive systems. The system $\mathcal{A}'$ *simulates* the system $\mathcal{A}$ if there exists a relation $R \subseteq S \times S'$ such that:

- $(s_0, s_0') \in R$;
- $(s, s') \in R \implies (s \in S_1 \leftrightarrow s' \in S_1')$;
- $\forall s, t \in S, s' \in S' : (s, s') \in R \wedge (s, \sigma, t) \in E \wedge s \in S_2 \implies (\exists t' : (s', \sigma, t') \in E' \wedge (t, t') \in R$; and
- $\forall s \in S, s', t' \in S' : (s, s') \in R \wedge (s', \sigma, t') \in E' \wedge s' \in S_1' \implies (\exists t : (s, \sigma, t) \in E \wedge (t, t') \in R$.

We can construct a game $\mathcal{G}^{\mathcal{A}, \mathcal{A}'}$ with a reachability objective such that $\mathcal{A}'$ simulates $\mathcal{A}$ if and only if Player 2 has a winning strategy. The game graph $\mathcal{G}^{\mathcal{A}, \mathcal{A}'}$ consists of the Player 1 states $S_1 \times \{\#\} \times S_1' \bigcup S_2 \times \{\#\} \times S_2'$ and Player 2 states $S_1 \times \mathcal{I} \times S_2' \bigcup S_1 \times \mathcal{O} \times S_2' \bigcup \{s_{err}\}$, the alphabet Σ, and the initial state $(s_0, \#, s_0')$. The transition set consists of the following transitions:

- $((s, \#, s'), \sigma, (t, \sigma, s'))$ where $(s, \sigma, t) \in E \wedge s \in S_2$;
- $((s, \#, s'), \sigma, (s, \sigma, t'))$ where $(s', \sigma, t') \in E' \wedge s \in S_1$;
- $((s, \sigma, s'), \sigma, (s, \#, t'))$ where $(s', \sigma, t') \in E' \wedge \sigma \in \mathcal{O}$;
- $((s, \sigma, s'), \sigma, (t, \#, s'))$ where $(s, \sigma, t) \in E \wedge \sigma \in \mathcal{I}$;
- $(s, \#, s_{err})$ for all Player 2 states s.

The objective for Player 1 is $Reach(\{s_{err}\})$.

Intuitively, in each step of the simulation game, either Player 1 chooses an input transition of $\mathcal{A}'$ and Player 2 matches it with an input transition of $\mathcal{A}$, or Player 1 chooses an output transition of system $\mathcal{A}$ and Player 2 matches it with an output transition of $\mathcal{A}'$. If Player 2 is not able to match a transition, s_{err} is visited and Player 2 loses the game. It is straightforward to show that $\mathcal{A}'$ simulates $\mathcal{A}$ if and only if Player 1 has a winning strategy.

Simulation Distances. In quantitative simulation games [6], Player 2 can simulate an $\mathcal{A}$ transition by an $\mathcal{A}'$ transition with a mismatching label. However, such mismatches have a cost and Player 2 tries to minimize the $LimAvg$ of costs. When simulation holds, there are no mismatches and the value of the game is 0. Here, we present a

(a) Standard Model   (b) Delayed Response

(c) No Spurious Response

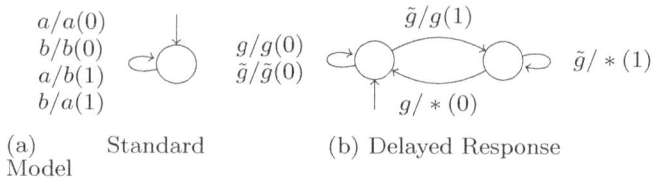

Figure 2: Sample error models

$d = 2, s = 1$	$\mathcal{S}_1$	$\mathcal{S}_2$	$d = 1, s = 10$	$\mathcal{S}_1$	$\mathcal{S}_2$
$\mathcal{I}_1$	0	2	$\mathcal{I}_1$	0	1
$\mathcal{I}_2$	1	1	$\mathcal{I}_2$	10	10
$\mathcal{I}_3$	1	1	$\mathcal{I}_3$	$\frac{1}{2}$	$\frac{1}{2}$

Table 1: Simulation distances for Example 2.1

generalization of quantitative simulation games for reactive systems with richer error models.

Error Models. The modification schemes used in [6] to model the permitted errors during the simulation game do not cover some natural error schemes. For example, the criteria used for request-grant systems in Section 1 is not expressible as a modification scheme from [6]. Hence, we define more general error models. An *error model* over an alphabet $\Sigma = \mathcal{I} \cup \mathcal{O}$ is a deterministic weighted transition system over $\mathcal{O} \times \mathcal{O}$. Intuitively, a transition on label (σ_1, σ_2) (henceforth denoted as σ_1/σ_2) represents that a transition on label σ_1 in the simulated system can be simulated by a transition on label σ_2 in the simulating system with the accompanying cost. We also require that each word over symbols of the form σ/σ is assigned cost 0 to ensure that correct simulations have a cost 0.

Given an error model $M = \langle S^e, \mathcal{O} \times \mathcal{O}, E^e, s_0^e \rangle$ with weight function ν and an ATS $\mathcal{A} = \langle S, \Sigma, E, s_0, (S_1, S_2) \rangle$, the *modified system* is the weighted transition system $\mathcal{A}_M = \langle S \times S^e, \Sigma, E^M, (s_0, s_0^e), (S_1^M, S_2^M) \rangle$ with weight function ν^e where:

- $((s, s^e), \sigma_1, (t, t^e)) \in E^M \Leftrightarrow s \in S_2, (s, \sigma_2, t) \in E \wedge (s^e, (\sigma_1, \sigma_2), t^e) \in E^e$,
- $((s, s^e), \sigma_1, (t, s^e)) \in E^M \Leftrightarrow s \in S_1 \wedge (s, \sigma_1, t) \in E$; and
- $\nu^e(((s, s^e), \sigma_1, (t, t^e))) = \nu((s^e, (\sigma_1, \sigma_2), t^e))$.

The modified transition system includes erroneous behaviors along with their costs. Note that we do not consider errors in the inputs as all our reactive systems are input enabled. We present a few natural error models here.

- *Standard Model.* (Figure 2a) Every replacement can occur during simulation with a constant cost and can be used to model errors like bit-flips. This model was defined and used in [6].
- *Delayed Response Model.* (Figure 2b) This model measures the timeliness of responses (g). Here, when the implementation outputs $\tilde{g}$ when a grant g is expected, all transitions have a penalty until the missing grant g is seen.
- *No Spurious Response Model.* (Figure 2c) This model is meant to ensure that no spurious grants are produced. If an implementation produces a grant not required by the specification, all subsequent transitions get a penalty.
- *Qualitative Model.* (Figure 5) This model recovers the

boolean simulation games. The distance is 0 if and only if the simulation relation holds.

- *Delayed-vs-Spurious Responses Model.* (Figure 3) We formalize the informal preference conditions from the discussion of the motivating example in Section 1 in the this error model. Delayed and spurious grants get penalties of d and s, respectively.

Of the above models, the standard model and the qualitative model can be expressed as modification schemes from [6], whereas the delayed response, the spurious response model, and the Delayed-vs-Spurious response model cannot be cast as modification schemes.

Quantitative Simulation Games. Given a modified specification system $\mathcal{A}'^M$ and an implementation system $\mathcal{A}$, the quantitative simulation game $\mathcal{Q}_M^{\mathcal{A}, \mathcal{A}'}$ is a game with the game-graph of $\mathcal{G}^{\mathcal{A}, \mathcal{A}'_M}$, and a weight function that maps:

- Each Player 1 transition to 0, and
- Each Player 2 transition to 4 times weight of the corresponding transition in $\mathcal{A}'_M$ (The constant 4 is for normalization). The objective of the game for Player 1 is to maximize the $LimAvg$ of weights.

In a quantitative simulation game, the implementation system is simulated by the modified specification system and for each simulation error, penalty is decided by the error model. The value of the quantitative simulation game $\mathcal{Q}_M^{\mathcal{A}, \mathcal{A}'}$ is the *simulation distance* (denote as $d_M(\mathcal{A}, \mathcal{A}')$).

EXAMPLE 2.1. *Consider the specifications and implementations from the motivating example in Section 1 (Figure 1), and the Delayed-vs-Spurious Response Model in Figure 3.*

By varying the penalties, we obtain different distances. The simulation distances of implementations $\mathcal{I}_1$, $\mathcal{I}_2$ and $\mathcal{I}_3$ to specifications $\mathcal{S}_1$ and $\mathcal{S}_2$ (Figure 1) are summarized in Table 1 for two valuations of d and s. For example, when $d = 2$ and $s = 1$, $\mathcal{I}_2$ and $\mathcal{I}_3$ have equal distances to $\mathcal{S}_1$ and $\mathcal{S}_2$. However, when $d = 1$ and $s = 10$, the distances of $\mathcal{I}_3$ are lower than that of $\mathcal{I}_2$.

Note that in the example of Figure 1, the specifications $\mathcal{S}_1$ and $\mathcal{S}_2$ specify what happens if the two requests r_1 and r_2 come at the same time. If we wanted to change this example and make the specifications completely independent (i.e. $\mathcal{S}_1$ only mentions r_1 and $\mathcal{S}_2$ only mentions r_2), we would need to modify our notion of product construction to allow two input symbols at the same time. Our results would still hold for this modified product construction.

2.2 Properties of Simulation Distances

Directed metric requires reflexivity and triangle inequality to hold. These are perhaps the minimal requirements that allow us to match the intuitive notion of distance. In [6], it is shown that simulation distances with restricted error models are directed metrics.

For our general error models, reflexivity follows from definition. However, the triangle inequality does not hold for all models. We provide a necessary and sufficient condition for the triangle inequality to hold.

An error model M is *transitive* if the following holds: For every triple of infinite lasso (i.e., ultimately periodic) words generated by the error model M of the form $\alpha = \frac{a_0}{b_0}\frac{a_1}{b_1}\ldots$, $\beta = \frac{b_0}{c_0}\frac{b_1}{c_1}\ldots$ and $\gamma = \frac{a_0}{c_0}\frac{a_1}{c_1}\ldots$, the $LimAvg(\alpha) + LimAvg(\beta) \geq LimAvg(\gamma)$.

LEMMA 2.2. *An error model M is transitive if and only if $\forall \mathcal{S}_1, \mathcal{S}_2, \mathcal{S}_3 : d_M(\mathcal{S}_1, \mathcal{S}_3) \leq d_M(\mathcal{S}_1, \mathcal{S}_2) + d_M(\mathcal{S}_2, \mathcal{S}_3)$.*

The proof of the triangle inequality for transitive error models can be derived from the proof of Theorem 1 in [6] with slight modifications. For a non-transitive error model, the three systems whose only behavior outputs the lasso-words which witness the non-transitivity violate the triangle inequality. All the error models from Figures 2 and 3 are transitive.

THEOREM 2.3. *The simulation distance d_M is a directed metric if and only if the error model M is transitive.*

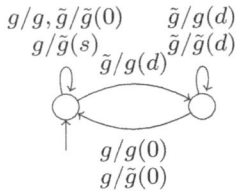

$g/g, \tilde{g}/\tilde{g}(0) \qquad \tilde{g}/g(d)$
$g/\tilde{g}(s) \qquad \tilde{g}/\tilde{g}(d)$
$\qquad \tilde{g}/g(d)$

$g/g(0)$
$g/\tilde{g}(0)$

Figure 3: Delayed-vs-spurious response error model

The transitiveness of an error model can be checked in polynomial time.

PROPOSITION 2.4. *It is decidable in polynomial time whether an error model $M = \langle S^e, \mathcal{O} \times \mathcal{O}, E^e, s_0^e \rangle$ is transitive.*

The result follows by constructing the product $M \times M \times M$ where the transitions with labels $\frac{\sigma_1}{\sigma_2}$, $\frac{\sigma_2}{\sigma_3}$ and $\frac{\sigma_1}{\sigma_3}$ and weights w_1, w_2 and w_3 are replaced with a transition of weight $w_1 + w_2 - w_3$. The model M is transitive iff there is no negative cycle in this graph (checkable in polynomial time).

3. THE INCOMPATIBLE SPECIFICATIONS PROBLEM

Specifications $\mathcal{S}_i$ and error models M_i for $1 \leq i \leq k$ are said to be *incompatible* if $\neg \exists \mathcal{I} : \bigwedge_i d_{M_i}(\mathcal{I}, \mathcal{S}_i) = 0$. Note that our definition may judge specifications compatible, even if there is no common implementation which is simulated classically by each specification. This happens if there exists an implementation with the distance 0 to each of the specifications, which is possible if the specifications share long-term behavior, but differ in the short-term initial behavior.

We formalize the synthesis from incompatible specifications problem as follows.
Incompatible Specifications Decision Problem. Given $\mathcal{S}_i$ and M_i for $1 \leq i \leq k$ as above, and a threshold vector $\mathbf{v} = \langle v_1, v_2, \ldots v_k \rangle \in \mathbb{Q}^k$, incompatible specifications decision problem asks if $\exists \mathcal{I} : \forall 1 \leq i \leq k : d_{M_i}(\mathcal{I}, \mathcal{S}_i) \leq v_i$.
Incompatible Specifications Optimization Problem. Given specifications $\mathcal{S}_i$ and error models M_i for $1 \leq i \leq k$ and a bound $\epsilon > 0$, the incompatible specifications optimization problem is to find an implementation $\mathcal{I}^*$ such that $\forall \mathcal{I} : \max_{i \in \{1,2,\ldots k\}} d_{M_i}(\mathcal{I}^*, \mathcal{S}_i) \leq \max_{i \in \{1,2,\ldots k\}} d_{M_i}(\mathcal{I}, \mathcal{S}_i) + \epsilon$. We call such an implementation $\mathcal{I}^*$ an ϵ-optimal implementation.

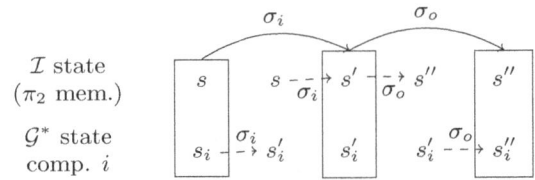

Figure 4: Working of π_2: Solid edges are transitions in $\mathcal{G}^*$ and dashed edges are transitions in $d_{M_i}(\mathcal{I}, \mathcal{S}_i)$

THEOREM 3.1. *The incompatible specifications decision problem is CONP-complete for a fixed k.*

PROOF. First, we prove that the incompatible specifications decision problem is in CONP. We reduce the problem to the decision problem in 2-player games with $MLimAvg$ objectives.

Given a specification $\mathcal{S}_i$ and an error model M_i for $1 \leq i \leq k$, consider the following game graph $\mathcal{G}^*$ with:
- Player 1 states $S_1 = S_1^1 \times \ldots \times S_1^k$ where S_1^i are the Player 1 states of $\mathcal{S}_i^{M_i}$;
- Player 2 states $S_2 = S_2^1 \times \ldots \times S_2^k$ where S_2^i are the Player 2 states of $\mathcal{S}_i^{M_i}$;
- A transition from state $(s_1, s_2, \ldots, s_k)$ to $(s_1', s_2', \ldots, s_k')$ on symbol σ if and only if each of $(s_i, \sigma, s_i') \in E^i$ where E^i is the transition set of $\mathcal{S}_i^{M_i}$; and
- Weight function ν with the ith component being $\nu^i((s_1, s_2, \ldots, s_k), \sigma, (s_1', s_2', \ldots, s_k')) = 2 * \nu((s_i, \sigma, s_i'))$ for $1 \leq i \leq k$.

Intuitively, Player 1 chooses the inputs and Player 2 chooses output transitions from $\mathcal{S}_i^{M_i}$. We prove that a witness implementation exists if and only if there exists a finite memory Player 2 strategy in $\mathcal{G}^*$ for the $MLimAvg$ objective.
(a) For any implementation $\mathcal{I}$, consider the games $\mathcal{Q}_{M_i}^{\mathcal{I}, \mathcal{S}_i}$ and the optimal Player 2 strategy π_2^i in each. By standard results on $LimAvg$ games, we have that each π_2^i is memoryless. From these strategies, we construct a finite-memory Player 2 strategy π_2 in $\mathcal{G}^*$ with the state space of $\mathcal{I}$ as the memory. The memory update function of π_2 mimics the transition relation of $\mathcal{I}$. Let s be the current state of π_2 memory and let $(s_1, s_2, \ldots, s_k)$ be the current state in $\mathcal{G}^*$. By construction, s is Player 1 state in $\mathcal{I}$ iff $(s_1, \ldots, s_k)$ is Player 1 state in $\mathcal{G}^*$.
- If $(s_1, s_2, \ldots, s_k)$ is a Player 1 state, Player 1 chooses an input symbol $\sigma_i \in \mathcal{I}$ and updates the $\mathcal{G}^*$ state. The memory of π_2 is updated to s' which is the unique successor of s on σ_i.
- Next, if the current state $(s_1', s_2', \ldots, s_k')$ is a Player 2 state, the memory of π_2 is updated to the unique successor s'' of s' in $\mathcal{I}$ (Player 2 states have unique successors in implementations). If (s', σ, s'') is the corresponding $\mathcal{I}$ transition, the chosen $\mathcal{G}^*$ state is $(s_1'', s_2'', \ldots, s_k'')$ where each $s_i'' = \pi_2^i((s'', \sigma, s_i'))$.

The construction of π_2 is explained in Figure 4.

For every path ρ conforming to π_2, we can construct a path ρ^i in $\mathcal{Q}_{M_i}^{\mathcal{I}, \mathcal{S}_i}$ conforming to π_2^i from the memory of π_2 and the projection of ρ to i^{th} component (See Figure 4). Furthermore, the weights of the ith component of ρ have the same $LimAvg$ as the weights of ρ^i. Therefore, the $LimAvg$ value of the ith component of ρ is bound by $d_{M_i}(\mathcal{I}, \mathcal{S}_i)$. This shows that the $MLimAvg$ value of π_2, $Val(\pi_2)$ is at most the maximum of $d_{M_i}(\mathcal{I}, \mathcal{S}_i)$.

(b) For every finite-memory strategy π_2 of Player 2 in $\mathcal{G}^*$, we can construct an implementation $\mathcal{I}$ such that $Val(\pi_2) \geq \max_{i \in \{1,2,\dots k\}} d_{M_i}(\mathcal{I}, \mathcal{S}_i)$, by considering the product of $\mathcal{G}^*$ and the memory of π_2 and by removing all transitions originating from Player 2 states which are not chosen by π_2.

From the results of [7], we have that solving $MLimAvg$ games for the threshold $\{0\}^k$ for finite memory strategies is CONP-complete. However, we can reduce the problem of solving $MLimAvg$ games for a threshold $\mathbf{v} \in \mathbb{Q}^k$ to a problem with threshold $\{0\}^k$ by subtracting $\mathbf{v}$ from each of the edge weights. This reduction is obviously polynomial. Therefore, the inconsistent specifications decision problem can be solved in CONP time in the size of $\mathcal{G}^*$, which in turn is polynomial in the size of the input for fixed k. To show the CONP hardness, we can use a modification of the proof of CONP hardness of $MLimAvg$ games by reduction from the complement of 3-SAT. $\square$

Now, we can find an ϵ-optimal implementation for the optimization problem by doing a binary search on the space of thresholds.

COROLLARY 3.2. *The incompatible specifications optimization problem can be solved in* NEXP *time for a fixed k, ϵ and W, where W is the absolute value of the maximum cost in the error models.*

PROOF. Without loss of generality, let $\epsilon = \frac{1}{q}$ for $q \in \mathbb{N}$. As the simulation distances are between 0 and W, we do a binary search on vectors of form $\{t\}^k$ to find $\{N/Wq\}^k$, the highest threshold for which an implementation exists. Since, the accuracy required is ϵ, the number of search steps is $O(\log(W/\epsilon)) = O(\log(Wq))$. We find an implementation (equivalently, a Player 2 finite memory strategy) with a value of at least this threshold. We reduce the problem to an equivalent threshold problem with integer weights and threshold $\{0\}^k$ by multiplying weights by Wq and subtracting $\{N\}^k$. From [7], we have that memory of size $O(|\mathcal{G}^*|^2 \cdot (|\mathcal{G}^*|qW)^k)$ is sufficient. For one such finite-memory strategy, checking whether it is sufficient can be done in polynomial time. Therefore, by guessing a strategy and checking for sufficiency, we have an NEXP time algorithm. $\square$

EXAMPLE 3.3. *For the specifications and error models from Example 2.1 (Section 2.1), we compute ϵ-optimal implementations for different values of d and s. In this case, we obtain optimal implementations by taking a small enough ϵ. We have that $\mathcal{I}_2$ is one of the optimal implementations for the case of $d = 2$ and $s = 1$. The implementation $\mathcal{I}_3$ and its dual (i.e., r_1, g_1 interchanged with r_2, g_2) are optimal for the case when $d = 1$ and $s = 10$. As expected, $\mathcal{I}_2$, which outputs many spurious grants, is worse when the cost of a spurious grant is higher.*

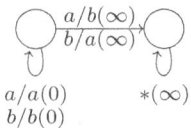

Figure 5: Qualitative error model

For the qualitative error model (Figure 5) and any set of incompatible specifications, for all implementations the distance to at least one of the specifications is ∞. However, for the standard error model of [6], we show for the case of two specifications that it always is possible to do better.

PROPOSITION 3.4. *For specifications $\mathcal{S}_1$ and $\mathcal{S}_2$ with the standard error model M, let $\delta = \min(d_M(\mathcal{S}_1, \mathcal{S}_2), d_M(\mathcal{S}_2, \mathcal{S}_1))$. There exists an implementation $\mathcal{I}^*$ with $d_M(\mathcal{I}^*, \mathcal{S}_1) < \delta$ and $d_M(\mathcal{I}^*, \mathcal{S}_2) < \delta$.*

PROOF. Without loss of generality, let $d_M(\mathcal{S}_1, \mathcal{S}_2) \leq d_M(\mathcal{S}_2, \mathcal{S}_1)$. Consider the game graph of $\mathcal{Q}_M^{\mathcal{S}_1, \mathcal{S}_2}$ and modify it by letting Player 2 choose the $\mathcal{S}_1$ output transitions, i.e., Player 1 chooses the inputs and Player 2 chooses both $\mathcal{S}_1$ and $\mathcal{S}_2$ outputs. Let π_2^* be the optimal Player 2 strategy in this game. From π_2^*, we construct two different implementations $\mathcal{I}_1$ and $\mathcal{I}_2$ having as the state space the product of the state spaces of $\mathcal{S}_1$ and $\mathcal{S}_2$. In the transition set,

- There exists an input transition from (s_1, s_2) to (s_1', s_2') on the input symbol σ_i if and only if (s_1, σ_i, s_1') and (s_2, σ_i, s_2') are input transitions of $\mathcal{S}_1$ and $\mathcal{S}_2$;
- There exists an output transition $((s_1, s_2), \sigma_o, (s_1', s_2'))$ in $\mathcal{I}_1$ iff π_2^* chooses the $\mathcal{S}_1$ transition (s_1, σ_o, s_1') from state $(s_1, \#, (s_2, e))$ and the $\mathcal{S}_2^M$ transition (s_2, σ_o, s_2') in state $(s_1', \sigma_o, (s_2, e))$; and
- There exists an output transition $((s_1, s_2), \sigma_o, (s_1', s_2'))$ on σ_o in $\mathcal{I}_2$ iff π_2^* chooses the $\mathcal{S}_1$ transition (s_1, σ_o', s_1') from state $(s_1, \#, (s_2, e))$ and the $\mathcal{S}_2^M$ transition (s_2, σ_o', s_2') in state $(s_1', \sigma_o', (s_2, e))$ and $\mathcal{S}_2^M$ transition corresponds to the $\mathcal{S}_2$ transition (s_2, σ_o, s_2') and the error model transition $(e, \sigma_o'/\sigma_o, e)$.

Intuitively, π_2^* chooses the most benevolent $\mathcal{S}_1$ behavior and $\mathcal{I}_1$ implements this $\mathcal{S}_1$ behavior, while $\mathcal{I}_2$ is the $\mathcal{S}_2$ behavior used to simulate this game.

Now, we construct $\mathcal{I}^*$ by alternating between $\mathcal{I}_1$ and $\mathcal{I}_2$. For each Player 1 state (s_1, s_2) in $\mathcal{I}_i$, let $TU((s_1, s_2))$ be the tree unrolling of $\mathcal{I}_i$ from (s_1, s_2) to a depth $N \in \mathbb{N}$ and let $\mathcal{T}(\mathcal{I}_i)$ be the disjoint union of such trees. Let $\mathcal{I}^*$ be the union of $\mathcal{T}(\mathcal{I}_1)$ and $\mathcal{T}(\mathcal{I}_2)$ where each transition to a leaf state (s_1, s_2) in $\mathcal{T}(\mathcal{I}_1)$ is redirected to the root of $TU((s_1, s_2))$ in $\mathcal{T}(\mathcal{I}_2)$, and vice versa.

We now show that $d_M(\mathcal{I}^*, \mathcal{S}_i) < \delta$. Consider the Player 2 strategy π_2 in $\mathcal{Q}_M^{\mathcal{I}^*, \mathcal{S}_2}$: to simulate an $\mathcal{I}^*$ transition from (s_1, s_2) to (s_1', s_2') on σ_o, π_2 chooses the $\mathcal{S}_2^M$ transition $((s_2, e), \sigma_o, (s_2', e))$. If $((s_1, s_2), \sigma_o, (s_1', s_2'))$ was from $\mathcal{T}(\mathcal{I}_2)$, the cost of the simulation step is 0, and otherwise it is equal to the corresponding transition from $\mathcal{Q}_M^{\mathcal{S}_1, \mathcal{S}_2}$. Now, fix π_2 in $\mathcal{Q}_M^{\mathcal{I}^*, \mathcal{S}_2}$ and let C be the cycle of the path obtained by fixing the optimal Player 1 strategy. Cycle C is composed of paths through $\mathcal{I}_1$ and $\mathcal{I}_2$ each of length N. The cost of the path through $\mathcal{I}_2$ is 0. The cost of the path through $\mathcal{I}_1$ is equal to the cost of the corresponding cycle in $\mathcal{Q}_M^{\mathcal{S}_1, \mathcal{S}_2}$. If N is large enough, the path through $\mathcal{I}_1$ is composed of an acyclic part of length at most $n = 2 \cdot |\mathcal{Q}_M^{\mathcal{S}_1, \mathcal{S}_2}|$ and of cyclic paths of average cost less than $d_M(\mathcal{S}_1, \mathcal{S}_2) = \delta$. Therefore, for all $\epsilon > 0$ and $N > \frac{nW}{\epsilon}$ we have

$$d_M(\mathcal{I}^*, \mathcal{S}_2) \leq Val(\pi_2) \leq \frac{(N-n) \cdot \delta + n \cdot W}{2N} \leq \frac{\delta}{2} + \epsilon < \delta$$

Similarly, we can show $d_M(\mathcal{I}^*, \mathcal{S}_1) < \delta$ to complete the proof. $\square$

4. QUANTITATIVE ALPHABETS

We have handled the case of controller synthesis from incompatible situations where all controlled variables are from a finite domain. However, often in practice, the controlled variable can take values from an infinite continuous domain. For example, an output representing voltage might take any value between 0 volts to 5 volts. Furthermore, in many cases, although the underlying controlled variable ranges over a continuous domain, due to practical reasons, the only viable controllers are the ones which have discretized outputs, i.e., allow the variable to assume values from a finite subset of the domain. In the case of voltages, it might be the case that the controller can only choose the values from one of 0 volts, 1 volt, 3 volts and 5 volts. Here we present results on synthesis for incompatible specifications with the controlled output variables ranging either over a continuous domain, or a finite discretization of a continuous domain.

Firstly, the notion of simulation distances can be generalized to systems with output alphabets that are infinite and quantitative. The assumptions about the output alphabet are that: (a) it is a metric space with the metric $m_{\mathcal{O}}$; and (b) it has a *midpoint function*, i.e., there exists a computable function $\mu : \mathcal{O} \times \mathcal{O} \to \mathcal{O}$ such that $\forall o_1, o_2 \in \mathcal{O}$: $m_{\mathcal{O}}(o_1, \mu(o_1, o_2)) = m_{\mathcal{O}}(o_2, \mu(o_1, o_2)) = \frac{m_{\mathcal{O}}(o_1, o_2)}{2}$. For example, any interval $I \subseteq \mathbb{R}$ with $m_I(a, b) = |a - b|$ and the midpoint function $\mu_I(a, b) = \frac{a+b}{2}$ satisfies our assumptions.

For simplicity, we consider only the standard error model from Section 2 (constant penalty for each mismatch), with the cost of an edge labeled σ/σ' being $m_{\mathcal{O}}(\sigma, \sigma')$. The resultant simulation distance is a directed metric.

4.1 Continuous Control Problem

For quantitative outputs with continuous control, i.e., when the controller can choose the output values from the whole continuous domain, the problem of synthesis from incompatible specifications can be solved with a simple construction. Intuitively, the reason is that when the two specifications differ, we can always find a "middle ground", due to our assumption on the existence of the midpoint function μ. The following theorem states that we can obtain an implementation which is no farther from either of the specification than half the original distance between the specifications.

THEOREM 4.1. *Let $\mathcal{S}_1$ and $\mathcal{S}_2$ be specifications over a finite input alphabet $\mathcal{I}$ and a quantitative output alphabet $\mathcal{O}$. Let $\delta = \min(d(\mathcal{S}_1, \mathcal{S}_2), d(\mathcal{S}_2, \mathcal{S}_1))$. There exists an implementation $\mathcal{I}^*$ such that:*

- $\forall \mathcal{I} : \max_{i \in \{1,2\}} d(\mathcal{I}^*, \mathcal{S}_i), \leq \max_{i \in \{1,2\}} d(\mathcal{I}, \mathcal{S}_i)$;
- $d(\mathcal{I}^*, \mathcal{S}_1) \leq \frac{\delta}{2}$ *and* $d(\mathcal{I}^*, \mathcal{S}_2) \leq \frac{\delta}{2}$; *and*
- *The number of states of $\mathcal{I}^*$ is in $O(n_1 n_2)$ where n_i is the number of states of $\mathcal{S}_i$.*

Proof Idea. Consider the game graph $\mathcal{G}^*$ whose states are the product of the state space of $\mathcal{S}_1$ and $\mathcal{S}_2$. For transitions (s_1, σ_1, s_1') and (s_2, σ_2, s_2') in $\mathcal{S}_1$ and $\mathcal{S}_2$, $\mathcal{G}^*$ contains the transition $((s_1, s_2), \mu(\sigma_1, \sigma_2), (s_1', s_2'))$ having the weight $m(\sigma_1, \sigma_2)$. We can show that the optimal Player 2 strategy to minimize the $LimAvg$ of the weights in this game corresponds to the implementation $\mathcal{I}^*$.

4.2 Discretized Control Problem

In the case where a continuous output variable is forced to take discrete values, the problem of synthesis from incompatible specifications is considerably more complex.

We call a finite set $\mathcal{O}' \subseteq \mathcal{O}$ a *discretization* of $\mathcal{O}$. For any $o \in \mathcal{O}$, we let $o|\mathcal{O}' = \{o' \in \mathcal{O}' | \forall o'' \in \mathcal{O}' m(o, o') \leq m(o, o'')\}$.

Now, we make a further assumption about the metric-space of outputs $\mathcal{O}$ and the encoding of transitions in the specifications. For a pair of states, s and s' in the specification, let $\Delta(s, s') \subseteq \mathcal{O}$ be the set of outputs o such that

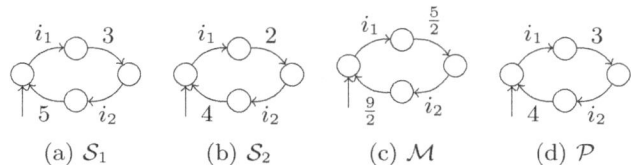

(a) $\mathcal{S}_1$ (b) $\mathcal{S}_2$ (c) $\mathcal{M}$ (d) $\mathcal{P}$

Figure 6: Example for synthesis using Projection Theorem

a transition (s, o, s') exists in the specification. We assume that for every $o' \in \mathcal{O}'$ and for every pair of states s, s', the value $\min_{o \in \Delta(s, s')} m(o', o)$ is computable. This is the case for example if the output alphabet represents a real-valued variable and the transitions in the specifications are given in terms of intervals.

We remark that due to the assumption on computability, we can use the synthesis algorithms for finite alphabets from Section 3 for the discretized control problem. However, we present a more efficient polynomial heuristic. It is based on the following theorem for solving the discretized synthesis problem for a single specification, i.e., finding the optimal discretized implementation for a single quantitative specification.

THEOREM 4.2 (PROJECTION). *Given a specification $\mathcal{S}$ over the output alphabet $\mathcal{O}$, and a discretization $\mathcal{O}' \subseteq \mathcal{O}$, there exists an implementation $\mathcal{I}^*$ over the output alphabet $\mathcal{O}'$ such that for all implementations $\mathcal{I}$ over the $\mathcal{O}'$, $d(\mathcal{I}^*, \mathcal{S}) \leq d(\mathcal{I}, \mathcal{S})$. Furthermore, the number of states of $\mathcal{I}^*$ is $O(n)$, where n is the number of states of $\mathcal{S}$.*

Proof Idea. Consider the game $\mathcal{G}^*$ with the same state space as $\mathcal{S}$ and each transition of $\mathcal{S}$ with label o has been replaced with a transition with label o' such that $o' \in o|\mathcal{O}'$. The weight of such a transition is $m(o, o')$. It is easy to show that $\mathcal{I}^*$ corresponds to an optimal Player 2 strategy to minimize the $LimAvg$ of the weights in $\mathcal{G}^*$.

Heuristic Synthesis using Projection For incompatible specifications, the algorithms for the finite alphabet case have a high complexity. However, Theorems 4.1 and 4.2 suggest a simple (albeit non-optimal) construction for the case of discretized alphabets. Given specifications $\mathcal{S}_1$ and $\mathcal{S}_2$ with output alphabet $\mathcal{O}$ or $\mathcal{O}'$, using Theorem 4.1, one could synthesize an optimal implementation over $\mathcal{O}$, and then use Theorem 4.2 to get the best approximation over the finite alphabet $\mathcal{O}'$. Though there is no guarantee that we get the optimal implementation, it can serve as a good heuristic.

In Figure 6, implementation $\mathcal{P}$ (on the discretized $\mathcal{O}' = \{2, 3, 4, 5\} \subseteq \mathbb{R} = \mathcal{O}$ is synthesized from $\mathcal{S}_1$ and $\mathcal{S}_2$ using this method. The system $\mathcal{M}$ is the optimal implementation for outputs in $\mathbb{R}$ produced by Theorem 4.1 and $\mathcal{P}$ is a projection of $\mathcal{M}$ to the discretization $\mathcal{O}'$. In this case, the projection happens to be the optimal system for discretized outputs.

We leave two questions open: (i) characterizing the implementation obtained in this way w.r.t. an implementation obtained by synthesis for the finite alphabet directly, and (ii) deriving heuristics for choosing a projection in case there are several projections available (e.g. $\mathcal{P}$ is only one of the possible closest projections of $\mathcal{M}$ to $\mathcal{O}'$).

To illustrate the second question, consider specifications $\mathcal{S}_1$ and $\mathcal{S}_2$ from Figure 7. The implementation $\mathcal{I}_1$ is given by the construction of Theorem 4.1. Any of $\mathcal{S}_1$, $\mathcal{S}_2$ or $\mathcal{P}_1$ can serve as a projection of $\mathcal{I}_1$ on the alphabet $\{0, 1\}$. However, for $\mathcal{S}_1$ and $\mathcal{S}_2$, the distance to the other specification

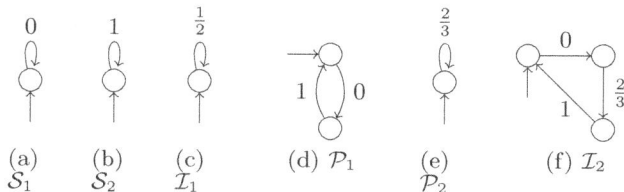

Figure 7: Incompatible Specifications and Projection

is 1, whereas for $\mathcal{P}_1$, the distance to both specifications is $\frac{1}{2}$. Hence, $\mathcal{P}_1$ is the better (in fact, optimal) projection.

Furthermore, the optimal solution might not be a projection of the one obtained from the construction in Theorem 4.1. For $\mathcal{S}_1$ and $\mathcal{S}_2$, instead of the discretization $\{0,1\}$, consider the discretization $\{0, \frac{2}{3}, 1\}$. Implementation $\mathcal{P}_2$ (a projection of $\mathcal{I}_1$) has distances $\frac{2}{3}$ and $\frac{1}{3}$ to $\mathcal{S}_1$ and $\mathcal{S}_2$ respectively. However, $\mathcal{I}_2$ (which is not a projection of $\mathcal{I}_1$) has distances $\frac{4}{9}$ and $\frac{5}{9}$ to $\mathcal{S}_1$ and $\mathcal{S}_2$, respectively.

5. CASE STUDIES

We present two case studies to demonstrate the use of simulation distances for modeling conflicting requirements. These case studies do not consider large-scale examples, but rather serve to demonstrate that simulation distances and the synthesis from incompatible specifications framework are in principle suitable for specifying real-world problems.

5.1 Case study: Synthesis of Forward Error Correcting Codes

Consider the task of sending messages over an unreliable network. Forward Error Correcting codes (FECs) are encoding-decoding schemes that are tolerant to bit-flips during transmission, i.e., the decoded message is correct in-spite of errors during transmission. For example, the well-known Hamming (7,4) code can correct any one bit-flip that occurs during the transmission of a bit-block. The Hamming (7,4) code transmits 7 bits for every 4 data bits to be transfered, and the 3 additional bits are parity bits.

Suppose bit-blocks of length 3 are to be transfered over a network where at most 1 bit-flip can occur during transmission. We want to minimize the number of transmitted bits. Furthermore, we also allow some errors in the decoded block. Therefore, we have two incompatible specifications:

- *Efficiency.* To minimize the number of bits transmitted, we add a requirement that only 3 bits are transmitted and an error model that has a constant penalty of e for each additional bit transmitted.
- *Robustness.* We want the decoded block to be as correct as possible. In a standard FEC scheme, all bits are given equal importance. However, to demonstrate the flexibility of our techniques, we consider the first bit to be the most significant one, and the third to be the least significant one. We add a requirement that the decoded bit block is the same as the original, with the following error model: An error in the first, second, and third bit have a cost of $4d$, $2d$, and d, respectively.

Formal modeling. The output and input alphabets are $\{T_0, T_1, R_0, R_1, O_0, O_1, \perp\}$ and $\{I_0, I_1, F, \neg F, \perp\}$ where T_i, R_i, I_i and O_i stand for transmission, receiving, input and output of bit i respectively. Symbols F and $\neg F$ denote if a

bit-flip occurs or not during the current transmission. Symbol $\perp$ is used whenever the input/output does not matter.

EXAMPLE 5.1. *For example, the diagram below represents the transmission of bit-block* 010 *through a system without any error correction.*

In	I_0	I_1	I_0	$\perp$	F	$\perp$	$\neg F$	$\perp$	$\neg F$	$\perp$	$\perp$	$\perp$
Out	$\perp$	$\perp$	$\perp$	T_0	R_1	T_1	R_1	T_0	R_0	O_1	O_1	O_0

First, three bits are input. Next, each of the three bits is transmitted and received. The environment decides that the first bit is flipped and the value received is 1 *even though* 0 *is transmitted. Finally, the bit block* 110 *is output.*

In addition to *Efficiency* and *Robustness* requirements above, we need the following. For these, we use the qualitative error model where even a single error is not allowed.

- *Encoding and Decoding.* For any input (resp., received) bit-block, the same sequence of bits should be transmitted (resp. output). The specification remembers the transmitted (resp., output) bits for each input (resp., transmitted) bit-block and ensures that the same bits are transmitted (resp., output) in the future.
- *Reception.* The received bit should be correctly flipped or not based on whether the input is F or $\neg F$.

Results. For different relative values of efficiency penalty e and robustness penalty d, different optimal FEC schemes are obtained. Suppose $b_1 b_2 b_3$ is the input bit-block.

- $e = 1 \wedge d = 100$. The implementation is fully robust, i.e., always outputs the right bit-block. For example, one of the optimal strategies transmits b_1, b_2, b_3, $b_2 \oplus b_3$, $b_1 \oplus b_3$ and $b_1 \oplus b_2$. The bit-block can always be recovered from the received bits. This has a total error of 3 for efficiency and 0 for robustness per round.
- $e = 100 \wedge d = 1$. The implementation transmits only the three input bits and in the worst case outputs the most significant bit wrong. The worst-case errors are 0 for efficiency and 4 for robustness per round.
- $e = 10 \wedge d = 10$. The implementation ensures the correctness of the most significant bit by transmitting it thrice (triple modular redundancy), i.e., transmits b_1, b_1, b_1, b_2 and b_3. In the worst case, the second bit is output wrong and the error for efficiency is 20 and for robustness is 20 per round.

These results show how we can obtain completely different FECs just by varying the costs in the error models.

5.2 Case study: Optimal Scheduling for Overloads

Consider the task of scheduling on multiple processors, where processes have definite execution times and deadlines. Deadlines are either "soft", where a small delay is acceptable, but undesirable; or "hard", where any delay is catastrophic. During overload, processes are either delayed or dropped completely; and usually these processes are chosen based on priorities. Our techniques can be used to schedule based on exact penalties for missing deadlines or dropping processes.

Each process repeatedly requests execution and scheduling is based on time-slices with each processor executing a single process in a time-slice. A process $\mathcal{P}(t, d, c)$ represents:

- the time-slices t needed for the computation;
- the deadline d from invocation time; and

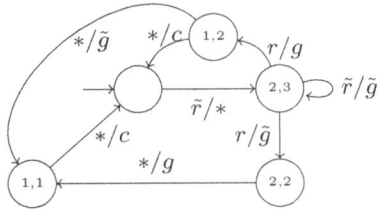

Figure 8: Modelling processes: $\mathcal{P}(2,3,1)$

- the minimum time c between the completion of one invocation and the next request.

We model a process as a reactive system with inputs $\{r, \tilde{r}\}$ and outputs $\{g, \tilde{g}, c\}$. The input r represents an invocation, the output g represents a single time-slice of execution, and the output c indicates completion of the invocation.

In Figure 8, all states (except the initial) are labeled by two numbers (t, d) representing, respectively, remaining execution steps, and time to deadline. Once request r is issued, execution starts at the state labeled $(2, 3)$ (input and output transitions are drawn together for readability). If the first time slice is granted, the execution goes to state $(2, 1)$ (i.e., deadline in two steps, and one step of work remaining). If the time slice is not granted, the execution transitions to a state labeled by $(2, 2)$. The model (specification) ensures that the task is completed before the deadline. After it is completed, the control is in the initial state, where a request cannot be issued for at least one time step.

We define both hard and soft deadline error models. In the hard deadline error model, a missed deadline leads to a one-time large penalty p_l, whereas in the soft deadline error model, a small recurring penalty p_s occurs every step until the process is finished. Furthermore, we have a specification that no more than n processes can be scheduled in each step, with the qualitative failure model (Figure 5). We describe some optimal implementations obtained for various inputs.

- For two $\mathcal{P}(3, 6, 3)$ processes and one processor, we obtain a 0 cost schedule where each process is alternately scheduled till completion. This schedule is obtained independently of whether the deadlines are hard or soft.
- For $P_1 = \mathcal{P}(5, 5, 5)$, $P_2 = \mathcal{P}(3, 5, 5)$, and $P_3 = \mathcal{P}(2, 5, 5)$ with P_1 on a soft deadline (i.e. with the soft deadline error model described above), P_2 on a hard deadline, and P_3 on a hard deadline. With $p_s = 1$ and $p_l = 10$, we get a scheduler where P_2 and P_3 are treated as having a higher priority. Whenever P_2 or P_3 requests arrive, P_1 is preempted till P_2 and P_3 finish.
- For the same processes, but with $p_s = 5 \wedge p_l = 10$, we get a scheduler where P_1 is preferred over P_2 and P_3.

6. CONCLUSION

There are several possible directions for future research. From the theoretical side, we will investigate extending the simulation distances framework to probabilistic systems (to model probabilistically distributed inputs). The second possible extension is using bisimulation (as opposed to simulation) as the basis of distances between systems. From the practical side, we plan to do a larger case study to test whether quantitative metrics lead to simpler, more robust, or easier to maintain real specifications.

7. REFERENCES

[1] R. Alur, T. Henzinger, O. Kupferman, and M. Vardi. Alternating refinement relations. In *CONCUR*, pages 163–178, 1998.

[2] R. Bloem, R. Cavada, I. Pill, M. Roveri, and A. Tchaltsev. Rat: A tool for the formal analysis of requirements. In *CAV*, pages 263–267, 2007.

[3] R. Bloem, K. Chatterjee, T. Henzinger, and B. Jobstmann. Better quality in synthesis through quantitative objectives. In *CAV*, pages 140–156, 2009.

[4] P. Caspi and A. Benveniste. Toward an approximation theory for computerised control. In *EMSOFT*, pages 294–304, 2002.

[5] P. Černý, K. Chatterjee, T. Henzinger, A. Radhakrishna, and R. Singh. Quantitative synthesis for concurrent programs. In *CAV*, pages 243–259, 2011.

[6] P. Černý, T. Henzinger, and A. Radhakrishna. Simulation distances. In *CONCUR*, pages 253–268, 2010.

[7] K. Chatterjee, L. Doyen, T. Henzinger, and J.-F. Raskin. Generalized mean-payoff and energy games. In *FSTTCS*, pages 505–516, 2010.

[8] K. Chatterjee, T. Henzinger, and B. Jobstmann. Environment assumptions for synthesis. In *CONCUR*, pages 147–161, 2008.

[9] E. Clarke and E. Emerson. Design and synthesis of synchronization skeletons using branching-time temporal logic. In *Logic of Programs, Workshop*, pages 52–71, 1982.

[10] L. de Alfaro, M. Faella, and M. Stoelinga. Linear and branching system metrics. *IEEE Trans. Software Eng.*, 35(2):258–273, 2009.

[11] J. Desharnais, V. Gupta, R. Jagadeesan, and P. Panangaden. Metrics for labelled Markov processes. *TCS*, 318(3):323–354, 2004.

[12] S. Divakaran, D. D'Souza, and R. Matteplackel. Conflict-tolerant specifications in temporal logic. In *ICSE*, pages 103–110, 2010.

[13] D. D'Souza and M. Gopinathan. Conflict-tolerant features. In *CAV*, pages 227–239, 2008.

[14] C. Heitmeyer, M. Archer, R. Bharadwaj, and R. Jeffords. Tools for constructing requirements specifications: the SCR toolset at the age of nine. *Comput. Syst. Sci. Eng.*, 20(1), 2005.

[15] R. Könighofer, G. Hofferek, and R. Bloem. Debugging formal specifications using simple counterstrategies. In *FMCAD*, pages 152–159, 2009.

[16] I. Pill, S. Semprini, R. Cavada, M. Roveri, R. Bloem, and A. Cimatti. Formal analysis of hardware requirements. In *DAC*, pages 821–826, 2006.

[17] N. Piterman and A. Pnueli. Synthesis of reactive(1) designs. In *VMCAI*, pages 364–380, 2006.

[18] A. Pnueli and R. Rosner. On the synthesis of a reactive module. In *POPL*, pages 179–190, 1989.

[19] F. van Breugel. An introduction to metric semantics: operational and denotational models for programming and specification languages. *TCS*, 258(1-2):1–98, 2001.

Timed Model Checking with Abstractions: Towards Worst-Case Response Time Analysis in Resource-Sharing Manycore Systems

Georgia Giannopoulou*   Kai Lampka†   Nikolay Stoimenov*   Lothar Thiele*
*Computer Engineering and Networks Laboratory, ETH Zurich, 8092 Zurich, Switzerland
† Information Technology Department, Uppsala University, Sweden
{giannopoulou, stoimenov, thiele}@tik.ee.ethz.ch   lampka@it.uu.se

ABSTRACT

Multicore architectures are increasingly used nowadays in embedded real-time systems. Parallel execution of tasks feigns the possibility of a massive increase in performance. However, this is usually not achieved because of contention on shared resources. Concurrently executing tasks mutually block their accesses to the shared resource, causing non-deterministic delays. Timing analysis of tasks in such systems is then far from trivial. Recently, several analytic methods have been proposed for this purpose, however, they cannot model complex arbitration schemes such as FlexRay which is a common bus arbitration protocol in the automotive industry. This paper considers real-time tasks composed of superblocks, i. e., sequences of computation and resource accessing phases. Resource accesses such as accesses to memories and caches are synchronous, i. e., they cause execution on the processing core to stall until the access is served. For such systems, the paper presents a state-based modeling and analysis approach based on Timed Automata which can model accurately arbitration schemes of any complexity. Based on it, we compute safe bounds on the worst-case response times of tasks. The scalability of the approach is increased significantly by abstracting several cores and their tasks with one arrival curve, which represents their resource accesses and computation times. This curve is then incorporated into the Timed Automata model of the system. The accuracy and scalability of the approach are evaluated with a real-world application from the automotive industry and benchmark applications.

Categories and Subject Descriptors

C.3 [**Special-purpose and application-based systems**]: Real-time and embedded systems; C.4 [**Performance of systems**]: Modeling techniques

Keywords

multi-core systems, worst-case response time analysis, resource contention

1. INTRODUCTION

Multicore systems have become increasingly popular as they allow increase in performance by exploiting parallelism in hardware and software without sacrificing too much on power consumption and cost. However, the reduction in cost is achieved by sharing resources between the processing cores. Such shared resources can be for example buses, caches, scratchpad memories, main memories, and DMA.

In safety-critical embedded systems, such as controllers in the Automotive Open System Architecture (AutoSAR) [1], accesses to the shared resources can be non-periodic and bursty, which means that the system may miss its real-time deadlines. Therefore, a designer needs to consider the interference due to contention on the shared resources in order to verify the real-time properties of the system. At the same time, the interference-induced delays need to be tightly bounded to avoid an extreme over-provisioning of the platform.

However, performing timing analysis for such systems is quite challenging because the number of possible interleavings of resource accesses from the different processing cores can be very large. Additionally, resource accesses can be asynchronous such as message passing or synchronous such as memory accesses due to cache misses. For the asynchronous accesses, the timing analysis needs to take into account the arrival pattern of accesses from the processing cores and the respective backlogs. In this case, traditional timing analysis methods such as Real-Time Calculus [24] and SymTA/S [11] can compute accurate bounds on the worst-case response times (WCRT) of tasks and the end-to-end delays of accesses. For the synchronous case, however, an access request stalls the execution of a processing core until the access is completed, i.e. an access increases the tasks' WCRT. Once an access starts being served, it cannot be preempted by other accesses. Bounding the waiting time for an access under these assumptions is challenging as one has to take into account the currently issued accesses from other cores and the state of the resource sharing arbiter. In this paper, we deal with the second case of synchronous accesses.

Schliecker et al. [20], have recently proposed methodologies to analyze the worst-case delay a task suffers due to accesses to shared memory, assuming synchronous resource accesses. The authors consider a system where the maximum and the minimum numbers of resource accesses in particular time windows are assumed to be known. The arbiter to the shared resource uses a first-come first-served (FCFS) scheduling scheme and tasks are scheduled according to fixed priority. The authors evaluate the approach with a system with two processing cores. In [15] Negrean et al.

consider the multiprocessor priority ceiling protocol where tasks have globally assigned priorities, but similarly use a system with two processing cores. None of the above results consider complex scheduling policies such as FlexRay [4] or systems with high number of processing cores as analyzed in this paper.

Recent results in [18, 21, 23] have proposed methods for WCRT analysis in multicore systems where the shared resource is arbitrated according to FCFS, Round Robin (RR), Time Division Multiple Access (TDMA) or a hybrid time-/event-driven strategy, the latter being a combination of TDMA and FCFS/RR. The presented analysis, however, uses over-approximations which result in overly pessimistic results, particularly in cases of state-based arbitration mechanisms, like FCFS or RR. This shortcoming is of concern, as industrial standards like the FlexRay [4] bus protocol explicitly exploit state-dependent behaviors. In this paper, we rely on model checking techniques in order to model accurately the behavior of such state-dependent arbiters.

Note that the FlexRay protocol is considered in our work as an example of a complex state-based arbitration policy, even though it is not originally designated for e. g., bus arbitration in shared-memory distributed systems. FlexRay has been analyzed by Pop et al. [19] and by Chokshi et al. [7] but these approaches deal only with the asynchronous case of resource accesses. On the other hand, FlexRay with synchronous accesses has never been modeled with analytic approaches. In [23], Schranzhofer et al. have modeled a hybrid arbitration mechanism as a combination of a static (TDMA) and a dynamic segment, the latter behaving according to FCFS or RR. Model checking enables us, however, to model and analyze FlexRay with synchronous accesses for the first time.

Model checking techniques have been applied for timing analysis in resource-sharing multicore systems in [14, 10]. The methods deal accurately with complex arbitration schemes, however, none of them can scale efficiently beyond two cores. In order to alleviate the state-explosion problem which is inherent to model checking techniques, in this paper we combine model checking with several abstractions. First being that tasks are composed of superblocks. Second being that some of the processing cores can be substituted by simpler models that represent only their resource accesses.

The superblock model for structuring real-time tasks has been proposed by industry as part of the EU sponsored project Predator [3], since it fits very well signal-processing and control applications. The model assumes that tasks are composed of sequentially executed superblocks for which the minimum/maximum number of resource accesses and execution times are known. The model has been extensively used in several methods [18, 21, 23] for deriving worst-case response times of tasks in resource-shared multicore systems with synchronous accesses. Different variants of the model are compared in [22]. They differ mostly in that superblocks may have phases where resource accesses are not required (computation-only phases). Such phase structure can be actually enforced by a compiler as shown in [16]. Additionally, [8] shows how this model of resource accessing can be mapped to an AutoSAR system for automotive applications.

Arrival curves as known from Network and Real-Time Calculus [24] are used to bound the maximum number of events arriving in any time interval of any given length. Several methods [15, 18, 20] have utilized them before to represent the maximum number of resource accesses from a task. The novelty of this paper is their integration into a Timed Automata model of the system in order to com-bine accurate modeling of complex arbitration schemes with analysis scalability.

It should be noted that we consider only hardware platforms without timing anomalies, such as the fully timing compositional architecture proposed by Wilhelm et al. [25], and we assume that a task partitioning is pre-defined, i.e. tasks are mapped to dedicated processing cores.

The contribution of this paper is summarized as follows:

- For the proposed system model, we introduce a state-based WCRT analysis approach. Timed automata (TA) are used to model (a) concurrent execution of processing cores and their tasks and (b) resource access arbitration according to an event-driven (FCFS, RR), time-driven (TDMA), hybrid (FlexRay) policy or any other policy of arbitrary complexity. The Uppaal model checker is then used to compute the exact WCRT of each task in the system.

- To increase the scalability of the approach, an abstraction based on arrival curves is introduced. Tight curves that bound the number of resource accesses in the time-interval domain are derived for each core from the actual accesses specified in the superblocks of the tasks mapped on the core. Using the interfaces between Real-Time Calculus and TA presented in [12], the TA model of the system is reduced by replacing the models of several processing cores with a single model that can generate non-deterministic streams of access requests according to the arrival curves of the abstracted cores.

- The accuracy and efficiency of the approach are demonstrated using a set of embedded benchmark applications (EEMBC) and a real-world application from the automotive industry. The WCRT bounds obtained with the proposed method are compared to those of state-of-the-art analytic approaches.

In the remainder of the paper, Section 2 shortly introduces some of the necessary theory on TA and Real-Time Calculus. Section 3 defines the considered system models. Section 4 introduces the new state-based analysis method, addressing explicitly the challenge of scalability. Finally, Section 5 presents the empirical evaluation of the proposed approach and Section 6 concludes the paper.

2. BACKGROUND THEORY

In this section we briefly introduce some important concepts from the theories of Timed Automata and Real-Time Calculus which will be needed throughout the paper. For more details, the reader is referred to the respective literature.

2.1 Timed Automata

Let C be a set of clocks and let $ClockCons$ be a set of constraints on these clocks. With Timed Automata (TA) [5] the clock constraints are conjunctions, disjunctions and negations of atomic (clock) guards of the form $x \bowtie n, x \in C, n \in \mathbb{N}_0$ with $\bowtie \in \{<, \leq, >, \geq, =\}$. A TA $\mathcal{T}$ is then defined as a tuple $\mathcal{T} := (Loc, Loc_0, Act, C, \hookrightarrow, I)$ where Loc is a finite set of locations, $Loc_0 \subseteq Loc$ is the set of initial locations, Act is a (finite) set of action (or edge) labels, C is the finite set of clocks, $\hookrightarrow \subseteq Loc \times ClockCons(C) \times Act \times 2^C \times Loc$ is an edge relation and $I : Loc \rightarrow ClockCons(C)$ is a mapping of locations to clock constraints, where the latter are referred to as location invariants.

Let the active locations be the locations the TA currently resides in. The operational semantics associated with a TA can be informally characterized as follows:

- *Delay transitions.* As long as the location invariants of the active location(s) are not violated, time may progress, where all clocks increase at the same speed.

- *Edge executions.* The traversal of an edge (one at a time) potentially changes the set of active locations; self-loops are possible. The traversal, or "edge execution" is instantaneous and possible as long as the source location of the edge is marked active and the guard of the edge evaluates to true. Upon edge executions, clocks can be reset.

This operational semantics yields that for a TA one may observe infinitely many different behaviors. This is because edge executions may occur at any time, namely as long as the edge guard evaluates to true. However, with the concept of clock regions [5] it is possible to capture all possible behaviors in a finite state graph, such that timed reachability is decidable. In fact, modern timed model checkers incorporate *clock zones* [13] as they often result in a coarser partitioning of the clock evaluation space in comparison to the original definition of clock regions.

In this paper we will exploit the timed model checker Uppaal [6], which implements timed safety automata extended with variables. Similarly to clocks, variables can be used within guards of edges and location invariants. Upon an edge execution, a variable can be updated. The used variable values must build a finite set, which, however, does not need to be known beforehand, i.e., it can be constructed on-the-fly upon the state space traversal. For conciseness, we omit further details, and refer the interested reader to the literature [5, 26, 6].

2.2 Real-time Calculus

Real-time calculus (RTC) [24] is a compositional methodology for system-level performance analysis of distributed real-time systems. We briefly recapitulate the basic concepts that are used in this paper.

In the context of real-time systems design, the timing behavior of event streams is usually characterized by real-time traffic models. Examples of such typically used models are periodic, sporadic, periodic with jitter, and periodic with burst. RTC provides an alternative characterization of streams: a pair (α^l, α^u) of arrival curves bounds the number of events seen on the stream for any interval of length $\Delta \in [0, \infty)$. Let $R(t)$ be a stream's cumulative counting function which reports the actual event arrivals for the time interval $[0, t)$. The upper and lower arrival curves bound $R(t)$, i.e., the possible event arrivals in the time interval domain, as follows:

$$\alpha^l(t - q) \le R(t) - R(q) \le \alpha^u(t - q) \text{ with } 0 \le q \le t. \quad (1)$$

In this work we restrict our attention to the case of *discrete amounts* of events. In RTC, such scenarios are modeled as staircase curves. In particular, the upper arrival curve $\alpha^u(\Delta)$ in this case is defined as the staircase function:

$$\alpha^{st}(\Delta) := B + \left\lfloor \frac{\Delta}{\delta} \right\rfloor \cdot s \quad (2)$$

Parameter $B > 0$ models the burst capacity, namely it is the number of events that can arrive at the same time instant in the stream bounded from above by $\alpha^{st}(\Delta)$. Parameters δ and s are related to the maximum long-term arrival rate of events in the stream and the step size (y-offset), respectively.

The timing behavior of streams modeled as staircase arrival curves (Eq. 2) can be correctly and completely modeled with timed automata models as described in [12].

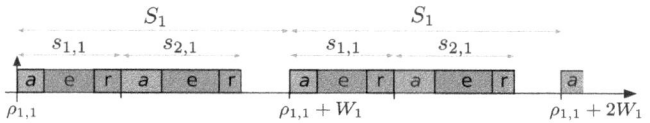

Figure 1: Dedicated sequential superblock model

3. SYSTEM MODEL

This section presents the real-time task model that was considered in our analysis and introduces the arbitration mechanisms for coordinating access to the shared resource.

3.1 Tasks and Processing Cores

A system consists of multiple *processing cores* $p_j \in P$. The cores in P execute independent tasks but can access a common resource, such as an interconnection bus to a shared memory. We assume a given task partitioning, in which a task set T_j is assigned to a predefined processing core $p_j \in P$. The *tasks* in T_j are specified by a sequence of *superblocks* S_j, which are non-preemptable execution units with known lower/upper bounds on their computation time and the number of resource accesses that they may require.

For each core p_j, we assume a static schedule of the assigned tasks, which is repeated periodically with period W_j. Periods of the processing cycles may be different among the cores. In the first processing cycle, the first superblock $s_{1,j}$ of the task set T_j starts executing at time $\rho_{1,j}$. The static schedule provides an order of the superblock set S_j [1]. Therefore superblocks in S_j are repeatedly executed in $[\rho_{1,j}, \rho_{1,j} + W_j)$, $[\rho_{1,j} + W_j, \rho_{1,j} + 2W_j)$, and so forth, with each superblock $s_{i+1,j}$ being triggered upon completion of its predecessor, $s_{i,j}$ [2] (see, e.g., execution of superblock sequence $S_1 = \{s_{1,1}, s_{2,1}\}$ on core p_1, Figure 1). The starting times of processing cycles on different cores may be synchronized, i.e., the first superblock in all first processing cycles starts at time 0 ($\rho_{1,j} = 0, \forall j$), or non-synchronized, i.e., $\rho_{1,j} \in [0, W_j)$.

In order to reduce non-determinism w.r.t. the occurrence of access requests, superblocks are separated into three phases, known as *acquisition*, *execution*, and *replication* which are denoted with a, e, and r in Figure 1. The model represents that a superblock reads the required data during the acquisition phase and writes back the modified/new data in the replication phase, after computations in the execution phase have been completed. This is a common model for signal-processing and control real-time applications. For our analysis, we consider in particular the dedicated superblock model, in which resource accesses are performed (sequentially) in the acquisition and the replication phase, while no accesses are required in the execution phase.

The dedicated superblock structure is the first abstraction proposed in this paper, since the restriction of resource accesses to dedicated phases leads to increased predictability when analyzing the system's timing behavior. In particular, Schranzhofer et al. have shown in [22] that the schedulability of the dedicated sequential superblock model dominates that of other models, in which accesses may occur any time during computation.

As a result of the discussed structure, a superblock is fully defined by the following parameters: (a) the minimum and maximum number of access requests during its acquisition and replication phase, $\mu_{i,j}^{min,\{a,r\}}$ and $\mu_{i,j}^{max,\{a,r\}}$, and (b) the minimum and maximum computation time during its

---

[1] Mixing of superblocks of different tasks, i.e., preemption on task level, is possible.

[2] Idle intervals between successive superblocks may also exist.

execution phase, $exec_{i,j}^{min}$ and $exec_{i,j}^{max}$. Note that the necessary computation to initiate the accesses during the dedicated phases is considered negligible compared to the time required for their completion and hence, can be ignored. For a superblock with logical branches, the above numbers might be overestimated, but the worst-case execution time will be safely bounded. We assume that the access request parameters can be derived either by profiling and measurement for the case of soft real-time systems, as shown in [17], or by applying static analysis when hard safe bounds are necessary.

3.2 Shared Resource and Arbiter

In the considered systems, task execution is suspended every time an access request is issued, until the latter is completely processed by the resource arbiter. Once the arbiter grants access of a request, the accessing time is (bounded by) C time units. That is, if a superblock $s_{i,j}$ could access the shared resource at any time, its worst-case execution time would be $exec_{i,j}^{max} + (\mu_{i,j}^{max,a} + \mu_{i,j}^{max,r}) \cdot C$. It is assumed that access can be granted to at most one request at a time and that processing of an ongoing access cannot be preempted. Once a pending access request is served, either task execution on the corresponding core is resumed by performing computations or a new access request is issued or the core remains idle until the start of a new processing cycle (or the next superblock). Access to the shared resource is granted by a dedicated arbiter. The implemented arbitration policy can be time-driven, e.g., TDMA, event-driven, e.g., FCFS or RR or hybrid, e.g., the FlexRay bus protocol. A more detailed discussion on the possible arbitration schemes follows.

3.2.1 TDMA Arbiter

In a TDMA arbitration scheme, access to the shared resource is statically organized by assigning time slots to each core. That is, access to the resource is partitioned over time and only a single core can acquire it at any moment. TDMA arbitration policies are widely used in timing- and safety-critical applications to increase timing predictability and alleviate schedulability analysis, since they eliminate mutual interferences of the tasks through their time isolation.

A TDMA arbiter uses a predefined cycle of fixed length, which is specified as a sequence of time slots. The time slots can be of variable lengths and there is at least one slot for each core $p_j \in P$ in every schedule. An access request issued by the current task of core p_j during the i-th time slot of the TDMA cycle is enabled immediately if the latter slot is assigned to core p_j and the remaining time of the slot is enough to accommodate processing of the new access. Requests that arrive "too late" have to wait until the next allocated slot. To provide meaningful results, we assume that all slots in a TDMA schedule are at least of length C.

3.2.2 RR Arbiter

RR-based arbitration can be seen as a dynamic version of TDMA with a varying arbitration cycle. This is because the unused slots of the cycle are skipped whenever the respective cores do not need to access the shared resource. To implement this behavior, the RR arbiter checks repeatedly (circularly) all cores in P, starting with the first identifier, p_1, up to the last one, p_N. If the core with the currently considered identifier p_i has a pending request, access is granted to it immediately. Otherwise, the arbiter checks the next identifier, and so forth.

3.2.3 FCFS Arbiter

The resource arbiter, in this case, is responsible for maintaining a first-in first-out (FIFO) queue with the identifiers of the cores which have a pending access request. Access is granted based on the time ordering of their occurrence, i.e., the oldest request is served first. This scheme guarantees fairness given that, if core p_i issues an access request before core p_j, p_i's request will be served at an earlier point in time, without considering any priorities between the two cores.

3.2.4 FlexRay Arbiter

The FlexRay protocol [4] has been introduced by a large consortium of automotive manufacturers and suppliers. It enables sharing of a resource (usually interconnection bus among the processing cores of an automotive system), featuring both time- and event-driven arbitration.

In the FlexRay protocol, a periodically repeated arbitration cycle is composed of a static (ST) and a dynamic (DYN) segment. The ST segment uses a generalized TDMA arbitration scheme, whereas the DYN segment applies a flexible TDMA-based approach. The lengths of the two segments may not be equal, but they are fixed across the arbitration cycles. Both segments are defined as sequences of time slots. The ST segment includes a fixed number of slots, with constant and equal lengths, d. Each slot is assigned to a particular core and one or more access requests from this core can be served within its duration. The DYN segment is defined as a sequence of *minislots* of equal length, $\ell \ll d$. The actual duration of a slot depends on whether access to the shared resource is requested by the corresponding core or not: if no access is to be performed, then the slot has a very small length (*minislot length*, ℓ). Otherwise, it is resized to enable the successful processing of the access (*access length*, here equal to C). To obtain reasonable results, we assume that each ST slot as well as the DYN segment are at least equal to C. The assignment of ST or DYN (mini)slots to the processing cores is static. However, since the introduction of FlexRay 2.0, cycle multiplexing has become also possible for the DYN segment, i.e., some minislots may be assigned to different cores in different cycles, resulting in more than one alternating arbitration schedule.

The above description implies that in the ST part of FlexRay, like in TDMA, interference can be neglected due to isolation. In the DYN part, however, the actual delay of an access is interference-dependent, which makes it difficult to analyze without a state-based approach. The accurate modeling and analysis of such an arbitration policy for the case of synchronous resource accessing has been one of the major motives of our developed approach.

4. TIMING ANALYSIS USING MODEL CHECKING

For the state-based analysis of resource contention scenarios in multicores, the system specification of Sec. 3 can be modeled by a network of cooperating TA. This section presents the TA that were used to model the system components. We discuss how the temporal properties of the system can be verified using the Uppaal timed model checker and we introduce a set of abstractions to reduce the required verification effort.

4.1 Multicore System as a TA Network

4.1.1 Modeling Concurrent Execution

The parallel execution of superblock sets S_j on the system's cores is modeled using instances of two TA for each core, mentioned in the following as *Scheduler* and *Superblock*, and depicted in Figure 2. In a system with N cores and a total of M superblocks executed on them, $(N + M)$ TA are needed to model execution.

The *Scheduler* TA (Figure 2(b)) specifies the scheduling mechanism of each core p_j. It is responsible for activating the superblocks in S_j sequentially, according to the predefined execution order (static schedule), which is repeated every W_j time units. Whenever a new superblock must be scheduled, the *Scheduler* emits a `start[sid]` signal. Due to the underlying composition mechanism, this yields a synchronization between the *Scheduler* and the respective *Superblock* instance. When the superblock's execution is completed, the *Scheduler* receives a `finish[sid]` signal. If this superblock was not the last of the current processing cycle (condition checked through user-defined function `last_sb()`), the *Scheduler* triggers the next superblock. Otherwise, it moves to location `EndOfPeriod`, where it lets time pass until the processing cycle's period is reached.

A *Superblock* TA (Figure 2(a)) models the three phases of each superblock and is parameterized by the lower and upper bounds on access requests and computation times. Once a *Superblock* instance is activated, it enters the `Acq` location, where the respective TA resides until a non-deterministically selected number of resource accesses (within the specified bounds) has been issued and processed. Access requests are issued through channel `access[pid]`, whereas notification of their completion is received by the arbiter through channel `accessed[pid]` (see 'loop transitions' over `Acq` in Figure 2(a)). For location `Acq`, we use Uppaal's concept of urgent locations to ensure that no computation time passes between successive requests from the same core, which complies with the specification of our system model. Subsequently, the *Superblock* TA moves to the `Exec` location, where computation (without resource accesses) is performed. The clock `x_exec` measures the elapsed computation time to ensure that the superblock's upper and lower bounds, $exec^{max}$ and $exec^{min}$, respectively, are guarded. The behavior of the TA in the following location `Rep` is identical to that modeled with location `Acq` (successive resource accesses).

For the case of a single superblock in S_j, clock `x` is used to measure its total execution time. Checking the maximum value of clock `x` while the TA resides in its 'final' location, i. e., `Rep`, allows to obtain the WCRT of the whole superblock. With Uppaal this is done by specifying the lowest value of `WCRT`, for which the safety property `A[] Superblock(i).Rep imply Superblock(i).x <= WCRT` holds[3]. This way we ensure that for all reachable states, the value of superblock s_i's clock `x` is never greater than `WCRT`. To find the lowest `WCRT` satisfying the previous query, binary search can be applied. Upon termination, the binary search will deliver a safe and tight bound of the superblock's WCRT. Similarly, we can compute a WCRT bound on a sequence S_j (a task) by adapting the TA of Figure 2(a) to model more than 3 phases.

4.1.2 Modeling Resource Arbitration

The TA modeling the four suggested arbitration policies of Sec. 3.2 are depicted in Figure 3. Depending on the implemented policy, the respective model is included in the TA network of our system.

The *FCFS* and the *RR Arbiter* share a similar TA, depicted in Figure 3(a). Both arbiters maintain a queue with the identifiers of the cores that have a pending access request. In the case of FCFS, this is a FIFO queue with capacity N, since each core can have at maximum one pending request at a time. When a new request arrives, the arbiter

---
[3] Query `sup{Superblock(i).Rep}:Superblock(i).x` could be also used for the same purpose.

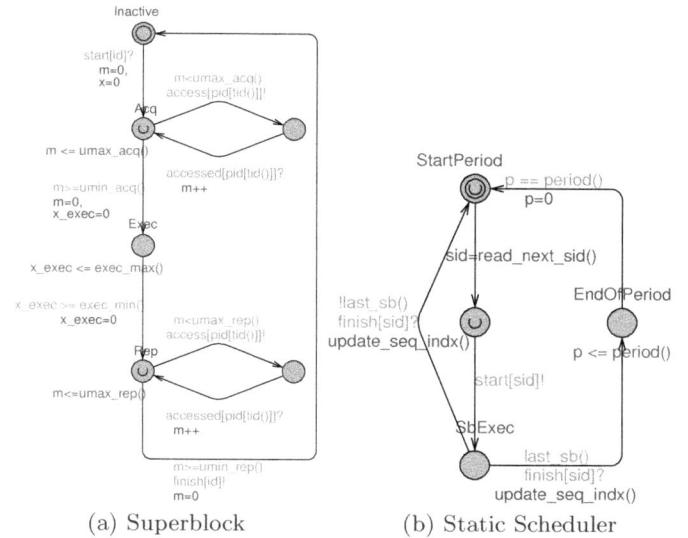

(a) Superblock   (b) Static Scheduler

Figure 2: Superblock and Static Scheduler TA

identifies its source, i. e., the emitting core, and appends the respective identifier to the tail of the FIFO queue. If the queue is not empty, the arbiter enables access to the shared resource for the oldest request (`active()` returns the queue's head). After time C, the access is completed, so the arbiter removes the head of the FIFO queue and notifies the *Superblock* TA that the pending request has been processed.

For the RR arbiter a bitmap is maintained instead of a FIFO queue. Each position of it corresponds to one of the cores and pending requests are flags with the respective bit set to 1. As long as at least one bit is set, the arbiter parses the bitmap sequentially granting access to the first request it encounters (return value of `active()`).

The *TDMA Arbiter* of Figure 3(b) implements the predefined TDMA arbitration cycle, in which each core has one or more, sequential or non-deterministically assigned time slots. It is assumed that the cores (*Scheduler* instances) and the arbiter initialize simultaneously such that the first slot on the shared resource and the first superblock on each core start at time 0 (assuming synchronized processing cycles among the cores). The arbiter's clock `slot_t` measures the elapsed time since the beginning of each TDMA slot. When `slot_t` becomes equal to the duration of the current slot, the clock is reset and a new time slot begins. According to this, a new access request from core `eid` is served as soon as it arrives at the arbiter on condition that (a) the current slot is assigned to `eid` and (b) the remaining time before the slot expires is large enough for the processing of the access. If at least one condition is not fulfilled, the pending request remains 'stored' in the arbiter's queue and is granted as soon as the next dedicated slot to `eid` begins.

The *FlexRay Arbiter* in Figure 3(c) is substantially an extension over the TDMA arbiter. This extension models the DYN segment of the FlexRay arbitration cycle that is executed after each ST segment. Once the ST segment is completed (`EndStatSegment()`), the arbiter checks if the core assigned to the first DYN minislot has a pending request. If this is true (`inQueue(proc_indx)`), the DYN minislot is resized to `C` time units to accommodate the access. Otherwise, the arbiter waits until expiration of the minislot and then, it checks for pending requests from the core assigned to the next minislot. This procedure is repeated until the DYN segment expires. According to this model, during the FlexRay DYN segment, a new access request from core `eid` is served

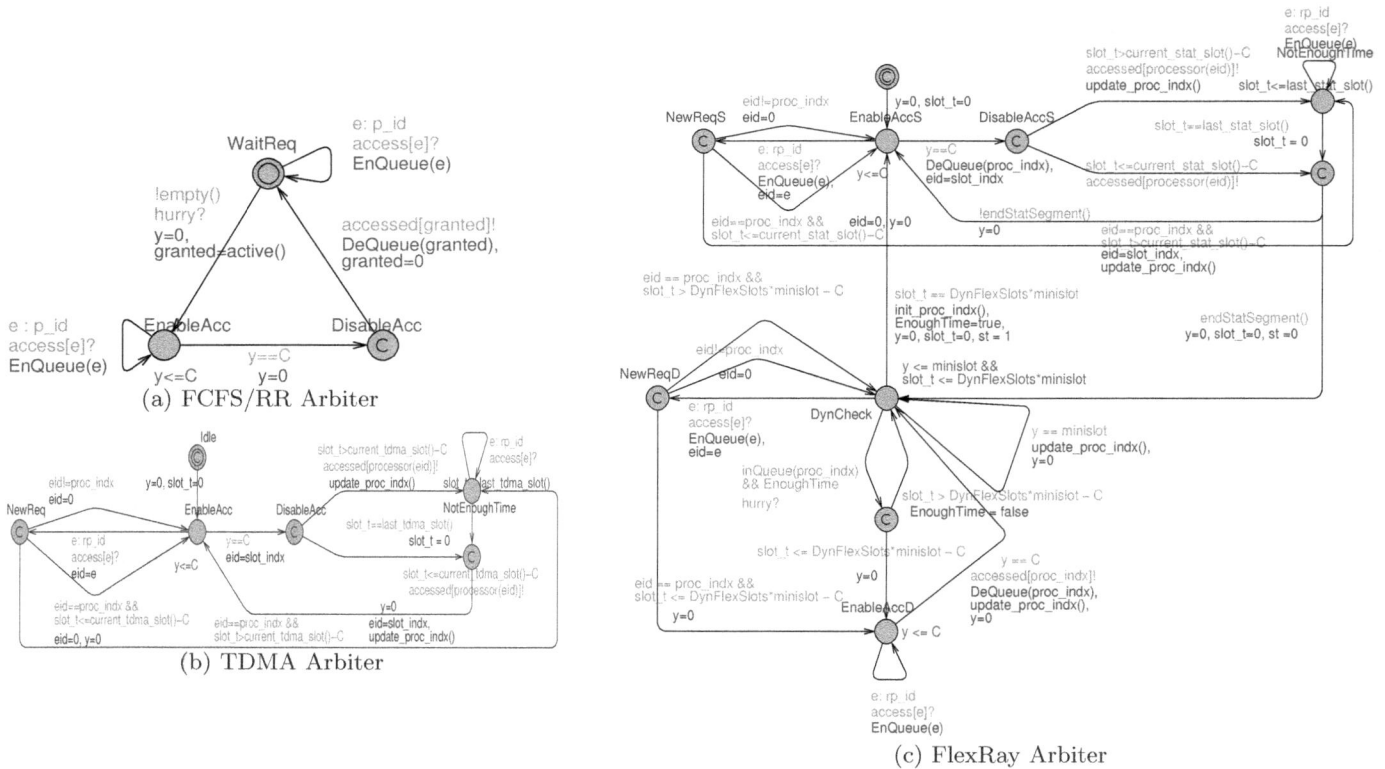

Figure 3: TA representation of arbitration mechanisms

immediately on condition that (a) the current minislot is assigned to eid and (b) the remaining time until the DYN segment expires is at least equal to C, so that the DYN segment cannot interfere with the upcoming ST segment. If a condition is not fulfilled, then serving eid's access request is postponed until its following ST or DYN (mini)slot.

In all *Arbiter* TA, new access requests can be received any time, either when the queue is empty or while the resource is being accessed. Multiple requests can also arrive simultaneously.

4.2 Reducing the Number of TA-based Component Models

A network consisting of N *Scheduler*, M *Superblock* and 1 *Arbiter* TA is used to model the multicore architectures under analysis. By verifying appropriate temporal properties in Uppaal, we can derive WCRT estimates for each superblock or superblock sequence that is executed on a processing core. However, scaling is related to the number of TA-based component models as the verification effort of the model checker depends on the number of clocks and clock constants used in the overall model. Particularly, the more the processing cores, the more the required clocks for modeling execution on them, which leads gradually to state space explosion. In the following sections, we propose safe abstractions for achieving a better analysis scalability.

In the proposed abstractions, only one processing core (core under analysis, CUA) is considered at a time, while all remaining cores, which compete against it for access to the shared resource, are abstracted away (not ignored). To model the access requests of abstracted cores we use arrival curves (Sec. 2.2). This way an arrival curve capturing the aggregate interference pattern of the abstracted cores can be constructed and then, modeled using TA. Eventually, the

network of TA that models our system will include only 1 *Scheduler*, M_i *Superblock* ($M_i = |S_i|$: number of superblocks executing on CUA p_i), 1 *Arbiter* and 2 *Request Generator* TA, i.e., the number of TA components will **not** depend on the number of abstracted cores.

4.2.1 Abstract representation of access request patterns

Representation of the access pattern of a core's periodically executed superblock sequence, using an arrival curve in the time-interval domain (as known from Real-Time Calculus), was introduced by Pellizzoni et al. in [18]. Their method for the arrival curve construction was based on the assumptions that (a) superblocks are general, i.e., computation and accesses can be performed any time, and (b) access requests from the same core can be buffered on the arbiter. The following part describes an extension to that method, namely it presents how to compute an upper arrival curve α_j which bounds the amount of access requests that a core p_j can issue in any time interval, while accounting for the dedicated superblock structure and the synchronous access requests that are assumed in our system model.

To derive this arrival curve for a core p_j, the core is considered in isolation, i.e., as if it had immediate exclusive access to the shared resource. For the curve construction, the following steps are necessary: (i) computation of all possible ordered phase subsets of the core's superblock sequence S_j, (ii) computation of the feasible time windows for each subset and the maximum number of access requests that can be issued during them, and (iii) construction of the arrival curve as a periodic function. These steps are elaborated briefly in the following. For a more detailed presentation and examples, the reader is referred to technical report [9].

(i) We first consider two subsequent instances of S_j (to account for the transition phase between successive processing cycles on p_j) and we specify all possible subsets of phases that can be executed during these instances. To do this, we reduce the superblocks in S_j to their three constituent phases, i.e., each superblock is specified as $s_{i,j} = \{f_{3 \cdot (i-1)+1,j}, f_{3 \cdot (i-1)+2,j}, f_{3 \cdot (i-1)+3,j}\}$. Then, the superblock sequence $\{SjSj\} = \{s_{1,j}...s_{|Sj|,j}, s_{1,j}...s_{|Sj|,j}\}$ can be redefined as the phase sequence $\{f_{1,j}...f_{3 \cdot |Sj|,j}, f_{1,j}...f_{3 \cdot |Sj|,j}\}$, which yields a set of $\frac{3 \cdot |Sj|(9 \cdot |Sj|+1)}{2}$ unique ordered subsets of superblock phases. Each of these ordered subsets, denoted as $F_{m,d}$, is described by the index m of the first phase it contains and the distance d to the last phase, such that:

$$F_{m,d} = \{f_{m,j}, ..., f_{m+d,j}\} \quad , \quad \forall d \in [0...6 \cdot |S_j| - 1],$$
$$\forall m \in [1...3 \cdot |S_j|] \quad (3)$$

where $m + d \leq 6 \cdot |S_j|$.

(ii) Every phase subset $F_{m,d}$ can be associated with several time windows, during which new access requests are considered. We can compute these time windows such that they are as short as possible while they contain as many access requests as possible. This way the windows represent the worst-case interference that a phase subset can cause to any other task attempting to access the shared resource within their duration. The time windows $\Delta_{m,d,k}^{x,y}$ of $F_{m,d}$ and the respective numbers of access requests $\gamma_{m,d,k}^{y}$ during them are computed in Eq. 4 and 5, for all $k \in [1, \mu_{m+d,j}^{max}]$, such that each time window differs from the others by at least one access request. The superscripts $x = max$ or $x = min$ denote maximum or minimum computation time, and $y = max$ or $y = min$ denote maximum or minimum number of access requests, respectively, indicating a total of up to $4 \cdot \mu_{m+d,j}^{max}$ new time windows for each subset $F_{m,d}$. Note that parameters $exec$ and μ in this case specify the computation time and access requests of each phase (rather than each superblock). The time windows are then computed as follows:

$$\Delta_{m,d,k}^{x,y} = \sum_{i=m+1}^{m+d-1} exec_{i,j}^{x} + \left(\sum_{i=m}^{m+d-1} \mu_{i,j}^{y} + k - 1 \right) \cdot C \quad (4)$$

$$\gamma_{m,d,k}^{y} = \sum_{i=m}^{m+d-1} \mu_{i,j}^{y} + k \quad (5)$$

It is important to note that the time windows are computed only for those phase subsets $F_{m,d}$, whose destination $f_{m+d,j}$ is an accessing phase ($\mu_{m+d,j}^{max} > 0$), since no new access requests can be issued during an execution phase. Additionally, for the computation of the time windows, we neglect the computation time of the first and the last phase of each subset, so as to minimize the window length. This is allowed because if any of these phases is an accessing phase, then its computation time is 0 whereas if it is an execution phase, then access requests will occur only after it.

Computing the time windows for subsets $F_{m,d}$, whose phase sequence spans over the period, needs to consider the gap g between the last phase of S_j and the period W_j of the processing cycle. During real-time execution, when interferences actually occur over the shared resource, this gap between two consecutive executions of S_j can be arbitrarily small. Therefore, to derive a conservative arrival curve, we need to consider its minimal feasible length (under any possible runtime scenario), g_{min}, while computing the time windows. If no information about it is available, we consider $g_{min} = 0$, which implies that in the worst case a new execution of S_j starts immediately after the previous one is completed.

Based on the above, each phase subset $F_{m,d}$ in $\{SjSj\}$ is characterized by a set of tuples $t_{m,d,k}^{x,y}$ (Eq. 6), i.e., a set of time windows and the respective number of access requests that can be issued by p_j within them. The tuples are defined as follows (for $k \in [1, \mu_{m+d,j}^{max}]$):

$$t_{m,d,k}^{x,y} = (\gamma_{m,d,k}^{y}, \Delta_{m,d,k}^{x,y} + g_{min}) \quad (6)$$

(iii) The computed tuples of each phase subset will be used to derive the core's access request arrival curve. In particular, by retrieving the maximum number of access requests for every time window of length $\Delta = \{0...W_j\}$ from the computed tuples[4], we can obtain the first part of the arrival curve, $\tilde{\alpha}_j$. Formally, if function $\delta(t)$ returns the length of the time window and $\nu(t)$ the number of access requests for each tuple $t_{m,d,k}^{x,y}$, then the first part of the arrival curve, for $\Delta \in [0, W_j]$, is computed as:

$$\tilde{\alpha}_j(\Delta) = \underset{\forall t_{m,d,k}^{x,y}; \delta(t_{m,d,k}^{x,y}) = \Delta}{\text{argmax}} \nu(t_{m,d,k}^{x,y}) \quad (7)$$

The infinite arrival curve α_j is eventually constructed as a concatenation of the initial part, $\tilde{\alpha}_j$, and a periodic part, i.e., a scaled version of $\tilde{\alpha}_j$ which is repeated infinitely. The obtained arrival curve α_j provides then a safe upper bound on the number of access requests issued by the superblock sequence S_j on p_j in any time window Δ (proof similar to [18]).

It is interesting to notice that adding the individual arrival curves α_j of the cores that are abstracted in our system model yields a safe upper bound on the worst-case interference α that these cores may cause on the arbiter in any time interval Δ:

$$\alpha(\Delta) = \sum_{p_j \in P \setminus \{p_{i(CUA)}\}} \alpha_j(\Delta) \quad (8)$$

The sum of the abstracted cores' arrival curves is mentioned in the following as interference curve α.

4.2.2 Embedding an interference curve into the TA-based analysis

For embedding the worst-case interference arrival curve α of the abstracted processing cores into the TA-based system model, we exploit the results of Lampka et al. in [12]. The goal is to transform α into a meaningful set of TA that will model the emission of interfering access requests at such a rate so that α is never violated.

Initially, to reduce the complexity of the embedding, we over-approximate curve α by a single staircase function $\alpha^{st}(\Delta) \geq \alpha(\Delta), \forall \Delta \in [0, \infty)$ (Eq. 2), as shown in Figure 4. The staircase function is selected so that (a) it coincides with the original α on the long-term rate and (b) it has the minimum vertical distance to it. The event streams that are specified by this new arrival curve can be generated by two TA, as depicted in Figure 5. These TA are adapted versions of the ones presented in [12], so as to comply with our system specification. The *Upper Bound* TA (UTA) is responsible for guarding the upper staircase function α^{st} (with fixed parameters Bmax, Delta and s), whereas the *Access Request Generator* (ARG) emits access requests 'on behalf of' the abstracted cores on condition that UTA permits it.

UTA models partly what is known from the computer networks field as a 'leaky bucket'. When the leaky bucket contains at least one token (unreleased access request), a corresponding event (request emission) can take place. If the

---

[4]Note that the linear approximations required in the method of [18] are obsolete, since the computed tuples capture already all possible access request arrivals.

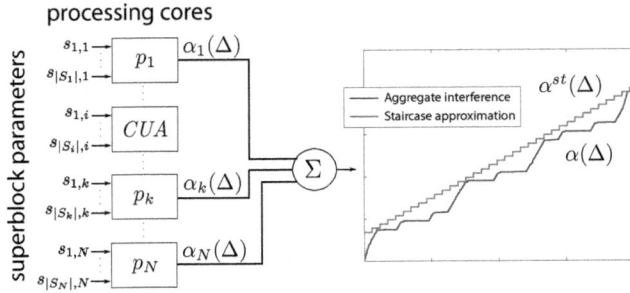

Figure 4: RTC Interference representation

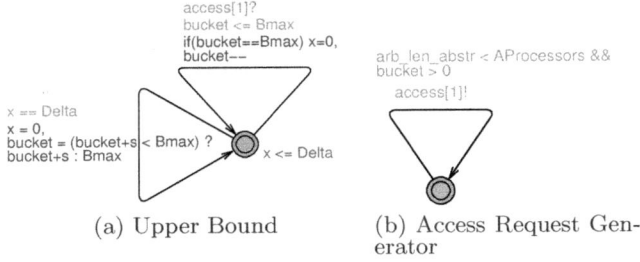

(a) Upper Bound   (b) Access Request Generator

Figure 5: Interference generating TA

leaky bucket is, however, empty, no requests can be emitted before new tokens are generated. The leaky bucket is configured so as to implement the upper staircase function α^{st}. Namely, it has a maximal capacity of B, being full in its initial state. An amount of s new tokens is produced every δ time units and one token is consumed every time a request is emitted by ARG.

Request emission by ARG is enabled as long as (a) at least one token is contained in the leaky bucket and (b) the current amount of pending interfering requests is lower than the number of abstracted cores (to consider only realistic scenarios). If both conditions are valid, then ARG may issue a new request, without restriction on the time point when the latter occurs (to account for all traces below α^{st}). Note that in the TA of Figure 5, '1' refers to the default 'identifier' of the access request generator as seen by the arbiter (representing without distinction any of the abstracted cores' identifiers).

Substitution of the $(N-1)$ *Scheduler* and the $(M-M_i)$ *Superblock* TA instances of the abstracted cores with the presented pair of interference generating TA is expected to alleviate significantly the verification effort for the WCRT estimation of the superblocks executing on CUA (core p_i). This comes with the cost of over-approximation, since the interference arrival curve α provides a conservative upper bound of the interfering access requests in the time-interval domain and a^{st} over-approximates it. As shown in Sec. 5, though, the pessimism in the WCRT estimates for the superblocks of CUA is limited.

4.2.3 Further Abstractions

On top of the two basic abstraction steps, i.e., the superblock model of execution and the interference representation with arrival curves, more abstractions and optimizations of our system specification can be considered. Some of them are briefly discussed in the following:

1. In the case of exact system specification (without interference abstraction) with a FCFS/RR arbiter, the state space exploration for the verification of a superblock's WCRT can be restricted to the duration of one hyper-period of the cores' processing cycles (least common multiple of their periods). Within a hyper-period, all possible interference patterns are exhibited, hence a safe WCRT estimate for each superblock can be computed.

Table 1: EEMBC benchmarks as superblocks

Benchmark	Acq (μ^a)	Exec (*exec*, ns)	Rep (μ^r)	Period (μs)
canrdr01	187	2734.2	9	44
cacheb01	91	1544.9	10	24
tblook01	267	5061.3	7	62
a2time01	129	1514.7	9	30
rspeed01	94	1331.6	7	24
bitmnp01	171	100064.0	48	160

2. In the case of system specification with the interference abstraction and a FCFS/RR arbiter, the *Superblock* TA can be simplified to model not periodic execution, but a single execution. Since all possible interference streams (bounded by α^{st}) can be explored for the time interval of one superblock execution and due to the property of sub-additivity of the arrival curves, the WCRT observed during it is a safe bound of the overall WCRT.

3. The previous optimization can be also applied for systems with a TDMA/FlexRay arbiter when we consider (enumerate and model) all possible offsets for the starting time of the superblock within the respective arbitration cycle.

4. For system models with a TDMA arbiter, the interference from the competing cores can be ignored (not modeled). This is because, it does not affect the WCRT of the superblocks executing on CUA. The same holds also for the ST segment of the FlexRay arbitration cycle.

Further abstractions and optimizations can be found in the technical report [9].

5. EMPIRICAL EVALUATION

This section presents two case studies, where the proposed state-based WCRT analysis approach was applied in order to evaluate its scalability and accuracy (pessimism) of the obtained results. In the following, we refer to the WCRT analysis with TA exploiting the superblock structure as *TAS*, and to the WCRT analysis with TA exploiting the superblock structure and the arrival curve abstraction as *TASA*. All presented verifications were performed with Uppaal v.4.1.7 on a system with a Dual-Core AMD Opteron CPU @2.7GHz and 8 GB RAM.

Comparing Accuracy of TAS to Analytic Methods. In the first scenario, we compare the accuracy of the WCRTs computed with TAS to those computed with state-of-the-art analytic approaches which also exploit the superblock structure. As reference, we have selected the approach from [18] which can be considered representative and similar to other analytic approaches [21, 23].

For this purpose, we use six applications from the industry-standard EEMBC 1.1 embedded benchmark suite [2]. These applications, which are typical for the automotive domain, were programmed and compiled using the PREM framework [16] so as to comply with the superblock model of execution. In particular, four sequential executions of each application are specified by one dedicated superblock. The derived memory access requests due to cache misses for the acquisition (Acq) and replication (Rep) phases, and the worst-case computation times for the execution phase (Exec) of the respective superblocks on the target architecture are shown in Table 1.

Each application is assumed to be executed periodically and mapped to a dedicated core. All cores have access to a shared memory in case of cache misses. The processing cycles of cores are considered synchronized (same starting time of first cycle). The application periods are specified

Table 2: WCRT results of EEMBC benchmarks

Cores	Benchmark Set	WCRT(TAS) FCFS/RR	Avg.Verif.Time FCFS/RR	WCRT([18]) FCFS/RR	Pessimism of [18](%)
1	canrdr01	9711.8	0.06 sec	9711.8	0
2	canrdr01	13307.4	0.64 / 0.65 sec	13307.4	0
	cacheb01	8722		8736.1	0.2
3	canrdr01	20078.4		20285	1
	cacheb01	12317.6/12282	3.9 / 4.0 sec	12331.7	0.1/0.4
	tblook01	25459.6		25638.1	0.7
4	canrdr01	25489.6		28900.2	13.4
	cacheb01	15913.2/15877.6	31.8 / 30.4 sec	15927.3	0.1/0.3
	tblook01	31164.1		38988.1	25.1
	a2time01	19829.2		19848.7	0.1
5	canrdr01	30936.4		37622.2	21.6
	cacheb01	19402/19366.4		19522.9	0.6/0.8
	tblook01	42454.7	102.4 / 58.7 sec	53833.3	**26.8**
	a2time01	23424.8		26078.7	11.3
	rspeed01	19188.4/19152.8		19309.6	0.6/0.8
6	canrdr01	41758.8/41794.4		43709.8	4.7/4.6
	cacheb01	22997.6		23118.5	0.5
	tblook01	53150.8/53222.0		61629.7	15.9/15.8
	a2time01	29690.4/29654.8	14.2 / 5.2 min	30991.5	4.8/4.5
	rspeed01	22784/22712.8		22905.2	0.5/0.8
	bitmnp01	141253.2/141288.8		146842.4	4.0/3.9

Table 3: Verification time for a superblock's WCRT

Cores	FCFS TAS	FCFS TASA	RR TAS	RR TASA	TDMA TAS/TASA	FlexRay TAS	FlexRay TASA
2	1.2 sec	1 sec	1.2 sec	0.5 sec	0.1 sec	0.7 sec	27.1 sec
4	-	1.7 sec	-	1.1 sec	0.2 sec	0.9 sec	28.5 sec
8	-	31.3 sec	-	1.2 sec	0.5 sec	2.8 sec	17.8 sec
16	-	4.9 min	-	1.3 sec	0.9 sec	-	10.4 sec
24	-	18.8 min	-	1.6 sec	1.1 sec	-	26.8 sec
32	-	-	-	1.9 sec	1.2 sec	-	57.4 sec
64	-	-	-	2.7 sec	1.7 sec	-	7 min

Table 4: Accuracy of TASA compared to state-of-the-art methods

Cores	FCFS(%)	RR(%)	TDMA(%)	FlexRay(%)
2	0	0	0	0
4	11.1	11.1	0	0
8	13.8	13.8	0	1.8
16	17.2	17.2	0	-
24	**17.3**	17.3	0	-
32	-	16.8	0	-
64	-	**25.4**	0	-

such that execution will be completed within them. That is, each superblock's period is at least equal to its conservative WCRT estimate, $WCRT_{cons} = (\mu^a + \mu^r) \cdot N \cdot C + exec$, which assumes that every access request experiences the worst possible serving delay, i.e., $N \cdot C$ in the case of FCFS or RR resource arbitration (e.g., for $N = 6$ and $C = 35.6$ns, we have $WCRT_{cons} = 146.8\mu$s for benchmark bitmnp01).

The comparison considers first a single core on which benchmark canrdr01 is executed. Gradually, the system is expanded by including one more core with a different application mapped to it on every step (up to 6 cores). The analysis is being performed once for FCFS arbitration and once for RR arbitration on the shared memory controller. Table 2 presents the derived WCRT estimates and the required verification times to obtain them (using the sup:Superblock.x query in Uppaal).

The results show that for the considered benchmark suite, tight WCRT estimates (up to 26.8% better than those of a state-of-the-art analytic method) can be verified in a few minutes for systems with up to 6 cores when TAS is employed. This indicates that the first proposed abstraction (superblock structure with dedicated phases) already provides a considerable benefit regarding scalability (w.r.t. the number of cores) compared to earlier model checking-based analysis methods, in which analysis did not scale efficiently beyond 2 cores for event-driven resource arbitration scenarios.

Evaluating Scalability and Accuracy of TASA. In the second case study, we explore the scalability of the proposed approach when resource accesses of some of the processing cores are abstracted with an arrival curve, i.e., the TASA approach. We also evaluate the accuracy of TASA w.r.t. state-of-the-art methods.

For this scenario, we use a real-world automotive application provided by an automotive supplier, which consists of 4 independent tasks. Each task is defined as a sequence of 2-8 general superblocks, whose access requests and computation parameters (bounds) were derived with static analysis techniques[5].

We now consider systems with 2, 4, 8, 16, 24, 32 or 64 cores and a shared memory that can be arbitrated according to any of the policies addressed in this paper. Each of the application tasks is executed periodically on one core

---

[5]The superblock and system parameters cannot be disclosed due to confidentiality restrictions.

(for systems with more than 4 cores, tasks are replicated), and depending on the arbitration policy of the memory controller, we make the following additional assumptions:

- When the shared memory arbitration is FCFS or RR, the processing cycles of different cores are considered non-synchronized, i.e., execution of superblock $s_{1,j}$ can start at any time within $[0, W_j]$. On the other hand, for TDMA and FlexRay, the processing cycles are considered synchronized to each other and also to the arbitration cycle, i.e., all tasks and the arbitration cycle start at time 0.

- The DYN segment of FlexRay makes 20% of the total arbitration cycle and enables cycle multiplexing. Namely there are two minislot assignments which alternate with each other in consecutive arbitration cycles.

The system model, in this case, exploits the interference abstraction (TASA). Therefore, we analyze the WCRT of a selected task running on a particular core (CUA), while all other cores are modeled by an access request generator that emits request streams bounded by their aggregate interference curve (Sec. 4.2.2). Additionally, abstractions 2 to 4 of Sec. 4.2.3 are applied whenever possible.

Table 3 shows the verification time required for each WCRT estimate for the different system configurations and arbitration policies. For comparison reasons, the respective verification times for TAS are also included, when available. For the FCFS and RR cases, the analysis scalability for TAS gets severely challenged due to the complexity of the considered industrial application and the assumption of non-synchronized processing cycles among the cores. Particularly, non-determinism w.r.t. the starting time of each task's first execution causes the analysis not to scale beyond 2 cores. The introduction of the interference abstraction (TASA), however, enables us to overcome this obstacle and obtain safe upper bounds on the WCRT of the considered tasks in a few minutes for systems with up to 24 cores for FCFS and 64 cores for RR and FlexRay. This is a major step forward compared to any of the existing approaches, opening the way for efficient interference analysis even in manycore systems.

In the case of TDMA arbitration, analysis scales very efficiently for any number of cores due to abstraction 4 of Sec. 4.2.3, i.e., the non-representation of interference in the system model. Because of this, the verification time in Table 3 is the same for both systems with (TASA) and without (TAS) the interference abstraction.

Furthermore, Table 4 shows the accuracy of TASA. For FCFS and RR arbitration schemes in systems with up to 2 cores, accuracy is compared against the best current results which are given by TAS. For systems with more than 2 cores, however, accuracy is compared against the methods presented in [18]. A value of '0', in this case, means that the results of both TASA and the analytic methods exhibit the same degree of pessimism. For TDMA systems, accuracy is evaluated against results obtained with the method in [21]. Since for FlexRay arbitration no analytic methodology is known, the accuracy of the obtained WCRTs is compared to the results of TAS when the latter are available.

For FCFS and RR, comparison shows that the results of TASA can be more pessimistic (up to 25.4%) in particular cases. As main source of this pessimism, we identified the behavior of the ARG TA in the abstract system specification (Sec. 4.2.2), which emits interfering requests nondeterministically over time, thus enabling the exploration of several request streams that are bounded by α^{st}, but may never be encountered in the real-time system.

For systems with a FlexRay arbiter, the WCRT estimates are identical for the TAS and TASA approaches for systems with 2 and 4 cores, and only slightly more pessimistic (1.8%) for TASA for systems with 8 cores. Note that beyond 8 cores, pessimism could not be evaluated as no other approach can compute tight WCRT bounds for tasks with synchronous access requests to a FlexRay-arbitrated resource.

Results in this second case study point out that the gain in scalability of the analysis is not severely compromised by the accuracy of the obtained results.

6. CONCLUSION

The paper presents a framework for state-based WCRT analysis of tasks that are executed in parallel on a multicore platform and have synchronous accesses to a shared resource under FCFS, RR, TDMA, or FlexRay arbitration schemes. For achieving scalability, tasks are organized in dedicated superblocks, namely sequences of resource access and computation phases. Empirical evaluations with benchmark applications show that the proposed approach delivers safe results, which due to its exact TA-based system specification (TAS) are tighter than those of state-of-the-art analytic methods. On a next step, we abstractly represent access requests of tasks, which compete for the shared resource against a task under analysis, by an RTC arrival curve and integrate it into the TA-based system specification (TASA). A case study based on a real-world industrial application shows that this method scales much better than previous state-based approaches without sacrificing on the accuracy of the results. What is more, the presented methods are the first to analyze WCRT of tasks with synchronous accesses to a shared resource arbitrated by FlexRay.

Acknowledgments

This work is supported by EU FP7 under grant agreement no. 288175. We would like to thank R. Pellizzoni for providing us with the EEMBC benchmark parameters for the evaluation of our method.

7. REFERENCES

[1] AutoSAR. Release 4.0. http://www.autosar.org.
[2] EEMBC 1.1 Embedded Benchmark Suite. http://www.eembc.org/benchmark/automotive_sl.php.
[3] European commission's 7th framework programme: Design for predictability and efficiency. www.predator-project.eu.
[4] Flexray communications system protocol specification, version 2.1, revision a. http://www.flexray.com/.
[5] R. Alur and D. L. Dill. Automata For Modeling Real-Time Systems. In *Automata, Languages and Programming*, pages 322–335. Springer, 1990.
[6] G. Behrmann, A. David, and K. G. Larsen. A tutorial on UPPAAL. In *Formal Methods for the Design of Real-Time Systems*, pages 200–236, 2004.
[7] D. B. Chokshi and P. Bhaduri. Performance analysis of flexray-based systems using real-time calculus, revisited. In *ACM Symposium on Applied Computing*, pages 351–356, 2010.
[8] A. Ferrari, M. Di Natale, G. Gentile, G. Reggiani, and P. Gai. Time and memory tradeoffs in the implementation of AUTOSAR components. In *Design, Automation, Test in Europe Conference*, pages 864 –869, 2009.
[9] G. Giannopoulou, N. Stoimenov, A. Schranzhofer, and L. Thiele. Derivation of access request arrival curves for dedicated superblock sequences. TIK-rep. 347, Computer Engineering & Networks Laboratory, ETH Zurich, 2012.
[10] A. Gustavsson, A. Ermedahl, B. Lisper, and P. Pettersson. Towards WCET Analysis of Multicore Architectures Using UPPAAL. In *Workshop on Worst-Case Execution Time Analysis*, pages 101–112, 2010.
[11] R. Henia, A. Hamann, M. Jersak, R. Racu, K. Richter, and R. Ernst. System Level Performance Analysis - The SymTA/S Approach. *Computers and Digital Techniques*, 152(2):148–166, 2005.
[12] K. Lampka, S. Perathoner, and L. Thiele. Analytic real-time analysis and timed automata: A hybrid methodology for the performance analysis of embedded real-time systems. *Design Automation for Embedded Systems*, 14(3):193–227, 2010.
[13] K. G. Larsen, C. Weise, W. Yi, and J. Pearson. Clock difference diagrams. *Nordic Journal of Computing*, 6(3):271–198, 1999.
[14] M. Lv, W. Yi, N. Guan, and G. Yu. Combining abstract interpretation with model checking for timing analysis of multicore software. In *Real-Time Systems Symposium*, pages 339–349, 2010.
[15] M. Negrean, S. Schliecker, and R. Ernst. Response-time analysis of arbitrarily activated tasks in multiprocessor systems with shared resources. In *Design, Automation, Test in Europe Conference*, pages 524–529, 2009.
[16] R. Pellizzoni, E. Betti, S. Bak, G. Yao, J. Criswell, M. Caccamo, and R. Kegley. A predictable execution model for cots-based embedded systems. In *Real-Time and Embedded Technology and Applications Symposium*, pages 269–279, 2011.
[17] R. Pellizzoni, B. D. Bui, M. Caccamo, and L. Sha. Coscheduling of cpu and i/o transactions in cots-based embedded systems. In *Real-Time Systems Symposium*, pages 221–231, 2008.
[18] R. Pellizzoni, A. Schranzhofer, J.-J. Chen, M. Caccamo, and L. Thiele. Worst case delay analysis for memory interference in multicore systems. In *Design, Automation, Test in Europe Conference*, pages 741–746, 2010.
[19] T. Pop, P. Pop, P. Eles, Z. Peng, and A. Andrei. Timing analysis of the FlexRay communication protocol. *Real-Time Systems*, 39(1):205–235, 2008.
[20] S. Schliecker, M. Negrean, and R. Ernst. Bounding the shared resource load for the performance analysis of multiprocessor systems. In *Design, Automation, Test in Europe Conference*, pages 759–764, 2010.
[21] A. Schranzhofer, J.-J. Chen, and L. Thiele. Timing analysis for TDMA arbitration in resource sharing systems. In *Real-Time and Embedded Technology and Applications Symposium*, pages 215–224, 2010.
[22] A. Schranzhofer, R. Pellizzoni, J.-J. Chen, L. Thiele, and M. Caccamo. Worst-case response time analysis of resource access models in multi-core systems. In *Design Automation Conference*, pages 332–337, 2010.
[23] A. Schranzhofer, R. Pellizzoni, J.-J. Chen, L. Thiele, and M. Caccamo. Timing analysis for resource access interference on adaptive resource arbiters. In *Real-Time and Embedded Technology and Applications Symposium*, pages 213–222, 2011.
[24] L. Thiele, S. Chakraborty, and M. Naedele. Real-time calculus for scheduling hard real-time systems. In *Symposium on Circuits and Systems*, volume 4, pages 101–104, 2000.
[25] R. Wilhelm, D. Grund, J. Reineke, M. Schlickling, M. Pister, and C. Ferdinand. Memory hierarchies, pipelines, and buses for future architectures in time-critical embedded systems. *IEEE Transactions on Computer-Aided Design of Integrated Circuits and Systems*, 28(7):966 –978, 2009.
[26] S. Yovine. Model checking timed automata. In *Lectures on Embedded Systems*, pages 114–152. Springer, 1998.

Server-based Scheduling of Parallel Real-Time Tasks

Luís Nogueira and Luís Miguel Pinho
CISTER/INESC-TEC
School of Engineering (ISEP), Polytechnic Institute of Porto (IPP)
Porto, Portugal
lmn@isep.ipp.pt, lmp@isep.ipp.pt

ABSTRACT

Multicore platforms have transformed parallelism into a main concern. Parallel programming models are being put forward to provide a better approach for application programmers to expose the opportunities for parallelism by pointing out potentially parallel regions within tasks, leaving the actual and dynamic scheduling of these regions onto processors to be performed at runtime, exploiting the maximum amount of parallelism.

It is in this context that this paper proposes a scheduling approach that combines the constant-bandwidth server abstraction with a priority-aware work-stealing load balancing scheme which, while ensuring isolation among tasks, enables parallel tasks to be executed on more than one processor at a given time instant.

Categories and Subject Descriptors

D.4.1 [**Operating Systems**]: Process Management—*Scheduling*

General Terms

Design, Algorithms, Theory

Keywords

Real-time systems, Task-level parallelism, Constant-bandwidth servers, Capacity sharing, Work-stealing

1. INTRODUCTION

In contrast to the conventional real-time scheduling theory that focus upon the worst-case analysis of systems that are restricted to execute in strictly controlled environments, there is now the understanding that not all applications need the same degree of real-time support. The constant-bandwidth server abstraction [1] has proved very useful in designing, implementing, and reasoning on systems where tasks can dynamically enter or leave at any time, a paradigm

that has been somewhat formalised in the concept of *open real-time* environments [17]. In this approach, each real-time task is assigned a fraction of the computational resources and it is handled by an abstract entity called server to achieve the goals of temporal isolation and real-time execution.

With multicore processors quickly becoming the norm, there have been significant efforts to extend reservation-based real-time scheduling theory to make it applicable to multiprocessor systems as well [5, 39, 18, 24]. Nevertheless, all these works consider task models where real-time tasks use at most a single core at each time instant. The advent of multicore technologies has also resulted in a renewed interest on parallel programming. In fact, dynamic task parallelism is steadily gaining popularity as a programming model for multicore processors. Parallelism is easily expressed by spawning threads that the implementation is allowed, but not mandated, to execute in parallel, using frameworks such as OpenMP [3], Cilk [19], Intel's Parallel Building Blocks [14], Java Fork-join Framework [27], Microsoft's Task Parallel Library [15], or StackThreads/MP [42]. The idea is to allow application programmers to expose the opportunities for parallelism by pointing out potentially parallel regions within tasks, leaving the actual and dynamic scheduling of these regions onto processors to be performed at runtime, exploiting the maximum amount of parallelism.

However, while several models of parallelism have been used in programming languages and Application Programming Interfaces (APIs) few of them have been studied in real-time systems. Recent work on real-time scheduling of parallel tasks define a parallel task as a collection of several regions, both sequential and parallel, with synchronisation points at the end of each region [26, 41]. A task always starts with a sequential region, which then forks into several parallel independent threads (the parallel region) that finally join in another sequential region. However, these models require that each region of a task contains threads of execution that are of equal length.

In contrast, in this paper we consider a more general model of *fork-join* parallel real-time tasks, where threads within a parallel region can take arbitrarily different amounts of time to execute. Indeed, many real-time applications, such as radar tracking, autonomous driving, and video surveillance, have a lot of potential parallelism which is not regular in nature and which varies with the data being processed. As the problem sizes scale and processor speeds saturate, the only way to meet deadlines in such systems is to parallelise the computation.

Irregular parallelism in these applications is often expressed in the form of dynamically generated threads of work that can be executed in parallel, generally represented as a Directed Acyclic Graph (DAG). Applications with these properties pose significant challenges for high-performance parallel implementations, where equal distribution of work over cores and locality of reference are desired within each core. For task graphs where the number of threads and their actual execution times are not known in advance one must use a dynamic approach to efficiently load-balance the computation. One of the simplest, yet best-performing, dynamic load-balancing algorithms for shared-memory architectures is work-stealing [7]. Blumofe and Leiserson have theoretically proven that the work-stealing algorithm is optimal for scheduling fully-strict computations, *i.e* computations in which all join edges from a thread go to its parent thread in the spawn tree [7]. Under this assumption, an application running on P processors achieves P-fold speedup in its parallel part, using at most P times more space than when running on one CPU. These results are also supported by experiments [40].

Motivated by these observations, this paper breaks new ground in several ways. It proposes p-CSWS (Parallel Capacity Sharing by Work-Stealing), a novel scheduling approach for parallel real-time runtimes that will coexist with a wide range of other complex independently developed applications, without any previous knowledge about their real execution requirements, number of parallel regions, and when and how many those parallel threads will be generated. Schedulers in these type of systems are therefore required to maintain a certain (quantifiable) level of service for each application, with the exact guarantee depending upon the CPU reservation's parameters. p-CSWS combines a multiprocessor residual capacity reclaiming scheme with a priority-based work-stealing policy which, while ensuring isolation among tasks, allows a task to be executed in more than one processor at a given time. To the best of our knowledge, no research has ever focused on this subject.

The remainder of this paper is structured as follows. The next section discusses the current challenges in supporting task-level parallelism in open real-time systems. Section 3 presents the system model. Sections 4 and 5 present the main principles of the proposed approach, while the p-CSWS scheduler is formally presented in Section 6 and proved correct in Section 7. Section 8 validates the effectiveness of p-CSWS through extensive simulations. Finally, Section 9 concludes the paper and discusses future work.

2. TASK-LEVEL PARALLELISM IN OPEN REAL-TIME SYSTEMS

Most results in multiprocessor real-time scheduling concentrate on sequential tasks running on multiple processors or cores [16]. While these works allow several tasks to execute on the same multicore host and meet their deadlines, they do not allow individual tasks to take advantage of a multicore machine. It is essential to develop new approaches for real-time intra-task parallelism, where real-time tasks themselves are parallel tasks which can run on multiple cores at the same time instant.

Different scheduling algorithms and assumptions in parallel real-time scheduling can be found in [32, 25, 28, 13, 23]. Most early work in parallel real-time scheduling makes simplifying assumptions about task models, assuming that the parallelism degree of jobs is known beforehand and using this information when making scheduling decisions. In practice, this information is not easily discernible, and in some cases can be inherently misleading.

Recently, Lakshmanan et al. [26] proposed a scheduling technique for synchronous parallel tasks where every task is an alternate sequence of parallel and sequential regions with each parallel region consisting of multiple threads of equal length that synchronise at the end of the region. In their model, all parallel regions are assumed to have the same number of parallel threads, which must be no greater than the number of processors. In [41], Saifullah et al. considered a more general task model, allowing different regions of the same parallel task to contain different numbers of threads and regions to contain more threads than the number of processor cores. Nevertheless, it still requires that each region of a task contains threads of execution that are of equal length.

In contrast, in this paper we consider a more general model of parallel real-time tasks where parallel jobs are represented as a DAG and threads (nodes) can take arbitrarily different amounts of time to execute. Also, to the best of our knowledge, we are the first to consider the scheduling of multithreaded real-time jobs in open environments, without any previous knowledge about their real execution requirements, number of parallel regions, and when and how many threads will be generated at each parallel region.

The design and implementation of open real-time environments is an active research area in the discipline of real-time computing. As an increasing number of users runs both real-time and traditional desktop applications in the same system, it is necessary to isolate and protect the temporal behaviour of one application from the others.

Conventional real-time scheduling theory has tended to focus upon the worst-case execution time (WCET) analysis of systems that are restricted to execute in strictly controlled environments. This traditional perspective of real-time scheduling theory has served the safety-critical embedded systems community well. However, even on single-core systems, WCET analysis is highly problematic and pessimistic WCET estimates are used. This leads to an under-utilisation of computing resources in practice and severely limits the computational workload that can be supported by the system. The problem is exacerbated on a multicore processor, where the worst-case scenario may be even less likely but even more costly. Such a waste of resources can only be justified for critical systems in which a single missed deadline may cause catastrophic consequences.

Therefore, over the last years, there is a new perspective towards being able to provide significant real-time support within the context of general-purpose operating systems with the understanding that not all applications need the same degree of real-time support. For soft real-time tasks, processing capacities are then typically allocated based on average-case execution times, with the result that the expected (mean) tardiness of a task is bounded [35].

Most open real-time environments that have been implemented are based upon two-level scheduling schemes, commonly known as bandwidth servers. In [34], Mercer et al. propose a scheme based on capacity reserves to remove the need of knowing the WCET of each task under the Rate Monotonic [31] scheduling policy. A reserve is a couple

(C_i, T_i) indicating that a task τ_i can execute for at most C_i units of time in each period T_i. If a task instance needs to execute for more than C_i, the remaining portion of the instance is scheduled in background.

Based on a similar idea of capacity reserves, Abeni and Buttazo [1] proposed the Constant Bandwidth Server (CBS) scheduler to handle soft real-time requests with a variable or unknown execution behaviour under the Earliest Deadline First (EDF) [31] scheduling policy. To avoid unpredictable delays on hard real-time tasks, soft tasks are isolated through a bandwidth reservation mechanism, according to which each soft task gets a fraction of the CPU and it is scheduled in such a way that it will never demand more than its reserved bandwidth, independently of its actual requests. This is achieved by assigning each soft task a deadline, computed as a function of the reserved bandwidth and its actual requests. If a task requires to execute more than its expected computation time, its deadline is postponed so that its reserved bandwidth is not exceeded. As a consequence, overruns occurring on a served task will only delay that task, without compromising the bandwidth assigned to other tasks.

However, the performance of CBS is highly dependent on the correct allocation of resource shares [9]. If a server completes a task in less than its budgeted execution time no other server is able to efficiently reuse the amount of computational resources left unused. In order to make effective use of the available computational bandwidth, a scheduling methodology that makes use of this residual processing capability is desirable. Therefore, CBS has been extended with several resource reclaiming schemes [30, 10, 33, 11, 29, 38] proposed to support an efficient sharing of computational resources left unused by early completing tasks. Such techniques have been proved to be successful in improving the response times of soft real-time tasks while preserving all hard real-time constraints.

Unfortunately, due to well-known multiprocessor scheduling anomalies [2], adopting the same rules as the uniprocessor case would lead to deadline violations in spite of the fact that the considered task set is schedulable by using a global EDF scheduler. As such, the extension of these reclaiming schemes for the multiprocessor case is not trivial and only a few works have address this subject.

M-CASH [39] is a resource reclaiming mechanism for identical multiprocessor platforms built on top of the M-CBS algorithm [5], an extension for the multicore case of the original CBS algorithm. It holds a global queue of residual capacities ordered by non decreasing absolute deadline. Each time a server becomes idle with an execution capacity greater than zero, a new residual capacity is inserted into the global queue with the current server's deadline and remaining capacity. Each time there is a residual capacity at the head of the queue and one or more servers with deadline greater than or equal to the capacity's deadline are scheduled for execution, those servers consume the capacity instead of their own reserved capacity. Thus, residual capacities are equally distributed across all processors, including idle ones.

EDF-HSB [8] uses a similar residual capacity redistribution method. Jobs that finish early donate their unused capacity to a global capacity queue. These capacities are treated as schedulable entities by the top-level scheduler, *i.e.* they compete for processor time as regular jobs with a deadline d. Whenever a capacity is selected to execute,

its processor time is donated to soft real-time tasks that are likely to be tardy and best-effort jobs.

However, while these resource reclaiming schemes allow tasks to efficiently execute on the same multicore host, they do not allow an individual task to take advantage of the several cores. In multicore platforms, an application can rely on increasing its concurrency level to maximise its performance, which often requires the application to divide its work into several short-living work units, which can be mapped to threads or other appropriate scheduling representation, increasing the scheduler's flexibility when distributing work evenly across processors. The downside of such fine-grain parallelism is that if the total scheduling cost is too large, then parallelism is not worthwhile.

Therefore, having many short-lived threads requires a simple and fast scheduling mechanism to keep the overall overhead low. Since many details of execution, such as the number of iterations in a loop and the number of threads that will created in a parallel region are often not known in advance, much of the actual work of assigning threads of parallel tasks to cores must be performed dynamically. Unlike static policies, dynamic processor-allocation policies allow the system to respond to load changes, whether they are caused by the arrival of new jobs, the departure of completed jobs, or changes in the parallelism of running jobs - the last case is of particular importance to us in this paper. One technique commonly employed to attempt to accomplish this dynamic load balancing is work-stealing.

As such, although previous works have previously considered residual capacity reclamation schemes in the context of multiprocessors, we are the first to do so within a scheme where reclamation is combined with a work-stealing policy to support parallel multithreaded tasks. Different scheduling algorithms and assumptions in parallel real-time scheduling can be found in [32, 25, 28, 13, 23, 26, 41]. Most work in parallel real-time scheduling assumes that the parallelism degree of jobs is known beforehand and uses this information when making its decisions. In practice, this information is not easily discernible, and in some cases can be inherently misleading. In contrast, p-CSWS allows the system to dynamically respond to load changes, whether they are caused by the arrival of new jobs, the departure of completed jobs, or changes in the parallelism degree of running jobs.

p-CSWS extends M-CBS with a novel residual capacity reclaiming scheme and a priority-aware work-stealing policy which, while ensuring isolation among tasks, enables parallel tasks to be executed on more than one processor at a given time instant. This way, it is possible to have parallel and non-parallel tasks with different levels of temporal criticality coexisting in the same system, while achieving the goals of temporal isolation and real-time execution. To ease the algorithm's discussion, the system model and the main principles of the proposed approach are discussed in the next sections while the p-CSWS scheduler is formally presented in Section 6.

3. SYSTEM MODEL

We consider the scheduling of sporadic independent servers on m identical processors $p_1, p_2, \ldots, p_m$ using global EDF. With global EDF, each server ready to execute is placed in a system-wide queue, ordered by nondecreasing absolute deadline, from which the first m servers are extracted to execute on the available processors.

We primarily consider a parallel implicit-deadline task model where each task τ_i in the system can generate a virtually infinite number of multithreaded jobs. A multithreaded job is modelled as a dynamic DAG, defined as $\mathcal{G} = (\mathcal{V}, \mathcal{E})$, where $\mathcal{V}$ is a set of nodes and $\mathcal{E}$ is a set of directed edges, both created on the fly at runtime. A node represents a thread, a set of instructions which must be executed sequentially. Jobs may dynamically create an arbitrary number of threads, which may have different execution requirements. Therefore, the worst case execution time (WCET) for the jth job of task τ_i is the sum of the execution requirements of all of its threads, if all threads are executed sequentially in the same core.

A directed edge $(a, b) \in \mathcal{E}$ represents the constraint that b's computation depends on results computed by a. Therefore, a living thread may either be ready or stalled due to an unresolved dependency. Because multithreaded jobs with arbitrary dependencies can be impossible to schedule efficiently, we limit our study to fully-strict computations. Any multithreaded computation that can be executed in a depth-first manner on a single processor can be made fully-strict by altering the dependency structure, possibly affecting the achievable parallelism, but not affecting the semantics of the computation [7].

All multithreaded jobs generated by a task τ_i are dedicated to a p-CSWS server S_i, an extension for the parallel case of the M-CBS algorithm [5]. Each p-CSWS server S_i is characterised by a pair (Q_i, T_i), where Q_i is the server's maximum reserved capacity and T_i its period. The ratio $U_i = \frac{Q_i}{T_i}$ is known as the server's bandwidth and denotes the fraction of the capacity of one processor that is assigned to the server. We further define $U_\Pi = \sum_i^n U_i$ as the system utilisation on the identical multiprocessor platform Π comprised of m unit-capacity processors and $u_\Pi = max_{1 \leq i \leq n} U_i$ as the maximum server bandwidth.

If the needed execution time and the minimum inter-arrival time of jobs are known beforehand, it is possible to guarantee the deadline of hard tasks by assigning its server a proper pair (Q_i, T_i). As such, t_i refers to the minimum inter-arrival time between successive jobs of τ_i so that $a_{i,j+1} \geq a_{i,j} + t_i$ and its execution requirements $e_{i,j}$ are characterised by the task's WCET. Thus, for a hard real-time task τ_i, its dedicated server S_i has a reserved capacity Q_i equal to the task's WCET and a period T_i equal to the task's period.

For soft real-time tasks, the timing constraints are more relaxed. In particular, for a soft task τ_i, t_i represents the expected inter-arrival period between successive jobs. As such, the arrival time $a_{i,j}$ of a particular job is only revealed at runtime and the exact execution requirements $e_{i,j}$ can only be determined by actually executing the job to completion until time $f_{i,j}$. Thus, as with M-CBS, we do not require an a priori upper bound on the value of $e_{i,j}$ and for soft real-time tasks, Q_i and T_i are set based on the served tasks' expected average values. Recall that our goal with respect to designing the global scheduler is to be able to provide complete isolation among the servers and to guarantee a certain degree of service to each individual server. If a job does not receive an allocation of $e_{i,j}$ time units before its implicit deadline $d_{i,j}$, then it is tardy. If a job executes for $e_{i,j} < Q_i$ time units, the resulting unused capacity $Q_i - e_{i,j}$ is referred to as dynamic residual capacity.

At each instant t, the following values are associated with a p-CSWS server S_i: (i) its currently assigned deadline d_k^i; and (ii) its remaining execution capacity $0 \leq c_k^i \leq Q_i$. Each time a new job of τ_i arrives, it is enqueued in a FCFS job queue held by S_i. The server is said to be active if its job queue is not empty, otherwise it is idle. Whenever the server is active, the job at the top of the queue is released with deadline equal to d_k^i. Upon reaching 0, the execution capacity of a server S_i is recharged to Q_i and its deadline is incremented by T_i.

Dynamically generated ready threads are maintained in a local work-stealing double-ended queue (deque) of the server where the job is currently being executed, thus reducing contention on the global queue. For any busy server, parallel threads are pushed and popped from the bottom of the deque and these operations are synchronisation free.

At runtime, the performance of the system is enhanced through a novel redistribution of residual capacities that not only lessens tardiness for soft real-time tasks and quickly adapts to load changes, but also enables parallel tasks to be executed on more than one processor at a given time instant. For that, the p-CSWS scheduler considers a second type of servers named residual capacity work-stealing servers. A residual capacity server is a p-CSWS server that applies a priority-based work-stealing policy whenever its local deque its empty.

4. SHARING RESIDUAL CAPACITIES

Although the server abstraction is an essential method in open real-time systems for achieving predictability in the presence of tasks with variable execution times, the overall system's performance becomes quite dependent on a correct resource allocation. To overcome this limitation, an efficient reclaiming of unused computation times generated by earlier completions is fundamental in order to relax the bandwidth constraints enforced by isolation and efficiently manage overruns.

By the very dynamic nature of open real-time systems, the availability of residual capacities is unknown beforehand and can only be scheduled dynamically when it is detected. Therefore, the proposed algorithm considers two different types of servers: (i) a p-CSWS server for managing the execution of each task in the system; and a (ii) residual capacity work-stealing server for managing each residual capacity that is dynamically generated by the earlier completion of jobs.

A p-CSWS server extends the M-CBS server with a work-stealing deque for supporting the parallel execution of multithreaded jobs. Dynamically generated threads are maintained in a local work-stealing deque of the server where the job is currently being executed. Each p-CSWS server successively dequeues a thread from the head of its deque, executes it, and continues with the next thread unless the deque is empty. If at time t, S_i finishes the execution of its currently served job without exhausting its reserved execution capacity Q_i and it has no pending work, a residual capacity of $min(c_k^i, d_k^i - t)$ and deadline d_k^i is dynamically generated. By pending work we refer to the case when there exists at least a served job such that its release time is $s_{i,j} \leq t < f_{i,j}$.

Residual capacities greater than a lower bound Q_{min} are released to the global queue as a new residual capacity work-stealing server. A residual capacity server is a p-CSWS server that applies a priority-based work-stealing policy whenever its local deque its empty. Whenever a residual capacity server S_j^r is enqueued in the global queue it competes for processor time as if it were a regular active server with pending work and deadline at time d_j^r. If a residual capacity server is selected for execution, then it may execute only prior to time d_j^r and the processor time it receives can be consumed by any eligible thread with a current deadline at least d_j^r, through work-stealing. This subject will be detailed in the next section.

Whenever a residual capacity server is executing a thread, the execution capacity of the threads's dedicated server remains unchanged. If the thread completes while consuming the residual capacity and if that residual capacity is neither expired nor exhausted, the leftover capacity $c_j^r > 0$ may be used to execute another thread.

If the available execution capacity of a residual capacity server is either expired or exhausted it is not replenished. If there is pending work, the residual capacity server remains active until all work has been reclaimed back by the respective dedicated server. Otherwise, it becomes idle and is erased from the system.

Due to work-stealing overheads, not every amount of residual capacity can be efficiently released as a new residual capacity server. Thus, residual capacities smaller than Q_{min} are assigned to the processor on which it was generated and will be consumed by the next server with a later deadline that executes on that processor, in a similar fashion of the residual capacity reclaiming scheme of M-CASH. This allows small capacities to accumulate into usable chunks, avoiding excessive overheads.

If a processor ever idles and there is any residual capacity server in the global queue, then it dequeues the earliest deadline residual capacity server and executes it without donating the resulting execution to any job/thread. The processor continues to execute the residual capacity server as long as it would otherwise be idle or the capacity is neither exhausted nor expired.

5. PRIORITY-BASED WORK-STEALING

Dynamic scheduling of parallel computations by work-stealing [7] has gained popularity in academia and industry for its good performance, ease of implementation and theoretical bounds on space and time. Work-stealing has proven to be effective in reducing the complexity of parallel programming, especially for irregular and dynamic computations, and its benefits have been confirmed by several studies [37, 36]. Therefore, it has been widely adopted in both commercial and open-source software and libraries, including Cilk++, Intel TBB, Microsoft Task Parallel Library (TPL) in the .NET framework, and the Java Fork/Join Framework.

A work-stealing scheduler employs a fixed number of workers, usually one per core. Each of those workers has a local double-ended queue (deque) to store ready threads. Workers treat their own deques as a stack, pushing and popping threads from the bottom, but treat the deque of another randomly chosen busy worker as a queue, stealing threads only from the top, whenever they have no local threads to execute. This reduces contention, by having stealing workers operate on the opposite end of the queue than the worker they are stealing from, and also helps to increase locality, since stealing a thread also migrates its future workload [19]. All queue manipulations run in constant-time $(O(1))$, independently of the number of threads in the queues. Furthermore, several works (e.g. [4, 12, 22]) have addressed how a non-blocking deque can be implemented to limit overheads.

However, the need to support tasks' priorities fundamentally distinguishes the problem at hand in this paper from other work-stealing extensions previously proposed in the literature [45, 21, 44]. With classical work-stealing, threads waiting for execution in a deque may be repressed by new threads, which are enqueued at the bottom of the worker's deque. As such, a thread at the tail of a deque might never be executed if all workers are busy. Consequently, there is no upper bound on the response time of a multithreaded real-time job. Therefore, considering threads' priorities and using of a single deque per core would require, during stealing, that a worker iterate through the threads in all deques until the highest priority thread to be stolen was found. This cannot be considered a valid solution since it greatly increases the theft time and, subsequently, the contention on a deque.

Our proposal is to replace the single per-core deque of classical work-stealing with the concept of a per-server *virtual deque*. A virtual deque of a p-CSWS server S_i is composed by its local deque and by all the deques of active residual capacity servers that have stolen some thread from S_i at some time instant. Thus, all parallel threads of job $j_{i,k}$ continue to be dedicated to the same server S_i, ensuring isolation among tasks. The concept is detailed in the next paragraphs.

Whenever a residual capacity server with execution capacity $c_k^r > 0$ finds its local deque empty, c_k^r can be used to execute any eligible thread with a current deadline at least d_k^r through work-stealing.

DEFINITION 1. *The set of active servers A_r eligible for work-stealing is given by $A_r = \{A_r | A_r \in A, d_l^j \geq d_k^r, c_k^r > 0\}$, where A is the set of all active p-CSWS servers with parallel threads in their local deques, d_l^j is the current deadline of parallel threads on the top of a deque, and d_k^r is the currently assigned deadline of server S_r.*

Having A_r, a residual capacity server S_r with available capacity and an empty local deque steals the thread from the top of the deque of the earliest deadline active server S_{edf} from the set of eligible servers P_r, following a deterministic approach as opposed to the random selection of classical work-stealing.

DEFINITION 2. *The earliest deadline active server S_{edf} from the set of eligible servers P_r is defined as $\exists^1 S_r \in P_r : min_{d_k^r}(P_r), P_r \neq \emptyset$.*

Note that the $\exists^1$ relation is guaranteed by the *min* function which, whenever there is more than one server with the same earliest deadline, always returns the first server on the list.

As with any p-CSWS server, a residual capacity server dequeues a thread from the head of its deque, executes it, and continues with the next thread unless the deque is empty. Similarly, all dynamically generated ready threads are pushed to the bottom of the residual server's deque. Therefore, a residual capacity server follow the same rules of operation as a regular p-CSWS server, except when (i) it finds its local deque empty, since it tries to work-steal; and (ii) when its capacity is exhausted or expired, since it is not replenished.

Thus, in order to efficiently manage the virtual deque of a p-CSWS server, whenever a steal occurs, a pointer to the bottom of the residual capacity stealing server's deque is added to a *thief list* of the stolen server. This pointer remains in the list until all work dedicated to the stolen server, currently in the residual capacity server's deque, has been executed. Recall that a residual capacity server only remains active if there is some pending work, even if its capacity is exhausted or expired. Otherwise, the residual capacity server no longer exists.

Whenever a server S_i finds its local deque empty, it verifies its thief list. If not empty, S_i follows the first pointer in the thief list, iteratively removing and executing the parallel threads from the top of the pointed residual capacity server's deque. Whenever a pointed deque has no more parallel threads dedicated to S_i, the pointer is removed from the server's thief list, and the next pointer is followed, until no more pointers exist.

6. THE P-CSWS SCHEDULER

The p-CSWS scheduler extends the Multiprocessor Constant Bandwidth Server (M-CBS), first introduced by Baruah et al. [5], with a powerful residual capacity reclaiming scheme combined with a work-stealing load balancing policy used to allow parallel tasks to execute on more than one processor at the same time instant. Recall that our goal with respect to designing the global scheduler is to be able to provide complete isolation among the servers, and to guarantee a certain degree of service to each individual server.

A single ready queue exists in the system, ordered by non-decreasing absolute deadlines. At each instant, the higher priority (with shorter absolute deadline) servers are scheduled for execution. Execution capacities and deadlines are managed using the following rules:

- **Rule A:** whenever a server S_i changes its state from idle to active at some time t, a test is executed. If $c_k^i < (d_k^i - t)U_i$, no update of deadline and budget is necessary. Otherwise, c_k^i is recharged to Q_i and the new value $d_k^i = t + T_i$ is assigned to its deadline.

- **Rule B:** whenever a server S_i is selected for execution, it picks the thread at the bottom of its deque, dynamically generated by its kth job. While executing it, its budget c_k^i is decreased by the same amount. If the server's capacity is either expired or exhausted, it is recharged to Q_i and its deadline d_k^i is incremented by T_i.

- **Rule C:** whenever a server S_i finds its local deque empty, it verifies its thief list. If non-empty, S_i follows the first pointer in the list, iteratively removing and executing those parallel threads. Whenever a pointed deque has no more parallel threads dedicated to server S_i, the pointer is removed from the thief list, and the next pointer (if present) is followed, until no more pointers exist.

- **Rule D:** whenever a server S_i completes its kth job at time $t < d_k^i$, after having consumed $e_k^i < Q_i$ time units, and it has no pending work, a new residual capacity with capacity $min(c_k^i, d_k^i - t)$ and deadline d_k^i is generated. S_i becomes idle and its remaining reserved capacity c_k^i is set to zero.

- **Rule E:** a new residual capacity less than a lower bound Q_{min} is assigned to the processor in which it was generated. The next active server S_j with a later deadline that executes on that processor consumes the

earliest deadline residual capacity prior to consuming its own dedicated capacity. When consuming a residual capacity, server S_j runs with the deadline of the residual capacity. If the processor idles beforehand, or if the capacity expires or is exhausted, it is disposed of.

- **Rule F:** a new residual capacity consisting of at least Q_{min} is released to the global ready queue as a new residual capacity server with an execution capacity of $min(c_k^i, d_k^i - t)$ and deadline d_k^i. Whenever a residual capacity server is enqueued, it immediately competes for processing time as if it were a regular server with deadline d_k^r.

- **Rule G:** if a residual capacity server is selected for execution, it may only execute until time d_k^r and the processor time c_k^r it receives is used to steal and execute the earliest deadline eligible thread with a current deadline at least d_k^r. Whenever a steal occurs, a pointer to the bottom of the deque of the residual capacity server is added to the thief list of the stolen server.

- **Rule H:** whenever a thread is executed by a residual capacity server, it is scheduled using the residual server's capacity c_k^r and deadline d_k^r. As such, the execution capacity c_k^i of its dedicated server S_i remains unchanged. If the execution capacity of the residual capacity server is either expired or exhausted, it is not recharged. If there is pending work, the residual capacity server remains active. Otherwise, it is removed from the system.

- **Rule I:** If a processor ever idles and there is any residual capacity server in the global queue, then it dequeues the earliest deadline residual capacity server and executes it without donating the resulting execution to any thread. The processor continues to execute the residua capacity server as long as it would otherwise be idle or the capacity of the residual capacity server is neither exhausted nor expired.

Note that from the point of view of the global scheduler a p-CSWS server performs the same three actions as a M-CBS server: (i) it inserts an execution request in the ready queue each time the server transitions from idle to active; (ii) it removes the execution request when it transitions from active to idle; and (iii) it postpones the deadline of its execution request once its capacity is depleted. Postponing a deadline is effectively equal to removing the current execution request and inserting a new one. Hence, as in [5], we can also abstract the execution requirements of a p-CSWS server as a series of server jobs. However, as opposed to M-CBS, with p-CSWS the computation time of a served multithreaded job can actually be greater than the reserved capacity of its dedicated server and it can be executed in more than one processor at a time, since parallel threads can be stolen and executed by residual capacity servers as well as by its dedicated server.

7. CORRECTNESS

In [5], it is proven that a M-CBS server with parameters (Q_i, T_i) cannot occupy a bandwidth greater than $\frac{Q_i}{T_i}$.

That is, if $D_{S_i}(t_1, t_2)$ is the server's bandwidth demand in the interval $[t_1, t_2]$, it is shown that $\forall t_1, t_2 \in N : t_2 > t_1, D_{S_i}(t_1, t_2) \leq \frac{Q_i}{T_i}(t_2 - t_1)$. This isolation property allow us to use a bandwidth reservation strategy to allocate a fraction of the processor to a task whose demand is not known a priori. The most important consequence of this property is that soft real-time tasks, characterised by average values, can be scheduled together with hard tasks, even in the presence of overloads.

Here, we show that the residual capacity reclaiming scheme and work-stealing policy of p-CSWS do not compromise the real-time correctness of the system.

We start by proving that each p-CSWS server S_i never miss its deadlines, or equivalently, whenever a server deadline d_k^i is reached, its reserved execution capacity is zero. Hence, S_i is able to guarantee an execution time Q_i every T_i time units to its served task.

THEOREM 1. *A server S_i executed on the identical multiprocessor platform Π comprised of m unit-capacity processors never misses its scheduling deadline under the following conditions:*

$$u_\Pi \leq 1;$$
$$U_\Pi \leq m - u_\Pi(m - 1)$$

Proof Sketch

The scheduling condition is equivalent to the schedulability bound expressed in [20] for periodic task sets scheduled by global EDF. It has been shown, *e.g.* in [1, 39], that the resulting schedule of a resource reservation-based system is the same as the one of a set of periodic real-time tasks, one per server, each with an utilisation equal to the server's reserved capacity Q_i and period equal to the server's period T_i.

Since the computation time of task τ_i is equal to Q_i, its job $j_{i,k}$ will complete before its deadline leaving zero execution capacity. Then, by following the same reasoning, job $j_{i,k+1}$ will be released to the ready queue at $a_{i,k+1} = d_k^i$, and will therefore meet its deadline as well. Hence, the theorem follows by induction. $\square$

We now ensure that all generated capacities under p-CSWS are either consumed or exhausted before their respective deadlines.

LEMMA 1. *Given a set of p-CSWS servers, each execution capacity generated during scheduling is either consumed or discharged until its deadline.*

Proof sketch

Let $a_{i,k}$ denote the instant at which a new job $J_{i,k}$ arrives and its associated p-CSWS server $S_i \in I$ is inactive. At $a_{i,k}$, a new capacity $c_k^i = Q_i$ is generated and S_i is released to the ready queue.

Let $\forall_{i,k} \ d_k^i = max\{a_{i,k}, d_{k-1}^i\} + T_i$ be the deadline associated with the generated execution capacity c_k^i.

Let $[t, t + \Delta_t[$ denote a time interval during which server S_i is executing, consuming its own capacity c_k^i. Consequently, S_i has used an amount equal to $c_k^{i'} = c_k^i - \Delta_t \geq 0$ of its own

capacity during Δ_t. As such, the server's reserved capacity c_k^i must be decreased to $c_k^{i'}$, until it is exhausted.

Let $f_{i,k}$ denote the time instant at which server S_i completes its job $J_{i,k}$. Assume that there are no pending jobs for server S_i at time $f_{i,k}$ and $c_k^i > 0$. According to rule D, a new residual capacity with capacity $min(c_k^i, d_k^i - t)$ and deadline d_k^i is generated.

According to Rule E, small capacities are assigned to the processor in which they were generated and are consumed by the next server with a later deadline that executes on that processor prior to its own reserved capacity. Assume that, at instant $f_{i,k}$, another active server S_j is scheduled for execution on the same processor. According to Rule E, if the inequality $d_k^i \leq d_l^j$ holds, let $[t, t + \Delta_t[$ denote the time interval during which server S_j is executing, consuming the residual capacity. Consequently, c_k^i must be decreased to $c_k^{i'} = c_k^i - \Delta_t \geq 0$, until the residual capacity is exhausted or the currently assigned deadline d_k^i is reached. In this later case, the residual capacity is depleted.

As for larger capacities that are dealt with via Rule F, the residual capacity dynamically generated on a early job completion can immediately be released as a new residual capacity server S_r. Assume now that, at instant $f_{i,k}$, S_r is scheduled for execution. According to Rule G, if the inequality $d_l^j \geq d_k^r$ holds, let $[t, t + \Delta_t[$ denote the time interval during which server S_r is executing the stolen thread with deadline d_l^j, consuming its own capacity c_k^r. Consequently, c_k^r must be decreased to $c_k^{r'} = c_k^r - \Delta_t \geq 0$, until the capacity of server S_r is exhausted or the currently assigned deadline d_k^r is reached. At deadline d_k^r, any remaining residual capacity c_k^r of server S_r not used is discharged. $\square$

THEOREM 2. *The dynamic residual capacity reclaiming scheme of p-CSWS does not invalidate the timing guarantees made in Theorem 1.*

Proof Sketch

The theorem follows immediately from Lemma 1. In fact, Lemma 1 ensures that each generated capacity is always exhausted before or discharged at its deadline.

Small residual capacities that are dealt with Rule E may merely cause the consuming job to consume less of its dedicated execution capacity, which cannot increase tardiness.

As for larger residual capacities that are dealt with via Rule F, then the reasoning is also straightforward. The execution capacity of the residual capacity server is scheduled essentially as it would have been included as part of the execution of the donating job.

Since the worst case response time of a task is independent of whether the reserved capacity of some server is being used by that server to execute its dedicated task or it is being consumed to execute any other task in the system, the system's schedulability is independent of whether the proposed dynamic residual capacity reclaiming mechanism of p-CSWS is in operation or not. In the worst case, the longest time a residual capacity can be used to execute tasks dedicated to other servers is bounded by the original server's capacity and deadline. $\square$

8. EXPERIMENTAL EVALUATION

Both M-CBS, M-CASH, and p-CSWS have been implemented in Linux, at user-space level, to measure the performance of the proposed approach to support parallel real-time tasks in open real-time systems through extensive simulations. In particular, we have considered a system of 4 processors with 15 periodic tasks where $\tau_1, \ldots, \tau_5$ were hard real-time tasks, each served by a server with maximum budget equal to the task's worst-case execution time, and $\tau_6, \ldots, \tau_{15}$ were parallel soft real-time tasks that could experience overload conditions.

Each task was a simple fork-join application whose actual work was limited to a series of NOP instructions to avoid memory and cache interferences. Each of the task's jobs (i) executes sequentially; (ii) splits into multiple parallel threads (a random number between $[2, 10]$); and (iii) synchronises at the end of the parallel region, resuming the execution of the master thread. This sequence could occur a random number of times between $[1, 3]$.

The actual execution time of each hard task varied between $[0.3 * Q_i, Q_i]$ of its dedicated server's reserved capacity Q_i, according to a Gaussian distribution. Hence, this variation provides a measure of the amount of bandwidth left free by early completing hard real-time jobs. For parallel multithreaded soft tasks, the total execution time varied between $[0.7 * Q_i, 1.8 * Q_i]$ of their respective dedicated server's reserved capacity Q_i, with sequential and parallel execution times being randomly distributed as a function of the chosen total execution time. All periods were chosen to be uniformly distributed in the interval $[600, 6000]$ ms.

In each simulation run, the performance of each algorithm was evaluated by computing the average tardiness for all soft real-time tasks. The global tardiness was computed by averaging over all soft real-time jobs executed in the simulation run.

Since both M-CBS and M-CASH do not support the parallel execution of multithreaded jobs, all dynamically generated threads were sequentially executed by their dedicated server when scheduled by these two algorithms. On the other hand, with p-CSWS, a multithreaded job could be simultaneously executed by both its dedicated server and one or more residual capacity work-stealing servers at the same time instant. Figure 1 shows the obtained results.

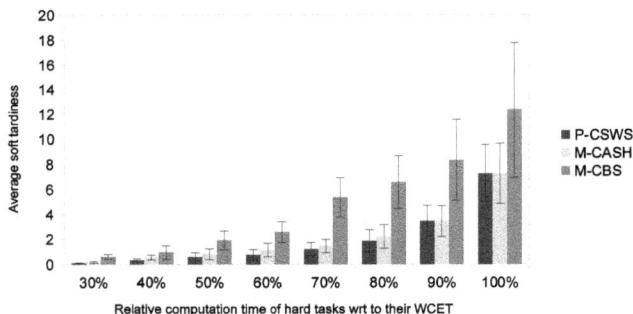

Figure 1: Average tardiness for parallel soft real-time tasks

As expected, the tardiness of soft tasks is smaller when hard tasks execute for less time, thus leaving more residual capacity. Thus, M-CASH significantly outperforms M-CBS, clearly justifying the use of a residual capacity reclaiming mechanism to significantly reduce the average tardiness of soft tasks. However, p-CSWS is always able to obtain better performance than M-CASH. One can conclude that p-CSWS: (i) is indeed able to exploit the available residual bandwidth, thus lowering the average tardiness of soft tasks significantly; and (ii) is able to exploit work-stealing to improve the performance of parallel programs, dynamically balancing the work load among processors. This is particularly for larger amounts of available residual capacity. Naturally, since no residual capacity is left free by hard tasks when they need to execute for the totally of their WCET, the tardiness of parallel soft real-time tasks grows rapidly.

A second study measured the impact of the chosen work-stealing policy on the tardiness of soft real-time tasks. The study considered two work-stealing policies applied to p-CSWS: (i) the classical random choice [7] of a stolen thread; and (ii) the proposed deterministic priority-based selection of the stolen thread. Figure 2 shows the obtained results.

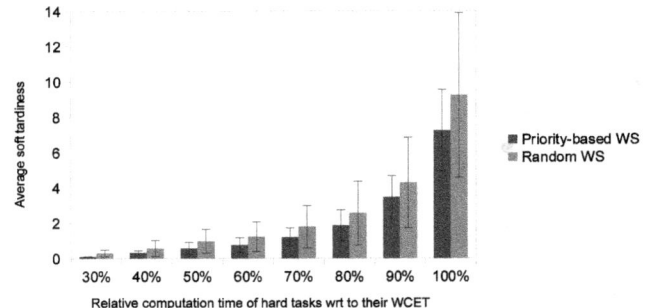

Figure 2: Average tardiness as a function of the chosen work-stealing policy

Similar trends exists for the several relative computation times of hard tasks with respect to their WCET. The bound on average tardiness is by far tighter when stolen threads are chosen according to their deadline rather than randomly. One can conclude that random selection, while fast and easy to implement, may not always select the best victim to steal from. Furthermore, as core counts increase, the number of potential victims also increases, and the probability of selecting the best victim decreases. This is particularly true under severe cases of work imbalance, where a small number of cores may have more work than others [6]. Moreover, when a thief cannot obtain tasks quickly, the unsuccessful steals it performs waste computing resources, which could otherwise be used to execute waiting threads. In fact, if unsuccessful steals are not well controlled, applications can easily be slowed down by 15%–350% [7].

9. CONCLUSIONS AND FUTURE WORK

Multiple programming models are emerging to address an increased need for dynamic task parallelism in applications for multicore processors and shared-address-space parallel computing, both in the general purpose and real-time embedded software development. Scheduling algorithms based on work-stealing are gaining in popularity but also have inherent limitations for real-time systems. This paper proposed and proved correct a novel scheduling approach that combines a priority-based work-stealing load balancing policy with a multicore reservation-based approach to support dynamic task-level parallelism in real-time systems.

p-CSWS is particularly suitable to open systems, where independently developed applications can enter and leave the system at any time but, nevertheless, it is important to achieve the goals of temporal isolation and real-time execution among tasks whose resource demands are only know at runtime. The performance of the proposed approach was demonstrated by extensive simulation studies. We are currently pursuing an evaluation of its efficiency in real-world scenarios by implementing it as new scheduling class in the Linux kernel.

Although it is possible to guarantee the schedulability of parallel hard real-time tasks with p-CSWS, in the worst-case we must consider all threads to execute sequentially on its dedicated server, since parallel execution is only possible when some other server releases residual capacity. This kind of guarantee is very pessimistic and leads to an overall-location of resources. We plan to consider the possibility to pre-allocate empty servers with some reserved capacity to immediately take care of spawned threads, so that it could be possible to provide less pessimistic guarantees to hard real-time tasks. Naturally, if only soft real-time tasks are considered, servers may miss their deadlines by bounded amounts, eliminating such restrictive utilisation limits. It has been shown that, when using global EDF to schedule sporadic real-time tasks on m processors, deadline tardiness is bounded, provided total utilisation is at most m [43].

Acknowledgements

This work was partially supported by National Funds through FCT (Portuguese Foundation for Science and Technology) and by ERDF (European Regional Development Fund) through COMPETE (Operational Programme 'Thematic Factors of Competitiveness'), within REGAIN and VipCore projects, refs. FCOMP-01-0124-FEDER-020447 and FCOMP-01-0124-FEDER-015006.

10. REFERENCES

[1] L. Abeni and G. Buttazzo. Integrating multimedia applications in hard real-time systems. In *Proceedings of the 19th IEEE Real-Time Systems Symposium*, page 4, Madrid, Spain, December 1998.

[2] B. Andersson and J. Jonsson. Preemptive multiprocessor scheduling anomalies. In *Proceedings of the 16th International Parallel and Distributed Processing Symposium*, page 271, April 2002.

[3] O. ARB. Openmp. Available at http://www.openmp.org/.

[4] N. S. Arora, R. D. Blumofe, and C. G. Plaxton. Thread scheduling for multiprogramed multiprocessors. In *Proceedings of the 10th annual ACM symposium on Parallel algorithms and architectures*, pages 119–129, New York, NY, USA, 1998. ACM.

[5] S. Baruah, J. Goossens, and G. Lipari. Implementing constant-bandwidth servers upon multiprocessor platforms. In *Proceedings of the 8th IEEE Real-Time and Embedded Technology and Applications Symposium*, pages 154–163, September 2002.

[6] A. Bhattacharjee, G. Contreras, and M. Martonosi. Parallelization libraries: Characterizing and reducing overheads. *ACM Transactions on Architecture and Code Optimization*, 8(1):5:1–5:29, February 2011.

[7] R. D. Blumofe and C. E. Leiserson. Scheduling multithreaded computations by work stealing. *Journal of the ACM*, 46(5):720–748, September 1999.

[8] B. Brandenburg and J. Anderson. Integrating hard/soft real-time tasks and best-effort jobs on multiprocessors. In *Proceedings of the 19th Euromicro Conference on Real-Time Systems*, pages 61 –70, Pisa, Italy, July 2007.

[9] G. Buttazzo and E. Bini. Optimal dimensioning of a constant bandwidth server. In *Proceedings of the 27th IEE International Real-Time Systems Symposium*, pages 169–177, Rio de Janeiro, Brasil, December 2006.

[10] M. Caccamo, G. Buttazzo, and L. Sha. Capacity sharing for overrun control. In *Proceedings of 21th IEEE RTSS*, pages 295–304, Orlando, Florida, 2000.

[11] M. Caccamo, G. C. Buttazzo, and D. C. Thomas. Efficient reclaiming in reservation-based real-time systems with variable execution times. *IEEE Transactions on Computers*, 54(2):198–213, February 2005.

[12] D. Chase and Y. Lev. Dynamic circular work-stealing deque. In *Proceedings of the 17th ACM Symposium on Parallelism in Algorithms and Architectures*, pages 21–28, 2005.

[13] S. Collette, L. Cucu, and J. Goossens. Integrating job parallelism in real-time scheduling theory. *Information Processing Letters*, 106:180–187, May 2008.

[14] I. Corporation. Parallel building blocks. Available at http://software.intel.com/en-us/articles/intel-parallel-building-blocks/.

[15] M. Corporation. Task parallel library. Available at http://msdn.microsoft.com/en-us/library/dd460717.aspx.

[16] R. I. Davis and A. Burns. A survey of hard real-time scheduling for multiprocessor systems. *ACM Computing Surveys*, 43(4):35:1–35:44, October 2011.

[17] Z. Deng and J. W.-S. Liu. Scheduling real-time applications in an open environment. In *Proceedings of the 18th IEEE RTSS*, page 308, Washington, DC, USA, 1997.

[18] D. Faggioli, G. Lipari, and T. Cucinotta. The multiprocessor bandwidth inheritance protocol. In *Proceedings of the 22nd Euromicro Conference on Real-Time Systems*, pages 90–99, July 2010.

[19] M. Frigo, C. E. Leiserson, and K. H. Randall. The implementation of the cilk-5 multithreaded language. *ACM SIGPLAN Notices*, 33(5):212–223, 1998.

[20] J. Goossens, S. Funk, and S. Baruah. Priority-driven scheduling of periodic task systems on multiprocessors. *Real-Time Systems Journal*, 25:187–205, September 2003.

[21] Y. Guo, J. Zhao, V. Cave, and V. Sarkar. Slaw: a scalable locality-aware adaptive work-stealing scheduler for multi-core systems. In *Proceedings of the*

24th IEEE International Symposium on Parallel and Distributed Processing, pages 1–12, April 2010.

[22] D. Hendler, Y. Lev, M. Moir, and N. Shavit. A dynamic-sized nonblocking work stealing deque. *Distributed Computing*, 18:189–207, February 2006.

[23] S. Kato and Y. Ishikawa. Gang edf scheduling of parallel task systems. In *Proceedings of the 30th IEEE Real-Time Systems Symposium*, pages 459 –468, December 2009.

[24] S. Kato, R. Rajkumar, and Y. Ishikawa. Airs: Supporting interactive real-time applications on multicore platforms. In *Proceedings of the 22nd Euromicro Conference on Real-Time Systems*, pages 47–56, July 2010.

[25] O.-H. Kwon and K.-Y. Chwa. Scheduling parallel tasks with individual deadlines. In *Algorithms and Computations*, volume 1004 of *Lecture Notes in Computer Science*, pages 198–207. Springer Berlin / Heidelberg, 1995.

[26] K. Lakshmanan, S. Kato, and R. Rajkumar. Scheduling parallel real-time tasks on multi-core processors. In *Proceedings of the 31st IEEE Real-Time Systems Symposium*, pages 259 –268, December 2010.

[27] D. Lea. A java fork/join framework. In *Proceedings of the ACM 2000 conference on Java Grande*, pages 36–43, 2000.

[28] W. Y. Lee and H. Lee. Optimal scheduling for real-time parallel tasks. *Transactions on Information and Systems*, E89-D:1962–1966, June 2006.

[29] C. Lin and S. A. Brandt. Improving soft real-time performance through better slack reclaiming. In *Proceedings of the 26th IEEE RTSS*, pages 410–421, 2005.

[30] G. Lipari and S. Baruah. Greedy reclamation of unused bandwidth in constant-bandwidth servers. In *Proceedings of the 12th EuroMicro Conference on Real-Time Systems*, pages 193–200, Stockholm, Sweden, 2000.

[31] C. L. Liu and J. Layland. Scheduling algorithms for multiprogramming in a hard-real-time environment. *Journal of the ACM*, 1(20):40–61, 1973.

[32] G. Manimaran, C. S. R. Murthy, and K. Ramamritham. A new approach for scheduling of parallelizable tasks inreal-time multiprocessor systems. *Real-Time Systems Journal*, 15:39–60, July 1998.

[33] L. Marzario, G. Lipari, P. Balbastre, and A. Crespo. Iris: A new reclaiming algorithm for server-based real-time systems. In *Proceedings of the 10th IEEE Real-Time and Embedded Technology and Applications Symposium*, page 211, Toronto, Canada, 2004.

[34] C. W. Mercer, S. Savage, and H. Tokuda. Processor capacity reserves: Operating system support for multimedia applications. In *Proceedings of the IEEE International Conference on Multimedia Computing and Systems*, pages 90–99, May 1994.

[35] A. Mills and J. Anderson. A stochastic framework for multiprocessor soft real-time scheduling. In *Proceedings of the 16th IEEE Real-Time and Embedded Technology and Applications Symposium*, pages 311 –320, Stockholm, Sweden, April 2010.

[36] A. Navarro, R. Asenjo, S. Tabik, and C. Caşcaval. Load balancing using work-stealing for pipeline parallelism in emerging applications. In *Proceedings of the 23rd International Conference on Supercomputing*, pages 517–518, New York, NY, USA, 2009. ACM.

[37] D. Neill and A. Wierman. On the benefits of work stealing in shared-memory multiprocessors. Technical report, Department of Computer Science, Carnegie Mellon University, 2009.

[38] L. Nogueira and L. M. Pinho. A capacity sharing and stealing strategy for open real-time systems. *Journal of Systems Architecture*, 56(4-6):163–179, 2010.

[39] R. Pellizzoni and M. Caccamo. M-cash: A real-time resource reclaiming algorithm for multiprocessor platforms. *Real-Time Systems*, 40:117–147, 2008.

[40] B. Saha, A.-R. Adl-Tabatabai, A. Ghuloum, M. Rajagopalan, R. L. Hudson, L. Petersen, V. Menon, B. Murphy, T. Shpeisman, E. Sprangle, A. Rohillah, D. Carmean, and J. Fang. Enabling scalability and performance in a large scale cmp environment. *ACM SIGOPS Operating Systems Review*, 41(3):73–86, June 2007.

[41] A. Saifullah, K. Agrawal, C. Lu, and C. Gill. Multi-core real-time scheduling for generalized parallel task models. In *Proceedings of the 32nd IEEE Real-Time Systems Symposium*, pages 217 –226, Vienna, Austria, December 2011.

[42] K. Taura, K. Tabata, and A. Yonezawa. Stackthreads/mp: integrating futures into calling standards. *ACM SIGPLAN Notices*, 34(8):60–71, 1999.

[43] P. Valente and G. Lipari. An upper bound to the lateness of soft real-time tasks scheduled by edf on multiprocessors. In *Proceedings of the 26th IEEE International Real-Time Systems Symposium*, pages 311–320, December 2005.

[44] v. Vrba, H. Espeland, P. Halvorsen, and C. Griwodz. Limits of work-stealing scheduling. In *Proceedings of the 14th International Workshop on Job Scheduling Strategies for Parallel Processing*, pages 280–299, May 2009.

[45] Z. Vrba, P. Halvorsen, and C. Griwodz. A simple improvement of the work-stealing scheduling algorithm. In *Proceedings of the 4th International Conference on Complex, Intelligent and Software Intensive Systems*, pages 925–930, February 2010.

Operating System Support for Redundant Multithreading

Björn Döbel
TU Dresden
Dresden, Germany
doebel@tudos.org

Hermann Härtig
TU Dresden
Dresden, Germany
haertig@tudos.org

Michael Engel
TU Dortmund
Dortmund, Germany
michael.engel@tu-dortmund.de

ABSTRACT

In modern commodity operating systems, core functionality is usually designed assuming that the underlying processor hardware always functions correctly. Shrinking hardware feature sizes break this assumption. Existing approaches to cope with these issues either use hardware functionality that is not available in commercial-off-the-shelf (COTS) systems or poses additional requirements on the software development side, making reuse of existing software hard, if not impossible.

In this paper we present Romain, a framework that provides transparent redundant multithreading[1] as an operating system service for hardware error detection and recovery. When applied to a standard benchmark suite, Romain requires a maximum runtime overhead of 30 % for triple-modular redundancy (while in many cases remaining below 5 %). Furthermore, our approach minimizes the complexity added to the operating system for the sake of replication.

Categories and Subject Descriptors

D.4.5 [**Reliability**]: Fault-tolerance

General Terms

Design,Reliability

Keywords

Microkernel, Redundant Multithreading

1. INTRODUCTION

Modern processor development exploits smaller hardware feature sizes to provide more functional units on the same die size in order to increase processors' performance and feature sets. This trend has a major drawback: chips become more

---

[1]Note that the term *redundant multithreading* refers to using multiple threads for replication, not necessarily to support multithreaded applications.

error prone and constantly or temporarily exhibit incorrect behavior.

Sources for hardware-related errors are manyfold. The lithographic process used for implementing hardware features at sizes as small as 22 nm still uses wavelengths of 193 nm. This may result in processors that don't work right from the start [7] or expose a large variety in terms of gate switch delays [25]. Furthermore, functional units may suffer from heat-induced errors [37], aging effects, or errors caused by undervolting or frequency scaling [49]. Finally, radiation originating from space or the packaging of the chip may lead to *single-event upsets (SEU)* [24], transient errors that manifest as bit-flips at the software level.

Coping with these problems at the hardware level has the advantage that software does not need to be aware of them. However, such solutions often involve specialized hardware circuitry, making these solutions infeasible in commercial-off-the-shelf (COTS) systems. In contrast, software-implemented fault tolerance can easily be adapted by patching the involved applications and integrating with operating system (OS) resource scheduling. This flexibility comes at a price: Software developers need to be aware of potential hardware errors and use the right techniques to handle them. This requirement decreases developers' productivity. Therefore, we argue that it should be the operating system's responsibility to deal with hardware errors and provide resilience guarantees to user-level applications.

OS support for handling errors has been extensively researched with respect to software errors [15, 19, 29]. Hardware errors have been investigated with respect to I/O devices and device drivers [18, 30]. However, tolerance against CPU failures is often limited to systems that can make use of specialized hardware components or employ dedicated software techniques [5, 12].

Our goal is to have the operating system provide fault tolerance against transient hardware errors in the CPU while still running on cheap COTS hardware and without restraining the software developers to using dedicated compilers or programming techniques.

In this paper we make the following contributions:

- We present our implementation of Romain, an operating system service using *software-implemented transparent redundant multithreading* [33] (RMT) to detect hardware errors during the execution of user-level applications. Romain recovers from detected errors using n-way modular redundancy.

To minimize runtime overhead, replicas are distributed across all available CPU cores. Application state is only compared before externalizing state, e.g. when performing system calls. In the current implementation, Romain is restricted to replicate single-threaded applications. We discuss how to extend our approach to handle multithreaded programs.

- Romain is implemented within a state-of-the-art capability-based operating system and we show how capabilities can efficiently be managed for replicated applications.

- Shared memory needs special treatment with respect to replicated execution. We investigate trap & emulate techniques for shared memory accesses and present a solution that works without a complex instruction emulator.

- We discuss how Romain fits into ASTEROID, an operating system architecture designed with the possibility of hardware errors in mind. ASTEROID provides a critical core of software components, that must be trusted to work correctly and that need to be hardened using other techniques than the rest of the system. We refer to this critical core as the *reliable computing base* (RCB). Romain adds less than 3,000 lines of code to this RCB

After giving an overview of the broad spectrum of available research in our area in Section 2, we discuss our assumptions about the hardware fault model in Section 3. Section 4 introduces the ASTEROID OS architecture and gives a short introduction to the Fiasco.OC kernel, which provides the necessary operating system services in our RCB. In Section 5 we then discuss the implementation of Romain, before we evaluate Romain with experiments based on the MiBench benchmark suite [13] in Section 6.

2. RELATED WORK

Research into operating systems fault tolerance often focuses on preventing or recovering from software errors, because these occur at a much higher frequency than hardware errors in today's systems. The Minix3 operating system [15] provides fault-tolerant execution by monitoring state-less applications for crashes and restarting them if necessary. David and colleagues extended this concept with kernel-protected state storage that can survive restarts [10]. Vogt et al. added Minix3-like restartability to the L4/Fiasco microkernel, focusing on the reintegration of restarted services into a capability-based system [46]. The SeL4 microkernel aims at fault avoidance by formally verifying that certain software errors can never happen [19]. All these approaches focus on software errors, whereas our approach aims at detecting and recovering from errors in computational hardware.

The existence of faulty hardware has been researched by the OS community in the context of I/O devices. Hard disks and network communication were hardened using redundancy at the data and device level [30,31] and these approaches were widely adopted in practical systems. Apart from that, most research on device-related issues focuses on software errors, especially in device drivers [29,35]. In contrast to these works, this paper is mainly concerned with hardware errors occurring in the CPU instead of I/O devices. As a notable exception, Kadav and colleagues proposed a tool to validate device driver code to not trust data read from hardware without proper validation [18].

Operating systems for highly available mainframe computers are designed to cope with all potential malfunctions at the hardware and software level [5,6,17]. These systems rely on tight integration with specialized hardware [16,32]. In our work, we provide tolerance against hardware faults using a commodity operating system running on COTS hardware.

Chip manufacturers produce hardware that masks errors, so they never become visible to software. A prominent example for such technologies is the application of error-correcting codes (ECC) [24] to protect memory and CPU registers. Researchers also proposed hardware extensions to handle errors in functional units: The DIVA architecture suggested to augment a non-reliable CPU core with a checker core built in a less complex and less error-prone way [4]. IBM's Power6 CPUs enhanced the processor pipeline with signature checks [32]. IBM's PowerPC 750GX allows executing software redundantly on lockstep processors [16].

Hardware error detection, masking and recovery is attractive, because it simplifies the lives of software developers. However, integrating these measures into a platform is costly and it takes a long time (if it happens at all) until these solutions reach the COTS market. We therefore develop an operating system architecture that solely relies on hardware features available in COTS hardware.

A range of software-only solutions dealing with hardware errors have been proposed. Oh et al. implemented checking of application control-flow using compiler-generated signatures [26] and duplicated instructions to detect computational errors [27]. Reis et al. integrated control-flow checking and error detection into one compiler, SWIFT [34]. SWIFT still had a couple of vulnerabilities that were addressed by Fetzer et al. [11] using arithmetic coding techniques.

Software-only solutions work without any support from the underlying hardware. However, they usually come as compiler extensions and require the whole software stack to be recompiled, which is impossible for proprietary third-party software. Our solution replicates execution at the binary code level and therefore works for all kinds of applications. Furthermore, it is transparent and does not require cooperation by the replicated application.

Hardware-level redundant multithreading executes the same code on multiple hardware threads and validates the order and content of memory accesses [33]. Wang et al. presented a compiler solution that achieves the same without the need for specialized hardware [47], but requires to recompile the whole software stack with their compiler. Shye and colleagues presented a runtime approach to RMT [38]. Their solution runs applications redundantly and uses binary recompilation to redirect system calls and accesses to shared memory to a master process that compares replica states. We chose the same approach with Romain and take Shye's approach to the operating system level, but provide three advantages: First, we also inspect OS-level events such as page faults, increasing the amount of monitored events for the sake of earlier error detection. Second, we do not rely on a binary recompiler to replicate applications, and thereby can come up with a solution less complex to comprehend. Third, by using a microkernel as the basis of our work, we enable to use replication to harden OS services, such as device drivers and protocol stacks.

3. FAULT MODEL

The design and experiments described in this paper assume a *single event upset* (SEU) fault model [50]. SEUs are *transient* errors caused by cosmic or environmental radiation, which can cause a transistor state change, resulting in a bit turning from 0 to 1 or vice versa.

Computer memory was the first device found to suffer from SEUs [50]. ECC techniques have been developed to detect and recover from memory SEUs and we observe these techniques to be widely available in today's COTS systems [24]. Hence, we focus our efforts on SEUs that affect the functional units of the CPU.

The probability of radiation effects depends on the geographical location (natural radiation levels vary) and the height above sea level [24,41]. Time does not influence SEU probabilities. Therefore, we assume SEUs to be distributed uniformly over time. In line with related research we assume that SEUs occur rarely enough so that only a single error in a single functional unit is active at a given point in time [34].

Several studies show that a significant amount of SEUs are masked either by the hardware or by application code before they manifest as observable deviation in program behavior. Saggese injected microarchitectural faults in a simulator and found hardware to mask between 0.5 and 30 percent of all SEUs before they propagate to the software level [36]. Arlat et al. injected faults into a microkernel operating system and found between 25 and 30 percent of all faults to be masked by the hardware or the OS [2]. Wang and colleagues identified programming constructs that make the application execute correctly even if SEUs cause the CPU to take a wrong branch. These outcome-tolerant branches were found to make up between 20 and 30 percent of all branches in the SPEC CPU 2000 benchmarks [48]. Romain benefits from these observations and delays state comparisons between replicas until the point where this state becomes visible to external applications.

Despite focusing on SEUs, we believe that the error detection mechanisms used in Romain will also detect other fault classes, such as permanent errors, as well as semi-permanent errors that occur for instance when heat crosses a certain threshold and vanish once the chip cools down. We think the difference between these error models is not in detection but in the way recovery works. While SEUs can be fixed by overwriting faulty state with correct state, non-transient errors need more complex recovery such as migrating the faulty job to another hardware node [8] or switching to an alternative implementation that does not make use of faulty hardware circuitry [23].

4. SYSTEM ARCHITECTURE

The ASTEROID system architecture is depicted in Figure 1. The hardware consists of COTS components, which are manufactured to come at a cheap price and for this reason do not incorporate specialized hardware fault tolerance mechanisms. As an exception, we assume memory hardware to be protected by ECC, which is a widespread feature of COTS memory devices these days.

The software stack is split into two layers. The critical core includes all services user-level applications need to rely on. These services include fundamental operating system services such as resource scheduling, multi-tasking and address space isolation. Additionally, the core also provides functionality that allows higher-level components to correctly execute in the presence of hardware faults. In our case, this includes the Romain framework.

The higher-level *application layer* comprises all applications running on top of the ASTEROID system and making use of its services. These applications are implemented by

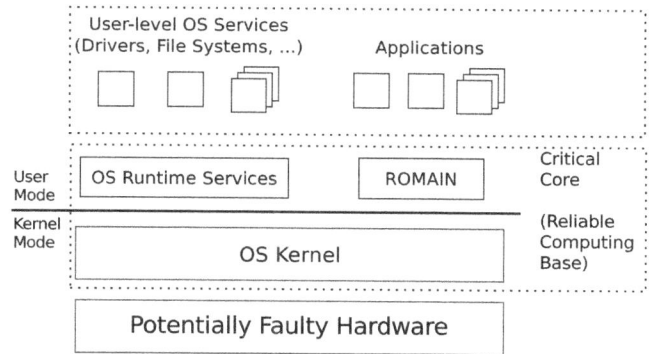

Figure 1: ASTEROID System Overview

developers without specific knowledge about system and hardware internals. Furthermore, we observe a growing body of software that is delivered only in binary form, ranging from mobile applications downloaded from AppStores to device drivers that are distributed without their source code. Therefore, our goal is to run unmodified applications and have the critical core provide the necessary mechanisms to transparently detect and recover from hardware errors.

While the critical core provides all means to safely execute applications in the application layer, the core's fault tolerance mechanisms cannot be used to protect core software itself. Therefore, other mechanisms need to be used at this level to ensure correct execution. In contrast to the application layer, we have full control over the software stack running in the critical core. This allows us to make use of potentially expensive techniques available at the software level such as applying basic block signatures [26], operand encoding [11], and compiler-inserted assertions [45].

4.1 Reliable Computing Base

In the context of secure systems, the term *trusted computing base* (TCB) refers to the set of hardware and software components an application needs to trust in order to maintain certain security goals [14]. To reduce testing and validation efforts, it has been proposed to minimize the TCB as much as possible [9,39]. Similar to the TCB, we think of the critical core as the software components that are necessary to provide transparent replication to applications and that itself need to be hardened using different means. Hence, we coined the term *reliable computing base* (RCB) for the critical core.

The mechanisms used to harden the RCB will be potentially expensive in terms of implementation effort or runtime overhead [11]. Therefore, we strive to minimize the amount of time spent executing in the RCB as well as the amount of code requiring special treatment. To this end, we make three design decisions: First, we minimize interaction between a replicated application and the RCB during normal runtime by only inspecting replica states at points where this state is externalized. Second, we minimize the amount of code that is added to the system by Romain. This rules out using large code bases, such as a binary recompilation tool used in Shye's work [38]. The runtime recompiler alone would add about 100,000 lines of code to the RCB. Instead, we use facilities that already exist in the operating system and augment them for our purposes where needed.

Third, the operating system kernel is part of the RCB. However, not all OS functionality lies on the critical path for providing fault tolerant execution. By using a componentized microkernel, we minimize the RCB and additionally enable Romain to be applied to system-level components such as device drivers and protocol stacks, so that these components are executed outside the RCB.

4.2 Fiasco.OC: Minimizing the RCB

The ASTEROID operating system is based on the Fiasco.OC microkernel [43]. Software running on top of Fiasco.OC consists of objects implemented in dedicated processes.

Similar to other third-generation microkernels such as Nova [40] and SeL4 [19], Fiasco.OC enables fine-grain access control over kernel objects by implementing object references as kernel-protected capabilities. A thread of execution can only use functionality of an object if it possesses a capability for this object. Capabilities are managed by the kernel on a per-process basis and are stored in a capability table. Similar to file descriptors in POSIX operating systems, a process only references its capabilities using indices into this capability table, but it never knows where the object behind this capability is implemented and cannot forge capabilities it did not explicitly obtain.

If owning an object capability, an application can use its functionality through a system call, which translates a function call into a message sent through the kernel's inter-process communication (IPC) mechanism. The parameters for a system call are passed through architectural registers and through the user-level thread control block (UTCB), a thread-specific memory region shared between the kernel and the user process. Fiasco.OC's IPC mechanism does not only support sending messages, but also attaching capabilities to a message. This is called a mapping and can be used to transfer access rights to memory pages or object capabilities between processes.

Memory management for Fiasco.OC applications is performed at the user-level using an implementation of hierarchical paging which has been derived from SawMill [3]. Every process runs a dedicated memory manager that is responsible for managing this process's address space. The memory manager knows about all sources of memory mappings (dataspaces in SawMill's terms). Whenever another thread of this process raises a page fault, the kernel reflects this fault to the memory manager, which in turn resolves the page fault by obtaining a memory mapping from the proper memory source.

Fiasco.OC has another feature, which aids our goal of transparently replicating binary applications: A thread can execute user-level code within an address space. If at any point in time, this thread causes a CPU exception, for instance by issuing a system call or raising a page fault, it is migrated to another process, where this exception can be handled before resuming execution. This whole mechanism [20] is fully transparent to the thread in question.

5. TRANSPARENT REDUNDANT MULTI-THREADING

Romain provides tolerance against hardware SEUs by using software-implemented redundant multithreading to replicate program execution. The replication approach is transparent to user-level applications and allows execution of any program written to run on Fiasco.OC without relying on source code availability or cooperation. Our prototype implementation was done on x86/32, but there are only

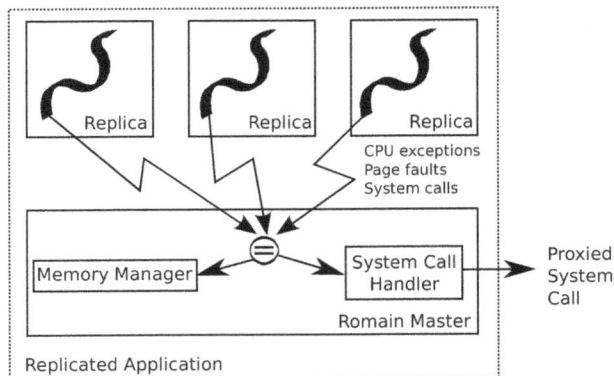

Figure 2: Romain architecture

few platform-specifics in Romain and we are convinced that it will in the end work on all platforms that Fiasco.OC is running on, which includes "real" embedded platforms, such as ARM.

Figure 2 depicts the internal layout of an application replicated using Romain. Every *replica* is run in a separate address space, leveraging hardware memory isolation to avoid propagation of an error from one replica to others. The amount of replicas is configurable and allows for n-way modular redundancy. A *master* process is responsible for managing the replicas of a single application, comparing their states, and performing recovery if necessary. It is furthermore the only part of the replicated application that performs any communication with other applications. This master is part of the RCB as defined in Section 4.1.

At application startup, the master serves as the program loader for the replicated application. It creates the initial replica address spaces and sets up an environment consisting of an initial stack, environment variables, and an initial set of capabilities. These actions are identical to those a program loader performs in the Fiasco.OC environment.

After the initial setup phase, the master creates one initial thread for each replica and configures it to start running within the respective replica address space. Whenever the replica thread raises a CPU exception, such as a page fault or a system call, the Fiasco.OC kernel migrates this thread to the master address space, where an exception handler is executed.

This handler function is the entry point to the second role performed by the master: runtime state comparison. A faulting replica thread is blocked until all other replica threads raise their next exception. The master then compares their states to make sure that all replicas raised the same exception and their architectural states match. The state comparison includes architectural registers, kernel-level exception state, and UTCB contents.

If the master finds the replica states to be identical, it is responsible for handling the respective exception. In Romain this handling is implemented by *observer modules*, which get notified whenever an exceptional situation is encountered. An observer handles the exception by inspecting the state of one replica and acting upon it. Then, the result of this operation (e.g., system call return values) are injected into the other waiting replicas by overwriting their thread states. This allows the master to remain in full control of all interactions between the replicated application and the rest of the system. After successful exception handling, every re-

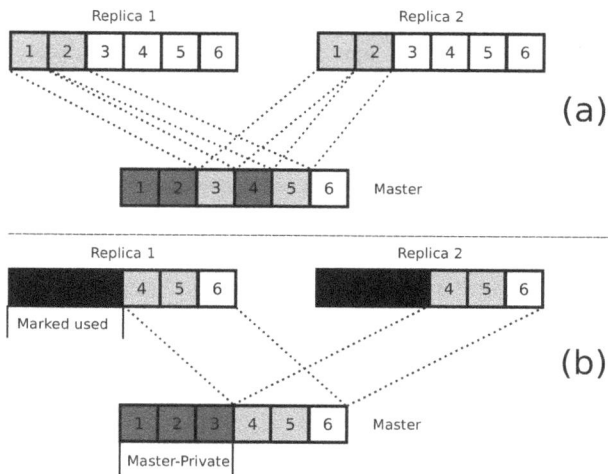

Figure 3: Matching capability tables between master and replicas

plica thread is migrated back to its respective address space and continues execution.

While the master is able to determine that the replicas' outputs to the external world match, it still needs to maintain control over inputs reaching the replicas. In Fiasco.OC this exclusively happens through synchronous system calls, which are covered by the exception handling mechanism. This is slightly different for shared memory, as we will discuss in Section 5.2.

5.1 Replica Resource Management

The exceptions caused by replicas and handled by the master fall into one of two categories: operations on kernel objects and operations on memory. Kernel objects are represented by capabilities, which Fiasco.OC maintains in a per-process capability table. To remain in control of all actions performed by a replica, the master needs to possess a capability to every object the replicas access. In addition, the master also requires capabilities to objects that are only used by itself. This means that over time the master's capability table will diverge from the replicas' ones.

To handle a replica's system call, the master needs to identify the kernel object the replica is referring to. This requires a data structure virtualizing each replica's capability table and mapping its entries to those owned by the master as shown in Figure 3 a). This approach complicates system call handling: for every system call, the master needs to identify all capabilities within the replica's architectural state and its UTCB. Then it must translate them to master capabilities and execute the system call. As the system call reply may also contain capabilities, these need to get translated back to replica capabilities before resuming execution.

To avoid the complexity of translating capabilities, Romain partitions the master's capability table as shown in Figure 3 b). One part is used by the master to obtain private capability mappings. This part is marked as reserved when setting up the initial environment for each replica, thereby making sure that replicas will only obtain mappings in the remainder of their capability tables. Due to this partitioning scheme, the master can carry out system calls on behalf of a replica and receive capability mappings into the replica-specific partition of its capability table. Capabilities

are mapped to the same index in the master and the replicas. The master does not have to perform any translation upon a system call.

While this approach allows redirecting all system calls without modifying their parameters or emulating their behavior, there remains a subset of system calls that need to be emulated by the master. First, some objects exist locally in the replicated task and are therefore existent in every replica. Modifications to these objects need to be applied in all replicas. Second, all system calls relating to the layout of the replicas' address spaces and requests for memory mappings are executed by the master as well.

To manage memory at the user level, Fiasco.OC assigns every thread a memory manager capability, which is provided during application startup. This capability is used a) by a thread to attach a memory object to its address space in order to use it, and b) by the Fiasco.OC kernel to reflect page faults occurring at runtime. The Romain master virtualizes this capability for the replicas in order to remain in control of how replica address spaces are laid out.

The master maintains a representation of every replica's address space and distinguishes between read-only and writable regions. As discussed in Section 4 we rely on memory to be protected by ECC techniques. This allows the master to use a single copy of every read-only memory region and share it among all replicas. In contrast, the master allocates a dedicated copy of writable memory regions for each replica. This increases the memory overhead imposed by Romain. However, the alternative would be to maintain a single copy of the region, map it to replicas read-only and emulate the write operation whenever a write page fault occurred in this region. This *trap & emulate* approach would drastically increase the runtime overhead for replication.

5.2 Shared Memory

The mechanisms discussed so far provide replicated execution under the assumption that all interactions between the replicated application and the outside world can be trapped and handled by the master. This assumption does not hold in the case of shared memory, as its content may be modified by a thread outside of the master's control at any time. The master still needs to make sure that whenever replicas access shared memory, they read the same data regardless of the timing or order of access. Therefore, in contrast to anonymous memory that is only used internally by the replicated application, a trap & emulate approach is required for handling shared memory regions.

Trap & emulate

Fiasco.OC applications obtain anonymous memory by invoking a memory allocator capability. The returned anonymous memory region is thereafter attached to the local address space by invoking the previously discussed memory manager capability. Romain virtualizes the memory allocator capability in order to keep track of all memory regions that have been allocated through it. Thereby the master is able to distinguish between anonymous memory that can be directly mapped to the replicas' address spaces and shared memory objects that require special handling.

When a replica attaches a shared memory region to its address space, the master does not add a memory mapping, but lets the replica continue execution as if a mapping had been established. Thereby every future memory access to

```
pushad
mov eax, [replica->eax]
mov ebx, [replica->ebx]       Prefix
mov ecx, [replica->ecx]
[...]
mov esp, [replica->esp]

nop
nop
nop                            NOP sled
[...]
nop

mov [replica->esp], esp
[..]
mov [replica->ebx], ebx        Suffix
mov [replica->eax], eax
popad
```

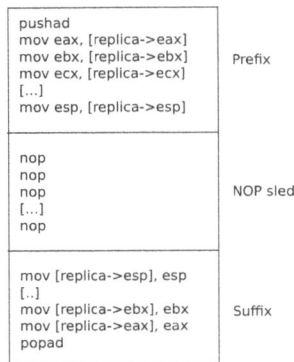

Figure 4: Executing a replica's instruction in the master

the respective region will lead to a page fault that is then handled by the master in a trap & emulate observer module.

Emulating read and write operations on shared memory regions is expensive in terms of overhead and implementation complexity. It requires an instruction emulator which in our case needs to cope with the full semantics of x86/32 memory operations and addressing modes. As a matter of fact, we started implementing such an emulator using the `udis86` disassembler library [42], which consists of about 6,000 lines of code. We added an instruction emulator of about 500 lines of code, restricting it to handle the instructions `mov`, `push`/`pop`, `stosd`, `movsd`, and `call`. This emulator was by far not complete, but allowed to replicate a tiny Fiasco.OC application using trap & emulate for accessing memory. Still, a full emulator would add thousands of lines of code to the RCB. This does not fit well with our goal of minimizing the RCB.

Copy & Execute

Looking closer at shared memory accesses, an instruction emulator needs to perform two tasks: First, it needs to translate virtual addresses in the replica's address space to virtual addresses in the master's address space so that emulation operates on the proper region. Second, the emulator needs to perform the memory operation.

As the master is in full control of the replica's address space layout, it can make sure that shared memory regions are mapped to the same virtual address in the master and replica address spaces. Thereby, if a replica raises a page fault in shared memory, the master can directly deduce where to perform this operation in its own address space. To additionally avoid the complexity and overhead of emulating the current instruction, we decided to make the master execute this instruction on the fastest and most complete instruction emulator available to us: the physical CPU.

To execute the replica's instruction locally in the master, the master maintains a buffer as shown in Figure 4. It contains prefix code, a NOP sled, and suffix code. The prefix code is responsible for storing the master's architectural registers on the stack (using `pushad`) and copying the trapping thread's register state to the architectural registers. The suffix code is responsible for reverting these actions. The NOP sled is patched with the instruction from the remote replica. To do so, we determine the instruction length using the `MLDE32` instruction length decoder [44] and then copy the instruction into the NOP sled, before executing the instruction sequence in the buffer. Implementing this approach

requires less than 300 lines of code and therefore minimizes the RCB complexity for emulating remote memory accesses.

Our solution has two limitations: if the remote instruction executed within the master performed a memory-indirect branch (such as 'jmp [eax]'), execution would divert and never reach the suffix code. This can be mitigated by using CPU support for single-stepping to ensure that only one instruction is executed before control is handed back to the master's code. However, this would increase runtime overhead because of the need for handling the additional single-step interrupt. So far we did not find any use case, where an application makes use of indirect branch targets that are stored in shared memory and we assume that this would already be an exceptional case for non-replicated execution. Therefore, we chose to not address this limitation in our implementation of Romain yet.

Furthermore, executing the shared memory access directly in the master does not replicate this single instruction. Therefore, execution is vulnerable against hardware errors for this single instruction.

Leveraging application knowledge

As we will see in Section 6.2, executing the replica's shared memory instruction in the master yields a better performance than emulating the instruction using a custom-built emulator. Nevertheless, it is still much slower than letting the replica execute shared-memory access directly without any interaction with the master.

In some scenarios, it is possible to leverage application knowledge to decrease the replication overhead in the presence of shared memory usage. One such scenario is the use of shared memory regions that are used mostly for static, read-only data.

The Fiasco.OC kernel provides applications with a kernel info page (KIP), which contains mostly static information, such as the kernel version number and configured features. Its most prominent content, is the code for entering the kernel, which is provided by Fiasco.OC similar to Linux' vsyscall page. The KIP also contains dynamic data: whenever the kernel decides to schedule a thread, it updates a time field within the KIP, which the thread can then use to obtain the current wall clock time through the C library's `gettimeofday` function. In a replicated application, the master needs to consider the dynamic time an external input and only if we can make sure that all replicas see the same value upon an access, we can make sure that their behavior will be consistent after this event.

The static nature of its content and the requirement to access the KIP for every system call prohibit emulating accesses to it. Instead, we currently statically analyse the replicated binary for memory accesses to the well-known clock address within the KIP. We then place a software breakpoint on these instructions and provide an observer module that emulates accesses to the clock field. While patching with interrupt instructions is a generic solution, which can be applied to an arbitrary amount of mostly-static shared memory regions, it still requires the binary to be analysed beforehand. An alternative would be to use hardware breakpoints provided by most of today's CPUs. Then, one could set a data breakpoint on the addresses of interest and provide handler code to emulate the corresponding accesses. However, we did not do so yet, because hardware breakpoints are a limited resource.

5.3 Recovery

Romain uses n-way modular redundancy and can therefore perform majority voting if it detects replica states to mismatch. Faulty replica state can then be overwritten with the state of a correct replica. This approach has the advantage of nearly instant recovery and does not require a combination with sophisticated checkpoint and rollback techniques, which could impose additional overhead.

As we will see in Section 6, replicated execution leads to runtime overhead. Therefore, it depends on the workload and usage scenario, whether a user is willing to run the minimum amount of three replicas necessary for using majority voting. One might instead opt to use double-modular redundancy and only detect errors. In this case, we believe Romain can be paired with restart strategies such as the one used by Minix [15], or application-level checkpointing [1].

6. EVALUATION

One fundamental assumption we based our work on was that a substantial amount of SEUs does not lead to erroneous behavior and it therefore makes sense to delay state comparison between replicas in order to decrease our solution's runtime overhead. We validate this assumption using fault injection experiments in Section 6.1. Thereafter, we evaluate Romain's overhead for double- and triple-modular redundancy in Section 6.2 and give an overview of our solution's code complexity in Section 6.3.

6.1 Fault Injection Experiments

We implemented a fault injection suite as an observer module within Romain. Using this suite, we simulated SEU injections of four types of errors in functional units. The error types were selected to mimic the hard error types injected by Li [21]:

- *Register flip:* We set a breakpoint on a random instruction from the application's code section and in the breakpoint handler trigger a flip of a random bit in a random general-purpose register to simulate SEUs in the register file.

- *Decode:* We simulate an SEU during instruction decoding by sampling a random instruction, flipping a bit in this instruction, single-stepping over the newly generated instruction and reverting the bit flip afterwards.

- *ALU:* We select a random arithmetic instruction and upon encountering it, randomly do one of three things: (1) modify the instruction to perform another arithmetic operation, (2) randomly flip a bit in one of the input operands, or (3) modify the output target. This simulates SEUs occurring in the arithmetic-logic unit.

- *RAT:* The register-allocation table (RAT) maintains a mapping between the general purpose registers (GPRs) exposed to an application and the physical register file provided by the underlying CPU. We simulate an SEU in the RAT by randomly intercepting an instruction that uses register operands. We then modify this instruction to use a random index within the RAT – in 10 % of the cases another register from the available GPRs is selected, in the other 90 % the register access is skipped, simulating writing to an unused register file index. This is a simplification: the register file entry might be used by another hardware

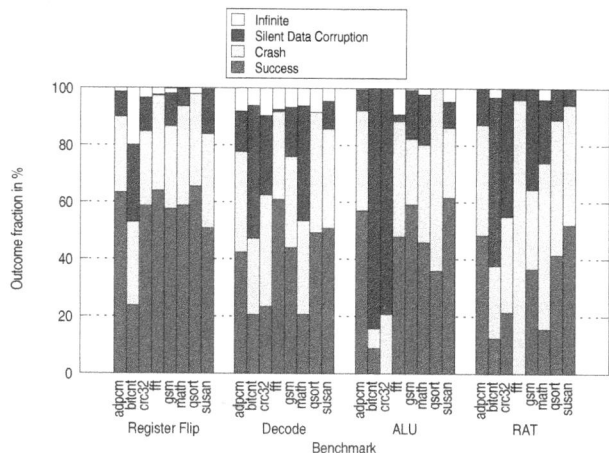

Figure 5: Distribution of benchmark outcomes for fault injection experiments

thread and thereby the write would influence the computations of this thread.

As Romain's purpose is to handle hardware errors occurring during the execution of user-level applications, we performed fault injection experiments targetting such applications. We ran fault injection campaigns on applications from the MiBench [13] embedded benchmark suite, observed the outcome of the experiments and classified them into four categories:

- *Success:* Execution continued and produced a correct result. This indicates that the SEU did not influence the outcome of execution at all.

- *Crash:* Execution terminated prematurely with an abnormal result. Such SEUs represent fail-crash errors which Romain immediately detects.

- *Infinite:* Execution did not terminate within a specified amount of time. This amount was selected to be double the amount of an error-free benchmark run. Such errors most likely represent the program being stuck in an infinite loop. Romain can detect them using a watchdog mechanism.

- *Silent data corruption (SDC):* Execution continued and produced an incorrect result. Romain detects such errors at the point the results are externalized, e.g., by making a system call.

We selected 8 benchmarks from the MiBench suite for fault injection experiments and performed injection runs for each of the error types and applications. On average we ran 7,000 GPR injections, 3,000 instruction flips, 2,000 ALU flips, and 750 RAT flips for each benchmark. The results in Figure 5 show that depending on the benchmark up to 60 % of the fault injections resulted in no observable misbehavior by the application.

It should be noted, that our fault injection campaigns targetted applications of little complexity (leading to few potential candidates for fault injection) and were biased in the way we selected the fault injection point, because we always injected a fault on the first hit of an instruction. We believe that these properties make our results appear overly optimistic in comparison to the studies we cited in Section 3. Nevertheless, the combination of our experiments and those

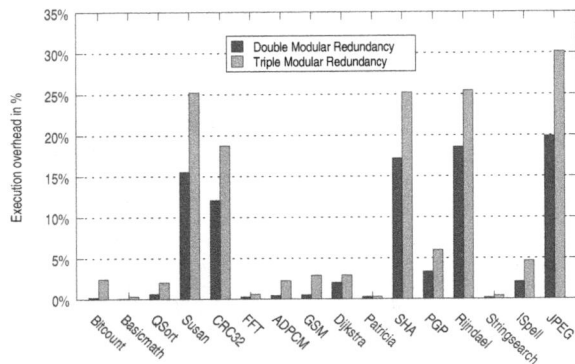

Figure 6: MiBench execution overheads for double- and triple-modular redundancy using Romain

Access type	Execution time	
Direct mapping	0.16	s
Trap & emulate	400.39	s
Copy & execute	219.20	s

Table 1: Execution times for writing a 256 MB memory chunk word-wise using direct mapping and the two evaluated shared memory access mechanisms

studies confirms the assumption that a significant amount of transient faults causes no visible application misbehavior.

Instruction-level state comparison, such as lock-stepping or compiler-generated signatures, would detect mismatches between replicas here and trigger recovery (implying additional runtime overhead), whereas Romain continues execution unnotified. Crashes and SDC, which Romain also detects at the system call level, make up most of the remainder of the failures.

6.2 Execution overhead

To evaluate Romain's overhead, we ran the benchmarks from the MiBench suite as a single instance, as well as in double- (DMR) and triple-modular redundancy (TMR) mode and compared their runtimes. We executed this test on a computer with 12 physical Intel Core2 CPUs running at 2.6 GHz. Hyperthreading was turned off and every replica as well as the master were pinned to a dedicated CPU. Figure 6 shows the normalized runtime overheads, which vary between 0.5 % and 30 %, and in many cases are below 5 %. These results are comparable with Shye's PLR work [38].

We further investigated what behavioral difference causes a benchmark to exhibit 30 % TMR overhead in comparison to having less than 5 % overhead. We counted the amount of memory management requests the master handles during a benchmark run and normalized the results with respect to benchmark execution times. Benchmarks allocating lots of dynamic memory cause higher rates of memory-related exceptions (page faults, mapping requests) that need to be handled. As can be seen in Figure 7, these benchmarks yield higher runtime overheads when running replicated.

Also in line with other replication approaches, CPU utilization and memory overhead are multiplied when using replication. We try to limit memory overhead by sharing read-only regions among replicas.

We additionally performed a microbenchmark to estimate the overhead of trap & emulate on shared memory accesses.

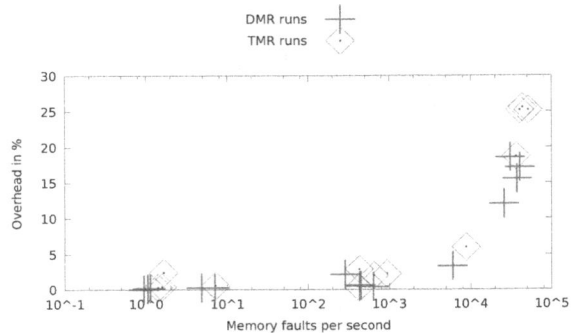

Figure 7: Normalized overhead is related to the amount of memory management requests (logarithmic x scale)

Base code (main, logging, locking)	325
Application loading	375
Replica management	628
Redundancy	153
Memory management	445
System call handling	311
Shared memory handling	281
Total Romain	**2,518**
Fault injection module	668
GDB server stub	1,304

Table 2: Romain complexity in lines of code

We measured the time for `memsetting` 256 MB of memory with a) the memory directly mapped to the replica, b) the memory accesses emulated with our trap & emulate approach, and c) the memory accesses handled using the copy & execute mechanism discussed in Section 5.2. We see that handling each memory access as an exception in a different process is much more expensive than direct accesses. However, we also see that our copy & execute approach is not only less complex, but also faster than using an instruction emulator.

6.3 Complexity

The main reason to implement Romain as an OS service was to keep the solution's complexity, and thus the RCB, minimal. Table 2 gives an overview about our tool's complexity in terms of lines of code. The features described in this paper amount to 2,518 lines of code. To put these numbers into a context, we also show the lines of code needed for the fault injection module used in Section 6.1 and for a GDB stub we implemented to aid debugging on top of Romain.

Especially for the system call handling module, we added code only as far as it was required by our test applications. We expect the lines of code to grow over time as we explore further use cases. Additionally, adding multithreading support to Romain will realistically also add several hundreds of lines of code.

7. LIMITATIONS AND FUTURE WORK

In its current implementation, Romain has three major limitations, which we intend to address in future work. First, so far we enabled replicated execution only for the single-threaded applications from the MiBench benchmark suite.

While this is in line with other related work [11,33,34,38,47] and while these benchmarks represent widespread workloads, it is insufficient with respect to our goal of addressing operating system services.

To successfully replicate OS services, Romain needs to support multithreaded execution, which is inherently non-deterministic, complicating state comparison between replicated threads. Additionally, multithreading also includes the problem of handling memory shared between threads of a replica. Both issues can be addressed by making execution of replicated threads deterministic, because then the events generated by replicated threads will match their replicated counterparts and racy memory accesses will produce the same outcome in all replicas. (Note, that we don't want to fix data races, we only want to verify that racy accesses produce the same outcome in all replicas.)

These problems are similar to the issues solved by deterministic multithreading [22, 28]. They rely on instrumenting synchronization events to make sure that all executions chose the same path. In terms of Fiasco.OC, these synchronization points are exposed through kernel objects, which Romain is able to instrument at the system call boundary.

Enhancing Romain to support device driver software, requires taking care of I/O memory and registers. These are represented by kernel objects and memory pages, both of which are in control of the master process. However, performing replicated I/O accesses implies all kinds of troubles because I/O devices' behavior may differ from traditional memory. We think that the copy&execute method presented in Section 5.2 may be used to handle I/O operations.

We will furthermore look into decreasing memory-related overhead. To decrease space overhead, we will use copy-on-write mappings of writable memory regions instead of dedicated copies as they are used right now. To reduce the runtime overhead related to handling memory exceptions, we will look into memory management strategies that allow handling page-faults at a coarser granularity. For instance mapping super-pages instead of single 4 kB pages might decrease the amount of exceptions that need to be handled and therefore decrease the related runtime overhead.

Close integration with Fiasco.OC enables us to minimize Romain with respect to the RCB, but leaves open the question whether our approach can be transferred to other systems. We will investigate whether similar mechanisms to ours can be implemented based on Linux' `ptrace` or virtualization features.

8. CONCLUSION

In this paper we presented Romain, a framework that provides software-implemented redundant multithreading to unmodified binary-only applications on top of the Fiasco.OC operating system. The framework allows to detect and recover from hardware single-event upsets. The induced runtime overhead is less than 30 %, and in most cases even less than 5 % for the MiBench benchmark suite. The required additions to reliable computing base could be minimized to less then 3,000 lines of code. Romain therefore provides the same features as previous works at lower complexity.

Romain is part of the L4 Runtime Environment (L4Re) running on Fiasco.OC. Download and build instructions can be obtained from `http://www.tudos.org/l4re`.

Acknowledgment

This work was partially supported by the German Research Foundation (DFG) as part of the priority program "Dependable Embedded Systems" (`spp1500.itec.kit.edu`). We furthermore thank our colleagues Carsten Weinhold, Adam Lackorzynski, Michael Roitzsch and Thomas Knauth for their feedback on drafts of this paper.

9. REFERENCES

[1] ANSEL, J., ARYA, K., AND COOPERMAN, G. DMTCP: Transparent checkpointing for cluster computations and the desktop. In *23rd IEEE International Parallel and Distributed Processing Symposium* (Rome, Italy, May 2009).

[2] ARLAT, J., FABRE, J.-C., SOCIETY, I. C., RODRIGUEZ, M., AND SALLES, F. Dependability of COTS microkernel-based systems. *IEEE Transactions on Computers 51* (2002), 138–163.

[3] ARON, M., DELLER, L., ELPHINSTONE, K., JAEGER, T., LIEDTKE, J., AND PARK, Y. The SawMill framework for virtual memory diversity. In *Proceedings of the 8th Asia-Pacific Computer Systems Architecture Conference* (Bond University, Gold Coast, QLD, Australia, Jan. 29–Feb. 2 2001).

[4] AUSTIN, T. DIVA: a reliable substrate for deep submicron microarchitecture design. In *Microarchitecture, 1999. MICRO-32. Proceedings. 32nd Annual International Symposium on* (1999), pp. 196–207.

[5] BARTLETT, J. F. A nonstop kernel. In *Proceedings of the Eighth ACM Symposium on Operating Systems Principles* (New York, NY, USA, 1981), SOSP '81, ACM, pp. 22–29.

[6] BERNICK, D., BRUCKERT, B., VIGNA, P., GARCIA, D., JARDINE, R., KLECKA, J., AND SMULLEN, J. Nonstop: Advanced architecture. In *Dependable Systems and Networks, 2005. DSN 2005. Proceedings. International Conference on* (june-1 july 2005), pp. 12–21.

[7] BORKAR, S. Designing reliable systems from unreliable components: the challenges of transistor variability and degradation. *IEEE Micro 25*, 6 (Nov.-Dec. 2005), 10–16.

[8] BRESSOUD, T. C., AND SCHNEIDER, F. B. Hypervisor-based fault tolerance. In *Proceedings of the Fifteenth ACM Symposium on Operating Systems Principles* (New York, NY, USA, 1995), SOSP '95, ACM, pp. 1–11.

[9] BROWN, J., AND KNIGHT, T. F. A minimal trusted computing base for dynamically ensuring secure information flow. Tech. rep., 2001.

[10] DAVID, F. M., CHAN, E. M., CARLYLE, J. C., AND CAMPBELL, R. H. CuriOS: Improving Reliability through Operating System Structure. In *USENIX Symposium on Operating Systems Design and Implementation* (San Diego, CA, December 2008), pp. 59–72.

[11] FETZER, C., SCHIFFEL, U., AND SÜSSKRAUT, M. AN-encoding compiler: Building safety-critical systems with commodity hardware. In *Proceedings of the 28th International Conference on Computer Safety, Reliability, and Security* (Berlin, Heidelberg, 2009), SAFECOMP '09, Springer-Verlag, pp. 283–296.

[12] GRAY, J. Why do computers stop and what can be done about it? In *Symposium on Reliability in Distributed Software and Database Systems* (1986), pp. 3–12.

[13] GUTHAUS, M. R., RINGENBERG, J. S., ERNST, D., AUSTIN, T. M., MUDGE, T., AND BROWN, R. B. MiBench: A free, commercially representative embedded benchmark suite. In *Proceedings of the Workload Characterization, 2001. WWC-4. 2001 IEEE International Workshop* (Washington, DC, USA, 2001), IEEE Computer Society, pp. 3–14.

[14] HENDRICKS, J., AND VAN DOORN, L. Secure bootstrap is not enough: shoring up the trusted computing base. In *Proceedings of the 11th workshop on ACM SIGOPS European workshop* (New York, NY, USA, 2004), EW 11, ACM.

[15] HERDER, J. N. *Building a dependable operating system: Fault Tolerance in MINIX3*. Dissertation, Vrije Universiteit Amsterdam, 2010.

[16] IBM. PowerPC 750GX Lockstep facility. IBM Application Note, 2008.

[17] IBM. z/OS – a smarter operating system for smarter computing. http://www-03.ibm.com/systems/z/os/zos/, 2011.

[18] KADAV, A., RENZELMANN, M. J., AND SWIFT, M. M. Tolerating hardware device failures in software. *Proceedings of the ACM SIGOPS 22nd Symposium on Operating Systems Principles* (2009), 59.

[19] KLEIN, G., ELPHINSTONE, K., HEISER, G., ANDRONICK, J., COCK, D., DERRIN, P., ELKADUWE, D., ENGELHARDT, K., KOLANSKI, R., NORRISH, M., SEWELL, T., TUCH, H., AND WINWOOD, S. seL4: Formal verification of an OS kernel. In *Proc. 22nd ACM Symposium on Operating Systems Principles (SOSP)* (Big Sky, MT, USA, Oct. 2009), ACM, pp. 207–220.

[20] LACKORZYNSKI, A., WARG, A., AND PETER, M. Generic Virtualization with Virtual Processors. In *Proceedings of Twelfth Real-Time Linux Workshop* (Nairobi, Kenya, October 2010).

[21] LI, M.-L., RAMACHANDRAN, P., SAHOO, S. K., ADVE, S. V., ADVE, V. S., AND ZHOU, Y. Understanding the propagation of hard errors to software and implications for resilient system design. In *Proceedings of the 13th International Conference on Architectural Support for Programming Languages and Operating Systems* (New York, NY, USA, 2008), ASPLOS XIII, ACM, pp. 265–276.

[22] LIU, T., CURTSINGER, C., AND BERGER, E. D. Dthreads: efficient deterministic multithreading. In *Proceedings of the Twenty-Third ACM Symposium on Operating Systems Principles* (New York, NY, USA, 2011), SOSP '11, ACM, pp. 327–336.

[23] MEIXNER, A., AND SORIN, D. J. Detouring: Translating software to circumvent hard faults in simple cores. In *Proceedings of the International Conference on Dependable Systems and Networks (DSN)* (2008), pp. 80–89.

[24] MUKHERJEE, S. *Architecture Design for Soft Errors*. Morgan Kaufmann Publishers Inc., San Francisco, CA, USA, 2008.

[25] NASSIF, S. R. The light at the end of the CMOS tunnel. In *Int. Conf. on Application-specific Systems Architectures and Processors* (july 2010), pp. 4–9.

[26] OH, N., SHIRVANI, P., AND McCLUSKEY, E. Control-flow checking by software signatures. *IEEE Transactions on Reliability 51*, 1 (mar 2002), 111–122.

[27] OH, N., SHIRVANI, P. P., AND McCLUSKEY, E. J. Error detection by duplicated instructions in super-scalar processors. *IEEE Transactions on Reliability 51* (Mar 2002), 63–75.

[28] OLSZEWSKI, M., ANSEL, J., AND AMARASINGHE, S. Kendo: efficient deterministic multithreading in software. *SIGPLAN Not. 44* (Mar. 2009), 97–108.

[29] PALIX, N., THOMAS, G., SAHA, S., CALVÈS, C., LAWALL, J., AND MULLER, G. Faults in Linux: Ten years later. In *Proceedings of the Sixteenth International Conference on Architectural Support for Programming Languages and Operating Systems* (New York, NY, USA, 2011), ASPLOS '11, ACM, pp. 305–318.

[30] PATTERSON, D. A., GIBSON, G., AND KATZ, R. H. A case for redundant arrays of inexpensive disks (RAID). In *Proceedings of the 1988 ACM SIGMOD International Conference on Management of Data* (New York, NY, USA, 1988), SIGMOD '88, ACM, pp. 109–116.

[31] POSTEL, J. Transmission Control Protocol. RFC 793 (Standard), Sept. 1981. Updated by RFCs 1122, 3168, 6093.

[32] REICK, K., SANDA, P., SWANEY, S., KELLINGTON, J., MACK, M., FLOYD, M., AND HENDERSON, D. Fault-tolerant design of the IBM Power6 Microprocessor. *IEEE Micro 28*, 2 (march-april 2008), 30–38.

[33] REINHARDT, S. K., AND MUKHERJEE, S. S. Transient fault detection via simultaneous multithreading. *SIGARCH Comput. Archit. News 28* (May 2000), 25–36.

[34] REIS, G. A., CHANG, J., VACHHARAJANI, N., RANGAN, R., AND AUGUST, D. I. SWIFT: Software implemented fault tolerance. In *Proceedings of the International Symposium on Code Generation and Optimization* (2005), IEEE Computer Society, pp. 243–254.

[35] RYZHYK, L., CHUBB, P., KUZ, I., LE SUEUR, E., AND HEISER, G. Automatic device driver synthesis with Termite. *Proceedings of the ACM SIGOPS 22nd Symposium on Operating Systems Principles SOSP '09* (2009), 73.

[36] SAGGESE, G. P., WANG, N. J., KALBARCZYK, Z. T., PATEL, S. J., AND IYER, R. K. An experimental study of soft errors in microprocessors. *IEEE Micro 25* (November 2005), 30–39.

[37] SCHRODER, D. K. Negative bias temperature instability: What do we understand? *Microelectronics Reliability 47*, 6 (2007), 841–852.

[38] SHYE, A., MOSELEY, T., REDDI, V. J., BLOMSTEDT, J., AND CONNORS, D. A. Using process-level redundancy to exploit multiple cores for transient fault tolerance. In *Proceedings of the 37th Annual IEEE/IFIP International Conference on Dependable Systems and Networks* (Washington, DC, USA, 2007), DSN '07, IEEE Computer Society, pp. 297–306.

[39] SINGARAVELU, L., PU, C., HÄRTIG, H., AND HELMUTH, C. Reducing TCB complexity for security-sensitive applications: three case studies. *SIGOPS Oper. Syst. Rev. 40* (April 2006), 161–174.

[40] STEINBERG, U., AND KAUER, B. NOVA: a microhypervisor-based secure virtualization architecture. In *Proceedings of the 5th European conference on Computer systems* (New York, NY, USA, 2010), EuroSys '10, ACM, pp. 209–222.

[41] TABER, A., AND NORMAND, E. Single event upset in avionics. *IEEE Transactions on Nuclear Science 40*, 2 (apr 1993), 120–126.

[42] THAMPI, V. udis86 - disassembler library for x86 and x86-64. http://udis86.sourceforge.net/, 2009.

[43] TU DRESDEN OS GROUP. L4/Fiasco.OC microkernel. http://www.tudos.org/fiasco, 2012.

[44] uNDErX. Micro length-disassembler engine 32. http://vx.netlux.org/vx.php?id=em24, 2004.

[45] VENKATASUBRAMANIAN, R., HAYES, J., AND MURRAY, B. Low-cost on-line fault detection using control flow assertions. In *On-Line Testing Symposium, 2003. IOLTS 2003. 9th IEEE* (july 2003), pp. 137–143.

[46] VOGT, D., DÖBEL, B., AND LACKORZYNSKI, A. Stay strong, stay safe: Enhancing reliability of a secure operating system. In *Proceedings of the Workshop on Isolation and Integration for Dependable Systems (IIDS 2010), Paris, France, April 2010* (New York, NY, USA, 2010), ACM.

[47] WANG, C., KIM, H.-s., WU, Y., AND YING, V. Compiler-managed software-based redundant multi-threading for transient fault detection. In *Proceedings of the International Symposium on Code Generation and Optimization* (Washington, DC, USA, 2007), CGO '07, IEEE Computer Society, pp. 244–258.

[48] WANG, N., FERTIG, M., AND PATEL, S. Y-branches: when you come to a fork in the road, take it. In *Parallel Architectures and Compilation Techniques, 2003. PACT 2003. Proceedings. 12th International Conference on* (sept.-1 oct. 2003), pp. 56–66.

[49] ZHU, D., MELHEM, R., AND MOSSE, D. The effects of energy management on reliability in real-time embedded systems. In *IEEE/ACM International Conference on Computer-Aided design* (Washington, DC, USA, 2004), ICCAD '04, IEEE Computer Society, pp. 35–40.

[50] ZIEGLER, J. F., AND LANFORD, W. A. Effect of cosmic rays on computer memories. *Science 206*, 4420 (1979), 776–788.

Flattening Hierarchical Scheduling

Adam Lackorzyński, Alexander Warg, Marcus Völp, Hermann Härtig
Technische Universität Dresden
Department of Computer Science
Operating Systems Group
{adam,warg,voelp,haertig}@os.inf.tu-dresden.de

ABSTRACT

Recently, the application of virtual-machine technology to integrate real-time systems into a single host has received significant attention and caused controversy. Drawing two examples from mixed-criticality systems, we demonstrate that current virtualization technology, which handles guest scheduling as a black box, is incompatible with this modern scheduling discipline. However, there is a simple solution by exporting sufficient information for the host scheduler to overcome this problem. We describe the problem, the modification required on the guest and show on the example of two practical real-time operating systems how flattening the hierarchical scheduling problem resolves the issue. We conclude by showing the limitations of our technique at the current state of our research.

Categories and Subject Descriptors

C.3 [**Computer Systems Organization**]: Real-time and embedded systems

Keywords

Virtualization, real-time, scheduling, embedded systems

1. INTRODUCTION

Given that we want to integrate two or more real-time systems as guests onto a single host system, what are the challenges and opportunities that we are faced with? How do we maintain timeliness properties, such as meeting all deadlines in such a system when using virtual machines (VMs)? Different if not contradictory answers are given to those questions in the recent real-time literature. One side, for example well represented by Heiser's paper on "The Role of Virtualization in Embedded Systems" [14], claims a "mismatch between embedded-systems requirements and the virtual-machine model is evident in scheduling." He argues "The integrated nature of embedded systems requires that scheduling priorities of different subsystems must be

interleaved. This is at odds with the concept of virtual machines." On the other side, an argument well presented by Sisu Xi et al. on RT-Xen [38] claims, that using bandwidth servers with small enough and frequently replenished budgets (1 ms) is sufficient for most real-time systems and that the performance overhead is negligible. In another recent publication, Masrur et al. motivate [25], "VMs are rewarding in the context of mixed-criticality applications to provide isolation between critical and non-critical tasks running on the same processor.", and "propose a method for selecting optimum time slices and periods for each VM in the system. Our goal is to configure the VM scheduler such that not only all tasks are schedulable but also the minimum possible resources are used."

The short dispute between the two sides following the presentation of Sisu Xi's paper at EMSOFT 2011 remained inconclusive. As a key point — apart from Heiser's doubt regarding Xen's suitability as a real-time kernel — issues with additional non-real-time tasks in *practical* real-time guests, causing problems, were brought forward. In this paper, we want to clarify the arguments.

We argue that at the root of the problem lies the insight that mixed-criticality systems across guests in virtual machines are not compatible with current virtualization technology. We describe two example task sets and show the limitations once they are integrated without using run-time knowledge of scheduling events in the task sets. We then describe a small modification of virtualization technology that allows to overcome these limitations: through a small enhancement of the scheduler in the guest operating system we export sufficient information about the guest task sets for the host scheduler to integrate these workloads onto a single system (e.g., by interleaving guest priorities). Having applied our approach in two practical real-time operating systems (RTOSs), we are confident that the modification to the guests are well in line with widely used virtualization techniques such as paravirtualization and the use of enlightened drivers for simplified virtualized devices. The contributions of this paper are:

- Two practical scheduling examples, which cannot be solved using a plain hierarchical scheduling approach.

- A mechanism to export relevant scheduling information from virtualized subsystems to allow the host to integrate these subsystems while preserving their timing requirements.

The remainder of this paper is organized as follows: after introducing the terminology, we construct two examples using the task sets of two virtual machines that are to be integrated into a single host in Section 3. We demonstrate that the assignment of a single budget (i.e., treating the VM-internal scheduling as a black box) does not suffice to meet the timing requirements of both VMs. Section 4 presents in greater detail how guest scheduling information can be exported to the host in order to flatten the hierarchical schedule and resolve the issue of integrating these subsystems. Section 5 demonstrates these modifications on the example of FreeRTOS and Linux-RT. In Section 6, we evaluate our approach with regards to the lines of code that had to be changed for these case studies and the performance implications that resulted form these changes. With Section 7 we conclude the paper by discussing the limitations and preliminary ideas how to overcome them.

2. TERMINOLOGY

Mixed-criticality systems [5] integrate tasks of different importance (criticality) into a single system while preserving run-time robustness. That is, they drop tasks in the order of increasing criticality if not all tasks can be serviced. In safety-critical settings, assurance in the execution of critical tasks is typically established by certifying more critical tasks at higher assurance levels and with tools that are more pessimistic in the characterization of these tasks. As usual, we assign each task τ_i the assurance (or criticality) level L_i up to which τ_i is certified and assume that it is also analyzed with the tools of all lower criticality levels. More precisely, we assume that for any two VMs (A and B), the criticality levels of the tasks that execute inside these VMs are comparable (i.e., $L_i^A \geq L_j^B \vee L_j^B \geq L_i^A$) and that all tasks are analyzed at all lower criticality levels (including those of tasks in other VMs).

For real-time systems, we obtain a task model for τ_i by replacing the worst-case execution time C_i of τ_i with a vector of worst-case execution times —one per criticality level— such that $\mathbb{C}_i(L) \geq \mathbb{C}_i(L')$ for $L \geq L'$. For better readability, we set $\mathbb{C}_i(L) := \mathbb{C}_i(L_i)$ for $L \geq L_i$. In the remainder of this paper, we shall use the sporadic task model. That is, a task τ_i is characterized by its period (minimal interarrival time), relative deadline, criticality level and worst-case execution time vector: $(T_i, D_i, L_i, \mathbb{C}_i)$. We assume implicitly constrained tasks (i.e., $D_i = T_i$). The *mixed-criticality* (MC) scheduling problem can be phrased as follows: *for each criticality level L, if no job of a task (τ_j) with criticality level $L_j \geq L$ executes longer than $\mathbb{C}_j(L)$, find a schedule such that all jobs of all tasks with criticality level $\geq L$ complete by their deadline.*

As usual, we say a schedule is *feasible* if it is a solution to the scheduling problem. A scheduler is *optimal* if it finds a feasible schedule whenever there exists one. The MC scheduling criterion gives rise to schedulers that deny the kth job $\tau_{i,k}$ of a lower-criticality task τ_i its requested service if a job $\tau_{j,l}$ of a higher-criticality task τ_j executes longer than $\mathbb{C}_j(L_i)$. In this case, we say $\tau_{j,l}$ denies $\tau_{i,k}$ and call the earliest point in time by which $\tau_{j,l}$ has executed longer than $\mathbb{C}_j(L_i)$ without completing the *criticality decision point* of L_i.

Virtualization is a technology to run legacy systems, that is operating systems and their applications on a Virtual Machine Monitor (VMM), sometimes also called hypervisor. Following commonly used terminology, we refer to the entities provided by the VMM as Virtual Machines (VM), the legacy systems running in VMs as guest (operating) systems and the (operating) system running the VMM as host. We encounter two forms of virtualization technology, one that runs guests without any modification, sometimes called faithful virtualization, the other using small changes to guest operating systems, usually called paravirtualization. Examples for paravirtualization systems are Xen [4][1], L^4Linux [13] and OKLinux [28]. Faithfully virtualized systems require certain hardware properties that have been added to many common architectures, for example the Intel-VT and AMD-SVM to the x86 architectures. Embedded platforms like ARM will also get virtualization functionality [27]. Current virtualization technology comes in two architectural variants often referred to as type I and type II: type I (bare metal) uses a small kernel and runs the VMM and most of its hosting software on top of this kernel, examples being Xen [4], OKL4 Microvisor [16], the NOVA microhypervisor [33] and the VMware vSphere Hypervisor™ [36]. Type II (hosted) includes the VMM/Hypervisor in a fully-fledged operating system, examples are KVM [23] and VirtualBox [34] running on Linux. In this paper, we reserve the term hypervisor for the small kernel in type I systems and discuss our approach in the setting of a hypervisor-based system with deprivileged virtual machine monitors. Figure 1 illustrates this setting and highlights the components that are important for our work. Deprivileged VMMs execute guest operating systems and their applications inside virtual machines. The hypervisor offers virtual CPUs (vCPUs) as an abstraction of physical CPUs (pCPUs). The host scheduler in the hypervisor schedules vCPUs. On top of vCPUs, the guest scheduler runs the tasks of its VM. An extension to Type II VMMs is straightforward.

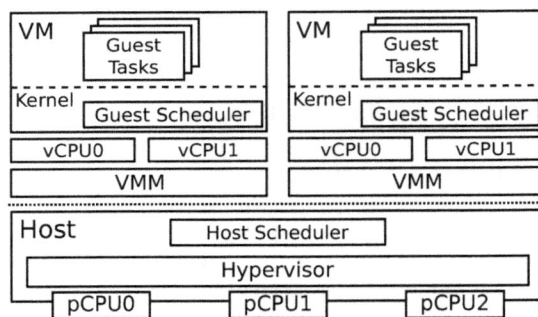

Figure 1: System architecture showing a system with two running VMs.

Scheduling in virtualized systems is typically strictly hierarchical. Each VM contains a scheduler whose responsibility it is to meet all the deadlines of the tasks that belong to this VM. The host scheduler then combines these guest schedules by assigning each VM a fraction of the CPU time. This fraction is typically characterized by a budget.

Besides having to meet the timeliness guarantees of the VMs, the host is also responsible for enforcing a certain degree of isolation between all guests. For safety-critical systems, the host must at least ensure that:

(R1) Scheduling in VM A must not depend on another VM

---

[1]Current versions of Xen also support faithful virtualization.

B providing information about the tasks it schedules; and

(R2) The scheduling and, in particular, the feasibility of a schedule in a VM *A* must not depend on the correctness of any component (including the scheduler) in any other VM *B*.

Because a guest scheduler in a virtual machine must be certified at least up to the criticality level of the tasks it schedules, we can relax the latter requirement for mixed-criticality systems:

(R2') The feasibility of a schedule produced by VM *A* for a certain criticality level L_i must not depend on the correctness of lower than L_i certified schedulers and components in other VMs.

Referring again to Figure 1, the hypervisor including the host scheduler must necessarily be trusted by all guests and hence certified at the highest criticality level. The VMMs must be trusted only up to the extent that the guest OS and its scheduler have to be trusted. That is, they must be certified at the highest criticality level of the tasks in the task set of the VM.

Other settings may impose further constraints on the isolation of VMs such as for instance the complete absence of covert channels [32]. However, for this paper, we restrict ourselves only to the above two constraints for mixed-criticality systems.

3. MOTIVATING EXAMPLES

The following two examples illustrate the need for multiple and, at the level of the host scheduler, interleaved budgets. In the first example, this need arises with as low as two mixed-criticality virtual machines (VM *A* and *B*), which schedule task sets comprised of two respectively three sporadic tasks with two criticality levels $HI > LO$ and different periods. All tasks in the second example share the same period of 8 units of time. The criticality levels of these tasks are $HI > MED > LO$. Table 1 contains the parameters for Example I, Table 2 for Example II. All units are normalized to the host system. We assume optimal mixed-criticality schedulers in both VMs and neglect all times spent in the host or guest operating systems. Both examples assume that the hypervisor schedules VMs strictly hierarchically. That is, it assigns exactly one budget to each of the two virtual machines VM *A* and VM *B*.

Sisu Xi et al. [38] propose to meet guest system timeliness properties by running each VM as a bandwidth server and allocate budgets proportional to the utilization. To ensure that even systems with very small periods can be handled, the budgets are allocated in very small portions. The paper reports that splitting up budgets into chunks of 1ms do not lead to significant performance problems, but state that with much smaller chunks the additional scheduling overhead becomes prohibitive. In our examples, we ignore the overheads introduced by small chunks and assume, arbitrarily small chunks can be selected without penalty. For our first example, we shall further allow the host scheduler to adjust budgets dynamically. In this way, the examples we give describe idealized systems.

VM	Task	T_i	L_i	WCET
A	τ_1	8	HI	$\mathbb{C}_1(HI) = 4, \mathbb{C}_1(LO) = 1$
	τ_2	4	LO	$\mathbb{C}_2(LO) = 1$
	τ_3	16	LO	$\mathbb{C}_3(LO) = 4$
B	τ_4	16	HI	$\mathbb{C}_4(HI) = 6, \mathbb{C}_4(LO) = 2$
	τ_5	4	LO	$\mathbb{C}_5(LO) = 1$

Table 1: Task parameters for Example I.

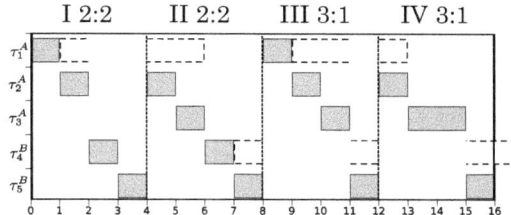

Figure 2: Schedule for the simultaneous release of the task set in Table 1 on top of a mixed-criticality hypervisor. Filled bars show LO WCETs ($\mathbb{C}_i(LO)$), dashed bars show the time $\mathbb{C}_i(HI) - \mathbb{C}_i(LO)$ that is required to complete high tasks that do not complete before $\mathbb{C}_i(LO)$.

3.1 Example I

Figure 2 shows a schedule for the simultaneous release of the task sets of Example I. We can distinguish four phases which correspond to the periods of the tasks τ_2^A and τ_5^B. Irrespective of when the hypervisor switches to VM *A* or VM *B* in the first phase, VM *A* and VM *B* cannot both execute τ_1^A for $\mathbb{C}_1(LO)$ and τ_4^B for $\mathbb{C}_4(LO)$ while meeting the low deadlines of τ_2^A and τ_5^B if both τ_1^A and τ_4^B would complete before their criticality decision points. For the same reason τ_1^A cannot completely be delayed to Phase II. As a consequence, *A* needs at least a budget of 2 in Phase I and *B* a budget of at least 1. Figure 2 illustrates the case where both VMs receive the same budget of length 2. It is easy to see that the arguments that we give hold also for all other sensible budget assignments. With a $2 : 2$ budget assignment in Phase I, VM *A* can execute τ_1^A for one unit of time, which allows the scheduler in VM *A* to decide whether τ_2 is released or, if τ_1^A does not complete by $\mathbb{C}_1(LO)$, whether to allow further execution of τ_1^A. Remember the mixed-criticality scheduling rule gives no further guarantees to LO tasks if a HI task executes longer than its LO WCET. VM *B* has to execute τ_5^B because VM isolation (R1) prevents *B*'s scheduler from knowing whether or not τ_1^A has already completed by $\mathbb{C}_1(LO)$. It may drop τ_5^B only after τ_4^B has executed longer than $\mathbb{C}_4(LO)$. Following Baruah et al. [6], we call the situation caused by τ_5^B *criticality inversion*. Following a $2 : 2$ budget in Phase I, *A* needs at least a budget of 2 in Phase II to guarantee completion of τ_1^A in the situation when τ_1^A did not complete by $\mathbb{C}_1(LO)$. An assignment of a larger budget to *A* is counterproductive as this would result in a remaining LO utilization for the two remaining phases of 1 and a remaining HI utilization of 9/8 (i.e., > 1). If both τ_1^A and τ_4^B are not completed by their LO WCETs, a completion by their HI WCETs can therefore no longer be guaranteed. The key insight that completes this example is that any execution of τ_3^A for longer than 1 unit of time may result in τ_4^B missing its deadline if it has executed longer than $\mathbb{C}_4(LO)$. However, without knowing the progress of τ_4^B, VM A cannot decide whether or not to execute τ_3^A at time 14 in Phase IV. Following the same line of argumentation, it is easy to see that also for other budget assignments the taskset in Table 1 is not feasible for mixed-criticality hypervisors that assign only one budget per VM. A priority assignment π with $\pi(\tau_3^A) < \pi(\tau_4^B) < \pi(\tau_5^B) \le \pi(\tau_2^A) \le \pi(\tau_1^A)$, that is two budgets for VM A to execute τ_3^A and τ_2^A, τ_1^A interleaved with the tasks of VM B, however leads to a feasible (fixed-priority) schedule if we assume that VM A stops τ_2^A latest after $\mathbb{C}_2(LO) = 1$ and that it switches to its low budget if τ_1^A completes before $\mathbb{C}_1(LO)$. To fulfill the Isolation Requirement (R2'), we do not have to require a similar precaution for τ_3^A.

3.2 Example II

Example II demonstrates the possibility of infeasible schedules when integrating two task sets with two tasks each and where all tasks share a single global strict period of 8 units of time. Table 2 contains the parameters of these task sets.

VM	Task	T_i	L_i	WCET
A	τ_1	8	HI	$\mathbb{C}_1(HI) = 4$, $\mathbb{C}_1(MED) = 2$, $\mathbb{C}_1(LO) = 2$
	τ_2	8	LO	$\mathbb{C}_2(LO) = 1$
B	τ_3	8	HI	$\mathbb{C}_3(HI) = 4$, $\mathbb{C}_3(MED) = 2$, $\mathbb{C}_3(LO) = 2$
	τ_4	8	MED	$\mathbb{C}_4(MED) = 3$, $\mathbb{C}_4(LO) = 3$

Table 2: Task parameters for Example II.

To ensure that all high-criticality tasks meet their deadlines, a minimum of four execution units per period must be allocated to each VM. Otherwise, τ_1^A, τ_3^B, or both may miss their deadline if they fully need the execution time $\mathbb{C}_i(HI) = 4$ ($i \in \{1, 2\}$) determined by the high WCET analysis tools. However, if τ_1^A executes only for $\mathbb{C}_1(MED) = 2$ of the four allocated units, the local scheduler of VM A will run τ_2^A on the remaining time (2 units) because it has only a local view on its task set (see Isolation Requirement (R1)). If τ_2^A then uses more than its low-criticality execution time $\mathbb{C}_2(LO) = 1$, for example because of an error or because the scheduler in VM A does not enforce $\mathbb{C}$ for low-criticality tasks, then the medium-criticality task τ_4^B may miss its deadline if both τ_3^B requires $\mathbb{C}_3(MED) = 2$ units and if τ_4^B requires the third unit as predicted by the medium WCET analysis tool ($\mathbb{C}_4(MED) = 3$). Notice, the violation of the mixed-criticality scheduling criterion does not depend on a particular guest or host scheduler but merely on the assigned budgets. For as long as the host scheduler allows VM A to consume 4 units, τ_3^B or τ_4^B may miss their deadlines because the remaining 4 units do not always suffice for $\mathbb{C}_3(MED) + \mathbb{C}_4(MED)$.

An assignment of multiple interleaved budgets again resolves this violation. Table 3 lists the global (i.e., host) priorities, parameters and tasks to run on these budgets. Like for Example I, we have to assume the scheduler in VM A to switch to its low budget if τ_1^A completes before $\mathbb{C}_1(MED)$.

Our general approach to enable the interleaved execution of virtual machines is to flatten the hierarchical scheduling problem by exporting some parts of the guest scheduling to the host. At the current state of our research, exporting

VM	Budget	Time	Priority	Tasks to run on
A	A_1	4	1	τ_1^A
	A_2	1	3	τ_2^A
B	B_1	5	2	τ_3^B, τ_4^B

Table 3: Example II priority/budget allocation (smaller numbers denote higher priority).

the required information to the host scheduler requires small modifications of the guest operating system. Moreover, we have to require that the results of the real-time analysis and hence the parameters of all real-time tasks in the task sets of all guests are available to the host scheduler for the purpose of a global admission. We believe that both requirements are adequate given that the host has to guarantee that all VMs meet the deadlines of all their tasks. In particular, deployment of binary guests remains possible after they have been enlightened for hosts that support flattening.

4. EXPORTING GUEST SCHEDULING TO THE HOST SCHEDULER

A scheduling property common to virtualization technologies is that schedulers in guest operating systems operate independently from the schedulers in other guests and in the host: The host schedules VMs by selecting the budget that it has associated with the virtualized CPU (vCPU). The schedulers in the guest operating systems make use of this budget to schedule their tasks.

In our approach, we attenuate this strict separation of schedulers by introducing an interface in the host, which allows VMs to allocate multiple budgets and to switch between these budgets on their demand. More precisely, during the startup phase of a virtual machine or later upon request from the VM, the host scheduler allocates the budgets in the form of *scheduling contexts* (SCs). After it has validated the schedulability of the system, it attaches the SCs to the virtual CPUs of the requesting VM. A virtual CPU (vCPU) may have multiple SCs attached in which case the guest can select the SC to run on. The set of parameters of a SC includes at least a global priority π and a budget b that is subject to some replenishment rule. In this sense, our approach is generally applicable to all host scheduling policies that select VMs (in our case SCs) from the set of highest prioritized VMs (SCs) with a positive remaining budget. In particular, our approach extends to scheduling schemes such as RT-Xen with small and frequently replenished budgets (if we limit the selection to the highest prioritized SCs) and to more classical global or partitioned fixed-priority schemes where each SC has a period T to denote when budgets are replenished and after which time the next job of a task is released. Of course, for a partitioning host scheduler, the physical CPU becomes an additional parameter of an SC and all SCs that are associated with a vCPU must agree on this parameter.

In addition to an interface for requesting an SC, which the host scheduler is able to validate before it associates this SC with a vCPU of the VM, the interface offered to guest schedulers consists of the following two functions:

`set_sc(id_sc)` deactivates the current SC of the vCPU that invokes this function and activates the SC referred to by `id_sc`. Identifiers like `id_sc` are local to the invoking VM and have to be translated by the host to the actual SC. During this translation, the host scheduler also validates that the referred SC is associated with the requesting vCPU of this VM.

`register_event(id_sc, event, function)` associates the specified event (e.g., an interrupt) with the SC. Upon occurrence of this event, the host activates this SC and, if this SC gets selected, invokes the VM at the specified function.

We defer the discussion of `register_event(id_sc, event, function)` and its use for triggering interrupt service routines to Section 4.2. For now, let us focus on `set_sc(id_sc)` to see how voluntary switches between SCs help resolve the scheduling problems raised in Section 3.

To keep the operation of the above two functions simple, it is convenient to assign each vCPU a default scheduling context (Default-SC). The priority of this Default-SC is the lowest host priority level. The budgets and in particular the replenishment and switching times of course depend on the host scheduling policy. However, to ensure progress of the non-real-time tasks of the individual VMs a Round-Robin or weighted Round-Robin scheme suggests itself. That is, VMs running on the Default-SC receive an equal or weighted proportional share of the time that remains after scheduling the real-time workload of all VMs.

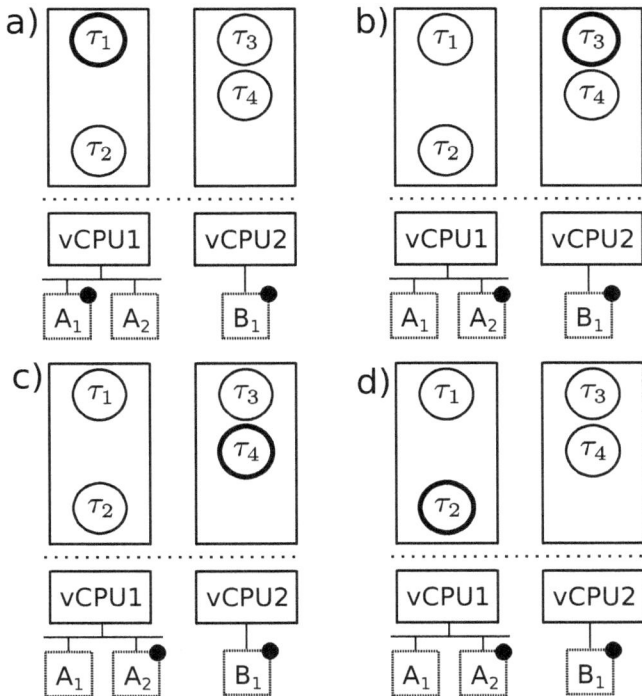

Figure 3: **Step-by-step illustration of a sequence of scheduler context switches (`set_sc()`). Bold circles indicate the active task and the currently active and highest prioritized scheduling contexts.**

Figure 3 illustrates the use of `set_sc()` to resolve the mixed-criticality scheduling problem of Example II. Of course, the three budgets in Table 3 already resolve this problem if the host creates three SCs with the same parameters as the budgets in this table and if the guest scheduler in VM A invokes `set_sc()` to switch from the SC for budget A_1 to the SC for budget A_2 in the event that τ_1^A completes before $\mathbb{C}_1(LO)$. However, more insights in our approach can be drawn from a discussion of this scenario with two budgets for each of the two VMs (i.e., one SC (SC_i) for each of the four tasks (τ_i) parametrized as described in Table 2). The priorities π of these SCs are $\pi(SC_1^A) = \pi(SC_3^B) = 1$, $\pi(SC_4^B) = 2$, and $\pi(SC_2^A) = 3$. Smaller numbers stand for higher priorities. We explain the solution for Example II for the simultaneous release of all tasks. At time 0 (relative to this simultaneous release), both SC_1^A for τ_1^A and SC_3^B for τ_3^B are active. Irrespective of the host scheduling policy, both VMs receive a share of 4 units at the highest priority to complete τ_1^A and τ_3^B in the event that not both complete before $\mathbb{C}_1(LO)$, respectively before $\mathbb{C}_3(MED)$. If one of these tasks completes latest after 2 units, the corresponding guest scheduler invokes `set_sc(SC_2^A)` (for VM A) or `set_sc(SC_4^B)` (for VM B) to switch to the respective lower prioritized scheduling context. Fig. 3a and b depict this situation for the case where τ_1^A completes first. After both VMs have dropped to their lower prioritized budgets (Fig. 3c), SC_4^B has a higher priority than SC_2^A, which allows τ_4^B to complete even in the case that τ_1^A exceeds its budget. Finally τ_2^A runs (Fig. 3d), completing the sequence.

4.1 Guest Task to Host SC Mapping

The two examples and in particular the two solutions to Example II show that the number of exported SCs heavily depends on the host and guest scheduling policies and on the workload to be scheduled. For fixed-priority schedulers in all guests and in the host and for criticality monotonic priority assignment [6], a relatively easy mapping of guest tasks to host SCs is demonstrated in the 4 SC variant of Example II: The scheduling parameters of every task are directly exported and the local priorities are interleaved in such as way that criticality levels are preserved. That is, the priorities of all high-criticality tasks are strictly higher than the priorities of all medium-criticality tasks and all low-criticality tasks, etc. The interleaving within these priority bands must of course be validated by the admission test performed by the host.

The two examples also show possibilities for reducing the number of SCs. For example, Table 3 shows a mapping for Example II with one SC per criticality level. As the focus of this paper is on introducing an easy to use mechanism for integrating VM workloads by flattening the hierarchical scheduling problem, we leave an exhaustive analysis of guest task to host SC mapping for future work.

4.2 Interrupt Service Routines

We now turn our attention to the second function `register_event()` and on one specific implementation detail of VM internal scheduling: interrupt service routines. At the same time, we relax our assumption that host and guest scheduling comes at no cost.

Scheduling decisions in VMs are triggered by injecting interrupts such as timer or device interrupts. Upon receiving these interrupts, the guest runs the corresponding interrupt service routine to decide how to react on these asynchronous events and how to adjust the VM internal scheduling. For example, a guest with one-shot timer may have programmed a timer to the minimum of the absolute deadline of the currently active task and to the point in time when the budget of this task will be depleted. Upon receiving this timer, the timer service routine invokes the scheduler to select the next task to switch to. From the perspective of the VM, this service routine runs non-preemptively, that is, effectively at a priority above the priorities of all tasks. However, to limit the interference from these events on other VMs and to maintain the principle operation of the VMs in the first place, the host must be able to integrate interrupts into the SC scheme and activate SCs in the course of injecting interrupts into the VM. The `register_event()` function serves the purpose of informing the host about which SC to activate for which event. The connection between the interrupt and the to-be-invoked service routine is already known to today's VMMs. Our implementation therefore differs in that the SC-to-event assignment and the event-to-function assignment are realized as two separate functions.

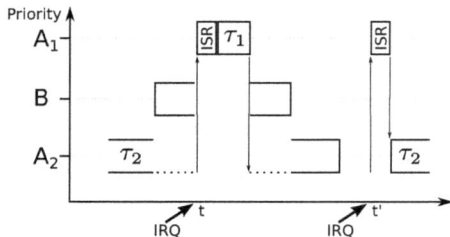

Figure 4: Scheduling context activation at the occurrence of asynchronous events such as interrupts or the expiration of a timer. The interrupt service routine always runs on A_1 until the guest scheduler, which it invokes, decides which task to run.

Figure 4 shows a detail of the release of τ_1 and the activation of the interrupt service routine that follows. Fig. 5 presents the same step-by-step illustration as Fig. 3 but for the scenario of Fig. 4, which includes interrupts. At time t, the host receives an interrupt (IRQ), which triggers the release of τ_1 and later (at time t') of τ_2 in VM A. The hypervisor therefore switches to the VMM of VM A, which in turn injects the interrupt into this VM. Because the interrupt is associated with SC_1^A (i.e., budget A_1), the interrupt service routine always runs on this highest prioritized scheduling context. In the first situation (at time t), the guest scheduler releases τ_1 and drops to SC_2^A (i.e., budget A_2) only if τ_1 completed before $\mathbb{C}_1(LO)$. In the second event (at time t'), the guest scheduler immediately switches to SC_2^A to release the second job shown for τ_2.

4.3 Required Guest OS Modifications

At the current state of our research, small modifications to guest operating systems are required to make use of multiple scheduling contexts. For an arbitrary guest, we have to add the following functionality:

- After every priority change, the corresponding SC must be activated by means of `set_sc()` (if this SC is not already active). A common place where this call to `set_sc()` must be made is after the invocation of the scheduler before the code for switching tasks is invoked.

- For every interrupt service routine that has an SC as-

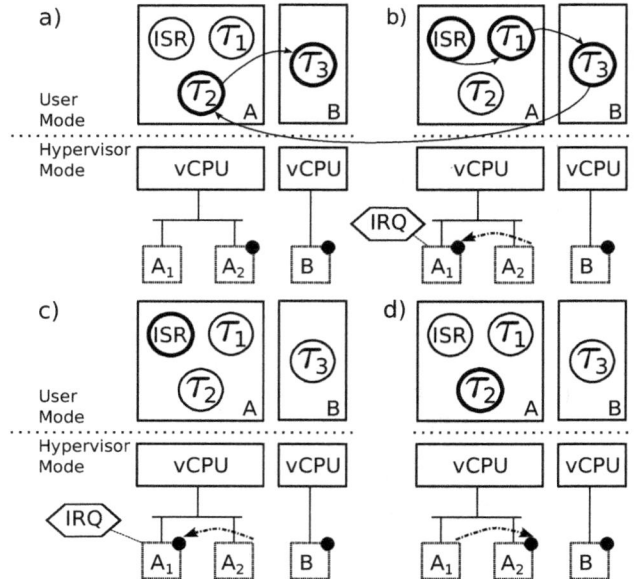

Figure 5: Example sequence of actions as depicted in Figure 4. a) and b) illustrate the first ISR invocation, after τ_3 has finished, the state of a) is restore. The second ISR invocation is depicted by c) and d).

sociated with it, `set_sc()` must be called when the service routine returns to the currently active task in the guest. Otherwise, the task would continue executing at the level of the interrupt routine, which in many guests corresponds to a non-preemptive execution.

For specific guests a subset of these modifications may suffice depending on the features the guest already provides. In the next section we discuss how the functionality is added to two real-time guest operating systems (RTOSs).

5. CASE STUDIES

For our experiments, we implemented flattening support in the Fiasco.OC microkernel [1] and into two operating systems, which we run as guests. Fiasco offers virtualization support in the form of specialized threads called *virtual CPUs* (vCPUs), which in addition to the user accessible registers provides also storage for the state that is typically accessible only from the kernel. That is, vCPUs abstract from the implementation details of the virtualization support in modern hardware architecture (for example, from the Virtual Machine Control Structure (VMCS) of Intel x86 CPUs [17]). Virtualization events are, as common for microkernel-based systems, reflected as messages and delivered with the inter-process communication (IPC) mechanism to application level virtual machine monitors. Therefore, taken together, the unprivileged VMMs and the microkernel serve as a type I VMM in the scenario depicted in Figure 1. The VMM for faithful virtualization was built using the Palacios VMM library [24].

Fiasco implements a generic interface, which allows application level schedulers to set the parameters for the in-kernel scheduling policy. Building upon the internal infrastructure of the kernel, exposing multiple SCs and attaching them to interrupts was straightforward. Regarding the handling of multiple SCs by the in-kernel scheduler, there are two principle ways this can be accomplished: Either the scheduler selects threads (or vCPUs) based on their position in the ready list, which is determined by the highest prioritized active SC that is attached to this thread; or active SCs occupy the ready list in the first place and the scheduler selects first the SC and then the thread attached to it. Both variants have their benefits and drawbacks depending on the frequency of SC switches and on the likelihood of finding a blocked thread, which in the second variant implies a lazy dequeue operation of all its SCs.

For this paper, we used Fiasco's fixed-priority scheduler. That is, the parameters for SCs are periods (implicit deadlines), budgets and priorities and SCs are scheduled according to these fixed priorities with a Round Robin scheduler for those SCs with the same priority.

In the remainder of this section, we describe some important details on the changes required to two popular operating systems: FreeRTOS and Linux-RT. In the examples, `set_sc(ID)` denotes a switch of the SC of the calling vCPU. The ID identifies the SC for activation. The specific implementation varies because of the different implementations of hypercalls. Faithfully virtualized guest operating systems invoke the hypervisor and hence the VMM through a special machine instruction (`vmcall` on x86), which in turn the hypervisor reflects as an IPC message to the VMM. Paravirtualized guests can directly invoke system-calls of the hypervisor to communicate with their VMM. As both techniques build upon vCPUs, the detailed implementation is transparent to the host scheduler.

Depending on the host scheduler, it is possible to implement optimizations for deferred scheduling when `set_sc(ID)` gets invoked. For example, the switch to a higher prioritized SC may be deferred to the point in time of the next preemption or the switch could be dropped if the current SC gets activated.

To simplify the presentation of our guest OS modifications, we restrict our examples to two SCs: the Default-SC and one SC to handle high priority work. Elevation of a VM to a higher host priority (i.e., to the SC for the high priority work) is triggered by a single interrupt. Switching away from this SC targets the Default-SC. An extension to multiple different SCs at different priorities is straightforward.

5.1 FreeRTOS

The real-time operating system FreeRTOS typically comes with no memory protection between tasks[2]. The scheduler in FreeRTOS allows multiple tasks to run concurrently at static priorities. Preemptive and non-preemptive variants of this scheduler exist. In our implementation, we exclusively use the preemptive version, which calls the internal scheduler for each timer tick. This timer tick is associated with the high priority SC. After the new task to be run has been chosen, the function listed in Figure 6 is called, handing over the new priority. Referring to FreeRTOS v6 and v7, the function must be added as `xvPortPostSchedule(uxTopReadyPriority)` in the function `vTaskSwitchContext()` after the while loop, which calculates the new priority. The function uses a barrier priority `RT_BASE_PRIO` to split FreeRTOS tasks into a real-time and a time-sharing category.

Based on this barrier priority, the FreeRTOS scheduler decides whether the selected task should continue to use the high priority SC or fall down to the default one (with `set_sc(ID_SC_DEFAULT)`).

```
void xvPortPostSchedule(unsigned prio)
{
  if (prio < RT_BASE_PRIO)
    set_sc(ID_SC_DEFAULT);
}
```

Figure 6: SC switching function for FreeRTOS.

5.2 Linux

Linux is a widely used and popular operating system that can be used for a wide range of use cases. With the ongoing work on improving the preemptiveness of the kernel and with the merge of a significant part of the Linux-RT patch, it is also increasingly used for real-time workloads. Linux priorities are divided into a range for time-sharing and an exclusive range for real-time processes. This distinction makes the implementation of the SC switching function straightforward as listed in Figure 7. Referring to Linux kernel version 3.3, the function `post_sched_sc(current)` is called within the function `finish_task_switch()` in `kernel/sched/core.c`[3].

To switch back to the Default-SC in the case no scheduling decision will be made after an interrupt has occurred, we introduce the function `irq_no_sched()`. It is called in the code paths for exiting interrupts as shown in Figure 8. Referring to Linux 3.3, a convenient location to call `irq_no_sched()` is the function `irq_exit()` in `kernel/softirq.c`. The synchronization in `irq_no_sched()` is required to atomically check the rescheduling condition with the actual operation. Otherwise, if an interrupt occurred meanwhile, a possible RT-task would be switched back to the default SC.

Using and mapping multiple RT-tasks within Linux to different SCs is also possible by enhancing the two presented functions.

6. EVALUATION

6.1 Further Use Cases of Flattening

Although we draw examples from mixed-criticality scheduling, the application field of flattening and of the mechanism to switch between multiple interleaved-prioritized SCs is broader. We now introduce two further use cases, which benefit from these enhancements.

The "rare-alarm" example includes two subsystems: $S1$ consisting of τ_{alarm} and τ_{book} and $S2$ consisting of τ_2^M. τ_{alarm} is a sporadic task and τ_{book} is a best-effort task, which gathers statistics for maintenance purposes. τ_{alarm} has a low minimum inter-arrival time and a WCET nearly as high as the inter-arrival time leading to very high utilization. τ_2^M is a high-utilization task. τ_{alarm} has an extremely low probability for high-frequency alarm showers, but the importance

---

[2] FreeRTOS support memory protection units (MPUs) however their use is not typical for the application fields of FreeRTOS.

[3] `kernel/sched.c` prior to version 3.3.

```
void post_sched_sc(struct task_struct *p)
{
        if (!rt_task(p))
                set_sc(ID_SC_DEFAULT);
}
```

Figure 7: Post scheduling function for Linux.

```
void irq_no_sched(void)
{
        unsigned long flags;
        local_irq_save(flags);
        if (!need_resched()
            && !rt_task(current))
                set_sc(ID_SC_DEFAULT);
        local_irq_restore(flags);
}
```

Figure 8: Function to be called in case no scheduling decision has been made upon interrupts.

of meeting the deadline in these rare situations is very high. τ_2^M is much less important than τ_{alarm}, but more important than the maintenance task τ_{book}. Without guest-host interaction in the form described in this paper, τ_{book} will use budgets reserved for the rare occasions of alarm showers and block τ_2^M in most situations.

Another example are systems with interactive processes. Common desktop operating systems have means to discover highly interactive tasks and use this information to boost their priorities. If several virtual machines with such interactive tasks change focus, single-budget allocation schemes cannot consider these priority boosts without knowledge of guest-task priorities. A way of solving this issue is to use a high switching frequency between the VMs. However, this increases the overhead as the VM switching has to be done periodically. The assignment of multiple (keyboard and mouse) interrupt triggered SCs allows to minimize these switches to when they are needed.

6.2 Guest Modifications

To quantify the changes required on the guest operating system, we count the number of lines that had to be added to each of the guest variants for switching SCs. We count here only the changes required for SC switching, not for paravirtualization itself. Moreover, we assume the availability of basic infrastructure code, for example, to issue hypervisor calls. Table 4 summarizes these changes.

FreeRTOS requires only the addition of one function plus the calls activating this function after scheduling decisions. Both sum up to a 10 line patch. We applied the two virtualization techniques to the same Linux version. The same modification was required to switch SCs after scheduling. That is, the modification differs only in the IRQ exit paths, however, not in the amount of code that has to be added.

SC setup requires additional code during the startup of the VM or in the event that additional real-time tasks arrive.

Guest	Added Source Code Lines
FreeRTOS (para-virtualized)	10
Para-virtualized Linux	22
Fully-virtualized Linux	22

Table 4: Added source lines of code to each guest variant.

However, because this code is largely dependent on the guest and host scheduling policy, lines-of-code statistics would not easily be comparable.

6.3 Runtime Costs

The modifications to the guest operating system incur no measurable overhead when SCs are not switched. Assuming that `set_sc()` will call out only when the SC must actually be changed, the overhead is negligible because in this situation `set_sc()` boils down to a simple check for equality between the IDs of the current and the targeted SC. In addition, inlining of `set_sc()` eliminates the function call overhead.

6.4 Scheduler Context Activation Latency

The costs for actually switching to a new SC are dominated by the costs to call out of the VM into the hypervisor. We have evaluated these costs in a benchmark running on an AMD Phenom 8450 based system clocked at 2.1GHz.

	Cycles	µs
Para-virtualized	795	0.4
Fully-virtualized	5863	2.8

Table 5: Average SC activation latencies. Cycles were measured using processor's time stamp counter (TSC), times are given for comparison.

Table 5 lists the average SC activation cost for the two types of virtualization used. A call from within a faithfully virtualized environment is more costly than in a paravirtualized guest. In a faithfully virtualized system, the hypercall consists of a `vmcall` instruction. Calls our of paravirtualized guests can directly use the host system call interface and hence benefit from the faster kernel entry.

7. LIMITATIONS AND FUTURE WORK

Currently, we require explicit call-outs of the guests to trigger SC switches. This of course only works if the source code of the guest is available for modification and can be recompiled. As this possibility might not always exist, a way to run unmodified guests would be desirable. The challenge of such a solution is to detect the locations where priorities change within the guest. Whether or not these limitation can be overcome, for example using techniques such as binary rewriting, has to be subject to further research. Considerable knowledge of guest OS kernels is required to identify those locations and it remains open whether or not this can be achieved.

For the overall system an admission must be performed which decides whether a VM, or more general, a subsystem, can be admitted to run on the system. Due to a possibly dynamic nature of subsystems, the admission should be done at runtime. Finding ways to dynamically generate a set of scheduling parameters that can be handled practically is a challenging task. Connected with that is the challenge of extracting runtime information out of guests by techniques such as profiling and event logging.

So far our guests and the host use static-priority based scheduling, which allows the construction of a mapping from guest to host priorities and especially to consider priorities across multiple VMs. Dynamic-priority based algorithms in the guest do not map as easily to a host with static priorities. Guests may use algorithms such as Earliest Deadline First (EDF) if the task set, which is scheduled according to this algorithm, is only exposed to the host as a single parameter set. Interleaving tasks scheduled with EDF across VMs or treating tasks from a single VM differently would require an EDF scheduler in the host as well. This also raises the challenge of mapping EDF guest tasks to another set of EDF host parameters.

It remains to be seen whether the presented technique is applicable for other resources, such as disk, network, or graphics. Generally, multiple scheduling parameters are not only useful for VMs but can also be beneficial for work loads with – for example – differing quality levels. Primary targets might be video decoding and game engines.

8. RELATED WORK

Virtualization of timing-critical systems has been considered before. In the commercial context several vendors offer real-time operating systems that also allow running virtualized guest operating systems in compartments, among them being VirtualLogix [35], PikeOS [29] and OKL4 [28]. The virtualized operating system needs to be adopted to run in those environments. For example, this has been implemented on a commercially deployed mobile phone, running a Linux and the UMTS software stack side by side [15]. Forthcoming hardware support for virtualization on the ARM architecture will improve currently used virtualization techniques [27]. Time partitioning is a popular method to ensure temporal isolation. PikeOS uses a certified time partitioning technique to isolate subsystems and those partitions can run a paravirtualized Linux version [18]. In the research community virtualization in embedded systems has also been worked on. Proteus [3, 19] is using periodic task-sets to fully virtualize operating systems without the need to modify them on the PowerPC architecture. Xen [4] is a popular virtualization solution for servers but has also been ported to the ARM architecture [37] and then evaluated for real-time use [7, 31]. Kinebuchi et al. [20] implemented a hypervisor to host an RTOS and commodity operating systems and evaluated against an L4 solution. Using an L4-based system, it has been researched which costs are induced by introducing address space isolation in Linux-RT environments [26] by building real-time applications using an improved environment that implements real-time threads using host threads. Using specific features of ARM CPUs and their utility in real-time environments has been evaluated in [12]. Kiszka evaluated the use of Linux and KVM as a real-time hypervisor [21] by measuring scheduling latencies and introducing a paravirtualized scheduling interface for guests. Follow-up work examined Linux-KVM for use in embedded systems [22]. Zuo et al. also examined a KVM-based solution for low-latency virtualization [40]. Cucinotta

et al. applied hierarchical real-time theory in a system with KVM by scheduling VMs with reservations [8]. In IRMOS an EDF scheduler in Linux is used to schedule KVM VMs with a guaranteed share [9].

Virtualization inevitably includes stacked scheduling which has been researched in form of hierarchical schedulers. Real-time tasks are grouped into applications with their own local scheduler, multiple applications run on the host. Applications are modelled as servers. Zhang et al. investigated hierarchical scheduling on single processors with earliest deadline first schedule being used as the local scheduler and EDF or fixed-priority as the global one, using independent local tasks [39]. Saewong et al. analyse fixed-priority scheduling in hierarchical configurations [30]. Feng et al. propose a multi-level approach to partition subsystems [11]. Davis et al. investigate hierarchical scheduling on uni-processors with fixed-priority preemptive scheduling in both the global and local schedulers [10]. Time-demand analysis techniques [2] can be used to express waiting times of subsystems.

9. CONCLUSIONS

Some scheduling problems that arise from the integration of real-time systems as guests in a real-time capable virtualization system cannot be solved without VMM control over guest tasks. More generally, in a hierarchical scheduling setup an outer stage must have knowledge about an inner stage configuration, possibly flattening the scheduling. The core of the problem turns out to be a mixed-criticality problem. We showed, how central control exercised over guests tasks can be used to overcome these problems. We also demonstrated how such controlling mechanisms can be provided using several scheduling contexts for real-time guest schedulers in the host scheduler. At the current stage of our research, tiny modifications of the guest OS are needed and a mapping must exist from guest to host scheduling.

10. REFERENCES

[1] Fiasco.OC. http://tudos.org/fiasco.
[2] N. Audsley, A. Burns, M. Richardson, K. Tindell, and A. J. Wellings. Applying new scheduling theory to static priority pre-emptive scheduling. *Software Engineering Journal*, 8:284–292, 1993.
[3] D. Baldin and T. Kerstan. Proteus, a hybrid virtualization platform for embedded systems. In A. Rettberg and F. J. Rammig, editors, *Analysis, Architectures and Modelling of Embedded Systems*. IFIP WG 10.5, Springer-Verlag, 14 - 16 Sept. 2009.
[4] P. Barham, B. Dragovic, K. Fraser, S. Hand, T. Harris, A. Ho, R. Neugebauer, I. Pratt, and A. Warfield. Xen and the art of virtualization. In *Proceedings of the nineteenth ACM symposium on Operating systems principles*, SOSP '03, pages 164–177, New York, NY, USA, 2003. ACM.
[5] S. Baruah, V. Bonifaci, G. D'Angelo, H. Li, A. Marchetti-Spaccamela, N. Megow, and L. Stougie. Scheduling real-time mixed-criticality jobs. *Computers, IEEE Transactions on*, PP(99):1, 2011.
[6] S. Baruah, A. Burns, and R. Davis. Response-time analysis for mixed criticality systems. In *Real-Time Systems Symposium (RTSS), 2011 IEEE 32nd*, pages 34 –43, 29 2011-dec. 2 2011.
[7] Chuck Yoo and team. Real-Time and VMM -

Real-Time Xen for Embedded Devices. `http://www.xen.org/files/xensummit_oracle09/RealTime.pdf`.

[8] T. Cucinotta, G. Anastasi, and L. Abeni. Respecting temporal constraints in virtualised services. In *Computer Software and Applications Conference, 2009. COMPSAC '09. 33rd Annual IEEE International*, volume 2, pages 73 –78, july 2009.

[9] T. Cucinotta, F. Checconi, G. Kousiouris, D. Kyriazis, T. Varvarigou, A. Mazzetti, Z. Zlatev, J. Papay, M. Boniface, S. Berger, D. Lamp, T. Voith, and M. Stein. Virtualised e-learning with real-time guarantees on the irmos platform. In *Service-Oriented Computing and Applications (SOCA), 2010 IEEE International Conference on*, pages 1 –8, dec. 2010.

[10] R. I. Davis and A. Burns. Hierarchical fixed priority pre-emptive scheduling. In *Proceedings of the 26th IEEE International Real-Time Systems Symposium*, pages 389–398, Washington, DC, USA, 2005. IEEE Computer Society.

[11] X. Feng and A. Mok. A model of hierarchical real-time virtual resources. In *Real-Time Systems Symposium, 2002. RTSS 2002. 23rd IEEE*, pages 26 – 35, 2002.

[12] T. Frenzel, A. Lackorzynski, A. Warg, and H. Härtig. ARM TrustZone as a Virtualization Technique in Embedded Systems. In *Proceedings of Twelfth Real-Time Linux Workshop*, Nairobi, Kenya, October 2010.

[13] H. Härtig, M. Hohmuth, J. Liedtke, S. Schönberg, and J. Wolter. The performance of μ-kernel-based systems. In *Proceedings of the 16th ACM Symposium on Operating System Principles (SOSP)*.

[14] G. Heiser. The role of virtualization in embedded systems. In *Proceedings of the 1st workshop on Isolation and integration in embedded systems*, IIES '08, pages 11–16, New York, NY, USA, 2008. ACM.

[15] G. Heiser. The Motorola Evoke QA4, A Case Study in Mobile Virtualization. *OK-Labs Technology White Paper*, 2009.

[16] G. Heiser and B. Leslie. The OKL4 microvisor: convergence point of microkernels and hypervisors. In *Proceedings of the first ACM asia-pacific workshop on Workshop on systems*, APSys '10, pages 19–24, New York, NY, USA, 2010. ACM.

[17] Intel Corporation. *Intel® 64 and IA-32 Architectures Software Developer's Manual, Volume 3, Chapter 24*, December 2011.

[18] R. Kaiser and S. Wagner. Evolution of the PikeOS Microkernel. In *Proceedings of the 1st International Workshop on Microkernels for Embedded Systems*, pages 50–57, Sydney, Australia, January 2007.

[19] T. Kerstan, D. Baldin, and S. Grösbrink. Full Virtualization of Real-Time Systems by Temporal Partitioning. In S. M. Petters and P. Zijlstra, editors, *Proceedings of the 6th International Workshop on Operating Systems Platforms for Embedded Real-Time Applications*, pages 24–32, 6 - 9 July 2010. in conjunction with the 22nd Euromicro Intl Conference on Real-Time Systems Brussels, Belgium, July 7-9, 2010.

[20] Y. Kinebuchi, M. Sugaya, S. Oikawa, and T. Nakajima. Task grain scheduling for hypervisor-based embedded system. In *Proceedings of the 2008 10th IEEE International Conference on High Performance Computing and Communications*, pages 190–197, Washington, DC, USA, 2008. IEEE Computer Society.

[21] J. Kiszka. Towards Linux as a Real-Time Hypervisor. In *Proceedings of the Eleventh Real-Time Linux Workshop*, Dresden, Germany, 2009.

[22] J. Kiszka. KVM in Embedded: Requirements, Experiences and Open Challenges. In *KVM Forum 2010*, August 2010.

[23] Kernel Based Virtual Machine for Linux. `http://http://www.linux-kvm.org/`.

[24] J. Lange and P. Dinda. An Introduction to the Palacios Virtual Machine Monitor—Release 1.0. Technical Report NWU-EECS-08-11, Department of Electrical Engineering and Computer Science, Northwestern University.

[25] A. Masrur, T. Pfeuffer, M. Geier, S. Drössler, and S. Chakraborty. Designing VM Schedulers for Embedded Real-Time Applications. In *Proceedings of the 11th International Conference on Embedded Software*, EMSOFT, 2011.

[26] F. Mehnert, M. Hohmuth, and H. Härtig. Cost and benefit of separate address spaces in real-time operating systems. In *Proceedings of the 23rd IEEE Real-Time Systems Symposium (RTSS)*, pages 124–133, Austin, Texas, USA, Dec. 2002.

[27] R. Mijat and A. Nightingale. Virtualization is Coming to a Platform Near You. *ARM White Paper*, 2010.

[28] Open Kernel Labs. `http://www.ok-labs.com/`.

[29] SYSGO PikeOS. `http://www.sysgo.com/`.

[30] S. Saewong, R. Rajkumar, J. Lehoczky, and M. Klein. Analysis of Hierarchical Fixed-Priority Scheduling. In *Proceedings of the 14th Euromicro Conference on Real-Time Systems (ECRTS'02)*, pages 152 –160, 2002.

[31] Seehwan Yoo and Chuck Yoo. Real-time support for Xen. `http://www.xen.org/files/xensummit_intel09/Real-timesupportforXen.pdf`.

[32] J. Son and J. Alves-Foss. Covert Timing Channel Analysis of Rate Monotonic Real-Time Scheduling Algorithm in MLS Systems. In *7th Annual IEEE Information Assurance Workshop*, West Point, NY, USA, June 2006.

[33] U. Steinberg and B. Kauer. NOVA: a microhypervisor-based secure virtualization architecture. In *EuroSys '10: Proceedings of the 5th European conference on Computer systems*, pages 209–222, New York, NY, USA, 2010. ACM.

[34] Oracle Virtualbox. `http://www.virtualbox.org/`.

[35] VirtualLogix. `http://www.virtuallogix.com`.

[36] VMware vSphere Hypervisor™ (ESXi). `http://www.vmware.com/products/vsphere-hypervisor/overview.html`.

[37] Xen ARM Project. `http://wiki.xensource.com/xenwiki/XenARM`.

[38] S. Xi, J. Wilson, C. Lu, and C. Gill. RT-Xen: Towards Real-time Hierarchical Scheduling in Xen. In *Proceedings of the 11th International Conference on Embedded Software*, EMSOFT, Oct. 2011.

[39] F. Zhang and A. Burns. Analysis of Hierarchical EDF Pre-emptive Scheduling. In *Real-Time Systems Symposium, 2007. RTSS 2007. 28th IEEE International*, pages 423 –434, Dec. 2007.

[40] B. Zuo, K. Chen, A. Liang, H. Guan, J. Zhang, R. Ma, and H. Yang. Performance Tuning Towards a KVM-Based Low Latency Virtualization System. In *Information Engineering and Computer Science (ICIECS), 2010 2nd International Conference on*, pages 1 –4, Dec. 2010.

Trigger Memoization in Self-Triggered Control

Indranil Saha
UCLA
indranil@cs.ucla.edu

Rupak Majumdar
MPI-SWS
rupak@mpi-sws.org

ABSTRACT

Self-triggered implementations of controllers have been proposed as an alternative to traditional *time-triggered* implementations. In a self-triggered implementation, the control task computes the actuator signal as well as a triggering time that specifies the next time instant at which the control task should be run. Self-triggered implementations have the potential to decrease communication costs and CPU requirements over time-triggered ones, e.g., by running the steady-state plant in open loop for long intervals if there is no disturbance. We show that commonly claimed gains for self-triggered implementations are too optimistic. The analysis of most self-triggering algorithms ignore the execution times for computing the trigger times. We show, using implementations of several self-triggering algorithms proposed in the literature on common embedded platforms, that the execution time to compute the trigger time can be non-negligible compared to the trigger times, and may even be higher than the trigger time itself, rendering a naive implementation infeasible.

We propose a hybrid implementation scheme for self-triggered control using state quantization and memoization of trigger times in a cache. We perform trigger-time computation tasks with low priority, and fall back on a time-triggered implementation when the trigger time computations are not guaranteed to finish in time (but use the computed results to update the cache). Our implementation achieves communication costs similar to self-triggered implementations and computation costs close to time-triggered implementations, while providing a bound for the region of practical stability.

Categories and Subject Descriptors

D.2.10 [**Software**]: Software Engineering—*Design-Methodologies*

Keywords

Control System, Self-Triggered Implementation, Stability, Memoization, WCET

EMSOFT'12, October 7-12, 2012, Tampere, Finland.

1. INTRODUCTION

Self-triggered implementations of digital controllers have been proposed recently as a computation- and communication-efficient technique for the software realization of a control law [26, 17, 19, 27, 18, 20, 4, 6]. In a self-triggered implementation, the control task computes, in addition to the actuation signal, the next instant of time at which the control law should be recomputed (the *trigger time*). In between the control updates, the actuation signal is held constant and the plant evolves in open loop. The appropriate choice of trigger time ensures that the resulting system is still stable and has required performance.

Self-triggering is an attractive technique for integrated architectures of cyber-physical systems, in which multiple control loops and non-critical applications share the same resources (CPU or communication network) [21]. Unlike the traditional *time-triggered* approach, where the control computation is performed periodically with a fixed period, it has the potential of making many fewer computations and lower use of the communication bandwidth. This is because the period in a time-triggered approach is chosen under a worst-case assumption, and control computations are performed at this rate even when the plant is in steady state and there are no disturbances [8]. Unlike *event-triggered* approaches [7, 25, 12], in which the state of the plant is continuously monitored using dedicated hardware to detect an event that triggers control re-computation, self-triggered approaches do not require the computation costs or extra hardware for continuous sensing. Indeed, simulations of some benchmark control systems demonstrate that self-triggered implementations can provide significant savings in both computation and communication [18, 20, 4, 6].

We show in this paper that savings estimates claimed for self-triggered implementations are somewhat optimistic. In most simulations of self-triggered implementations, it is assumed that the execution time required to compute the trigger time is negligible. We show that this assumption is not realistic for a number of common embedded platforms, and that the time required to compute the trigger time can indeed be more than the trigger time itself, making a direct implementation infeasible.

We propose an implementation scheme for self-triggered controllers using memoization of trigger times. We demonstrate that our implementation can provide similar savings in communication bandwidth as the naive self-triggered implementation, while keeping computation costs low. We maintain a *memoization region*: a subset of the state space around a given operating point for the controller. We quantize the memoization region into a grid of chosen precision, and compute the trigger times for states on the grid on demand. To compute the trigger time of a state ξ, we compute its quantization on the grid and see if the trigger time has been cached from a previous computation. If so, we return the pre-computed value. If not, instead of computing the trigger time with the same priority as the control task, we schedule it as a background task of lower priority, and fall back on a time-triggered implementation in case it is not computed in time. If the operating point is fixed, the entire memo table can be pre-computed and there is no runtime overhead. However, in many cases the operating points can change dynamically and may not be known statically, or the space required to keep the entire grid may be too high. In these cases, we compute the entries of the memo table incrementally and on demand, falling back on a time-triggered implementation if the computation does not finish in time.

Memo table based implementations for explicit model predictive control have been suggested before [9, 3], where the control signals for a compact state space, computed by solving an optimization problem, are stored in a lookup table for fast actuation. We show memo tables allow fast implementation of self-triggered controllers as well, even with dynamic computations in case it is not feasible to pre-compute the entire table.

The quantization of states in computing trigger times introduces an error in the implementation of the controller, since the trigger time may not be computed for the given state, but for its approximation on the grid. We show how we can bound the effects of this error, and provide a bound on the practical stability of the controlled system [16, 22, 5] based on results on self-triggered controllers for control systems with bounded disturbances [4]. While we focus on trigger times, quantization and memoization can also be applied to the computation of the control law, and a similar error analysis can be performed. (In our examples, the computation of the control law takes negligible time in comparison to the computation of the trigger time, so we focus only on memoizing trigger times.)

We have developed a framework to evaluate self-triggered implementations of control systems. Our framework uses Truetime [10] for the simulation of control applications and aiT [11] for the computation of worst case execution times. We evaluate our implementation on the example of a batch reactor process, a standard linear system benchmark used in previous papers on self-triggered control [18, 20, 4], and an example of a jet engine compressor, a standard nonlinear control benchmark [6]. Experimental results show that our hybrid implementation attains communication costs close to that of naive self-triggered implementations, and simultaneously reduces computation costs significantly.

2. SELF-TRIGGERED CONTROL

We denote by $\mathbb{N}$, $\mathbb{R}$ and $\mathbb{R}_0^+$ the set of natural numbers, the set of real numbers, and the set of nonnegative real numbers, respectively. We denote by $\mathbb{R}^n$ the set of vectors of real numbers of length n. For a vector $x \in \mathbb{R}^n$, we use x_i, $1 \leq i \leq n$, to denote the i-th element of x. We write $\|x\|$ for the *Euclidean norm* of x, given by $\|x\|^2 = x_1^2 + x_2^2 + \ldots + x_n^2$. We denote by $\mathbb{R}^{n \times m}$ the set of real matrices with n rows and m columns. We write I_n for the $n \times n$ identity matrix. For a matrix $X \in \mathbb{R}^{n \times m}$, we write X^T for the transpose of X, $\lambda_{max}(X)$ and $\lambda_{min}(X)$ for its maximum and minimum

eigenvalues, respectively, and $\|X\|$ for its norm, given by $\sqrt{\lambda_{max}(X^T X)}$. For a signal $u : \mathbb{R}_0^+ \to \mathbb{R}^n$, the $\mathcal{L}_\infty$ norm is denoted by $\|u\|_\infty$ and is given by $\|u\|_\infty = \sup_{t>0} \|u(t)\|$.

2.1 Controlled Dynamical Systems

The evolution of a dynamical system with time is captured by a differential equation:

$$\dot{\xi} = f(\xi, v), \ \xi(0) = \xi_0 \tag{1}$$

where $\xi(t) \in \mathbb{R}^n$ denotes the state of the system at time t and $v(t) \in \mathbb{R}^m$ denotes the external input to the system at time t. The curve $\xi : \mathbb{R} \to \mathbb{R}^n$ is said to be a *solution* or *trajectory* of (1) when there exists a piecewise continuous input curve $v : \mathbb{R} \to \mathbb{R}^m$ such that the time derivative of ξ at time t equals $f(\xi(t), v(t))$. The control system is called *linear time invariant* if there are matrices $A \in \mathbb{R}^{n \times n}$ and $B \in \mathbb{R}^{n \times m}$ such that

$$\dot{\xi}(t) = A\xi(t) + Bv(t), \qquad \xi(t) \in \mathbb{R}^n, v(t) \in \mathbb{R}^m. \tag{2}$$

A controller

$$v(t) = k(\xi(t)) \tag{3}$$

computes the input $v(t)$ as a function of the state $\xi(t)$. The goal of controller synthesis is to compute a controller so that the closed loop system $\dot{\xi} = f(\xi, k(\xi(t)))$ exhibits some desirable properties. Below we define different stability criteria that are widely used as desirable properties of a closed loop control system. For more detailed analysis, we refer the readers to the book by Khalil [13].

The closed loop system is *stable* with respect to the origin $\xi = 0$, if for every $b > 0$ there exists a $a > 0$ such that

$$\|\xi(0)\| \leq a \quad \Rightarrow \quad \|\xi(t)\| \leq b \qquad \text{for all } t \geq 0$$

The closed loop system is called *asymptotically stable* if it is stable and a can be chosen so that

$$\|\xi(0)\| \leq a \quad \Rightarrow \quad \xi(t) \to 0 \quad \text{as} \quad t \to \infty.$$

If the above condition holds for any $a > 0$, the closed loop system is called *globally asymptotically stable* with respect to the origin. The closed loop system is called *exponentially stable* if there exist positive constants a, c and λ such that for all $\|\xi(0)\| \leq a$, $\xi(t)$ satisfies the inequality

$$\|\xi(t)\| \leq c\|\xi(0)\|e^{-\lambda t}, \qquad \forall t \geq 0.$$

If the above inequality holds for any a, the closed loop system is called *globally exponentially stable*.

The stability of a closed loop control system in the presence of a piecewise continuous disturbance input $d(t)$ is given by the concept of *input-to-state stability*. A closed-loop dynamical system with a *disturbance input* is represented as

$$\dot{\xi} = f(\xi, k(\xi(t)), d(t)).$$

The system is called *input-to-state stable* (ISS) if there exists a $\mathcal{K}_\infty$ function α, and a $\mathcal{KL}$ function β,[1] such that for

---

[1] A continuous function $\gamma : \mathbb{R}_0^+ \to \mathbb{R}_0^+$, is said to belong to class $\mathcal{K}$ if it is strictly increasing and $\gamma(0) = 0$. A $\mathcal{K}$-function γ is said to belong to class $\mathcal{K}_\infty$ if $\gamma(s) \to \infty$ as $s \to \infty$. A continuous function $\beta : \mathbb{R}_0^+ \times \mathbb{R}_0^+ \to \mathbb{R}_0^+$ is said to belong to class $\mathcal{KL}$ if $\beta(r, t)$ belongs to class $\mathcal{K}_\infty$ for each fixed $t \geq 0$ and $\beta(r, t)$ is decreasing with respect to t and $\beta(r, t) \to 0$ as $t \to \infty$ for each fixed $r \geq 0$.

any initial state $\xi(0)$, the state $\xi(t)$ satisfies the following inequality:

$$\|\xi(t)\| \leq \beta(\|\xi(0)\|, t) + \alpha(\|d\|_\infty), \qquad \forall t \geq 0$$

Sufficient conditions on different stability criteria are given using Lyapunov functions. A *Lyapunov function* is a continuously differentiable function $V : D \to \mathbb{R}$, $D \subset \mathbb{R}^n$, for which the following conditions hold:

$$V(0) = 0, \qquad V(\xi) > 0 \quad \text{for all } \xi \neq 0.$$

The derivative of V along the solution of the closed loop system is given by

$$\dot{V}(\xi) = \frac{\partial V}{\partial \xi} f(\xi, k(\xi(t)))$$

The closed loop system is stable with respect to $\xi = 0$ if there exists a Lyapunov function V such that $\dot{V}(\xi) \leq 0$ for all $\xi \neq 0$. The closed loop system is asymptotically stable with respect to origin if there is a Lyapunov function V such that $\dot{V}(\xi) < 0$ for all $\xi \neq 0$. The closed loop system is globally asymptotically stable if there exists a radially unbounded[2] Lyapunov function with $\dot{V}(\xi) < 0$. The closed loop system is exponentially stable if there exists a Lyapunov function V and a positive constant λ such that

$$V(\xi(t)) \leq V(0)e^{-\lambda t}, \qquad \text{for all } t \geq 0.$$

The largest constant that can be used for λ in the above inequality is called the *rate of decay*. The closed loop system is ISS if there exists a radially unbounded Lyapunov function V and two $\mathcal{K}_\infty$ functions α_1 and α_2 such that

$$\dot{V}(\xi, d) \leq -\alpha_1(\|\xi\|) + \alpha_2(\|d\|) \qquad \text{for all } \xi, d.$$

2.2 Self-Triggered Implementation

To implement the control law (3) on a digital computer, the state of the plant is sampled at a sequence of time instants $t_0 = 0, t_1, t_2, \ldots$ The state of the plant at time instant t_i is $\xi(t_i)$. The computed control signal is given by $u(t_i) = k(\xi(t_i))$. The time instant t_i is called the *trigger time*. The control signal is applied to the plant immediately after it is available, and is held constant until the next trigger time t_{i+1}. The control signal computation time is generally in the microsecond range and can be considered to be negligible. Thus the control signal in the digital implementation of the system in (1) is given by

$$v(t) = v(t_i) \quad \text{for } t \in [t_i, t_{i+1}[\tag{4}$$

In a *time-triggered* implementation, the control engineer fixes a sampling period $T > 0$, and selects a periodic sequence of trigger times $t_i = iT$, for $i \in \mathbb{N}$. For *self-triggered* implementations, the sequence $\{t_i\}_{i \in \mathbb{N}}$ is computed online. At time t_i, in addition to the control signal, the next time instant t_{i+1} when the plant's state would be sampled is computed based on the current state $\xi(t_i)$. This computation is done based on a rule that is designed to ensure stability and desired performance of the control system.

We focus on linear control systems and briefly recall the self-triggered implementation of a linear controller achieving exponential stability as proposed in [18, 20]. Consider the

---
[2]A function $F : \mathbb{R}^n \to \mathbb{R}$ is called *radially unbounded* if $F(x) \to \infty$ as $\|x\| \to \infty$.

linear time-invariant control system (2). The system is rendered closed loop exponentially stable by using a controller

$$v(t) = -K\xi(t). \tag{5}$$

where $\xi(t)$ is the solution of (2) at time t, and matrices A, B, and K are of appropriate dimensions. The closed loop system is given by

$$\dot{\xi} = (A - BK)\xi \tag{6}$$

As the closed loop system is stable, there exists a Lyapunov function

$$V(\xi(t)) = \xi(t)^T P \xi(t) \tag{7}$$

where P is a symmetric positive definite matrix. The matrix P can be obtained by solving the following Lyapunov equation:

$$(A - BK)^T P + P(A - BK) + Q = 0 \tag{8}$$

where Q is a given symmetric positive definite matrix.

The Lyapunov function in (7) admits an exponential decay. Let V be a Lyapunov function satisfying (8) and let $\lambda_0 > 0$ denote its rate of decay. For self-triggered implementations, we fix $0 < \lambda < \lambda_0$ and define a function S upper-bounding the evolution of V:

$$S(t, \xi(t_k)) = V(\xi(t_k))e^{-\lambda(t - t_k)}. \tag{9}$$

Thus, at $t = t_k$, we have $S(t, \xi(t_k)) = V(\xi(t_k))$ and for $t_k < t < t_{k+1}$, we have $S(t, \xi(t_k)) > V(\xi(t))$. The constant λ in the function S specifies the desired performance of the control system.

The self-triggered implementation has to ensure that the value of $V(\xi(t))$ never goes beyond the value of $S(t, \xi(t_k))$. To ensure this, a *triggering function* is defined as

$$h(t, \xi(t_k)) = V(\xi(t)) - S(t, \xi(t_k)) \qquad \text{for all } t \geq t_k \tag{10}$$

Triggering happens when $h(t, \xi(t_k)) = 0$. At that moment, the plant's state is sampled again. The triggering scheme ensures that there exists a positive constant $\tau_{\min}$ such that for any i, we have $\tau_i = t_{i+1} - t_i \geq \tau_{\min}$. The value of $\tau_{\min}$ is effectively computable from the parameters of the control system and the Lyapunov function (see Theorem 5.1 in [18]).

To implement self-triggered control, the designer fixes two design parameters: a maximum duration $\tau_{\max}$ between two triggering instants that determines how long the system is allowed to operate in open loop, and a discretization parameter $\Delta > 0$ that puts a grid on the interval $[\tau_{\min}, \tau_{\max}]$. Then, a discrete version of the triggering function h from (10) is defined:

$$\widetilde{h}(n, \xi(t_k)) = V(\xi(t_k + n\Delta)) - S(n\Delta, \xi(t_k)) \tag{11}$$

The self-triggered implementation $\Gamma_l : \mathbb{R}^n \to \mathbb{R}^+$, $\Gamma_l(\xi(t_k)) = t_{k+1}$ for linear control systems is given by:

$$t_{k+1} = \max\{t_k + \tau_{\min}, t_k + n_k\Delta\} \tag{12}$$

$$n_k = \max\{s \leq \lfloor \frac{\tau_{\max}}{\Delta} \rfloor \mid \text{ for all } n \in [0, s] : \widetilde{h}(n, \xi(t_k)) \leq 0\}$$

Note that the worst case execution time depends on n_k and n_k depends on $\tau_{\max}$ and Δ. The self-triggered implementation scheme is feasible only if the time required to compute the trigger time t_{k+1} is less than $t_{k+1} - t_k$.

2.3 Problem: Trigger Time Computation

We now illustrate the problem of implementing the self-triggering scheme defined above through a motivating example of a batch reactor process originally described in [24] and used in [18, 20, 4] as a benchmark. The model of the plant is given by

$$\dot{\xi} = \begin{bmatrix} 1.38 & -0.20 & 6.71 & -5.67 \\ -0.58 & -4.29 & 0 & 0.67 \\ 1.06 & 4.27 & -6.65 & 5.89 \\ 0.04 & 4.27 & 1.34 & -2.10 \end{bmatrix} \xi + \begin{bmatrix} 0 & 0 \\ 5.67 & 0 \\ 1.13 & -3.14 \\ 1.13 & 0 \end{bmatrix} v.$$

The feedback controller

$$v = -\begin{bmatrix} 0.1006 & -0.2469 & -0.0952 & -0.2447 \\ 1.4099 & -0.1966 & 0.0139 & 0.0823 \end{bmatrix} \xi$$

renders the system exponentially stable. Let us denote the worst case execution time (WCET) of the computation of the trigger time t_{k+1} by τ_c. The rate of decay is $\lambda_0 = 0.41$. Setting $\lambda = 0.9\lambda_0$, we get $\tau_{min} = 18ms$. The authors of [20] chose $\tau_{max} = 358ms$ and $\Delta = 10ms$. The maximum possible value for n_k is thus 35. With these choices, we implement the trigger time computation given by (12) using the discrete triggering function (11) as a C program and cross-compile it using a GNU-based cross-compiling system. We then compute the WCET of the trigger time computation using aiT [11], a state-of-the-art worst case execution time analysis tool. The WCET of the trigger time is $29.793ms$ on a Leon 2 processor, assuming the processor frequency to be $100MHz$ (Most of the commercial implementations of Leon 2 processor have clock frequency below $100MHz$ [2]). As we see, the WCET is greater than τ_{min}. This implies that there may be cases where the controller will produce the next trigger time at an instant when the trigger time has already passed. This clearly shows the infeasibility of the implementation of the triggering rule provided in [20]. (In simulating the performance of their controller, the authors of [20] ignore trigger computation times.)

Note that we cannot increase the value of τ_{min} as it depends on the parameters of the control system, and increasing τ_{min} may cause the self-triggered implementation of the control system to violate stability requirements. The self-triggered implementation may be made feasible by decreasing the value of τ_{max}, as τ_{max} is a design parameter and the worst case execution time is directly proportional to τ_{max}. Decreasing the value of τ_{max} does not have any effect on the performance of the control system. However, it causes the trigger of the controller to occur more frequently than what the designer in [20] expected, and thus increases communication between the controller and the actuators (negating much of the benefits of self-triggering). Thus, the performance advantages of self-triggered implementations must be evaluated taking the computation time for the trigger time into account.

3. HYBRID IMPLEMENTATION

We now present a hybrid implementation scheme for self-triggered control systems. Our implementation utilizes a time-vs-space tradeoff, and memoizes trigger times for future reuse. We assume that a fixed-size piece of memory is available to store the *memoization table*, which maps a state of the system (a vector in $\mathbb{R}^n$) to a trigger time. The memoization table can be accessed using indices computed from a state as described later.

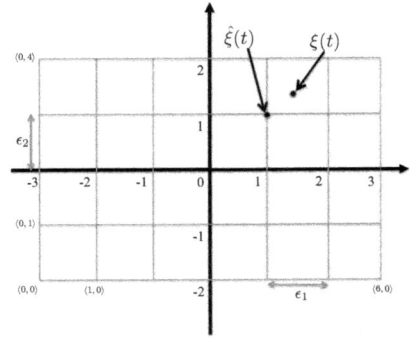

Figure 1: Memoization region and table

3.1 Memoized Trigger Time Computation

For the implementation, we fix a *memoization region* $[-w, w] \subseteq \mathbb{R}^n$ of the control system around the origin. We want to memoize the computed trigger time for any state in this region. Since the memoization table is finite, we discretize the memoization region using a *quantization factor* $\epsilon \in \mathbb{R}^n$. We describe the choice of ϵ in Section 3.3. The memoization region is represented as a multi-dimensional array, where each element is a trigger time. The number of entries in the table is given by

$$N = \prod_{i=1}^{n} \frac{2w_i}{\epsilon_i} \qquad (13)$$

As an example, Figure 1 shows an example system with two state variables and the memoization region $[-3, 3] \times [-2, 2]$. The quantization factor $\epsilon = (1, 1)$, that is, each state is divided into intervals of size one unit. There are 24 different entries in the memoization table, and they are indexed as shown in the figure, from $(0, 0)$ at the bottom left corner to $(5, 3)$. The quantized value of a state ξ is the state corresponding to the closest grid point to its left and bottom, e.g., the state $\xi = (1.3, 1.3)$ is quantized to $\hat{\xi} = (1.0, 1.0)$, with index $(4, 3)$. Note that the difference between $\hat{\xi}(t)$ and $\xi(t)$ is bounded by the quantization factor ϵ, thus $\hat{\xi}(t) \geq \xi(t) - \epsilon$.

Algorithm 3.1 shows the pseudo-code for trigger-time computation with memoization. The function **findTriggerTime** takes as input the system state $\xi(t_k)$ at the kth sample time t_k and returns t_{k+1}, the next time the plant should be sampled. The memoization table **Memo** stores trigger times. The function **findIndex** takes the state $\xi(t_k)$ and returns the index of its discretization, if within the memoization region, or a special value denoting that the current state is outside the memoization region. In case the current state is outside the memoization region, the trigger time computation is scheduled (line 5). In case the current state is within the memoization region, the memoization table is first checked (line 7). If the trigger time has been pre-computed, it is returned (line 11). Otherwise, the trigger time computation is scheduled with the discretized state (line 9). When the computation is done, the memoization table is updated with the computed value.

The statement

$$\min(\tau_{min}, \text{schedule trigger}(\hat{\xi}))$$

Algorithm 3.1: Trigger Time Computation with Memoization.

Input: $\xi(t_k)$, the state of the system at time instant t_k

Output: t_{k+1}, the next trigger time of the controller

```
1  ;
2  function findDeliveryTime(ξ);
3  begin
4     ⟨s₁ ... sₙ⟩ = findIndex(ξ);
5     if outsideRange(⟨s₁ ... sₙ⟩) then
6        return min(τ_min, schedule trigger(ξ));
7     else
8        if Memo[s₁ ... sₙ] is not found then
9           ξ̂ = quantizeState(⟨s₁ ... sₙ⟩);
10          return min(τ_min, schedule trigger(ξ̂));
11       else
12          return Memo[s₁ ... sₙ];
13       end
14    end
15 end
```

indicates that the task of computing the trigger time is scheduled as a background task of lower priority than the control loop. If the task finishes before $\tau_{\min}$, its value is returned, otherwise, the plant is sampled again at $t_k + \tau_{\min}$. That is, if the background task is not finished in time, the controller reverts to a time-triggered implementation with period $\tau_{\min}$. On completion of the task to compute the trigger time, the memoization table Memo is updated with the computed value (in case the state was within the memoization region). Moreover, in our implementation, when one trigger time computation is running, no other **trigger** task is spawned, and the controller works in a time-triggered mode using the minimum trigger time τ_{min} as the sampling period. We call this implementation scheme *hybrid*.

3.2 Dynamic Choice of Memoization Region

In Section 3.1 we assume that in the steady state the control system operates at the origin, and we fix the memoization region to be $[-w, w] \subseteq \mathbb{R}^n$. If a control system has only one operating point, the memoization table can be precomputed offline for all the states in the memoization region around the operating point instead of computing the table online. However, in reality, a control system may have a number of operating points, and the system can move from one operating point to another during its life cycle. All these operating points may not be known to the designer of the system a priori. For example, one of the states of the batch reactor process introduced in Section 2.3 is the temperature of the reactor. The desired temperature of the reactor is different during the different reaction phases. It is not possible to store the memoization table for all operating points in the memory.

We handle the change in operating point during runtime by online reconfiguration of a parameter used in Algorithm 3.1. Suppose the operating point changes from ξ_1 to ξ_2. We assume that the size of the memoization region remains the same for any operating point. Thus, the memoization region changes from $[\xi_1 - w, \xi_1 + w]$ to $[\xi_2 - w, \xi_2 + w]$. Even though there may be an overlap between the old and new memoization regions, the data in the overlapped region is not reused, as that data needs to be moved to a new location in the memoization table, and this operation

may take many CPU cycles. The findIndex function in Algorithm 3.1 depends on an offset vector that maps a state in the memoization region to a particular position in the memoization table. When the operating point changes, we perform the following two actions. First, the memoization table is cleared. Second, the offset parameter is reconfigured to reflect the new memoization region.

3.3 Effect of State Quantization

As our memoization based implementation employs quantization of the state of the control system, we need to take into account the effect on the quantization on the triggering time. Since the trigger time computation does not have a closed form formula, correcting the triggering rule to take into account the quantization error is not straightforward. Rather, we show how the quantization error influences the behavior of the closed loop system in the steady state.

To show how the quantization error on the states effect the overall behavior of a linear control system, we resort to a result proved by Almeida, Silvestre, and Pascoal [4]. Consider the following linear time-invariant control system:

$$\dot{\xi}(t) = A\xi(t) + Bv(t) + \delta(t), \qquad \xi(t) \in \mathbb{R}^n, v(t) \in \mathbb{R}^m, \quad (14)$$

where $\delta(t)$ is exogenous disturbance with bounded $\mathcal{L}_\infty$ norm δ_b. Note that the system in (14) is obtained by introducing an additive disturbance term $\delta(t)$ in the system in (2). In the presence of disturbance it is not possible to render the system (14) asymptotically stable to the origin. Rather, it was shown in [4] that by appropriately modifying the triggering rule in (10), it is possible to ensure that the system is exponentially stable with respect to a region around the origin.

Consider the Lyapunov function in (7). It can be shown that in the presence of bounded disturbance, the feedback law in (5) can render the states of the system (2) exponentially in a region defined by

$$V(\xi(t)) \leq \max\{V(\xi(t_0))e^{-\gamma_0(t-t_0)}, V_b\}, \quad (15)$$

where $\xi(t_0)$ denotes the initial state of the evolution at time t_0. Note that as $t \to \infty$, $V(\xi(t))$ is inside a region defined by V_b. For the system (14), V_b is given by

$$V_b = \frac{4\lambda_{\max}^3(P)\delta_b^2}{(\lambda_{\min}(Q) - \gamma_0\lambda_{\max}(P))^2}, \quad (16)$$

where P and Q are matrices in the Lyapunov Equation (8).

Now the performance function in (9) need be modified according to the behavior of $V(\xi(t))$ in (15). The modified specification function is given by

$$S'(t, \xi(t_k)) = \max\{V(\xi(t_k))e^{-\gamma(t-t_k)}, V_b\}, \quad (17)$$

where $0 < \gamma < \gamma_0$. The triggering function in (10) is now modified as follows:

$$h(t, \xi(t_k)) = U(t, \xi(t)) - S'(t, \xi(t_k)), \quad (18)$$

where $U(t, \xi(t))$ is given by

$$U(t, \xi(t_k)) = V(\xi(t_k)) + \mu(t, \xi(t_k)), \quad (19)$$

with $\mu(t, \xi(t_k)) = \beta(t)(2\|P\xi(t_k)\| + \lambda_{\max(P)}\beta(t))$ and $\beta(t) = \frac{\delta_b}{\sigma}(e^{\sigma(t-t_k)} - 1)$. The value of σ can be chosen as any value between $\|A\|$ and $\frac{1}{2}\lambda_{\max}(A + A^T)$.

As shown in [4], the self-triggered implementation in (12) with the triggering function given in (18) renders the states of the system (14) in finite time to the set $\{\xi(t) \in \mathbb{R}^n : V(\xi(t)) \leq V_b\}$. We call this set the *stability region*.

We model the quantization error arising from the memoization based implementation of a self-triggered linear control system as the disturbance δ in (14). For a state $\xi(t)$ the control signal and the trigger time is computed by its quantized value $\hat{\xi}(t)$, where $\xi(t) - \hat{\xi}(t) = \bar{\epsilon}(t)$. The computed control signal is given by

$$\hat{v}(t) = -K\hat{\xi}(t) = v(t) + K\bar{\epsilon}(t).$$

Plugging the value of the control signal in (2) we get

$$\dot{\xi}(t) = A\xi(t) + Bv(t) + BK\bar{\epsilon}(t), \qquad \xi(t) \in \mathbb{R}^n, v(t) \in \mathbb{R}^m. \tag{20}$$

Comparing (20) with (14) we get that the disturbance arising due to quantization in the states is given by

$$\delta(t) = BK\bar{\epsilon}(t). \tag{21}$$

Suppose we have been given an upper bound $V_b^{\max}$ on V_b as the specification. To find the upper bound of the quantization factor we proceed as follows: The upper bound on the $\mathcal{L}_\infty$ norm of $\delta(t)$ is given by

$$\delta_b^{\max} = \sqrt{\frac{(\lambda_{min}(Q) - \gamma_0 \lambda_{\max}(P))^2}{4\lambda_{\max}^3(P)} V_b^{\max}}. \tag{22}$$

The upper bound on the quantization factor ϵ is found by solving the following optimization problem:

$$\begin{aligned} \text{maximize} \quad & \epsilon_1 \\ \text{subject to} \quad & \|BK\epsilon_1[1\ 1\ 1\ 1]^T\| \leq \delta_b^{\max}, \end{aligned} \tag{23}$$

where $\bar{\epsilon}(t) = \epsilon_1[1\ 1\ 1\ 1]^T$. Here we have chosen the quantization factors in all dimensions to be equal. The optimization problem in (23) is a convex one. The solution of the optimization problem provides the upper bound on the quantization factor of the state.

THEOREM 1. *Consider the linear control system (2) with stabilizing controller (5) and Lyapunov function V obtained from (7) and (8). Let $V_b^{\max}$ be a given bound on the stability region. Suppose the controller is implemented using the hybrid implementation using Algorithm 3.1, using a discretization ϵ given by (23). Then, the state ξ is guaranteed to converge to the set $\{\xi \in \mathbb{R}^n \mid V(\xi) \leq V_b^{\max}\}$.*

3.4 Fixed-point Representation

The trigger time is computed in (12) as a floating point entity. A single precision floating point value needs four bytes of space in memory. To save memory, we can store the trigger time as a fixed-point number. The trigger times are always positive, thus we do not need to deal with the sign of a number. The fixed-point representation of a trigger time is given as a pair $\langle n, m \rangle$ consisting of a *length* $n \in \mathbb{N}$, and a *length of the fractional part* $m \in \mathbb{N}$. The length of the integer part is $n - m$, if $n > m$, and 0 otherwise. To achieve the highest precision for a chosen length m of the representation, the length of the fractional part m is chosen such that the maximum trigger time $\tau_{\max}$ satisfies $2^{n-m-1} \leq \tau_{\max} < 2^{n-m}$. In this case, the maximum error in the fixed-point representation is given by 2^{-m}. For example, if the range of the trigger time to be represented is given by $[0.020, 0.400]$ and we choose $n = 8$, then $m = 9$ and the bound on the error in the representation is given by 2^{-9}.

Given a computed trigger time t, its fixed-point representation can be stored as an integer given by $\hat{t} = \lfloor(t \times 2^m)\rfloor$. From the fixed-point representation $\hat{t}$, the floating point value $\tilde{t}$ of the trigger time is obtained by $\tilde{t} = 2^{-m}\hat{t}$. To use fixed-point representations in Algorithm 3.1, line 9 and line 11 are adapted appropriately. Note that it is always safe to use $\tilde{t}$ obtained from the memoization table instead of using t, as $\tilde{t} \leq t$.

4. NONLINEAR SYSTEMS

We now extend the hybrid implementation to self-triggered implementations of nonlinear control systems.

Triggering Rule. Consider the nonlinear dynamical system (1). We recall the setting of [6]. The objective of the controller is to ensure that an invariant on the state of the plant, given as the specification, is never violated. Henceforth, we will refer to this specification as *invariant specification*. The idea behind a self-triggered implementation is that at any time instant t, the difference between the current state $x(t)$ and the last measured state $x(t_i)$ for $i \in \mathbb{N}$ is bounded in such a way that the invariant specification on the closed loop system is not violated. This error is referred as the *measurement error* and is given by

$$e(t) = \xi(t_i) - \xi(t) \quad \text{for } t \in [t_i, t_{i+1}]. \tag{24}$$

The dynamics of the closed loop control system is given by:

$$\dot{\xi} = f(\xi, k(\xi + e)). \tag{25}$$

Now if the control law is designed to render the system (1) ISS with respect to measurement error, there exists a Lyapunov function V for the system satisfying the following inequality:

$$\dot{V} \leq -\alpha_1(\|x\|) + \alpha_2(\|e\|). \tag{26}$$

where α_1 and α_2 are $\mathcal{K}_\infty$ functions. To maintain stability of the closed loop system (25), we have to ensure that $\dot{V} < 0$. This can be ensured if the following condition holds:

$$\alpha_2(\|e\|) \leq \kappa\alpha_1(\|x\|), \qquad \kappa > 0. \tag{27}$$

The triggering strategy in a nonlinear control system is designed based on the invariant specification on the states of the system around the equilibrium point. If a Lyapunov function satisfying the inequality in (26) can be discovered for the system, then an invariant on the admissible error can be derived from the invariant on the states using (27). As shown in [6], these two invariants can be used to derive a closed form formula z to compute the next sampling time t_{k+1} from the sampled state $\xi(t_k)$ at the current sampling time t_k.

The self-triggered implementation $\Gamma_{nl} : \mathbb{R}^n \to \mathbb{R}^+$, $\Gamma_{nl}(\xi(t_k)) = t_{k+1}$ for nonlinear control systems is given by:

$$t_{k+1} = z(\xi(t_k)). \tag{28}$$

Hybrid Implementation. Given the triggering rule (28), the hybrid implementation is similar to the implementation of linear controllers, where we discretize the state space and memoize computed trigger times.

Since there is a closed form formula to compute the triggering time, we can correct the triggering times by taking into account the maximum possible error introduced by quantizing the states. To find the maximum possible error introduced in the trigger time, we solve the following optimization problem:

$$\begin{aligned}
\text{maximize} \quad & \tau_e \\
\text{Subject to} \quad & \tau = z(\xi) \quad \hat{\tau} = z(\hat{\xi}) \\
& \tau_e = \tau - \hat{\tau} \\
& \xi - \hat{\xi} \le \epsilon \quad \xi \ge \hat{\xi}.
\end{aligned} \tag{29}$$

In this optimization problem, ξ denotes the sampled state and $\hat{\xi}$ denotes the quantized state obtained from ξ. We denote by τ and $\hat{\tau}$ the trigger time computed based on ξ and $\hat{\xi}$ respectively. We maximize τ_e, the difference between τ and $\hat{\tau}$, subject to additional constraints that the difference between ξ and $\hat{\xi}$ is bounded by the quantization factor ϵ and $\xi \ge \hat{\xi}$.

For a given state $\xi(t_k)$, if the maximum value of τ_e is obtained as τ_e^{max} then the triggering time is computed by the following modified form of (28):

$$t_{k+1} = z(\hat{\xi}(t_k)) - \tau_e^{max}. \tag{30}$$

Note that unlike linear control systems, the control signal in a nonlinear control system is computed based on $\xi(t_k)$ instead of $\hat{\xi}(t_k)$.

5. EXPERIMENTS

Experimental Setup. In our experiments we have used the Truetime simulator [10] to implement the control tasks for our example control systems and simulate the systems under different conditions. We choose PowerPC MPC5xx [1] and Leon2 [2] processors as the two target platforms on top of which the embedded control applications are built. The PowerPC MPC5xx is widely used in Delphi Corporation and Robert Bosch GmbH to develop engine controllers. The Leon 2 processor was developed by European Space Research and Technology Centre to be used for European space projects. The worst-case execution times [28] for control computation and trigger time computation on the target processors have been obtained using the worst-case execution time analysis tool aiT [11]. The control computations and trigger time computations are implemented in C, and then cross-compiled for respective processors using GNU-based cross compilation systems. The worst-case execution times are computed by aiT based on the compiled binary code. The computation of trigger time involves computation of square root function and exponential function. We implement the square root computation using the *Babylonian method* [14]. The exponential function is computed by expanding it as a Taylor series.

We report CPU times and communications costs. Given a time interval, CPU times are reported as the total CPU time required by all control tasks over the time interval. The communication cost is the number of control tasks run over a time interval. This captures the cost of communication, since each control task requires transmitting the plant state from the sensors to the controller and the actuation signal from the controller to the actuators.

5.1 Examples

We demonstrate our results on a benchmark linear control system: a *batch reactor processor*, and a benchmark nonlinear control system: a *jet engine compressor*.

Linear System: Batch Reactor Process. First, we present our results on the batch reactor process from Sec-

tion 2.3. The Lyapunov function for the closed loop system has been computed using (8) with $Q = I_4$. With this choice of Q, we have $\lambda_{\max}(P) = 1.2185$ and $\lambda_{\min}(Q) = 1$. The other parameters are chosen in accordance with [4]: $\tau_{\min} = 39.8ms$, $\tau_{\max} = 720ms$, $\Delta = 10ms$, $\gamma_0 = 0.08207$, $\gamma = 0.008207$. We compute the values of $\tau_{\max}$ on both PowerPC and Leon2 processors to ensure that the trigger computation time τ_c does not exceed the minimum trigger time $\tau_{\min}$. The values of modified $\tau_{\max}$ are $510ms$ and $270ms$ on PowerPC and Leon2, respectively.

Suppose we want the state of the system to converge in a stability region $V_b^{\max}$ of size 0.5 when the system is free from any external disturbance. The upper bound on the quantization factor can be found to be 0.04346 by first finding the value of $\delta_b^{\max}$ for $V_b^{\max} = 0.5$ using (22), and then solving the optimization problem in (23). We choose the quantization factor to be 0.04 in each dimension. We store the trigger times in the memoization table as a 8-bit fixed-point number. The fixed-point representation is given by $\langle 8, 8 \rangle$, as $0.5 < \tau_{\max} < 1$. The trigger time retrieved from the memoization table may by at most 2^{-8} less than its computed value. We choose the memoization region to be $[-0.5, 0.5]$ in each dimension. With the quantization factor to be 0.04, the number of entries in the memoization table is computed by (13) to be 390625. As each entry of the memoization table takes 1 byte, the memoization table requires at most 381.47KB. Note that if this amount of memory is not available, we have two options. First, we may increase the value of the quantization factor which in turn increases the bound on the size of the stability region. Second, we may shrink the memoization region without changing the quantization factor. The second option ensures that the specification on the size of the stability region is met, but we memoize trigger time for the states in a narrower region, thus the computation time grows.

We compare three different implementations for the batch reactor processor: (i) a time-triggered implementation using the sampling period $\tau_{\min}$, (ii) a self-triggered implementation using the triggering rule (12), where the triggering function is given by (18). The maximum trigger time $\tau_{\max}$ is updated to ensure that the computation of the trigger time is guaranteed to be finished before the minimum trigger time $\tau_{\min}$ ($\tau_{max} = 510ms$ for PowerPC and $\tau_{max} = 270ms$ for Leon2 processor), and (iii) our hybrid implementation, without decreasing the maximum trigger time ($\tau_{max} = 720ms$). We fall back to the time-triggered implementation using trigger time $\tau_{\min}$ when the trigger time computation takes more than $\tau_{\min}$ time.

We simulate the self-triggered batch reactor process on three scenarios: (a) the system is free from any external disturbance (Disturbance free), (b) the system is subjected to a periodic external disturbance signal of pulse shape with amplitude 8, period 800 samples, pulse width 40 samples, zero phase delay, and sample time $10ms$ (Disturbance scenario 1), and (c) the system is subjected to a normally distributed random disturbance signal with mean 0, variance 1, and sample time $1ms$ (Disturbance scenario 2).

The evolution of the state of the batch reactor process with initial state $\langle 2, 2, 2, 2 \rangle$ is shown in Figure 2 for the case when no external disturbance is present. While the state of the time-triggered implementation and the self-triggered implementation eventually go to the origin, the state of the

(a) TT

(b) ST

(c) Hybrid

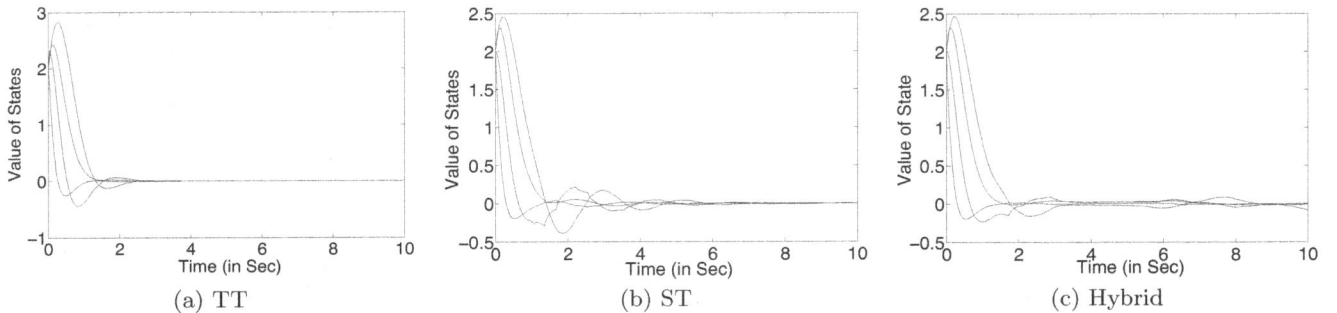

Figure 2: Evolution of states of a batch reactor process from initial state $\langle 2, 2, 2, 2 \rangle$ for (a) time-triggered (TT), (b) self-triggered (ST), and (c) Hybrid implementation

Implementation	Disturbance Free		Disturbance Scenario 1		Disturbance Scenario 2	
	PowerPC	Leon2	PowerPC	Leon2	PowerPC	Leon2
TT	0.164s	0.226s	0.164s	0.226s	0.164s	0.226s
ST	167.514s	342.554s	167.188s	341.117s	167.691s	342.541s
Hybrid	0.959s	1.824s	4.039s	7.336s	31.322s	57.360s

Table 1: CPU time required for different implementations of the controller of the batch reactor process running for 2000s

hybrid implementation eventually enters the region defined by $V_b^{\max}$ and remains there forever.

Table 1 and Table 2 show the CPU time and communication cost for different implementations of the controller for the batch reactor process for 2000s runtime. From Table 1, we see that the naive self-triggered implementation takes significantly more CPU time in comparison to the time-triggered implementation. The hybrid implementation brings the required CPU time close to that of the time-triggered implementation. Table 2 shows that the number of communications from the plant to the controller improves significantly in self-triggered implementations, as claimed in the existing literature on self-triggered control systems. The Hybrid implementation maintains similar communication cost as the naive self-triggered implementations. For self-triggered implementation, the number of communications is always more for Leon2 processor, as τ_{max} for Leon2 is less than that for PowerPC. For Hybrid implementation, the number of communications is more for Leon2 processor than that for PowerPC as the trigger time computation takes more time with the Leon2 processor than with the PowerPC processor and the system remains in time-triggered mode when the trigger time computation is running.

Figure 3 shows how the CPU time required for the controller of the batch reactor process for different implementations using Leon2 processor vary for different duration of runtime between $500s$ and $5000s$ when there is no external disturbance acting on the system. The figure shows that the naive self-triggered implementation always takes significantly more computation time than the time-triggered implementation. However, our hybrid implementation is always close to the time-triggered implementation in terms of computation time, and as time progresses and the memoization table gets filled up with trigger times, the difference between the computation time for our hybrid implementation and that of the time-triggered implementation slowly decreases.

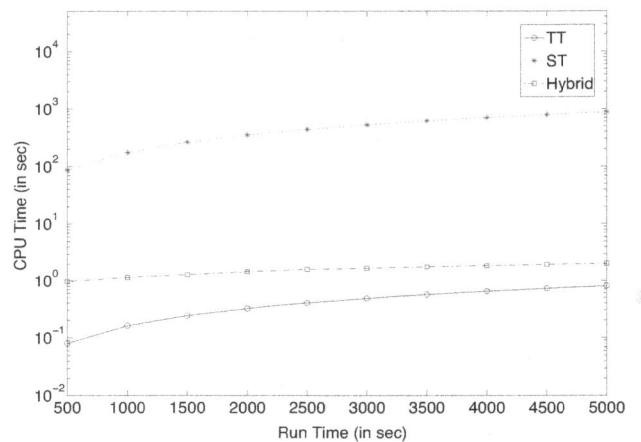

Figure 3: CPU time required for batch reactor process for different implementations using the Leon2 processor for different running times in the disturbance-free scenario

Nonlinear System: Jet Engine Compressor. We illustrate our experimental results on nonlinear self triggered control systems using the standard benchmark of a jet engine compressor. The model of the system originally appeared in [15]. In [6], it was adapted to translate the desired equilibrium point to the origin as follows:

$$\dot{\xi}_1 = -\xi_2 - \frac{3}{2}\xi_1^2 - \frac{1}{2}\xi_1^3$$
$$\dot{\xi}_2 = \frac{1}{\beta^2}(\xi_1 - u) \tag{31}$$

where ξ_1 and ξ_2 denote the mass flow and pressure rise in the compressor respectively. The symbol β is a constant

Implementation	Disturbance Free		Disturbance Scenario 1		Disturbance Scenario 2	
	PowerPC	Leon2	PowerPC	Leon2	PowerPC	Leon2
TT	50251	50251	50251	50251	50251	50251
ST	5731	7422	14735	15786	5974	7422
Hybrid	5868	5891	15847	15868	6932	7343

Table 2: Communication cost for different implementations of the controller of the batch reactor process running for 2000s

positive parameter. The output of the controller u denotes the throttle mass flow.

A control law $u = k(\xi_1, \xi_2)$ was designed in [6] to render the system in (31) globally asymptotically stable. The control law is given by:

$$u = \xi_1 + \frac{\beta^2}{4}(z(\xi_1^2 + 1) + 3\xi_1^2 y + \xi_1^3 + \xi_1 + 3y) \quad (32)$$

where $\quad y = (3\xi_1^2 + 2\xi_2 - \xi_1)/(\xi_1^2 + 1) \quad$ and $z = 2\xi_1 y(y - 3) + \xi_1^2(4y - 6)$. By substituting u with its corresponding expression, the closed loop system becomes

$$\dot{\xi_1} = -\frac{1}{2}(\xi_1^2 + 1)(\xi_1 + y)$$
$$\dot{\xi_2} = -(\xi_1^2 + 1)y \quad (33)$$

The following ISS Lyapunov function is provided in [6]

$$V = 1.46\xi_1^2 - 0.35\xi_1 y + 1.16y^2,$$

which is computed using SOStools [23]. Using this Lyapunov function, this can be shown that the state of the closed loop system $\xi = (\xi_1, y)^T$ and the measurement error on the state $e = (e_1, e_2)^T$ are related by the following inequality:

$$0.90\|e\|^2 \leq 0.74\nu^2\|\xi\|^2$$

Now based on the specification that the state ξ is contained in the invariant set $\{\xi \in \mathbb{R}^n | V(\xi) = 27.04\}$, the following formula is provided in [6] to compute the trigger time:

$$t_{k+1}(\xi(t_k)) = \frac{29\xi_1(t_k) + \|\xi(t_k)\|^2}{5.36\|\xi(t_k)\|\xi_1(t_k)^2 + \|\xi(t_k)\|^2}\tau^*,$$

where $\tau^* = 7.63ms$ for $\nu = 0.33$.

The operating point of the jet engine is $\xi_1 = 0, \xi_2 = 0$. The state ξ_1 is mass flow, which is a positive quantity. The state ξ_2 is pressure rise, which may be both positive and negative. We choose the memoization region to be $\langle \xi_1 \in [0, 0.5], \xi_2 \in [-1, 1]\rangle$. The minimum trigger time $\tau_{min} = \tau^* = 7.63ms$. We choose the maximum trigger time $\tau_{max} = 250ms$, and store the trigger times in the memoization table as a fixed-point number with representation $\langle 8, 10\rangle$. This enables us to store the trigger time in 1 byte. We assume that we have 256KB memory available to store the memoization table. With this amount of memory, the quantization factor can be chosen to be 0.002 in each dimension, using (13). For this quantization factor, we solve the optimization problemn (29) to find out the value of τ_e^{max}. The optimization problem is not convex and we solve the problem numerically by dividing the region $\langle \xi_1 \in [0, 0.5], \xi_2 \in [-1, 1]\rangle$ into a grid with precision 0.0001 and exhaustively searching all the points on the grid. We find that the value of τ_e^{max} for the values of ξ_1 in the range $[0, 0.25]$ is fairly high (greater than the minimal trigger time 7.63ms). We shift the memoization region in the ξ_1 direction

to exclude the region from the memoization region. Thus our memoization region is $\langle \xi_1 \in [0.25, 0.75], \xi_2 \in [-1, 1]\rangle$. In the memoization region, τ_e^{max} is 6.634ms.

We consider two scenarios to compare the performance of the hybrid implementation with the time-triggered and self-triggered implementations without memoization. In both scenarios we consider the evolution of the system for $2000s$ in the presence of external disturbances. In the first scenario, the disturbance signal is a periodic pulse signal with amplitude 8, period 400 samples, pulse width 40 samples, zero phase delay and sample time $10ms$. In the second scenario, the disturbance is a normally distributed random signal with mean 1, variance 1, and sample time $1ms$. We do not show results for the scenario when no external disturbance is present, as the memoization-based implementation does not provide any benefit due to not including a region around the origin (ξ_1 is in the range $[0, 0.25]$). Table 3 shows the CPU time and the communication cost for the two processors for different implementations of the controller for runs of length $2000s$. The results show that a self-triggered implementation without memoization itself gives significant savings on both the CPU time and number of communications. However, with memoization, we can gain even more in CPU time with a slight increase in the number of communications. The number of communications increases in the hybrid implementation as we need to decrease the trigger time to correct any error arising due to quantization of states in the trigger time computation. On both processors, the time to compute the trigger time is always less than the minimum trigger time τ_{min}. Thus the hybrid implementation never falls back to the time-triggered implementation, and the number of communications for both the processors are the same.

Figure 4 shows how the CPU time required for jet engine compressor for different implementations using PowerPC processor vary in the disturbance scenario 2 for different duration of runtime between $500s$ and $5000s$. The figure shows that the savings in CPU time grows with time from the time-triggered implementation to self-triggered implementation without memoization, and also from the self-triggered implementation without memoization to the hybrid implementation. As time progresses, more and more trigger times are memoized, and the ratio of cache hit to cache miss also increases. Thus the CPU time requirement keeps on decreasing with time for the hybrid implementation.

Acknowledgements. We thank AbsInt for making the aiT tool available to us for free. We thank Adolfo Anta, Manuel Mazo Jr., Paulo Tabuada, and Majid Zamani for helpful discussions. We thank Toyota Motors for partially sponsoring the research.

Implementation	Disturbance Scenario 1			Disturbance Scenario 2		
	Computation		Commu-	Computation		Commu-
	PowerPC	Leon2	nication	PowerPC	Leon2	nication
TT	1.094s	1.732s	262122	1.094s	1.732s	262122
ST	0.338s	0.473s	18729	0.303s	0.422s	16447
Hybrid	0.190s	0.315s	19009	0.117s	0.211s	16464

Table 3: CPU time and communication cost for different implementations of the controller of the jet engine compressor running for 2000s

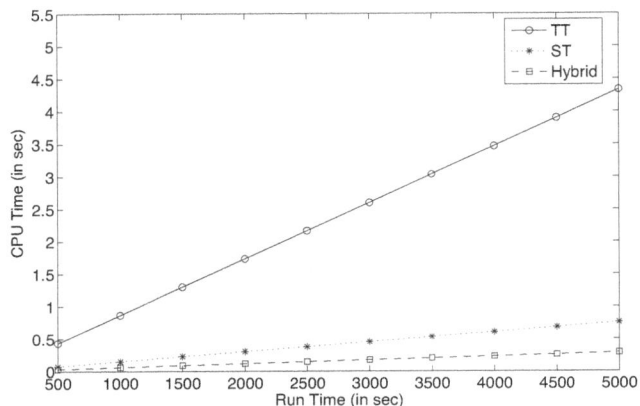

Figure 4: CPU time required for the jet engine compressor for different implementations on the PowerPC processor for different running times for disturbance scenario 2

6. REFERENCES

[1] Powerpc 5xx controllers. http://www.freescale.com/webapp/sps/site/taxonomy.jsp?code=DRMCRMPC500MC.

[2] Leon2 processor. http://vlsicad.eecs.umich.edu/BK/Slots/cache/www.gaisler.com/products/leon2/leon.html.

[3] A. Alessio and A. Bemporad. A survey on explicit model predictive control. In *Nonlinear Model Predictive Control*, volume 384 of *LNCIS*, pages 345–369. Springer, 2009.

[4] J. Almeida, C. Silvestre, and A. M. Pascoal. Self-triggered state feedback control of linear plants under bounded disturbances. In *Proc. CDC*, pages 7588–7593, 2010.

[5] A. Anta, R. Majumdar, I. Saha, and P. Tabuada. Automatic verification of control system implementations. In *Proc. EMSOFT*, pages 9–18, 2010.

[6] A. Anta and P. Tabuada. To sample or not to sample: Self-triggered control for nonlinear systems. *IEEE Transaction on Automatic Control*, 55(9):2030–2042, 2010.

[7] K.-E. Årzén. A simple event-based PID controller. In *Proc. IFAC*, volume 18, pages 423–428, 1999.

[8] K. J. Åström and B. Wittenmark. *Computer-controlled systems: theory and design*. Prentice-Hall, Inc., 2nd edition, 1990.

[9] A. Bemporad, M. Morari, V. Dua, and E. N. Pistikopoulos. The explicit linear quadratic regulator for constrained systems. *Automatica*, 38(1):3–20, 2002.

[10] A. Cervin, D. Henriksson, B. Lincoln, J. Eker, and K.-E. Årzén. How does control timing affect performance? Analysis and simulation of timing using Jitterbug and TrueTime. *IEEE Control Systems Magazine*, 23(3):16–30, 2003.

[11] R. Heckmann and C. Ferdinand. Worst-case execution time prediction by static program analysis. White paper, AbsInt Angewandte Informatik GmbH, 2009.

[12] W. P. M. H. Heemels, J. H. Sandee, and P. P. J. Van Den Bosch. Analysis of event-driven controllers for linear systems. *Intl. J. of Control*, 81(4):571–590, 2008.

[13] H. K. Khalil. *Nonlinear Systems*. Prentice Hall, 2002.

[14] O. Kosheleva. Babylonian method of computing the square root: Justifications based on fuzzy techniques and on computational complexity. In *Annual Meeting of the North American Fuzzy Information Processing Society (NAFIPS)*, pages 1–6, 2009.

[15] M. Krstic and P. Kokotovic. Lean backstepping design for a jet engine compressor model. In *Proceedings of IEEE Conf. Control App.*, pages 1047–1052, 1995.

[16] J. LaSalle and S. Lefschetz. *Stability by Lyapunov's Direct Method*. Academic Press, Inc., 1961.

[17] M. Lemmon, T. Chantem, X. S. Hu, and M. Zyskowski. On self-triggered full information H-infinity controllers. In *Proc. HSCC*, pages 371–384, 2007.

[18] M. Mazo Jr., A. Anta, and P. Tabuada. On self-triggered control for linear systems: Guarantees and complexity. In *Proc. ECC*, 2009.

[19] M. Mazo Jr. and P. Tabuada. On event-triggered and self-triggered control over sensor/actuator networks. In *Proc. CDC*, pages 435–440, 2008.

[20] M. Mazo Jr. and P. Tabuada. Input-to-state stability of self-triggered control systems. In *Proc. CDC*, pages 928–933, 2009.

[21] R. Obermaisser, C. E. Salloum, B. Huber, and H. Kopetz. From a federated to an integrated architecture. *IEEE Transaction on Computer-Aided Design of Integrated Circuits and Systems*, 28(7):956–965, 2009.

[22] A. Podelski and S. Wagner. Region stability proofs for hybrid systems. In *Proc. FORMATS*, pages 320–335, 2007.

[23] S. Prajna, A. Papachristodoulou, P. Seiler, and P. A. Parrilo. SOSTOOLS: Control applications and new developments. In *Proc. IEEE CASC*, pages 315–320, 2004.

[24] H. H. Rosenbrock. *Computer-Aided Control System Design*. Academic Press, 1974.

[25] J. Sandee. *Event-driven control in theory and practice: Tradeoffs in software and control performance*. PhD thesis, Technische Universeteit Endhoven, 2006.

[26] M. Velasco, P. Martí, and J. M. Fuertes. The self-triggered task model for real-time control systems. In *Work In Progress Proceedings of RTSS*, pages 67–70, 2003.

[27] X. Wang and M. Lemmon. Self-triggered feedback control systems with finite gain $\mathcal{L}_2$ stability. *IEEE Transaction on Automatic Control*, 54(3):452–467, 2009.

[28] R. Wilhelm, J. Engblom, A. Ermedahl, N. Holsti, S. Thesing, D. Whalley, G. Bernat, C. Ferdinand, R. Heckmann, T. Mitra, F. Mueller, I. Puaut, P. Puschner, J. Staschulat, and P. Stenström. The worst-case execution-time problem – overview of methods and survey of tools. *ACM Trans. Embed. Comput. Syst.*, 7(3):36:1–36:53, 2008.

Feedback Thermal Control of Real-time Systems on Multicore Processors

Yong Fu[1], Nicholas Kottenstette[2], Chenyang Lu[1], Xenofon D. Koutsoukos [2]
[1] Dept. of CSE, Washington University, St. Louis, Mo
[2] Dept. of EECS, Vanderbilt University, Nashville, TN
{fuy, lu}@cse.wustl.edu, {nkottens, Xenofon.Koutsoukos}@vanderbilt.edu

ABSTRACT

Embedded real-time systems face significant challenges in thermal management. While earlier research on feedback thermal control has shown promise in dealing with the uncertainty in thermal characteristics, multicore processors introduce new challenges that cannot be handled by previous solutions designed for single-core processors. Multicore processors require the temperature and real-time performance of *multiple* cores be controlled simultaneously, leading to multi-input-multi-output control problems with inter-core thermal coupling. Furthermore, current Dynamic Voltage and Frequency Scaling (DVFS) mechanisms only support a finite set of states, leading to *discrete* control variables that cannot be handled by standard linear control techniques. This paper presents *Real-Time Multicore Thermal Control (RT-MTC)*, a novel feedback thermal control framework specifically designed for multicore real-time systems. RT-MTC dynamically enforces both the desired temperature set point and the schedulable CPU utilization bound of a multicore processor through DVFS. RT-MTC employs a rigorously designed, efficient controller that can achieve effective thermal control with the small number of frequencies commonly supported by current processors. The robustness and advantages of RT-MTC over existing thermal control approaches are demonstrated through both experiments on an Intel Core 2 Duo processor and simulations under a wide range of uncertainties in power consumption.

Categories and Subject Descriptors

C.3 [**Computer Systems Organization**]: Real-time and embedded systems; H3.4 [**Information Systems**]: System and Software—*performance evaluation*

General Terms

Algorithm

Keywords

real-time systems, multicore, thermal control

1. INTRODUCTION

Embedded real-time systems face significant challenges in thermal management as they adopt modern computing platforms with increasing power density. While traditional embedded real-time systems typically run on single-core low-power microcontrollers, the increasing complexity of real-time applications demands the adoption of modern multicore microprocessors to leverage their computing power. Such systems must avoid processor overheating while maintaining desired real-time performance. The need to enforce temperature bounds can conflict with the need to meet real-time performance requirements, because thermal management mechanisms such as Dynamic Voltage and Frequency Scaling (DVFS) reduce processor speed resulting in prolonged execution times for real-time tasks. While modern processors usually rely on hardware throttling mechanisms to prevent overheating, such mechanisms can cause severe performance degradation unacceptable to real-time applications. Moreover, modern processors can exhibit significant *uncertainties* in their power and thermal characteristics. For instance, the power consumption of a processor may vary significantly when running different applications due to the different sets of instructions executed [18].

In recent years, control-theoretic thermal management approaches have shown promise in [8, 11, 12, 21, 34, 35, 37] handling uncertainties in thermal characteristics. In contrast to heuristic-based design relying on trial-and-error, control-theoretic approaches provide a scientific framework for systematic design and analysis of thermal control algorithms. However, previous research on feedback thermal control for embedded real-time systems focused on single-core processors and cannot handle the practical limitations of multicore processors. Thermal management mechanisms such as DVFS only support a finite set of states, leading to *discrete* control variables that cannot be handled by standard linear control techniques. Moreover, multicore processors require the temperatures and real-time performance of *multiple* cores to be controlled simultaneously, leading to multi-input-multi-output (MIMO) control problems with inter-core thermal coupling.

We present *Real-Time Multicore Thermal Control (RT-MTC)*, a novel feedback thermal control algorithm specifically designed to meet the challenges posed by multicore processors. RT-MTC employs a feedback control loop that enforces the desired temperature and CPU utilization bounds of embedded real-time systems through DVFS. RT-MTC employs an efficient and robust control design that integrates three components.

- a robust nonlinear proportional controller that deals with uncertainties in power consumption;

- a saturation block for the controller output that enforces the schedulable utilization bound;

- a Pulse Width Modulation (PWM) component that achieves desired control input by dynamically switching between discrete voltage/frequency levels.

RT-MTC combines a control-theoretic approach and a practical design. In contrast to heuristics-based solutions relying on extensive testing and hand tuning, we provide control-theoretic analysis of the stability and robustness of RT-MTC under uncertainties in power consumption. At the same time, RT-MTC employs a simple and efficient control algorithm suitable for run-time execution. Moreover, RT-MTC can be easily implemented in the user space without modification to the OS kernel which is usually required by traditional thermal-aware real-time scheduling approaches. The robustness and advantages of RT-MTC over existing thermal control approaches are demonstrated through implementation on Linux and experiments on an Intel Core 2 Dual processor as well as extensive simulations with varying power consumption.

2. RELATED WORKS

There has been significant work on thermal aware real-time scheduling for both single-core processors [7, 33] and multicore processors [5, 6, 9]. Those algorithms rely on accurate models about the thermal characteristics of the processors, and hence cannot effectively deal with uncertainties in thermal characteristics such as power consumption and ambient temperature. Moreover, they usually require fine-grained scheduling decisions that require kernel-level implementations. In contrast, our feedback control approach is implemented in user space without modifications to the kernel and therefore can be easily deployed in existing systems.

Control-theoretic thermal management has been explored for non-real-time systems. Donald and Martonosi present a general framework of dynamic thermal management for multicore processors [8]. Essentially, the proposed framework is a hierarchical feedback control loop with PI controllers, but it does not provide real-time performance guarantees. Several papers [26, 34–37] have adopted model predictive control or online convex optimization for dynamic thermal management. None of these works is concerned with maintaining real-time performance. In addition, control approaches based on model predictive control and convex optimization has higher computation complexity than our efficient proportional control approach. Moreover, our approach deals with *discrete* voltage/frequency levels, a practical issue associated with DVFS which is ignored by the aforementioned control solutions [26, 35, 37].

Control-theoretic approaches have recently been proposed for thermal management of real-time systems [12, 21]. Our previous work [12] proposed a feedback control algorithm that enforces thermal and real-time constraints simultaneously. That work adjusts the rate of periodic real-time tasks as the control knob, whereas RT-MTC employs DVFS

that does not require applications to support variable rates. Lindberg [21] proposed a feedback control framework to manage both temperature and media performance. Both algorithms [12, 21] are designed for single-core processors and cannot deal with multicore processors as they are not cognizant of inter-core thermal coupling in multicore processors.

Different from prior research handle thermal management on hardware level [4, 16, 30, 31], RT-MTC mainly focus on system level thermal management of multicore processors. Two aspects differentiate hardware and system level thermal management. First, thermal dynamics on hardware level is faster, with time constant at milliseconds [4]. In contrast at system level thermal dynamics of the processor is relative slow and with time constant in seconds [15]. Second, hardware thermal management usually adopt low level control knobs, e.g., clock gating or pipeline throttling, which can not be exposed as system level interfaces. In contrast, system level thermal management employs high-level knobs, e.g., DVFS, that are supported by most operating systems.

3. PROBLEM FORMULATION

We assume a common embedded real-time system model where the workload consists of real-time tasks released periodically. A embedded real-time system comprises a set of periodic real-time tasks running on a multicore processor with m homogeneous cores. The processor supports Dynamic Voltage and Frequency Scaling (DVFS). We assume two common characteristics of DVFS in mainstream multicore processors (e.g., Intel Core2, i5, i7 and Atom). First, the frequency and voltage of all the cores can only be scaled *uniformly*, i.e., all cores always share the *same* frequency and voltage. Second, the processor only supports a *discrete* set of frequencies. New challenges are posed by The dicretization and nonlinearity introduced by both assumptions pose key challenges to thermal control design that were not addressed in previous works [26, 34–37].

We assume *partitioned* multicore real-time scheduling, under which tasks are statically partitioned and bound to processor cores. There is a real-time tasks set $\mathbb{S}$ with n independent, periodic real-time tasks for the processor. For core l, there is a task set $\mathbb{S}_l \subseteq \mathbb{S}$ with n_l real-time tasks. Each task s_i in the task set $\mathbb{S}_l$ has a period p_i, a soft deadline d_i, and a worst-case execution time c_i. The utilization of an individual core l is thus $U_l = \sum_{s_j \in \mathbb{S}_l} \frac{c_j}{p_j}$.

We assume the tasks on a core are scheduled locally based on a real-time scheduling policy with a known schedulable utilization bound U_b, e.g., Rate Monotonic (RM) or Earliest Deadline First (EDF) under certain conditions [22]. The tasks on a core l meet their deadlines if $U_l \leq U_b$. The system can therefore guarantee the schedulability of all the tasks on a core by enforcing the schedulable utilization bound. [1]

Given a embedded real-time system running on a multicore processor, our problem is to control the temperature of the processor such that the *maximum* temperature among all the cores tracks a temperature set point, y_s, subject to the constraint of utilization bound U_b on each processor core. The temperature set point y_s is the desired temperature below the maximum temperature tolerable by the proces-

---

[1] Our approach can be extended to support a mixed task set containing periodic and soft real-time aperiodic tasks via well known aperiodic server mechanisms [23] by enforcing appropriate schedulable utilization bounds.

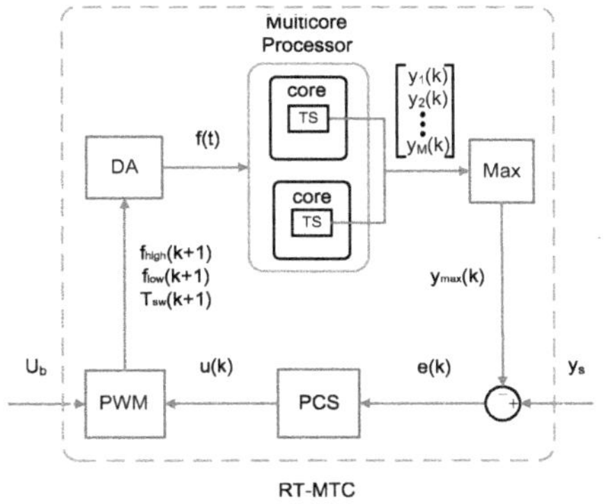

Figure 1: Feedback Control Loop of RT-MTC

sor. Our control problem formulation therefore aims to meet both the thermal and real-time performance requirements of a embedded real-time system.

4. OVERVIEW OF RT-MTC

The feedback control loop of RT-MTC, shown in Fig. 1, consists of a Temperature Sensor (TS) for each core, a Proportional Controller with Saturation (PCS), Pulse Width Modulation (PWM), and a DVFS Actuator (DA). The user input to RT-MTC is the desired temperature set point y_s and the utilization bound U_b. The feedback control loop is invoked periodically at the end of every sampling period. Specifically, at the end of kth sampling period, RT-MTC performs the following operations:

1. The TS on each core measures the temperature of the core i, $y_i(k)$. The Max function calculates the maximum temperature among all cores and feeds the maximum temperature $y_{\max}(k)$ among all the cores to the PCS.

2. The PCS computes the controller output $u(k)$ as follows:

$$u(k) = \begin{cases} 1, & \text{if } k_p e(k) > 1, \\ -1, & \text{if } k_p e(k) < -1, \\ k_p e(k), & \text{otherwise}; \end{cases} \quad (1)$$

where k_p is the coefficient of proportional control and $e(k) = y_s - y_{\max}(k)$. The output of the controller is limited to the range $[-1, 1]$. The PCS design is discussed in more details in Section 6.1.

3. The PWM receives the controller output $u(k)$ and calculates a pair of frequencies $f_{high}(k+1)$, $f_{low}(k+1)$ and the switching time $T_{sw}(k+1)$. Details of calculating $f_{high}(k+1), f_{low}(k+1), T_{sw}(k+1)$ are presented in Section 5.2.

4. The DA adjusts the frequency of the multicore processor via the DVFS interface according to the $(f_{high}(k+1), f_{low}(k+1), T_{sw}(k+1))$ input from the PWM. Specifically, at $T_{sw}(k+1)$ seconds after the beginning of the current sampling period, the processor switches its frequency from $f_{high}(k+1)$ to $f_{low}(k+1)$. The implementation of DA is detailed in Section 7.

5. THERMAL DYNAMIC MODEL

As the first step of control design and analysis, we now present a difference equation model to characterize the relationship between the frequency and the temperature. We construct the model in three steps. We first caputre the power consumption. Based on a well known power model, we then characterize the impact of PWM on the power consumption model. Finally, we complete the system model by incorporating a widely used thermal RC model that characterizes the relationship between power consumption and temperature.

We note that our system model is necessarily a simplification of the actual system's thermal behavior for the purpose of control-theoretic design and analysis. The inherent robustness of feedback control enables our system to handle considerable modeling errors in model parameters, as demonstrated in our evaluation (Sec. 8.1.2).

5.1 Power Model

As shown in [12], the average power $\bar{P}(k)$ of a core in the kth sampling period can be modeled as

$$\bar{P}(k) = U(k)P_{\text{act}}(k) + (1 - U(k))P_{\text{idle}}(k)$$

where $U(k)$ is the CPU utilization of the core, $P_{\text{act}}(k)$ is the active power, and $P_{\text{idle}}(k)$ is the idle power in k^{th} sampling period. $P_{\text{idle}}(k)$ can be approximated by a piecewise linear model $P_{\text{idle}} = (C_0(V(k)) + C_1(V(k))y(k))V(k)$ [28]. A well-known model of the active power is $P_{\text{act}}(k) = C_2 V^3(k)$, where C_2 is a constant coefficient and $V(k)$ is the supply voltage [29].

We can rewrite the average power as

$$\bar{P}(k) = \bar{P}_a(k) + C_y y(k) \quad (2)$$

where $\bar{P}_a(k) = U(k)C_2 V^3(k) + C_0(V(k))V(k)$ and $C_y = C_1(V(k))$. $\bar{P}_a(k)$ and C_y can be expressed in terms of the frequency, based on the relationship between supply voltage and frequency, $V(k) = Kf(k) + V_{\text{th}}$ [20] and $\frac{U(k)}{f(k)} = \frac{U_0}{f_0}$ where U_0 and f_0 are the initial CPU utilization and frequency. Note we assume that the processor utilization scales proportionally with the frequency which usually hold for those CPU bound applications.

5.2 Pulse Width Modulation (PWM)

As each core of the multicore processor runs under a discrete set of frequencies, the power $\bar{P}_a(k)$ in equation (2) can only switch between discrete levels. To track the temperature set point closely, PWM is employed to map desired average power in each sampling period to the discrete frequency levels supported by the processor.

The continuous input to the PWM in the kth sampling period is $u(k) \in [-1, 1]$. The PWM computes $(f_{high}(k+1), f_{low}(k+1), T_{sw}(k+1))$ based on $u(k)$. The upper limit of the output corresponds to the maximum frequency supported by the processor. The lower limit of the output corresponds to the lowest frequency that satisfies the utilization bound or the minimum frequency, whichever is higher. Let the frequency corresponding to the upper and lower limit of $u(k)$ be $f_{\max}, f_{\min}$, and let $f_u(k) = f_{\min} + (f_{\max} - f_{\min})\frac{u(k)+1}{2}$. To minimize the change in CPU speed, PWM first chooses a pair of *consecutive* frequency levels f_i and f_{i+1} which satisfy $f_i \leq f_u(k) \leq f_{i+1}$ from the supported discrete frequency set; these are designated $f_{low}(k+1)$ and

$f_{high}(k+1)$ respectively. The time to switch from $f_{high}(k+1)$ to $f_{low}(k+1)$ is computed as

$$T_{sw} = \frac{f_u(k) - f_{low}(k+1)}{f_{high}(k+1) - f_{low}(k+1)} T_s,$$

where T_s is the sampling period. Note if $f_u(k)$ equals any frequency in the supported frequency set, both $f_{high}(k+1), f_{low}(k+1)$ will exactly equals that frequency and $T_{sw} = 0$.

Let $\bar{P}_{a,max}, \bar{P}_{a,min}$ be the upper and lower bound of $\bar{P}_a$, which are the average power consumption at f_{max} and f_{min}, respectively. We can rewrite the power model to incorporate PWM based on (2) as

$$\bar{P}(k) = G_p(P_{ap}u(k) + P_{am}) + C_y y(k) \quad (3)$$

where $P_{ap} = (\bar{P}_{a,max} - \bar{P}_{a,min})/2$, $P_{am} = (\bar{P}_{a,max} + \bar{P}_{a,min})/2$, and G_p is the gain to represent the uncertainty caused by power variation.

The power consumption model (3) approximates the power behavior of the processor, since it derives the average power rather than actual power. However, as we shown in our stability analysis (Section 6.1) and experiments (Section 8.1.2), the inherent robustness of our feedback control design can tolerate considerable modeling error without compromising system stability.

5.3 Thermal Dynamic Model

Our control design is based on a well-established thermal RC model for multicore processors with M cores and a heat sink [9]. Compared to architecture-level thermal models such as Hotspot [17], the model presented here is simpler but more suitable for control design of thermal management. The effectiveness of the model has been validated in [9, 29].

Symbol	Meaning
$R_i, R_h, R_a, R_{i,j}$	thermal resistance of the core i, the heat sink, environment and thermal resistance between the core i and j
C_i, C_h	thermal capacitance of the core i and the heat sink
y_0, y_i, y_h	temperature of environment, the core i and the heat sink
P_i	power of the core i
$\mathbb{N}_i$	the set of cores adjacent the core i

Table 1: Symbols in Thermal Dynamic Model

Based on the symbols listed in Tab. 1, the thermal dynamic model of the multicore processor can be written in the following compact form:

$$\dot{\mathbf{Y}}(t) = A\mathbf{Y}(t) + B_P\mathbf{P}(t) + B_y y_0 \quad (4)$$

where $\mathbf{Y}(t) = [y_1(t), \ldots, y_M(t), y_h(t)]^\mathsf{T} \in \mathbb{R}^{M+1}$, $\mathbf{P}(t) = [P_1(t), \ldots, P_M(t)]^\mathsf{T} \in \mathbb{R}^M$ and y_0 is the ambient temperature, $A \in \mathbb{R}^{(M+1)\times(M+1)}$, $B_P \in \mathbb{R}^{(M+1)\times M}$ and $B_y \in \mathbb{R}^{(M+1)}$. The matrices A, B_P and B_y are computed

as follows:

$$A(i,j) = \begin{cases} \frac{-1}{C_i}\left(\frac{1}{R_i} + \sum_{m\in\mathbb{N}_i} \frac{1}{R_{i,m}}\right), & \text{if } i = j \neq (M+1) \\ \frac{1}{R_{i,j}C_i}, & \text{if } j \in \mathbb{N}_i \\ \frac{1}{R_iC_i}, & \text{if } i \neq (M+1) \text{ and } j = (M+1) \\ \frac{1}{R_jC_h}, & \text{if } i = (M+1) \text{ and } j \neq i \\ \frac{-1}{C_h}\left(\frac{1}{R_a+R_h} + \sum_{m=1}^M \frac{1}{R_m}\right) & \text{if } i = j = (M+1) \\ 0, & \text{otherwise.} \end{cases},$$

$$B_P(i,j) = \begin{cases} \frac{1}{C_i}, & \text{if } i = j \\ 0, & \text{otherwise.} \end{cases},$$

$$B_y(i) = \begin{cases} \frac{1}{C_h(R_a+R_h)}, & \text{if } i = M+1 \\ 0, & \text{otherwise.} \end{cases}.$$

We use a Zero Order Hold (ZOH) equivalent model [10] in which the average power-model for $\bar{P}(k)$ is assumed to be held constant and the average environmental temperature is $y_0(k) = \frac{1}{T_s}\int_{kT_s}^{(k+1)T_s} y_0(t)dt$ during the kth sampling period. The ZOH equivalent of (4) is

$$\mathbf{Y}(k+1) = \Phi_o\mathbf{Y}(k) + \Psi_P\bar{P}(k) + \Psi_y y_0(k) \quad (5)$$

where $\Phi_o = e^{AT_s}$, $\Psi_P = \left(\int_0^{T_s} e^{A\tau}d\tau\right)B_P$, $\Psi_y = \left(\int_0^{T_s} e^{A\tau}d\tau\right)B_y$ and $\bar{\mathbf{P}}(k) = [\bar{P}_1(k), \ldots, \bar{P}_M(k)]^\mathsf{T} \in \mathbb{R}^M$. Substituting the power model (3) for $\bar{P}(k)$ in (5) results in:

$$\mathbf{Y}(k+1) = \Phi\mathbf{Y}(k) + P_{ap}\Psi_P G_p u(k) + \Psi_y y_0(k) + P_{am}\Psi_P G_p \quad (6)$$

in which $\Phi = \left(\Phi_o + C_y\Psi_P \begin{bmatrix} I_M & 0 \end{bmatrix}\right)$ where $\begin{bmatrix} I_M & 0 \end{bmatrix} \in \mathbb{R}^{M\times(M+1)}$ and $I_M \in \mathbb{R}^{M\times M}$ denotes the identity matrix. The term involving $y_0(k)$ relates how environmental temperature changes can perturb the system. The last term represents a fixed-disturbance due to the mean active power resulting from our proposed modulation approach.

In practice the model parameters can be estimated using well-known system identification method. Essentially, there are two methods to acquire the parameters of the compact thermal model. We can either extract the parameters based on fine grain thermal RC models, for example Hotspot [17] or estimate the parameters using realistic operational data, which is also the method we used in this paper. The detailed description of model identification is presented in Section 8.1.1.

6. CONTROL DESIGN

We propose a low-complexity controller to tackle the problem of thermal management of real-time systems on multicore processors. Our control design ensures that the maximum temperature of the cores tracks the thermal set-point without violating the utilization constraints. Although the control structure shown in Fig. 1 only has single input, the PCS must control the temperature of multiple cores simultaneously. Previous approaches to thermal control for the single core processor [12] is not suitable to multicore thermal control because their control design do not handle the interaction among the thermal dynamics of different cores. In this section we present a control design which can handle not only thermal coupling among cores but also other nonlinearities induced by the multicore processors.

6.1 Stability Analysis and Control Design

The PCS is designed based on passivity [27] and can accommodate the nonlinearities induced by the *Max* function and the saturation. There are various precise mathematical definitions for passive systems that essentially state that the output energy must be bounded so that the system does not produce more energy than was initially stored. Under certain technical conditions, strictly input and strictly output passive systems are Lyapunov stable [32]. In this case, passivity offers advantages for computing a Lyapunov function that is used to prove stability of the closed-loop system.

In order to analyze the stability of RT-MTC, we assume that the set-point $T_b = 0$ and we consider the unperturbed system where $y_0 = 0$, $\Psi_P G_P = 0$ in (6). We provide sufficient conditions that ensure the existence of a Lyapunov function for the closed loop system, and thus, stability of the RT-MTC. A detailed proof can be found in [13]. The disturbance in the power model arises because of (1) the ambient temperature that can change but is measurable and (2) the mean active power introduced by the PWM. We can minimize the steady-state error by taking into account these terms in the set-point T_b (the detailed derivation of T_b can be found in [13]).

THEOREM 1. *Consider the closed-loop system shown in Fig. 1 with $T_b = 0$ and assume that the power model of the multicore processor is described by (6) with $y_0(k) = 0$ and $P_{am}\Psi_P G_P = 0$. If there exists a matrix $P = P^\mathsf{T} > 0$ and $-\infty < \delta < 0$ such that the following LMI is satisfied:*

$$\begin{bmatrix} \Phi^\mathsf{T} P \Phi - P & \Phi^\mathsf{T} P P_{ap}\Psi_P G_p - \frac{1}{2}C_l^\mathsf{T} \\ (\Phi^\mathsf{T} P P_{ap}\Psi_P G_p - \frac{1}{2}C_l^\mathsf{T})^\mathsf{T} & \delta + P_{ap}^2 G_p^\mathsf{T}\Psi_P^\mathsf{T} P \Psi_P G_p \end{bmatrix} \leq 0$$
(7)

for all $l \in \{1, \ldots, M\}$, where C_l is the coefficient for the measured temperature of the core l, then the closed-loop system is passive and stable.

By exploring the solution of the LMI (7) given in Theorem 1, we can acquire the stability condition of the system under modeling error. Specifically, for items in the search space of power gain, thermal resistance and capacitance, we can check whether the LMI is solvable and then decide whether the closed-loop system is stable with the parameters. Accordingly we derive robustness of the system in terms of the range of uncertain parameters, power gain and thermal related parameters resulting in stable systems.

The above theorem can also be used for designing the controller. This is achieved by finding the smallest value of δ that satisfies the LMI (7), The controller gain of the PCS (equation (6)) is defined as $k = -\frac{1}{\delta}$. This is the highest proportional gain that guarantees stability of the closed-loop system. In general, higher controller gain improves control performance. If there is deviation from the set point, high gain controller ensures that the system will converge to the set-point as fast as possible. The LMI shown in the theorem can be solved efficiently using standard LMI tools such as the Matlab LMI toolbox and the Scilab lmitool.

7. IMPLEMENTATION OF RT-MTC

We have implemented RT-MTC on top of Linux, using a combination of Python, MATLAB, and C. The PCS, PWM, DVFS Actuator, and Max components shown in Fig. 1 are written in Python.

All the components in the feedback control loop are implemented in one process assigned the highest real-time process priority so that RT-MTC can be executed periodically with minimum interference from real-time tasks.

Thermal Sensor: Most modern multicore processors are equipped with hardware thermal sensors for each individual core, which are supported by the operating system or third-party libraries. For example, the temperature of cores can be read from the interface provided by *lmsensor* [3] via the coretemp driver (/sys/bus/platform/drivers/coretemp/) in Linux. The thermal information can also be acquired from standard ACPI interfaces. For those multicore processors without thermal sensors on each core, such as those used in embedded systems, soft thermal sensors [19] can be employed to estimate the temperature of a single core.

PCS and PWM: The implementations of PCS and PWM are straightforward, based on the description in Sec. 6 and Sec. 5.2.

DVFS Actuator: We implemented the DVFS Actuator using the *signal* mechanism provided by POSIX interface. First, an alarm is set to be fired at the switching time T_{sw} by using the POSIX *alarm* function. When the alarm expires, a $SIGALRM$ signal is sent to the process's signal handler set by the function *sigact*. The signal handler calls a procedure to switch the frequency of the multicore processor from the high level f_{high} to the low level f_{low} via a interface which can access the processor's DVFS function, for examples, ACPI, lmsensor or Machine Specific Register. The delay between PWM output switching time T_{sw} and the time that the frequency is actually switched relies on the resolution of clock interrupt of the underlying operating system. For example, the Linux kernel uses a configurable time resolution (known as *jiffy*) which ranges from $1ms$ to $10ms$. Even at a resolution of $10ms$, the delay has negligible effect on the control performance, since it is comparatively much shorter than the sampling period. We choose $10s$ as the sampling period in our implementation because it is short enough to control the thermal behavior of the processor , which has time constant greater than $100s$, without imposing singnificant overhead from frequency switching and computation.

8. EVALUATION

We first evaluate RT-MTC through experiments based on above implementation and then perform extensive simulations with parameters acquired from model identification experiments. An Intel Core 2 Duo two core processor is used to run the experiments and be the target of simulations as it provides discrete DVFS mechanism. Moreover thermal parameters, especially thermal capacitance, of Intel Core2 Duo are acquired directly as shown later. The simulations complement experimental results by allowing us to examine RT-MTC's performance under stress-test conditions (such as fan failure) which are difficult or dangerous to run on real hardware.

8.1 Experiments

The hardware platform used for the experiments is a Lenovo W500 laptop with an Intel T9400 Core 2 Duo dual core processor and the Linux kernel 2.6.32 distributed with Fedora 12.[2] The T9400 processor has 2 digital thermal sensors lo-

---

[2]Although we only present the results of experiments for a dual core processor, the methodology and implementation can be ex-

cated on each core and supports processor-wide DVFS, that is, the two cores' frequencies must be set uniformly. The DVFS frequencies and the thermal properties of the T9400 are listed in Table 2.

Frequency	2.53, 1.6, 0.8 GHz
Voltage	1.175, 1.00, 0.900 V
T_{junc}	$105°C$
Thermal Design Power (TDP)	35W

Table 2: Frequencies and Thermal Properties of the T9400 Processor

8.1.1 Model Identification

To acquire the parameters of the thermal RC model, we first run a set of real-time workloads to profile the processor's thermal behavior. Then the thermal parameters is identified from the experiments results by Matlab Model Identification Toolbox. The real-time workloads used for model identification involves two micro benchmarks, CRC and Bzip2. CRC is a data verification application chosen from Mibench [14], a test suite for embedded systems. Bzip2 is a data compression tool chosen from SPEC CPU 2006 [2], a standard benchmarks suite. We implement three kinds of workloads: CRC alone, Bzip2 alone and a Mixed workload containing both microbenchmarks. The workload for each core is identical and involves 5 periodic tasks which are either CRC or Bzip2 according to the type of the workload. The deadlines of the tasks are set to the same as their periods. The periods and execution time of the tasks are listed in Table 3.

	Task 1	Task 2	Task 3	Task 4	Task 5
Period	250	300	450	500	1000
Exe. Time	23	27	41	45	90

Table 3: Workload Tasks Period and Execution Time@$2.53GHz$ (ms)

To capture the comprehensive thermal behavior for different frequencies, we employ a pseudo-sequence of frequency as input, where frequency switches between $2.53GHz$ and $0.8GHz$. Considering the large time constant of the processor's thermal behavior, we run each workload for 5400s. Table 4 shows the results of the model identification via Matlab Model Identification Toolbox. Fig. 2 illustrates the temperature and frequency of the Mixed workload; the other two workloads are omitted here due to space constraints.

There are two important observations from Table 4. First, it indicates the efficacy of the thermal dynamic model, as the estimated model parameters result in fitness levels above 80% for all three workloads. Second, the model parameters estimated under different workload differ considerably. This entails that thermal control must be robust against uncertainties of model parameters caused by different workloads since it is unrealistic to expect users to re-estimate the parameters via system identification for every workload. Such robustness against modeling errors is an important advantage of RT-MTC, as shown in both the empirical results and the simulation study presented below.

---

tended to the processor with more than two cores easily since control design proposed in this paper is based on a general multicore processor model.

Thermal Parameters (Mixed, Fit*: 82%)					
$R_1(\Omega)$	1.61	$C_h(F)$	216.74	$R_{12}(\Omega)$	16.16
$R_2(\Omega)$	1.46	$C_2(F)$	1.25	$C_1(F)$	1.25
$R_a + R_h$	1.05				
Thermal Parameters (Bzip2, Fit:83%)					
$R_1(\Omega)$	1.35	$C_h(F)$	263.02	$R_{12}(\Omega)$	15.23
$R_2(\Omega)$	1.13	$C_2(F)$	1.61	$C_1(F)$	1.61
$R_a + R_h$	1.35				
Thermal Parameters (CRC, Fit: 81%)					
$R_1(\Omega)$	1.78	$C_h(F)$	242.23	$R_{12}(\Omega)$	16.83
$R_2(\Omega)$	1.56	$C_2(F)$	1.35	$C_1(F)$	1.35
$R_a + R_h$	1.08				

*: the accuracy index in Matlab Model Identification Toolbox.

Table 4: Results of Model Identification

8.1.2 Experiment Results

In this section we present the experimental results of RT-MTC on the real hardware platform. We run RT-MTC under the workload of the CRC and the Mixed for 10 minutes each. The controller parameters of RT-MTC are computed using the thermal RC model parameters of the Mixed workload. In this experiment we choose the temperature set point as $60°C$ to ensure that internal thermal throttling circuit is not activated even when there is overshoot during temperature adjustment.

Two important observations can be made from the results plotted in Fig. 3. First, RT-MTC enforces both the temperature set point and the utilization bound. As seen in Fig. 3(b), after $280s$ the temperature is steady at the temperature set point, $60°C$. The average upper limit of the utilization is 74%, which is below the utilization bound. Second, RT-MTC (with the same control parameters) can control the thermal behavior of the processor effectively under *both* test workloads. As shown in Table 4, there is difference between the parameters identified by the Mixed and the CRC workloads, which induces modeling error. Ensuring temperature set point in both cases shows RT-MTC robustness against modeling error induced by different workloads. Although there are spikes in temperature during the CRC workload caused by background services (which cannot be manipulated by our user-space implementation), RT-MTC quickly counteracts these spikes.

8.2 Simulation

We perform extensive simulations based on the model parameters identified from the experiments in Sec. 8.1.1. Although we wish to explore the performance of RT-MTC in extreme scenarios, it is often impractical to carry such experiments out on real hardware. For example, an experiment int RT-MTC's performance in the face of fan failure would be likely to damage the processor. For this reason, we stress-test the performance of RT-MTC under simulation, as discussed in this section.

8.2.1 Simulation Setup

There are two components in our simulation environment:

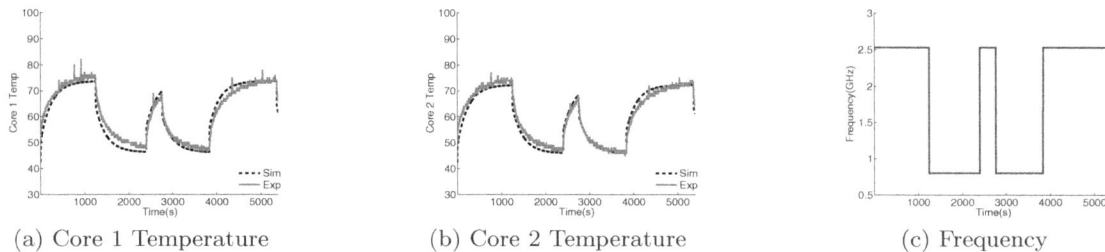

(a) Core 1 Temperature   (b) Core 2 Temperature   (c) Frequency

Figure 2: Model Identification Data (Mixed Workload)

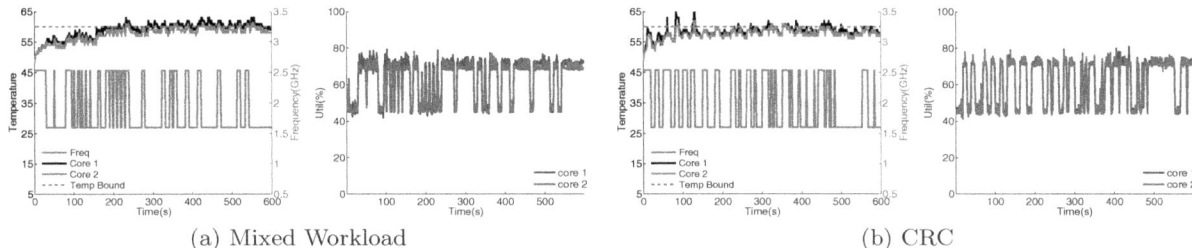

(a) Mixed Workload   (b) CRC

Figure 3: Experimental Results of RT-MTC

an event driven simulator implemented in C++ and a Simulink module implemented in MATLAB (R2008a). The C++ simulator simulates embedded real-time systems over multicore processors and calculates the processor utilization according to the frequency output by the controller. The Simulink module performs the controller's computation. And the Simulink module also calculates the temperatures of multicore processors based on the utilization generated by the C++ simulator. The C++ simulator and the Simulink module communicate with each other through a TCP connection.

The target multicore processor in our simulation is the dual core processor, Intel Core 2 Duo T7200 [1]. The power and thermal related parameters of T7200 are shown in Table 5. The parameters of the leakage power model are acquired by linear approximation of an accurate leakage power model [24]. The active power and available frequencies are obtained from Intel T7200 data sheet [1]. Note that although the evaluation is only preformed on the dual-core processor, our approach for thermal management is developed for general multicore processors and therefore can handle the processors with more cores.

We use the same methodology and tools for model identification as described in Sec. 8.1.1. The acquired thermal parameters are listed in Table 5. As thermal design is different between manufacturers, it is reasonable that these parameters identified vary significantly from those identified for the T9400.

In the simulations we use a fine-grained workload which runs 10 periodic soft real-time tasks on each core. We assume partitioned scheduling for the multicore embedded real-time systems. The Rate Monotonic (RM) scheduling algorithm [22] is employed to schedule all tasks on each core. The utilization bound is set to 0.71. At the beginning of the experiment, the period of each task T_i is randomly generated in the range $[100ms, 200ms]$. The execution time of each task is generated to keep each task's utilization nearly equal and the sum of all tasks' utilization at 0.7, just below the utilization bound.

Power Parameters				
f(GHz)	0.8,	1.2,	1.6,	2.0
C_0	-0.3638,	-0.3687,	0.1071,	2.3367
C_1	0.0191,	0.0342,	0.0608,	0.1066
C_2	7.7378			
Thermal Parameters				
$R_1(\Omega)$	0.53	$C_h(F)$	390	$R_{12}(\Omega)$	5.5
$R_2(\Omega)$	0.57	$C_2(F)$	39.14	$C_1(F)$	50.38
$R_a + R_h$	0.2				

Table 5: Simulation Parameters

In the following simulations, we set the temperature bound to $60°C$, below the temperature achieved by the Thermal Design Power (TDP) of T7200 so as not to activate the internal hardware thermal regulation. Note that the effectiveness of our approach does not rely on the specific temperature bound.

We compare RT-MTC against four other baseline algorithms, OPEN, Reactive, MPC-QUAN and MPC-PWM. The algorithm OPEN statically sets the processors' frequency at beginning of the simulation and does not change it while the simulation runs.

MPC-QUAN and MPC-PWM are control-theoretic approaches and based on the algorithm proposed in [35]. The control algorithms of both baselines are the solutions of the following constraint optimizing problem with the optimizing objective as follows:

$$J(k) = \sum_{i=1}^{H_p} |y_{max}(k+i) - y_s|^2 \qquad (8)$$

where H_p is the prediction horizon and y_s is the temperature set point. The solution of the optimizing problem also needs to satisfy the constraints of the utilization bound, the thermal bound, and the frequency limit. Note that $T(k)$ must follow the thermal model (5). The solution of the constraint optimizing problem (8) is a vector with length of H_p. The first element of the solution is employed as control output. The pulse width modulation transforms the control output of the power to the duty cycle of the power signal. MPC-QUAN rounds off the control output, aforementioned as the final output while MPC-PWM employs a PWM mechanism described in the previous section to approximate the control output.

The baseline Reactive (Reactive Thermal Control) is a modified version of reactive speed control of embedded real-time systems [33]. The key design point of Reactive is that whenever the thermal threshold is hit, the frequency corresponding to equilibrium temperature (thermal bound in our case) is applied. Otherwise, the highest available frequency is applied. The original version of reactive speed control works at the level of tasks, that is, the frequency changes during the duration of one task running. Reactive, however, only changes frequency at the end of a sampling period. If all the parameters, both power and thermal related, are accurate, Reactive can enforce the thermal threshold effectively. However if there are uncertainties of parameters, the equilibrium temperature cannot precisely enforce the temperature bound.

8.2.2 Constant Power Variation

This set of simulations is designed to evaluate the performance of RT-MTC when there is constant deviation between the estimated and the real tasks power. In these simulations, we compare RT-MTC to the other baselines when the power ratio of all tasks running on the target multicore processor is 4.0, that is, the real power of the tasks is 4 times that of the estimated power. The value of power ratio is chosen intentionally to show the capability of RT-MTC to counteract heavy disturbances, a major benefit of control-theoretic thermal control. In this simulation, we expect RT-MTC to work resiliently under constant power variation.

Fig. 4 compares the performance of RT-MTC, Reactive, MPC-QUAN, and MPC-PWM when the power ratio is 4. We exclude OPEN from the comparison intentionally because it violates the thermal bound during the experiment. Without thermal management, the processor cannot handle the thermal bound violation, and the steady temperature of the two cores reaches $84°C$; this significantly exceeds the $60°C$ temperature threshold and likely to trigger the internal hardware thermal control.

As shown in the top figure in Fig. 4(a), the temperature under RT-MTC converges to the temperature set point $60°C$. The slight oscillation in converged temperature, which can be seen in Fig. 4(d), is caused by the sampling period. If the temperature surpasses the bound within the sampling period ($10s$ in this experiment) RT-MTC cannot respond to enforce the thermal bound. Meanwhile, we also observe the frequency switches between 3 levels guided by PWM according to RT-MTC's output.

The bottom half of Fig. 4(a) shows the utilization of the multicore processor. As seen in the figure, the utilization is always below the utilization bound, validating that RT-MTC can enforce the real-time utilization bound. Because of RT-MTC saturation component, the frequency never switches to the lowest level, which confines utilization under the real-time bound.

Fig. 4(b) illustrates the simulation results under Reactive. After two frequency switches, Reactive forces the frequency to stay at $1.6GHz$ even though the temperature violates the thermal bound. Recall the algorithm of Reactive: if the thermal bound is hit, the frequency will change to the predefined level to enforce the equilibrium temperature, which, otherwise, is calculated based on the nominal model. In this case, the predefined frequency level is $1.6GHz$. However, in this simulation, the power ratio is 4.0 rather than 1.0 used by Reactive. Hence, at the same frequency, more power is generated and the predefined frequency level in Reactive cannot prohibit the temperature from surpassing the bound. This experiment shows clearly that Reactive is not able to handle thermal management accurately under power uncertainty.

Compared to Reactive, RT-MTC follows the temperature set point more precisely under power uncertainty. When the power generated by the processor is overestimated, the processor runs at higher frequency in RT-MTC than Reactive, so that throughput of the systems is improved. When the power is underestimated, likewise, RT-MTC adjusts the processor frequency to consume less power than Reactive, which can not only save power consumption of the workload but also reduce power consumed by the cooling system. Moreover, in this case, Reactive is more likely to trigger internal thermal throttling.

Fig. 4(c) and 4(d) show the simulation results of MPC-QUAN and MPC-PWM. Both baselines can ensure the temperature set point. However, there is oscillation in both cases. For MPC-QUAN, because of the effect of quantization, the temperature frequently violates the bound slightly. Although MPC-PWM can alleviate the effect of quantization by PWM, the sampling period that we analyzed in RT-MTC also induce oscillation around the thermal bound. Moreover, since MPC works on the margin of constraints, it behaves in a complex, nonlinear way. That makes the oscillation of MPC-PWM greater than that of RT-MTC. On the other hand, MPC can handle effectively the real-time constraints embedded in the constrain optimizing problem (8), which then enforces the real-time constraints, that is, the utilization bound.

The major advantage of RT-MTC over MPC-like methods is the reduction of running overhead and implementation complexity. When employing MPC, the controller must solve online the constrained optimization problem, which is notably computation intensive [25]. In contrast, RT-MTC only involves computation of a linear function. Moreover, although there are a few of commercial or open source optimization solver, porting them to solve MPC is still a difficult task.

8.2.3 Dynamic Power Variation

This set of simulations is designed to evaluate the case when the power ratio of tasks deviate from the estimation dynamically. Since tasks often experience different stages of processing, the power of tasks changes frequently. Thus, dynamic power variation is a common source of uncertainty for thermal management. In this simulation, we also assume asymmetric power ratio variation: that is, cores consuming different power when running. For the simulations in this section, we assume the power ratio of Core 1 rises to 4.0 at $200s$ and then decreases to 0.5 at $300s$ while Core 2 keeps the power unchanged.

Similarly to the case of constant power variation, OPEN

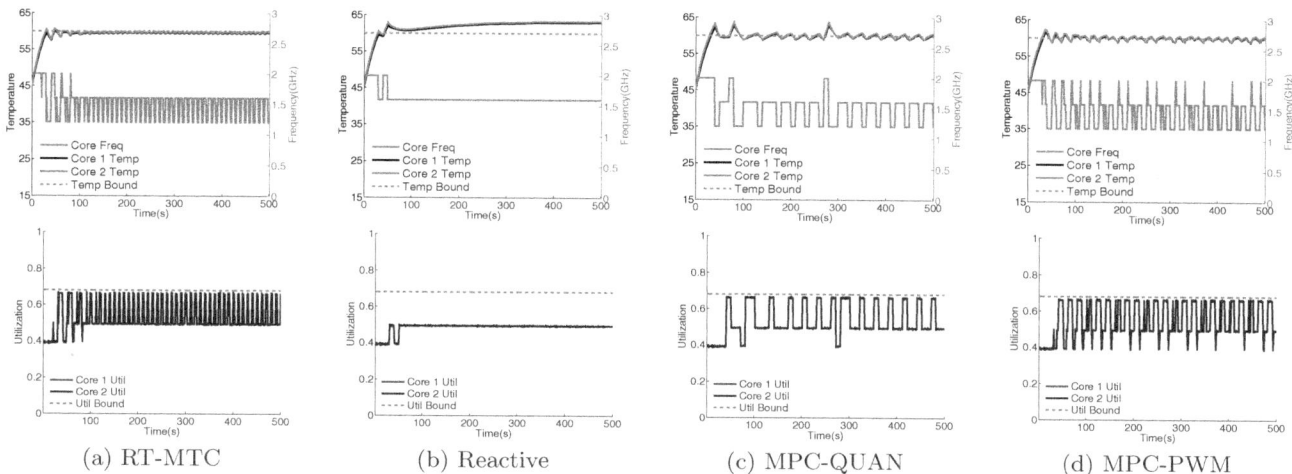

Figure 4: Constant Power Variation (Power Ratio = 4)

violates the thermal bound under dynamic power variation. However, since only the power of core 1 increases, the temperature of both cores rises less than if the power of both cores varied.

Fig. 5 shows the simulation results of different algorithms under dynamic power variation. Fig 5(a) shows that the temperature of core 1 is below the temperature bound under RT-MTC, validating that RT-MTC is able to ensure the thermal bound under dynamic power variation. We observe that RT-MTC responds to the abrupt temperature increase from $200s$ to $300s$. So when power decreases, the temperature is still able to stay near the temperature bound.

Unlike the previous experiments, Reactive has no steady temperature error in the simulation, as shown in Fig. 5(b). As only one core's power rises, the heat generated by the processor is less than that when both cores' power rise; hence the predefined frequency level can enforce the thermal bound. However, we observes spikes in temperature which violates the thermal bound. These spikes occur because the reactive mechanism only responds to thermal violation passively, compared to RT-MTC where the feedback controller is designed intentionally to accommodate a temperature variation so as to offset thermal violation.

Fig. 5(c) and 5(d) show the results under MPC-QUAN and MPC-PWM, respectively. When subjected to dynamic power variation, both MPC baselines can keep the temperature around the thermal bound. But similarly to the case of constant power variation, quantization and nonlinear control behavior cause oscillation.

To explore the limits of robustness of RT-MTC, we also perform additional simulation experiments under wider uncertainty than the two simulations discussed here. The results also indicate that RT-MTC is more robust than other algorithms when subjected to uncertainties. More details on these experiments may be found in [13].

9. CONCLUSION

Embedded real-time systems face significant challenges in thermal management with their adoption of multicore processors of increasing power density. Such systems require the temperatures and real-time performance of *multiple* cores to be controlled simultaneously, leading to multi-input-multi-output control problems with inter-core thermal coupling. This paper presents *Real-Time Multicore Thermal Control (RT-MTC)*, the first feedback thermal control algorithm specifically designed for multicore embedded real-time systems. RT-MTC dynamically enforces both the temperature and the CPU utilization bounds of a multicore processor through DVFS. The strength of RT-MTC lies in both its control-theoretic approach and its practical design. RT-MTC employs a highly efficient controller that integrates saturation and proportional control components rigorously designed to enforce the desired core temperature and CPU utilization bounds. Moreover, It handles discrete frequencies through Pulse Width Modulation (PWM) that enables RT-MTC to achieve effective thermal control with only a small number of frequencies typical in current processors. The robustness and advantages of RT-MTC over existing thermal control approaches are demonstrated through extensive simulations under a wide range of power consumptions.

10. ACKNOWLEDGMENTS

The research of Yong Fu and Chenyang Lu is supported in part by NSF CAREER Award CNS-0448554 and CNS-1035773 (CPS). The research of Nicholas Kottenstette and Xenofon Koutsoukos is supported in part by NSF Award NSF-CCF-0820088.

11. REFERENCES

[1] http://ark.intel.com/Product.aspx?id=27255.
[2] http://www.spec.org/.
[3] www.lm-sensor.org.
[4] D. Brooks and M. Martonosi. Dynamic thermal management for high-performance microprocessors. In *HPCA*, 2001.
[5] T. Chantem, R. P. Dick, and X. S. Hu. Temperature-aware scheduling and assignment for hard real-time applications on MPSoCs. In *DATE*, 2008.
[6] J.-J. Chen, C.-M. Hung, and T.-W. Kuo. On the minimization fo the instantaneous temperature for periodic real-time tasks. In *RTAS*, 2007.
[7] J.-J. Chen, S. Wang, and L. Thiele. Proactive speed scheduling for real-time tasks under thermal constraints. In *RTAS*, 2009.
[8] J. Donald and M. Martonosi. Techniques for multicore

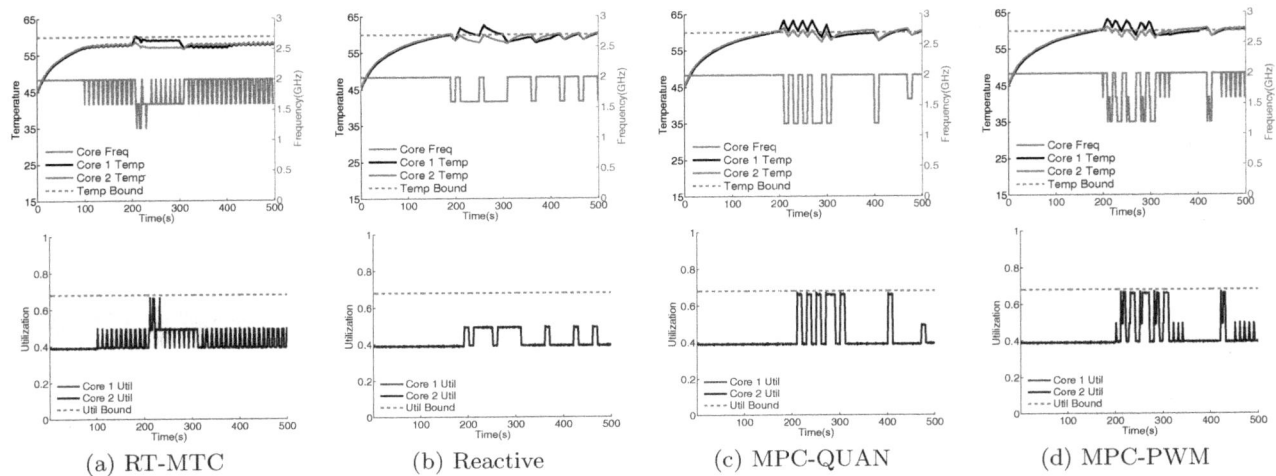

| (a) RT-MTC | (b) Reactive | (c) MPC-QUAN | (d) MPC-PWM |

Figure 5: Dynamic Power Variation

thermal management: Classification and new exploration. *SIGARCH Comput. Archit. News*, 34(2):78–88, 2006.

[9] N. Fisher, J.-J. Chen, S. Wang, and L. Thiele. Thermal-aware global real-time scheduling on multicore systems. In *RTAS*, 2009.

[10] G. F. Franklin, J. D. Powell, and M. Workman. *Digital Control of Dynamic Systems*. Addison Wesley Longman, Inc., 1998.

[11] X. Fu, X. Wang, and E. Puster. Dynamic thermal and timeliness guarantees for distributed real-time embedded systems. In *RTCSA*, 2009.

[12] Y. Fu, N. Kottenstette, Y. Chen, C. Lu, X. D. Koutsoukos, and H. Wang. Feedback Thermal Control for Real-time Systems. *RTAS*, 2010.

[13] Y. Fu, N. Kottenstette, Y. Chen, C. Lu, X. D. Koutsoukos, and H. Wang. Feedback Thermal Control of Real-time Systems on Multicore Processors. Technical Report WUCSE-2011-3, Washington University in St. Louis, 2011.

[14] M. R. Guthaus, J. S. Ringenberg, D. Ernst, T. M. Austin, T. Mudge, and R. B. Brown. Mibench: A free, commercially representative embedded benchmark suite. In *WWC*, 2001.

[15] T. Heath, A. P. Centeno, P. George, L. Ramos, Y. Jaluria, and R. Bianchini. Mercury and freon: temperature emulation and management for server systems. In *ASPLOS*, 2006.

[16] M. Huang, J. Renau, S.-M. Yoo, and J. Torrellas. A framework for dynamic energy efficiency and temperature management. In *MICRO*, 2000.

[17] W. Huang, M. R. Stan, K. Skadron, K. Sankaranarayanan, S. Ghosh, and S. Velusam. Compact thermal modeling for temperature-aware design. In *DAC*, 2004.

[18] C. Isci and M. Martonosi. Runtime power monitoring in high-end processors: Methodology and empirical data. In *MICRO*, 2003.

[19] J. S. Lee, K. Skadron, and S. W. Chung. Predictive temperature-aware DVFS. *IEEE Transactions on Computers*, 59(1):127–133, 2010.

[20] W. Liao, L. He, and K. M. Lepak. Temperature and supply voltage aware performance and power modeling at microarchitecture level. *IEEE Trans. Comput.-Aided Design Integr. Circuits Syst.*, 24(7):1042–1053, 2005.

[21] M. Lindberg and K.-E. Årzén. Feedback control of cyber-physical systems with multi resource dependencies and model uncertainties. In *RTSS*, 2010.

[22] C. Liu and J. Layland. Scheduling Algorithms for Multiprogramming in a Hard-Real-Time Environment. *JACM*, 20(1):46–61, 1973.

[23] J. Liu. *Real-Time systems*. Prentice Hall, 2000.

[24] Y. Liu, H. Yang, R. P. Dick, H. Wang, and L. Shang. Thermal vs energy optimization for dvfs-enabled processors in embedded systems. In *ISQED*, 2007.

[25] J. M. Maciejowski. *Predictive Control with Constraints*. Pearson Eduction Limited, Edinburg Gate, England, 2002.

[26] A. Mutapcic, S. Boyd, S. Murali, D. Atienza, G. De Micheli, and R. Gupta. Processor speed control with thermal constraints. *Circuits and Systems I: Regular Papers, IEEE Transactions on*, 56(9):1994–2008, 2009.

[27] R. Ortega, A. J. Van Der Schaft, I. Mareels, B. Maschke, and L. G. Y. Supelec. Putting energy back in control. *Control Systems Magazine, IEEE*, 21(2):18–33, 2001.

[28] G. Quan and Y. Zhang. Leakage aware feasibility analysis for temperature-constrained hard real-time periodic tasks. In *ECRTS*, 2009.

[29] R. Rao, S. B. K. Vrudhula, and C. Chakrabarti. Throughput of multi-core processors under thermal constraints. In *ISLPED*, pages 201–206, 2007.

[30] K. Skadron, T. F. Abdelzaher, and M. R. Stan. Control-theoretic techniques and thermal-rc modeling for accurate and localized dynamic thermal management. In *HPCA*, 2002.

[31] J. Srinivasan and S. V. Adve. Predictive dynamic thermal management for multimedia applications. In *ICS*, 2003.

[32] A. J. van der Schaft. *L2-Gain and Passivity in Nonlinear Control*. New York:Springer-Verlag, 1999.

[33] S. Wang and R. Bettati. Reactive speed control in temperature-constrained real-time systems. *Real-Time Systems*, 39(1-3):73–95, 2008.

[34] Y. Wang, K. Ma, and X. Wang. Temperature-constrained power control for chip multiprocessors with online model estimation. *SIGARCH Comput. Archit. News*, 37(3):314–324, 2009.

[35] F. Zanini, D. Atienza, L. Benini, and G. De Micheli. Multicore Thermal Management with Model Predictive Control. In *ECCTD 2009*, 2009.

[36] F. Zanini, D. Atienza, and G. De Micheli. A control theory approach for thermal balancing of MPSoC. In *ASP-DAC*, pages 37–42, 2009.

[37] F. Zanini, C. N. Jones, D. Atienza, and G. De Micheli. Multicore thermal management using approximate explicit Model Predictive Control. In *ISCAS*, 2010.

Synthesis of Minimal-Error Control Software

Rupak Majumdar
MPI-SWS
rupak@mpi-sws.org

Indranil Saha
UCLA
indranil@cs.ucla.edu

Majid Zamani
UCLA
zamani@ee.ucla.edu

ABSTRACT

Software implementations of controllers for physical systems are at the core of many embedded systems. The design of controllers uses the theory of dynamical systems to construct a mathematical control law that ensures that the controlled system has certain properties, such as asymptotic convergence to an equilibrium point, and optimizes some performance criteria such as LQR-LQG. However, owing to quantization errors arising from the use of fixed-point arithmetic, the implementation of this control law can only guarantee practical stability: under the actions of the implementation, the trajectories of the controlled system converge to a bounded set around the equilibrium point, and the size of the bounded set is proportional to the error in the implementation. The problem of verifying whether a controller implementation achieves practical stability for a given bounded set has been studied before. In this paper, we change the emphasis from verification to automatic synthesis. We give a technique to synthesize embedded control software that is Pareto optimal w.r.t. both performance criteria and practical stability regions. Our technique uses static analysis to estimate quantization-related errors for specific controller implementations, and performs stochastic local search over the space of possible controllers using particle swarm optimization. The effectiveness of our technique is illustrated using several standard control system examples: in most examples, we find controllers with close-to-optimal LQR-LQG performance but with implementation errors, hence regions of practical stability, several times as small.

Categories and Subject Descriptors

D.2.10 [**Software**]: Software Engineering—*Design-Methodologies*

Keywords

Embedded control software, synthesis, stochastic optimization, fixed-point arithmetic

1. INTRODUCTION

Software implementations of controllers for physical systems are the core of many critical cyber-physical systems. The design of these systems usually proceeds in two steps. First, starting with a mathematical model of the system, one designs a mathematical control law that ensures that the physical system, equipped with this control law, has certain desirable properties such as asymptotic stability (convergence to an ideal behavior) and performance. Second, the control law is implemented as a software task on a specific hardware architecture. Since the implementation has quantization errors due to the use of fixed-precision representation of real numbers, the quantization of a stabilizing controller may lead to limit cycles and chaotic behavior [12]. Hence, the implemented system usually guarantees the weaker property of *practical* stability, where the system is guaranteed to converge to a bounded set around the ideal behavior and the size of the bounded set is proportional to the quantization error.

Much recent research has focused on verifying that a given implementation of a control law guarantees that the practical stability region lies within a given set [21, 22, 6, 1, 4]. In this paper, we change the emphasis from verification to synthesis. We provide a design methodology to synthesize a control implementation for which the effect of implementation errors on system performance is minimized.

We focus on linear systems in this paper. For linear systems, a standard optimal control design approach uses the *linear quadratic regulator* (LQR) and *linear quadratic Gaussian* (LQG) algorithms [8], which find a feedback controller stabilizing the plant while minimizing quadratic cost functions. The LQR cost function takes into account the deviations of the state and control inputs from ideal values and the LQG cost function takes into account the deviation of the state from its estimation. However, they usually do not take implementation errors arising from fixed-precision arithmetic into account. Thus, a controller optimizing only the LQR-LQG cost may have a large implementation error because its implementation on a fixed-precision platform has large numerical errors, but a controller "close" to the optimal performance may have much lower numerical errors when implemented on the same platform.

In our methodology, we modify the performance criterion of LQR-LQG to additionally minimize the error due to quantization in the implementation. Technically, we answer the following two challenges. First, how can we estimate the error due to quantization in a given implementation? Second, how can we find Pareto-optimal points for the two objectives given by the LQR-LQG and quantization error cost functions? We proceed as follows.

For the first step, for a given linear feedback controller and the operating intervals of the states of the plant and the controller, we first perform a precise range analysis of the controller variables, and use the computed ranges to allocate bitwidths to each controller variable. We implement our range analysis based on linear programming. Using the allocated bitwidths, we generate code for a fixed-precision program implementing the control law. Finally, we use an algorithm based on mixed-integer linear programming to find a bound on the maximum difference between the ideal control law and the output of the fixed-precision program.

For the second step, we optimize a weighted linear combination of the two cost functions using a stochastic local search technique. LQR-LQG is attractive because it gives rise to a convex optimization problem, for which efficient solutions are known. Unfortunately, additionally tracking the quantization error results in a non-convex optimization problem. We solve the non-convex optimization problem using *particle swarm optimization* (PSO), a population-based stochastic optimization approach [13, 17, 10]. PSO iteratively solves an optimization problem by maintaining a population (or *swarm*) of candidate controllers, called *particles*, and moving them around in the search-space of possible controllers, trying to minimize the objective function. In our setting, a particle represents gain parameters for a controller.

In more detail, our algorithm proceeds as follows. Given a linear control design problem, we set up a non-convex optimization problem to minimize a weighted combination of the LQR-LQG cost function and the implementation error. We minimize this cost function using PSO. In each step of PSO, given a new controller, we perform the following checks. First, we check if the controller is stabilizing (by examining the eigenvalues of the controlled system). If not, we assign the controller an infinite cost. If it is stabilizing, we generate the best possible fixed-point code for this controller under a hardware budget and perform static analysis to estimate a bound on the implementation error. We compute the value of the objective function by taking the weighted sum of the LQR-LQG cost and this bound. We continue PSO until convergence or until some iteration bound is met. At this point, we output the controller that minimized the objective function.

We have implemented this methodology on top of Matlab's Control Theory Toolbox, using an implementation of PSO proposed in [5], and a custom static analysis using the lp_solve linear programming tool. In our experiments, we compare the LQR-LQG cost and implementation errors of controllers generated by conventional LQR-LQG optimization (implemented in Matlab) with controllers generated by PSO using our methodology. In most cases, our controllers have LQR-LQG costs close to the optimal LQR-LQG controllers, but have implementation errors that are reduced by a factor of 4 or more. Thus, we generate controllers with guaranteed bounds on practical stability regions that are 4 times or more smaller than the pure LQR-LQG optimal controllers. Our work provides an integrated analysis to take quantization errors into account in model-based design and implementation of controllers. While we have instantiated the methodology using the LQR and LQG costs and quantization errors, our algorithm is more generally applicable to other performance criteria and other sources of modeling or implementation error.

Other Related Work Besides the related work mentioned above, we mention the results in [24, 25, 18] which provide controller synthesis approaches minimizing some performance criteria where controllers are implemented using fixed-point arithmetic. The results in [24, 25, 18] assume some excitation conditions under which the quantization error can be modeled as a zero mean uniform white noise. Furthermore, they do not provide any bounds on regions of practical stability. Our results do not make any assumptions on the quantization error and provide an explicit bound on the region of practical stability.

Static analysis for range analysis has been studied extensively in the context of optimum bitwidth allocation to intermediate variables in a fixed-point program, mostly in the DSP domain [15, 14, 20]. These approaches employ abstractions based on interval arithmetic [19] or affine arithmetic [23]. Jha [9] gives an algorithm for optimal fixed-point program synthesis based on inductive sythesis. Jha's algorithm is general, but takes several minutes for each synthesis step. We found our mixed-integer linear programming approach to be both precise and reasonably fast for our application.

2. PRELIMINARIES

2.1 Controllers and Observers

We use $\mathbb{N}_0$, $\mathbb{R}$, and $\mathbb{R}_0^+$ for the set of nonnegative integers, real, and nonnegative real numbers, respectively. For a vector $x \in \mathbb{R}^n$, we denote by x_i the i-th element of x, and by $\|x\|$ the Euclidean norm of x. Recall that $\|x\| = \sqrt{x_1^2 + x_2^2 + \cdots + x_n^2}$. We write I_n and $0_{n \times m}$ for the identity and zero matrices in $\mathbb{R}^{n \times n}$ and $\mathbb{R}^{n \times m}$, respectively.

A continuous function $\gamma : \mathbb{R}_0^+ \to \mathbb{R}_0^+$, is said to belong to class $\mathcal{K}$ if it is strictly increasing and $\gamma(0) = 0$; γ is said to belong to class $\mathcal{K}_\infty$ if $\gamma \in \mathcal{K}$ and $\gamma(r) \to \infty$ as $r \to \infty$. A continuous function $\beta : \mathbb{R}_0^+ \times \mathbb{R}_0^+ \to \mathbb{R}_0^+$ is said to belong to class $\mathcal{KL}$ if, for each fixed s, the map $\beta(r, s)$ belongs to class $\mathcal{K}_\infty$ with respect to r and, for each fixed nonzero r, the map $\beta(r, s)$ is decreasing with respect to s and $\beta(r, s) \to 0$ as $s \to \infty$.

In this paper, we focus on *linear* control systems given by the differential equation:

$$\begin{cases} \dot{\xi} = A\xi + Bv + \overline{B}\omega, \\ \eta = C\xi + \nu, \end{cases} \tag{2.1}$$

where, for any $t \in \mathbb{R}$, $\xi(t) \in \mathbb{R}^n$, $v(t) \in \mathbb{R}^m$, $\omega(t) \in \mathbb{R}^q$, $\eta(t) \in \mathbb{R}^p$, and A, B, $\overline{B}$, and C are matrices of appropriate dimensions. The curve $\xi : \mathbb{R} \to \mathbb{R}^n$ is a *trajectory* of (2.1) if there exist curves $v : \mathbb{R} \to \mathbb{R}^m$ and $\omega : \mathbb{R} \to \mathbb{R}^q$ such that the time derivative of ξ satisfies (2.1). In the rest of the paper, we assume that all curves v and ω have some regularity assumptions, guaranteeing existence and uniqueness of the solutions of (2.1). Note that v, ω, η, and ν denote control input, disturbance, output of the system and measurement noise, respectively. We assume that $\omega(t)$ and $\nu(t)$, for any $t \in \mathbb{R}$, are zero-mean Gaussian noise processes (uncorrelated from each other). For all curves ω, we also write $\xi_{xv}(t)$ to denote the points reached at time t under the input v from initial condition $x = \xi_{xv}(0)$.

To describe the mismatch between the controller specifications and its software implementations such as digital sampling and finite precision arithmetic, which is the focus of this paper, we consider the discrete-time version of (2.1), as follows:

$$\begin{cases} x[r+1] = A_\tau x[r] + B_\tau u[r] + \overline{B}_\tau d[r] + e_s, \\ y[r] = Cx[r] + v[r], \end{cases} \tag{2.2}$$

where the matrices A_τ, B_τ, and $\overline{B}_\tau$ are given by:

$$A_\tau = e^{A\tau}, \quad B_\tau = \int_{r\tau}^{(r+1)\tau} e^{A(\tau - t)} B dt,$$

$$\overline{B}_\tau = \int_{r\tau}^{(r+1)\tau} e^{A(\tau - t)} \overline{B} dt,$$

and τ is the sampling time. The function e^{At}, for any $t \in \mathbb{R}$, denotes the matrix function defined by the convergent series:

$$e^{At} = I_n + At + \frac{1}{2!} A^2 t^2 + \frac{1}{3!} A^3 t^3 + \cdots,$$

where e is Euler's constant. The signals x, u, d, y, and v describe the exact value of the signals ξ, v, ω, η, and ν, respectively, at the sampling instants $0, \tau, 2\tau, 3\tau, \ldots$. Mathematically, we have:

$$x[r] = \xi(r\tau), \; u[r] = \upsilon(r\tau), \; d[r] = \omega(r\tau),$$
$$y[r] = \eta(r\tau), \; v[r] = \nu(r\tau), \; \forall r \in \mathbb{N}_0.$$

The term e_s in (2.2) is the sampling error. It can be shown that by sampling sufficiently fast, the error e_s can be made arbitrarily small [3]. Since typical embedded controller implementations use sampling time in the range of milliseconds to microseconds, we will make the assumption that quantization errors dominate the sampling errors, and assume that $e_s = 0$.

We assume that only output y of the system is measurable and not the full state x. Hence, a (proportional) *feedback* $K : \mathbb{R}^n \to \mathbb{R}^m$ defines the input $u[r] = -K\widehat{x}[r]$ based on an estimation $\widehat{x}$ of the state x. As explained in [8], the estimation $\widehat{x}$ can be constructed using the observer dynamic:

$$\begin{cases} \widehat{x}[r+1] = A_\tau \widehat{x}[r] + B_\tau u[r] + L\left(y[r] - \widehat{y}[r]\right), \\ \widehat{y}[r] = C\widehat{x}[r], \end{cases} \quad (2.3)$$

where $\widehat{y}$ should be viewed as an estimate of y and the linear map $L : \mathbb{R}^p \to \mathbb{R}^n$ is called an observer gain. By applying the feedback $u[r] = -K\widehat{x}[r]$ and combining the dynamics of control system in (2.2) and observer in (2.3), one obtains:

$$\begin{cases} x[r+1] = A_\tau x[r] - B_\tau K\widehat{x}[r] + \overline{B}_\tau d[r], \\ \widehat{x}[r+1] = (A_\tau - B_\tau K - LC)\widehat{x}[r] + LCx[r] + Lv[r]. \end{cases} \quad (2.4)$$

As shown in [1], using a fixed-point implementation of the feedback gain as well as the observer dynamic, one gets the following overall dynamics:

$$\begin{cases} x[r+1] = A_\tau x[r] - B_\tau K\widehat{x}[r] + \overline{B}_\tau d[r] + B_\tau e_{q2}, \\ \widehat{x}[r+1] = (A_\tau - B_\tau K - LC)\widehat{x}[r] + LCx[r] + Lv[r] + e_{q1}, \end{cases} \quad (2.5)$$

where e_{q1} and e_{q2} are quantization errors in observer dynamic and feedback gain codes, respectively. Now, one can rewrite the control system in (2.5) as follows:

$$w[r+1] = Gw[r] + H_1 e_1[r] + H_2 e_2[r], \quad (2.6)$$

with:

$$w = \begin{bmatrix} x \\ \widehat{x} \end{bmatrix}, \; e_1 = \begin{bmatrix} d \\ v \end{bmatrix}, \; e_2 = \begin{bmatrix} e_{q1} \\ e_{q2} \end{bmatrix},$$

and:

$$G = \begin{bmatrix} A_\tau & -B_\tau K \\ LC & A_\tau - B_\tau K - LC \end{bmatrix}, \; H_1 = \begin{bmatrix} \overline{B}_\tau & 0_{n \times p} \\ 0_{n \times q} & L \end{bmatrix},$$
$$H_2 = \begin{bmatrix} 0_{n \times n} & B_\tau \\ I_n & 0_{n \times m} \end{bmatrix}.$$

Since states of the control system (2.1) are bounded physical quantities, such as temperature, pressure, and so on, their estimations and the output of the control system are bounded quantities as well. Hence, in the rest of the paper, we assume that $y \in Y$, and $\widehat{x} \in \widehat{X}$ for compact sets $Y \subset \mathbb{R}^p$ and $\widehat{X} \subset \mathbb{R}^n$.

2.2 Stability of Perturbed Systems

We recall the notion of uniform global asymptotic stability with respect to a set [16].

Definition 2.1 ([16]). *A control system of the form (2.1) is uniformly globally asymptotically stable (UGAS) with respect to a set $\mathcal{A}$ if there exists a $\mathcal{KL}$ function β such that for any $t \in \mathbb{R}_0^+$, any $x \in \mathbb{R}^n$, any control input $\upsilon : \mathbb{R}_0^+ \to \mathsf{D}_1 \subseteq \mathbb{R}^m$, and for any*

possible disturbance $\omega : \mathbb{R}_0^+ \to \mathsf{D}_2 \subseteq \mathbb{R}^q$, where D_1, and D_2 are compact sets, the following condition is satisfied:

$$\|\xi_{x\upsilon}(t)\|_{\mathcal{A}} \leq \beta(\|x\|_{\mathcal{A}}, t), \quad (2.7)$$

where the point-to-set distance $\|x\|_{\mathcal{A}}$ is defined by $\|x\|_{\mathcal{A}} = \inf_{y \in \mathcal{A}} \|x - y\|$.

When $\mathcal{A}$ is a singleton $\{x_0\}$, we speak of an asymptotically stable equilibrium point x_0 rather than a UGAS set. The notion of UGAS for discrete-time control systems is obtained from Definition 2.1 by replacing $t \in \mathbb{R}_0^+$ with $r \in \mathbb{N}_0$.

We recall the following result describing how stability properties are affected by additive disturbances.

Proposition 2.2 ([1]). *Consider the discrete-time linear system:*

$$x[r+1] = Ax[r]$$

and assume that the origin is an asymptotically stable equilibrium point. Then, for any signal $d : \mathbb{N}_0 \to \mathbb{R}^m$ satisfying $\|d[r]\| \leq b(d)$ for any $r \in \mathbb{N}_0$ and some constant $b(d) \in \mathbb{R}_0^+$, the system:

$$x[r+1] = Ax[r] + Bd[r] \quad (2.8)$$

is UGAS with respect to the set:

$$\mathcal{A} = \{x \in \mathbb{R}^n \mid \|x\| \leq \gamma b(d)\},$$

where γ is given by:

$$\gamma = \max_{\theta \in [0, 2\pi[} \left\| \left(\mathrm{e}^{i\theta} I_n - A\right)^{-1} B \right\|, \quad (2.9)$$

with $i = \sqrt{-1}$. Moreover, the output $y = Cx$ is guaranteed to converge to the set:

$$\mathcal{A}_y = \{y \in \mathbb{R}^p \mid \|y\| \leq \gamma_y b(d)\}, \quad (2.10)$$

with:

$$\gamma_y = \max_{\theta \in [0, 2\pi[} \left\| C\left(\mathrm{e}^{i\theta} I_n - A\right)^{-1} B \right\|.$$

In control theory, γ_y is known as the $\mathcal{L}_2$ *gain* of the control system in (2.8) with the output $y = Cx$. The following proposition follows from Proposition 2.2 and describes the stability properties of linear control systems in (2.6) with respect to disturbance, measurement noise, and implementation errors in the feedback gain and observer dynamic.

Proposition 2.3. *Consider the discrete-time linear system in (2.6). For any input e_1 and e_2 satisfying $\|e_1[r]\| \leq b(e_1)$ and $\|e_2[r]\| \leq b(e_2)$ for any $r \in \mathbb{N}_0$ and some constants $b(e_1), b(e_2) \in \mathbb{R}_0^+$, the system is UGAS with respect to the set:*

$$\mathcal{A} = \{x \in \mathbb{R}^n \mid \|x\| \leq \gamma_1 b(e_1) + \gamma_2 b(e_2)\},$$

where γ_1 and γ_2 are given by:

$$\gamma_j = \max_{\theta \in [0, 2\pi[} \left\| \left(\mathrm{e}^{i\theta} I_{2n} - G\right)^{-1} H_j \right\|, \; \text{for } j = 1, 2,$$

with $i = \sqrt{-1}$. Moreover, the output $y = [C \; 0_{p \times n}] w \in \mathbb{R}^p$ is guaranteed to converge to the set:

$$\mathcal{A}_y = \{y \in \mathbb{R}^p \mid \|y\| \leq \gamma_{1y} b(e_1) + \gamma_{2y} b(e_2)\}, \quad (2.11)$$

where γ_{1y} and γ_{2y} are given by:

$$\gamma_{jy} = \max_{\theta \in [0, 2\pi[} \left\| [C \; 0_{p \times n}] \left(\mathrm{e}^{i\theta} I_{2n} - G\right)^{-1} H_j \right\|, \; \text{for } j = 1, 2. \quad (2.12)$$

The error vector e_1 includes disturbance and measurement noise, depending for example on the environment and the quality of the sensors collecting measurements. Hence, the controller designer does not have any control on the value of $b(e_1)$. However, one can reduce the amount of γ_{1y} by appropriately choosing gains K and L. On the other hand, one can reduce the amount of not only γ_{2y} but also $b(e_2)$ by appropriately choosing gains K and L. We use Proposition 2.3 in the following way. Given a feedback gain K and an observer gain L, we compute $\mathcal{L}_2$ gains γ_{1y} and γ_{2y} and an upper bound $b(e_2)$ on the implementation error e_2. Then the output of the controlled system (with implementation error) must converge to set $\mathcal{A}_y$ in (2.11). We show later that appropriate choices of gains K and L can shrink the size of the set $\mathcal{A}_y$ and hence, provide a tighter bound on the set to which the output of the system converges.

2.3 LQR-LQG Performance

In addition to asymptotic stability, controller designers also consider the *performance* of the controller, that is, of the controllers ensuring asymptotic stability of the origin, one desires the controller that minimizes a given cost function. A common approach for optimal output feedback controller are the *linear quadratic regulator* (LQR) and *linear quadratic Gaussian* (LQG). The LQR cost function to be minimized is given by:

$$J_{LQR} = \sum_{r=0}^{+\infty} \left\{ x[r]^T Q x[r] + u[r]^T R u[r] \right\}, \qquad (2.13)$$

for some chosen weight matrices Q and R that are positive definite and of appropriate dimensions.

The LQG cost function to be minimized is given by:

$$J_{LQG} = \lim_{r \to +\infty} \mathrm{E} \left[\|e[r]\|^2 \right], \qquad (2.14)$$

where E stands for expected value and e is the estimation error for the control system in (2.4) whose dynamic is given by:

$$e[r+1] = x[r+1] - \widehat{x}[r+1] = (A_\tau - LC)e[r] + \overline{B}_\tau d[r] - Lv[r]. \qquad (2.15)$$

As mentioned before, d and v are assumed to be zero-mean Gaussian noise process (uncorrelated from each other) with covariance matrices:

$$\mathrm{E}\left(d[r]d[r]^T\right) = \widehat{Q}, \ \mathrm{E}\left(v[r]v[r]^T\right) = \widehat{R}, \ \forall r \in \mathbb{N}_0, \qquad (2.16)$$

where $\widehat{Q}$ and $\widehat{R}$ are some positive semi-definite matrices of appropriate dimensions.

A standard control-theoretic construction rewrites the cost function (2.13) as $J_{LQR} = x[0]^T S(K) x[0]$, where $u = -Kx$, and $S(K) \in \mathbb{R}^{n \times n}$ is a positive definite matrix that is the unique solution for S to the Lyapunov equation:

$$(A_\tau - B_\tau K)^T S (A_\tau - B_\tau K) - S + Q + K^T R K = 0, \quad (2.17)$$

where K is a controller making $A_\tau - B_\tau K$ Hurwitz.[1] See [8] for detailed information. Additionally, we have

$$\lambda_{\min}(S(K))\|x[0]\|^2 \leq J_{LQR} \leq \lambda_{\max}(S(K))\|x[0]\|^2, \quad (2.18)$$

where $\lambda_{\min}(S(K)) \in \mathbb{R}^+$ and $\lambda_{\max}(S(K)) \in \mathbb{R}^+$ are minimum and maximum eigenvalues of $S(K)$, respectively. Therefore, J_{LQR} can be minimized for all possible choices of initial conditions by just minimizing the maximum eigenvalue of $S(K)$. Note

that since S is a positive definite and symmetric matrix, its maximum eigenvalue is equal to its induced 2 norm[2] $\|S\|$.

Similarly, the cost function (2.14) can be rewritten as $J_{LQG} = \|P(L)\|$, where $P(L) \in \mathbb{R}^{n \times n}$ is a positive definite matrix that is the unique solution for P to the Lyapunov equation:

$$(A_\tau - LC) P (A_\tau - LC)^T - P + \overline{B}_\tau \widehat{Q} \overline{B}_\tau^T + L\widehat{R}L^T = 0, \qquad (2.19)$$

where L is an observer gain making $A_\tau - LC$ Hurwitz. See [8] for more detailed information. Therefore, J_{LQG} can be minimized by just minimizing $\|P(L)\|$.

Note that the optimal feedback $u = -Kx$ minimizing the LQR cost in (2.13) is computed using the deterministic dynamic:

$$x[r+1] = A_\tau x[r] + B_\tau u[r].$$

On the other hand, the optimal gain L minimizing the LQG cost in (2.14) is computed using the stochastic dynamic in (2.15). Thanks to the separation principle for linear control systems [8], one concludes that the overall closed loop system in (2.4) is $UGAS$ even though the gains K and L are designed separately.

2.4 The Effect of Errors

Example We now present a simple motivating example showing how different choices of controllers may result in different steady state errors due to their fixed-point implementations, yet providing approximately the same LQR-LQG performance. Consider the following simple physical model of a bicycle, borrowed from [2]:

$$\left\{ \begin{array}{l} \begin{bmatrix} \dot{\xi_1} \\ \dot{\xi_2} \end{bmatrix} = \begin{bmatrix} 0 & \frac{g}{h} \\ 1 & 0 \end{bmatrix} \begin{bmatrix} \xi_1 \\ \xi_2 \end{bmatrix} + \begin{bmatrix} 1 \\ 0 \end{bmatrix} (v + \omega), \\ \eta = \begin{bmatrix} \frac{av_0}{bh} & \frac{v_0^2}{bh} \end{bmatrix} \begin{bmatrix} \xi_1 \\ \xi_2 \end{bmatrix} + \nu, \end{array} \right. \qquad (2.20)$$

where ξ_1 is the steering angular velocity, ξ_2 is the steering angle, η is the role angle, v is the torque applied to the handle bars, $g = 9.8m/s^2$ is the acceleration due to gravity, $h = 1.5m$ is the height of the center of mass, $v_0 = 2m/s$ is the velocity of the bicycle at the rear wheel, $a = 0.5m$ is the distance of the center of mass from a vertical line through the contact point of the rear wheel and $b = 1m$ is the wheel base.

The control objective is to design a feedback gain $K \in \mathbb{R}^{1 \times 2}$ and an observer gain $L \in \mathbb{R}^{2 \times 1}$ such that the feedback control law $u = -K\widehat{x}$, where $\widehat{x} = [\widehat{x}_1, \ \widehat{x}_2]^T$ is the state of the observer in (2.3), makes the closed loop system UGAS. By choosing the matrices $Q = I_2$ and $R = 1$ inside the LQR cost function and $\widehat{Q} = 1$ and $\widehat{R} = 1$ in (2.16), the feedback and observer gains minimizing the LQR and LQG costs are given by $K_1 = [5.1538, \ 12.9724]$, and $L_1 = [0.0317, \ 0.0118]^T$, respectively. Consider a second pair of feedback and observer gains given by $K_2 = [3.0253, \ 12.6089]$ and $L_2 = [0.0132, \ 0.1021]^T$. For the initial condition $x = (0.2, \ 0.2)^T$, the value of the LQR cost function is 264.1908 for feedback gain K_1 and 284.1578 for K_2. Moreover, the value of the LQG cost function is 0.0229 for observer gain L_1 and 0.0246 for L_2. So, the gains K_2 and L_2 give cost functions about 7% greater than the optimal gains K_1 and L_1.

We now show how different choice of feedback and observer gains result in different fixed-point implementation errors. For now, let us assume that $\omega(t) = 0$ and $\nu(t) = 0$, for any $t \in \mathbb{R}_0^+$. In Figure 1, we show the output of the closed-loop system starting from the initial condition $x = (0.2, \ 0.2)^T$, when the feedback gain and

---

[1] We call the matrix $A_\tau - B_\tau K$ Hurwitz if its eigenvalues are inside the unit circle, centered at the origin.

[2] We recall that induced 2 norm of a matrix $A \in \mathbb{R}^{n \times m}$ is given by: $\|A\| = \sqrt{\lambda_{\max}\left(A^T A\right)}$.

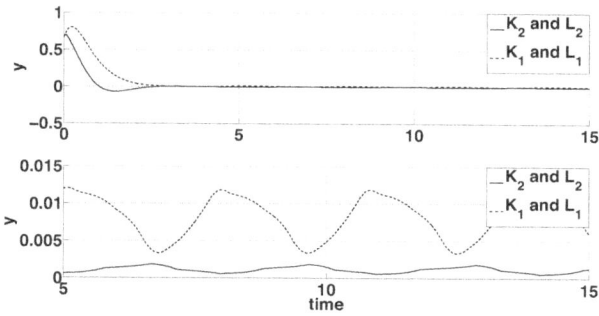

Figure 1: Evolution of the output y with initial state $(0.2, \, 0.2)^T$ for the pair of gains K_1, L_1 and K_2, L_2 using 16-bit implementation. Upper panel: evolution of y from 0 to 15 seconds. Lower panel: evolution of y from 5 to 15 seconds (magnified version).

observer dynamic are implemented using 16-bit fixed-point representation. As can be observed from Figure 1, the output of the controlled system does not converge to the equilibrium point at the origin because of the fixed-point implementation error in the controllers. Furthermore, the practical stability region using gains K_2 and L_2 is much smaller than the one using gains K_1 and L_1.

Using bounds on implementation errors for the two controllers (described in Section 3) and Proposition 2.3, we can prove that the output of the system with feedback and observer gains K_1 and L_1 (resp. K_2 and L_2) converges to a ball centered at the origin with radius 0.5486 (resp. 0.0513), whenever the output of the system and the state of the observer take values in the interval $[-1, \, 1]$ and the feedback gain and observer dynamic are implemented using 16-bit fixed-point implementation. As can be seen, given a 16-bit implementation, feedback and observer gains K_2 and L_2 may be preferred to gains K_1 and L_1 because they have guaranteed bounds on practical stability region that is 10 times smaller than gains K_1 and L_1 and provide approximately similar performance. If one considers the effect of disturbance and measurement noise, it can be proved that the output of the system with feedback and observer gains K_1 and L_1 (resp. K_2 and L_2) converges to a ball centered at the origin with radius $5.0489 b(e_1) + 0.5486$ (resp. $2.5341 b(e_1) + 0.0513$), where $b(e_1)$ is an upper bound on the size of the vector e_1 introduced in (2.6).

Optimization objectives The above example suggests that the control design should optimize for the following objectives: the LQR and the LQG costs for performance, error caused by disturbance and measurement noise, and the implementation error given by a fixed-precision encoding. Accordingly, we define a cost function that is weighted sum of the four factors:

$$\mathcal{J}(K, L) = w_1 \frac{\|S(K)\|}{\|S^*\|} + w_2 \frac{\|P(L)\|}{\|P^*\|} + w_3 \frac{\gamma_{1y}}{\gamma_{1y}^*} + w_4 \frac{\gamma_{2y} b(e_2)}{\gamma_{2y}^* b^*(e_2)}, \quad (2.21)$$

where $w_1, \ldots, w_4$ are weighting factors, S^* and P^* are matrices, computed from Lyapunov equations in (2.17) and (2.19) using standard LQR and LQG gains (K_{LQR} and L_{LQG}), γ_{1y} and γ_{2y} (resp. γ_{1y}^* and γ_{2y}^*) are the $\mathcal{L}_2$ gains in (2.12) using feedback and observer gains K and L (resp. K_{LQR} and L_{LQG}) and $b(e_2)$ (resp. $b^*(e_2)$) is the bound on the implementation error of given feedback and observer gains K and L (resp. K_{LQR} and L_{LQG}). Minimizing the terms γ_{1y} and $\gamma_{2y} b(e_2)$ inside (2.21) results in a tighter bound on the set $\mathcal{A}_y$ in Proposition 2.3. Since the four factors in (2.21) have different scales, we normalized them by their values using the stan-

dard gains K_{LQR} and L_{LQG}. The designer can choose $w_1, \ldots, w_4$ based on the priorities on LQR and LQG performances and steady state error. Our objective is to find feedback and observer gains that minimize the cost function $\mathcal{J}$.

We focus on implementation errors arising out of fixed-precision arithmetic. The bound $b(e_2)$ is computed using the strategy explained in Section 3. Since the cost function $\mathcal{J}$ is not necessarily convex with respect to the feedback and observer gains K and L, we cannot reduce the design problem to a convex optimization problem. We use a heuristic stochastic optimization approach to find feedback and observer gains K and L minimizing $\mathcal{J}$.

In our exposition, we consider the plant model to be precise, and only consider quantization effects as the source of error. Our methodology can consider both additive and multiplicative uncertainties in the plant model as well [7]. We can take those uncertainties into account by adding appropriate extra terms to the cost function in (2.21), using the results provided in [29, 27]. We omit the details for simplicity.

3. COMPUTING QUANTIZATION ERROR

In this section we show how to compute a bound on the fixed-point implementation error for given feedback and observer gains K and L. We assume that the outputs of the controlled system and the state of the observer are restricted to compact subsets $Y \subset \mathbb{R}^p$ and $\widehat{X} \subset \mathbb{R}^n$, respectively.

3.1 Best Fixed-point Implementation

A *fixed-point representation* of a real number is a triple $\langle s, n, m \rangle$ consisting of a *sign bit indicator* $s \in \{1, 0\}$ (for *signed* and *unsigned*), a *length* $n \in \mathbb{N}$, and a *length of the fractional part* $m \in \mathbb{N}$. The length of the integer part is $n - m - 1$. Intuitively, a real number is represented using n bits, of which m bits are used to store the fractional part. Clearly, the largest integer portion has to fit in $n - m - 1$ bits.

A variable with a fixed-point type is represented as an integer. We associate an integer variable $\widehat{x}$ with the fixed-point representation of a real variable x. An integer variable $\widehat{x}$ that represents a fixed-point variable with type $\langle 0, n, m \rangle$ can be interpreted as the rational number $2^{-m} \widehat{x}$. We deal with a signed number by separately tracking the sign and the magnitude, performing the operations on the magnitudes using unsigned arithmetic, and finally putting the appropriate sign bits back.

An operation using real arithmetic may have different fixed-point implementations depending on how many bits are allocated to hold the integer part and the fraction part of the variables. Allocating fewer number of bits than required to hold the integer part may lead to overflow. On the other hand, if more than the required number of bits are allocated to the integer part, the quantization error can increase because fewer bits are assigned to the fractional part. When we compare fixed-point implementations of different controllers, we first synthesize the best possible implementation of a controller, relative to an analysis.

Let us fix the total number of bits to be n for the implementation of a controller. Let us fix a program analysis that computes an upper bound on the quantization error for a fixed-point implementation. Given a controller, let b be the upper bound on the quantization error computed by the analysis in a fixed-point implementation I of a controller using n bits in all for a given range of the inputs. The fixed-point implementation I is the *best implementation* if there does not exist another implementation I' using n bits, for which the bound on the quantization error computed by the analysis is b' and $b' < b$.

If the ranges of the variables in the real arithmetic computation can be computed exactly, it is possible to synthesize the best fixed-point implementation. In the best fixed-point implementation, the number of bits allocated to the integer part is just enough to hold the integer part of any value in that range. For example, if the range of a variable is [-35.55, 48.72], the datatype for the variable in the best 16-bit fixed-point representation is $\langle 1, 16, 9 \rangle$.

The range computation problem of variable y in an operation $y = f(x_1, \ldots, x_n)$ involves solving a maximization and a minimization problem, where f is the objective function and the ranges on $x_1, \ldots, x_n$ form the set of constraints. If the function f is convex, the range of y can be computed exactly, and it is also straightforward to find the best fixed-point implementation for the operation.

3.2 Error Bound Computation

We apply a mixed-integer linear-programming-based optimization technique to find out the error bound between a computation in real arithmetic and its best fixed-point implementation. Suppose we have an arithmetic operation $s : a = b \; op \; c$, where $op \in \{+, -, *\}$, where we assume that if $op = *$, then either b or c is a constant. If $op = +$ or $op = -$, then b and c can both be variables. We associate an integer variable $\widehat{x}$ with the fixed-point representation of a real variable x. Let the range of the values for a and b and c are $[l_a, u_a]$, $[l_b, u_b]$, and $[l_c, u_c]$, respectively. Let the fixed-point representation of a, b and c be $\langle 1, n_a, m_a \rangle$, $\langle 1, n_b, m_b \rangle$, and $\langle 1, n_c, m_c \rangle$, respectively. Let $b(e_b)$ and $b(e_c)$ be bounds on the quantization errors of b and c, respectively. The optimization problem to find the bound on the error is given by:

$$
\begin{aligned}
\text{maximize} \quad & \left| a - 2^{-m_a} \widehat{a} \right| \\
\text{subject to} \quad & l_a \le a \le u_a, \quad l_b \le b \le u_b \\
& \left| b - 2^{-m_b} * \widehat{b} \right| \le b(e_b) \\
& \left| c - 2^{-m_c} * \widehat{c} \right| \le b(e_c) \\
& a = b \; op \; c \\
& \Phi(\mathsf{fp}(s))
\end{aligned}
\tag{3.1}
$$

where $\mathsf{fp}(s)$ is the fixed-point representation of the statement s and $\Phi(\mathsf{s})$ denotes a logical formula that relates the inputs and outputs of the fixed-point representation s. Technically, Φ is the *strongest postcondition* [26] of s with respect to *true*. We compute Φ using an arithmetic encoding of a fixed-point computation [1]. Here we illustrate the computation of the strongest postcondition Φ using an example.

Example. Suppose we have the following arithmetic operation

$$s : y = -7.2479 * x .$$

Assume the compact set for x is [-1, 1]. The fixed-point expression corresponding to s in the best fixed-point implementation is

$$\mathsf{fp}(s) : -\widehat{y} = (-115 * \widehat{x}) \gg 6 .$$

The strongest postcondition $\Phi(\mathsf{fp}(s))$ of $\mathsf{fp}(s)$ is given by:
$$
\begin{aligned}
\Phi(\mathsf{fp}(s)) := \quad & tmp = -115 * \widehat{x} \wedge \\
& tmp \ge 0 \to tmp1 = tmp \wedge \\
& tmp < 0 \to tmp1 = -tmp \wedge \\
& tmp1 = 2^6 * divisor + remainder \wedge \\
& remainder \ge 0 \wedge remainder < 2^6 \wedge \\
& tmp \ge 0 \to \widehat{y} = divisor \wedge \\
& tmp < 0 \to \widehat{y} = -divisor ,
\end{aligned}
$$
where tmp, $tmp1$, $divisor$, and $remainder$ are integer variables.

Depending on the arithmetic operation, we need to solve at most four instances of mixed integer linear programming problems to solve the optimization problem in (3.1), and the maximum among all of these instances gives the bound on the error in the fixed-point implementation.

We use the above technique to compute the bound on the error in one operation in the fixed-point implementation of a gain. The implementation of a gain involves a series of arithmetic operations. We compute the error bound for the output of one arithmetic operation at a time. Let $s : a = b \; op \; c$ is an arithmetic operation in the implementation of a gain. In the arithmetic operation, b and c may either be a constant, a state variable or a temporary variable which captures the result of some previous operation. If b (or c) represents a constant, and the fixed-point representation contains m bits for the fraction part, then the error in the fixed point representation is bounded by $\frac{1}{2^m}$. If b (or c) represents a state variable, then the fixed-point datatype can be determined from the given compact set for the state, and the fixed-point datatype can be determined accordingly. Then the error in the fixed-point representation is bounded by $\frac{1}{2^m}$, where m is the number of bits to represent the fraction part in the fixed-point datatype of the variable. If b (or c) is a temporary variable used to hold the result of an earlier computation, then the range and error bound for the variable are already known.

4. OPTIMAL CONTROLLER SYNTHESIS

We now describe our controller synthesis algorithm that minimizes the cost function (2.21) combining LQR and LQG performance, disturbance, measurement noise, and implementation errors. Since the cost function is non-convex, we use a stochastic local search technique.

4.1 Particle Swarm Optimization

We use a stochastic local search approach called particle swarm optimization (PSO). It maintains a set of potential solutions (called "particles") in a compact d-dimensional search space $D = \prod_{j=1}^{d} [y_{\min}^j, y_{\max}^j] \subset \mathbb{R}^d$, minimizing a given cost function. The particles move in this space according to their velocity. Each particle, indexed by $i \in \mathbb{N}$, has a position $y_i \in \mathbb{R}^d$, changing between $y_{\min}$ and $y_{\max}$, and a velocity vector $v_i \in \mathbb{R}^d$, changing between some vectors $v_{\min}$ and $v_{\max}$. The terms $v_{\min}$ and $v_{\max}$ are often set to the maximum dynamic range of the variables on each dimension [28]: $-v_{\min}^j = v_{\max}^j = |y_{\max}^j - y_{\min}^j|$. Every particle remembers its own best position (i.e., the lowest value of the cost function achieved so far by this particle) in a vector $P_i \in \mathbb{R}^d$. The best position with respect to the cost function among all of the particles so far is stored in a vector $P_g \in \mathbb{R}^d$.

PSO updates the positions and velocities of all particles iteratively. The new velocity and position for particle i are determined as:

$$
v_i^{l+1} = w^l v_i^l + c_1 r_1 \left(P_i^l - y_i^l \right) + c_2 r_2 \left(P_g^l - y_i^l \right),
\tag{4.1}
$$

$$
y_i^{l+1} = y_i^l + v_i^{l+1},
\tag{4.2}
$$

where the superscript l denotes the iteration number, the subscript $i = 1, \ldots, N$ denotes the index of the particle, and N is the number of particles. The constant w^l in (4.1) is updated using the inertia weight approach [5] as the following:

$$
w^l = w_{\max} - \frac{w_{\max} - w_{\min}}{l_{\max}} (l - 1),
\tag{4.3}
$$

where $w_{\max}$ and $w_{\min}$ are adjusted to 1 and $\frac{c_1 + c_2}{2} - 1$ and $l_{\max}$ is the maximum number of iterations. The constants c_1 and c_2 in (4.1) are the acceleration constants, influencing the convergence speed of particles toward its own and global best positions and set to 0.5 and 1, respectively [5]. The constants r_1 and r_2 in (4.1) are uniformly distributed random numbers on the interval $[0, 1]$.

4.2 Overall Algorithm

The PSO algorithm is used to search for feedback and observer gains $K \in \mathbb{R}^{m \times n}$ and $L \in \mathbb{R}^{n \times p}$ for the control system (2.5), minimizing (2.21). Note that a particle in PSO represents a feedback and an observer gain K and L, respectively, moving in an $m \times n + n \times p$ dimensional search space. To discard those gains that make the controlled system unstable, we penalize unstable gains by including a penalty term $\widetilde{P}$ in the cost function such that $\widetilde{P} = 0$ if $A_\tau - B_\tau K$ and $A_\tau - LC$ are Hurwitz and $\widetilde{P} = +\infty$ otherwise. The cost function for PSO is then $F(K, L) = \mathcal{J}(K, L) + \widetilde{P}(K, L)$.

The design steps are as follows:

(1) Initialize positions of N feedback gains K_i and observer gains L_i by K_{LQR} and L_{LQG}, respectively, and uniformly randomly initialize their velocities, for $i = 1, \ldots, N$.

(2) Given any feedback gain K_i and observer gain L_i, compute the cost function $F(K_i, L_i)$. To compute $\widetilde{P}$, check if $A_\tau - B_\tau K$ and $A_\tau - LC$ are Hurwitz. There are some steps to compute $\mathcal{J}$. First, compute $S(K_i)$ and $P(L_i)$ by solving the Lyapunov equations (2.17) and (2.19), respectively, and find their induced 2-norm. Second, compute the $\mathcal{L}_2$ gains γ_{1y} and γ_{2y}. Third, compute $b(e_2)$ by solving the optimization problems from Section 3.

(3) Compare $F(K_i, L_i)$ to its own best position P_i so far and the global best position P_g so far. If $F(K_i, L_i)$ is less than the previous personal best (resp. the global best), update the best position (resp. the global best) to K_i and L_i.

(4) Modify the velocity and position of each pair K_i and L_i according to (4.1) and (4.2).

(5) If the number of iterations, denoted by l, reaches the maximum, denoted by $l_{\max}$, or the value of F does not change for the global best position P_g for 50 consecutive iterations up to error 10^{-6} then go to Step (6), otherwise go to Step (2);

(6) The latest P_g is an estimate for the optimal controller.

5. EXTENSION: PID CONTROLLERS

PID controllers are a common class of controllers in many industries, such as automotive, power systems, servomotors, and so on. We now extend the analysis of Section 2 to PID controllers. A PID controller generalizes a proportional feedback controller, and includes three terms: a proportional term, an integrator, and a differentiator. For an input v, the output η of the PID controller is computed as follows:

$$\eta(t) = K_P v(t) + K_I \int_0^t v(s)ds + K_D \frac{dv(t)}{dt}, \ \forall t \in \mathbb{R}_0^+, \ (5.1)$$

where K_P, K_I, and K_D are called proportional, integrator, and differentiator gains, respectively. To describe the mismatch between the PID specifications and its software implementation, we consider the discrete-time version of (5.1). An integrator term:

$$\eta(t) = \int_0^t v(s)ds, \ \forall t \in \mathbb{R}_0^+,$$

can be discretized based on the trapezoidal approximation as follows:

$$y[r+1] = y[r] + \frac{\tau}{2} \left(u[r+1] + u[r] \right), \ \forall r \in \mathbb{N}_0, \quad (5.2)$$

where τ is the sampling time, $y[r] = \eta(r\tau) + e_1$ and $u[r] = v(r\tau)$, for any $r \in \mathbb{N}_0$. A common way of discretizing a differentiator, is based on the backward Euler method. A differentiator term:

$$\eta(t) = \frac{dv(t)}{dt}, \ \forall t \in \mathbb{R}_0^+,$$

can be discretized as follows:

$$y[r+1] = \frac{u[r+1] - u[r]}{\tau}, \ \forall r \in \mathbb{N}_0, \quad (5.3)$$

where $y[r] = \eta(r\tau) + e_2$ and $u[r] = v(r\tau)$, for any $r \in \mathbb{N}_0$. By using the fast sampling time assumption, we can ignore the errors e_1 and e_2 in the discretized versions of the integrator and differentiator in comparison with quantization errors. To follow the same analysis as in Section 2, we need a state space realization of PID controller. By resorting to control theoretic results (see, e.g., [11]) and using the discretization rules in (5.2) and (5.3), the state space realization of discretized PID controller with input $\widehat{u}[r]$ and output $\widehat{y}[r]$ are obtained as follows:

$$\begin{cases} \widehat{x}[r+1] = \widehat{A}\widehat{x}[r] + \widehat{B}\widehat{u}[r], \\ \widehat{y}[r] = \widehat{C}\widehat{x}[r] + \widehat{D}\widehat{u}[r], \end{cases} \quad (5.4)$$

where

$$\widehat{A} = \begin{bmatrix} 0 & 1 \\ 0 & 1 \end{bmatrix}, \ \widehat{B} = \begin{bmatrix} 0 \\ 1 \end{bmatrix}, \ \widehat{C} = \begin{bmatrix} \dfrac{K_D}{\tau} & K_I\tau - \dfrac{K_D}{\tau} \end{bmatrix},$$

$$\widehat{D} = \left(K_P + \frac{K_I\tau}{2} + \frac{K_D}{\tau} \right).$$

Without loss of generality, consider a single-input ($m = 1$) single-output ($p = 1$) discrete-time linear control system of the form:

$$\begin{cases} x[r+1] = Ax[r] + Bu[r], \\ y[r] = Cx[r]. \end{cases}$$

Since the input of the PID controller is equal to the negative of the output of the plant ($\widehat{u} = -y$) because of negative feedback and the output of the PID controller is equal to the input of the plant ($u = \widehat{y}$), one obtains:

$$\begin{cases} x[r+1] = \left(A - B\widehat{D}C \right) x[r] + B\widehat{C}\widehat{x}[r], \\ \widehat{x}[r+1] = -\widehat{B}Cx[r] + \widehat{A}\widehat{x}[r]. \end{cases} \quad (5.5)$$

Similar to what has been explained in Section 2, by fixed-point implementation of the PID controller, one gets the following overall dynamic:

$$\begin{cases} x[r+1] = \left(A - B\widehat{D}C \right) x[r] + B\widehat{C}\widehat{x}[r] + Be_{q2}, \\ \widehat{x}[r+1] = -\widehat{B}Cx[r] + \widehat{A}\widehat{x}[r] + e_{q1}, \end{cases} \quad (5.6)$$

where e_{q1} and e_{q2} are quantization errors in computing the PID controller. Now, we can use the same strategy, as explained in Subsection 4.2, to design parameters K_P, K_I, and K_D of PID controllers minimizing a performance-based cost function as well as the effect of quantization error. For example, one can consider:

$$\mathcal{J}(K_P, K_I, K_D) = \frac{w_1}{\text{PM}} + \frac{w_2}{\text{GM}} + w_3\gamma(b(e_{q1}) + b(e_{q2})), \ (5.7)$$

where PM and GM are phase and gain margins, w_1, w_2, w_3 are weighting factors, γ is the $\mathcal{L}_2$ gain of the linear control system (5.6) and $b(e_{q1})$ and $b(e_{q2})$ are the bounds on the implementation errors e_{q1} and e_{q2}. Note that control over PM and GM guarantees robust stability of the closed-loop systems [8]. The phase and gain margins measure the system's tolerance to the time delay and the steady state gain, respectively.

Control systems	# bits	Synthesized gains		Time cost
		K	L	
Bicycle	16	$[3.0253\ 12.6089]$	$[0.0132\ 0.1021]^T$	1h36m41s
DC motor position	16	$[0.1129\ 0.0211\ 0.0093]$	$[0.0390\ 0.3700\ -0.0175]^T$	1h39m06s
Pitch angle control	32	$[\ -0.1202\ 42.5655\ 1.0001]$	$[0.0001\ 0.0000\ 0.0017]^T$	8h31m53s
Inverted pendulum	32	$[-1.5362\ -2.0254\ 16.5192\ 2.7358]$	$\begin{bmatrix} 0.0017 & 0.0021 & 0.0012 & 0.0000 \\ 0.0001 & 0.0018 & 0.0122 & 0.0770 \end{bmatrix}^T$	9h54m17s
Batch reactor process	16	$\begin{bmatrix} 0.0583 & 0.9093 & 0.3258 & 0.8721 \\ -2.4638 & -0.0504 & -1.7099 & 1.1653 \end{bmatrix}$	$\begin{bmatrix} 0.0774 & -0.0022 & 0.0267 & 0.0356 \\ -0.0103 & 0.0227 & 0.0398 & 0.0001 \end{bmatrix}^T$	3h08m29s

Table 1: Synthesized gains and required time for synthesizing them.

Control systems	lub of LQR cost		LQG cost		Steady state error	
	LQR	Synthesized K	LQG	Synthesized L	LQR-LQG	Synthesized gains
Bicycle	$3956.3\|x\|^2$	$4331.7\|x\|^2$	0.0229	0.0246	$5.0489b(e_1)+0.5486$	$2.5341b(e_1)+0.0513$
DC motor position	$1001.6\|x\|^2$	$1376.7\|x\|^2$	36.6315	36.6731	$30.566b(e_1)+0.16$	$15.421b(e_1)+0.011$
Pitch angle control	$2.9732 \times 10^6\|x\|^2$	$2.9887 \times 10^6\|x\|^2$	0.0013	0.0018	$2.6781b(e_1)+0.4746$	$1.4453b(e_1)+0.0807$
Inverted pendulum	$4.2988 \times 10^4\|x\|^2$	$5.3471 \times 10^4\|x\|^2$	0.3600	0.3897	$83.4217b(e_1)+0.0432$	$30.3801b(e_1)+0.0086$
Batch reactor process	$223.1773\|x\|^2$	$223.1825\|x\|^2$	0.0731	0.0949	$2.9309b(e_1)+0.4194$	$2.1216b(e_1)+0.1642$

Table 2: Least upper bound (lub) on the LQR cost (2.13), for a given initial condition x, the LQG cost (2.14), and the Euclidean norm of the steady state error for the LQR-LQG and the synthesized gains.

6. EXPERIMENTAL RESULTS

We implemented the algorithm presented in Section 4.2 in Matlab. We use a PSO function in Matlab from [5]. We implemented a static analyzer in OCaml that synthesizes the best fixed-point program and computes the bound on the fixed-point implementation error for given feedback and observer gains K and L, respectively. The tool gets the number of bits in the fixed-point datatype, compact subsets $Y \subset \mathbb{R}^p$ and $\widehat{X} \subset \mathbb{R}^n$, and feedback and observer gains K and L, respectively, as inputs. The optimization problems in computing the error bound are solved using the mixed-integer linear programming tool lp_solve [30]. All the experiments were done on a laptop with CPU Intel Core 2 Duo at 2.4 GHz.

We applied the proposed controller synthesis approach to a number of linear control systems. In all of the experiments, the number of particles in PSO is $N = 24$, the maximum number of iterations is $l_{\max} = 100$, and we choose the matrices $Q = I_n$ and $R = I_m$ in (2.13) and $\widehat{Q} = I_q$, and $\widehat{R} = I_p$ in (2.16). The value of $l_{\max}$ was chosen in such a way that appropriate gains are obtained in terms of the cost function (2.21) (or (5.7)) for all control systems. Moreover, we assume that the search space is $D = \prod_{i=1}^{n \times m + n \times p}[-150, 150] \subset \mathbb{R}^{n \times m + n \times p}$, which contains the standard LQR and LQG gains for all the examples. Further, we work on the compact subsets $Y = \prod_{i=1}^{p}[-1, 1] \subset \mathbb{R}^p$ and $\widehat{X} = \prod_{i=1}^{n}[-1, 1] \subset \mathbb{R}^n$. All constants and variables are expressed in SI units.

Our unstable examples include a bicycle [2], a DC motor position control [31], a pitch angle control [31], an inverted pendulum [31], a batch reactor process [7], and another inverted pendulum for PID synthesis [31]. See Table 1 and 2 for experimental results. Note that for those examples for which a 32-bit implementation is chosen, the 16-bit one provides a stability region which is even larger than the range of the variables inside the controller. As can be seen from Table 2, in comparison with the conventional LQR-LQG approach, the synthesis approach proposed in this paper worsens the LQR and LQG performances by at most 1.37 times (for DC motor position) and 1.38 times (for Pitch angle control), respectively. However, the proposed synthesis approach improves

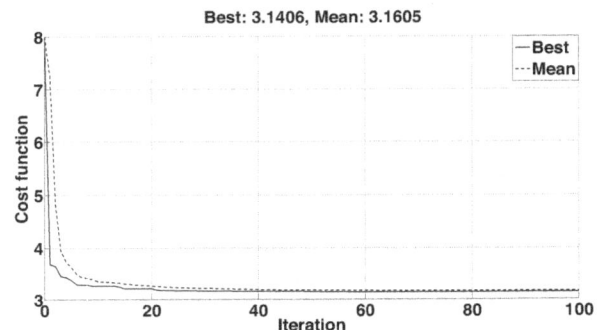

Figure 2: Cost of the best particle and average cost of all population vs iteration.

the size of the region of practical stability due to quantization error by at least 2.55 times. For certain examples, the improvement goes beyond the factor of 10. For the bicycle and DC motor position control, the region of practical stability due to quantization error improves by a factor of 10.69 and 14.55, respectively.

The detailed descriptions of the systems are as follows.

Bicycle The model of a bicycle is shown in (2.20). The weighting factors in (2.21) are chosen as $w_1 = w_2 = w_3 = 1$ and $w_4 = 5$. The results of the LQR, LQG, and the method in this paper are shown in Tables 1 and 2. To assess the quality of the proposed stochastic search method, we run the algorithms 10 times. The resulted standard deviation of the cost function $\mathcal{J}$ in (2.21) of all runs was 0.2806 which is around 9% of the best cost 3.1406. Figure 2 shows how the value of the cost function improves monotonically with the number of iteration for the best run. The fixed-point C code for the synthesized controller is shown in Figure 3.

DC motor position control The dynamic of a DC motor position

```
float output(float yin)
{
    static int x1 = x1₀;  // fixdt(1,16,14)
    static int x2 = x2₀;  // fixdt(1,16,14)
    int x1_new;           // fixdt(1,16,14)
    int x2_new;           // fixdt(1,16,14)
    int u;                // fixdt(1,16,11)

    // Intermediate variables
    int Gain1;            // fixdt(1,16,15)
    int Gain2;            // fixdt(1,16,15)
    int Gain3;            // fixdt(1,16,15)
    int Add1;             // fixdt(1,16,14)
    int Gain4;            // fixdt(1,16,15)
    int Gain5;            // fixdt(1,16,15)
    int Gain6;            // fixdt(1,16,15)
    int Add2;             // fixdt(1,16,15)
    int Gain7;            // fixdt(1,16,13)
    int Gain8;            // fixdt(1,16,11)

    y = convert_to_fixedpoint(yin);
    Gain1 = (31499 * x1) >> 14;
    Gain2 = (-3145 * x2) >> 14;
    Add1 = (Gain1 + Gain2) >> 1;
    Gain3 = (432 * y) >> 14;
    x1_new = ((Add1 << 1) + Gain3) >> 1;
    Gain4 = (-1907 * x1) >> 14;
    Gain5 = (23835 * x2) >> 14;
    Add2 = Gain4 + Gain5;
    Gain6 = (3345 * y) >> 14;
    x2_new = (Add1 + Gain6) >> 1;
    Gain7 = (24783 * x1_new) >> 14;
    Gain8 = (25823 * x2_new) >> 14;
    u = (Gain7 + (Gain8 << 2)) >> 2;
    return(float(u));
}
```

Figure 3: synthesized fixed-point controller C code for Bicycle.

control, borrowed from [31], is given by:

$$
\begin{cases}
\begin{bmatrix} \dot{\xi}_1 \\ \dot{\xi}_2 \\ \dot{\xi}_3 \end{bmatrix} = \begin{bmatrix} 0 & 1 & 0 \\ 0 & \frac{-b}{J} & \frac{K}{J} \\ 0 & \frac{-K}{L} & \frac{-R}{L} \end{bmatrix} \begin{bmatrix} \xi_1 \\ \xi_2 \\ \xi_3 \end{bmatrix} + \begin{bmatrix} 0 \\ 0 \\ \frac{1}{L} \end{bmatrix} (v + \omega) \\
\eta = \begin{bmatrix} 1 & 0 & 0 \end{bmatrix} \begin{bmatrix} \xi_1 \\ \xi_2 \\ \xi_3 \end{bmatrix} + \nu,
\end{cases}
$$

where ξ_1 is the angle of the motor's shaft, ξ_2 is the angular velocity of the motor's shaft, ξ_3 is the armature current, $b = 3.508 \times 10^{-6}$ is the damping ratio of the mechanical system, $J = 3.228 \times 10^{-6}$ is the moment of inertia of the rotor, $K = 0.027$ is the electromotive force constant, $R = 4$ is the electric resistance, $L = 2.75 \times 10^{-6}$ is the electric inductance, and v is the source voltage. The weighting factors in (2.21) are chosen as $w_1 = w_2 = w_3 = 1$ and $w_4 = 5$. The LQR and LQG gains are given by $K_{LQR} = [0.4055\ 0.3782\ 0.0022]$ and $L_{LQG} = [0.0288\ 0.3858\ -0.0026]^T$ and the gains, computed by the approach in this paper, are given in Table 1. Tables 1 and 2 show the detailed results.

Pitch control The dynamic of the longitudinal motion of an aircraft, borrowed from [31], is given by:

$$
\begin{cases}
\begin{bmatrix} \dot{\xi}_1 \\ \dot{\xi}_2 \\ \dot{\xi}_3 \end{bmatrix} = \begin{bmatrix} -0.313 & 56.7 & 0 \\ -0.0139 & -0.426 & 0 \\ 0 & 56.7 & 0 \end{bmatrix} \begin{bmatrix} \xi_1 \\ \xi_2 \\ \xi_3 \end{bmatrix} \\
\quad + \begin{bmatrix} 0.232 \\ 0.0203 \\ 0 \end{bmatrix} (v + \omega) \\
\eta = \begin{bmatrix} 0 & 0 & 1 \end{bmatrix} \begin{bmatrix} \xi_1 \\ \xi_2 \\ \xi_3 \end{bmatrix} + \nu,
\end{cases}
$$

where ξ_1 is the angle of attack, ξ_2 is the pitch rate, ξ_3 is the pitch angle, and v is elevator deflection angle. The weighting factors in (2.21) are chosen as $w_1 = w_2 = w_3 = 1$ and $w_4 = 5$. The LQR and LQG gains are given by $K_{LQR} = [-0.1141\ 49.1428\ 0.9995]$ and $L_{LQG} = 10^{-3} \times [0.6407\ 0.0039\ 0.6655]^T$ and the gains, computed by the approach in this paper, are given in Table 1. Tables 1 and 2 show the detailed results.

Inverted pendulum Consider a simple physical model of an inverted pendulum on a cart, borrowed from [31]. The dynamics of the system is given by:

$$
\begin{cases}
\begin{bmatrix} \dot{\xi}_1 \\ \dot{\xi}_2 \\ \dot{\xi}_3 \\ \dot{\xi}_4 \end{bmatrix} = \begin{bmatrix} 0 & 1 & 0 & 0 \\ 0 & \frac{-(I+ml^2)b}{K} & \frac{m^2gl^2}{K} & 0 \\ 0 & 0 & 0 & 1 \\ 0 & \frac{-mlb}{K} & \frac{mgl(M+m)}{K} & 0 \end{bmatrix} \begin{bmatrix} \xi_1 \\ \xi_2 \\ \xi_3 \\ \xi_4 \end{bmatrix} \\
\quad + \begin{bmatrix} 0 \\ \frac{I+ml^2}{K} \\ 0 \\ \frac{ml}{K} \end{bmatrix} v + \begin{bmatrix} 1 \\ 1 \\ 1 \\ 1 \end{bmatrix} \omega, \\
\eta = \begin{bmatrix} 1 & 0 & 0 & 0 \\ 0 & 0 & 1 & 0 \end{bmatrix} \begin{bmatrix} \xi_1 \\ \xi_2 \\ \xi_3 \\ \xi_4 \end{bmatrix} + \nu,
\end{cases}
$$

where ξ_1, and ξ_2 are the position and velocity of the cart, respectively, ξ_3, and ξ_4 are the angular position and velocity of the mass to be balanced, v is the applied force to the cart, $K = I(M + m) + Mml^2$, $g = 9.8$ is the acceleration due to gravity, $l = 0.3$ is the length of the rod, $m = 0.2$ is the mass of the system to be balanced, $M = 0.5$ is the mass of the cart, $b = 0.1$ is the coefficient of friction of the cart, and $I = 0.006$ is the inertia of the pendulum. The weighting factors in (2.21) are chosen as $w_1 = w_2 = w_3 = 1$ and $w_4 = 5$. The LQR and LQG gains are given by $K_{LQR} = [-0.9929\ -2.0276\ 20.2819\ 3.9126]$ and

$$
L_{LQG} = \begin{bmatrix} 0.0016 & 0.0011 & 0.0007 & 0.0034 \\ 0.0007 & 0.0051 & 0.0111 & 0.0618 \end{bmatrix}^T,
$$

and the gains, computed by the proposed approach in this paper, are given in Table 1.

Batch reactor process Consider an unstable batch reactor process, borrowed from [7]. The dynamic of the system is given by:

$$
\begin{cases}
\begin{bmatrix} \dot{\xi}_1 \\ \dot{\xi}_2 \\ \dot{\xi}_3 \\ \dot{\xi}_4 \end{bmatrix} = \begin{bmatrix} 1.38 & -0.2077 & 6.715 & -5.676 \\ -0.5814 & -4.29 & 0 & 0.675 \\ 1.067 & 4.273 & -6.654 & 5.893 \\ 0.048 & 4.273 & 1.343 & -2.104 \end{bmatrix} \begin{bmatrix} \xi_1 \\ \xi_2 \\ \xi_3 \\ \xi_4 \end{bmatrix} \\
\quad + \begin{bmatrix} 0 & 0 \\ 5.679 & 0 \\ 1.136 & -3.146 \\ 1.136 & 0 \end{bmatrix} v + \begin{bmatrix} 1 \\ 1 \\ 1 \\ 1 \end{bmatrix} \omega, \\
\eta = \begin{bmatrix} 1 & 0 & 1 & -1 \\ 0 & 1 & 0 & 0 \end{bmatrix} \begin{bmatrix} \xi_1 \\ \xi_2 \\ \xi_3 \\ \xi_4 \end{bmatrix} + \nu.
\end{cases}
$$

The weighting factors in (2.21) are chosen as $w_1 = w_3 = 1$, $w_2 = 2$, and $w_4 = 5$. The LQR and LQG gains are given by:

$$
K_{LQR} = \begin{bmatrix} 0.0376 & 0.9157 & 0.3262 & 0.8226 \\ -2.4884 & -0.0734 & -1.7461 & 1.1438 \end{bmatrix},
$$

$$
L_{LQG} = \begin{bmatrix} 0.0447 & -0.0003 & 0.0170 & 0.0127 \\ 0 & 0.0020 & 0.0058 & 0.0059 \end{bmatrix}^T,
$$

and the gains, computed by the approach in this paper, are given in Table 1.

PID controller In this example, we provide a PID controller for an inverted pendulum whose dynamic is given by a transfer function.

Consider the transfer function of an inverted pendulum, borrowed from [31], given by:

$$\frac{\Phi(s)}{U(s)} = \frac{\frac{ml}{q}s}{s^3 + \frac{b(I+ml^2)}{q}s^2 - \frac{(M+m)mgl}{q}s - \frac{bmgl}{q}}, \qquad (6.1)$$

where $q = (M + m)(I + ml^2) - (ml)^2$, output ϕ is the angular position of the mass to be balanced, input v is the force applied to the cart, $g = 9.8$ is the acceleration due to gravity, $l = 0.3$ is the length of the rod, $m = 0.2$ is the mass of the system to be balanced, $M = 0.5$ is the mass of the cart, $b = 0.1$ is the coefficient of friction of the cart, and $I = 0.006$ is the moment of inertia of the pendulum. Using standard results in control theory [11], one obtains the following state space realization for the inverted pendulum:

$$\begin{cases} \begin{bmatrix} \dot{\xi}_1 \\ \dot{\xi}_2 \\ \dot{\xi}_3 \end{bmatrix} = \begin{bmatrix} -0.1818 & 3.8977 & 0.5568 \\ 8.000 & 0 & 0 \\ 0 & 1 & 0 \end{bmatrix} \begin{bmatrix} \xi_1 \\ \xi_2 \\ \xi_3 \end{bmatrix} + \begin{bmatrix} 1 \\ 0 \\ 0 \end{bmatrix} v \\ \phi = [0 \ 0.5682 \ 1] \begin{bmatrix} \xi_1 \\ \xi_2 \\ \xi_3 \end{bmatrix}. \end{cases}$$

Our objective is to design PID gains K_P, K_I, and K_D minimizing the cost function (5.7) with weighting factors $w_1 = w_2 = w_3 = 1$ and such that the closed loop system has a settling time (t_s) of less than 5 seconds and such that the pendulum does not move more than 0.05 radians away from the vertical axis. The latter two constraints are treated the same as the stability constraint in Subsection 4.2 by penalizing the cost function (5.7). The synthesized gains are $K_P = 109.032$, $K_I = 1.2268$, and $K_D = 13.9945$. The closed loop system has $PM = +\infty$, $GM = 26237$, $\gamma(b(e_{q1}) + b(e_{q2})) = 4.1705 \times 10^{-4}$, settling time $t_s = 0.4790$, and ensures that the pendulum does not move more than 0.0098 radians away from the vertical axis.

7. CONCLUSION

We have presented a generic methodology to search for optimal controller implementations that minimize implementation errors in addition to traditional controller performance criteria. While we have instantiated the methodology using the LQR and LQG costs and quantization errors, our algorithm is more generally applicable to other performance criteria and other sources of modeling or implementation error.

Acknowledgments. This research was funded in part by Toyota Motors.

8. REFERENCES

[1] A. Anta, R. Majumdar, I. Saha, and P. Tabuada. Automatic verification of control system implementations. *In proceedings of EMSOFT*, pages 9–18, October 2010.

[2] K. J. Astrom and R. M. Murray. *Feedback systems*. Princeton University Press, 2008.

[3] T. Chen and B. A. Francis. *Optimal sampled-data control systems*. Springer-Verlag, New York, 1995.

[4] P. Duggirala and S. Mitra. Abstraction-refinement for stability. In *Proc. ICCPS*, 2011.

[5] S. Ebbesen, P. Kiwitz, and L. Guzzella. A generic particle swarm optimization function for Matlab. *American Control Conference (to appear)*, June 2012.

[6] E. Feron. From control systems to control software. *IEEE Control Systems Magazine*, 30(6):50–71, 2010.

[7] M. Green and D. J. N. Limebeer. *Linear robust control*. Prentice Hall, August 1994.

[8] J. P. Hespanha. *Linear systems theory*. Princeton University Press, September 2009.

[9] S. Jha. *Towards Automated System Synthesis Using SCIDUCTION*. PhD thesis, University of California at Berkeley, 2011.

[10] M. Jiang, Y. P. Luo, and S. Y. Yang. Stochastic convergence analysis and parameter selection of the standard particle swarm optimization algorithm. *Information Processing Letters*, 102(1):8–16, April 2007.

[11] T. Kailath. *Linear systems*. Prentice-Hall, Inc., 1980.

[12] R. E. Kalman. Nonlinear aspects of sampled-data control systems. *in Proceedings of the Symposium on Nonlinear Circuit Analysis, edited by J. Fox, Polytechnic Institute of Brooklyn*, pages 273–313, 1956.

[13] J. Kennedy and R. Eberhart. Particle swarm optimization. *In Proceedings of IEEE International Conference on Neural Networks*, pages 1942–1948, 1995.

[14] J. A. López, C. Carreras, and O. Nieto-Taladriz. Improved interval-based characterization of fixed-point LTI systems with feedback loops. *IEEE Trans. on CAD of Integrated Circuits and Systems*, 26(11):1923–1932, 2007.

[15] D. Lee, A. A. Gaffar, R. C. C. Cheung, O. Mencer, W. Luk, and G. A. Constantinides. Accuracy-guaranteed bitwidth optimization. *IEEE Trans. on CAD of Integrated Circuits and Systems*, 25(10):1990–2000, 2006.

[16] Y. Lin, E. D. Sontag, and Y. Wang. A smooth converse lyapunov theorem for robust stability. *SIAM Journal on Control and Optimization*, 34(1):124–160, 1996.

[17] H. Liu, A. Abraham, and V. Snasel. Convergence analysis of swarm algorithm. *World congress on Nature and Biologically Inspired Computing*, pages 1714–1719, December 2009.

[18] K. Liu, R. E. Skelton, and K. Grigoriadis. Optimal controllers for finite wordlength implementation. *IEEE Transactions on Automatic Control*, 37(9):1294–1304, September 1992.

[19] R. Moore. *Interval Analysis*. Prentice Hall, 1966.

[20] W. G. Osborne, R. C. C. Cheung, J. G. F. Coutinho, W. Luk, and O. Mencer. Automatic accuracy-guaranteed bit-width optimization for fixed and floating-point systems. In *Proc. FPL*, pages 617–620, 2007.

[21] A. Podelski and S. Wagner. Model checking of hybrid systems: From reachability towards stability. In *Proc. HSCC*, pages 507–521, 2006.

[22] A. Podelski and S. Wagner. Region stability proofs for hybrid systems. In *Proc. FORMATS*, pages 320–335, 2007.

[23] J. Stolfi and L. H. Figueiredo. Self-validated numerical methods and applications. In *Monograph for 21st Brazilian Mathematics Colloquium, Rio de Janeiro: IMPA*, 1997.

[24] D. Williamson. Finite wordlength design of digital Kalman filters for state estimation. *IEEE Transactions on Automatic Control*, 30(10):930–939, October 1985.

[25] D. Williamson. Optimal finite wordlength linear quadratic regulation. *IEEE Transactions on Automatic Control*, 34(12):1218–1228, December 1989.

[26] G. Winskel. *The Formal Semantics of Programming Languages: An Introduction*. MIT Press, 1993.

[27] M. Zamani, M. Karimi-Ghartemani, and N. Sadati. FOPID controller design for robust performance using particle swarm optimization. *Journal of Fractional Calculus & Applied Analysis (FCAA)*, 10(2):169–188, 2007.

[28] M. Zamani, M. Karimi-Ghartemani, N. Sadati, and M. Parniani. Design of a fractional order PID controller for an AVR using particle swarm optimization. *Control Engineering Practice*, 17(12):1380–1387, December 2009.

[29] M. Zamani, N. Sadati, and M. Karimi-Ghartemani. Design of an H_∞ PID controller using particle swarm optimization. *International Journal of Control, Automation, and Systems (IJCAS)*, 7(2):273–280, April 2009.

[30] lp_solve, a Mixed Integer Linear Programming (MILP) solver. Available online at http://lpsolve.sourceforge.net/.

[31] Control tutorial for Matlab and Simulink. Available online at http://www.library.cmu.edu/ctms/ctms/.

Shared Hardware Data Structures
for Hard Real-Time Systems

Gedare Bloom
Dept. of Computer Science
George Washington University
Washington, DC 20052
gedare@gwu.edu

Gabriel Parmer
Dept. of Computer Science
George Washington University
Washington, DC 20052
gparmer@gwu.edu

Bhagirath Narahari
Dept. of Computer Science
George Washington University
Washington, DC 20052
narahari@gwu.edu

Rahul Simha
Dept. of Computer Science
George Washington University
Washington, DC 20052
simha@gwu.edu

ABSTRACT

Hardware support can reduce the time spent operating on data structures by exploiting circuit-level parallelism. Such hardware data structures (HWDSs) can reduce the latency and jitter of data structure operations, which can benefit real-time systems by reducing worst-case execution times (WCETs). For example, a hardware priority queue (HWPQ) can enqueue and dequeue prioritized items in constant time with low variance; the best software implementations are in logarithmic-time asymptotic complexity for at least one of the enqueue or dequeue operations. The main problems with HWDSs are the limited size of hardware and the complexity of sharing it. In this paper we show that software support can help circumvent the size and sharing limitations of hardware so that applications can benefit from a HWDS. We evaluate our work by showing how the choice of software or hardware affects schedulability of task sets that use multiple priority queues of varying sizes. We model task behavior on two applications that are important in real-time and embedded domains: the grey-weighted distance transform for topology mapping and Dijkstra's algorithm for GPS navigation. Our results indicate that HWDSs can reduce the WCET of applications even when a HWDS is shared by multiple data structures or when data structure sizes exceed HWDS size constraints.

Categories and Subject Descriptors

D.4.7 [**Operating Systems**]: Real-time systems and embedded systems; B.3.3 [**Memory Structures**]: Worst-case analysis; E.1 [**Data Structures**]

General Terms

Algorithms, Performance

Keywords

Hardware data structures, schedulability, priority queue

1. INTRODUCTION

Throughout the history of computing there has been a performance gap between CPUs and main memory. Wilkes [28] points out that memory started out different from and underperforming processing, and the performance gap persisted despite the use of semiconductors for both since the 1970s. Indeed, the performance gap has steadily increased since the 1980s, leading Wulf and McKee [30] to coin the term *memory wall* to describe the bottleneck caused by the gap. The memory wall arises from processor performance improving faster than memory bandwidth and latency.

A common technique to delay the impact of the memory wall is caching. Unfortunately data caches are difficult to model in hard real-time systems; in particular obtaining an accurate worst-case execution time (WCET) is hard [8]. One well-known approach to dealing with the data cache is to attempt to partition it among the system's tasks [24]. However data sharing and RTOS services can make cache partitioning problematic and workarounds lead to locking or other strategies that frustrate real-time analysis. (The instruction cache is easier to handle and well-known techniques can accommodate it in a WCET analysis [20].)

Another common approach to reducing the effect of memory latency is to reduce the complexity and operating frequency of processing cores while maintaining high throughput by replicating multiple cores on one chip: the chip multiprocessor or multicore. Multicore platforms have become common due to the continued growth of chip space predicted by Moore's law. For real-time systems, problems with using multicore platforms include the difficulties of parallelizing applications, managing shared caches, partitioning tasks across cores, and synchronizing shared resources among cores; these problems drive up the complexity (and therefore cost) to develop real-time systems using multicore platforms. We suggest an alternative approach for using the spare chip space.

In this paper we introduce hardware data structures (HWDSs) as an approach for hard real-time systems to improve the predictability of memory accesses. HWDSs represent an alternate use of chip space compared to replicating processing cores. The devotion of chip space to HWDSs is a promising direction for time-predictability in hard real-time systems. The contributions of this work include: fitting HWDSs into traditional response time analysis by identifying variables that affect WCET when using a HWDS; deriving two novel assignment algorithms for choosing which tasks should use a HWDS as opposed to a software DS; exploring the parameter space of the variables that affect HWDS WCET in order to quantify the effectiveness of those algorithms; and demonstrating how real-world applications can benefit from this work.

The advantage that HWDS have over alternatives such as scratchpad memory is that a HWDS exploits hardware parallelism to reduce the algorithmic complexity of data structure operations while also improving memory access predictability. The primary disadvantage for HWDSs is that chip designers need to devote a fixed size of hardware resources for the benefit of DS operations, and the limited size causes problems both for sharing the hardware and for using the HWDS when DS size exceeds HWDS capacity. We circumvent hardware size constraints by using exceptions triggered in hardware and handled in software; amortizing exception costs across multiple non-excepting operations puts bounds on the cost of HWDS operations for schedulability analysis. For sharing a HWDS we present two simple algorithms and two novel algorithms that determine which tasks and data structures can use HWDS resources subject to task, data structure, and HWDS parameters.

2. HARDWARE DATA STRUCTURES

A *hardware data structure* (HWDS) is an implementation of a data structure with hardware mechanisms to improve the performance and asymptotic complexity of data structure operations. A HWDS organizes the memory hierarchy in terms of data structure operations instead of cache line fetches. By avoiding the cache a HWDS has the potential to deliver consistent, predictable timing.

So far most work on HWDSs has ignored the interface between the HWDS and programmer, with existing HWDSs having limited interactions with operating system (OS) and application software. This paper shows how such interactions are crucial to realize efficient HWDSs. In particular, we investigate HWDSs from a holistic view that incorporates processor architecture, OS, and applications. OS support extends the capabilities of HWDSs beyond prior art with support for large data structures and sharing a HWDS.

2.1 Priority queue: an example HWDS

A priority queue (PQ) is a data structure with *enqueue* (insert), *dequeue* (delete-min), and *peek* (read first) operations. Dequeue removes and returns the highest priority node in the queue; peek is similar to dequeue, but without removing the node. Applications of PQs include graph problems like finding the minimum spanning tree or shortest path, discrete event simulation [9], network routing [19], OS scheduling [5], and image analysis [16].

Although many software implementations of PQs exist, the implicit binary heap remains one of the best due to its simplicity, logarithmic worst-case time complexity, and low memory overhead [15, 16]; these points especially are valid in real-time systems [18]. In this paper we consider only the implicit binary heap as a representative software-implemented PQ.

A hardware priority queue (HWPQ) is a hardware implementation of the PQ data structure. An example of a HWPQ is the shift register PQ, which is shown in Figure 1. The shift register PQ is an array of priority and data payload tuples that the hardware sorts by priority value. A shift register block encapsulates each tuple, and each block connects to its two neighbors. Global lines connect all the blocks to the input and control. Global broadcast lines limit the scalability of the shift register PQ, but each block makes a decision locally based on inputs from its neighbors and the single global input so the design is simple. The latency of this HWPQ primarily comes from the wire delays of the global signals, especially for a

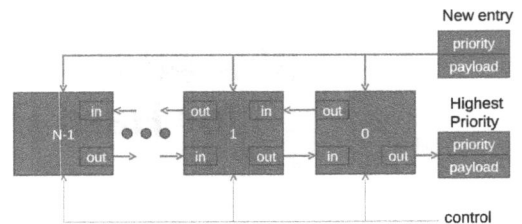

Figure 1: A shift-register based hardware priority queue of priority-payload tuples in a double-linked hardware list.

large number of blocks [19]. Fanout of the comparators is also a concern if there is a wide range of priority values. Other HWPQ implementations eliminate the global lines—see Moon et al. [19]. The choice of HWPQ implementation makes a difference in terms of hardware size, power cost, scalability, and maximum operating frequency, but we defer the reasoning behind such choice.

Both adding and removing nodes with the shift register HWPQ are efficient because priority comparisons occur in parallel and every block determines its action upon receiving global signals. The insert operation broadcasts a new tuple to all blocks. Each block sends its current tuple to the left and compares its current priority value, new priority, and priority from the right. If the new priority is less than the current priority, then the block keeps its current data. If the new priority is between the current priority and the priority from the right, then the block latches the tuple. Otherwise, the block latches the right neighbor's tuple. Removing the highest priority node is simple, with each block sending its tuple to the right and latching from the left.

HWPQs motivate the HWDS approach. Enqueue and dequeue happen in constant time: the fastest software implementations take logarithmic time for at least some operations. Unfortunately the size constraints and lack of support for sharing the HWPQ among multiple PQs present problems for general-purpose application use of a HWPQ. To address these problems we introduce novel mechanisms for spilling and filling data between the HWPQ and main memory. We start with the established work on fixed-size unshared HWPQs and evolve a new approach that combines reasonable hardware and OS modifications to support application use of a HWPQ.

2.2 Spilling and Filling

Applications require support for PQs of arbitrary size. Since hardware has a fixed capacity, arbitrarily large data sets eventually will cause overflow. In addition, chip space allocated to the HWPQ steals from other features such as cache, so minimizing the HWPQ size is important.

We solve the problem of arbitrarily large PQs using an exception-based approach for handling overflow inspired by work in fine-grained threading [14, 23]. HWPQ control logic and software services handle overflow by spilling HWPQ data to secondary storage (memory). A HWPQ generates an overflow exception when the number of nodes it contains meets some threshold; the maximum threshold is the size of the HWPQ. Similarly, the hardware raises an exception when there exist spilled nodes and either the HWPQ holds less than some threshold of nodes or the highest priority node in the HWPQ has lower priority than some spilled node.

The ordering of nodes in the HWPQ has meaning—based on the interpretation of priority—so the overflow exception handler removes low-priority nodes from the HWPQ. As the exception handler removes nodes the HWPQ marks the lowest priority node remaining in the HWPQ with an *invalid* bit. The hardware will mark invalid any node that the application subsequently enqueues with a lower priority than an existing invalid node. When the head of the HWPQ is invalid the HWPQ raises an underflow exception because a higher priority node might exist among the spilled nodes. The underflow exception handler fills the HWPQ, which mark nodes valid if they have higher priority than those the exception handler fills from the spilled nodes. During an underflow exception the handler may also need to spill nodes because of invalid nodes.

The choice of algorithm for storing the spilled nodes will affect the time required by both the overflow and underflow exception handlers. Because the HWPQ nodes are already sorted we chose to maintain a sorted linked list for the spilled nodes. The overflow handler merge sorts the spilled nodes into the linked list, and the underflow handler fills from the head of the linked list. Other software PQs would likely show advantages for certain PQ sizes, HWPQ sizes, priority value distributions, and PQ access patterns.

For real-time systems the execution time and rate of overflow and underflow exceptions is important because those two parameters affect a task's WCET when using a HWPQ. Exception handler execution time depends on the size of the PQ and the number of nodes spilled (equivalently filled). The rate of exceptions depends on two factors: the rate of PQ operations and the number of nodes spilled. The PQ size and rate of operations are application-dependent, but if they are bounded then the exception WCET and rate depends on the amount of work done—the number of nodes spilled.

Tuning the number of nodes spilled to be any number k less than or equal to half of the HWPQ size limits the number of exceptions to at most one overflow and one underflow per k PQ operations. If the handler spills 4 nodes then there could be two exceptions for every 4 PQ operations; spilling 8 nodes allows 8 PQ operations with at most two exceptions, and so on. In any window of k PQ operations the worst case is that the entire HWPQ is full of invalid nodes and the HWPQ reads the head node and then enqueues a node. The read induces an underflow exception since the head is invalid. The underflow handler fills the HWPQ with k valid nodes and spills at least k nodes, leaving the HWPQ in a state with at least k valid nodes and possibly invalid nodes filling the rest of the HWPQ. (The HWPQ can then satisfy at least k operations without another underflow.) The subsequent enqueue may cause an overflow exception which will spill k nodes. At this point the HWPQ can satisfy at least k operations without another exception. We minimize the number of exceptions that get taken by tuning the handlers to spill half of the PQ size because each exception that gets taken adds extra fixed processing overhead to invoke the handler.

Spilling HWPQ data causes a problem for operations that target spilled nodes: software must implement the operation on the nodes in the spill area. Peek, enqueue, and dequeue operations work fine, but some applications violate the priority abstraction to access PQ nodes at random; for example Dijkstra's algorithm benefits from a change-key operation that can change the priority of an enqueued item, or task schedulers may need to delete a task from the PQ when the task suspends or is killed. Currently we ignore these cases, but we could solve them by introducing an exception to emulate the operation in software; assuming these exceptions are rare or bounded we can analyze them similarly to the overflow and underflow exceptions. For Dijkstra's algorithm change-key can be ignored at the cost of extra storage and processing when dequeueing [7].

2.3 Sharing

Sharing is a traditional OS problem of managing contention for a limited hardware resource. We implement an offline assignment algorithm that decides which task's PQs are allocated the HWPQ. At runtime a HWPQ context switch swaps one PQ for another.

Sharing the HWPQ adds a little more complexity to both hardware and software support. The main addition is that the HW needs to distinguish PQs, so the PQ operations must identify which PQ to use; in prior work there was a one-to-one mapping between PQ and HWPQ. Loosening that mapping to many-to-one introduces the problem that the HWPQ must have some way to separate or distinguish data belonging to different PQs. As with other facets of HWPQ design many possible solutions exist for this problem. Our solution is to add an identifier to every instruction that accesses the HWPQ and for the HWPQ to track which PQ currently is using the HWPQ based on the identifier. The exception handlers use the identifiers to store the spilled nodes for each PQ in a separate data structure. We chose this approach because the hardware cost is small (an extra register and some comparators) while supporting a wide range of policies for how PQs share the HWPQ. The main drawback is that each software PQ must have a unique identifier.

The HWPQ context switch involves spilling all of the nodes for the currently loaded PQ and filling nodes for the PQ the application is accessing. To simplify WCET analysis our HWPQ context switch handler tracks how many nodes it spills from the HWPQ while emptying and refills that PQ so that the same number of nodes are present in the HWPQ before and after a PQ is context switched. We also restrict each task to use at most one PQ; when a task uses more than one PQ only one should use the HWPQ otherwise the number of HWPQ context switches may be large. With our restriction the HWPQ context switch aligns with the task context switch, which is important when analyzing a task's WCET. The worst case cost of a HWPQ context switch is when the HWPQ is full and the handler is refilling from a PQ that had a full HWPQ previously; then the context switch spills and fills the entire HWPQ. Similar to spilling and filling the cost of a HWPQ context switch depends on PQ size and spill data structure implementation.

3. RESPONSE TIME ANALYSIS

A hardware data structure (HWDS) affects task response time by decreasing WCET due to reducing DS operation times, but exceptions caused by overflow/underflow conditions increase WCET. Sharing the HWDS among tasks also increases the response time. In the following we evolve a standard response time analysis [3] to include variables that affect WCET when using a HWDS. We only consider periodic tasks.

We adopt the notation

- τ: the set of all tasks
- T_i: the i'th task
- p_i: period of T_i
- e_i: the worst-case execution time (WCET) of T_i.
- c_i: the maximum context switch latency of T_i

Usually c_i is equal for all tasks and is included twice in e_i: once for the task preempted by T_i and once for resuming that task.

The response time R_i of T_i is the minimum value of t satisfying

$$t = e_i + \sum_{k=1}^{i-1} \left\lceil \frac{t}{p_k} \right\rceil e_k. \tag{1}$$

Equation 1 considers the WCET of T_i plus the sum of processor time of higher priority tasks overlapping with the time interval t. We find R_i by solving the recurrence

$$t^{(l+1)} = e_i + \sum_{k=1}^{i-1} \left\lceil \frac{t^{(l)}}{p_k} \right\rceil e_k$$

starting with $t^{(0)} = e_i$. τ is schedulable if $R_i < p_i$ for all $T_i \in \tau$.

Adding HWDSs splits the periodic tasks into two sets

- $\widehat{\tau}$: the set of tasks using a HWDS

- $\widetilde{\tau}$: the set of tasks not using a HWDS

so $\tau = \widehat{\tau} \cup \widetilde{\tau}$. HWDS assignment is the problem of choosing whether to place T_i in $\widehat{\tau}$ or in $\widetilde{\tau}$ for every i.

Task response times depend on HWDS assignment. Each task's WCET is now

$$e_i = \begin{cases} \widehat{e_i} + \widehat{x_i} + \widehat{c_i} + \max_{j>i} \widehat{c_j} & \text{if } T_i \in \widehat{\tau} \\ \widetilde{e_i} & \text{otherwise} \end{cases}$$

where

- $\widehat{e_i}$ is the WCET of T_i when the HWDS replaces DS operations

- $\widehat{x_i}$ is the cost of exceptions taken due to using a HWDS

- $\widehat{c_i}$ is the maximum cost to context switch the HWDS for T_i

- $\widetilde{e_i}$ is the WCET of T_i using a software-only DS

$\widehat{x_i}$ depends primarily on how many DS operations can cause exceptions during p_i (i.e. during any job of T_i) and the time needed to handle the exceptions: because $\widehat{x_i}$ depends on the HWDS implementation no generic formula exists for e_i.

$\widehat{e_i}$ depends on $\widehat{c_j}$ for $j > i$, that is the maximum time needed to empty and fill the HWDS of a lower priority task. Preempting a lower priority task j empties j's HWDS and fills i's, whereas resuming j empties i's HWDS and fills j's.

Equation 1 still gives R_i but now e_i depends on whether $T_i \in \widehat{\tau}$ or not; that is, on the assignment algorithm. Assignment for just one task depends on whether

$$\widetilde{e_i} > \widehat{e_i} + \widehat{x_i}.$$

Assuming that $\widehat{x_i}$ is bounded then finding the T_i that maximizes

$$\widetilde{e_i} - (\widehat{e_i} + \widehat{x_i})$$

gives the task that will benefit most from using the HWDS.

Including multiple tasks that share the HWDS complicates the assignment problem. In particular $\widehat{c_i}$ varies depending on the cost of emptying and filling the HWDS (i.e. a context switch), so—unlike with traditional response time analysis—a low priority task can affect the response time of higher priority tasks. Conversely higher priority tasks already affect the response time of lower priority tasks. So putting any T_i into $\widehat{\tau}$ necessitates checking whether it negatively affects the rest of the tasks already in $\widehat{\tau}$ in order to find an optimal assignment (see Section 4).

3.1 Hardware Priority Queues

When using a hardware priority queue (HWPQ) as a HWDS the costs of $\widehat{x_i}$ and $\widehat{c_i}$ are upper-bounded as follows.

Let $\widehat{S}$ be the size of the HWPQ. Tuning the number of nodes that the overflow (underflow) exception handler spills (fills) to be $w < \widehat{S}/2$ guarantees that at most one overflow (underflow) exception will occur for every w priority queue operations (enqueues or dequeues). Let O_i be the maximum number of PQ operations that can occur for any job of T_i, and let $A(w)$ be the WCET of the overflow (underflow) algorithm to handle w nodes. Then

$$\widehat{x_i} < A(w) * \lceil O_i/w \rceil. \tag{2}$$

When the context switch invokes the overflow routines to empty the HWPQ and the underflow routines to fill the HWPQ then the bound on $\widehat{c_i}$ depends on how much of the HWPQ T_i uses. Let $\widehat{s_i} <= \widehat{S}$ be the maximum usage of the HWPQ by T_i. Then

$$\widehat{c_i} < A(\widehat{s_i}) * \widehat{s_i}. \tag{3}$$

For example if N_i is the maximum size of the priority queue (i.e. maximum number of overflow nodes) then a binary heap implementation of the overflow nodes will have $A(w) \approx w * \log_2 N_i$ (approximating the WCET of the heap by its asymptotic behavior). Then $\widehat{x_i}$ and $\widehat{c_i}$ come directly from Equations 2 and 3 respectively. In Section 5 we measure software and hardware implementations of priority queues for the WCET of their enqueue and dequeue operations and—for HWPQs—context switch, spill, and fill. We evaluate HWDS assignment algorithms with those measurements.

4. HWDS ASSIGNMENT

Assigning the HWDS attempts to assign tasks to use either a HWDS or a software DS. We use terminology from scheduling—indeed the assignment problem is similar to the problem of task scheduling. An assignment is feasible if a solution to Equation 1 can be found for every task (equivalent to finding a feasible schedule). If an assignment algorithm exists that produces a feasible assignment for a set of tasks then we say those tasks are schedulable. An assignment algorithm is optimal if it always produces a feasible assignment for a set of tasks when one exists.

We evaluate four assignment algorithms for HWDSs: software-only assignment (SOA), hardware-only assignment (HOA), priority-aware assignment (PAA), and context switch cost-aware assignment (CSCAA). The first two algorithms are naïve and represent two extremes, and the latter two are greedy algorithms employing different heuristics to make choices about when to use a HWDS. None of these algorithms is optimal, and the PAA and CSCAA algorithms do not permit tasks to change their priorities.

Some aspects of these algorithms are dependent on DS behavior in particular on the WCET of DS operations, HWDS exceptions, and the HWDS context switch time. We established in Section 3.1 that a HWPQ has a bounded WCET if the maximum DS size, maximum number of DS operations per period, and the HWPQ size are bounded. In general these algorithms will work for any HWDS that has bounded WCET based on the DS size and DS operations. If a HWDS requires more information to bound its WCET then new algorithms may be required.

The SOA algorithm simply assigns every task to use a software-implemented DS: the SOA algorithm ignores the HWDS. The HOA algorithm assigns every task to use the largest possible HWDS. Usually the largest available HWDS gives the best performance out of all the available HWDS sizes, but not always. As the usage of the HWDS increases the rate of exceptions should go down assuming that the work done during the exception handler increases. However the latency of the exception handlers will increase, and so will the HWDS context switch due to needing to move more data. For small numbers of DS operations per period the larger HWDSs underperform smaller HWDSs; at such small sizes of DS operations the software DS typically performs better than any HWDS.

The PAA algorithm (Algorithm 1) iterates through tasks from the lowest priority to the highest priority choosing at each task whether to use the HWDS by comparing the WCET of the software DS with the WCET of the HWDS. This algorithm tracks the maximum HWDS context switch of the tasks that it has assigned to the HWDS so that it can compute the WCET accurately taking into account the context switch costs of lower-priority tasks. Iterating from low to high priorities allows the algorithm to move in one direction. The reason that this algorithm is not optimal is that higher-priority tasks that use the HWDS have a WCET that depends on whether (and which) lower-priority tasks use the HWDS. Because the algorithm only moves in one direction it does not allow for re-evaluating the assignment of lower-priority tasks and therefore can miss feasible assignments.

Algorithm 1: Priority-Aware Assignment (PAA)

Input: n: number of tasks, τ: task set, N: max DS sizes, O: max DS operations, S: max HWDS size

1   $\widehat{\tau} = \emptyset$
2   $\widetilde{\tau} = \emptyset$
3   $\widehat{c_m} = 0$
4   **for** i *from* n *to* 0 **do**
5      $\widehat{e_i} = \texttt{get\_hwds\_wcet}\,(N_i, O_i, S, \widehat{c_m})$
6      $\hat{S_i} = S$
7   **for** $s < S$ **do**
8         $\widehat{e_i} = \texttt{get\_hwds\_wcet}\,(N_i, O_i, s, \widehat{c_m})$
9   **if** $e < \widehat{e_i}$ **then**
10            $\widehat{e_i} = e$
11            $S_i = s$
12   **end**
13   **end**
14      $\widetilde{e_i} = \texttt{get\_swds\_wcet}\,(N_i, O_i)$
15   **if** $\widehat{e_i} < \widetilde{e_i}$ **then**
16         $\texttt{add\_to\_set}\,(\widehat{\tau}, T_i)$
17   **if** $\widehat{c_i} > \widehat{c_m}$ **then**
18            $\widehat{c_m} = \widehat{c_i}$
19   **else**
20         $\texttt{add\_to\_set}\,(\widetilde{\tau}, T_i)$
21   **end**
22   **return** $\widehat{\tau}, \widetilde{\tau}$

Algorithm 2: Context Switch Cost-Aware Assignment (CSCAA)

Input: n: number of tasks, τ: task set, N: max DS sizes, O: max DS operations, S: max HWDS size

1   $\widehat{\tau} = \emptyset$
2   $\widetilde{\tau} = \emptyset$
3   $\widehat{c_m} = 0$
4   **for** i *from* n *to* 0 **do**
5      $\widehat{e_i} = \texttt{get\_hwds\_wcet}\,(N_i, O_i, S, \widehat{c_m})$
6      $\widehat{S_i} = S$
7   **for** $s < S$ **do**
8         $e = \texttt{get\_hwds\_wcet}\,(N_i, O_i, s, \widehat{c_m})$
9   **if** $e < \widehat{e_i}$ **then**
10            $\widehat{e_i} = e$
11            $S_i = s$
12   **end**
13   **end**
14      $\widetilde{e_i} = \texttt{get\_swds\_wcet}\,(N_i, O_i)$
15   **if** $\widehat{e_i} + \texttt{get\_cost}\,(i, n, S_i, \widehat{c_m}) < \widetilde{e_i}$ **then**
16         $\texttt{add\_to\_set}\,(\widehat{\tau}, T_i)$
17   **if** $\widehat{c_i} > \widehat{c_m}$ **then**
18            $\widehat{c_m} = \widehat{c_i}$
19   **else**
20         $\texttt{add\_to\_set}\,(\widetilde{\tau}, T_i)$
21   **end**
22   **return** $\widehat{\tau}, \widetilde{\tau}$

CSCAA (Algorithm 2) is similar to PAA except for the cost heuristic that gets added to the HWDS WCET. We introduce the cost heuristic to penalize low-priority tasks for using the HWDS. This heuristic tries to offset the effect of lower-priority tasks on higher-priority tasks. In particular, the WCET of high-priority tasks affects low-priority task response times, so reducing high-priority task WCETs should benefit response times for a set of tasks. Of course the penalty may prevent low-priority tasks from using the HWDS when they could (and should), so this algorithm can miss feasible assignments. The cost heuristic can be any function that gives a penalty to a task that—if it uses the HWDS—would increase the maximum HWDS context switch time compared to tasks with a lower-priority. For this work we used a cost heuristic that multiplies the amount a task will increase the maximum HWDS context switch latency times the number of tasks with a higher priority. So in Algorithm 2 the function $\texttt{get\_cost}$ would return $(c_i - c_m) * (n - i)$ or 0, whichever is greater.

5. EXPERIMENTS

We conducted a series of experiments to evaluate HWDSs in the context of hard real-time systems. These experiments use a HWPQ as an example of a HWDS. We use synthetic task sets to explore the parameter space of the HWPQ as the parameters relate to WCET. We also demonstrate how this work can apply in the real-world by examining the benefits of our approach for workloads approximating real applications.

We implemented a HWPQ within Simics/GEMS [17]—a functionally correct cycle-accurate full system simulator for an out-of-order architecture (based on the ALPHA) that executes the SPARC v9 instruction set. We implemented OS support for HWPQs in the Real-Time Executive for Multiprocessor Systems (RTEMS) [1] open source real-time operating system, which can run on Simics/GEMS. The architectural parameters we chose are representative of an embedded system: 75 MHz CPU, 80 cycle memory latency, and a 4-issue 5-stage pipeline. We extended the SPARC instruction set to support new HWPQ operations directly and added a

functional unit to execute the new instructions. This functional unit operates atomically and non-speculatively. Although the HWPQ can achieve single-cycle latencies for PQ operations, restricting the unit to be atomic and non-speculative increases the latency to around 12 cycles for the simulated architectural parameters.

The values we measured for WCET parameters underlie all of the experimental results we present. To estimate the WCET of PQ operations we implemented an implicit binary heap as a representative software PQ. We designed a series of measurement tests that build a PQ up to a specified size and then measure the cost of a PQ operation at that size. We measured five specific events in isolation: enqueue, dequeue, overflow exception, underflow exception, and HWDS context switch. The latter three are only relevant and measured for a HWPQ. We turned off all caching to obtain the WCET of PQ operations. Our approach is pessimistic, but lacking a time-predictable cache leaves few options. As a result the measurements we take are dominated by the memory access latency.

To force the worst-case conditions for the software PQ we measure an enqueue of a node with priority less than the highest-priority node in the heap so that the enqueue operation must move the new node to the top of the heap resulting in a maximum number of swaps (equal to the log base-2 of the PQ size). A dequeue of the minimum value causes a maximum amount of work in a heap.

For the HWPQ enqueue and dequeue WCET the HWPQ must be in a state that will not cause an exception. Before measuring enqueue we ensure the HWPQ has enough spare capacity to accept the new node, and before measuring dequeue we ensure at least one valid node is at the head of the HWPQ. To generate the WCET overflow the nodes that get spilled must cause the spill algorithm to do maximum work. We implemented a merge-sorted linked list that iterates from the tail of the spilled nodes to the head (which has highest priority), so to cause the WCET overflow we empty the HWPQ and then fill it with new nodes that have priority less than the head of the linked list. Thus we ensure that the spill algorithm iterates through the entire linked list before completing. The underflow handler has a special condition under which it has to spill nodes; when the HWPQ is full of invalid nodes it must fill from the spilled nodes and also spill some of its invalid nodes. We generated the worst-case condition of an underflow by enqueueing nodes with priority less than the head of the spilled nodes (as with the overflow case), invalidated the HWPQ, and then dequeued. The dequeue causes an underflow exception, and the exception handler finds that no capacity exists to fill the HWPQ and so spills nodes. The spills will take maximum time because the handler spills nodes with higher priority than the nodes already in the spill data structure. Finally the underflow handler will fill the HWPQ. To cause the WCET of the HWPQ context switch we filled the HWPQ to its maximum size using two separate PQs ensuring the HWPQ contains nodes with priority less than the head of the spilled nodes. Then we cause a HWPQ context switch by issuing an operation for the PQ that is not currently loaded in the HWPQ. The context switch handler spills all of the nodes in the HWPQ which (because of the ordering of nodes) takes maximum time, and then fills the HWPQ with nodes from the next PQs spill data structure.

5.1 Schedulability

To characterize the HWPQ parameter space and evaluate the HWPQ assignment algorithms we designed a series of experiments using synthetic task sets generated as follows. Create a set of n tasks by choosing integer task periods p_i uniformly from $[1, 1000]$. Choose task utilizations u_i uniformly at random from $[0.001, 1)$ implicitly selecting task execution times e_i. After assigning all n tasks a utilization, normalize each u_i so that $\sum_{i=0}^{n} u_i = U$, where U is some target utilization value. This method of generating tasks provides a variety of task sets while controlling the number of tasks and the task set utilization. We use response time analysis (Equation 1) to ensure the generated task set is schedulable, and regenerate any sets that fail the schedulability test.

We then modify each generated task set to include PQ operations parametrized by a max PQ size, max HWPQ size, PQ implementa-

tion, and number of operations to complete in a period. Using the task's period and utilization we calculate its compute time and add the WCET determined by the PQ parameters. PQ size and implementation determine the WCET for any given operation and the PQ size with the number of operations determines the WCET for the HWPQ exceptions. The HWPQ and PQ sizes determine the WCET for the HWPQ context switch.

We varied the parameters of max PQ size, PQ implementation, and number of operations in a controlled way. For each particular assignment of parameters we generated 10000 task sets and attempted to assign PQ usage for each task set using all four of the algorithms (SOA, HOA, PAA, and CSCAA) presented in Section 4. For each task set and assignment algorithm we determine whether the task set is schedulable after PQ assignment. For these experiments we set the max HWPQ size at 1024 and let PAA and CSCAA choose to limit individual tasks to a smaller size; in practice these algorithms typically—but not always—use the largest possible HWPQ size.

Figure 2 shows the results of our experiments as both the max PQ size and the number of PQ operations per period vary by powers of 2 from 16 to 8192. For this particular figure we set the task set utilization U to 0.6 and the number of tasks per task set to 8. The plot shows the percent of task sets (out of 10000) that are schedulable after PQ assignment for each combination of PQ size and number of PQ operations. We also plot a line below which each combination feasibly schedules at least 90% of its task sets. These results show how the different assignment algorithms work, and in particular show that PAA dominates SOA and HOA for much of the explored space. The threshold line also shows that differences exist between the schedulability of task sets assigned using PAA versus

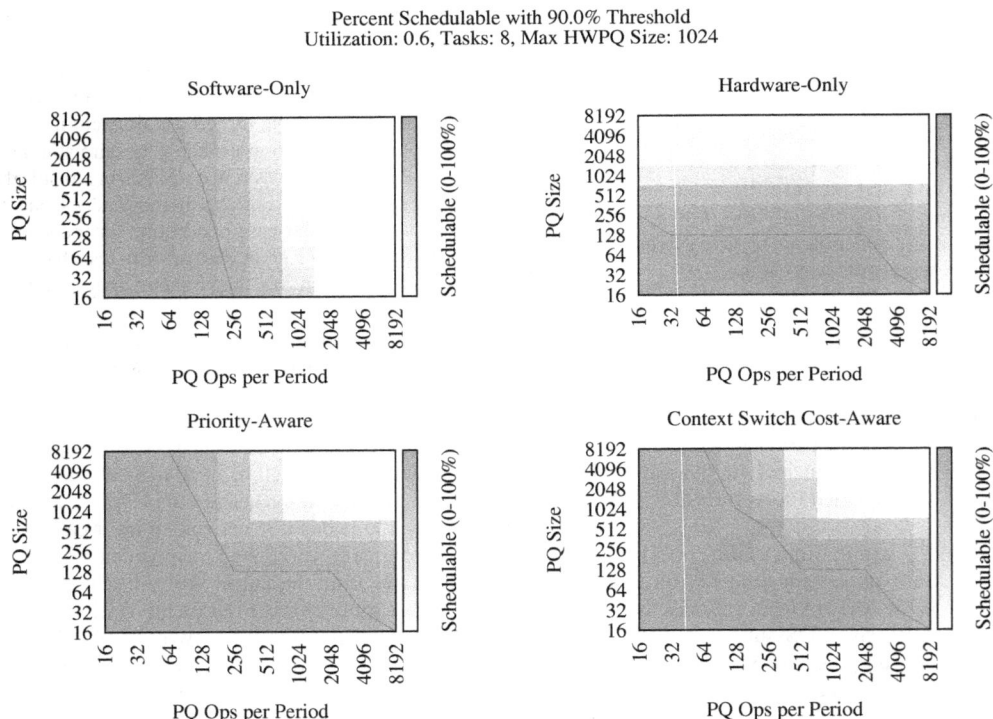

Percent Schedulable with 90.0% Threshold
Utilization: 0.6, Tasks: 8, Max HWPQ Size: 1024

Figure 2: Schedulability of random task sets for utilization without PQ operations fixed at 0.6 and task set size at 8. Varying utilization and the number of tasks moves the threshold lines, which we show in later figures.

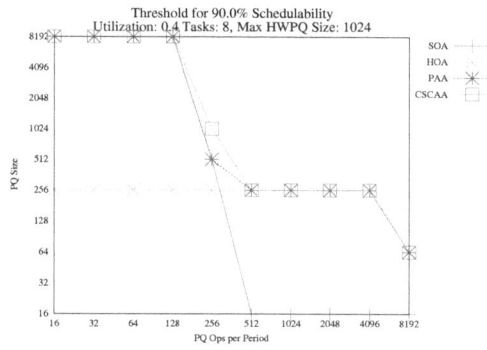

Figure 3: Schedulability with $U = 0.4$. As utilization decreases threshold lines move up because applications have greater spare utilization for larger PQs and more PQ operations.

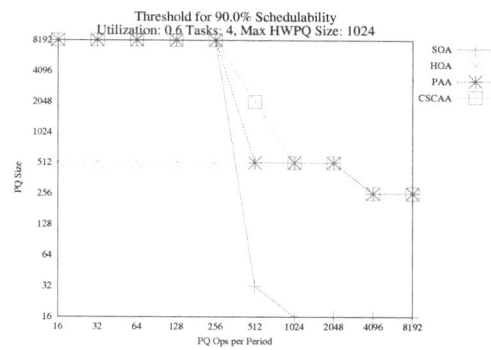

Figure 5: Schedulability with 4 tasks. As the number of tasks decreases the threshold lines move up. Halving the number of tasks more than doubles the number of schedulable task sets.

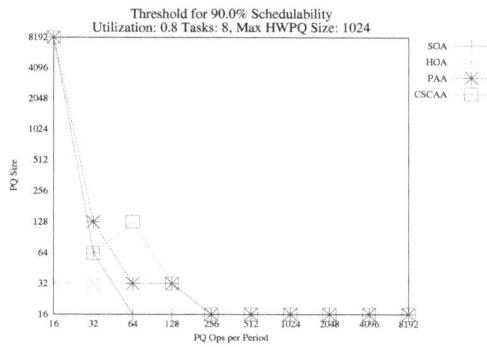

Figure 4: Schedulability with $U = 0.8$. As utilization increases threshold lines move down because applications cannot accommodate extra work induced by PQ operations.

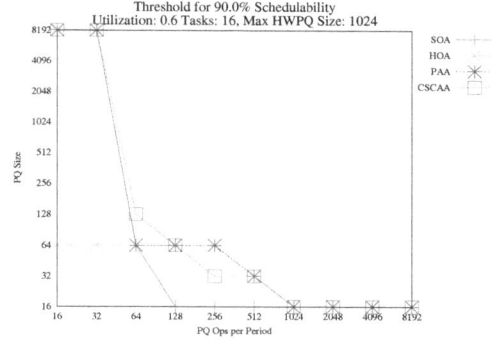

Figure 6: Schedulability with 16 tasks. As the number of tasks increases the threshold lines move down. Doubling the number of tasks reduces the number of schedulable task sets by more than half.

CSCAA with neither outperforming the other for all parameters although CSCAA generally does better than PAA.

Figure 3 shows just the threshold lines this time for a task set utilization U at 0.4 and again with the tasks fixed at 8; Figure 4 shows how increasing U affects schedulability by measuring schedulability with U at 0.8 and with 8 tasks. When system utilization is low the extra slack available in the system allows for PQ operations to use more time which leads to more task sets being schedulable. In general the threshold lines move up indicating that for a given number of PQ operations the task sets having PQ sizes twice as large are schedulable over 90% of the time with the extra 20% available CPU time.

Figure 5 again shows the threshold lines, this time with U at 0.6 and with 4 tasks; Figure 6 shows how increasing the number of tasks with fixed U affects schedulability by keeping U at 0.6 and increasing the number of tasks to 16. The extra tasks increase the global number of PQ operations (since every task does the same PQ workload). Doubling the tasks has the effect of reducing by a factor of two the PQ sizes of tasks sets that are schedulable at least 90% of the time for a given number of PQ operations (two factors if compared to half as many tasks and 20% more CPU time).

5.2 Real-world Applications

The synthetic task sets demonstrate HWPQs with the PAA and CSCAA algorithms can decrease utilization hence increase schedulability of applications that use priority queues. In this section we consider how HWPQs might benefit real-world applications, which may not exhibit behavior that is similar to the synthetic task sets. Two important application domains in real-time and embedded systems are navigation and terrain mapping. Both of these domains contain applications that use a PQ as a central data structure in their main algorithms. From the navigation domain we use a version of Dijkstra's algorithm that is executed on real-world maps taken from the DIMACS shortest path implementation challenge benchmarks [2]. From the terrain mapping domain we have an implementation of the grey-weighted distance transform that executes on a random 3D image; this application has been used previously to evaluate a variety of software PQs [16]. We call these applications GPS and GWDT respectively. Both applications and their inputs are available online, see [16, 2].

In order to simulate these real-world applications we measured their behavior with respect to PQ parameters that affect HWPQ WCET; table 1 summarizes the measurements. We instrumented these applications with additional performance counters in order to measure the maximum PQ size, number (and type) of PQ operations, and the time taken by the PQ operations. For the GWDT application we included the peek, enqueue, and dequeue operations and also PQ allocation and freeing; the software PQ we used for the measurements was the 4-heap [16]. For the GPS application we included only enqueue and dequeue operations.

We executed these applications without modifications using timing mechanisms that are provided with the applications. These

App.	Input	PQ Size	PQ Operations	PQ time
GWDT	32 pixels	16303	168840	31.4%
	64 pixels	56447	1353326	33.5%
GPS	NYC	925	528693	28.5%
	S.F. BAY	886	642540	27.1%
	Colorado	945	871332	30.1%
	Florida	1413	2140753	28.4%
	NW US	1723	2415891	29.2%
	NE US	1796	3048907	26.7%
	California	2355	3781631	27.4%
	Great Lakes	1810	5516239	27.9%
	Eastern US	2336	7197247	24.6%
	Western US	4281	12524209	24.3%
	Central US	5086	28163632	22.4%

Table 1: PQ behavior in real-world applications

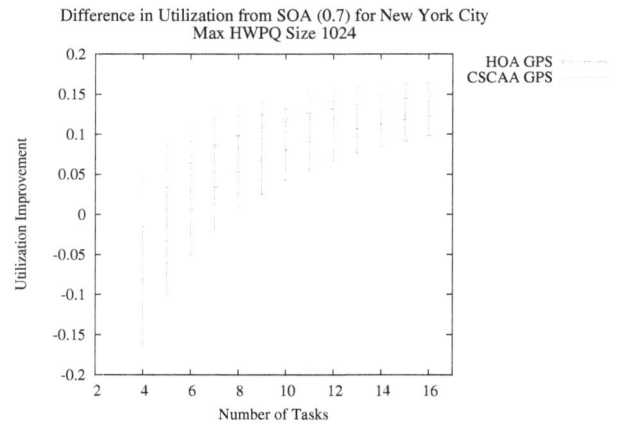

Figure 7: Utilization improvements for GPS application with increasing number of tasks executing local search in New York City.

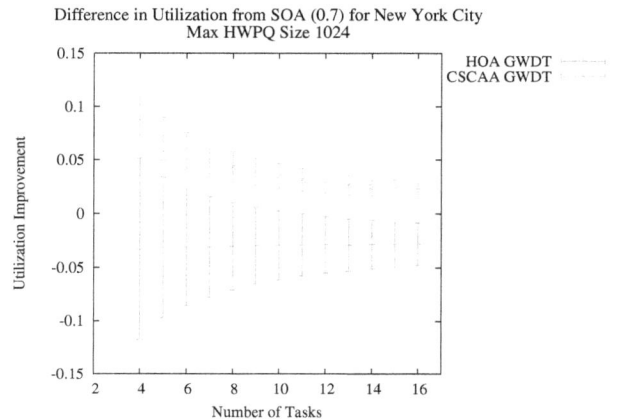

Figure 8: Utilization improvements for grey-weighted distance transform application with increasing numbers of tasks executing small GWDT.

timers query the host system for the user time of the process running the application. The timing elides all startup and shutdown costs. To time individual operations we added timer calls before and after each PQ operation and ran the application both unmodified and with the timer calls. The difference in total time taken between the two runs is the overhead for making the extra timer calls, half of which we deducted from the sum of the time taken for PQ operations (because the time accounted toward the PQ operations includes half of the timer overhead). Then the ratio of the time taken for PQ operations to the total time taken of the unmodified application is a measure for the amount of time spent by the application in the PQ.

Using the parameters that we measured from running the applications we model two new applications that simultaneously run x numbers of small (32 pixel) GWDT tasks, y numbers of local GPS search tasks, 1 large (64 pixel) image processing task, 1 regional GPS search task, and 1 long-distance GPS search task. One application lets x vary from 0 through 12 with y fixed at 1 (call it the GWDT application) and the other application lets y vary from 0 through 12 with x fixed at 1 (call it the GPS application). The total number of tasks in either application varies from 4 to 16.

For each application at a given number of tasks we generate 10000 random task sets with the utilization drawn randomly as before (uniform in $[0.001, 1]$ then normalized to a target U after all tasks have a utilization) but now with the period determined by the PQ parameters we obtained from measuring the applications. In particular we determine the WCET of a software PQ (using our numbers from the implicit binary heap) for the maximum PQ size and number of PQ operations for the task and use the percent of time the task should spend on the PQ to determine how long its total compute time should be. Then we compute the task's period by dividing its total compute time by its randomly generated utilization. We regenerate any task set that does not pass the response time analysis.

The result of task set generation is a set of tasks that use a software PQ and whose task set has a utilization equal to a known value U. We then remove the software PQ WCETs from the tasks and run each assignment algorithm (SOA, HOA, PAA, and CSCAA) on the task set. The SOA algorithm will result in a schedulable task set with a utilization equal to U. Instead of using schedulability as the metric for performance in these experiments we use the amount the assignment algorithm improves (reduces) task set utilization.

Figure 7 shows how HOA and CSCAA improve utilization over SOA for the application that varies the number of tasks running a local GPS search; each point is the arithmetic mean of the dif-

ference between the utilization of SOA—fixed at 0.7—and one of the assignment algorithms (either HOA and CSCAA) averaged across 10000 trials, and with error bars showing the sample standard deviation in both directions (one standard deviation up and one down). The local GPS search is executing the benchmark challenge for New York City, with the regional and long-range searches executing the northeastern US and eastern US benchmarks respectively. Larger numbers are better and represent the amount by which the utilization of the task set as a whole goes down; negative numbers indicate that the assignment algorithm does worse than SOA. Figure 8 shows the same measurements but taken as the number of tasks running the small (32 pixels) GWDT (32 pixels) increases. The results for PAA are not shown because they overlap closely with those for CSCAA. The gains for the GPS application are around 10–16% utilization which represents an improvement of 14–22% over the software PQ utilization.

The real-world applications demonstrate some interesting results. First is that just using a HWPQ (HOA) yields rather large swings in utilization; the smallest GWDT task has a standard deviation of around 7% utilization. Second is that for some applications the benefit of using HWPQs may actually increase as the number of tasks increases; conversely the benefits may decrease as shown by the GWDT results. Even so the CSCAA algorithm produces useful assignments of the HWPQ to tasks in these real-world task sets that improve task set utilization and therefore provide extra slack time in the system for other tasks to complete. The extra utilization can be useful for executing sporadic or background tasks.

6. RELATED WORK

This work builds on research in hardware queues, primarily of the FIFO and PQ varieties. HWPQs have been cited widely for both network routing and real-time scheduling. Moon et al. [19] compare four approaches to hardware PQs for high-speed networks and introduce an approach that melds two of the previous solutions. Kim and Shin [10] describe an architecture for EDF scheduling for ATM switch networks and introduce deadline folding to circumvent limitations in the range of priority values. Bhagwan and Lin [4] introduce a heap-based hardware PQ with pipelined stages of the enqueue and dequeue operations. The Spring Scheduling Coprocessor (SSCoP) [6] is one of the first examples of a hardware task scheduler and introduces simple queues for the set of scheduled tasks. Others have implemented hardware scheduling using some form of custom logic and a HWPQ [22, 12, 11, 5, 13]. In contrast to the prior work, which focuses on hardware support for a single fixed-size PQ, our work demonstrates how arbitrarily-large PQs can share a HWPQ.

Carbon by Kumar et. al [14] provides hardware acceleration for multicore task scheduling with task LIFOs, prefetchers, and work stealing in hardware to support fine-grained thread-level parallelism. Carbon exposes a task queue API in the form of ISA extensions, so it is similar to the HWDS paradigm. It differs in that the queues are used specifically for task scheduling, which means that applications only benefit if Carbon extracts sufficient fine-grained TLP. Carbon provides no benefit to serial workloads and requires small task sizes to see improvement over software scheduling. A HWDS configured as a LIFO would be similar to the single core configuration of Carbon. Otherwise, the two approaches are not directly comparable.

Chandra and Sinnen [7] investigate HWDSs in the context of integrating Java with reconfigurable computing. The authors use a shift-register PQ to speed up Prim's minimum spanning tree algorithm. Their work uses a single PQ and HWPQ. In addition to the usual PQ operations, the authors investigate how to increase the queue length, use non-integer priority values, and add new operations. Our work differs from theirs by supporting large queues with an exception model instead of relying on library interpositioning on PQ accesses; we also allow multiple PQs to share the HWPQ.

For real-time systems a promising approach for providing a time-predictable memory system is to use a scratchpad memory [21]. Scratchpads can provide predictable access times and software control over code [29] and data [25]. Some problems with scratchpads include its limited size and the difficulty in choosing which data to store. The scratchpad memory management unit (SMMU) [27] uses custom hardware to split a virtual address space between a scratchpad and traditional RAM. SMMU uses runtime mechanisms to copy objects between the two memories so that once an object is moved into the scratchpad that object is accessed with predictable timing. The SMMU provides time predictability for accesses to the scratchpad and achieves WCET approaching that of the average-case performance with caching [26]. A downside for the SMMU is that it can actually increase WCET when applications exhibit poor temporal locality for object references because the time taken to copy an object into the scratchpad may negate

any gain due to object reuse. Large objects also present a problem due to the spatial constraints of the scratchpad. HWDSs differ from scratchpads in that a HWDS relies on a high-level abstraction—the data structure—and provides support for high-level operations. Scratchpads rely on memory regions that contain an active working set without using any knowledge about application (data) behavior. So scratchpads may be generally more useful, yet HWDS have more knowledge available and are able to make use of known properties of data structures. HWDS uses these known properties to exploit parallelism and achieve speedup that scratchpads alone cannot. Combining the two approaches to use a HWDS with a scratchpad as the backing store—somewhat like how the SMMU splits storage between a scratchpad and RAM—may be an interesting research direction for reducing the WCET of overflow and underflow exception handlers.

7. CONCLUSION

In this paper we have demonstrated that HWDSs can benefit real-time systems by reducing worst-case execution times even when data structure sizes exceed the size of the HWDS. Systems software support provides flexibility to remove size and sharing limitations of hardware so that applications can benefit from using HWDSs. We devised two new algorithms that assign tasks to use either a HWDS or a software DS and show those algorithms outperform just using the software DS or just using the HWDS for much of the explored application and parameter space. We demonstrated a HWPQ as an example of a HWDS and showed how real-world applications for navigation and image processing could obtain practical improvements in the range of 5–15% of total utilization when using our approach. Our results show promise for the HWDS approach and open new avenues of research into new HWDSs, improvements in the hardware to ease the integration of hardware and software, and better DS abstractions for programming.

Acknowledgments

This work is supported in part by NSF grant CNS-1117243, NSF grant CNS-0934725, AFOSR grant FA9550-09-1-0194, and George Washington University Summer Disssertation Fellowship. The authors thank the anonymous reviewers for their helpful advice.

8. REFERENCES

[1] RTEMS: Real-Time executive for multiprocessor systems. http://www.rtems.com/, 2011.

[2] 9th DIMACS implementation challenge: Shortest paths. http://www.dis.uniroma1.it/challenge9/download.shtml, 2012.

[3] N. Audsley, A. Burns, M. Richardson, K. Tindell, and A. Wellings. Applying new scheduling theory to static priority pre-emptive scheduling. *Software Engineering Journal*, 8(5):284 –292, Sept. 1993.

[4] R. Bhagwan and B. Lin. Fast and scalable priority queue architecture for high-speed network switches. In *INFOCOM 2000. Nineteenth Annual Joint Conference of the IEEE Computer and Communications Societies. Proceedings. IEEE*, volume 2, pages 538–547 vol.2, 2000.

[5] G. Bloom, G. Parmer, B. Narahari, and R. Simha. Real-Time scheduling with hardware data structures. In *Work-in-Progress Session. IEEE Real-Time Systems Symposium*, Dec. 2010.

[6] W. Burleson, J. Ko, D. Niehaus, K. Ramamritham, J. A. Stankovic, G. Wallace, and C. Weems. The spring scheduling

coprocessor: a scheduling accelerator. *IEEE Trans. Very Large Scale Integr. Syst.*, 7(1):38–47, 1999.

[7] R. Chandra and O. Sinnen. Improving application performance with hardware data structures. Tech. Report Faculty of Engineering, no. 678, University of Auckland, May 2010.

[8] C. Ferdinand and R. Wilhelm. On predicting data cache behavior for Real-Time systems. In *Proceedings of the ACM SIGPLAN Workshop on Languages, Compilers, and Tools for Embedded Systems*, LCTES '98, pages 16–30, London, UK, UK, 1998. Springer-Verlag.

[9] D. W. Jones. An empirical comparison of priority-queue and event-set implementations. *Commun. ACM*, 29(4):300–311, Apr. 1986. ACM ID: 5686.

[10] B. K. Kim and K. Shin. Scalable hardware earliest-deadline-first scheduler for ATM switching networks. In *Real-Time Systems Symposium, IEEE International*, page 210, Los Alamitos, CA, USA, 1997. IEEE Computer Society.

[11] P. Kohout, B. Ganesh, and B. Jacob. Hardware support for real-time operating systems. In *Proceedings of the 1st IEEE/ACM/IFIP international conference on Hardware/software codesign and system synthesis*, pages 45–51, Newport Beach, CA, USA, 2003. ACM.

[12] P. Kuacharoen, M. A. Shalan, and V. J. M. III. A configurable hardware scheduler for Real-Time systems. *In Proceedings of the International Conference on Engineering of Reconfigurable Systems and Algorithms*, pages 96–101, 2003.

[13] C. Kumar, S. Vyas, J. Shidal, R. Cytron, C. Gill, J. Zambreno, and P. Jones. Improving system predictability and performance via hardware accelerated data structures. In *Dynamic Data Driven Application Systems (DDDAS)*, 2012.

[14] S. Kumar, C. J. Hughes, and A. Nguyen. Carbon: architectural support for fine-grained parallelism on chip multiprocessors. In *Proceedings of the 34th annual international symposium on Computer architecture*, pages 162–173, San Diego, California, USA, 2007. ACM.

[15] A. LaMarca and R. Ladner. The influence of caches on the performance of heaps. *J. Exp. Algorithmics*, 1, Jan. 1996. ACM ID: 235145.

[16] C. L. Luengo Hendriks. Revisiting priority queues for image analysis. *Pattern Recogn.*, 43(9):3003–3012, Sept. 2010. ACM ID: 1808374.

[17] M. M. K. Martin, D. J. Sorin, B. M. Beckmann, M. R. Marty, M. Xu, A. R. Alameldeen, K. E. Moore, M. D. Hill, and D. A. Wood. Multifacet's general execution-driven multiprocessor simulator (GEMS) toolset. *ACM SIGARCH Computer Architecture News*, 33:92–99, Nov. 2005. ACM ID: 1105747.

[18] N. Mhatre. *A Comparative Performance Analysis of Real-Time Priority Queues*. Master's thesis, The Florida State University, 2001.

[19] S. Moon, K. Shin, and J. Rexford. Scalable hardware priority queue architectures for high-speed packet switches. In *Real-Time Technology and Applications Symposium, 1997. Proceedings., Third IEEE*, pages 203–212, 1997.

[20] F. Mueller. Timing analysis for instruction caches. *Real-Time Syst.*, 18(2/3):217–247, May 2000.

[21] I. Puaut and C. Pais. Scratchpad memories vs locked caches in hard real-time systems: a quantitative comparison. In *Proceedings of the conference on Design, automation and test in Europe*, DATE '07, pages 1484–1489, San Jose, CA, USA, 2007. EDA Consortium.

[22] S. Saez, J. Vila, A. Crespo, and A. Garcia. A hardware scheduler for complex real-time systems. In *Industrial Electronics, 1999. ISIE '99. Proceedings of the IEEE International Symposium on*, volume 1, pages 43–48 vol.1, 1999.

[23] D. Sanchez, R. M. Yoo, and C. Kozyrakis. Flexible architectural support for fine-grain scheduling. In *Proceedings of the fifteenth edition of ASPLOS on Architectural support for programming languages and operating systems*, pages 311–322, Pittsburgh, Pennsylvania, USA, 2010. ACM.

[24] X. Vera, B. Lisper, and J. Xue. Data caches in multitasking hard real-time systems. In *Real-Time Systems Symposium, 2003. RTSS 2003. 24th IEEE*, pages 154–165, 2003.

[25] Q. Wan, H. Wu, and J. Xue. WCET-aware data selection and allocation for scratchpad memory. In *Proceedings of the 13th ACM SIGPLAN/SIGBED International Conference on Languages, Compilers, Tools and Theory for Embedded Systems*, LCTES '12, pages 41–50, New York, NY, USA, 2012. ACM.

[26] J. Whitham and N. Audsley. Investigating average versus Worst-Case timing behavior of data caches and data scratchpads. In *Real-Time Systems (ECRTS), 2010 22nd Euromicro Conference on*, pages 165–174, July 2010.

[27] J. Whitham and N. Audsley. Studying the applicability of the scratchpad memory management unit. In *Real-Time and Embedded Technology and Applications Symposium (RTAS), 2010 16th IEEE*, pages 205–214, Apr. 2010.

[28] M. V. Wilkes. The memory gap and the future of high performance memories. *SIGARCH Comput. Archit. News*, 29(1):2–7, Mar. 2001. ACM ID: 373576.

[29] H. Wu, J. Xue, and S. Parameswaran. Optimal WCET-aware code selection for scratchpad memory. In *Proceedings of the tenth ACM international conference on Embedded software*, EMSOFT '10, pages 59–68, New York, NY, USA, 2010. ACM.

[30] W. A. Wulf and S. A. McKee. Hitting the memory wall: implications of the obvious. *ACM SIGARCH Computer Architecture News*, 23:20–24, Mar. 1995. ACM ID: 216588.

A Low-overhead Dedicated Execution Support for Stream Applications on Shared-memory CMP

Paul Dubrulle, Stéphane Louise, Renaud Sirdey, Vincent David
CEA, LIST
Point Courrier 172
91191 Gif-sur-Yvette Cedex, France
<firstname.lastname>@cea.fr

ABSTRACT

The ever-growing number of cores in Chip Multi-Processors (CMP) brings a renewed interest in stream programming to solve the programmability issues raised by massively parallel architectures. Stream programming languages are flourishing (StreaMIT, Brook, ΣC, etc.). Nonetheless, their execution support have not yet received enough attention, in particular regarding the new generation of many-cores.

In embedded software, a lightweight solution can be implemented as a specialized library, but a dedicated micro-kernel offers a more flexible solution. We propose to explore the latter way with a Logical Vector Time based execution model, for CMP architectures with on-chip shared memory.

Categories and Subject Descriptors

D.4.1 [**Operating Systems**]: Process Management—*scheduling,synchronization*; D.1.3 [**Programming Techniques**]: Concurrent Programming—*parallel programming*

General Terms

Performance, Reliability, Algorithms, Theory, Experimentation, Measurement.

Keywords

Execution model, logical vector time, micro-kernel, chip multiprocessor, manycore, stream programming.

1. INTRODUCTION

1.1 Motivations

With the advent of multi-core processors as a pervasive reality, from supercomputing to embedded systems, programming concepts must also evolve toward new paradigms as massive parallelism in programs is becoming mandatory. This means that imperative programming does not fit this new area well. Several concepts of parallel programing are

competing for the status of being the most adapted language paradigm for many-core systems. Among them, a number of stream programming languages are emerging (StreaMIT [24], Brook, ΣC [12], ...). The advantages of stream programming relies for a part in their theoretical bases which make them amenable to formal verification of important application properties like dead-lock freeness, execution within limited memory bounds, or correctness of parallel applications including functional determinism, or absence of race conditions [18]. Even though stream programing does not fit all computation kinds, it is very well fitted to signal and image processing applications, which are among the killer applications for many-core systems.

The bases of stream programing rely on Kahn Process Networks (KPN [15]), more precisely on their special derivation, Data Process Networks [18], as well as their more restrictive variants such as Cyclo-Static Data Flows (CSDF, [10]). KPN and CSDF are deterministic and the possibility to run a CSDF in bounded memory is a decidable problem [4].

Most of current implementations of execution support for stream programming languages are threading libraries above off-the-shelf OS. This is a correct approach as a validation tool or for running streaming applications on full-size computers. However, in the embedded world, a lighter approach is needed as memory is usually a scarce facility, and embedded targets require special attention to power consumption and code performance.

A specialized micro-kernel would potentially provide a very light execution support with little overheads, along with more options for scheduling policies. It is an adequate answer for stream applications on multi-core and many-core embedded platforms as it provides a strict control over hardware resources and task execution, a necessity to achieve a negligible CPU and memory overhead.

1.2 Target architectures

The choice of the target architecture is of first importance regarding the design of a specialized micro-kernel. We choose to target multi-core systems with shared on-chip memory. This memory can either be a specialized local storage shared among several cores, or be a shared L2 or L3 on-chip cache.

A specialized micro-kernel targeting such architectures is scalable to embedded many-core chips, most such architectures being clustered (hence one instance of the micro-kernel runs on each cluster, which typically is a small SMP - cf. Figure 1). When it is not so, the set of cores can be partitioned.

These architectures are well fitted for stream program-

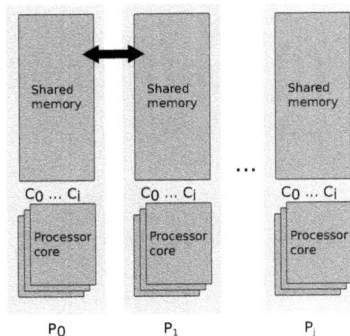

Figure 1: A multi-core micro-kernel is scalable to many-core by partitioning the many-core and executing an instance of the micro-kernel per partition; the multi-core partitions P_0 to P_j each host an instance of the micro-kernel, the double arrow represents the need of communication between partitions (e.g. partitions could be clusters and the double arrow a NoC for a hierarchical many-core target).

ing paradigms because channels between processes can be implemented as shared memory buffers (with low latencies) between processes running in parallel. If buffer sizes are correctly adjusted, the producing process in a channel can run in parallel with the consuming process(es), because the latter can work on data in a section already written by the producing process at the previous step of execution.

Moreover, such architectures allow for a global and dynamic scheduling of the tasks instead of a static scheduling, as what is often met nowadays: a shared task list in on-chip memory theoretically allows for a dynamic execution which can absorb variations in single task execution times, hence taking advantages of early release of processing cores/units to gain either on the average execution time or on the typical latency of a given multitasking application (or both).

1.3 Goals

We aim at providing a road-map from a stream programing language to an execution model on a multi-core with shared on-chip memory, with the following constraints:

1. light weight implementation of a specific micro-kernel, for the reasons expressed in subsection 1.1;

2. as low an overhead as possible to minimize the impact of the runtime on user computation;

3. constrained dynamic scheduling, because of its advantages on the chosen target platforms, as said in subsection 1.2.

For us the second constraint is nearly as important as the first, this is why we choose to focus on an asymmetric implementation of a multi-core micro-kernel. One execution resource is dedicated to task management, while inter-process communication and computation are left to the others.

2. RELATED WORKS

2.1 StreaMIT execution support

StreaMIT provides a support for the RAW multi-core architecture, as described in [2]. In this work, communications

are statically determined between cores, and tasks running on the same core are fused together by several compilation techniques (parallel fusion for split-join parallelism and vertical fusion for successive filters). This provides an overall static scheduling of the parallel application on the RAW multi-core target.

This work is the closest to what we aim to do with multi-core architectures. Nonetheless, the RAW architecture is quite different from our main target architecture since it does not provide a shared memory for all the cores. Moreover, the paper provides mostly performance benchmarks for an application on RAW making it quite difficult to compare with our approach on task switch latencies: on one hand the fusion and static scheduling means that there is no real task switch on a given core, on the other hand benchmark program results are also hard to compare because the RAW architecture is not comparable to ours (communication through shared memory vs. communication through core specific data channels, etc.).

Anyway, a static scheduling as implemented in support of StreaMIT for RAW is based on measures of user task execution times. If these execution times tend to vary a lot during execution (in dynamic applications such as video encoders for example), the static scheduling is much less efficient. A dynamic scheduling, as in our approach, takes advantage of early release of processing cores.

Another paper [29] shows an implementation of an execution layer for StreaMIT on the Cell BE processor. The Cell BE processor is a heterogeneous platform with one front-end dual threaded PPC core (with L1 and L2 cache) and 8 SPE core (which are mostly vectorial processors) with 256 KB of per core local on chip memory (local store). All the cores are connected through a double ring high speed NoC. The Multicore Streaming Layer described in this paper is close by its principles to ours. The aim is to have an execution abstraction layer that would be valid both in shared-memory multi-core and local-memory multi-core.

Nonetheless, the implementation is done for a local memory multi-core (CELL BE). Though the implementation we present in this paper is for shared-memory, its is ready to be extended to local memory paradigm (cf. subsection 1.2) by using double buffers to manage communication transparently between on-Chip local memory: the basic principle is to replace the shared-memory buffer with a source buffer and as many copy buffers as required by the application (depending on task clustering and assignation on cores or groups of cores).

The main difference with our approach is that Zhang approach provides a framework for dynamically running task and managing buffers (and send data to depending task when it is ready). Our approach is more static, and allows for off-line verifications whereas their approach depends on the correct firing of commands (or groups of commands) to the runtime library, especially in the dynamic scheduling scheme. Since this framework relies on Linux OS for CELL BE and is not a bare-bone implementation, the *filter_run* command is said to take a few hundreds of micro-seconds which is large compared to our task selection/commutation time. The benchmarks are, as in the previous case, hard to compare because the targeted architecture and software approach are quite different.

2.2 Array-OL

Array-OL is a Domain Specific Language which, by its constructs, can be easily parented or mapped to stream processing models of execution. Two works were specifically proposed toward this goal.

The first one mapped the language constructs to Khan Process Network (KPN) constructs [1]. It shows that Array-OL paradigms are easily projected onto KPN where they used arrays as basic tokens. KPN were then implemented with pipes on top of a CORBA framework. The aimed target systems are heterogeneous computing farms (networks of workstations) and MultiProcessor System on Chip (MP-SoC). Experiments where only conduct for the former target, so comparisons with our work are hard to make (networks of workstations are not shared memory systems). Moreover, performance should heavily depend on the CORBA implementation and no details are provided regarding how should such an implementation for MPSoC be achieved.

The second one applied a closely related technique with Multidimensional Synchronous Dataflows (MSDF) [7]. The model mapping is very close to the previous. Nonetheless, the evaluations are only made on the Ptolemy platform [17] which is a good target for research work, but would not provide real ground to compare with a specialized execution layer.

2.3 Brook

The Brook language [3] is an extension of standard C that provides notions of stream types. Streams are processed by kernels (*i.e.* specialized functions). Specialized functions and kernels provide the tools for splitting, joining or decimating stream values (so communication framework). Brook relies on a source to source compiler to generate *e.g.* code for GPGPU targets. It uses a generic runtime called Brook RunTime library (BRT) as execution support. Its main aim is to facilitate the transformation of legacy C code to exploit the power of GPU by accelerating the execution of compute intensive parts of the original code onto the GPU.

Although one of the long term goal of Brook is to support embedded multi-core target like PicoChip or RAW, nowadays environment is focused on general purpose workstation with GPU accelerators. Only the compute intensive kernels are accelerated and even the communication (scatter and gather especially) parts are mapped on the CPU since current GPU are not well fitted to these kinds of processing. Therefore the comparison with our work is hard to achieve, even on the pure stream parts of a Brook application.

Several other extension of C or C++ language families have been proposed to provide a mean to program GPU. One can cite openCL, CUDA or Cg. They are proposed for vertex shader or GPGPU kernel programming. But they remain low level compared to stream programming paradigms.

3. CONTRIBUTIONS

We propose a micro-kernel architecture for the support of stream applications on embedded multi-cores, based on a Logical Vector Time (LVT) execution model. We developed a prototype for this micro-kernel and provide a first evaluation on a set of stream processing applications. To the best of our knowledge, there is no micro-kernel approach to the execution support of stream applications, and the work we present here shows it is a safe and efficient approach.

The concept of vector clocks has been indirectly used before in many application fields (file consistency [22], distributed debugging [8], distributed mutual exclusion [23], ...). Yet the capability of vector clocks to capture causal relations between events has never been used for dynamic scheduling. It is quite adapted because it allows an efficient, deterministic and dynamic task status update at runtime, as exposed in the technical part of this paper in subsection 5.2. A major drawback, though, is the space such vectors use in memory, especially for embedded environments, but this problem was also addressed in the implementation of our prototype (cf. subsection 5.3).

Using the LVT execution model as a library over a POSIX system was our validation approach, but the present micro-kernel approach has always been our goal. A specialized micro-kernel uses much less resources (memory, CPU time) than a general purpose kernel, which is critical in the embedded platforms we target. It also avoids interactions between the user space scheduler (LVT based) and the host system's scheduling policy, which may decide a preemption without considering the impact on the application latency.

4. STREAM PROGRAMMING

Before describing our execution model and micro-kernel, we describe the stream programming paradigm and the task model it supports. Stream programming paradigm is based on the following two elements.

First, a series of *filters* which are computing units that take values as entries on specified read-only channels, use these values for processing and output values (obviously computation results) on predeclared write-mostly channels. Reading on input channels of filters is blocking. Output channels are theoretically not limited in size, but of course a desired property of the system is that it is amenable to run in finite memory.

Second, a *communication graph* which links either output channels or sources to either input channels or sinks. The communication graph can be quite complex, holding expression of data access patterns including but not limited to permutations, with possible duplication or decimation (without any change to the transfered data).

Among the desired properties of the system, the stream paradigm eliminates race conditions by construction, and the presence of dead-locks can be detected at compile time.

One possible restriction for stream programs is to conform to the Cyclo-Static Data Flow (CSDF) model [10], shortly introduced in subsection 4.2. Actually, the programing language ΣC [12] defines a superset of CSDF which remains decidable though allowing data dependent control to a certain extent. Nonetheless, as the focus is not set on the programming aspects in this paper, let us suppose that it is limited to CSDF.

4.1 Communication graph

Usual elements of communication graphs are simple channels (possibly with distinct production and consumption rhythms), splitters (including duplicators or dispatchers), joiners, and feed-back loops. Filters can have the same semantic as some graph elements (*e.g.* splitters) if defined accordingly. But one of the main advantages to express them in the communication graph is that properties such as deadlock freeness and execution in bounded memory can be automatically checked (with automatic sizing of the exchange buffers). Moreover, transformations can be inferred to produce an equivalent graph that would *e.g.* reduce the memory requirements or the throughput, as in [20], or as done in StreaMIT [24].

Channels and communication buffers

The goal of the compilation is to transform the communication through channels into efficient communication through shared memory-mapped circular buffers. The compilation tools are used to ensure that the application liveness property is fulfilled provided that task scheduling is correct. Mapping channels into circular buffers is a first step to provide a pointer equivalence (at the fist level), so that application code can access data as ordinary arrays in C language without having to compute complex index values for each access (this should hold true for sliding windows as well). Moreover, as only one filter is authorized to write a given value, while one or many filters can read it, flushing/invalidating L1 caches at design points can ensure memory coherency. This is one of the main advantages of stream programing for embedded targets where cache coherency mechanisms are often lacking because of their silicon surface and power consumption.

4.2 Filters

In this paper, we limit the task model to CSDF. In order to distinguish the task as seen in the CSDF model (so in the programing model) from the actual task that can run on a multi-core target system (hence in the execution model), the word *filter* is used here to refer to the CSDF tasks.

Therefore, in the CSDF model a filter has in general several input channels and several output channels. The number of data tokens produced (resp. consumed) in a channel are set at compile-time, and may change from one activation of the filter to the next following a static cycle. For example, if c is an input channel of a given filter, with an intake cycle defined by a suite of n_c positive integers x_j^c, then the number of data tokens consumed on channel c at cycle i is x_k^c with $k = i \mod n_c$ (cf. Figure 2).

Filters are in general stateful. They can do any kind of operation with the data they have in input channel and proceed them to the output channels. Nonetheless, they are not authorized to use shared variables and the channels are the only way a filter can communicate values to another (this can be formally enforced by an adequate link edition process).

Filters and tasks

The *tasks* are entities that actually run on a given platform. They differ from filters in the sense that their communication channels have been mapped to buffers in memory (on-chip Memory if available). Moreover, several filters may have been merged together to form one single task and usually when complex communication patterns are used (as expressed by composition of splitters, joiners, etc) they are also often merged with filters: this is done as part of the compilation optimization process, as in [5].

4.3 Extracting task dependencies

As said through this section and especially in subsection 4.1, the correct execution of the system relies on a correct partial order of execution of the compiled tasks so that the

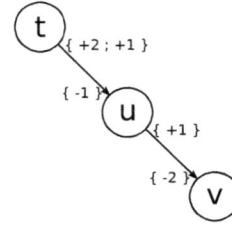

Figure 2: An example of a simple CSDF communication graph, with three pipelined filters t, u and v (the corresponding dependency graph is given in Figure 3); the production sequences on channels are presented on the right of the edges, the intake sequences on the left.

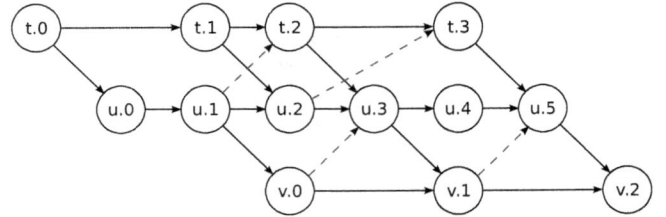

Figure 3: An example of dependency graph produced for the pipeline of Figure 2; node labels represent the owner filter and the rank of the corresponding activation, and the dashed arcs represent dependencies for a possible buffer dimensioning.

circular buffers become a simulation of the channels in the communication graph.

We said in 4.2 that filters had a cyclic communication behavior. The compilation process ensures that tasks (compiled filter or set of filters) also have such a cyclic behavior. For a compiled task, an *activation* is an event in the task's lifetime corresponding to its activation to produce and/or consume data as defined in its cyclic communication state machine.

The partial order is created from the constrains that a given task should not start an activation before its input buffers hold enough data (*i.e.* the task producing data in the buffer completed the producing activation), and its output buffers have free space as to prevent an overwrite of data still consumed by other tasks (*i.e.* all the consuming tasks have completed enough consuming activations).

The task activations that are not comparable with respect to this partial order can be executed in parallel. The other activations must wait until all preceding activations are completed before task activation is possible.

In the compilation process, we can encode the partial order in the form of a Directed Acyclic Graph (DAG), called the *dependency graph* (cf. Figure 3), denoted $G(V, A)$. A node $e_t^i \in V$ represents the ith activation of task t, and an arc $(e_t^i, e_u^j) \in A$ tells e_u^j depends on e_t^i (denoted $e_t^i \rightarrow e_u^j$). The subset of activations of one task t in the dependency graph is denoted V_t.

The dependency graph is a finite object, which gives the dependencies between activations of tasks such that, when all activations present in the graph are executed, the buffers return to their initial state (all produced data was consumed). It means that the application behavior described in the graph can be *replicated* as many times as needed in the analysis process.

5. LOGICAL VECTOR TIME BASED EXECUTION MODEL

The dependencies between task activations in the dependency graph can be used at runtime to decide whether a task is ready or not. To extract and use efficiently this information from the graph, we propose an execution model based on Logical Vector Time (LVT), providing deterministic and safe execution of stream programs.

It is based on assigning a vector clock to each task in the set T of all compiled tasks in the application. The clock is updated and compared at runtime to decide whether current activations of two tasks are ordered or causally independent. To achieve this, we need to compute off-line a partially ordered set (*poset*) of vector time-stamps, isomorphic to the partial order defined by the dependency graph. Further analysis on the vectors produced allows us to find a time-stamp defining an initial clock value for each task, and a finite set of vector increments to infinitely update this value.

5.1 Generating vector clocks

We first summarize here the elements from partially ordered set theory [6] necessary to describe our execution model, and the way to obtain the runtime data structures necessary to execute the application. Let X be a set of elements. A partial order on X is a relation, denoted $\sqsubseteq$, reflexive ($x \sqsubseteq x, \forall x \in X$), antisymmetric ($x \sqsubseteq y \wedge y \sqsubseteq x \Leftrightarrow x = y, \forall x, y \in X$), and transitive ($x \sqsubseteq y \wedge y \sqsubseteq z \Leftrightarrow x \sqsubseteq z, \forall x, y, z \in X$). The pair $(X, \sqsubseteq)$ defines a poset. We also define a relation $\sqsubset$ as $x \sqsubset y \Leftrightarrow x \sqsubseteq y \wedge x \neq y, \forall x, y \in X$.

To build the poset of vector time-stamps $(H, \sqsubseteq)$, each activation e in the dependency graph is affected a unique vector $h(e)$, with $|T|$ coordinates, using Algorithm 1, a variant of a well-known algorithm [9, 19].

ALGORITHM 1: Computing vector time-stamps in the dependency graph

---

Input: Dependency graph of the application($G(V, A)$)
Output: Set of vector time-stamps (H)
for *each activation* $e_t^i \in V$ **do**
    $\forall v, h(e)[v] = 0$
end
for *each activation* $e_t^i \in V$, *in topological order* **do**
    $h(e_t^i)[t] = i$;
    for *each direct successor* e_u^j *to* e_t^i **do**
        $\forall v, h(e_u^j)[v] = \max(h(e_u^j)[v], h(e_t^i)[v])$;
    end
end

This algorithm guarantees that a vector coordinate $h(e_t^i)[u]$ is monotonically increasing, and $e_t^i \rightarrow e_u^j \Leftrightarrow h(e_t^i)[v] \leq h(e_u^j)[v], \forall v$. This relation can be narrowed down to $e_t^i \rightarrow e_u^j \Leftrightarrow h(e_t^i)[t] \leq h(e_u^j)[t]$ when t and u are known, as shown in [16].

Thus, given H the set of the vector time-stamps, and given the relation $h(e_t^i) \sqsubseteq h(e_u^j) \Leftrightarrow h(e_t^i)[v] \leq h(e_u^j)[v], \forall v$, we

have a poset $(H, \sqsubseteq)$ isomorphic to the partial order defined by the dependency graph.

The cyclic property of task behavior implies that in the dependency graph, task dependencies repeat themselves following the same pattern over and over. So, by transitivity, once a task has received at least one dependency from every other task in the computation, it will receive them cyclically for ever after.

Considering the time-stamp of this initial activation and the task's cycle length, we can build a cyclic set of increment vectors. Incrementing the initial time-stamp using this finite cyclic increment set gives us a vector clock that can theoretically be infinitely incremented (see subsection 5.3 for details on how this is achieved).

To compute the initial clock values and the increment set, the algorithms have a quadratic complexity. Thus it is not a problem to generate runtime data structures even for thousands of tasks on an average workstation (less than 1 second for 1000 tasks on a workstation equipped with Intel Core i5 CPU M520).

5.2 Using vector clocks for task activation

To each task $t \in T$, we associate the following runtime data:

1. a vector clock d_t, of dimension $|T|$, representing its current availability date;

2. an integer k_t used as a dependency counter;

3. an incrementation rule, $\delta_t : \mathbb{Z}^{|T|} \longrightarrow \mathbb{Z}^{|T|}$, used at the end of every activation of t to update d_t.

A task with $k_t = 0$ is by construction ready for its execution. A simple sequence of clock comparisons can initialize the dependency counter of a task t: $k_t = 0$, for each task v in $T \setminus \{t\}$, if $d_v \sqsubset d_t$ then $k_t = k_t + 1$.

As the initial values of vector clocks encode a partial order, there must be at least one task t such that $k_t = 0$ (*i.e.* there is always at least one vertex without predecessor in the dependency DAG).

At the end of every activation of a task t, applying the Algorithm 2 updates the LVT and task dependencies. It is important to mention that this algorithm can be parallelized, and that the set of tasks used in update can be significantly reduced.

5.3 Optimizing vector clocks for embedded environments

Now we have to discuss complexity of the algorithms of this execution model. A direct implementation would certainly not show performance, as every activation termination costs $O(3T^2)$.

To reduce the cost of this operation, we can first reduce the set of tasks v to which vector clock of ended task t is compared. The transitivity of the relation $\sqsubseteq$ allow us to update t only using its direct neighbors N in the dependency graph. This reduces the complexity to $O(3T \times N)$, knowing that in usual graphs the average value of N is 4.

The second reduction is based on the fact that in our specific context, we know which tasks own the activations being compared. This allows us to take advantage of the vector clock property extracted from the LVT construction in subsection 5.1: $e_t^i \rightarrow e_v^j \Leftrightarrow h(e_t^i)[t] \leq h(e_v^j)[t]$. Thus

ALGORITHM 2: Updating task runtime data at end of activation

Input: Set of tasks in computation (T), task at end of activation ($t \in T$)

Output: Set of tasks in computation (T), task at start of next activation ($t \in T$)

for *each task* $v \in T \setminus \{t\}$ **do**
    if $d_t \sqsubset d_v$ **then**
        $k_v = k_v - 1$;
    end
end
$d_t = \delta_t(d_t)$;
for *each task* $v \in T \setminus \{t\}$ **do**
    if $d_t \sqsubset d_v$ **then**
        $k_v = k_v + 1$;
    end
    if $d_v \sqsubset d_t$ **then**
        $k_t = k_t + 1$;
    end
end

---

deciding $d_t \sqsubset d_v$ is a $O(1)$ operation, reducing complexity of end of activation update to $O(3N)$.

Another issue with vector clocks is their size in coordinates, the memory they use and the cost to increment such vectors. Many works aim at reducing the vector dimension [21, 13, 26, 27], but finding the smallest dimension is a NP-complete problem [28], it might give no reduction of initial vector size [25] and the existing methods are in general rather costly and more importantly remove the possibility to compare clocks in $O(1)$.

In our case, vector dimension can be significantly reduced by cutting the dependency graph into subgraphs before computing the time-stamps. This gives multiple vector clock posets, with incomparable elements across different posets (with sufficiently small subgraphs, we can achieve any vector dimension). The synchronization between activations of tasks across different posets can then be made through different methods, or using a hierarchical LVT. Actually, for most of the targets we studied, the chip consists of interconnected clusters over a Network on Chip (NoC), which forces the division of the global dependency graph anyway and allows synchronization using a simple network protocol.

Finally, we have to settle the need of infinite vector coordinates. We could use 64-bit integers to encode them, which would functionally prevent an overflow, but this is not satisfactory and ruins the effort to reduce memory usage. Instead, we increment and compare the coordinates using a global modulo M, computed off-line as $M > 2T$, T being the maximum advance a producing task can have on its consumers. We simply associate the relation $\preceq$ to the integer set $\{0, \ldots, M-1\}$ with $x \preceq y \Leftrightarrow (x \le y \wedge y - x \le T) \vee (x > y \wedge M + y - x \le T)$. This generally results in coordinates encoded on 8 bits or 16 bits, allowing acceleration using specialized vector instructions on some targets.

Figure 4 shows the complete dependency graph for the pipeline of Figure 2, with vector timestamps on each activation, from which the runtime data can be extracted.

6. KERNEL IMPLEMENTATION

We prototyped an implementation of this execution model, as a micro-kernel for two target platforms: 1) a non-public

domain embedded many-core architecture; 2) a x86 multicore PC.

6.1 Asymmetric kernel

The processor cores of the target are divided in two categories: 1) *Control Core* (CC), which is in charge of the main part of task scheduling, and supervises the other cores; 2) *Processing Core* (PC), which is in charge of user computation, inter-process communication and of a minor part of task scheduling.

There is always one CC, and at least one PC. This repartition takes benefit from the parallelism of target architectures to optimize the scheduling operations, by minimizing the scheduling overhead on the PC (they only perform small operations that do not imply race conditions on the different PC). Using wait-free algorithms [14], the CC can perform the remainder of the scheduling operations while the PC keep running ready tasks (if any left). The only explicit synchronization occurs when tasks are inserted or removed from a lock-free FIFO, and possibly when a core wakes an idle one on some targets when power saving is important.

The number of PC must be adequate to avoid making the CC a bottleneck. This is not a problem when partitionning the available cores into logical or physical computation clusters is considered (cf. subsection 1.2).

6.2 Cyclic buffers for channel implementation

The communication layer is totally handled on the PC. Each channel in the communication graph is implemented as an *exchange buffer* in the shared memory.

Though mapping the channels to cyclic buffers with firstlevel pointer equivalence has been an important part of our prototyping, it is only a detail in this paper focusing on the execution model. We only present here the description of the operations performed by the IPC mechanisms of our micro-kernel necessary to understand the results shown in the evaluation section.

The micro-kernel provides each task with *production access* (resp. *intake access*) to the exchange buffers, which are statically allocated. For each buffer it accesses, a task has an access descriptor. It gives a description of cyclic access behavior of the task in the memory region, and the current status in this cyclic behavior (including current *alias* pointer into the buffer). These access aliases allow an easy implementation of the complex acccess schemes described in the communication graph.

At the end of every activation of a task, the access descriptors of the buffers used at ended activation and used at next activation are updated. This update is a mere modulo incrementation of the alias pointer. In some rare cases, a shadow copy is performed to enforce pointer equivalence in user code.

The blocking read operations are not handled at buffer level. The scheduling used to build the dependencies between tasks (thus the LVT ruling the execution of the tasks) guarantees that there is no race condition in buffer access.

6.3 Task management

The PC is in charge of executing user code, and to provide services for inter-task communication and task activation supervision. The CC is in charge of hardware supervision and global system state updates.

Initially, a PC starts in the micro-kernel context and en-

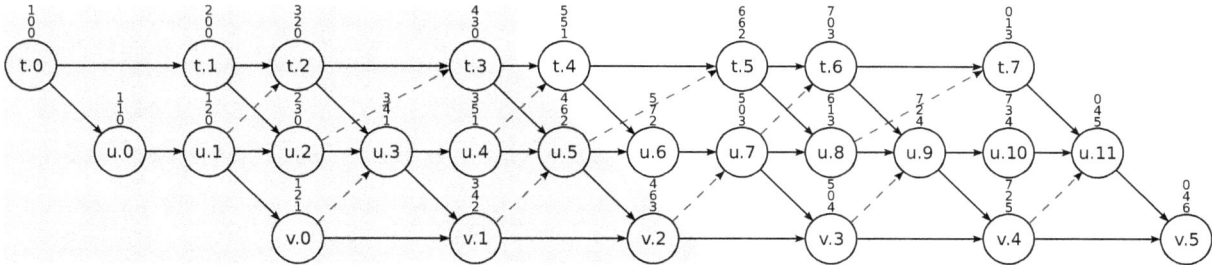

Figure 4: Two replications of the dependency graph shown in Figure 3, with the vector time-stamps over each activation, their coordinates are on a modulo 8; in this example, initial clock values are those of activations e_t^4, e_u^3 and e_v^0, the length of the incrementation cycles are respectively 4, 6, and 3.

ters an *idle state*, where it waits for at least one user task to be *ready* (no dependencies left for current activation) and *eligible* (available for PC to load its context). When one or more tasks change state to ready eligible, all idle PC are woken up by the CC and try to load a ready user context. If it succeeds, it loads the user context for execution and changes task's state to *running* (otherwise it returns to idle state). When a user context is loaded, the PC restore processor to protected mode and return to last position of the task in user code (or task entry at first load).

In user context, a task can have access to the communication interface through local pointers to buffers, retrieved using communication system calls (the calls are inlined and execute in protected mode, as they consist only in reading the application runtime data). At the end of an activation, the task must enter the end of transition procedure through an appropriate system call. The following operations are then performed: processor enters privileged mode; the next availability date of the task is computed by incrementing the current availability date; for each access descriptor, the exchange position must be updated for next activation; PC switches to the micro-kernel context, saves the execution context of the task and updates its status to ended activation; PC performs the same operations as when woken up from idle mode.

The CC never executes user code. It is the first execution resource to start, and is in charge to wake all PC which will enter idle mode and wait for kick off. It must also initialize any other hardware resource (*e.g.* the network interface to the NoC if any).

Once the hardware setup is over, the CC wakes all PC so they start to feed on the ready task set. The rest of its execution flow is an infinite loop, waiting for service requests from hardware resources (including PC).

When a PC requests end of task treatment for the task it finished, the CC performs LVT comparisons and updates dependency counters accordingly, and changes state to ready for every task whose dependency counter reached zero.

7. EVALUATION AND BENCHMARKS

This section gives some benchmarks, to evaluate the system overhead for a stream application executed over our LVT execution support. The measures are only given for an implementation on a x86 multi-core workstation. Another implementation targeting a non-public domain embedded

architecture has also been evaluated, but we cannot publish the results.

The x86 implementation has been evaluated using a workstation based on an Intel Xeon 2.53GHz with 8 hyper-threaded cores (dispatched as 1 CC, 7 PC), with a shared L3 cache of 12 MB. The micro-kernel was compiled using gcc 4.6 for x86 targets, with an optimization flag *-O3*.

The execution times were extracted by reading performance monitoring devices provided by the respective targets. On x86, the measures are based on the cycle-accurate time-stamp counter. The results we produce are average values, based on execution times collected during the execution of ten thousand replications of the dependency graph for each application.

The applications used were written or translated to the ΣC language (cf. section 4), from which we could generate runtime data and compile application binaries for the micro-kernel:

1. *FFT2* is a translation of the StreaMIT implementation of a Fast Fourrier Transform for benchmarking, this application was chosen to make a comparison to the static scheduling approach for RAW;

2. *BeamFormer* is a translation of the StreaMIT implementation of a beam former for benchmarking, it was chosen for the same reasons as FFT2;

3. *Laplacian* is an application that performs edge detection on a flow of input images by performing a convolution on lines and columns using Gaussian kernels, it was chosen because it is highly parallel and adapted to our targets;

4. *MotionDetection* is an application that performs target tracking on a flow of related input images (image differentiation, thresholding, connected component extraction and fusion as well as temporal target matching), it was chosen because task behavior is dynamic (due to the randomness in the effective number of targets) and thus exposes the advantages of our dynamic execution model.

Table 1 gives important information to describe the applications: count of tasks in application, size of clock vectors in coordinates and the average execution times for one activation of the tasks.

Table 1: Properties of the applications used for measurement (x86 target)

Application	Tasks	LVT	Average task activation	
			Cycles	Time (μs)
FFT2	15	16	767	0.307
BeamFormer	53	56	2019	0.808
Laplacian	16	16	6970	2.788
MotionDetect.	47	48	223777	89.510

7.1 System execution time

Table 2 gives measurement of the execution time of system operations (cf. subsection 6.3 for detailed description of the operations). The entry *Scheduling (CC)* gives the average execution time of the LVT update and task list management on the CC. The entry *Scheduling (PC)* gives the average execution time of the LVT update, task election and context switch on the PC. The entry *IPC (PC)* gives the average execution time of the buffer access descriptor updates on the PC.

Table 3 gives the overhead of the micro-kernel for each application, obtained from the division of the total time spent in the micro-kernel on the PC by the total time spent in user computation.

First of all, we can observe that though the applications have different granularities (from 15 to 53 tasks), the average time spent for system operations is almost the same. This is possible thanks to the optimizations we implemented for the comparison and incrementation of the clock vectors (cf. subsection 5.3). This demonstrates the scalability of our approach, and the good properties of vector time for dynamic scheduling.

Though the target architectures and scheduling approach are quite different, we compare our results to those of the static scheduling for StreaMIT on the RAW architecture. For StreaMIT benchmarks, the micro-kernel overhead is very high, and for these two specific examples the static scheduling is far better than our approach. This is due to the very short average execution time of the tasks in these applications. On the other hand, when executing applications with tasks performing complex and rather long operations, such as our Motion Detector, the micro-kernel inflicts a very low overhead, and the application can take full advantage of our dynamic scheduling. This demonstrates the importance of task granularity, which can be controlled by the compilation tools to merge several parallel tasks, in order to reach an appropriate minimum execution time (as in [11]).

7.2 Memory footprint

The measures of memory usage are given for the x86 binaries.

Figure 5 shows the memory usage for the runtime data generated for the tasks, which consist essentially of the vector clocks, the vector clock increments and the access descriptors. It also gives the memory used by the micro-kernel, whose size does not depend on the application, and the total memory overhead. The maximum memory overhead we measured is 64.4 KB (48,7 KB average), which represents an average memory overhead of about 2% of on-Chip shared memory on recent embedded multi-core designs (ranging from 2 to 4 MB). On the x86 platform used for evaluation, it represents 0.4% of the shared L3 cache of 12MB.

Table 2: Measurement of system operations (x86 target)

Application	System operations for a task activation		
	Operation	Cycles	Time (μs)
FFT2	Scheduling (CC)	704	0.281
	Scheduling (PC)	684	0.273
	IPC (PC)	167	0.067
BeamFormer	Scheduling (CC)	691	0.277
	Scheduling (PC)	811	0.324
	IPC (PC)	195	0.078
Laplacian	Scheduling (CC)	790	0.316
	Scheduling (PC)	781	0.294
	IPC (PC)	253	0.101
MotionDetect.	Scheduling (CC)	720	0.288
	Scheduling (PC)	803	0.321
	IPC (PC)	229	0.091

Table 3: Measurement of system overhead (x86 target)

Application	System overhead
FFT2	113.80%
BeamFormer	49.96%
Laplacian	14.17%
MotionDetect.	0.45%

Figure 6 shows the detailed memory usage for the x86 micro-kernel. The total memory usage is given, along with memory usage per module in the micro-kernel.

Compared to the library approach, the micro-kernel uses much less memory. When supporting stream programming with a library over on-the-shelf OS, one must pay memory for the library and the OS. An embedded Linux kernel alone, stripped of all unnecessary drivers, uses 197 KB. With our micro-kernel approach, we use 67.31% less, taking the runtime data into account.

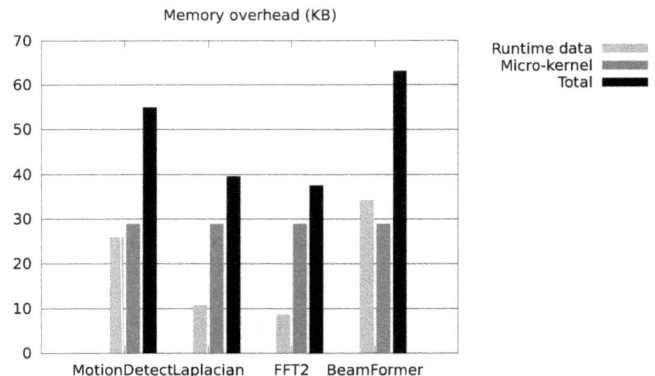

Figure 5: **Memory used by runtime data, and by micro-kernel in the x86 test binaries; the average memory overhead is 2% for recent embedded multi-core designs with 2MB of shared memory, which is at least 67.31% less than using a stream programming support library over a minimal Linux kernel.**

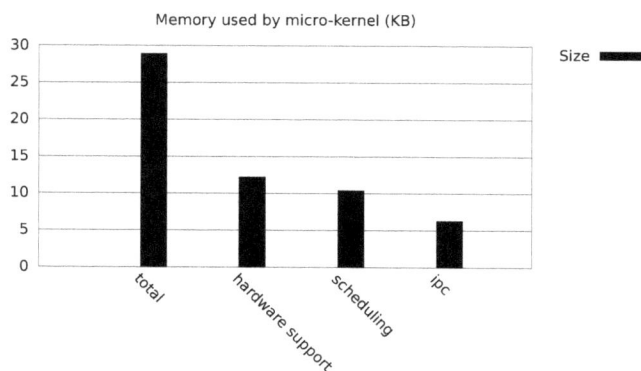

Memory used by micro-kernel (KB)

Figure 6: Detail of memory used by micro-kernel modules in the x86 test binaries; total size is 28.9 KB, which is 85.33% less than a minimal embedded Linux kernel.

8. CONCLUSION AND FUTURE WORKS

This paper showed that building a specialized micro-kernel gives an efficient execution support for the currently emerging generation of stream programming languages, with very low latencies on a first selection of mainstream applications. Our prototype will be improved with additional code optimizations and more subtle task list management (efficient scheduling policies would significantly improve performance and power saving).

With very fine grained applications, the control core may become a bottleneck (which is unlikely, as the latencies are very tight) and the micro-kernel overhead becomes too high. This is not a problem for most of the real applications targeting embedded multi-core (which have sufficiently high execution times per task), and it would anyway be quite easy for the compilation tools to avoid this situation (*e.g.* a fusion of several parallel tasks to reach an appropriate minimum execution time [11]).

Apart from code optimizations, our future work will be to extend the micro-kernel to non-shared memory systems, with efficient communication between physical or logical clusters. This raises several issues, as core and task migrations, which would be interesting to address.

9. REFERENCES

[1] A. Amar, P. Boulet, and P. Dumont. Projection of the Array-OL specification language onto the Kahn Process Network computation model. Technical Report RR-5515, LIFL, USTL, Mar 2005.

[2] S. Amarasinghe, M. I. Gordon, M. Karczmarek, J. Lin, D. Maze, R. M. Rabbah, and W. Thies. Language and compiler design for streaming applications. *International Journl of Parallel Programming*, 33(2/3), Jun 2005.

[3] I. Buck, T. Foley, D. Horn, J. Sugerman, K. Fatahalian, M. Houston, and P. Hanrahan. Brook for gpus: stream computing on graphics hardware. *ACM Trans. Graph.*, 23:777–786, August 2004.

[4] J. T. Buck and E. A. Lee. Scheduling dynamic dataflow graphs with bounded memory using the token flow model. Technical report, 1993.

[5] L. Cudennec and R. Sirdey. Parallelism reduction based on pattern substitution in dataflow oriented programming languages. In *Proceedings of the 12th International Conference on Computational Science*, ICCS'12, Omaha, Nebraska, USA, 2012. To Appear.

[6] B. A. Davey and H. A. Priestley. *Introduction to lattices and order.* Cambridge University Press, New York, NY, 2002.

[7] P. Dumont and P. Boulet. Another multidimensional synchronous dataflow: Simulating Array-OL in Ptolemy II. Technical Report RR-5516, LIFL, USTL, Mar 2005.

[8] C. J. Fidge. Partial orders for parallel debugging. In *Proceedings of the 1988 ACM SIGPLAN and SIGOPS Workshop on Parallel and Distributed Debugging*, pages 183–194, 1988.

[9] C. J. Fidge. Timestamps in message-passing systems that preserve the partial ordering. In *Proceedings of the 11th Australian Computer Science Conference*, pages 56–66, 1988.

[10] R. L. G. Bilsen, M. Engels and J. A. Peperstraete. Cyclo-static data flow. *IEEE Transactions on Signal Processing*, 44(2):397–408, 1996.

[11] M. I. Gordon, W. Thies, M. Karczmarek, J. Lin, A. S. Meli, A. A. Lamb, C. Leger, J. Wong, H. Hoffmann, D. Maze, and S. Amarasinghe. A stream compiler for communication-exposed architectures. *SIGOPS Oper. Syst. Rev.*, 36(5):291–303, Oct. 2002.

[12] T. Goubier, R. Sirdey, S. Louise, and V. David. ΣC: A programming model and language for embedded manycores. In Y. Xiang, A. Cuzzocrea, M. Hobbs, and W. Zhou, editors, *ICA3PP (1)*, volume 7016 of *Lecture Notes in Computer Science*, pages 385–394. Springer, 2011.

[13] M. Habib, M. Huchard, and L. Nourine. Embedding partially ordered sets into chain-products. In *Proceedings of the 1995 International Symposium on Knowledge Retrieval, Use, and Storage for Efficiency*, Santa Cruz, CA, 1995. University of California.

[14] M. Herlihy. Wait-free synchronization. *ACM Transactions on Programming Languages and Systems*, 13(2):124–149, 1991.

[15] G. Kahn. The semantics of a simple language for parallel programming. In J. L. Rosenfeld, editor, *Information processing*, pages 471–475, Stockholm, Sweden, Aug 1974. North Holland, Amsterdam.

[16] A. D. Kshemkalyani and M. Singhal. *Distributed Computing: Principles, Algorithms and Systems.* Cambridge University Press, Baltimore, MD, 2011.

[17] E. A. Lee. Finite state machines and modal models in Ptolemy II. Technical Report UCB/EECS-2009-151, EECS Department, University of California, Berkeley, Nov 2009.

[18] E. A. Lee and T. Parks. Dataflow process networks. In *Proceedings of the IEEE*, pages 773–799, 1995.

[19] F. Mattern. Virtual time and global states of distributed systems. In *Proceedings of the International Workshop on Parallel and Distributed Algorithms*, pages 215–226, 1988.

[20] P. Oliveira Castro, S. Louise, and D. Barthou. Reducing memory requirements of stream programs

by graph transformations. In *Proc. of the Int. Conf. of High Perf. Computing and Sim. (HPCS)*, pages 171–180, 2010.

[21] Ø. Ore. *Theory of graphs*, volume 38. American Mathematical Society Colloquium Publications, Providence, RI, 1962.

[22] D. Parker, G. J. Popek, G. Rudisin, A. Stoughton, B. J. Walker, E. Walton, J. M. Chow, D. Edwards, S. Kiser, and C. Kline. Detection of mutual inconsistency in distributed systems. *IEEE Trans. Software Ingineering*, 9:240–247, 1983.

[23] M. Singhal. A heuristically-aided algorithm for mutual exclusion in distributed systems. *IEEE Trans. on Computers*, 38(5), 1989.

[24] W. Thies, M. Karczmarek, and S. Amarasinghe. Streamit: A language for streaming applications. In R. Horspool, editor, *Compiler Construction*, volume 2304 of *Lecture Notes in Computer Science*, pages 49–84. Springer Berlin / Heidelberg, 2002. 10.1007/3-540-45937-5_14.

[25] W. T. Trotter. *Combinatorics and Partially Ordered Sets: Dimension Theory*. Johns Hopkins University Press, Baltimore, MD, 1992.

[26] P. A. S. Ward. An offline algorithm for dimension-bound analysis. In *Proceedings of the 1999 International Conference on Parallel Processing*. IEEE Computer Society, 1999.

[27] J. Yañez and J. Montero. A poset dimension algorithm. *Journal of Algorithms*, 30(1):185–208, 1999.

[28] M. Yannakakis. The complexity of the partial order dimension problem. *Journal on Algebraic and Discrete Methods*, 3(3):351–358, 1982.

[29] X. D. Zhang, Q. J. Li, R. Rabbah, and S. Amarasinghe. A lightweight streaming layer for multicore execution. In *Workshop on Design, Architecture and Simulation of Chip Multi-Processors*, Chicago, IL, Dec 2007.

Partitioned Scheduling for Real-Time Tasks on Multiprocessor Embedded Systems with Programmable Shared SRAMs *

Che-Wei Chang[1,2], Jian-Jia Chen[3], Waqaas Munawar[3], Tei-Wei Kuo[1,2] and Heiko Falk[4]

[1]Research Center for Information Technology Innovation, Academia Sinica, Taiwan
[2]Department of Computer Science and Information Engineering, National Taiwan University, Taiwan
[3]Department of Informatics, Karlsruhe Institute of Technology (KIT), Germany
[4]Institute of Embedded Systems/Real-Time Systems, Ulm University, Germany
f95093@csie.ntu.edu.tw, jian-jia.chen@kit.edu, munawar@kit.edu,
ktw@csie.ntu.edu.tw, Heiko.Falk@uni-ulm.de

ABSTRACT

This work is motivated by the advance of multiprocessor system architecture, in which the allocation of tasks over heterogeneous memory modules has a significant impact on the task execution. By considering two different types of memory modules with different access latencies, this paper explores joint considerations of memory allocation and real-time task scheduling to minimize the maximum utilization of processors of the system. For implicit-deadline sporadic tasks, a two-phase algorithm is developed, where the first phase determines memory allocation to derive a lower bound of the maximum utilization, and the second phase adopts worst-fit partitioning to assign tasks. It is shown that the proposed algorithm leads to a tight $(2 - \frac{2}{M+1})$-approximation bound where M is the number of processors. The proposed algorithm is then evaluated with 82 realistic benchmarks from MRTC, MediaBench, UTDSP, NetBench and DSPstone, and extensive simulations are further conducted to analyze the proposed algorithm.

Categories and Subject Descriptors

D.4.7 [**Operating Systems**]: Organization and Design—*Real-time systems and embedded systems*

Keywords

Shared SRAM, Multiprocessor partitioned scheduling, Real-time systems, Approximation algorithms

---

*This work was partially supported by the National Science Council of Taiwan, R.O.C., under grant 100-2221-E-002-120-MY3 and grant 101-2219-E-002-002, by the Excellent Research Projects of National Taiwan University under grant 10R80919-2, by Baden Württemberg MWK Juniorprofessoren-Programms and Karlsruhe House of Young Scientists (KHYS), and by Deutsche Forschungsgesellschaft (DFG) under grant FA 1017/1-1.

1. INTRODUCTION

In the past decade, we have witnessed the growing popularity of multiprocessor systems, due to their potential in resolving energy and thermal problems. It is of paramount importance that a multiprocessor system must be designed with effective hardware architecture to optimize its performance and utilization, such as the hierarchical memory designs for Intel i7 and AMD Phenom II. Moreover, real-time task scheduling should consider not only task scheduling over processors but also related resource allocation problems. Such an observation motivates the joint considerations of the task scheduling over processors and the memory allocation of task-execution images.

Real-time multiprocessor task scheduling could be roughly classified into three types: *partitioned*, *global*, and *semi-partitioned* scheduling algorithms. Partitioned scheduling statically assigns each task to a processor such that any arrival of a task instance only executes on its assigned processor. Global scheduling has a global queue to dynamically dispatch task instances in the queue to an available processor according to some criterion, such as their priorities. Semi-partitioned scheduling is a compromise between the above two. For example, we can divide a task into subtasks and assign these subtasks to processors statically under the guarantee that the subtasks of a task will not execute on two processors simultaneously. For more details of real-time multiprocessor task scheduling, we refer readers to a comprehensive survey by Davis and Burns [7].

This paper is interested in partitioned scheduling over multiple processors with heterogeneous memory modules. Unfortunately, real-time multiprocessor partitioned scheduling has been proven to be $\mathcal{NP}$-complete even for implicit-deadline sporadic tasks [17], in which the relative deadline of a task is equal to its minimum inter-arrival time. The closest related results are partitioned scheduling algorithms with a $\left(\frac{4}{3} - \frac{1}{3M}\right)$-approximation bound and a $\left(2 - \frac{1}{M}\right)$-approximation bound with the largest-utilization-first (LUF) task order and any arbitrary task order, respectively [9], where M is the number of processors.

In this paper, we are interested in real-time task scheduling over multiple processors with different access latencies for different memory modules, for which the worst-case execution time (WCET) of a task depends on its memory allocation. Examples are the platforms with the hierarchical memory architecture [10] or the shared scratchpad memory designs [11, 19] on embedded systems, where scratchpad memories are usually shared among all processors physically or virtually by direct-memory-access mechanisms [24], such as Intel 48-core SCC [21]. Scratchpad memories are small SRAMs (with relatively short access latencies compared to DRAMs) that are mapped onto the address space of processors at predefined and programmable address ranges so that software can explicitly access scratchpad memories with the supports of compilers or operating systems. Therefore, scratchpad memories have become popular for real-time embedded systems because of their predictable access latencies and lower power consumption [4] compared to caches.

Because of the considerations in the non-uniform memory access, the state-of-the-art results in partitioned scheduling could not be directly applied to the target problem of this paper. An algorithm is proposed in [23] for exploring energy-efficient task scheduling over heterogeneous processors, and the work in [18] further considers different memory footprints for tasks on different processors, where only one shared memory pool is considered. Another work studies the task memory allocation with heterogeneous multiple memory modules for real-time environments [20], but only single processor is considered. When each processor has its local memory, the work in [5] considers both computation, i.e., execution time, and local memory requirements for task partitioning. However, none of these approaches has considered the impact of allocating programmable shared local memory on the worst-case execution time.

In this paper, we consider the task scheduling over homogeneous processors with a shared fast memory pool (such as the shared scratchpad memories) and a global slow memory pool (such as the DRAMs). Given a set of implicit-deadline sporadic tasks, the WCETs of different memory allocation strategies are derived with the state-of-the-art static WCET analyzer aiT [1] for each task. The problem is to decide the memory block allocation (in the fast or slow memory pool) and the task assignment (to the processors) so that the maximum utilization of the processors is minimized. If the maximum utilization of the derived solution is no more than 100%, the system is guaranteed to meet the timing constraints. This paper develops an algorithm to solve this problem by two phases: (1) In the first phase, we decide memory allocation to derive a lower bound of the maximum utilization, regardless of task assignment; (2) in the second phase, we use worst-fit partitioning under the LUF order and any arbitrary ordering of tasks policy to assign tasks based on the derived memory allocation. It is shown that our algorithm with the LUF ordering has a tight $(2 - \frac{2}{M+1})$-approximation bound, and our algorithm with any arbitrary ordering has a tight $(2 - \frac{1}{M})$-approximation bound. Moreover, we also consider the mechanism of resource augmentation [12] to quantify the failure when our algorithm does not return a solution to meet the timing constraints. A case study with 82 realistic benchmarks from MRTC [2], MediaBench [14], UTDSP [3], NetBench [16] and DSPstone [25] is provided to evaluate the algorithm. A set of extensive simulations is also conducted to analyze the performance and limitation of the proposed algorithm.

The rest of this paper is organized as follows: Section 2 specifies the task and platform models and provides the problem definition. Section 4 presents two memory allocation algorithms with analysis, and the corresponding task partitioning algorithms are provided with approximation bounds in Section 5. Section 7 evaluates the proposed algorithm, and Section 8 concludes this work.

2. SYSTEM ARCHITECTURE AND PROBLEM DEFINITION

This section defines the memory and task models used in this paper. The problem definition is then provided, where its computational complexity is also briefly discussed.

2.1 Platform and Task Models

In this work, we consider the system architecture with a shared slow-and-large memory pool, such as DRAMs, and a shared fast memory pool, such as scratchpad memories. Examples are the Infineon TriCore TC1797 platform which consists of a 40 Kilo-Bytes scratchpad memory module and the Intel SCC platform which has multiple scratchpad memory modules (that are called message passing buffer) with a total size of 384 Kilo-Bytes. For more details of the shared scratchpad memory designs, we refer readers to the studies in [11].

This paper considers a platform, consisting of M identical processors $\mathbf{C} = \{c_1, c_2, \ldots, c_M\}$, a shared fast memory pool with B_f blocks, and a large slow memory pool, where a block is the basic unit to allocate memory for the software execution. In this paper, we explore how to assign a set $\mathbf{T} = \{\tau_1, \tau_2, \ldots, \tau_N\}$ of N independent implicit-deadline sporadic tasks to meet the timing constraints (arrival times and deadlines) with the considerations of memory access latencies. Each implicit-deadline sporadic task τ_i is characterized by its relative deadline D_i, where the minimum inter-arrival time (period) is assumed to be equal to D_i.

The execution of a task can be sped up if some proper blocks are mapped to the fast memory pool. When the blocks in the fast memory pool are allocated to host a task, such a configuration is fixed so that we can compute the WCET of a task. For task τ_i, the set of accessed memory blocks is denoted by $\mathbf{P}_i$, and $|\mathbf{P}_i|$ is the cardinality of the set $\mathbf{P}_i$. The static analysis is performed to obtain a *WCET mapping table*, which can provide the WCET W_i^ℓ of $\tau_i \in \mathbf{T}$ when the available blocks $\ell = 0, 1, 2, \ldots, |\mathbf{P}_i|$ of the fast memory pool of τ_i is given. For the simplicity of notations, we implicitly denote W_i^ℓ as $W_i^{|\mathbf{P}_i|}$ if $\ell > |\mathbf{P}_i|$.

2.2 Problem Definition

For such a platform, to meet the timing constraints, there are two major challenges: (1) allocating memory blocks for the task execution and (2) partitioning tasks onto the available processors. This paper considers partitioned scheduling, in which a task is statically assigned on a processor. Therefore, to decide whether the tasks assigned on a processor can meet their timing constraints, it has been shown that the necessary and sufficient condition is to test whether the total *utilization* of these tasks is no more than 100% by applying the earliest-deadline-first (EDF) strategy [15], where the utilization of a task is defined as its WCET divided by its period (minimum inter-arrival time). Therefore, if the number of available blocks ℓ in the fast memory pool of task τ_i is decided, the utilization u_i of task τ_i is $U_i^\ell = \frac{W_i^\ell}{D_i}$. For notational brevity, we define $U_i^\ell = \infty$ if $\ell < 0$. We do not discuss this scheduling in details, as the standard EDF policy is applied to give the task instance with the earliest absolute deadline the highest priority [15].

This paper studies how to assign the blocks of tasks onto the slow/fast memory pools and partition tasks onto processors such that the maximum utilization among the processors is minimized. Therefore, if the maximum utilization is no more than 100%, the solution can meet the real-time constraints. We define the problem as follows:

DEFINITION 1. **The Minimization of the Maximum Utilization (MMU) Problem**:
Consider a set $\mathbf{T}$ of implicit-deadline sporadic tasks running on a platform with M homogeneous processors, a fast memory pool with B_f blocks, and a large slow memory pool. Each task τ_i in $\mathbf{T}$ is with an implicit deadline D_i and has a WCET mapping table for mapping $0 \leq \ell \leq |\mathbf{P}_i|$ blocks to the fast memory pool to derive the WCETs W_i^ℓ. The problem is to allocate memory blocks

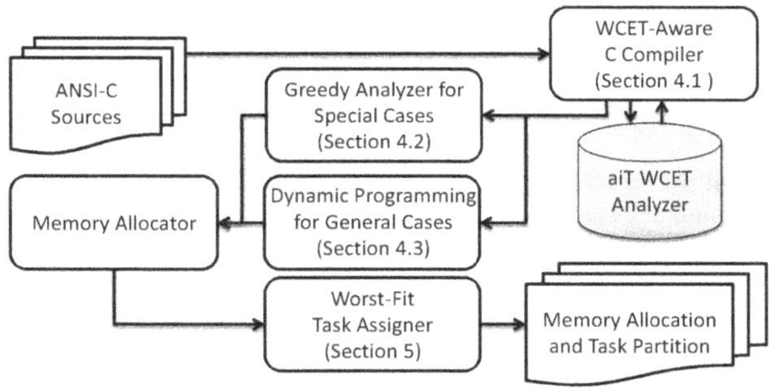

Figure 1: The overview of the proposed algorithm

in the fast and slow memory pools for the task execution and to partition the task set onto the processors such that the maximum utilization of the processors is minimized, the required amount of blocks of each memory pool does not exceed the size, and all tasks meet their deadlines. □

For the rest of this paper, we assume that the total space of the two memory pools can accommodate all the software blocks; otherwise, no feasible solution exists for memory allocation. The following theorem shows the complexity of this problem.

THEOREM 1. *The MMU problem is $\mathcal{NP}$-hard in the strong sense.*

PROOF. The special case with a constant WCET for a task regardless of memory allocation is the traditional schedulability problem over multiprocessor systems, which is $\mathcal{NP}$-hard in the strong sense [17]. □

As the MMU problem is $\mathcal{NP}$-hard, we look for polynomial-time approximation algorithms in this paper, in which *an algorithm is said to be with an α-approximation bound if it guarantees to derive a solution that is at most α times of the optimal solution for a minimization problem.*

3. OVERVIEW OF OUR APPROACH

This section briefly gives an overview of our algorithm for the MMU problem. The algorithm includes two phases. In the first phase, presented in Section 4, the objective is to find the memory allocation to provide a lower bound of the MMU problem. That is, we would like to decide how to assign the B_f blocks of the fast memory to real-time tasks and keep the remaining blocks of the tasks in the slow memory such that the maximal value between the maximum required utilization of each single task and the average utilization of processors is minimized. This property can be achieved by using a greedy strategy for special cases, or by using a dynamic-programming strategy for general cases. The following lemma shows the rationale behind this property:

LEMMA 1. *For an instance of the MMU problem, if the memory allocation is already given, $\max\left\{\max_{\tau_i \in \mathbf{T}}\{u_i\}, \frac{\sum_{\tau_i \in \mathbf{T}} u_i}{M}\right\}$ is a lower bound of the maximum utilization in any task partition, where u_i is the utilization of task τ_i under the given memory allocation, and M is the number of processors.*

PROOF. Since the total utilization of the tasks is $\sum_{\tau_i \in \mathbf{T}} u_i$, at least one processor has utilization no less than $\frac{\sum_{\tau_i \in \mathbf{T}} u_i}{M}$ by the pigeonhole principle. The utilization $\max_{\tau_i \in \mathbf{T}}\{u_i\}$ is also a lower bound of the maximum utilization in any task partition. Therefore, this lemma is proved. □

In the second phase, presented in Section 5, we use a worst-fit algorithm to partition tasks onto processors based on the memory allocation obtained in the first phase. The algorithm first sorts all tasks in a non-increasing order of their utilization under the computed fast memory allocation in the first phase. Then, tasks are sequentially assigned to the processor with the currently lowest utilization.

The flow of our algorithm is abstracted in Figure 1. To derive the WCETs for real-time tasks, Section 4.1 illustrates a mechanism to use a WCET-aware C compiler for producing the WCET mapping tables. To decide memory allocation, a greedy algorithm, presented in Section 4.2, and a dynamic-programming algorithm, presented in Section 4.3, are developed for the special case and general case of the MMU problem, respectively. Based on the derived memory allocation, a worst-fit algorithm produces feasible solutions with memory allocation and task scheduling, which is presented and proved to be with a 2-approximation bound for the MMU problem in Section 5.

4. MEMORY ALLOCATION STRATEGIES

This section presents our algorithms for the memory allocation to minimize $\max\left\{\max_{\tau_i \in \mathbf{T}}\{u_i\}, \frac{\sum_{\tau_i \in \mathbf{T}} u_i}{M}\right\}$, where u_i is the utilization of task τ_i under the memory allocation. For the rest of this paper, a memory allocation result is called an *optimal solution for memory allocation* if $\max\left\{\max_{\tau_i \in \mathbf{T}}\{u_i\}, \frac{\sum_{\tau_i \in \mathbf{T}} u_i}{M}\right\}$ is the minimum.

To derive the values of W_i^ℓ (which is the WCET of τ_i when ℓ proper blocks of τ_i are mapped to the fast memory pool) for all tasks, Section 4.1 shows a mechanism to construct the WCET mapping tables. With given WCET mapping tables, we start from the special case, in which $W_i^{\ell-1} - W_i^\ell$ is a non-negative and non-increasing function for $\ell = 1, 2, \ldots, |\mathbf{P}_i|$, in Section 4.2. We denote such a special case as *WCET Improvement Decreasing* (WID). Then, we will move to the general case in Section 4.3, in which the non-negative and non-increasing property does not hold.

4.1 WCET Mapping Tables

Our real-time scheduling and memory allocation algorithm takes the WCET mapping tables of tasks as the input. In order to derive the WCET mapping tables for a given task set under a hardware platform, we first have to set up the analysis mechanism to extract the WECTs of each task with different number of the available fast memory blocks. The state-of-the-art WCET analysis uses approximation to derive a safe upper-bound for the execution time of a program from the machine code. For example, the aiT [1] WCET analyzer uses static analysis and path analysis to provide a safe bound. For a basic block in a program, the aiT analyzer can decide the upper bound of execution time when this block is allocated to the fast memory pool or to the slow one. Therefore, as we can have different configurations in the fast memory allocation by selecting different blocks of a task into the fast memory pool, a *WCET-aware C compiler*, e.g., [8], can be adopted to produce the configuration of memory allocation with the minimum WCET for a given amount of available blocks in the fast memory pool. The basic idea of the WCET-aware C compiler is to inherently capture the current worst-case execution path of the task and its possible switches and to get the minimum WCET by an *integer linear programming* approach with the constraint of limited size of the fast memory pool. Therefore, to build the WCET mapping table for each task τ_i, we iteratively use the WCET-aware C compiler to derive the minimum WCETs with the numbers of available fast memory blocks from 0 to $\min\{|\mathbf{P}_i|, B_f\}$.

Algorithm 1: Partial WCET Profiling

Input: a task τ_i with $\mathbf{P}_i$ blocks, a target platform with B_f blocks of the fast memory pool and an approximation bound $1 \leq \beta$;

Output: a partial WCET mapping table with the approximation bound;

1   $b_{low} \leftarrow 0; b_{high} \leftarrow \min\{|\mathbf{P}_i|, B_f\}; b_{mid} \leftarrow \lfloor \frac{b_{low}+b_{high}}{2} \rfloor$;

2   conduct the WCET analysis to derive $W_i^{b_{low}}$ and $W_i^{b_{high}}$;

3   **if** $b_{high} - b_{low} = 1$ **then**

4 | break;

5   **else if** $\frac{W_i^{b_{low}}}{W_i^{b_{high}}} \leq \beta$ **then**

6 | $W_i^j \leftarrow W_i^{b_{low}}, \forall b_{low} < j < b_{high}$;

7 | break;

8   **else**

9 | conduct the WCET analysis to derive $W_i^{b_{mid}}$;

10 | go to Step 3 for recursively checking (b_{low}, b_{mid}) and (b_{mid}, b_{high});

Moreover, as the WCET table construction is with high complexity, to trade the optimality with the analyzing time of a WCET mapping table, we can use Algorithm 1 for a partial WCET mapping table with a given approximation bound $\beta \geq 1$ of the WCET tables. The basic idea of the algorithm is to derive the WCETs for selected numbers of available fast memory blocks instead of all the possible numbers. In Algorithm 1, for each task τ_i, if the mapping table has no other WCET analysis item from items $W_i^{b_{high}}$ to $W_i^{b_{low}}$, and $b_{high} - b_{low} > 1$ (the gap between the two fast memory sizes is more than one block), Step 5 would make sure that $\frac{W_i^{b_{low}}}{W_i^{b_{high}}}$ is no more than the bound β. If the condition is violated, some more WCET analysis items should be produced by the WCET-aware C compiler, and the checking should be recursively conducted, as shown in Steps 9 and 10. Therefore, as W_i^ℓ is a non-increasing function of ℓ, Algorithm 1 at most overestimates the WCETs by β times. Notice that if $W_i^{\ell_1} < W_i^{\ell_2}$ for some $\ell_1 < \ell_2$, $W_i^{\ell_2}$ can be set as $W_i^{\ell_1}$ by using only ℓ_1 blocks in the ℓ_2 available fast memory blocks. As a result, by using the approximated WCET values from partial WCET mapping tables, the lower bound (presented in Lemma 1) of an MMU problem instance at most increased by a factor β.

For the simplicity of presentation, we assume the WCET tables are given for the remaining algorithms in this paper. The analysis and optimization are both based on the given WCET tables, and the utilization $U_i^\ell = \frac{W_i^\ell}{D_i}$ is as the presented definition in Section 2.1.

4.2 Memory Allocation: Special Case - WID

This subsection develops an algorithm to solve the memory allocation issue of a special case of the MMU problem with the WID property. The optimal solution for memory allocation has a certain task τ_i^* with the maximum utilization among all the tasks by assigning its ℓ^* blocks in the fast memory pool. Based on this observation, the Lower Bound Minimization (LBM) algorithm is to find the memory allocation by searching the tuples of ℓ blocks and task τ_i such that task τ_i has exactly ℓ blocks in the fast memory pool, and τ_i is the task with the maximum utilization among all the tasks in $\mathbf{T}$.

Given τ_i and ℓ with $\ell \leq |\mathbf{P}_i|$, we know that its utilization is U_i^ℓ.

Algorithm 2: LBM

Input: an MMU problem instance with a task set $\mathbf{T}$, M processors, and two memory pools;

1   $LB \leftarrow \infty$;

2   **forall the** $\tau_i \in \mathbf{T}$ **do**

3 | **for** $\ell = 0$ to $\min\{B_f, |\mathbf{P}_i|\}$ **do**

4 | find ℓ_j with $U_j^{\ell_j-1} > U_i^\ell \geq U_j^{\ell_j}, \forall \tau_j \in \mathbf{T} \setminus \{\tau_i\}$;

5 | $B_{rm} \leftarrow B_f - (\ell + \sum_{\tau_j \in \mathbf{T} \setminus \{\tau_i\}} \ell_j)$;

6 | **if** $B_{rm} < 0$ **then**

7 | break;

8 | $\ell_i \leftarrow \ell; k_j \leftarrow 0, \forall \tau_j \in \mathbf{T}$;

9 | **while** $B_{rm} > 0$ **do**

10 | select $\tau_j \in \mathbf{T} \setminus \{\tau_i\}$ with maximum $U_j^{\ell_j+k_j} - U_j^{\ell_j+k_j+1}$;

11 | $k_j \leftarrow k_j + 1$ and $B_{rm} \leftarrow B_{rm} - 1$;

12 | $sol \leftarrow \max \left\{ U_i^\ell, \frac{\sum_{\tau_j \in \mathbf{T}} U_j^{\ell_j+k_j}}{M} \right\}$;

13 | **if** $LB > sol$ **then**

14 | $LB \leftarrow sol$;

15 | update the memory allocation by allocating the $\ell_j + k_j$ blocks of $\tau_j \in \mathbf{T}$ to the fast memory pool;

16   **return** the solution for memory allocation;

As τ_i is the task with the highest utilization by assigning exactly ℓ blocks to the fast memory pool, for task τ_j with $j \neq i$, we have to select at least ℓ_j blocks to the fast memory pool such that

$$U_j^{\ell_j-1} > U_i^\ell \geq U_j^{\ell_j}.$$

Clearly, if $\ell + \sum_{j \neq i} \ell_j > B_f$, it is not possible to satisfy the argument that τ_i has exactly ℓ blocks in the fast memory pool, and τ_i is the task with the maximum utilization. Otherwise, we proceed to reduce the average utilization, i.e., $\frac{\sum_{\tau_j \in \mathbf{T}} u_j}{M}$, by allocating more fast memory blocks for tasks in $\mathbf{T} \setminus \{\tau_i\}$. Let the amount of the remaining blocks in the fast memory pool $B_f - (\ell + \sum_{j \neq i} \ell_j)$ be B_{rm}. For the tasks in $\mathbf{T} \setminus \{\tau_i\}$, we iteratively increase the number k_j, with the initialization of k_j as 0, by selecting the task τ_j with the maximum utilization reducing $U_j^{\ell_j+k_j} - U_j^{\ell_j+k_j+1}$ for allocating one more block in the fast memory, until all the fast memory blocks are allocated.

Algorithm 2 presents the pseudo-code of the LBM algorithm. Let $P_{all} = \sum_{\tau_i \in \mathbf{T}} |\mathbf{P}_i|$ denote the number of all the blocks. A naïve implementation has time complexity $O(N \cdot B_f(P_{all} \cdot \log P_{all} + N + B_f))$, by using a sorting algorithm to perform the selection of B_{rm} blocks in the **while** loop in Step 9 for each iteration from Steps 4 to 15.

To reduce the time complexity, we can perform a global sorting with respect to $U_j^{\ell_j-1} - U_j^{\ell_j}$ for $1 \leq \ell_j \leq |\mathbf{P}_j|, \forall \tau_j \in \mathbf{T}$. For each task τ_i under considerations in the **forall** loop, we can duplicate the sorted list and remove the information associated with task τ_i. In the loop from Step 4 to Step 15, it is not difficult to see that an iteration for a given ℓ takes *amortized* $O(N)$ time complexity by implementing Step 4 and the **while** loop in Step 9 in an incremental manner. That is, for a given ℓ, the values ℓ_j and k_j are recorded so that they can be used in the next iteration when ℓ is set to $\ell + 1$. Therefore, the overall time complexity with such an implementation is $O\left(N^2 B_f + P_{all} N + P_{all} \log P_{all}\right)$. The following theorem shows the optimality of the derived solution from the LBM algorithm.

THEOREM 2. *The* LBM *algorithm derives the optimal solution for memory allocation for the special case with WCET Improvement Decreasing.*

PROOF. For a given tuple ℓ and τ_i, under the assumption that task τ_i has exactly ℓ blocks in the fast memory pool and is of the maximum utilization among all the tasks in $\mathbf{T}$, we will prove that the iteration of the loop in Algorithm 2: either (1) shows that the predicate is incorrect or (2) derives the memory allocation to minimize the lower bound under the assumption.

The LBM algorithm first reduces the utilization of all the other tasks by finding the minimum number of the required fast memory blocks until τ_i has the highest utilization among all the tasks. Therefore, if the LBM algorithm fails the test in Step 6, the assumption of this iteration must be incorrect.

Otherwise, the remaining blocks of the fast memory pool, i.e., B_{rm} blocks, are used to accommodate some more blocks in tasks in $\mathbf{T} \setminus \{\tau_i\}$ to reduce the average utilization, i.e., $\frac{\sum_{\tau_j \in \mathbf{T}} u_j}{M}$. Suppose that we are given a solution which assigns ℓ'_j blocks to the fast memory pool and $U_j^{\ell'_j} \leq U_i^{\ell}$ for all $\tau_j \in \mathbf{T} \setminus \{\tau_i\}$, i.e., $\sum_{\tau_j \in \mathbf{T}} \ell'_j \leq B_f$ and $\ell_j \leq \ell'_j$. If there exists τ_j with $\ell'_j > \ell_j + k_j$ for some τ_j, there must be a task τ_q with $\ell_q \leq \ell'_q < \ell_q + k_q$. We know that $U_j^{\ell'_j-1} - U_j^{\ell'_j} \leq U_j^{\ell_j+k_j} - U_j^{\ell_j+k_j+1} \leq U_q^{\ell_q+k_q-1} - U_q^{\ell_q+k_q} \leq U_j^{\ell'_q} - U_j^{\ell'_q+1}$, where the first and the last inequalities come from the assumption of the special case for WID since $\ell'_j - 1 \geq \ell_j + k_j$ and $\ell'_q + 1 \leq \ell_q + k_q$, and the second inequality is because τ_j (resp. τ_q) is only selected with $\ell_j + k_j$ (resp. $\ell_q + k_q$) blocks in the loop in Algorithm LBM for given τ_i and ℓ. Therefore, for the above case, increasing ℓ'_q by 1 and decreasing ℓ'_j by 1 can result in the average utilization reducing. As a result, by applying the above procedure repeatedly, we can conclude that $\sum_{\tau_j \in \mathbf{T} \setminus \{\tau_i\}} U_j^{\ell_j+k_j} \leq \sum_{\tau_j \in \mathbf{T} \setminus \{\tau_i\}} U_j^{\ell'_j}$.

As the LBM algorithm iterates all possible combinations of ℓ and τ_i, it is clear that the minimum solution among all these combinations is the optimal solution for memory allocation. □

4.3 Memory Allocation: General Cases

This subsection presents a strategy for the general cases without any specific property for the WCET reductions. The LBM algorithm requires some modifications to properly derive the optimal solution for memory allocation. The only change we need is to find the optimal solutions k_j for τ_j in $\mathbf{T} \setminus \{\tau_i\}$ to minimize $\sum_{\tau_j \in \mathbf{T} \setminus \{\tau_i\}} U_j^{\ell_j+k_j}$ under the constraint $\sum_{\tau_j \in \mathbf{T} \setminus \{\tau_i\}} k_j \leq B_{rm}$ and $k_j \geq 0$.

The following dynamic programming approach is proposed to replace the **while** loop in Step 9 of the LBM algorithm for the above optimization. For each iteration of a tuple of ℓ and τ_i, after Step 8, ℓ_j fast memory blocks are allocated to τ_j for all $\tau_j \in \mathbf{T}$.

Suppose that $\mathbf{T}'$ is a subset of the input task set $\mathbf{T}$. Let $u(\mathbf{T}', y)$ be the minimum total utilization of the set of tasks in $\mathbf{T}'$ when $\sum_{\tau_j \in \mathbf{T}'} k_j \leq y$. Therefore, iteratively, we can build the dynamic programming table by using the following recursive function:

$$u(\{\tau_j\}, y) = \min_{0 \leq x \leq y} \{U_j^{\ell_j+x}\}, \tag{1}$$

$$u(\mathbf{T}' \cup \{\tau_j\}, y) = \min_{0 \leq x \leq y} \{u(\mathbf{T}', y-x) + U_j^{\ell_j+x}\}. \tag{2}$$

The Dynamic Programming Approach (DPA) algorithm adopts the dynamic programming technique as shown in Algorithm 3 to

---

Algorithm 3: DPA

Input: an MMU problem instance with a task set $\mathbf{T}$, a task τ_i, an allocation of the fast memory pool $\ell_1, \ell_2, ..., \ell_N$, and the remaining B_{rm} blocks of the fast memory;

1 $\mathbf{T}' \leftarrow \emptyset, \mathbf{T}^{\dagger} \leftarrow \mathbf{T} \setminus \{\tau_i\}$;
2 **while** $\mathbf{T}^{\dagger} \neq \emptyset$ **do**
3   select and remove an arbitrary task τ_j from $\mathbf{T}^{\dagger}$;
4   **for each** y *from 0 to B_{rm} step by 1* **do**
5   build a table entry $u(\mathbf{T}' \cup \{\tau_j\}, y)$ by using Equation (1) when $\mathbf{T}'$ is $\emptyset$ or Equation (2) otherwise;
6   add task τ_j to $\mathbf{T}'$;
7 return $u(\mathbf{T}', B_{rm})$;

---

build a two-column table $u(\mathbf{T}', y)$. To build an entry in the table, it takes $O(B_{rm})$ time complexity. The number of entries in the table is $O(NB_{rm})$. Therefore, the total time complexity is $O(N(B_{rm})^2)$ for this dynamic programming. As a result, the time complexity by revising the LBM algorithm with the above dynamic programming is $O(N^2 B_f^3)$. To get the value of k_j for task τ_j to achieve the utilization returned from the DPA algorithm, we can use the standard backtracking approach in the dynamic programming.

LEMMA 2. *The recursive relation in Equations (2) and (1) is of optimal substructure.*

PROOF. We prove this property by using the mathematical induction. It is clear that $u(\{\tau_j\}, y)$ is $\min_{0 \leq x \leq y}\{U_j^{\ell_j+x}\}$ for any $0 \leq y \leq B_{rm}$, according to the definition of function $u()$. Suppose that $u(\mathbf{T}', y)$ stores the minimum value $\sum_{\tau_q \in \mathbf{T}'} U_q^{\ell_q+k_q}$ under the constraint $\sum_{\tau_q \in \mathbf{T}'} k_q \leq B_{rm}$ and $k_q \geq 0$, for a given subset $\mathbf{T}'$. For a given task $\tau_j \notin \mathbf{T}'$, we prove that Equation (2) leads to minimum value of $u(\mathbf{T}' \cup \{\tau_j\}, y)$ for any $0 \leq y \leq B_{rm}$.

Suppose for contradiction that there exists a better solution to set k_q for τ_q in $\mathbf{T}' \cup \{\tau_j\}$ with $\sum_{\tau_q \in \mathbf{T}' \cup \{\tau_j\}} k_q \leq y$, in which $u' = \sum_{\tau_q \in \mathbf{T}' \cup \{\tau_j\}} U_q^{\ell_q+k_q} < u(\mathbf{T}' \cup \{\tau_j\}, y)$. In such a solution, the tasks in $\mathbf{T}'$ allocate at most $y - k_j$ pages to the fast memory pool with total utilization $u' - U_j^{\ell_j+k_j}$, which is less than $u(\mathbf{T}', y-k_j)$. As a result, we reach the contradiction as $u(\mathbf{T}', y - k_j)$ stores the minimum utilization by allocating $y - k_j$ additional blocks for tasks in $\mathbf{T}'$ to the fast memory pool. □

THEOREM 3. *The* LBM *algorithm by using the* DPA *algorithm for deriving the values of k_j for $\tau_j \in \mathbf{T}$ derives the optimal solution for the memory allocation.*

PROOF. This comes directly from the *optimal substructure* property of Equation (2) and Equation (1), proved in Lemma 2. □

Note that for the rest of the paper, we assume that the LBM algorithm will check whether the WID property holds to decide whether the **while** loop in Step 9 in Algorithm 2 adopts the DPA algorithm.

5. TASK PARTITION

This section presents a worst-fit approach to partition the tasks onto the given processors. The Worst-Fit-Partition (WFP) algorithm first sorts all the tasks in a non-increasing order of their utilization based on the result derived from the LBM algorithm. Tasks are then sequentially assigned to the processor with the currently lowest utilization. Algorithm 4 illustrates the pseudo-code of the WFP algorithm. For the sorting in Step 2, it takes time complexity

$O(N \log N)$, by assuming $U_i^{\ell_i}$ is also calculated in Step 1. For the loop from Steps 4 to 6, a heap can be used to get the processor with the minimum utilization. As a result, excluding Step 1, the time complexity of the WFP algorithm is $O(N(\log N + \log M))$. The following theorems prove the approximation bound of the WFP algorithm and the tightness of the analysis.

THEOREM 4. *The* WFP *algorithm is a* $(2-\frac{2}{M+1})$-*approximation algorithm for the MMU problem.*

PROOF. Suppose that OPT is the maximum utilization among the processors in the optimal solution for the MMU problem, where LB is the optimal solution for memory allocation derived in the LBM algorithm. By Theorems 2 and 3 and Lemma 1,

$$LB \leq OPT. \qquad (3)$$

Let ℓ_i be the number of blocks for task $\tau_i \in \mathbf{T}$ in the fast memory pool by applying the LBM algorithm. Let c_{j*} be the processor with the maximum utilization after the WFP algorithm is invoked, where τ_k is the last task assigned to processor c_{j*}. According to the worst-fit and largest-task-utilization-first strategies of the WFP algorithm, if $k \leq M$, LB is the maximum utilization among the processors in the solution. As the LBM algorithm provides the optimal solution for memory allocation (with the minimum lower bound for the MMU problem), the WFP algorithm always returns the optimal solution when $k \leq M$.

For the rest of this proof, we consider only the case $k \geq M+1$. With the definition of task set $\mathbf{T}_j$ for $j = 1, 2, \ldots, M$, *before assigning task* τ_k, we know that $\sum_{\tau_i \in \mathbf{T}_{j*}} U_i^{\ell_i} \leq \sum_{\tau_i \in \mathbf{T}_j} U_i^{\ell_i}$ for any $c_j \in \mathbf{C}$, which implies

$$M \sum_{\tau_i \in \mathbf{T}_{j*}} U_i^{\ell_i} \leq \sum_{j=1}^{M} \sum_{\tau_i \in \mathbf{T}_j} U_i^{\ell_i} = \sum_{i=1}^{k-1} U_i^{\ell_i}. \qquad (4)$$

As tasks are ordered non-increasingly according to the utilization and $k \geq M+1$, we know that

$$U_k^{\ell_k} \leq \frac{\sum_{i=1}^{M+1} U_i^{\ell_i}}{M+1} \leq \frac{\sum_{i=1}^{k} U_i^{\ell_i}}{M+1}. \qquad (5)$$

By (4) and (5), we have

$$
\begin{aligned}
U_k^{\ell_k} + \sum_{\tau_i \in \mathbf{T}_{j*}} U_i^{\ell_i} &\leq U_k^{\ell_k} + \frac{\sum_{i=1}^{k-1} U_i^{\ell_i}}{M} \\
&= (1 - \frac{1}{M}) U_k^{\ell_k} + \frac{\sum_{i=1}^{k} U_i^{\ell_i}}{M} \\
&\leq \left((1 - \frac{1}{M})\frac{M}{M+1} + 1 \right) \frac{\sum_{i=1}^{k} U_i^{\ell_i}}{M} \\
&\leq (2 - \frac{2}{M+1}) \frac{\sum_{\tau_i \in \mathbf{T}} U_i^{\ell_i}}{M} \\
&\leq (2 - \frac{2}{M+1}) \max \left\{ \max_{\tau_i \in \mathbf{T}}\{U_i^{\ell_i}\}, \frac{\sum_{\tau_i \in \mathbf{T}} U_i^{\ell_i}}{M} \right\} \\
&= (2 - \frac{2}{M+1})LB \leq (2 - \frac{2}{M+1})OPT, \qquad (6)
\end{aligned}
$$

where the last inequality comes from (3). Therefore, we reach the conclusion by proving that the maximum utilization, i.e., the utilization of processor c_{j*} is at most twice of the optimal solution OPT. $\square$

THEOREM 5. *The* $(2-\frac{2}{M+1})$-*approximation bound of the* WFP *algorithm is tight for the MMU problem.*

Algorithm 4: WFP

Input: an MMU problem instance with a task set $\mathbf{T}$, M processors, and the memory allocation result of the LBM algorithm;

1   let ℓ_i be the number of blocks for task $\tau_i \in \mathbf{T}$ in the fast memory pool by applying the LBM algorithm;

2   re-index $\mathbf{T}$ in a non-increasing order of $U_i^{\ell_i}$;

3   $\mathbf{T}_j \leftarrow \emptyset, \forall c_j \in \mathbf{C}$;

4   **for** $i = 1$ to N **do**

5      $c_{min} \leftarrow \arg_{c_j \in \mathbf{C}} \min\{\sum_{\tau_i \in \mathbf{T}_j} U_i^{\ell_i}\}$;

6      $\mathbf{T}_{min} \leftarrow \mathbf{T}_{min} \cup \{\tau_i\}$;

7   **return** the memory allocation and task partition $\mathbf{T}_1, \mathbf{T}_2, \ldots, \mathbf{T_N}$;

PROOF. We prove this theorem with a concrete problem instance. There are M processors, M fast memory blocks, and $M+1$ tasks in the problem instance. Task τ_1 has M blocks with utilization $(U_1^0, U_1^1, \ldots, U_1^{M-1}, U_1^M) = (\frac{M}{M+1} + \epsilon, \frac{M-1}{M+1} + \epsilon, \ldots, \frac{1}{M+1} + \epsilon, \epsilon)$, where ϵ is a positive real number close to 0. The next M tasks have utilization $1 - \epsilon$ when no block is in the fast memory pool, i.e., $U_i^0 = 1 - \epsilon, \forall 2 \leq i \leq M+1$. There is one block in each of the last M tasks, and moving the block to the fast memory pool can reduce the task utilization by $\frac{1}{M+1} + \epsilon$, i.e., $U_i^1 = \frac{M}{M+1} - 2\epsilon, \forall 2 \leq i \leq M+1$. For this problem instance, by allocating all the M blocks of the fast memory pool to task τ_1, assigning task τ_i on processor c_{i-1} for all $i = 2, 3, \cdots, M+1$ and task τ_1 on any of the M processors leads to a solution with 100% utilization. By adopting the LBM algorithm, to reduce the lower bound, we will select one block in each of the last M tasks to the fast memory pool. Therefore, the WFP algorithm will return a solution which allocates τ_1 and τ_{M+1} on one processor and each of the other tasks on one individual processor. The maximum utilization of the resulting solution will be $(\frac{M}{M+1} + \epsilon) + (\frac{M}{M+1} - 2\epsilon) = 2 - \frac{2}{M+1} - \epsilon$, which implies the tightness of the approximation bound. $\square$

If Step 2 of Algorithm 4 is removed, i.e., the task set is examined in an arbitrary order for the worst-fit partition, the complexity will be reduced to $O(N \log M)$, excluding Step 1. The following corollary presents the corresponding approximation bound.

COROLLARY 1. *For the MMU problem, Algorithm* WFP *has a tight* $(2 - \frac{1}{M})$-*approximation bound if there is no sorting in Step 2 in Algorithm 4.*

PROOF. Let OPT, LB, c_{j*}, ℓ_i, and τ_k be defined in the same manner as the proof of Theorem 4. Therefore,

$$
\begin{aligned}
U_k^{\ell_k} + \sum_{\tau_i \in \mathbf{T}_{j*}} U_i^{\ell_i} &\leq U_k^{\ell_k} + \frac{\sum_{i=1}^{k-1} U_i^{\ell_i}}{M} \\
&= (1 - \frac{1}{M}) U_k^{\ell_k} + \frac{\sum_{i=1}^{k} U_i^{\ell_i}}{M} \\
&\leq (2 - \frac{1}{M}) \max \left\{ U_k^{\ell_k}, \frac{\sum_{i=1}^{k} U_i^{\ell_i}}{M} \right\} \\
&\leq (2 - \frac{1}{M}) \max \left\{ \max_{\tau_i \in \mathbf{T}}\{U_i^{\ell_i}\}, \frac{\sum_{\tau_i \in \mathbf{T}} U_i^{\ell_i}}{M} \right\} \\
&= (2 - \frac{1}{M})LB \leq (2 - \frac{1}{M})OPT. \qquad (7)
\end{aligned}
$$

The tightness comes from a similar input instance in [22, Example 10.4]. The memory allocation for this input instance does not affect the execution time. Let the utilization of the first $M(M-1)$ tasks and the last task be $\frac{1}{M}$ and 1, respectively. The optimal solution assigns the last task to one processor and share the remaining $M-1$ processors to the first $M(M-1)$ tasks, which leads to a solution with 100% utilization. However, if the worst-fit partition is conducted with the original task order, the last task will be assigned to a processor with other $M-1$ tasks. As a result, the utilization of the processor is $\frac{M-1}{M}+1=2-\frac{1}{M}$. $\square$

6. RESOURCE AUGMENTATION

If the maximum utilization of the solution derived from the WFP algorithm is no more than 100%, it is clear that the solution meets the timing constraint, as the schedulability condition for EDF is to ensure no more than 100% utilization on a processor [15]. This section is presented to quantify the failure when the WFP algorithm returns a solution with the maximum utilization more than 100%.

We adopt the concept of resource augmentation bound [6, 12]. For an algorithm with a ρ resource augmentation bound, the algorithm guarantees that *the solution derived from the algorithm always meets the timing constraints by speeding up the system (including the processor speed and the memory access latency) to ρ times as fast as the original platform, if there exists a solution that meets the timing constraint for the original platform.*

For the issues related to the *schedulability* for real-time tasks, the objective is to decide the memory allocation and the task partitioning such that the timing constraints can be satisfied, in which the resource augmentation bound can be adopted. The following theorem shows the resource augmentation bound of the WFP algorithm.

THEOREM 6. *The WFP algorithm has a tight $\left(2-\frac{2}{M+1}\right)$ resource augmentation factor.*

PROOF. For a problem instance, due to the optimality of EDF, if there exists a feasible solution to meet the timing constraints, the solution must have the maximum utilization no more than 100%. Moreover, we know that the maximum utilization of the solution derived from the WFP algorithm is no more than $\left(2-\frac{2}{M+1}\right)$ times of the optimal solution, which leads to a utilization upper-bound $\left(2-\frac{2}{M+1}\right)$. By speeding up the processor speed and the memory access latency by a factor $\left(2-\frac{2}{M+1}\right)$, we know that the resulting solution has maximum utilization no more than 100%. The tightness comes directly from Theorem 5. $\square$

In other words, if the WFP algorithm does not derive a feasible solution to meet the timing constraints, the input instance cannot be feasibly scheduled by slowing down to $\frac{1}{2-\frac{2}{M+1}}$ of the original platform speeds (including the processors and the memory pools).

7. PERFORMANCE EVALUATION

This section presents the performance evaluation of our algorithm for minimizing the maximum utilization of processors. Section 7.1 first presents the evaluation results of 82 real-life benchmarks with Infineon TriCore TC1797 and the corresponding WCET-aware C compiler, and Section 7.2 then shows a case study for large-scale applications with the benchmarks from SPEC2000 [13].

7.1 A Case Study for General Case Memory Allocation

In this subsection, two experiment sets are conducted to evaluate the performance of the proposed algorithm with different sizes of the fast memory pool and different numbers of processors, respectively. Based on the reference architecture Infineon TriCore

TC1797, we build the WCET mapping tables by a WCET-aware C compiler for the TriCore architecture with optimization level *-O2*, where the size of a block is set as 128 Bytes. For this case study, we exhaustively derive all items of the WCET mapping tables of all benchmark programs. For the Infineon TriCore TC1797 platform, 1 Mega-Bytes half-word addressable Flash, as the slow memory module, and 40 Kilo-Bytes scratchpad memory, as the fast memory module, are included. The latency to access the fast memory (the scratchpad memory) is 1 cycle and the latency to access the slow memory (the flash memory) is 7 cycles. Notice that there is 1 Kilo-Byte of the scratchpad memory reserved for system routines so that only 39 Kilo-Bytes of the scratchpad memory are available for application execution.

Our algorithm is applied to a total of 82 different real-life benchmarks from MRTC [2], MediaBench [14], UTDSP [3], NetBench [16] and DSPstone [25] where NetBench is with encoders, and DSPstone is partitioned into fixed-point and floating-point parts, as shown in Figure 2. In this experiment set, the minimum inter-arrival time of each task is properly configured such that the total utilization of a benchmark set is equal to 300% when using no scratchpad memory, and the number of processors is configured as 3 where each processor can independently provide 100% utilization (the processors are assumed to be dedicated for the benchmarks). Since the total size of the program codes of each benchmark set is less than the size of the available scratchpad memory (39 Kilo-Bytes), we artificially limit the size of the available scratchpad memory. For each benchmark set, the size of the scratchpad memory is limited as 0%, 20%, 40%, 60% and 80% of the total size of the program codes of each benchmark set. Figure 2 presents the results for the different configurations. For each benchmark set, the results are normalized to the maximum utilization of the setting with no scratchpad memory (0%).

From the experimental results in Figure 2, we can see that the maximum utilization of all the processors can be significantly reduced by using the scratchpad memory with the size only 20% of the total size of the program codes. That is because our LBM algorithm always selects the most important blocks into the fast memory pool to provide the minimum lower bound of the maximum utilization amount all processors with a given size of the fast memory pool. To enlarge the size of the scratchpad memory to more than 20% would not provide much improvement because in the real-life benchmarks, the frequently accessed part of a program usually takes a small footprint in the entire program. Therefore, we can say that the presented algorithm requires only a small pool of the fast memory to significantly improve the result of the MMU problem. For hardware environments with smaller fast memory pools, Figure 3 shows the results when the size of the scratchpad memory is limited as 1.25%, 2.5%, 5%, 10% and 20% of the total size of the program codes of each benchmark set. We can see that sometimes the maximum utilization is not significantly reduced when the fast memory size is slightly increased. It is because that the WCET of each task might be bound by multiple worst-case execution paths. To reduce the WCET, all worst-case execution paths have to be sped up.

In the second experiment set, we would like to discuss the influence of the number of processors to the presented algorithm. The sizes of the fast and slow memory pools are configured as 39 Kilo-Bytes and 1 Mega-Bytes, respectively. For the input task set, all the benchmarks are included, where the total number is 82 and the total size of the programs codes is 107.648 Kilo-Bytes. For each task, the minimum inter-arrival is set to repeat the task, such that the utilization of each task forms a uniform distribution from 1% to 20% when no scratchpad memory is used.

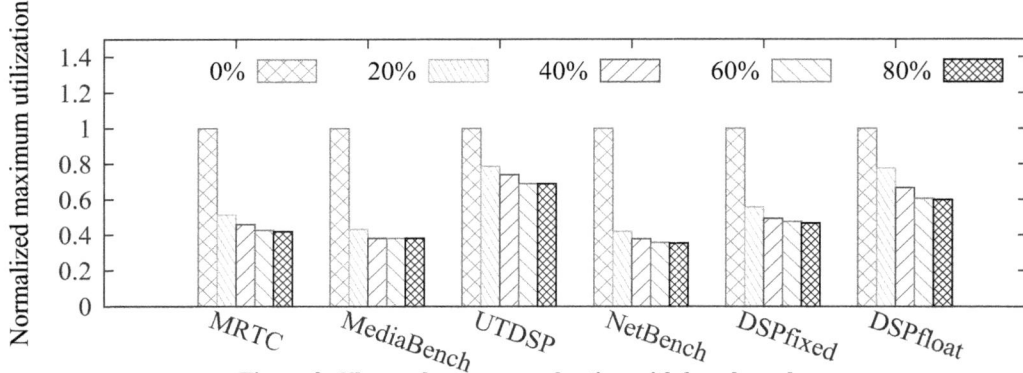

Figure 2: The performance evaluation with benchmarks.

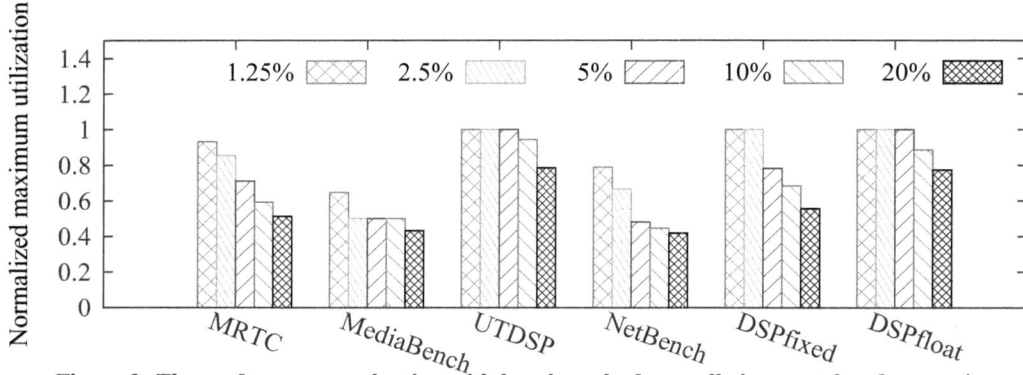

Figure 3: The performance evaluation with benchmarks for small-size scratchpad memories.

By varying the number of processors from 4 to 12 with 500 tests for each configuration, Figure 4 illustrates the average of the maximum utilization for the 500 tests. For the setting, we compare the following solutions:

- *WF-Arbitrary*: It only uses the worst-fit algorithm for the partitioned task scheduling. This gives a $(2 - \frac{1}{M})$ approximation bound [9] without considering the feature of the fast memory pool.

- *WF-LUF*: It uses the worst-fit algorithm with the LUF task ordering. This gives a $(\frac{4}{3} - \frac{1}{3M})$ approximation bound [9] without considering the feature of the fast memory pool.

- *LBM-Arbitrary*: It is the algorithm proposed in Sections 4 and 5 by using arbitrary task ordering.

- *LBM-LUF*: It is the algorithm proposed in Sections 4 and 5 by using the LUF task ordering.

It is clear that both LBM-Arbitrary and LBM-LUF reduce the maximum utilization significantly, compared to WF-Arbitrary and WF-LUF. When the number of processors is increasing, all of the solutions can provide lower maximum utilization, but we can see that the ratio of the maximum utilization in LBM-LUF (resp. LBM-Arbitrary) to that in WF-LUF (resp. WF-Arbitrary) is about 0.49 to 0.51. Moreover, for LBM-LUF and LBM-Arbitrary with 4 processors, among the 500 tests, there are 338 and 394 tests with maximum utilization more than 100%, respectively, whereas no test has timing violation for LBM-LUF and LBM-Arbitrary with more than 4 processors ($M \geq 5$). However, for WF-LUF and WF-Arbitrary even with 8 processors, there are still 333 and 463 tests with maximum utilization more than 100%, respectively.

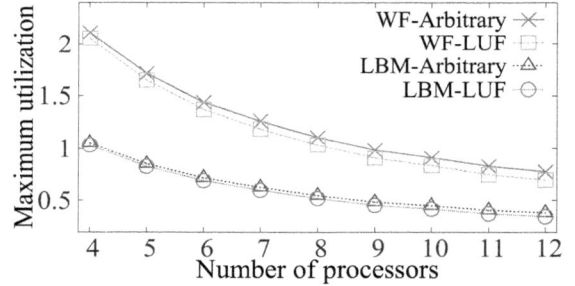

Figure 4: The evaluation with different numbers of processors.

7.2 A Case Study for Special Case Memory Allocation with the WID Property

In this subsection, three sets of experiments are conducted for the special case of the MMU problem with the WID property. The evaluations are then conducted with a model platform Intel 48-core SCC [21]. To the best of our knowledge, there is no WCET analyzer for such a platform. Therefore, instead of using static WCET analysis, we derive the upper bound of the execution times for benchmarks in the benchmark set SPEC2000 [13], by considering the traces. The timing analysis is also achievable by adopting minor changes in static WCET analyzers.

In this case study, based on the traces, the timing analysis is performed to obtain the following two types of parameters for each task τ_i: (1) the worst-case CPU execution time C_i by assuming that the memory (load/store) accesses require no latency, and (2) the worst-case number $A_{i,h}$ of the memory accesses to block $p_{i,h}$

160

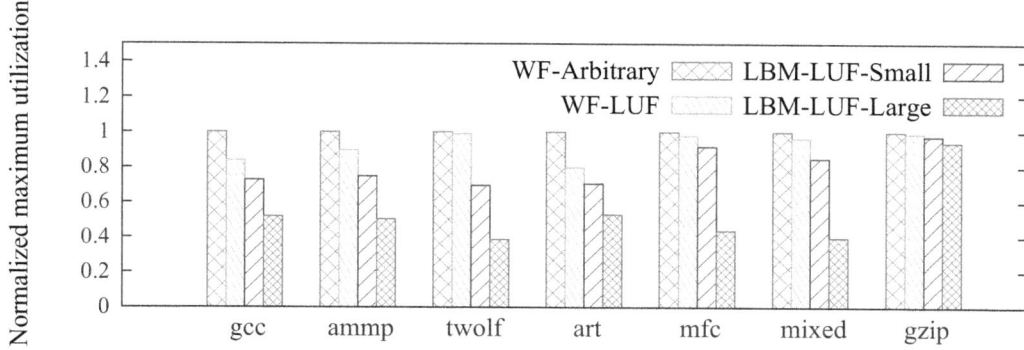

Figure 5: The performance evaluation with benchmarks.

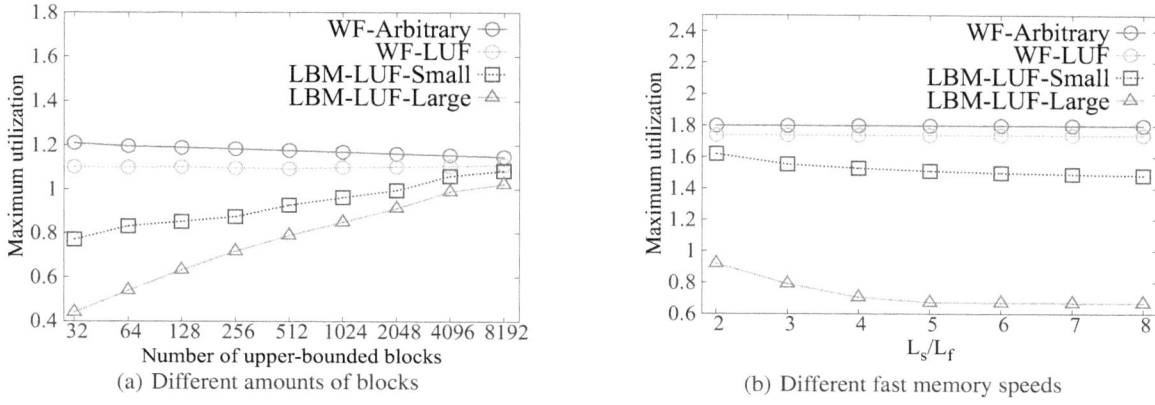

(a) Different amounts of blocks

(b) Different fast memory speeds

Figure 6: The simulations over different hardware configurations and workloads.

in $\mathbf{P}_i$, where $\mathbf{P}_i$ is defined as the set of the accessed blocks of τ_i. Without loss of generality, we order the blocks of each task τ_i such that $A_{i,h} \geq A_{i,g}$ when $h \leq g$. If a block $p_{i,h}$ is allocated in the fast memory pool, the worst-case latency to access this block is $L_f \cdot A_{i,h}$; otherwise, the worst-case latency is $L_s \cdot A_{i,h}$, where L_f and L_s are the access latency for one read/write operation to the fast and slow memory pool, respectively. Therefore, if a subset $\mathbf{P}_i'$ of the block set $\mathbf{P}_i$ of task τ_i is assigned to the fast memory pool, the utilization u_i of task τ_i is

$$\frac{C_i + \sum_{p_{i,h} \in \mathbf{P_i}'} A_{i,h} L_f + \sum_{p_{i,h} \in \mathbf{P_i} \setminus \mathbf{P_i}'} A_{i,h} L_s}{D_i}.$$

Based on the previous discussion, with the timing model for Intel 48-core SCC, the following evaluations target large-scale applications and many-core environments by considering 48 identical processors and four DRAMs with total size 16 Giga-Bytes as the slow memory pool. In the following simulations, the processors/cores are with 800 MHz, and the access latency to the slow memory pool (L_s) is bounded by 13.1 μ-seconds. The latency bound was measured from Intel SCC in our simulations. For the fast memory pool, to evaluate the impact of different sizes of the fast memory pool, we consider two different configurations: (1) 384 Kilo-Bytes (the total size of the shared message passing buffer of the Intel SCC testbed) and (2) 6144 Kilo-Bytes (16 times of 384 Kilo-Bytes). For the latency to access the fast memory pool, if not specified, we assume that it is 4 times faster than that to access the slow memory pool,

i.e., $\frac{L_s}{L_f} = 4$. A block here is configured as a page with the size of 4 Kilo-Bytes.

We consider four solutions as follows:

- *WF-Arbitrary*: It is the same as that in Section 7.1.

- *WF-LUF*: It is the same as that in Section 7.1.

- *LBM-LUF-Small*: It is the algorithm proposed in Section 4 and 5 with the LUF task ordering and a fast memory pool with 384 Kilo-Bytes.

- *LBM-LUF-Large*: It is the algorithm proposed in Section 4 and 5 with the LUF task ordering and a fast memory pool with 6144 Kilo-Bytes.

In the first set, we evaluate these four solutions based on the task sets generated from SPEC2000 benchmarks. To have variant execution times and accessed blocks of tasks, we conduct trace-based experiments here so that a task τ_i has known $C_i, A_{i,h}, \mathbf{P}_i$ based on its execution trace with a specific input. For each of the configurations with *gcc*, *ammp*, *twolf*, *art*, *mfc*, and *gzip*, we generate 100 independent sporadic tasks of a specified application. The benchmark *mixed* is constructed by including 20 tasks from each of *gcc*, *ammp*, *twolf*, *art*, and *mfc* benchmarks. For each task τ_i, the CPU utilization is set as a uniform distribution in [1%, 10%] so that the minimum inter-arrival time is C_i divided by the CPU utilization. Figure 5 reports the maximum utilization results of the solutions, normalized to the results of *WF-Arbitrary*. Except the *gzip* benchmark, our algorithm with joint considerations of memory allocation and task assignment produces significant improvement, compared to *WF-Arbitrary* and *WF-LUF*, since these tasks require several blocks with very frequent memory accesses. However, for *gzip*, the memory footprint is much larger than the others and our algorithm has no significant improvement because of the lack of blocks with extremely frequent memory accesses.

The effect of the *gzip* benchmark leads to the following simulations to identify the impact of memory footprints. The input task set is constructed with 100 synthetic tasks. The CPU utilization of a task is in uniform distribution between 1% and 20%. For each task τ_i, the memory footprint is in uniform distribution between 1 block to a given upper bound X, and the memory access utilization

$$\frac{\sum_{h \in \mathbf{P}_i} A_{i,h} L_s}{D_i}$$

by allocating only to the slow memory is uniformly distributed between 1% and 60%. Then, the access frequencies of blocks are distributed uniformly to the blocks. By varying X from 32 blocks to 8192 blocks with 500 tests for each configuration, the simulation results by averaging the 500 tests are presented in Figure 6(a). As shown in Figure 6(a), when the footprint is small, selecting correct blocks to the fast memory pool has significant impacts.

Moreover, Figure 6(b) illustrates the simulation results based on the benchmark *mixed* with different settings on the ratio of the slow memory access latency to the fast one, i.e., $\frac{L_s}{L_f}$. In general, the larger $\frac{L_s}{L_f}$ is, the better improvement our proposed algorithm can achieve. However, as shown in Figure 6(b), the improvement becomes saturated when $\frac{L_s}{L_f}$ is higher than 5 in this case, because the CPU execution time has dominated the task executions.

8. CONCLUSIONS AND FUTURE WORK

This paper studies the real-time scheduling problem with identical multiple processors and two different types of memory modules. For an implicit-deadline sporadic task set, a two-phase algorithm is developed to allocate blocks onto memory pools and to partition tasks onto processors. The quality of the proposed algorithm is discussed with the tight approximation bounds for minimizing the maximum utilization among all processors. The resource augmentation bound is presented to quantify the failure when our algorithm does not return a solution to meet the timing constraints. The case study and simulations are further conducted to illustrate the performance of our algorithm. For future research, we would like to continue exploring the memory-aware task scheduling under shared memory architecture with more than two types of modules and study more complex memory layouts.

9. REFERENCES

[1] AbsInt Angewandte Informatik GmbH. aiT: worst-case execution time analyzers. *http://www.absint.com/ait*, 2012.

[2] Malardalen WCET Research Group. WCET benchmarks. *http://www.mrtc.mdh.se/projects/wcet*, 2012.

[3] UTDSP Benchmark Suite. *http://www.eecg.toronto.edu/~corinna/DSP/infrastructure/UTDSP.tar.gz*, 2012.

[4] R. Banakar, S. Steinke, B.-S. Lee, M. Balakrishnan, and P. Marwedel. Scratchpad memory: design alternative for cache on-chip memory in embedded systems. In *CODES*, 2002.

[5] S. Baruah. Partitioning sporadic task systems upon memory-constrained multiprocessors. *to appear in ACM Transactions in Embedded Computing Systems*.

[6] J.-J. Chen and S. Chakraborty. Resource augmentation bounds for approximate demand bound functions. In *RTSS*, 2011.

[7] R. I. Davis and A. Burns. A survey of hard real-time scheduling for multiprocessor systems. *ACM Computing Surveys*, 43(4), October 2011.

[8] H. Falk and J. C. Kleinsorge. Optimal static WCET-aware scratchpad allocation of program code. In *DAC*, 2009.

[9] R. L. Graham. Bounds on multiprocessing timing anomalies. *SIAM Journal on Applied Mathematics*, 17(2):416–429, 1969.

[10] J. Guo, M. Lai, Z. Pang, L. Huang, F. Chen, K. Dai, and Z. Wang. Hierarchical memory system design for a heterogeneous multi-core processor. In *SAC*, 2008.

[11] Y. Guo, Q. Zhuge, J. Hu, M. Qiu, and E. H.-M. Sha. Optimal data allocation for scratch-pad memory on embedded multi-core systems. In *ICPP*, 2011.

[12] B. Kalyanasundaram and K. Pruhs. Speed is as powerful as clairvoyance. *Journal of the ACM*, 47(4):617–643, 2000.

[13] A. KleinOsowski, J. Flynn, N. Meares, and D. J. Lilja. Adapting the SPEC 2000 benchmark suite for simulation-based computer architecture research. *The Kluwer International Series in Engineering and Computer Science*, 610:83–100, 2002.

[14] C. Lee, M. Potkonjak, and W. H. Mangione-Smith. Mediabench: A tool for evaluating and synthesizing multimedia and communications systems. In *MICRO*, 1997.

[15] C. L. Liu and J. W. Layland. Scheduling algorithms for multiprogramming in a hard-real-time environment. *Journal of the ACM*, 20(1):46–61, 1973.

[16] G. Memik, W. H. Mangione-Smith, and W. Hu. Netbench: A benchmarking suite for network processors. In *ICCAD*, 2001.

[17] A. K. Mok. Fundamental design problems of distributed systems for the hard-real-time environment. Technical report, Cambridge, MA, USA, 1983.

[18] M. Niemeier, A. Wiese, and S. Baruah. Partitioned real-time scheduling on heterogeneous shared-memory multiprocessors. In *ECRTS*, 2011.

[19] O. Ozturk, M. Kandemir, and I. Kolcu. Shared Scratch-Pad memory space management. In *ISQED*, 2006.

[20] H. Takase, H. Tomiyama, and H. Takada. Partitioning and allocation of scratch-pad memory for priority-based preemptive multi-task systems. In *DATE*, 2010.

[21] R. F. van der Wijngaar, T. G. Mattson, and W. Haas. Light-weight communications on intel's single-chip cloud computer processor. *SIGOPS Operating Systems Review*, 45:73–83, February 2011.

[22] V. V. Vazirani. *Approximation Algorithms*. Springer, 2001.

[23] C.-Y. Yang, J.-J. Chen, T.-W. Kuo, and L. Thiele. An approximation scheme for energy-efficient scheduling of real-time tasks in heterogeneous multiprocessor systems. In *DATE*, 2009.

[24] L. Zhang, M. Qiu, W.-C. Tseng, and E. H.-M. Sha. Variable partitioning and scheduling for MPSoC with virtually shared scratch pad memory. *Journal of Signal Processing Systems*, 58:247–265, 2010.

[25] V. Zivojnovic, J. M. Velarde, C. Schlager, and H. Meyr. DSPstone: A DSP-oriented benchmarking methodology. In *ICSPAT*, 1994.

Code-Level Timing Analysis of Embedded Software*

EMSOFT'12 Invited Talk Session Outline

Heiko Falk
Institute of Embedded
Systems / Real-Time Systems
Ulm University
Ulm, Germany
Heiko.Falk@uni-ulm.de

Kevin Hammond
School of Computer Science
University of St. Andrews
St. Andrews, Scotland
kh@cs.st-andrews.ac.uk

Kim G. Larsen
Department of Computer
Science
Aalborg University
Aalborg, Denmark
kgl@cs.aau.dk

Björn Lisper
Department of Computer
Science
Mälardalen University
Västerås, Sweden
bjorn.lisper@mdh.se

Stefan M. Petters
School of Engineering
Polytechnic Institute of Porto
Porto, Portugal
smp@isep.ipp.pt

ABSTRACT

Embedded systems are often business- or safety-critical, with strict timing requirements that have to be met for the information-processing. Code-level timing analysis (used to analyse software running on some given hardware w.r.t. its timing properties) is an indispensable technique for ascertaining whether or not these requirements are met. However, recent developments in hardware, especially multi-core processors, and in software organisation render analysis increasingly more difficult, thus challenging the evolution of timing analysis techniques. This special session aims to give an overview over the current state of the art and the future challenges w.r.t. code-level timing analysis and introduces TACLe, a recently started EU-funded networking activity targeting these challenges.

Categories and Subject Descriptors

C.3 [**Real-time and embedded systems**]

General Terms

Algorithms, Performance

Keywords

Timing Analysis, WCET, Multi-Core Processors

Timing Analysis for Multicore / Manycore Architectures

Kevin Hammond, University of St. Andrews

Multicore / manycore architectures present significant new challenges to timing analysis. Since hardware resources are shared between processor cores, activities on one core can

---

*Supported by the European Community's ICT COST Action IC1202 (TACLe).

affect the timing of activities on other cores. It is no longer possible to consider execution times independently for each core: rather, timing analysis must take all possible simultaneous activities into account. These processor architectures thus lack timing composability, i.e., the ability to infer timing for a full system from the timing of its parts, which has a highly negative effect on the timing predictability of multicore / manycore systems. This talk introduces the research area, outlines the major challenges that must be overcome and highlights promising new approaches to timing analysis for multicore / manycore architectures.

Reconciling Compilation and Timing Analysis

Heiko Falk, Ulm University

The current state of the art in designing software for hard real-time systems is heavily unsafe. On the one hand, the actual industrial design practice relies on measurements or simulations so that no guarantees about the worst-case timing of a piece of software can be derived. On the other hand, current compilers usually optimise the average-case execution time (ACET) of a program, instead of the worst-case execution time (WCET). This talk presents a WCET-aware compiler for hard real-time systems. A WCET timing model provides valuable data about the worst-case behaviour of a program to be compiled and optimised. This timing model is then used by specialised optimisations which achieve a fully automatic minimisation of the WCET.

Early-Stage and Portable Timing Analysis

Stefan M. Petters, Polytechnic Institute of Porto

Since redesigning a software system is very costly, designers usually choose to over-specify the hardware initially and then just verify that it is indeed sufficiently powerful. However, as systems' complexity rises, these initial safety margins can prove to be very expensive. Undertaking lightweight (but less precise) analysis in the early stages of the design process has the potential to drastically reduce total hardware costs.

Analysis of Mixed-Critical Embedded Systems with Multiple Objectives

Kim G. Larsen, Aalborg University

We demonstrate how a combination of model checking and statistical model checking may be applied to analyse on the one hand hard real-time system response time requirements and on the other hand soft real time requirements allowing a trade-off between time and energy consumption.

TACLe – An EU COST Action on Timing Analysis on Code-Level

Björn Lisper, Mälardalen University

TACLe is a new COST Action that will coordinate and support European research in code-level timing analysis through a number of networking activities. The Action gathers all the prominent European groups in the area as well as groups in neighbouring areas. The coordinated research is organised in the following working groups:

WG1: Timing models for multi-cores and timing composability

WG2: Tooling Aspects

WG3: Early-stage timing analysis

WG4: Other resources than time

The Action is motivated particularly by the challenges to code-level timing analysis brought by the rapid transition to multi-core technology, and anticipated future evolution to many-core architectures. These challenges require a coordinated effort to be met. The purpose of TACLe is to provide this coordination.

Estimation of Probabilistic Bounds on Phase CPI and Relevance in WCET Analysis

Archana Ravindar   Y. N. Srikant
Department of Computer Science and Automation
Indian Institute of Science
Bangalore-560012, India
{archana,srikant}@csa.iisc.ernet.in

ABSTRACT

Estimating program worst case execution time(WCET) accurately and efficiently is a challenging task. Several programs exhibit *phase behavior* wherein cycles per instruction (CPI) varies in phases during execution. Recent work has suggested the use of phases in such programs to estimate WCET with minimal instrumentation. However the suggested model uses a function of mean CPI that has no probabilistic guarantees. We propose to use Chebyshev's inequality that can be applied to any arbitrary distribution of CPI samples, to probabilistically bound CPI of a phase.

Applying Chebyshev's inequality to phases that exhibit high CPI variation leads to pessimistic upper bounds. We propose a mechanism that refines such phases into sub-phases based on program counter(PC) *signatures* collected using profiling and also allows the user to control variance of CPI within a sub-phase. We describe a WCET analyzer built on these lines and evaluate it with standard WCET and embedded benchmark suites on two different architectures for three chosen probabilities, p={0.9, 0.95 and 0.99}. For p=0.99, refinement based on PC signatures alone, reduces average pessimism of WCET estimate by 36%(77%) on $Arch1(Arch2)$. Compared to *Chronos*, an open source static WCET analyzer, the average improvement in estimates obtained by refinement is 5%(125%) on $Arch1(Arch2)$. On limiting variance of CPI within a sub-phase to {50%, 10%, 5% and 1%} of its original value, average accuracy of WCET estimate improves further to {9%, 11%, 12% and 13%} respectively, on $Arch1$. On $Arch2$, average accuracy of WCET improves to 159% when CPI variance is limited to 50% of its original value and improvement is marginal beyond that point.

Categories and Subject Descriptors

C.3 [**Special-Purpose and Application-Based Systems**]: Real-time and embedded systems; C.4 [**Performance of Systems**]: Measurement techniques

General Terms

Measurement, Performance Evaluation

Keywords

phase behavior, CPI, WCET analysis, profiling, soft real-time systems, probabilistic bounds, Chebyshev inequality, confidence intervals

1. INTRODUCTION

The worst case execution time (WCET) of a program is the maximum time a program will ever take to execute on a given architecture. WCET estimates are necessary to design real-time systems where programs have deadlines to adhere to. WCET estimates help build an optimal schedule that ensures effective resource utilization. WCET analysis is non-trivial as it depends on several factors like program structure, input and complexity of the architecture.

Generally, WCET analyzers work on components of a program. Static WCET analyzers [19] estimate WCET of program components on an analytical model of the architecture built for this purpose. Measurement based WCET analyzers [11, 18, 20, 16, 22] measure execution time of these components directly on the architecture either by native execution or simulation. The overall program WCET is estimated by combining these costs using program structural analysis. Statistical WCET analyzers measure end to end execution times and fit models to estimate WCET [21, 12, 24, 23]. Instead of an absolute WCET estimate, one can estimate WCET at various probabilities, especially useful, when tasks with different priorities exist. Bernat et al [11] probabilistically combine worst case effects of basic blocks under three different scenarios and build the program worst case path to estimate probabilistic WCET.

Each WCET analysis technique is applicable in a specific domain and has its own set of concerns. While static WCET analysis guarantees safe WCET estimates, absence of runtime information forces the analysis to make conservative assumptions that might lead to pessimistic WCET estimates. Statistical WCET techniques need to make their model close to the real world as much as possible [10]. A measurements based WCET analyzer might make unsafe estimates of WCET due to incomplete coverage of functions, statements and conditions.

The amount of instrumentation remains a concern in measurement based analyzers which typically measure basic blocks or group of basic blocks of a program [5, 6]. Several programs exhibit *phase behavior* that refers to phase-like vari-

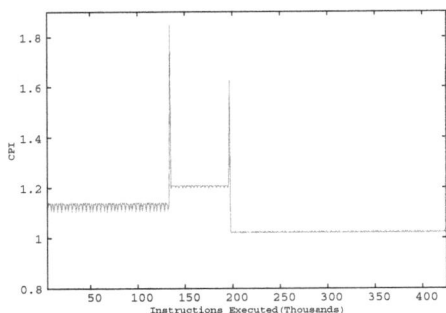

Figure 1: CPI variation in *Bitcount* over time on *Arch1*.

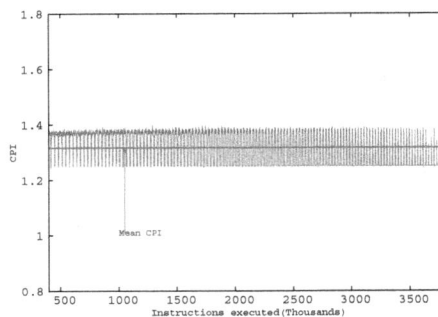

Figure 2: Deviation of CPI around the mean in *Bubble sort* on *Arch1*.

ation of CPI (cycles per instruction) observed during their dynamic execution. In [8], we have demonstrated that program phase behavior can be used to reduce instrumentation in measurement based WCET analysis. Figure 1 plots cycles per instruction(CPI) for every 1000 instructions executed for *Bitcount* (Table 2). Within each phase, CPI varies homogeneously and is distinct across phases as shown. In order to make use of phase behavior, we consider execution time (processor cycles) as a product of instructions executed(IC) and cycles per instruction(CPI).

The distinct CPI behavior of each phase drives the formulation of program WCET as a sum of WCET of it's constituent phases. The homogeneity and repeatability of CPI behavior within a phase helps in obtaining CPI of a phase with minimal instrumentation. Code structural analysis is used to mark phases in the program [14] that hold across different inputs. We instrument programs at every thousand instructions in [8] resulting in an instrumentation ratio of 0.1%. The product of worst case number of instructions executed within a phase, $Max(IC)$ and worst case CPI of a phase, $Max(CPI)$ is the WCET of that phase. Although the idea is simple and promising, the method uses maximum of mean CPI observed as $Max(CPI)$ resulting in an approximate WCET estimate that has no probabilistic guarantees[8].

Our objective is to improve the phase based WCET analyzer to yield WCET estimates associated with probabilistic guarantees. For this purpose, we compute probabilistic upper bound of phase CPI that is multiplied by Max(IC) to yield a probabilistic WCET estimate. For each phase, CPI samples are collected by measurement at numerous points by running benchmarks with a large number of test inputs. The true probability distribution of these CPI samples is not known. We know that the samples have finite mean and finite variance. Hence we use Chebyshev's inequality to bound CPI of a phase within a confidence interval for a probability, p. Applying Chebyshev's inequality to benchmarks with stable CPI behavior (coefficient of variation or CoV of CPI < 0.5%) results in accurate WCET estimates (that are within 1% of maximum observed cycles even at p=0.99).

Some benchmarks like *Bubble_sort* (Table 2) exhibit high variation in CPI during execution(Figure 2). Applying Chebyshev's inequality directly for such phases yields a wide confidence interval for CPI leading to highly pessimistic WCET estimates, as execution time is directly proportional to CPI. It is observed that deviations in CPI correspond to deviations in the program counter even at a granularity of a

few tens of instructions. Using this observation, we *refine* such phases into smaller sub-phases based on PC(program counter) signatures, collected using profiling. These signatures basically encode path information of loop iterations in a concise manner and are analyzed to isolate high deviations in CPI. Re-applying Chebyshev's inequality on CPI samples for each sub-phase gives us a tight bound on CPI thereby resulting in an accurate WCET estimate. The refinement process also allows the user to control CPI variance within a sub-phase and hence accuracy of WCET.

For evaluation, we choose two architectures, *Arch1* and *Arch2* as shown in Table 1 with benchmarks taken from Mälardalen WCET project suite [3] and embedded benchmark suite, Mibench [1] (Table 2). All measurements are carried out using cycle accurate simulator, *Simplescalar Version 3.0* [4]. We compute bounds on CPI for unrefined and refined phases respectively at three chosen probability values, p={0.9, 0.95, 0.99}.

For benchmarks that exhibit high variation of CPI, refinement is observed to reduce pessimism in WCET estimates by 36%(*Arch1*) and 77%(*Arch2*), on an average, compared to unrefined phases. Refinement of sub-phases further limiting CPI variance to {50%, 10%, 5%, 1%} of original sub-phase CPI variance is observed to improve accuracy of WCET further, on both architectures, compared to refinement based on PC signature alone. Compared to *Chronos*, at p=0.99, WCET estimates computed using phase refinement based on PC signature and limiting CPI variance of sub-phase to (50%, 10%, 5%, 1%) of original sub-phase CPI variance, are tighter by {5%, 9%, 11%, 12%, 13%} on *Arch1* and by {125%, 159%, 159%, 159%, 159%} on *Arch2* respectively.

We address the following questions in this paper.
1. How can we obtain robust WCET estimates that are also accurate in the phase based timing model?
2. How can we isolate points of high CPI variation within a phase?
3. How can we control CPI variation within a phase?
4. What is the impact of 2 and 3 on WCET accuracy?

The rest of the paper is organized as follows. Section 2 outlines the phase based WCET analyzer. Section 3 describes the basic framework to compute probabilistic bound on CPI of a phase. Section 4 describes phase refinement in detail and how refined phases can be used to estimate WCET. The proposed technique is evaluated in Section 5 and compared with related work in Section 6. The paper is finally concluded in Section 7.

Table 1: Architectural configurations used for experimentation.

Common Parameters	Issue, decode and commit width=1, Register update unit (RUU) size=8, Fetch Queue size=4
Arch1	8KB direct mapped Instruction cache, Out of order Issue, 2-level Branch Predictor
Arch2	In-order Issue, 8KB direct mapped Instruction Instruction cache, 8KB 2-way set associative Data cache, Unified 64KB 8-way associative, L2 cache, Perfect Branch Prediction

2. PHASE-BASED TIMING MODEL

In [8], we propose to estimate program WCET as a sum of WCET of it's phases. A phase corresponds to a static code region detected by code structure analysis [14]. The unit of analysis is a hierarchical call loop(HCL) graph, created out of the program binary. The program is executed with various inputs to ensure coverage of all functions and conditions. Profile data is used to annotate the HCL graph with hierarchical information regarding number of calls, loop iteration counts, variance in instructions executed every time each call/loop is executed. The HCL graph is analyzed to pick phase marker edges. The code region lying between a marker edge *e1* and the following marker edge *e2* comprises the phase associated with *e1*.

The WCET of a program is estimated as,

$$WCET = \Sigma_{i \in \{1..p\}} WCET_i \qquad (1)$$

where p is the number of phases of the program. WCET of the i-th phase, is estimated as,

$$WCET_i = T_i \times Max(IC_i) \times Max(CPI_i) \qquad (2)$$

where, $\mathbf{T}_i$: Maximum number of times phase i occurs during execution.

$\mathbf{Max(IC}_i\mathbf{)}$: Worst case instruction count(IC) of phase i. $Max(IC_i)$ is either the theoretical upper bound on IC derived using static analysis($SWIC_i$) or the maximum observed IC of phase $i(MIC_i)$ [8].

$\mathbf{Max(CPI}_i\mathbf{)}$: Worst case CPI of phase i. CPI is measured within each phase at various points and maximum of mean CPI across all tested inputs is taken as *Max(CPI_i)*. In this work, we use probabilistically bounded CPI instead of maximum of mean CPI to obtain a more robust WCET estimate.

A program depending on its structural complexity, can execute different code regions(phases) on execution with different inputs thereby exhibiting multiple phase sequences across inputs [8]. In that case, WCET is estimated as the maximum among WCET of all possible sequences.

3. COMPUTING BOUNDS ON PHASE CPI

We now describe how CPI of a phase is bounded for a given probability, p. To bound CPI, we collect n CPI samples for each phase(static code region) to form the sample set, $\widehat{S}_i$, by running the program with a large number of test inputs. CPI is measured at intervals ranging from 100 to 1000 instructions depending on the program dynamic execution length.

On an average, CPI samples are observed to be within 10% of the sample mean($\widehat{\mu}$) on both architectures. Our main objective is to quantify the amount by which a future CPI sample can be away from $\widehat{\mu}$ for a given probability(p). Had

we known the true probability distribution of the samples (ascertained only if true population set, S_i, built by exercising *all* paths within phase i is known), we could apply an appropriate probability density function to compute the confidence interval to contain a future CPI sample for probability p. Building S_i is computationally expensive. Hence we use Chebyshev's inequality as it can be applied to any arbitrary distribution. Chebyshev's inequality only requires the random variable(CPI) to have finite mean and finite variance. If variance is small, bounds obtained using Chebyshev's inequality are tight.

Chebyshev's inequality: The inequality states that p, probability of a future sample, cpi_x, being greater than mean of $S_i(\mu)$, is as follows,

$$P(|cpi_x - \mu| \geq C) \leq \frac{\sigma^2}{C^2} \qquad (3)$$

Where, C is an arbitrary constant, μ is true mean of the distribution and σ^2 is true variance of the distribution. We can use sample mean, $\widehat{\mu}$ and sample variance, $\widehat{\sigma}^2$ in Eq.3 provided variance of sample mean, $Var(\widehat{\mu})$ is small.

$$Var(\widehat{\mu}) = \frac{\sigma^2}{n} \qquad (4)$$

$Var(\widehat{\mu})$ is inversely proportional to the number of samples, n. Hence with increasing n, $Var(\widehat{\mu})$ decreases [25]. Since we have a large number of samples, we can confidently use $\widehat{\mu}$ and $\widehat{\sigma}^2$ in place of μ and σ^2 to give the following equation.

$$P(|cpi_x - \widehat{\mu}| \geq C) \leq \frac{\widehat{\sigma}^2}{C^2} \qquad (5)$$

Applying Chebyshev's inequality to $\widehat{S}_i$, we obtain a confidence interval $[CPI_{i,l}, CPI_{i,u}]$ within which a future CPI sample will lie with probability p. As WCET is to be estimated, we use the upper bound of the interval, $CPI_{i,u}$, which for probability p, is referred as $PrCPI_p$. Hence original timing equation, Eq.2 is modified to,

$$WCET_i = T_i \times Max(IC_i) \times PrCPI_p \qquad (6)$$

Since we use theoretically bounded $Max(IC_i)$, which is a constant and is multiplied by $PrCPI_p$, the probabilistic guarantee applies to the resultant WCET as well. For benchmarks that exhibit low variance in CPI, Chebyshev's inequality tightly bounds phase CPI. Applying the inequality to phases with high variance in CPI results in a wide confidence interval leading to higher $PrCPI_p$ values and hence pessimistic WCET estimates. In the next section, we will see how such phases can be divided into smaller sub-phases to obtain tighter CPI bounds and hence tighter WCET estimates.

4. PHASE REFINEMENT

Code structure analysis [14] ensures that variation in instructions executed within a phase is much lesser than the corresponding variation across different phases. However, presence of if-conditions in loops or calls can cause high variance in instructions executed across loop iterations or call invocations. The if-condition of the inner-loop in *Bubble_sort* (Figure 3), when *true*, executes additional code compared to when the condition is *false*. The HCL graph for the routine created by profiling with a set of 5 different inputs, is shown in the same figure. Each loop is represented by a loop head

Benchmark	Description	Phase Sequence	Static Length	Avg. Dynamic Length
Bezier (*Bez*)	Draws a set of 200 lines of 4 reference points on a 800×600 image [7].	P1 P2	114	107901512
Bitcount (*Bit*)	Performs bit operations on a 1K bit-vector a thousand times [1].	P1 P2 P3 P4 P5 P6	257	404910
Binary Search (*Bs*)	Search for a key in a 50K number vector [3].	single	51	6329
Bubble sort (*Bub*)	Sort an array of size 3K [3].	single	55	41472125
CNT (*Cnt*)	Counts positive numbers in a 200×200 matrix [3].	P1 P2	72	653672
CRC (*Crc*)	Cyclic redundancy check on a 16KB char vector [3].	P1 P2	84	583140
FIR (*Fir*)	Finite impulse response filter over a signal of size 400 [3].	single	272	148171
FFT (*Fft*)	Fast fourier transform on a wave of size 16K [1].	P1 P2	277	8508909
Insertion Sort (*Ins*)	Sort a 3K number vector [3].	single	38	24899477
Janne_complex (*Jan*)	A nested loop program, *a*, *b* are input parameters [3].	single	35	1201362
LMS (*Lms*)	Adaptive signal enhancement [3].	single	142	567565
Matmul (*Mat*)	Matrix multiplication of two 200×200 matrices [3].	P1 P2	106	105090836

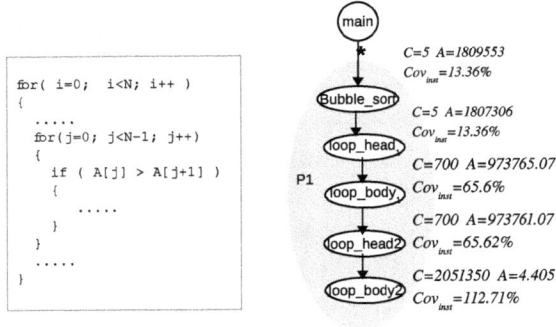

Figure 3: Code structure of *Bubble_sort* routine and the corresponding HCL graph.

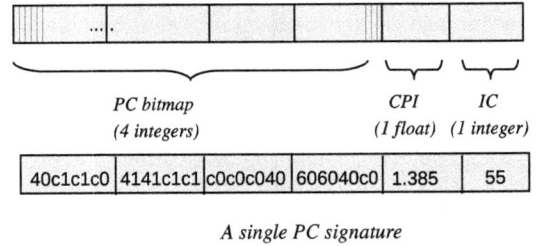

Figure 4: Format of a single PC signature.

node and a loop body node in the HCL graph. The edge associated with loop head node stores information about the number of times loop head was executed(**C**), hierarchical average number of instructions(**A**) and CoV in instructions executed(**CoV**$_{inst}$) over different executions. Similarly the edge associated with loop body node stores these information pertaining to a loop iteration. It can be observed that loop edges have a very high CoV$_{inst}$ hence do not qualify as software markers resulting in the whole routine being selected as a single phase [14]. Considering the entire loop as a single phase exhibits high variation in CPI(Figure 2).

In such cases, we could statically mark the code region associated with each iteration and hence each path per iteration as a different phase. But that would not work because, a) The underlying architecture is based on a pipeline consisting of several stages. Multiple instructions are in flight at the same time. A phase should be lengthy enough to allow at least few instructions to completely execute to facilitate calculation of CPI of the phase.
b) Instrumenting every few instructions can hamper performance of the program that we are trying to measure.
Hence it appears that we need to find a mid point where phases are big enough, at the same time, small enough to obtain tight bounds on CPI.

An intuitive approach is to consider every x consecutive iterations of a loop, L, as a potential phase, which we term as a *window*, W. We emit dynamic execution information of every window, W, in the form of a triple, defined as a *PC signature* (Figure 4), storing the following information.
PCbitmap: The bitmap is a vector of 4 integers (128 bits).

The simulator hashes every instruction PC encountered and stores it into the bitmap. 127 bits are sufficient to map PC addresses in each phase of the benchmarks considered in this paper.
CPI: CPI represents observed cycles per instruction while instructions belonging to W are executed.
IC: IC represents number of instructions executed that belong to W.

4.1 Refinement Based on PC Signature

Refinement consists of three steps: trace generation, trace compression and classification of compressed trace into subphases.
1) Trace Generation: In order to generate a trace, we first identify the branch instruction that iterates loop L of the phase. If L is nested with several levels, we select the innermost loop. The simulator is modified to count x consecutive executions of the branch instruction of L. If $Min(|L_i|)$ denotes the minimum number of instructions executed in each loop iteration i of L, number of iterations that make up a single window, x is defined as,

$$x = \left\lceil \frac{Phase\_length}{Min(|L_i|)} \right\rceil \quad (7)$$

where, *Phase_length* is the number of instructions that make up a phase. On a given architecture, *Phase_length* should be greater than the minimum number of instructions that have to be executed for at least one instruction commit. A *Phase_length* of *50* instructions suffices for both architectures considered in this paper (Table 1). x being a ceiling value, Eq.7 might cause some windows to be composed of more than *50* instructions. x will not always be an exact multiple of $|L|$. Hence the execution time of the last few

Trace of a single run of Bub

PC Bitmap	CPI	IC
. . . .		
202020002020202020	1.250000	64
202020002020202020	1.250000	64
202020002020202020	1.250000	64
202020002020202020	1.250000	64
202020002020202020	1.250000	64
2020200020202020300302020303030	1.451610	93
20202000202020202020202020	1.291140	79
202020002020202020	1.250000	64
202020002020202020	1.250000	64
202020002020202020	1.250000	64
202020002020202020	1.250000	64
. . . .		

Compressed trace of a single run of Bub

PC Bitmap	CPI	IC	#duplicates
. . . .			
202020002020202020	1.250000	64	147
2020200020202020300302020303030	1.451610	93	1
20202000202020202020202020	1.291140	79	1
202020002020202020	1.250000	64	93
. . . .			

Figure 5: Signature trace of a single run of *Bubble sort* and its compressed version.

iterations will have to be added separately. If the phase has multiple loops, the same procedure is repeated for all loops within the phase.

A loop with small $|L_i|$ will have windows comprising of a large number of iterations. If $|L_i|$ is greater than minimum *Phase_length*, every iteration forms a window. If $|L_i|$ is well beyond minimum *Phase_length*, we can use code structure analysis to break it into smaller phases. The benchmarks considered in this paper comprises of loops where $|L_i| \leq$ minimum *Phase_length*. The cycles taken by code preceding loop L of phase P, if any, is added separately.

When a program is simulated by *Simplesim-3.0* modified as explained above, we obtain a trace consisting of $\frac{|L|}{x}$ such signatures, where $|L|$ is the loop iteration count of L. The modifications to simulator do not impact execution cycles of the program as PC values are read off the pipeline and processed in parallel. In the worst case, for every 50 instructions executed, a trace comprising of 6 words, is emitted out and the 4-word hash table is reset.

An integer vector that stores occurrences of each PC encountered would be more accurate to represent path information of every window, instead of the existing bitmap. But that would clearly not scale with x and would lead to huge traces. The bitmap is imprecise as we shall now see with an example.

In Figure 3, assume the inner loop executes 18 instructions when if-condition evaluates to *true* and 10 instructions when it evaluates to *false*. Let window size, x be 4 iterations. Consider two such windows W_1 and W_2. Assume in W_1: if-condition is *true* once and false three times. In W_2, if-condition was *true* three times and *false* once. The PCbitmap will be identical in both cases but $IC(W_1) = 18 \times 1 + 10 \times 3 = 48$. $IC(W_2) = 18 \times 3 + 10 \times 1 = 64$. Hence IC serves to store extra information without bloating the trace. Although seeming imprecise, the combination of IC and PCbitmap is observed to be sufficient to isolate high CPI variations in most cases.

2) Trace Compression: Lengthy program runs can produce megabytes of trace. But they are easily compressible owing to the repetitive nature of phases. A large number of consecutive windows have identical PC signatures which can be compressed(Figure 5). We look for consecutive triples that repeat to compress them. The time complexity of the compression algorithm is linear to the trace size.

3) Trace Classification: A one-to-one correspondence is observed between <PCbitmap, IC> and CPI in the trace for program *Bubble sort* (Figure 5), which is observed in other

```
/****************    Refine sub-phase based on CPI ************/
/* Inputs:                                                    */
/* <CPI data for each sub-phase>                              */
/* <Variance_threshold>                                       */
/* Output:                                                    */
/* <New Bounds on CPI for each new sub-phase>                 */
/**************************************************************/

Procedure Split(sub-phase_CPI_vector)
  Compute variance of CPI;
  While (variance > Variance_threshold) do
    Split sub-phase_CPI_vector into two depending on range of values
    /* vector_1 range: [lower..mean] vector_2 range: [mean..upper] */
    Split(vector_1);
    Split(vector_2);
  end for
end Split
Procedure Bounds(sub-phase_CPI_file)
  Compute mean of CPI;
  Compute Variance of CPI;
  Compute Chebyshev bounds on CPI;
end Bounds
Procedure main
  for each sub-phase, i, do
    Split(i); // generates new sub-phases
    for each new-sub-phase, j, do
      Bounds(j);
    end for
  end for
end main
```

Figure 6: Algorithm to refine sub-phase based on CPI variance.

benchmarks as well. This happens because CPI is largely determined by the instructions that execute [14]. Based on this, we define a *sub-phase* as a unique pair of <PCbitmap, IC> values. All windows with the same <PCbitmap, IC> value belong to one sub-phase. For each such sub-phase, new confidence intervals are computed by applying Chebyshev's inequality on CPI samples pertaining to that sub-phase.

The time taken by the classification algorithm is $O(m \times n)$, where m is the number of unique <PCbitmap, IC> pairs (sub-phases) and n is the number of entries in the compressed trace. On an average, number of sub-phases, m, detected for benchmarks used in this paper is 15.04(15.33) for *Arch1(Arch2)* even if number of windows for some benchmarks go upto a few thousands. The size of compressed trace obtained across all inputs for a program, n, ranges from 2 MB to 1.8GB. The average sub-phase size observed across all benchmarks is 62 resulting in an average instrumentation overhead of 1.6%.

4.2 Refinement Based on CPI Variance

Inspite of refinement based on PC signature, certain sub-phases exhibit high variance of CPI. Hence we add another level of refinement wherein the user can control the variance of CPI within the sub-phase. The classification will now be based on <PCbitmap, IC, CPI-range>. The procedure repeatedly splits the sub-phase until the CPI values fall in the desired range giving rise to variance well within the specified limit(Figure 6). The time complexity of *Split* is $O(n \times log(n))$, where n is the number of entries in sub-phase CPI file. The overall time complexity of the refinement procedure is $O(m \times n \times log(n))$ where m is the number of original sub-phases.

4.3 WCET Estimation Using Sub-Phases

A phase represents a static code region. Whereas a sub-phase represents a group of consecutive loop iterations. Every single loop iteration is included in the analysis. Sub-phases do not overlap as each of them represent a different group of loop iterations. In order to estimate WCET in terms of sub-phases, Eq.6 has to be suitably modified. Different phases can occur on execution with different inputs[8]. The same holds for sub-phases. The set of sub-phases that occur for a particular program run with input i forms a sub-phase sequence $\mathcal{S}_i$. Note that we are not interested in the exact order in which sub-phases occur. A sub-phase sequence ($\mathcal{S}_i$) obtained with input i, takes the form of an integer vector, $[s_{i.0}, s_{i.1}, \ldots, s_{i.sp}]$ where sp is the total number of sub-phases appearing across all inputs. $s_{i.j}$ indicates the number of times sub-phase j occurs in the execution run of program with input i. Among two sequences, $\mathcal{S}_a$ and $\mathcal{S}_b$, obtained with inputs a and b, such that $s_{a.k} \geq s_{b.k}$ $\forall$ k $= \{0,..,sp\}$, we include only $\mathcal{S}_a$. The number of unique sub-phase sequences that can occur range from 1 to over a hundred.

For each sequence, $\mathcal{S}_i$, $WCET_i$, is estimated as-

$$WCET_i = \Sigma_{j \in \{0,..,sp\}} (s_j \times Max(IC_j) \times PrCPI_p) \quad (8)$$

s_j is the sub-phase counterpart of T_i(in Eq.6). Since sub-phase is a dynamic entity, we use maximum observed IC in a window, occurring for the bitmap corresponding to sub-phase j, across all inputs as $Max(IC_j)$. For s possible sequences, overall WCET is estimated as,

$$WCET = max(WCET_1, \ldots., WCET_s) \quad (9)$$

Equation 8 applies to loops that iterate the same number of times for all inputs. However, the loop can terminate sooner than intended depending on data. It is hence useful to compute WCET in a situation when iterations reach the loop bound. For this purpose, we calculate the theoretical upper bound on the number of windows, SWW, possible for a given loop making up a program phase. If $|L|$ denotes the loop bound of L, x denotes the number of iterations per window, SWW is computed as,

$$SWW = \frac{|L|}{x}$$

For each unique sub-phase sequence, $\mathcal{S}_i$, we calculate the weight of each sub-phase, k, occurring in that sequence as,

$$w_k = \frac{s_{i,k}}{\Sigma_{j \in \{0,..,sp\}} s_{i,j}}$$

And consequently, $WCET_i$ is estimated as,

$$WCET_i = \Sigma_{j \in \{0,..,sp\}} (w_j \times SWW \times Max(IC_j) \times PrCPI_p) \quad (10)$$

4.4 Context Sensitivity

An analysis of a program fragment is said to be context sensitive if it takes into account the context in which the fragment appears. Context sensitive analysis has been observed to improve precision of WCET analysis significantly[22]. Context sensitive analysis is typically applied for procedures and loops. In this paper, we treat a procedure appearing in two different contexts as two different procedures. It is observed that the first iteration of a loop takes more time to execute (greater CPI) than rest of the iterations[17]. Hence we treat the first window (that includes the first iteration) of a loop as a separate sub-phase.

5. EVALUATION

All our experiments are performed on benchmarks taken from *Mibench* and Mälardalen standard WCET project benchmark suite(Table 2), for architectures mentioned in Table 1. The benchmarks are compiled to MIPS PISA binaries with -O2 -static flags. *Simplescalar Version 3.0* is used to obtain CPI samples and generate traces of PC signatures with modifications described in Section 4.1. Input selection is done

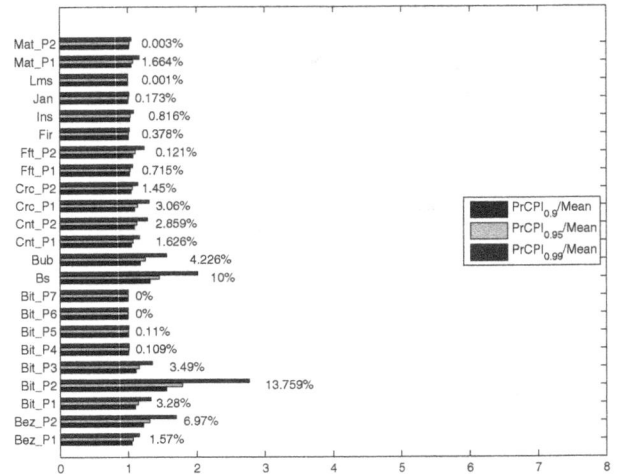

Figure 7: Ratio of probabilistic CPI upper bound to mean CPI at p={0.9, 0.95, 0.99} on *Arch1*. Percentages indicated next to bars refer to coefficient of variation of CPI.

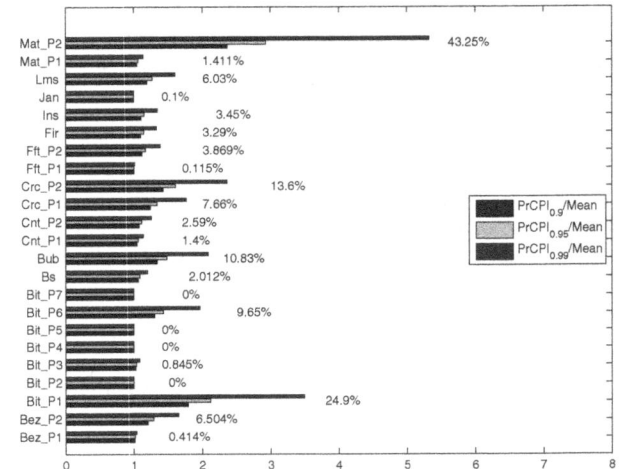

Figure 8: Ratio of probabilistic CPI upper bound to mean CPI at p={0.9, 0.95, 0.99} on *Arch2*. Percentages indicated next to bars refer to coefficient of variation of CPI.

primarily on the basis of MC/DC coverage criteria. Randomly generated inputs are also used. Each (benchmark, input) pair is executed with 500 different inputs multiple number of times to model different initial states [7] and atleast one million CPI samples per phase are generated. Invalid inputs and inputs that terminate execution early are not considered for analysis. The resulting estimates are compared with the open source static WCET analyzer *Chronos* as it models the MIPS architecture.

5.1 Impact of Coefficient of Variation of CPI on Probabilistic Upper Bound of CPI

Chebyshev's inequality yields tight CPI bounds for phases that exhibit low CoV(CPI) as can be seen from Figures 7 and 8 which plot $PrCPI_p$ at p={0.9, 0.95, 0.99}, normal-

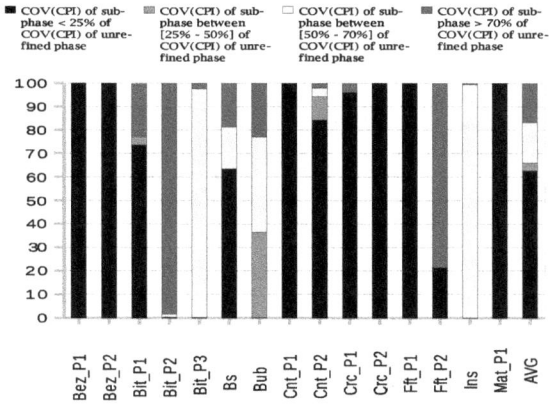

Figure 9: *Arch1:* Percentage breakup of sub-phases based on CoV(CPI).

ized to the mean CPI, for all program phases on *Arch1* and *Arch2* respectively. However, applying the inequality directly to phases like *Mat_P2(Arch2)* with high CoV(CPI) results in pessimistic upper bounds of CPI, as can be seen from Figure 8. Hence we need to refine such phases into smaller sub-phases. This will reduce CPI variance within a sub-phase and help yield tighter CPI bounds.

5.2 Impact of Refinement on Coefficient of Variation of CPI

We now compare sub-phases obtained using refinement based on unique <PCBitmap, IC> pairs with the corresponding unrefined phase based on their CoV(CPI). Figures 9 and 10 group sub-phases into four categories as shown. The breakup of only those unrefined phases that exhibit high CPI variance is shown. Post refinement, 63%(87%) of sub-phases exhibit CoV(CPI) that is less than 25% of the corresponding unrefined phase CoV(CPI) on *Arch1(Arch2)*. Sub-phases of *Bit_P2(Arch1)*, *Fft_P2*, *Bit_P6 (Arch2)* and *Ins(Arch2)* continue to exhibit high CoV(CPI). Such sub-phases are further refined into smaller sub-phases based on CPI variance as outlined in Section 4.2.

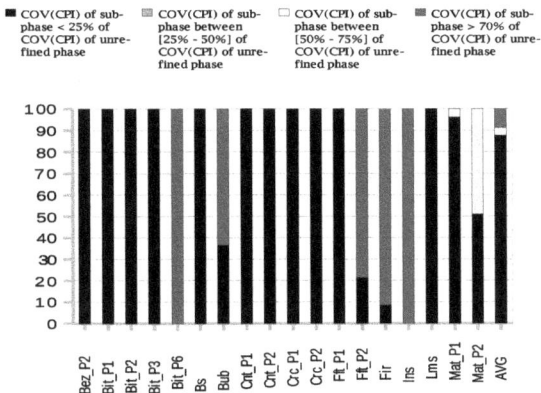

Figure 10: *Arch2:* Percentage breakup of sub-phases based on CoV(CPI).

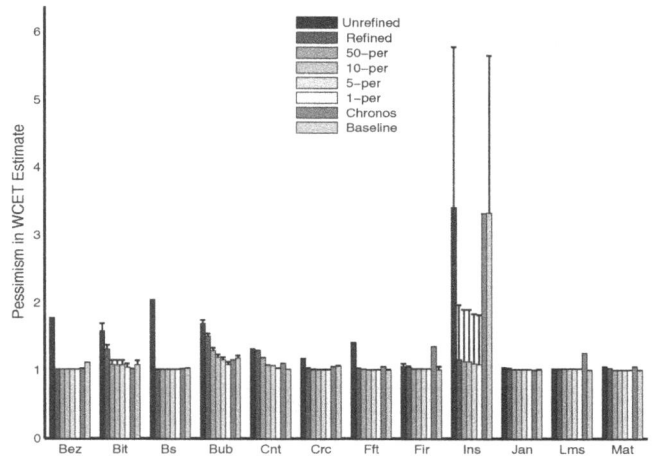

Figure 11: **Comparison of WCET estimates using proposed method with *Chronos* and Baseline estimates on *Arch1*.**

5.3 Accuracy of WCET

Figures 11 and 12 plot the ratio of estimated WCET to maximum observed cycles (*Pessimism in the WCET estimate*) observed when the proposed phases/sub-phases are used for p=0.99. *Unrefined* and *Refined* bars represent the pessimism observed using unrefined phases and phases refined based on PC signature respectively. The *50-per, 10-per, 5-per* and *1-per* bars indicate pessimism in WCET obtained using refined sub-phases with variance of CPI limited at {50%, 10%, 5% and 1%} of CPI variance of original sub-phase respectively. Alongside the bars, WCET estimated by *Chronos* and our original phase based model (Eq.2) [8] (*Baseline*) are also plotted.

The theoretical maximum IC executed coincides with maximum observed IC for benchmarks with straight line code. However they differ for programs with complex conditions and loops. The bars in Figures 11 and 12 are plotted using maximum observed IC (for phases) and maximum observed windows (for sub-phases) (Eq.8). Similarly the upper limit of the bar is plotted using theoretical upper bound on IC (for phases) and theoretical maximum windows (for sub-phases) (Eq.10). CoV(CPI) for benchmarks like *Fir(Arch1)*, *Lms(Arch1)* and *Jan(Arch2)* is less than 1%. As a result, the phase CPI bounds obtained by Chebyshev's inequality are tight enough and improvement by refinement is very marginal.

Applying Chebyshev's inequality to phases with high variation of CPI leads to pessimistic unrefined WCET estimates as shown in Figures 11 and 12. Refinement based on PC signature reduces pessimism considerably(Table 3). The reduction is less on *Arch1* as CPI variation is more scattered possibly due to an out-of-order pipeline and a realistic branch predictor. Refinement based on CPI variance continues to reduce pessimism further. The average improvement in accuracy of WCET estimate compared with *Chronos* for p=0.99 is also shown. As expected, Eq.10 gives a more pessimistic WCET as it uses theoretical upper limit of windows.

Figure 13 plots level of refinement needed to reach a point of zero CPI variance in every sub-phase of the benchmark. Refinement beyond this point will not improve accu-

Table 3: Impact of Refinement on pessimism of WCET and comparison with *Chronos.*

p	100-per	50-per	10-per	5-per	1-per
	(Arch1)				
% Reduction in pessimism compared to unrefined WCET					
0.9	20.13	21.81	22.3	22.66	23.25
0.95	23.3	25.64	26.39	26.82	27.56
0.99	35.74	40.63	42.48	43.19	44.82
% Average Pessimism of all refined estimates using Eq.8					
0.99	11.99	6.41	4.53	3.86	2.56
% Average Pessimism of all refined estimates using Eq.10					
0.99	19.84	13.85	11.97	11.06	9.63
% Improvement in accuracy compared to Chronos using Eq.8					
0.99	15.46	20.02	21.56	22.63	24.02
% Improvement in accuracy compared to Chronos using Eq.10					
0.99	4.91	9.25	10.75	11.57	12.84
	(Arch2)				
% Reduction in pessimism compared to unrefined WCET					
0.9	35.83	42.23	42.37	42.37	42.37
0.95	44.37	52.46	52.65	52.65	52.65
0.99	77.11	92.09	92.5	92.5	92.52
% Average Pessimism due to refinement using Eq.8					
0.99	20.66	4.82	3.97	3.97	3.96
% Average Pessimism due to refinement using Eq.10					
0.99	31.35	11.63	11.23	11.23	11.22
% Improvement in accuracy compared to Chronos using Eq.8					
0.99	148.88	191.62	191.62	191.62	191.65
% Improvement in accuracy compared to Chronos using Eq.10					
0.99	125.5	158.97	158.97	158.97	159

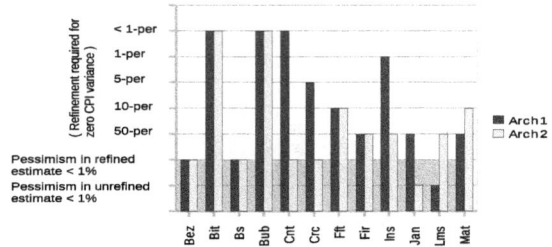

Figure 13: Amount of refinement required to reach zero variance of CPI within a sub-phase.

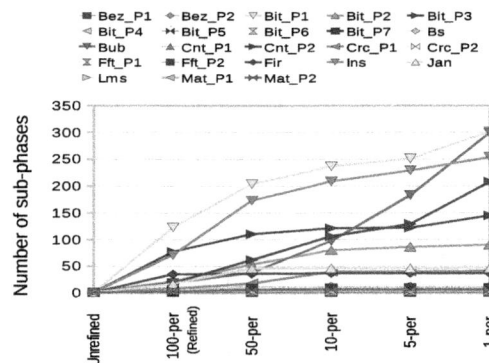

Figure 14: Impact of refinement on number of sub-phases on *Arch1.*

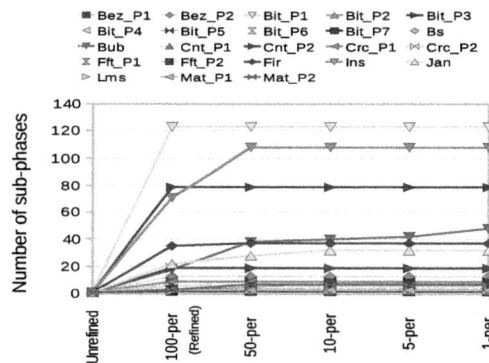

Figure 15: Impact of refinement on number of sub-phases on *Arch2.*

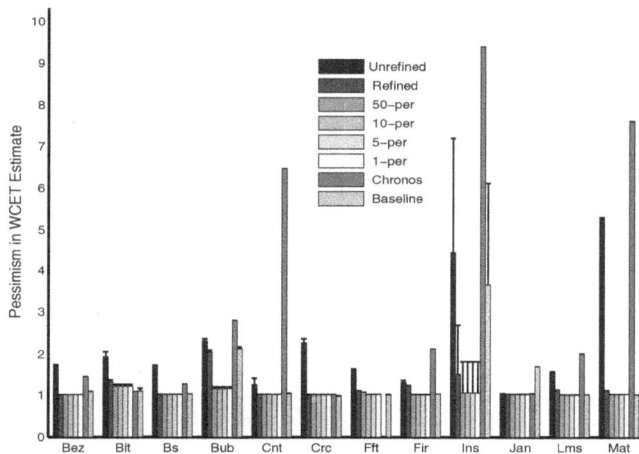

Figure 12: Comparison of WCET estimates using proposed method with *Chronos* and Baseline estimates on *Arch2.* (Chronos goes out of memory while analyzing *Fft(Arch2)*.)

racy of WCET. The benchmarks falling under the grey band have accurate WCET estimates either without refinement or when refined based on PC signatures alone and hence not considered for refinement based on CPI variance. *Bubble sort, Bitcount* and *Cnt(Arch1)* continue to show variance in CPI even beyond a point when CPI variance is limited to 1% of CPI variance of the original sub-phase. With CPI variance of a sub-phase limited to 10% of original sub-phase CPI variance, 4 out of 9(5 out of 7) benchmarks reach the point of maximum WCET accuracy on *Arch1(Arch2)*. The WCET estimates obtained by different kinds of refinement as described in the paper are evaluated with respect to *safety* by

running the benchmarks with a new set of 1000 inputs that were not considered for estimating CPI bounds. None of the estimates (refined based on PC signature, refined based on CPI variance) fall below maximum observed cycles at p={0.9, 0.95 and 0.99} on both architectures.

5.4 Impact of Refinement on Sub-phases

Refinement splits a phase into smaller sub-phases based on PC signature. When a sub-phase is refined based on CPI variance, many more smaller sub-phases are generated. Figures 14 and 15 plot the increase in number of sub-phases due to refinement based on PC signature(indicated by *100-per(Refined)* and refinement based on CPI variance (*50-per* to *1-per*). Number of sub-phases reaches a saturation point for 69%(96%) of phases by the time CPI variance of a sub-phase is limited to 50% of CPI variance in the sub-phase obtained by refinement based on PC signature alone on *Arch1*(*Arch2*). The reason could be that *Arch2* has an *in-order* processor with perfect branch prediction.

5.5 Compression

Table 4 compares the average sizes of trace obtained across all inputs before and after compression on both architectures. On an average, traces are compressed by a factor of 24.86(24.21) on *Arch1*(*Arch2*).

6. RELATED WORK

Program Phase Behavior: In this paper, we extend the phase based WCET analyzer that we proposed in [8] to use probabilistically bounded phase CPI to obtain more robust WCET estimates. The earlier model uses a function of mean CPI which has no probabilistic guarantees and is hence approximate. We also profile PC, CPI and IC of loop iterations to refine a phase with high CPI variation into smaller sub-phases. Phases described in [8] are architecture independent. The minimum sub-phase size in our case is architecture dependent. Although the PC bitmap which is determined by code structure is independent of the architecture, number of instructions executed within each sub-phase and CPI of a sub-phase is determined by the architecture.

Davies et al [9] record instruction pointers encountered during execution in the form of an integer vector(EIP) that are classified into phases based on grouping of EIP values. However their purpose is to have minimal error in estimating phase CPI by collecting least number of samples in a phase to reduce simulation effort. We consider all CPI samples in a phase, our objective being WCET estimation. Moreover we benefit from a large sample set, as confidence of Chebyshev bounds increases with the number of CPI samples(Eq.4). The phases in [9] are large($>=$100 million instructions) compared to our phases (50-100 instructions). The existence of phase behavior at different levels was first studied by [13] that use *sequitur* to classify the trace consisting of loop branch, procedure call and return instructions in the context of reducing simulation effort. In addition to PC Bitmap and IC of loop iterations, we classify phases based on measured CPI as well.

Measurement Based WCET Analysis: Measurements are taken either at the whole program level or at the level of basic blocks [11, 16, 22], program segments [18, 17] or paths [20]. Measurement usually generates a timing trace from which cost of each component is derived. These costs are combined using structural analysis and techniques like IPET [19] to estimate WCET. The location of instrumentation points influence trace size and accuracy of WCET estimate considerably [6]. Further, instrumentation should be least intrusive. The repetitive manner in which CPI varies in programs that exhibit phase behavior can be used to reduce instrumentation required in WCET analysis of such programs. We propose to instrument at the level of groups of loop iterations leading to a low instrumentation overhead of 1-2%. The number of iterations per group can be varied as per the requirement. Phases also help in compressing PC signatures considerably(Table 4). The issue of adequate program coverage is equally important in this work as it is for any other measurement based WCET analyzer.

Table 4: Average trace size across inputs before and after compression.

Phase	Trace size before compression	Trace size after compression		Compression factor	
		Arch1	Arch2	Arch1	Arch2
Bez_P1	1.8M	92K	68K	20:1	27:1
Bez_P2	50M	504K	312K	101:1	27:1
Bit_P1	24K	24K	24K	1:1	1:1
Bit_P2	48K	46K	23K	1.04:1	2.4:1
Bit_P3	160K	104K	96K	1.53:1	1.66:1
Bit_P4	28K	8K	8K	3.5:1	3.5:1
Bit_P5	32K	8K	8K	4:1	4:1
Bit_P6	32K	8K	8K	4:1	4:1
Bit_P7	32K	8K	8K	4:1	4:1
Bs	8K	8K	8K	1:1	1:1
Bub	23M	17M	11M	1.35:1	2.09:1
Cnt_P1	180K	28K	24K	6.42:1	7.5:1
Cnt_P2	212K	24K	24K	8.83:1	8.83:1
Crc_P1	8K	8K	8K	1:1	1:1
Crc_P2	780K	12K	8K	65:1	97.5:1
Fft_P1	220K	8K	20K	27.5:1	11:1
Fft_P2	220K	8K	20K	27.5:1	11:1
Fir	28K	8K	8K	3.5:1	3.5:1
Ins	21M	408K	328K	52.7:1	65.5:1
Jan	904K	4K	4K	223:1	223:1
Mat_P1	316K	48K	36K	6.58:1	8.77:1
Mat_P2	75M	5.2M	3.6M	14.4:1	20.8:1

Statistical WCET Analysis: Bernat et al [11] measure execution time of basic blocks(execution time profiles or ETPs) and note their relative frequencies. The ETPs are convolved together to give probabilistic WCET estimates using three different scenarios- ETPs are mutually independent, ETPs are dependent, dependency is not known. The phase based timing model views execution time as a product of instruction count(IC) and CPI and estimates program WCET in terms of phases instead of blocks, instructions, segments or paths. We use probabilistic bounds on phase CPI to compute WCET of a phase.

Edgar et al [21], Hansen et al [12] and Lu et al [24, 23] work with end to end program execution time samples and try to fit these samples into a *Gumbel* distribution using extreme value theory(EVT). Once the parameters of the distribution are computed, the estimate of WCET at various probabilities is available. Our work neither assumes any probability distribution of CPI samples nor tries to fit these samples into any distribution. We use Chebyshev's inequality that is applicable to *any* distribution, to compute bounds on CPI. The precision of our results will definitely improve if information regarding *true probability distribution* of CPI samples is available.

7. CONCLUSIONS AND FUTURE WORK

The repetitive manner in which CPI varies in programs exhibiting phase behavior can be used to reduce instrumentation in WCET analysis of such programs We propose a basic model in [8] that uses maximum of mean CPI observed across inputs to estimate WCET. However, WCET estimated thus, is approximate and has no probabilistic guarantees. In this paper, we extend this model to use probabilistically bounded phase CPI. Using CPI bound along with maximum IC results in a robust WCET that can be estimated at the desired probability. The proposed method assumes no probability distribution of CPI samples and uses Chebyshev's inequality to compute bounds of CPI. The accuracy of CPI bound will certainly improve if the true probability distribution is known. Chebyshev's inequality works well with phases that exhibit low variance in CPI resulting in tight CPI bounds and accurate WCET estimates (Examples: *Fir(Arch1)*, *Jan(Arch2)* and *Lms(Arch1)*). Some phases exhibit high variance in CPI. Applying Chebyshev's inequality for such phases results in pessimistic WCET estimates (*Mat(Arch2)*). To isolate points of high variation in CPI, we refine such phases into smaller sub-phases based on PC signatures collected using profiling. We observe the following results for p=0.99. Refinement based on signatures reduces average pessimism of WCET by 36%(77%) on *Arch1(Arch2)*. Refinement is designed to enable the user to control variance of CPI within a sub-phase, which is useful in programs like *Bubble sort* wherein CPI varies throughout program execution and points of high variation of CPI cannot be isolated based on PC signatures alone. We split a sub-phase into four levels (CPI variance within the sub-phase is limited to 50%, 10%, 5% and 1% of average CPI variance of the sub-phase obtained by refinement based on PC signature). Refining *Bubble sort (Arch1)* at these four levels reduces pessimism by 21%, 31%, 35% and 42% respectively.

The following improvements are with respect to *Chronos* at p=0.99. Average accuracy of WCET obtained by refinement based on signature improves by 15%(149%) on *Arch1(Arch2)* using maximum observed windows and by 5%(125%) on *Arch1(Arch2)* using theoretically bounded windows. Average accuracy of WCET continues to improve following refinement at each of these four levels of CPI variance on *Arch1* by {20%, 21%, 23% and 24%} using maximum observed windows and by {9%, 11%, 12% and 13%} using theoretical maximum windows). On *Arch2*, average accuracy improves by refinement at the first level(50%) by 192% (using maximum observed windows) and 159% using theoretical maximum windows. The improvement is marginal beyond the first level. The process of collecting PC signatures through profiling is completely independent of program phase detection and classification. It would be interesting to see if PC signatures can subsume program phase detection and classification. The amount of instrumentation in the proposed method can be varied by modifying the window size depending on the accuracy requirement and availability of resources. Future work will analyze the impact of window size on accuracy of WCET and evaluate the proposed method on larger programs and more complex architectures.

Acknowledgements: We thank Indrajit Bhattacharya, T. Matthew Jacob, Rupesh Nasre and Meghana Mande for their valuable suggestions on several aspects of this work. We are grateful for the financial support provided by the IMPECS project during the course of this research. We would also like to thank the anonymous reviewers for their suggestions to improve this paper.

8. REFERENCES

[1] http://euler.slu.edu/~fritts/mediabench.

[2] http://www.comp.nus.edu.sg/~rpembed/chronos/download.html.

[3] http://www.mrtc.mdh.se/projects/wcet/benchmarks.html.

[4] http://www.simplescalar.com.

[5] A. Betts et al. Hybrid Measurement-Based WCET Analysis at the Source Level using Object-level Traces. In *Proceedings of WCET 2010*, pages 54–63.

[6] A. Betts et al. WCET Analysis of Component-Based Systems using Timing Traces. In *Proceedings of ICECCS 2011*, pages 13–22.

[7] A. Colin et al. Experimental Evaluation of Code Properties for WCET Analysis. In *Proceedings of RTSS 2008*, pages 190–199.

[8] A. Ravindar et al. Implications of Program Phase Behavior on Timing Analysis. In *Proceedings of INTERACT 2011*, pages 71–79.

[9] B. Davies et al. iPART: An Automated Phase Detection and Recognition Tool. *Technical Report.*, IR-TR-2004-1.

[10] D. Griffin et al. Realism in Statistical Analysis of Worst Case Execution Times. In *Proceedings of WCET 2010*, pages 44–53.

[11] G. Bernat et al. WCET Analysis of Probabilistic Hard Real-Time Systems. In *Proceedings of RTSS 2002*, pages 279–288.

[12] J. Hansen et al. Statistical Based WCET Estimation and Validation. In *Proceedings of ECRTS 2009*, pages 123–133.

[13] J. Lau et al. Motivation for Variable Length Intervals and Hierarchical Phase Behavior. In *Proceedings of ISPASS 2005*, pages 135–146.

[14] J. Lau et al. Selecting Software Phase Markers with Code Structural Analysis. In *Proceedings of CGO 2006*, pages 135–146.

[15] K. Ghani et al. Automatic Test Data Generation for Multiple Condition and MC/DC Coverage. In *Proceedings of ICSEA 2009*, pages 152–157.

[16] M. Corti et al. Approximation of Worst-Case Execution Time for Preemptive Multitasking Systems. In *Proceedings of LCTES 2000*, pages 178–198.

[17] M. Zolda et al. Context-Sensitive Measurement-Based Worst-Case Execution Time Estimation. In *Proceedings of RTCSA 2011*, pages 243–250.

[18] M. Zolda et al. Towards Adaptable Control Flow Segmentation for Measurement-Based Execution Time Analysis. In *Proceedings of RTNS 2009*.

[19] R. Wilhelm et al. The Worst-Case Execution Time Problem - Overview of Methods and Survey of Tools. *ACM Trans. Embed. Syst.*, 7(3), April 2008.

[20] S. A. Seshia et al. Game-Theoretic Timing Analysis. In *Proceedings of ICCAD 2008*, pages 575–582.

[21] S. Edgar et al. Statistical Analysis of WCET for Scheduling. In *Proceedings of RTSS 2001*, pages 215–224.

[22] S. Stattelmann et al. On the Use of Context Information for Precise Measurement-Based Execution Time Estimation. In *Proceedings of WCET 2010*, pages 64–76.

[23] Y. Lu et al. A Trace-Based Statistical Worst-Case Execution Time Analysis of Component-Based Real-Time Embedded Systems. In *Proceedings of ETFA 2011*.

[24] Y. Lu et al. A New Way about using Statistical Analysis of Worst-Case Execution Times. *ACM SIGBED Review*, 8(2), September 2011.

[25] S. M. Ross. *Introduction to Probability and Statistics for Engineers and Scientists*. Wiley, 2009.

Assessing the Suitability of the NGMP Multi-core Processor in the Space Domain

Mikel Fernández[†]
mikel.fernandez@bsc.es

Roberto Gioiosa[†]
roberto.gioiosa@bsc.es

Eduardo Quiñones[†]
eduardo.quinones@bsc.es

Luca Fossati[‡]
luca.fossati@esa.int

Marco Zulianello[‡]
marco.zulianello@esa.int

Francisco J. Cazorla[†,*]
francisco.cazorla@bsc.es

[†] Barcelona Supercomputing
Center
C/Jordi Girona, 31
08034 Barcelona (Spain)

[‡] European Space Agency
ESTEC, Postbus 299
2200 AG Noordwijk (The
Netherlands)

[*] IIIA-CSIC
Campus UAB
08193 Bellaterra
Cerdanyola del Valles (Spain)

ABSTRACT

Multi-core processors are increasingly being considered as a means to provide the performance required by future safety-critical embedded systems. In this line, Aeroflex Gaisler has developed, in conjunction with the European Space Agency, the NGMP, a quad-core processor to be used in the future space missions of the Agency. Unfortunately, the use of multi-core processors in industrial domains is not straightforward since it poses various challenges on the timing behavior of the system. This is mainly due to the interferences tasks suffer when accessing hardware shared resources and which can affect their WCET. Although the effect of inter-task interferences in multi-core shared resources on real-time applications has received attention from academia, most of the solutions proposed require hardware changes. The lack of quantitative studies of the slowdown on applications' performance caused by inter-task interferences on real COTS multi-core processors, limit their use by industry.

As a first step to understand the effect of inter-task interference in real COTS processors, this paper evaluates the timing predictability properties of the NGMP. In particular, we measure the maximum variation on tasks' execution time due to inter-task interferences accessing NGMP's shared hardware resources. To that end, we use a set of specialized micro-benchmarks designed to stress specific processor shared resources. The results of this can be useful for developing interference-aware WCET estimation methodologies and scheduling algorithms for real-time applications running on embedded multi-core processors.

Categories and Subject Descriptors

C.3 [**Computer Systems Organization**]: Special Purpose and Application-based Systems—*Real-time and Em-bedded Systems*; C.4 [**Computer Systems Organization**]: Performance of Systems

General Terms

Experimentation, Measurement, Performance

Keywords

Multi-core, Real-time, WCET, COTS Processors

1. INTRODUCTION

The market for Critical Real-Time Embedded Systems (CRTES) has experienced an unprecedented growth in recent years, and is expected to grow in the foreseeable future [5][11]. Because of the competition on functional value, CRTES industry is faced with rising demands for greater performance and hence increased computing power, as well as to reduce the number of processing units used in the system [15]. Such high performance requirements could be met by designing more complex processors with longer pipelines, out of order execution, and higher clock frequency. However, using complex processor cores in CRTES designs is problematic because they could introduce timing anomalies [14] due to the their non-deterministic run-time behaviour. Moreover, the high energy requirements of such complex processors do not satisfy the low-power constraints and the severe cost limitations common in most embedded systems.

Another way to meet high performance requirements is by means of multi-core processors. Multi-cores offer better performance per watt than single-core processors, while maintaining a relatively simple processor design. Moreover, multi-core processors ideally enable co-hosting applications with different requirements (e.g. high data processing demand and stringent time criticality). Co-hosting non-safety and safety critical applications on a common powerful multi-core processor brings many advantages to the embedded system market, allowing to schedule a higher number of tasks on a single processor hence maximizing the hardware utilization while cost, size, weight and power requirements are reduced. This is especially important for the space industry where weight reduction is essential.

Even if multi-core processors may offer several benefits to embedded systems, their use is not straightforward. First of all, it is necessary to prevent that one application corrupts the state of other applications ensuring that low-criticality applications cannot affect high-criticality ones. This can be accomplished by providing software isolation and has been done within the space domain through the use of hypervisors [3]. CRTES also require guarantees on the timing predictability of the system. Unfortunately, multi-core processors are much harder to time analyse than single-core processors, because of inter-task interferences accessing hardware shared resources (shared bus, shared cache, main memory, etc.): Inter-task interferences appear when two or more tasks that share a resource try to access it at the same time. To handle this contention an arbitration mechanism is required, potentially affecting the execution time and WCET of running tasks. As a result, providing a meaningful timing analysis becomes extremely difficult because the execution time of a task may change depending on the other tasks running simultaneously. Hence, understanding and controlling inter-task interferences is mandatory to provide time analysability, so that the activity of tasks has a bounded effect on the execution of the most critical ones.

In this paper we evaluate the suitability for CRTES of the latest multi-core processor used by the European Space Agency, the NGMP (Next Generation Multi-Purpose Microprocessor). The NGMP is a LEON4-based quad-core processor, developed by Aeroflex Gaisler together with the European Space Agency [2]. The NGMP has private data and instruction caches per core. Each core access to the shared L2 through the AMBA AHB processor bus [1]. The memory bandwidth is also shared by all cores. In particular, this paper focuses on providing accurate figures on the execution time variation introduced by four of the main sources of inter-task interferences: the AMBA AHB processor bus, the shared L2 cache, the shared memory controller and the write-through policy of the L1 data cache.

Approach: To reach these objectives, we use a set of specialized micro-benchmarks [9][10][16][25] designed to stress each of the processors resources considered in this paper. The micro-benchmarks are designed to stress a particular processor resource like the L1 data cache, or the bus. By means of those micro-benchmarks we identify in which hardware shared resources the interaction among tasks significantly affects their execution time. The higher the variability due to inter-task interferences the lower the suitability of the architecture to real-time environments. We do our analysis on both Linux and RTEMS [29] with a two fold-objective: increasing the confidence on the results obtained in our study and determining whether inter-task interferences effects are the same under both operating systems.

Our results show that applications may experience high execution time variations due to inter-task interferences when executed in the NGMP under both RTEMS and Linux. In particular, we observe the following:

- When several bus-hungry tasks try to access at the same time the AMBA AHB processor bus, they may suffer a slowdown of up to 1.83x in Linux and 1.95x in RTEMS.

- The combined effect of the interaction in the memory controller and the AMBA AHB processor bus introduces a slowdown on applications' performance of 2.6x for Linux and 3.4x for RTEMS.

- The combined effect of the three resources, i.e. AMBA AHB processor bus, L2 cache and memory controller

makes the execution time of applications increase up to 4.3x for Linux and more than 9x for RTEMS.

- Finally, and more surprisingly, applications with high number of stores may suffer slowdowns higher than 19x. This is due to the fact that the first level data cache is write-through, so every single store has to go to L2, suffering significant slowdowns.

The different effect of inter-task interferences under Linux and RTEMS is due to the fact that under RTEMS tasks are less affected by the OS operation (noise), having higher performance when run in isolation. As a result, when the task runs with other micro-benchmarks its performance degradation is higher.

We confirm our results on the micro-benchmarks with real-time benchmarks, EEMBC Automotive, on which we observe a maximum slowdown of 5.5x. We identify the average number of stores per instruction as the main factor determining the sensitivity of an application to inter-task interferences in the NGMP architecture.

Contribution: Although the effect of inter-task interferences in multi-core hardware shared resources on real-time applications have received significant attention by the research community (e.g. [28] [15][19][6][23]), most of the works have focused on simulation environments or involve hardware changes. Currently, the lack of quantitative studies on inter-task interferences on real COTS multi-core processors, limit their potential use by industry. This paper represents an step in that direction: We evaluate, under heavy load conditions, the inter-task interference impact of NGMP shared resources on applications' execution time. On the one hand, this study is a first step towards providing safe WCET bounds to the execution time of applications in the NGMP. On the other hand, this can also help determining how applications have to be sheduled to reduce inter-task interferences effect on WCET bounds. Both these topics are left as future work.

The rest of this paper is organized as follows. In Section 2 we show introduce the NGMP architecture. In Section 3 we explain the micro-benchmarks we use in this study. Section 4 presents our experimental setup. Section 5 shows the main results we have obtained under Linux and Section 6 the ones we obtained under RTEMS. Section 7 discusses the applicability of the results of this study. Section 8 describes the related work. Finally, Section 9 summarizes the main conclusions of this study and future lines of research.

2. INTRODUCTION TO THE NGMP

The NGMP is a SPARC V8 quad-core processor, developed by Aeroflex Gaisler and the European Space Agency featuring the latest LEON core design, LEON4, which provides a significant performance increase compared to earlier LEON processors [8][4]. The LEON4 is a 32-bit 7-stage pipeline processor, comprising an always-taken branch predictor and private data and instruction caches of 16 KB each. Both the instruction and the data cahche have 32-byte lines and are 4-way associative. The data caches employs a write-through with no-allocate miss policy.

In the NGMP, each LEON4-core connects to a shared 256 KB L2 cache through an AMBA AHB processor bus [1] with a 128-bit data width and round-robin arbitration policy. The L2 cache uses the LRU replacement algorithm

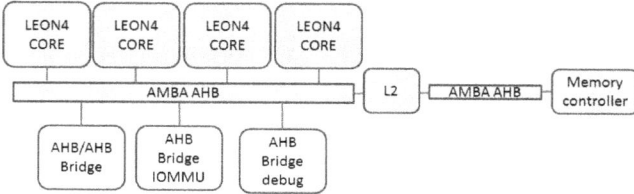

Figure 1: Block diagram of the part of the NGMP architecture studied in this paper

implementing a write-back, write-allocate policy. The L2 cache connects to the memory controller through a single memory channel shared by all cores (see Figure 1).

Three AHB bridges connect the AHB processor bus to other I/O and debugging specific AMBA buses: (1) a 128-bit to 32-bit unidirectional AHB-to-AHB bridge from debug bus to processor bus, (2) a 128-bit to 32-bit unidirectional AHB-to-AHB bridge from processor bus to slave I/O bus and (3) a 32-bit to 128-bit unidirectional AHB-to-AHB bridge with IOMMU from master I/O bus to processor bus. Although these three specific buses are not the focus of our study, they should be considered when providing timing analysis for the NGMP.

The NGMP provides a set of performance counters that enable collecting run-time information about certain events of the processors. In this study we have used the following performance counters: data and instruction cache misses, L2 cache misses, total number of executed instructions, number of memory operations, number of executed cycles, and processor AMBA bus usage.

3. MICRO-BENCHMARKS

In a multi-core architecture, the performance of one process tightly depends on the other processes running simultaneously and on their specific execution phases. Programs go through different execution phases in which the effect of inter-task interference may vary significantly. Evaluating all possible combinations of programs that might be running together and their different execution phases is not feasible.

Instead, in this paper we execute the application under analysis into different high-load inter-task interference scenarios. In order to build a basic knowledge of inter-task interference effects we developed a set of synthetic micro-benchmarks, each of them stressing a specific processor characteristic. Benchmarks are designed to cause high load on a specific hardware resource, allowing us to isolate independent behaviours of a specific shared resource. Furthermore, micro-benchmarks have been designed to provide higher flexibility and compatibility with other processor architectures due to their simplicity.

3.1 Stressing the cache hierarchy

In most shared-memory, symmetric multi-core architectures, like the NGMP, running tasks interact in the cache hierarchy. For this reason we have designed and implemented five micro-benchmarks which allow exercising the different hardware shared resource that form the cache hierarchy of the NGMP. Next, we define the characteristics of each micro-benchmark. Note that micro-benchmarks are independent tasks that do not share any data:

- *L1.* This micro-benchmark accesses a vector with a data footprint smaller than 16 KB, fitting completely

Table 1: code listing for $L2_{40}$, $L2_{200}$ and $L2_{miss}$

(a) Initialization of the array to be accessed by the micro-benchmark

```
for(cnt=0; cnt<array_size; cnt+=stride){
   if(cnt<array_size-stride)
      M[cnt] = (int*)&M[cnt+stride];
   else
      M[cnt] = (int*)M;
}
```

(b) Actual code of the micro-benchmark

```
a=&M[0];
for (i=0; i<it; i++) {
   b=*a; a=*b
   b=*a; a=*b
       ... // repeated 126 more times
}
```

inside the data cache. Hence, it does not stress the L2 of the AHB processor bus.

- $L2_{40}$. It accesses a vector with a data footprint of 40 KB, so most loads miss in data cache and hit in L2 cache. Hence, it stresses the data cache, the processor AHB AMBA bus and, to a lesser extent, the L2 cache.

- $L2_{200}$. It accesses a vector with a data footprint of 200KB with the purpose of generating L2 cache hits when run alone and L2 cache misses when run together with other L2 stressing micro-benchmarks. Hence, it stresses the data cache, the processor AHB AMBA bus and the L2 cache.

- $L2_{miss}$. It accesses a vector with a data footprint of 1 MB, generating systematic misses in the L2 cache. Hence, it stresses the data cache, the processor AHB AMBA bus, the L2 cache, the memory AHB AMBA bus and the memory controller.

- $L2_{st}$. This benchmark simply writes to a 40KB vector. Hence, it mainly executes store operations.

All micro-benchmarks, except $L2_{st}$, which uses direct addressing, employ *pointer chasing* to access memory: in each location of the vector we store the address of the next memory location to be accessed. By doing so, no instructions are required to compute the memory address to be accessed. Moreover, the data inside the vector is stored such that the stride controls which particular cache level (L1 or L2) is accessed. It is also important to remark that micro-benchmarks are small enough to fit inside the instruction cache. In fact, in this study we do not consider the effect of the L1 instruction cache, we rather focus on the L1 data and the L2 cache.

The first four micro-benchmarks have the same structure, see Table 1. They are mainly composed of loads (more than 95% of the total instruction count), that access a vector with a variable data footprint. The micro-benchmark code is contained inside a main loop.

In the initialization code, see Table 1(a), the *stride* and the *array_size* determine how often the micro-benchmark will hit/miss in each cache level: The stride is always set to prevent several accesses to the same cache line. The *array_size* is set to ensure that a benchmark hits/misses in a desired

Table 2: code listing for L2$_{st}$ microbencmarks

(a) Initialization of the array to
be accessed by the st microbenchmark

```
st_array     =
st_pointer = (int*)malloc(array_size);
```

(b) Actual code of the st microbenchmark

```
#define STRIDE 32
int data = 4;     // data may be any integer value
for (i=0; i<it; i++) {
    __asm__ __volatile__ (
        "st %0, [%1]"            "\n\t"
        "st %0, [%1+32]"         "\n\t"
        "st %0, [%1+64]"         "\n\t"
                  ...
        "st %0, [%1+4032]"       "\n\t"
        "add %1, 4064, %1"       "\n\t"
        "st %0, [%1]"            "\n\t"
        "st %0, [%1+32]"         "\n\t"
                  ... // total of 508 stores
    :
    : "r"(data), "r"(st_pointer)
    );

    if (st_pointer+509*STRIDE >=
        st_array+array_size)
            st_pointer = st_array;
    else
            st_pointer +=STRIDE;
}
```

cache level. In the code of the micro-benchmark, Table 1(b), every execution of the loop body, called a micro-iteration, contains 128 loads, 1 cmp, 1 br and 1 nop instructions. The number of micro-iterations is so that the percentage of control operations of the loop is less than 5%.

The structure of the L2$_{st}$ micro-benchmark is a bit different, see Table 2. For this benchmark GCC inline assembler syntax is used: *%0* is replaced by *data*, a variable containing the value to be stored, and *%1* is replaced by *st_pointer*, a pointer to access the allocated array. The destination memory address is defined by a pointer plus an immediate value (*st_pointer* plus the numeric value in Table 2).

Each store instruction has a different immediate value, where each immediate equals the previous one plus the stride. In Table 2, a 32-byte stride is used. This methodology presents the limitation that the maximum allowed immediate value in the target architecture is 4095. This limitation is overcame by resetting the immediate value and increasing *st_pointer*. After completion of an iteration, *st_array* bounds are checked to make sure it does not overflow during the next iteration.

All micro-benchmarks were compiled with gcc with the -O2 option and their object code was verified in order to guarantee that the benchmarks retain the desired characteristics. Note that that all micro-benchmarks are independent processes so they do not share data, even when several copies of the same benchmark run at the same time.

4. EXPERIMENTAL SETUP

4.1 Experimental Methodology

All the experiments presented in this paper have been obtained using a ML510 embedded development platform.

This platform contains a Virtex 5 FPGA that implements a preliminary design of the NGMP operating at 70Mhz. Due to FPGA space limitation, each core lacks the floating point unit. The NGMP under this implementation comprises a 64-bit data DDR2-800 memory interface with a channel frequency of 140 MHz. This frequency-ratio between the NGMP and the memory has important effect on our conclusions: the effect of memory controller interferences on the execution time of programs will be higher in the final implementation of NGMP than in our FPGA implementation. Unfortunately, at the time of carrying out this study, the only available implementation of an NGMP processor is on a FPGA.

We designed an Execution Infrastructure that allows the execution of workloads comprised of different applications and it is compatible with both operating systems, i.e. Linux and RTEMS. The Execution Infrastrcutre facilitates the study of Linux- and RTEMS-based applications under different inter-task interferences scenarios by measuring its execution time variation.

For the experiments on Linux we use Linux 2.6.36 operating system (OS). As our experiments were executed on a full-flegded OS, they were designed to provide reliable results and minimize the impact of the OS to our measurements [12, 21, 26]. To avoid task migration among different cores of a processor, we bound each benchmark to the corresponding core using the *sched_setaffinity* system call.

We also use RTEMS 4.10 provided by Aeroflex Gailser as part of the Development package for NGMP. For the experiments presented in this paper, RTEMS was configured as a multi-processor application with 4 cores, where each core was assigned a 8MB memory segment, 4MB of which were used as stack. Three global semaphores were used to synchronize cores, and a single global RTEMS partition was used to allocate output buffers. Each core uses a GPTIMER as a system clock generator, which is configured to provide millisecond resolution.

4.2 Application Workloads

In order to empirically evaluate the maximum application delay due to inter-task interferences, we have used two different types workloads: (1) *micro-benchmark workloads*, composed of only micro-benchmarks, and (2) *EEMBC workloads* composed of both EEMBC Autobench benchmarks [22] and micro-benchmarks. The former allows us to generate the worst possible delay *any* application might suffer due conflicts in the specific resource (or set of resources) exercised by the micro-benchmark. The latter allows us to see the effect that the specific resource (or set of resources) on a specific application, in this case an EEMBC benchmark.

The micro-benchmark workloads are formed by four different workloads that will continuously stress a given resource (or set of resources):

1. L2$_{40}$ workload to analyze processor AHB AMBA bus that connects cores to L2.

2. L2$_{miss}$ workload to analyze the memory controller and memory AHB AMBA bus that connects the L2 cache with the main memory and the processor AHB AMBA bus.

3. L2$_{200}$ workload to analyze the memory controller and memory AHB AMBA bus that connects the L2 cache

Table 3: L1 data cache miss ratio, L2 miss ratio and processor AHB AMBA bus utilization per process when we simultaneously run 1, 2 and 4 copies of the same micro-benchmark, each on a different core.

	Data cache miss (%)			L2 cache miss (%)			% of stores
No. of copies →	1	2	4	1	2	4	1
L1	0.01	0.01	0.01	0.01	0.01	0.01	0.04
$L2_{40}$	99.7	99.7	99.6	0.08	0.06	5.94	0.15
$L2_{200}$	99.5	99.0	98.1	31.5	88.4	98.6	0.20
$L2_{miss}$	99.2	99.0	98.1	100	99.6	98.5	0.36
$L2_{st}$	0.02	0.09	0.19	0.03	0.04	0.04	95.3

with the main memory, the shared L2 cache and the processor AHB AMBA bus.

4. $L2_{st}$, $L2_{40}$, $L2_{200}$ and $L2_{miss}$ workloads to analyze the effect of write-through policy in the L1 data cache.

The EEMBC workloads are formed by multiple copies of the same benchmark, as well as one EEMBC benchmark and multiple micro-benchmarks. EEMBC Autobench suite is a well-known benchmark suite that reflects the current real world demands of embedded systems.

Note that in this paper we are not interested in scheduling aspects so all the experiments we run comprise workloads of 4 or less applications running simultaneously, i.e. at most one application per core.

4.3 Metrics

In order to evaluate the impact that inter-task interferences have on the execution time, the application under study is, in a first step, run in isolation, i.e. without suffering any interferences coming from other tasks. In a second step, the application is run simultaneously with other applications, i.e. within a workload. Finally, we measure the inter-task interferences in shared resources and their effect in execution time as the ratio between the execution time of the program in isolation and its execution time when it runs as part of a workload, as shown in Equation 1, where $Exec.Time_{wokload}$ is the execution of the application under consideration when it runs in multi-core mode as part of a workload.

$$Execution\ Time\ Slodown = \frac{Exec.Time_{wokload}}{Exec.Time_{isolation}} \quad (1)$$

Execution time is measured using the *gettimeofday()* call for Linux. On RTEMS a single *GPTIMER* was used, and a different timer assigned to each core.

Other metrics are also considered such as L1 and L2 cache misses, processor AHB AMBA bus utilization, number of load and store instructions executed, and total number of instructions executed. Average cache miss rates are measured per 100 instructions.

5. RESULTS UNDER LINUX

This section evaluates the execution time variability of both workloads, i.e. micro-benchmarks and EEMBC workloads, running under Linux.

5.1 Micro-benchmark Validation

In order to guarantee that micro-benchmarks generate significant inter-task interferences, it is fundamental to provide arguments about the fact the they significantly stress shared

processor resources. To that end, we simultaneously executed several copies (1, 2 and 4) of each micro-benchmark, and measure the slowdown they suffer due to inter-task interferences using the performance monitoring support provided by the NGMP. For each benchmark we measure (1) the number of memory operations per instruction, (2) the miss rate in the data cache, (3) the miss rate in the L2 cache and (4) the processor AHB AMBA bus utilization. Table 3 summarizes the behaviour of each micro-benchmark.

As expected, the L1 micro-benchmark does not stress shared resources at all, having a data cache miss rate of almost 0. Instead, $L2_{40}$, $L2_{200}$ and $L2_{miss}$ access the processor bus frequently. As a result, the processor AHB AMBA bus utilization is almost 100% when running 4 copies of the benchmarks (this result is not shown in Table 3).

$L2_{40}$ does not stress much the memory controller, even four copies. In the worst case, $L2_{40}$ has 6% L2 cache miss rate since its data footprint is small enough to fit inside the L2 cache. $L2_{200}$ suffers some L2 misses in isolation that significantly increase when several copies are run (up to 88% with 2 copies and 99% with 4 copies). $L2_{miss}$ stresses always all shared resources, having roughly the same L2 cache miss rate (99%) regardless of the number of copies. Finally, the $L2_{st}$ benchmark executes store opeartions which, due to the write-through policy of the data L1 cache, are written into the L2 cache. As a result $L2_{st}$ is sensitive to L2 occupancy, suffering significant slowdowns when it runswith other L2 stressing benchmarks.

5.2 Processor AHB AMBA Bus

With this first experiment we want to determine the effect that interactions in the processor AHB AMBA bus have on program execution time. To that end, we use the $L2_{40}$ micro-benchmark that has a high data cache miss rate and hits in L2, as its data footprint is higher than the size of data cache but smaller than the L2. Moreover, when running up to four copies of $L2_{40}$, the overall data footprint, i.e. 160 KB, fits in the L2 cache, so in general it does not generate evictions in the L2 cache. As a result, under all core counts most access to cache goes to the L2 and the execution time slowdown experienced when several copies of $L2_{40}$ are run simultaneously is due to inter-task interferences in the processor AHB AMBA bus.

The first set of bars in Figure 2 shows the execution time slowdown of the $L2_{40}$ when we simultaneously run several copies of it in different cores. All values are normalized to $L2_{40}$ execution time when running in isolation. We observe that the worst delay due to sharing the AMBA bus is 12% when two tasks are executed and 83% when 4 tasks are executed. This slowdown is relatively moderate. These results are higher than those reported in [17]: 27% slowdown for a configuration comprising 4 cores. The may reason behind

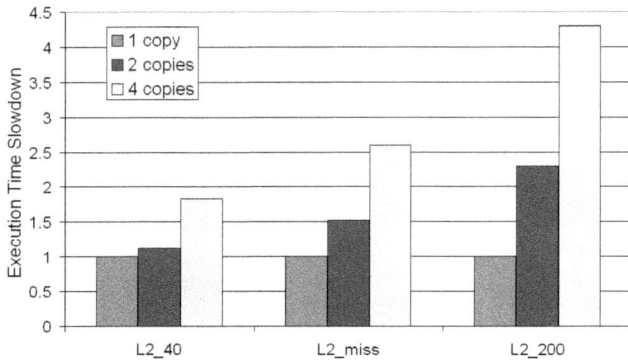

Figure 2: Execution time slowdown of $L2_{40}$, $L2_{miss}$ and $L2_{200}$ under different workloads

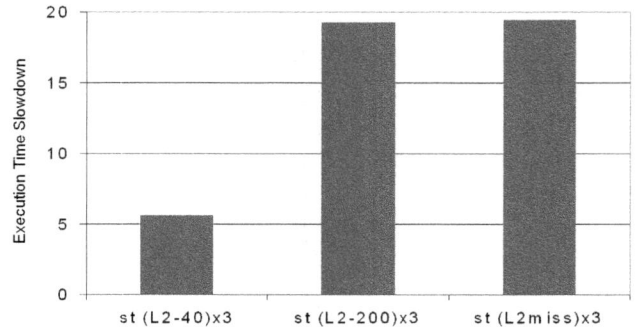

Figure 3: Execution time slowdown of $L2_{st}$ when run against $L2_{40}$, $L2_{200}$ and $L2_{miss}$ for Linux

this difference is that in [17] the bus model used is simpler, having low latency and hence less effect on applications' performance.

5.3 Memory Controller and Processor AHB AMBA Bus

This experiment aims at determining the effect of inter-task interferences generated at the memory controller, the memory AHB AMBA bus and the processor AHB AMBA bus on program's execution time. We use the $L2_{miss}$ micro-benchmark that misses in L1 and L2 frequently, regardless of the workload in which it runs. This is so because its data footprint is much higher than the L2 cache cache size. Hence, regardless of the workload within it runs, the $L2_{miss}$ generates systematic L2 misses without taking advantage of the L2 cache at all.

The second set of bars in Figure 2 shows the execution time slowdown that $L2_{miss}$ suffers when it runs with other copies of $L2_{miss}$. We observe that the access to the main memory introduces an execution time variation up to 1.5x and 2.6x when considering 2 and 4 $L2_{miss}$ micro-benchmarks respectively. These slowdowns due to interactions in the memory controller and the AHB AMBA bus are similator to those reported in [20], in which authors measured a WCET slowdown of 3x due to interferences in the access to memory.

By comparing the first and second set of bars in Figure 2 we can conclude that the main memory introduces significantly higher execution time variation that the AMBA AHB processor bus.

5.4 Memory Controller, L2 cache and Processor AHB AMBA Bus

In this experiment we want to determine the overall effect of inter-task interferences generated in each of the memory hierarchy components, i.e. the memory controller, the L2 cache and the processor AHB AMBA buses. To that end, we consider the $L2_{200}$ micro-benchmark with a data footprint of 200 KB. When running in isolation the $L2_{200}$ almost always misses in the data cache and hits in L2, taking profit of the L2 cache. However, when running within a workload composed of four copies of $L2_{200}$, the micro-benchmark does not take advantage of the L2 cache as each task may evict data from other tasks.

The third set of bars in Figure 2 shows the execution time

slowdown that $L2_{200}$ suffers when we run it simultaneously with other copies of $L2_{200}$. We observe that the inter-task interferences generated by memory hierarchy components, introduce an execution time variation up to 2.3x and 4.3x when considering 2 and 4 $L2_{200}$ micro-benchmarks respectively. By comparing the second and third set of bars in Figure 2 we conclude that in the worst case L2 cache interferences, makes the execution time vary from 2.6x to 4.3x, being still the memory controller and the bandwidth to memory the shared resources that introduces the highest execution time variation.

5.5 Effect of Store operations

Store operations introduce higher execution time variability than load operations due to the write policy implemented in the L1 data and L2 caches of the NGMP, i.e. write-through and write-back respectively. This makes every store instruction to always access to the AMBA AHB processor bus and the L2 cache, even if the data footprint of the program fits the L1. As a result, stores are delayed due to interferences accessing the AMBA AHB processor bus and the L2 cache and, in addition, stores create additional traffic on the bus. Moreover, if a store evicts a dirty line in L2 it is stalled until the data is copied to main memory.

In order to evaluate the impact of interferences caused by cache stressing benchmarks on store intensive benchmark ($L2_{st}$), we consider three instances of $L2_{40}$, $L2_{200}$ and $L2_{miss}$. Figure 3 shows the execution time slowdown of $L2_{st}$ when running it simultaneously with 3 instances of $L2_{40}$, $L2_{200}$ and $L2_{miss}$, respectively labelled as $st(L2_{40})x3$, $st(L2_{200})x3$ and $st(L2_{miss})x3$.

In case of the $st(L2_{40})x3$ workload, the slowdown suffered by $L2_{st}$ is 5x, mainly due to conflicts on the AMBA AHB Bus, as well as and dirty cache lines. $L2_{st}$ has a data footprint similar of $L2_{40}$ which make the overall footprint to fit in L2 cache (40 KB x 4). However, performance degradation increases up to 19x when running it with $L2_{200}$ and $L2_{miss}$ due to the fact that stores that miss in L2, may evict dirty lines. This cause the store operation to be stalled until the dirty line is written back to main memory and the new line is brought into the cache, before the store writes its value on the new line.

This shows that, even if the data footprint of the store micro-benchmark fits in the data cache, the fact that it has to access to the L2 and hence use the AMBA AHB Processor

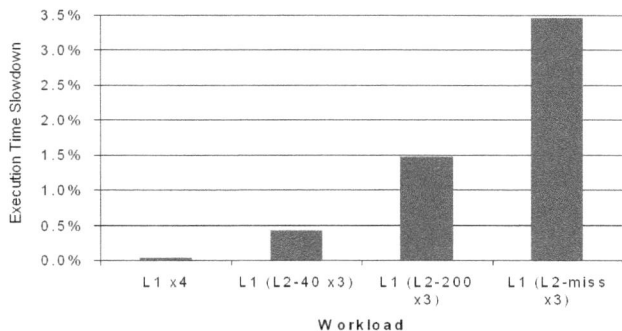

Figure 4: Execution time slowdown of L1 when running within several workloads composed of 3 L1, $L2_{40}$, $L2_{200}$ and $L2_{miss}$

bus on every store operation, as well as memory access at every dirty cache line eviction, make it quite sensitive to other benchmarks using the bus.

We conclude that programs with a high density of store instructions may suffer high slowdowns even if they fit in data cache, mainly if they are run concurrently with programs using the L2 cache or the AMBA processor bus extensively.

5.6 Effect of Intra-Core Resources

While previous sections evaluated the impact of using the shared resources of the cache hierarchy, this section evaluates the impact of not using them.

Figure 4 shows the execution time slowdown of the L1 benchmark when running it within several 4-application workloads, taking as a baseline its execution time running in isolation. In the experiment, L1 runs with three copies of L1, $L2_{40}$, $L2_{200}$ and $L2_{miss}$, labeled as L1 x4, L1 ($L2_{40}$ x3) L1 ($L2_{200}$ x3) and L1 ($L2_{miss}$ x3) respectively.

We observe no noticeable slowdown, having a maximum execution time variation of less than 3,5% when running within a workload composed of the $L2_{miss}$ micro-benchmarks.

5.7 Impact of inter-task interferences on EEMBC

In this section we consider the EEMBC AutoBench to confirm the results we obtained in previous section with micro-benchmarks. We run each EEMBC simultaneously with several copies of the different micro-benchmarks described in previous sections.

Figure 5 shows the execution time slowdown of different EEMBC benchmarks when running each with two copies of the same benchmark (labeled as x2), with four copies (labeled as x4), with three copies of the $L2_{40}$ (labeled as $L2_{40}$ x3), with three copies of the $L2_{200}$ (labeled as $L2_{200}$ x3) and with three copies of the $L2_{miss}$ (labeled as $L2_{miss}$ x3).

We start running workloads comprised of copies of the same EEMBC benchmark (x2 and x4). We do so, instead of putting different benchmarks in the same workload, because as shown in [25] the synchronized start of several instances of the same program shows higher slowdown than the parallel execution of different programs. Anyway, we observe that the inter-task interaction between several copies of the same EEMBC is very low.

However, when running each EEBMC with micro-benchmarks, the execution time increases significantly due to inter-task interferences. When running EEMBC together with 3 in-

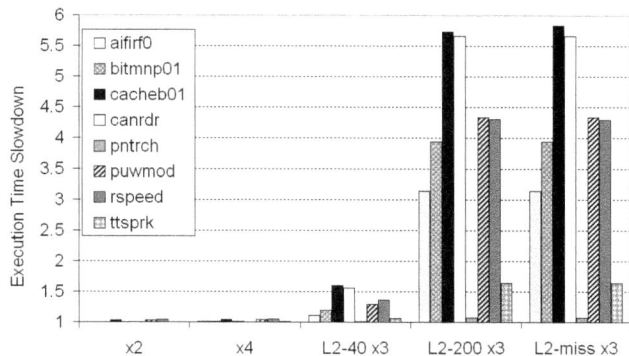

Figure 5: Execution time slowdown of EEMBC AutoBench when running them together with micro-benchmarks

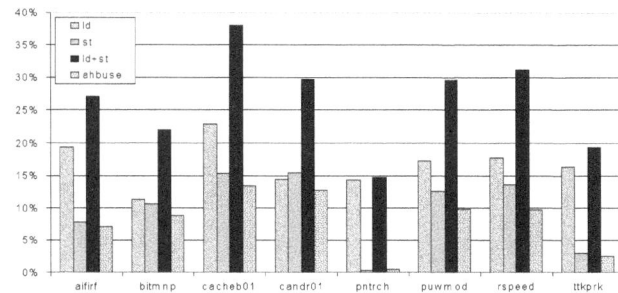

Figure 6: Characterization of EEMBC benchmarks

stances of the $L2_{40}$ benchmark, which have a 120KB data footprint in total, the execution time increases up to 60% in case of the cacheb. Such an slowdown is even higher when running EEMBC with $L2_{200}$ and $L2_{miss}$, observing an execution time slowdown of up to 5.5x (in case of cacheb and canrdr).

We have used PMC data to find the reason behind this behavior. Figure 6 shows the amount of load instructions (labeled as ld), the second column shows the amount of store instructions (labeled as st), the third column shows the sum of load and store instructions (labeled as ld+st), and the fourth column shows the bus utilization (ahbuse). We observe that the EEMBC with more load and store instructions and the ones with a higher bus utilization (*cacheb* and *candr*, followed by *puwmod* and *rspeed*) are the ones suffering from the highest inter-task interference. Specifically, there is a high correlation between the density of store instructions and the slowdown. This correlation is shown in Figure 7. The primary y-axis shows the Execution Time slowdown and the secondary y-axis the percentage of stores of each benchmark.

The grey line shows the percentage of stores per instruction. That is $\frac{Store\ Count}{Instruction\ Count} * 100\%$. The small variations are due to small noise that the system introduce in the measurements. The grey line measures the slowdown suffered by the different EEMBCs in each configuration. From the picture, we observe a clear possitive correlation between slowdown and store percentage. As a result, we conclude that store instruction count is the main source of inter-task interferences in the NGMP for the observed benchmarks.

We also run each EEMBC against workloads composed of

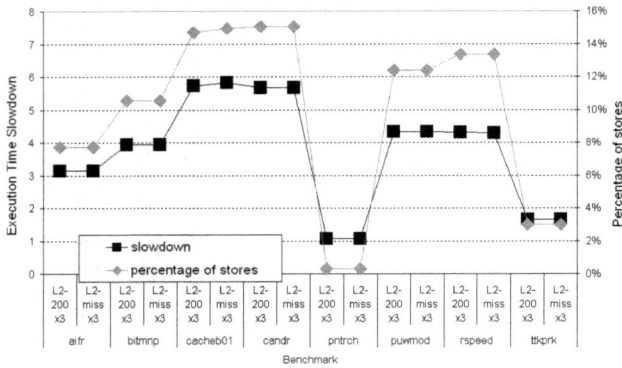

Figure 7: Correlation between percentage of stores (right x-axis) and slowdown (left x-axis) for all studied EEMBC benchmarks, when run together with 3 instances of either $L2_{200}$ or $L2_{miss}$.

different combinations of the $L2_{40}$, $L2_{200}$, $L2_{miss}$ and $L2_{st}$ benchmark. In particular, we bind each EEMBC to a core and run it with all possible combinations of the 4 micro-benchmarks in the other three cores, for a total of 20 experiments: AAA, BBB, CCC, DDD; AAB, AAC, AAD, BBA, BBC, BBD, CCA, CCB, CCD, DDA, DDB, DDC; ABC, ABD, ACD, BCD. Where A, B, C and D represent a different micro-benchmark. The slowdown observed in all cases for all EEMBC is less than the maximum reported in Figure 7.

6. RESULTS UNDER RTEMS

Though the use of adapted versions of COTS OS has recently been observed in the real-time industry, special-purpose OS, such as RTEMS, are still predominant. Hence, to increase the applicability of our study we have carried out under RTEMS the same study we did for Linux

Similarly to the experiments prepared for Linux, the main metric we take into account for RTEMS is the slowdown tasks suffer in the NGMP due to inter-task interferences. The Execution Infrastructure allows the the same type of experiment we have on Linux to be run on RTEMS: it allows running different 'workloads' binding tasks to the desired cores, periodically reading PMCs.

6.1 Validation

We analysed each micro-benchmark running simultaneously with multiple copies of itself (1, 2 and 4), using the performance monitoring support provided by the NGMP under RTEMS. The results are shown in Table 4.

By comparing Table 3 and Table 4 we observe that in general microbenchmarks have similar behavior. The main difference is $L2_{200}$ which under RTEMS has a much 'sharper' behavior: a single copy of $L2_{200}$ almost does not have any L2 cache miss under RTEMS, while under Linux the L2 miss rate is 31%. We checked that the object code executed in both cases is almost the same, and that the main difference in the behavior lies on the 'noise' introduced by the Operating System.

6.2 Results

Figure 8 shows the slowdown that $L2_{40}$, $L2_{200}$ and $L2_{miss}$

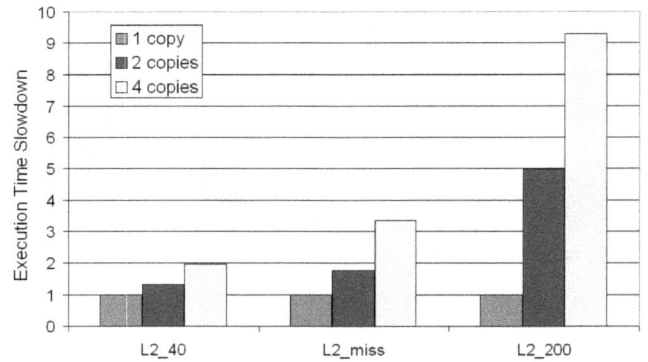

Figure 8: Execution time slowdown of $L2_{40}$, $L2_{200}$ and $L2_{miss}$ under differerent workloads in RTEMS

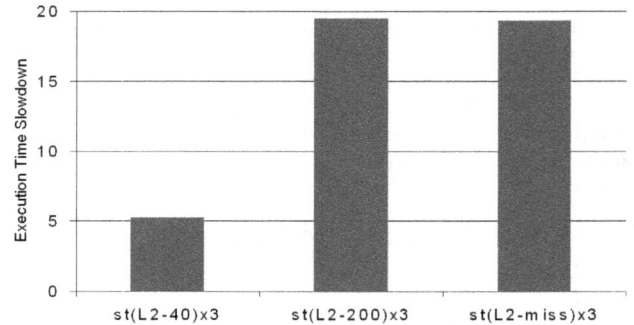

Figure 9: Execution time slowdown of $L2_{st}$ when run against $L2_{40}$, $L2_{200}$ and $L2_{miss}$ under rtems

suffer with respect to its execution in isolation when they are run under different workloads.

In the case of $L2_{40}$, which bounds the maximum inter-task interference caused by the AMBA bus, results are very similar to the ones obtained on Linux.

For $L2_{miss}$, the micro-benchmark that bounds the combined effect of the AMBA bus and the memory controller, results are again slightly worse, yet very similar to the results obtained on Linux.

For $L2_{200}$, the micro-benchmark that bounds the combined impact of L2 cache, AMBA bus, and memory controller, we observe a much bigger performance degradation than we observed on Linux (5x slowdown on 2 cores, 9x slowdown on 4 cores). The reason for this is that on RTEMS, the baseline $L2_{200}$ run in isolation causes very few L2 misses, thanks to the small memory footprint of the operating system.

Finally, in Figure 9 we observe the execution time slowdown of $L2_{st}$ when in runs in different workloads with 3 copies of $L2_{40}$, $L2_{200}$ and $L2_{miss}$. We observe that the slowdown is quite similar to the one obtained under Linux.

7. DISCUSSION

In this section we discuss some of the main applications of the results of this study.

Timing Verification of NGMP-based real-time systems. Verification is the process used to check that the requirements of a system are satisfied. The verification can be classified into functional verification and timing verification; the former checks that the system is functionally correct

Table 4: L1 data and L2 cache miss ratio, and processor AHB AMBA bus utilization per process of all micro-benchmarks, running simultaneously 1, 2 and 4 copies under RTEMS.

No. of copies $\rightarrow$	Data cache miss (%)			L2 cache miss (%)			% of stores
	1	2	4	1	2	4	1
L1	0	0	0	0	0	0	0.07
$L2_{40}$	99.5	99.5	99.6	0.25	0.24	0.16	0.21
$L2_{200}$	99.0	99.1	99.4	0.31	99.1	99.1	0.21
$L2_{miss}$	98.9	99.1	99.2	99.0	99.1	99.2	0.61
$L2_{st}$	0	0	0	0	0	0.06	96.9

while the latter verifies that timing constraints are met. For industry it is of primary importance to keep the costs of such verification low. In Integrated Architectures [13], currenlty used in automotive and avionics, a key design principle in order to contain the cost of timing verification is to guarantee that there is no interaction between the different functions sharing the resources. To that end, at functional level, it is necessary to provide functional isolation, such that a bug/misbehavior in a function does not affect the others. At timing level, it is necessary to provide timing isolation, such that the timing behavior of a task is not affected by the others. Incremental qualification [13] relies on each software and hardware component exhibiting the property of time composability. Such property dictates that the timing behavior of an individual component does not depend on the rest of the components, thus allowing the system to be composed of individually analyzed components. Time composability also helps reducing system integration cost.

In the case of the NGMP we observe that the main software features affecting time composability are (1) the percentage of store instructions and (2) in case the application has low number of stores, whether its data fits in the L1 data cache. Given an application with high percentage of stores, even if it fits in the L1 cache, we found it very sensitive to the overall workload of the system: small changes in the other application's behavior may significantly affect the execution time (up to a 19x slowdown). This because store operations always access a shared resource, the processors main bus. Such behavior seriously compromise time composability.

Software design. For application developers the main conclusion is to reduce the number of stores of their applications. Obviously, this is intrinsic to the functionality of the application and hence it can be difficult to change it. Otherwise, in order to ensure time composability, those store-intensive applications have to be scheduled in isolation or it has to be ensured that any other application that may simultaneously run on the other cores fit their data cache so they do not introduce traffic in the AHB processor bus or use the L2 cache.

Hardware design. At hardware level, a write-back policy for the L1 data cache may be considered as it will significantly reduce the overhead on applications execution time due to inter-task interferences. This will introduce several challenges that would need to be addressed. (1) In the implementation of the consistency protocol, as MESI/MOESI or directory-based protocols will be needed, and they are consistently more complex than snooping-based ones. (2) If write-back schemes were used, there would be some data for which only one copy would exist in the system, located indeed in the L1 cache. And the current implementation of the NGMP features error detection only in the L1 cache;

to maintain adequate protection from errors (frequent in space, the target environment for the NGMP) error correction schemes would have to be implemented in the L1 cache, potentially increasing the latency of read/write operations in such cache, thus lowering the maximum frequency of the overall system.

8. RELATED WORK

In this work we have used micro-benchmarks as the main tool to bound the effect of inter-task interferences in hardware shared resources. Micro-benchmarks have been also in prior studies in high-performance and real-time systems [9][10][16][25].

For hard real-time systems there have been several studies focused on new designs for multicore processors to make them more time predictable. This includes the cache and the processor bus [17] and the memory controller [18][7]. Also, there have been a series of projects working on the same direction [15][19][24][27][6]. Many of these works propose changes in the design of the multicore processors in order to make them more predictable. In this study, instead, we start from an existing processor architecture and provide software-only mechanisms to increase time predictability by bounding the effect of inter-task interferences in hardware shared resources.

9. SUMMARY AND CONCLUSIONS

In this paper we have evaluated the maximum variation that inter-task interferences may introduce in the execution time of applications when running in the NGMP multi-core processor, the latest multi-core processor used by the European Space Agency. Bounding the effect of inter-task interferences is of paramount importance to provide meaningful WCET estimations in safety critical systems.

Concretely, this paper provides accurate data on the impact of interferences arisen in the processor AHB AMBA bus, the L2 shared cache, the memory controller and the write-through policy in the data cache under both Linux and RTEMS. To do so, we use a set of specialized micro-benchmarks designed to stress each of the processor resources close to the worst-case scenario. Our results show that, when considering a workload composed of four micro-benchmarks, the interactions in the processor AHB AMBA bus may increase the execution time up to 1.83x (1.95 for RTEMS); the combined effect of the interaction in the processor bus and the memory controller may slowdown the execution time of applications up to 2.6x (3.4 for RTEMS); the combined effect of the processor bus, the L2 cache and the memory controller may can slowdowns of up to 4.3x (9x for RTEMS). Finally, the effect due to the write-through policy in the first level data cache can be as much as 19x for microbenchmarks and more than 5x for EEMBC benchmarks. For EEMBC we have also identified the average number of stores per instruction as the main factor determining the sensitivity of an application to inter-task interferences in the NGMP architecture.

Overall, the main software features affecting time composability are (1) the percentage of store instructions and (2) if the application has few number of stores, whether it fits in the first level data cache. We have proposed several hardware/software directions to improve the time composability of the NGMP. We expect that our in-depth evaluation of the effects of inter-task interferences in the NGMP for both Linux and RTEMS will benefit the real-time software community to develop interference-aware WCET estimation techniques and scheduling algorithms for NGMP and real multi-core processors in general.

Acknowledgements

This work has been mainly funded by the European Space Agency under Contract 4000102623. Eduardo Quiñones is partially funded by the Spanish Ministry of Science and Innovation under the grant Juan de la Cierva JCI2009-05455. The authors thank Jiri Gaisler and Jan Ardenson for their help with the ML510 platform.

10. REFERENCES

[1] *AMBA Bus Specification.* http://www.arm.com/products/system-ip/amba/amba-open-specifications.php.

[2] *ESA contract: 22279/09/NL/JK.*

[3] *ESA contract 4200023100, System Impact of Distributed Multi-core Systems.*

[4] *NGMP Preliminary Datasheet Version 1.6, August 2011 http://microelectronics.esa.int/ngmp/LEON4-NGMP-DRAFT-1-6.pdf.*

[5] *ARC Advisory Group. Process Safety System Worldwide Outlook. Market Analysis and Forecast through.* 2012.

[6] ACROSS. ARTEMIS CROSS-Domain Architecture. http://www.across-project.eu.

[7] Benny Akesson, Kees Goossens, and Markus Ringhofer. Predator: a predictable SDRAM memory controller. In *CODES+ISSS*, USA, 2007. ACM.

[8] Jan Andersson, Jiri Gaisler, and Roland Weigand. Next generation multipurpose microprocessor. In *DASIA*, 2010.

[9] C. Boneti, F. J. Cazorla, R. Gioiosa, A. Buyuktosunoglu, C.Y. Cher, and M. Valero. Software-controlled priority characterization of power5 processor. In *35th International Symposium on Computer Architecture (ISCA)*, 2008.

[10] V. Cakarevic, P. Radojkovic, J. Verdu, A. Pajuelo, F. J. Cazorla, M. Nemirovsky, and M. Valero. Characterizing the resource-sharing levels in the ultrasparc t2 processor. In *42nd International Symposium on Microarchitecture (MICRO)*, 2009.

[11] P. Clarke. *Automotive chip content growing fast, says Gartner (9/6/2010).* http://www.eetimes.com/electronics-news/4207377/Automotive-chip-content-growing-fast.

[12] R. Gioiosa, F. Petrini, K. Davis, and F. Lebaillif-Delamare. Analysis of system overhead on parallel computers. In *Proceedings of the 2003 ACM/IEEE conference on Supercomputing*, 2003.

[13] Henning Butz. Open Integrated Modular Avionic (IMA): State of the Art and future Development Road Map at Airbus Deutschland. Department of Avionic Systems at Airbus Deutschland GmbH.

[14] T. Lundqvist and P. Stenstrom. Timing anomalies in dynamically scheduled microprocessors. In *RTSS*, 1999.

[15] MERASA. *EU-FP7 Project: www.merasa.org.*

[16] Jan Nowotsch and Michael Paulitsch. Leveraging multi-core computing architectures in avionics. *Ninth European Dependable Computing Conference (EDCC 2012)*, 2012.

[17] Marco Paolieri, Eduardo Quinones, Francisco J. Cazorla, Guillem Bernat, and Mateo Valero. Hardware support for WCET analysis of hard real-time multicore systems. In *ISCA*, Austin, TX, USA, 2009.

[18] Marco Paolieri, Eduardo Quinones, Francisco J. Cazorla, and Mateo Valero. *An Analyzable Memory Controller for Hard Real-Time CMPs .* Embedded System Letters (ESL), 2009.

[19] parMERASA. *EU-FP7 Project:http://www.parmerasa.eu/.*

[20] Rodolfo Pellizzoni, Andreas Schranzhofer, Jian-Jia Chen, Marco Caccamo, and Lothar Thiele. Worst case delay analysis for memory interference in multicore systems. In *Proceedings of the Conference on Design, Automation and Test in Europe*, DATE '10, 2010.

[21] F. Petrini, D. J. Kerbyson, and S. Pakin. The case of the missing supercomputer performance: Achieving optimal performance on the 8,192 processors of ASCI Q. In *Proceedings of the 2003 ACM/IEEE conference on Supercomputing*, 2003.

[22] Jason Poovey. *Characterization of the EEMBC Benchmark Suite.* North Carolina State University, 2007.

[23] PRET. Precision Timed (PRET) Machines. http://chess.eecs.berkeley.edu/pret.

[24] PROARTIS. Probabilistically analyzable real-time systems. feb 2010. http://www.proartis-project.eu/.

[25] Radojković, Petar, Girbal, Sylvain, Grasset, Arnaud, Qui nones, Eduardo, Yehia, Sami, and Cazorla Francisco J. On the evaluation of the impact of shared resources in multithreaded cots processors in time-critical environments. *ACM Trans. Archit. Code Optim.*, 8(4):34:1–34:25, January 2012.

[26] P. Radojković, V. Cakarević, J. Verdú, A. Pajuelo, R. Gioiosa, F. Cazorla, M. Nemirovsky, and M. Valero. Measuring Operating System Overhead on CMT Processors. In *SBAC-PAD '08: Proceedings of the 2008 20th International Symposium on Computer Architecture and High Performance Computing*, 2008.

[27] T-CREST. *EU-FP7 Project:http://www.t-crest.org/.*

[28] http://www.predator-project.eu.

[29] http://www.rtems.org/.

Compositional Temporal Analysis Model for Incremental Hard Real-Time System Design

Joost P.H.M. Hausmans [§]
joost.hausmans@utwente.nl

Stefan J. Geuns [§]
stefan.geuns@utwente.nl

Maarten H. Wiggers [*] [‡]
maarten.wiggers@us.fujitsu.com

Marco J.G. Bekooij [§] [¶]
marco.bekooij@nxp.com

[§] University of Twente, Enschede, The Netherlands   [‡] Fujitsu Laboratories of America, Sunnyvale, CA, USA
[¶] NXP Semiconductors, Eindhoven, The Netherlands

ABSTRACT

The incremental design and analysis of parallel hard real-time stream processing applications is hampered by the lack of an intuitive compositional temporal analysis model that supports arbitrary cyclic dependencies between tasks.

This paper introduces a temporal analysis model for hard real-time systems, called the Compositional Temporal Analysis (CTA) model, in which arbitrary cyclic dependencies can be specified. The CTA model also supports hierarchical composition and incremental design of timed components. The internals of a component in the CTA model can be hidden without changing the temporal properties of the component. Furthermore, the composition operation in the CTA model is associative, which enables composing components in an arbitrary order. Besides all these properties, also latency constraints and periodic sources and sinks can be specified and analyzed.

We also show in this paper that for the CTA model efficient algorithms exist for buffer sizing, verifying consistency of compositions and to compute the temporal properties of compositions.

The CTA model can be used as an abstraction of timed dataflow models. The CTA model uses components with transfer rates per port, in contrast to dataflow models that use actors with firing rules. Unlike dataflow models, the CTA model is not executable.

An audio echo cancellation application is used to illustrate the applicability of the CTA model for a stream processing application with throughput and latency constraints, and to illustrate incremental design.

Categories and Subject Descriptors

D.2.2 [**Software Engineering**]: Design Tools and Techniques—*Modules and interfaces*; D.2.13 [**Software Engineering**]: Reusable Software

---

*This work was done while the author was at the University of Twente, Enschede, The Netherlands.

General Terms

Performance, Theory, Verification

Keywords

Compositionality, Hiding, Performance Analysis, Hard Real-Time and Dataflow

1. INTRODUCTION

Emerging software defined radio applications should be able to process multiple streams of different radio standards simultaneously on shared multiprocessor hardware. The design and verification of these systems is hampered by the lack of suitable compositional temporal analysis models that can handle arbitrary cyclic dependencies, and can also handle latency constraints in addition to throughput constraints. As a result, an incremental design style to reduce the complexity of the design and the analysis of these systems is hard to apply. Ideally, such an incremental design style would allow the grouping of components into subsystems that are characterized in isolation without loss of accuracy.

For the throughput analysis of stream processing applications, dataflow models are often used. However, a limitation of dataflow models is that they are not compositional in general. A model is compositional if the properties of a composition of components can be deduced from the properties of the individual components without knowing their internal hierarchy. In the Synchronous Dataflow (SDF) [5] model for example, composition is not always possible [13] because deadlock freedom and token rate consistency of an SDF graph can only be checked if the SDF graph contains no hierarchy.

Figure 1, taken from [13], illustrates that the SDF model is not compositional. In Figure 1a an SDF graph is shown that is deadlock free because there are always sufficient tokens in one of the queues to fire one of the actors. However, when actors A and B are composed into an actor P, an issue with defining the rate at which actor P transfers tokens arises. Using consistent rates, which guarantee that there is no infinite accumulation of tokens on the edges, gives the SDF graph shown in Figure 1b. However, this graph deadlocks because the numbers of initial tokens are insufficient. Even initially, no actor is enabled.

In this paper we introduce the Compositional Temporal Analysis (CTA) model. We show that an abstraction can be made from an SDF graph to a CTA model in which

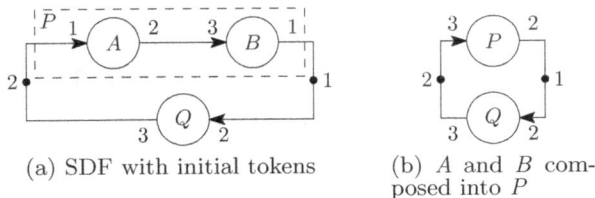

(a) SDF with initial tokens   (b) A and B composed into P

Figure 1: Composition of SDF actors

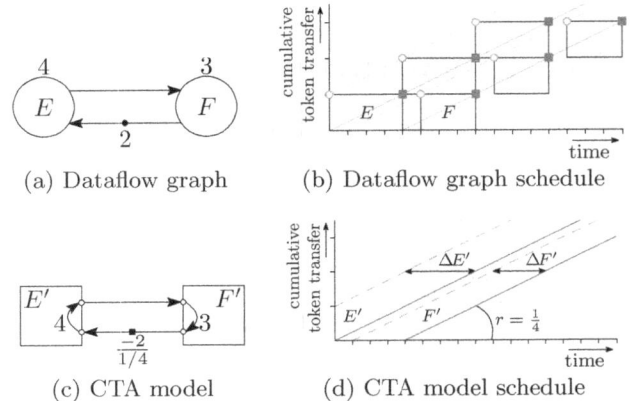

(a) Dataflow graph   (b) Dataflow graph schedule

(c) CTA model   (d) CTA model schedule

Figure 3: Dataflow graph and the corresponding CTA model with the schedules used for temporal analysis

hierarchical composition of components can be performed and incremental design is supported. It is also shown that the CTA model can model latency constraints and strictly periodic sources and sinks. The CTA model also supports arbitrary cyclic dependencies between components.

The outline of this paper is as follows. The basic idea behind the CTA model is presented in Section 2. Section 3 describes the CTA component model in detail. Composition of CTA components is discussed in Section 4. The use of the CTA model is illustrated in Section 5. Related work is discussed in Section 6 and the conclusions are presented in Section 7.

2. BASIC IDEA

In this section we provide an informal introduction to the CTA model which is formalized in subsequent sections.

Components in the CTA model consist of ports and directed connections between ports. Ports transfer data at a current rate r which is bounded by a maximum rate $\hat{r}$. Connections introduce a total delay of Δ which depends on the current transfer rate of the connection. This delay specifies the time it takes for data to go through the connection. When ports are connected, their transfer rates are coupled by a fixed ratio which is specified by the connection. An example of such a component in the CTA model can be found in Figure 2a. The example contains two components, A and B, with three and four ports respectively and which both have two connections between their ports. With the proposed CTA component description, we can conservatively model the periodic temporal behavior of dataflow graphs.

It has been shown that dataflow graphs can conservatively model the temporal behavior of streaming applications [5]. Thanks to the monotonicity property of dataflow graphs [15], earlier production times, can not lead to worse temporal results. Therefore, these production times can be chosen conservatively. Furthermore, we call a dataflow graph to be temporally conservative to a task graph when every data item arrives earlier in the buffer than the corresponding token arrives in the queue of the dataflow graph [2].

We propose the CTA model as an additional level of abstraction in which the arrival of data is modeled temporally conservative (pessimistic) to the arrival of tokens in the dataflow graph by bounding a possible schedule of the dataflow graph with linear bounds. The CTA model is then temporally conservative to an application if the dataflow graph is also temporally conservative to the application. It is guaranteed that in the application data arrives earlier than is assumed during the temporal analysis of the CTA model. Furthermore, compared to temporal analysis of dataflow graphs, the CTA model adds composition and hiding possibilities.

Figure 3a contains a dataflow graph and Figure 3c shows the CTA model that corresponds to this graph. An actor in the dataflow graph is translated to a component where each

incoming or outgoing queue of the actor becomes a port. Inside the component, all ports corresponding to an incoming queue are connected to all ports corresponding to an outgoing queue. The queues between actors in the dataflow graphs correspond with connections between components in the CTA model. In this example, the delays of the internal connections of the CTA components correspond with the firing durations of the corresponding actors. Initial tokens on a queue correspond with a negative, rate dependent, delay on the corresponding connection. This negative delay Δ represents data that can initially be used, i.e. data can be used Δ time units before data is produced on the connection. For illustration we have chosen a transfer rate of $\frac{1}{4}$ token per time unit.

Figures 3b and 3d show that the delays of the CTA model in Figure 3c, model the temporal behavior of the dataflow graph in Figure 3a conservatively. Figure 3b contains periodic schedules of actors E and F. The circles mark the consumption times of tokens and the squares mark the production times of tokens. On a queue, tokens can only be consumed after they are produced, which means that all the consumptions (circles) of F need to take place later than the corresponding productions (squares) of E. Purely for illustration purposes we have added time between these production and consumption times while they could occur at the same time.

The periodic schedules as shown in Figure 3b can be bounded by linear bounds which are illustrated with dashed and solid lines. Figure 3d contains only these linear bounds. The bound on the consumptions (dashed line) assumes earlier (or equal) consumption times of tokens and the production bound (solid line) assumes later (or equal) production times of tokens. We can use these linear bounds in the analysis because they assume later production times of data which leads to a conservative temporal analysis result [2]. The CTA model of a dataflow graph is based on these linear bounds.

In the CTA model periodic event sequences are used to express constraints. These periodic event sequences are specified using an offset and a distance between events. The delays in the CTA model shift such a periodic event sequence over the time axis and thus change the offset. The delays in the CTA model are therefore chosen to be equal to the horizontal difference between the linear consumption

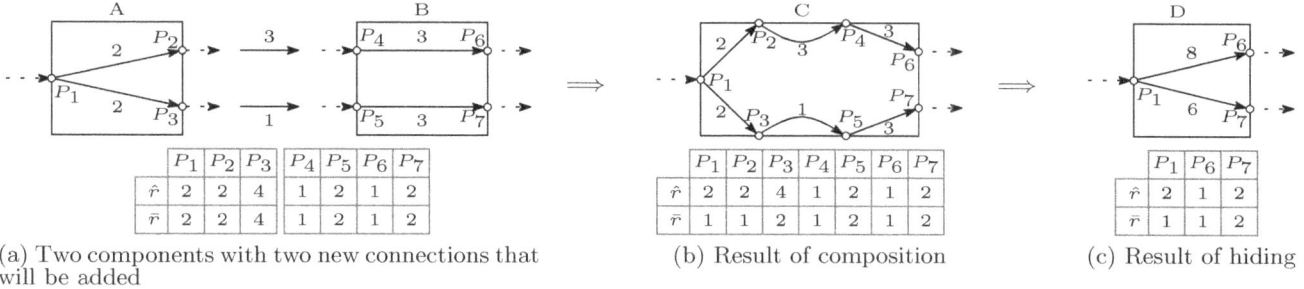

(a) Two components with two new connections that will be added   (b) Result of composition   (c) Result of hiding

Figure 2: Components, composition and hiding in the CTA model. The tables below the models contain the visible ports, their maximum rates $\hat{r}$ and their maximum current rates $\bar{r}$

and production bound on the schedules of the corresponding dataflow actors. This represents the maximum time between the consumption of data on one port and the production on the other port. The delay on the connection from F' to E' specifies the amount of initially available data, which can be computed with the number of initial tokens on the corresponding queue in the dataflow model. The time it takes to produce X tokens on a queue is in fact equal to X divided by the transfer rate of data on the connection. Actor E can transfer one token per four time units, i.e. the transfer rate is maximally $\frac{1}{4}$, and thus, component E' can start consuming events $\frac{-2}{1/4}$ time before F' starts producing events.

Connections in the CTA model can change the transfer rate with a fixed ratio. This can be seen as increasing or decreasing the distance between events of the periodic event sequence with a fixed amount of time.

Composition and hiding.

Figure 2a shows two CTA components, A and B. The ports of the components are drawn as small circles and are named P_x. The maximum rates of the ports are shown in the table below the components. When composing components, connections are added between the ports of the components. Arrows in this figure denote connections and the numbers written next to these arrows represent the delay introduced on the connection. The current rates of the ports connected by connections are coupled with a fixed transfer rate ratio which means that the maximum current rates of ports are adapted to the slowest port in the chain of connected ports. This transfer rate ratio is not shown in the figure, but can be found by dividing the maximum transfer rates ($\hat{r}$) from the table in Figure 2a. Between P_1 and P_3 the transfer rate ratio is equal to $\frac{\hat{r}(P_3)}{\hat{r}(P_1)} = 2$ which means that the transfer rate is doubled. The transfer rate ratios of the other connections in Figure 2a are equal to 1.

Figure 2b shows the composition of components A and B where the connections between P_2 and P_4 and between P_3 and P_5 are added. The maximum current rates that are possible given the transfer rate ratios of the connections are shown in the table denoted by $\bar{r}$. As shown in this figure, the composition of components is again a component.

The ports that are connected in the composition can also be hidden without changing the characteristics of the component. This can be done by iteratively removing an internal port and creating a connection for each pair of ports which had a connection via this port. The delays of these new connections can be found by adding the delays of the original two connections together. The result of hiding all the internal ports of the composition of Figure 2b is shown in

Figure 2c. The delays of the resulting connections are equal to the sum of the delays of the original connections.

Consistency.

Not all compositions are possible. A composition must be consistent, which means that it must be able to meet the constraints imposed on the resulting component. Adding connections can have the result that a port is connected by multiple connections which means that there can be a conflict in the ratios enforced by the different connections. This type of consistency is similar to the consistency check for SDF graphs and it indicates accumulation of data at a lower level of abstraction.

It must be enforced that data becomes available in time. The delay of a connection specifies the time it takes for data to go through the connection. There can be cyclic connections between ports. This means that if the total time it takes for data to travel through such a cycle of connections is positive, data arrives too late. Because delays can be rate dependent, we can calculate maximum transfer rates for which all cycles have a negative cumulative delay. If such rates can not be found, the composition is inconsistent. If a CTA model corresponds to an SDF graph, inconsistency of a composition usually indicates deadlock in that SDF graph.

3. COMPONENT MODEL

A component in the CTA model can be defined as a tuple $V = (P, \hat{r}, C, \gamma, \delta, \varepsilon)$. P specifies the ports of the component. Each port has a strictly positive maximum transfer rate which is specified by $\hat{r} : P \to \mathbb{R}^+$. We use $r(p) \leq \hat{r}(p)$ as the current rate at which port p transfer data.

The set of connections between ports of the component is defined by $C \subseteq P \times P$. A connection $(p, q) \in C$ is directed from port p to port q and we use c_{pq} as a shorthand for (p, q). For each connection in the component a specification of the delay introduced on the connection is given by δ and ε, where $\varepsilon : C \to \mathbb{R}$ specifies a constant delay on a connection and $\delta : C \to \mathbb{R}$ a rate dependent delay.

The transfer rates of ports of a connection (p, q) are coupled with a fixed ratio. This ratio is specified by $\gamma : C \to \mathbb{R}^+$. The current rate of port q of a connection (p, q) is coupled to the current rate of port p: $r(q) = \gamma(c_{pq}) \cdot r(p)$.

We define the transfer rate on a connection (p, q) to be equal to the transfer rate of the sending port: $r_c(c_{pq}) = r(p)$. The time that data is delayed over a connection (p, q) depends on the transfer rate of the connection and is equal to: $\Delta(c_{pq}) = \varepsilon(c_{pq}) + \frac{\delta(c_{pq})}{r_c(c_{pq})}$. The total delay of a connec-

$$\left(\gamma(c_{pq}), \epsilon(c_{pq}), \delta(c_{pq})\right)$$

$$p \circ \xrightarrow{} \circ q$$
$$(o_p, \lambda_p) \qquad\qquad\qquad (o_q, \lambda_q)$$

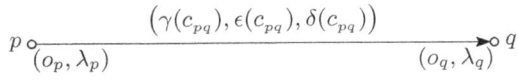

Figure 4: Periodic event sequences of a connection

tion can be negative to specify that when the corresponding application starts, data is available at the connection.

We introduce periodic event sequences as the unit of computation in the CTA model. A periodic event sequence can be specified as a tuple (o, λ). With o the offset of the event sequence and λ the distance between events. The time at which event n occurs in an event sequence (o, λ) is then equal to $\tau(n) = o + n \cdot \lambda$. The rate r of such a periodic event sequence is equal to $\frac{1}{\lambda}$.

The semantics of ports in the CTA model can be formalized using such periodic event sequences. A port p can produce event n on its outgoing connections at the moment that event n is available at all of its incoming connections. The moment that the first event can be produced is called the start time $s(p)$ of port p. This moment is larger than or equal to the maximum of the offsets of the incoming periodic event sequences. The rate at which port p can produce data from that moment on is smaller or equal to the minimum of the rates of the incoming periodic event sequences.

A connection in the CTA model can also be formalized using periodic event sequences. A connection is always directed from one port to another. Thus a connection (p, q) receives one periodic event sequence from port p and produces a periodic event sequence on port q. The semantics of the connection can be formalized as a transformation of the parameters of the incoming periodic event sequence. Consider the situation illustrated in Figure 4. Given a periodic event sequence (o_p, λ_p) at port p the periodic event sequence on port q is constrained by connection (p, q). The event sequence at port p is then equal to (o_q, λ_q) with $o_q \geq o_p + \varepsilon(c_{pq}) + \lambda_p \cdot \delta(c_{pq})$ and $\lambda_q = \frac{1}{\gamma(c_{pq})} \cdot \lambda_p$.

4. COMPOSITION

In this paper we use the following definition for compositionality which is taken from [6]:

Definition 1:
A system is called compositional, if the properties of a complex system can be deduced from the specifications of its component modules, without any further information about the exact internal structure of these modules.

In this section such a composition function is defined for the CTA model. The composition of components is again a component and the properties of this new component can be deduced from the individual components of the composition and the added connections between the components. Only consistent compositions are allowed as will be defined in subsequent sections. Furthermore, the connections between the external ports of a component, including their properties suffices for making a valid composition.

In Section 4.1 we describe the composition function itself and in Section 4.2 the consistency of a composition is discussed. Associativity of the composition function of the CTA model is presented in Section 4.3. The last section defines a function which can hide ports from the specification of a component without losing any information on the resulting ports of the component.

4.1 Specification

Composing two components in the CTA model adds connections between the two components. Consider two components $A = (P_A, \hat{r}_A, C_A, \gamma_A, \delta_A, \varepsilon_A)$ and $B = (P_B, \hat{r}_B, C_B, \gamma_B, \delta_B, \varepsilon_B)$ where P_A and P_B are disjoint sets of ports. The result of the composition $D = A \oplus B$ is a new component which is specified by A, B and $\oplus$. The compose function $\oplus$ adds connections $C_\oplus$ between components A and B with $C_\oplus \subseteq (P_A \cup P_B) \times (P_A \cup P_B)$. The ratio between the rates on the added connections is specified by the function $\gamma_\oplus : C_\oplus \to \mathbb{R}$, the rate dependent delay introduced on the new connections by the function $\delta_\oplus : C_\oplus \to \mathbb{R}$ and the constant delay by $\varepsilon_\oplus : C_\oplus \to \mathbb{R}$.

The result of the composition $D = A \oplus B$, is formalized as $D = (P_D, \hat{r}_D, C_D, \gamma_D, \delta_D, \varepsilon_D)$. The ports of D are equal to the union of the ports of A and B, i.e. $P_D = P_A \cup P_B$. The maximum rates $\hat{r}_D$ are defined using the maximum transfer rates of A and B:

$$\hat{r}_D(p) = \hat{r}_X(p) \qquad \text{for all } p \in P_X, \text{ with } X \in \{A, B\}$$

The set of connections between ports of D can be specified by $C_D = C_A \cup C_B \cup C_\oplus$. For each of these connections the rate ratio γ_D, the rate dependent delay, δ_D, and the constant delay, ε_D are specified as follows:

$$\gamma_D(c) = \gamma_X(c) \qquad \text{for all } c \in C_X, \text{ with } X \in \{A, B, \oplus\}$$

$$\delta_D(c) = \delta_X(c) \qquad \text{for all } c \in C_X, \text{ with } X \in \{A, B, \oplus\}$$

$$\varepsilon_D(c) = \varepsilon_X(c) \qquad \text{for all } c \in C_X, \text{ with } X \in \{A, B, \oplus\}$$

4.2 Consistency

A CTA component needs to meet a certain number of constrains. Rates of ports are coupled by connections between ports and the constraint on the start time of a port needs to be met. Because a port can be connected by multiple in- and/or outgoing connections, multiple constraints must be met for a port. We call a CTA component consistent if all the constraints for all the ports can be met.

Composing two consistent components can lead to inconsistencies because cyclic constraints that can not be met can be created between the two components. This section presents a method to verify the consistency of a component. This method can obviously also be used to check if a composition (which itself is also a component) is consistent. Inconsistent compositions and components are not allowed in the CTA model because they have ports on which it is not possible to transfer any data or connections on which data is accumulated.

A CTA component $V = (P, \hat{r}, C, \gamma, \delta, \varepsilon)$ describes the following set of constraints: The transfer rates of ports connected by connections are coupled:

$$\forall c_{ij} \in C : r(j) = \gamma(c_{ij}) \cdot r(i)$$

Furthermore, the start time $s(p)$ of a port p needs to be larger or equal than the offsets of all the periodic event sequences on the incoming connections. The offset on an incoming connection can be specified using the start time of the other port of the connection and the delay of the connection. The start time constraint for all the ports can thus be enforced with:

$$\forall c_{ij} \in C : s(j) \geq s(i) + \varepsilon(c_{ij}) + \frac{\delta(c_{ij})}{r(i)}$$

Next to that we have that the transfer rate of ports is larger than 0 and smaller or equal than its maximum rate:

$$\forall p \in P : 0 < r(p) \leq \hat{r}(p)$$

We now define a component to be consistent if a solution exist for the Linear Programming (LP) program, defined in Algorithm 1, in which we have substituted $r(p)$ by $1/\bar{\lambda}(p)$. Note that LP programs can be solved in polynomial time and thus checking the consistency of a component has a polynomial time-complexity.

Algorithm 1 : Consistency

$$\text{Minimize} \sum_{p \in P} \bar{\lambda}(p)$$

Subject to
$$\forall c_{ij} \in C : \bar{\lambda}(j) = \frac{1}{\gamma(c_{ij})} \cdot \bar{\lambda}(i) \qquad (1)$$

$$\forall c_{ij} \in C : s(j) \geq s(i) + \varepsilon(c_{ij}) + \delta(c_{ij}) \cdot \bar{\lambda}(i) \qquad (2)$$

$$\forall p \in P : \bar{\lambda}(p) \geq \frac{1}{\hat{r}(p)} \qquad (3)$$

Algorithm 1 not only checks consistency but also calculates for each port the minimum event distance. This corresponds with calculating, for each port p, the maximum possible transfer rate $\bar{r}(p) = 1/\bar{\lambda}(p)$ for which the component is consistent. These maximum possible transfer rates can be useful if one is interested in the temporal properties of the component.

The composition of components A and B equals the union of the set of constraints that describes A, the set of constraints that describes B, and the set of constraints that describes the connections between A and B.

The solution of LP programs is exact in the sense that there is no smaller solution for the LP for which the constraints are satisfied. Furthermore, we show that for each $p \in P$ there can be only one value for $\bar{\lambda}(p)$ for which the solution of the LP is optimal. This is shown as follows: the set of ports P of the component is split in k disjoint subsets of ports P_i such that all the ports in a subset are (indirectly) connected by connections and ports in different subsets are not connected by connections. All the distances between events of the ports in a subset are coupled, i.e. $\bar{\lambda}(q) = \xi \cdot \bar{\lambda}(p)$ with ξ a constant. For such a subset P_i, the sum of minimum distances between events is equal to: $\sum_{p \in P_i} \bar{\lambda}(p) = \bar{\lambda}(p_0) + \xi_1 \cdot \bar{\lambda}(p_0) + \ldots = \bar{\lambda}(p_0) \cdot (1 + \xi_1 + \ldots)$.

Now there can only be one assignment to the individual values for $\bar{\lambda}(p)$ that lead to the optimal solution for the minimum distances between events because smaller minimum distances for one connected disjoint subset of ports can not result in larger distances between events of another disjoint subset of ports. This is because by definition there is no connection between these subsets and thus also no constraint that couples the minimum distances of the two subsets.

4.3 Associativity

This section shows that the composition operation is associative. This means that the resulting CTA model, after performing multiple compositions, does not depend on the order in which these compositions take place. This allows for incremental design because the consistency of compositions can be checked even if not all components are fully specified. The consistency of a subsystem can thus be checked separately from the complete system because composing the

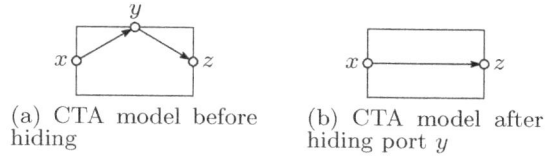

(a) CTA model before hiding

(b) CTA model after hiding port y

Figure 5: Example of a CTA component where port y is hidden

complete system does not depend on the order in which the different compositions are done.

Now consider two compositions of three components: $A \oplus_0 (B \oplus_1 C)$ and $(A \oplus_2 B) \oplus_3 C$. We require that the set of added connections and the corresponding functions, γ, ε and δ of $\oplus_0 \cup \oplus_1$ is equal to the connections and functions added by $\oplus_2 \cup \oplus_3$. We use the notation $\oplus_0 \cup \oplus_1 = \oplus_2 \cup \oplus_3$ for this.

With this requirement we prove the associativity of the composition operation for the CTA model with the following proposition:

Proposition 1:
If composition using $\oplus_0$, $\oplus_1$, $\oplus_2$ and $\oplus_3$ result in consistent compositions and $\oplus_0 \cup \oplus_1 = \oplus_2 \cup \oplus_3$ then $A \oplus_0 (B \oplus_1 C) = (A \oplus_2 B) \oplus_3 C$ holds.

Proof. With composition, the ports, their connections and the delays on the connections are not changed, see Section 4.1. Because also the added connections are equal for both compositions the resulting components are indeed equal.

As discussed in Section 4.2 composition of components is equal to taking the union of the constraints of the components with the added constraints for the connections between the components. Union of sets is an associative operation so the constraints imposed by both the compositions are also equal. Because the constraints are equal also the possible solutions are equal which means that the composition operation is associative. □

4.4 Hiding

Ports of a component that do not need to be connected from outside the component can be hidden from the component description. Hiding removes the port while maintaining the same constraints between the remaining ports of the component. It is therefore an exact operation in the sense that it does not change the temporal properties of the remaining ports. The transformation of Figure 2b into Figure 2c shows an example of hiding.

Often, when applying the compose function, $\oplus$, on two components A and B, the ports that become connected by $C_\oplus$ do not need to be visible to the outside anymore. These ports can be hidden from the interface description of a component with the method presented in this section. This leads to a smaller description of the component, it enables hierarchy and it enables the creation of valid black-box components for which only the external ports together with the connections between these external ports are known.

The idea of hiding a port p is that all the indirect constraints between ports which follow from connections from and to p are replaced by direct constraints. This is done by adding connections from all the ports with a connection to p to all the ports with a connection from p. We illustrate this with the example shown in Figure 5. Port y is hidden

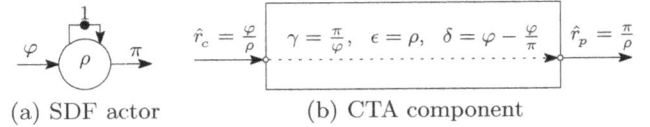

(a) SDF actor   (b) CTA component

Figure 6: Translation of an SDF actor to a CTA component

from the component description and the indirect constraints imposed by port y need to be redistributed. This is done by removing the two connections (x, y) and (y, z) and adding a new connection (x, z). The characterization of this new connection is as follows.

We have that $r(y) = \gamma(c_{xy}) \cdot r(x)$ and $r(z) = \gamma(c_{yz}) \cdot r(y)$ and thus $r(z) = \gamma(c_{xy}) \cdot \gamma(c_{yz}) \cdot r(x) = \gamma(c_{xz}) \cdot r(x)$. Therefore, we choose $\gamma(c_{xz}) = \gamma(c_{xy}) \cdot \gamma(c_{yz})$.

Next to that we have $\Delta(c_{xz}) = \Delta(c_{xy}) + \Delta(c_{yz}) = \varepsilon(c_{xy}) + \frac{\delta(c_{xy})}{r(x)} + \varepsilon(c_{yz}) + \frac{\delta(c_{yz})}{r(y)}$. Because $r(y) = \gamma(c_{xy}) \cdot r(x)$ we have that $\Delta(c_{xz}) = \varepsilon(c_{xz}) + \frac{\delta(c_{xz})}{r(x)}$ with $\varepsilon(c_{xz}) = \varepsilon(c_{xy}) + \varepsilon(c_{yz})$ and $\delta(c_{xz}) = \delta(c_{xy}) + \frac{\delta(c_{yz})}{\gamma(c_{xy})}$.

We can generalize this approach to the following method in which we hide a port $p \in P$ from a component $V = (P, \hat{r}, C, \gamma, \delta, \varepsilon)$ such that a new component $V' = (P', \hat{r}', C', \gamma', \delta', \varepsilon')$ is created. We have $P' = P \setminus \{p\}$ and $\hat{r}'(p) = \hat{r}(p)$ for every port $p \in P'$

We first add the following direct connections to bypass the indirect connections via p:

$$C' = C \cup C_n \qquad \text{with}$$
$$C_n = \{(i, j) \mid (i, p) \in C \land (p, j) \in C\}$$

The values for $\gamma'(c)$, $\varepsilon'(c)$ and $\delta'(c)$ for connections $c \in C$ are equal to $\gamma(c)$, $\varepsilon(c)$ and $\delta(c)$ respectively. The values for connections $c \in C_n$ are as follows:

$$\gamma'(c_{ij}) = \gamma(c_{ip}) \cdot \gamma(c_{pj}) \qquad \text{with} \quad c_{ip}, c_{pj} \in C$$
$$\varepsilon'(c_{ij}) = \varepsilon(c_{ip}) + \varepsilon(c_{pj}) \qquad \text{with} \quad c_{ip}, c_{pj} \in C$$
$$\delta'(c_{ij}) = \delta(c_{ip}) + \frac{\delta(c_{pj})}{\gamma(c_{ip})} \qquad \text{with} \quad c_{ip}, c_{pj} \in C$$

As a last step, the connections to and from port p can safely be removed from C'.

The presented method for hiding a port only redistributes constraints between the remaining ports and does not add or remove constraints. Hiding a port thus does not influence the consistency of the component and also the temporal properties of the component do not change.

5. PRACTICAL APPLICATIONS OF THE CTA MODEL

An analysis model becomes useful if it can be derived from a different level of abstraction. In this section we illustrate some of the applications of the CTA model and give some examples of how the CTA model can be used as an extra level of abstraction.

In the past it has been shown that different types of dataflow models can be used to model the temporal behavior of real-time applications [10]. In Section 5.1 we give an example of how an SDF graph can be temporally analyzed with a conservative CTA model. We use research performed on the linearized analysis of SDF graphs for this.

There are difficulties with expressing periodic sources and sinks in dataflow graphs. Section 5.2 shows how to include such periodic sources and sinks in the analysis of CTA models. Furthermore, we illustrate in Section 5.3 how the CTA model can be used to calculate the sizes of buffers of applications. Adding latency constraints to dataflow graphs is in general also difficult. In Section 5.4 we show that latency constraints can be analyzed with the CTA model.

This section is concluded with a case-study in which the

CTA model is used to model the temporal behavior of a car-radio application.

5.1 CTA abstraction of SDF graphs

This section shows that the CTA model can be used as an abstraction of SDF graphs. Exact analysis of SDF graphs often uses a transformation from the SDF graph to a corresponding Homogeneous Synchronous Dataflow (HSDF) graph. This transformation has a worst-case exponential blowup in the number of nodes and connections [8]. By using linear bounds to conservatively bound schedules of the SDF graph, the transformation to an HSDF becomes redundant. The abstraction from an SDF graph to a CTA model uses these linear bounds and thus results in an analysis method in which the transformation to an HSDF graph is superfluous. The analysis algorithms defined for the CTA model have a polynomial computational complexity which means that using the CTA model as an abstraction for an SDF graph, the SDF graph can be conservatively analyzed in polynomial time.

Given that a periodic schedule exists between such linear bounds, and given that the self-timed execution of SDF graphs has a monotonic temporal behavior, it can be concluded that tokens are produced earlier than in the periodic schedule [15]. Using linear bounds only leads to conservative analysis results because the bound on the production of tokens assumes later production times than the periodic schedule.

Figure 6 shows the abstraction of an SDF actor to a CTA component. Every incoming and every outgoing edge of the SDF actor corresponds with one port of the CTA component. Figure 6a illustrates the case for one incoming and one outgoing edge of the actor. The corresponding CTA component in Figure 6b has two ports. Every firing of the actor in Figure 6a takes ρ time and every firing φ tokens are consumed from the incoming edge and π tokens produced on the outgoing edge. The actor has a self-edge with one token to denote that its firings may not overlap which means that it can fire maximally once every ρ time units. The maximum transfer rates of the actor are thus equal to $\frac{\varphi}{\rho}$ for the incoming edge and $\frac{\pi}{\rho}$ for the outgoing edge. These transfer rates are used as the maximum rates of the corresponding ports in the CTA component. Note that if an actor does not have a self-edge, its maximum transfer rate would be equal to infinity. This can still be analyzed using a CTA component that does not have constraints on the maximum transfer rates of its ports.

The connections of the CTA component are as follows. For every port of the CTA component that corresponds to an incoming edge of the SDF actor, connections are added to every port that corresponds to an outgoing edge of the SDF actor. For example, if the SDF actor has 2 incoming edges and 3 outgoing edges, then the corresponding CTA component will consist of five ports and six connections between these ports.

Figure 6b shows the typical characterization of a connection in the created CTA component. The transfer rate ratio of the connection is equal to the number of tokens produced on the corresponding outgoing edge divided by the number of tokens consumed on the corresponding incoming edge. For the CTA component illustrated in Figure 6b this ratio is equal to $\frac{\pi}{\varphi}$.

For the calculation of the delay on the connection, we use the discussed linear bounds. Figure 7 shows a periodic schedule for the actor of Figure 6a. The vertical axis shows the cumulative token transfer and the horizontal axis the elapsed time. The consumptions of tokens is visualized with circles and every firing, $\varphi = 3$, tokens are consumed at the beginning of that firing. The productions of tokens are visualized with squares. The number of produced tokens in every firing equals $\pi = 2$ and the tokens are produced at the end of the firing. The duration of a firing is $\rho = 3$.

We have drawn the schedule with a consumption rate of $r_c = \frac{3}{6}$ and a production rate of $r_p = \frac{2}{6}$. The start time of each firing f is defined as: $s(f) = \frac{f \cdot \varphi}{r_c}$. The tokens of firing f are consumed at time $s(f)$ and produced at time $s(f) + \rho$. The maximum number of consumed tokens at time $s(f)$ is thus $(f+1) \cdot \varphi$ and the minimum number of produced tokens at time $s(f) + \rho$ is $f \cdot \pi + 1$. An upper bound on the consumption of tokens can be defined as $\hat{\alpha}_c = r_c \cdot t + \varphi$ and a lower bound on the production of tokens can be defined as $\check{\alpha}_p = r_p \cdot (t - \rho) + 1$. This is illustrated in Figure 7.

The delay of a connection can then be seen as the horizontal difference between the production bound, $\check{\alpha}_p$, and the consumption bound, $\hat{\alpha}_c$, on the x-axis ($\check{\alpha}_p = 0$ and $\hat{\alpha}_c = 0$). This corresponds with the difference in start times and is, as shown in Figure 7, equal to $\left(\frac{-1}{r_p} + \rho - \frac{-\varphi}{r_c} \right)$. With $r_p = r_c \cdot \frac{\pi}{\varphi}$ this can be rewritten to $\rho + \frac{\varphi - \frac{\varphi}{\pi}}{r_c}$. The constant delay of the connection in the CTA component is thus ρ and the rate dependent delay of the connection is $\varphi - \frac{\varphi}{\pi}$.

An edge in an SDF graph is formed by connecting an outgoing edge from an actor to an incoming edge of an actor. Such an edge can be abstracted in a CTA model with a connection from the port corresponding to the outgoing edge to the port corresponding to the incoming edge. The transfer rate ratio on such a connection is equal to 1 and the delay of the connection can be calculated by using the number of initial tokens on the corresponding edge. Initial tokens allow the consuming actor to start consuming tokens before the producing actor produces tokens. For d initial tokens and a transfer rate r on the edge, the consuming actor can start $\frac{d}{r}$ time before the first token is produced. This can be modeled in the CTA model with a delay of $\frac{-d}{r}$. The value $-d$ can thus be used as the rate dependent delay δ of the connection in the CTA model.

Note that the bounds on the schedules of the dataflow graph are completely in the time domain and there is no abstraction made to the time-interval domain, as is done in [11].

Example 1:
Figure 8 shows an SDF graph and the corresponding CTA model. Given the seven initial tokens of the SDF graph we can transform the SDF graph in an equivalent HSDF graph. On this HSDF graph it can be computed with an Maximum Cycle Mean (MCM) algorithm [9] that actor V_a can fire on average twice every seven time units. Because actor V_a consumes and produces 3 tokens per firing the average transfer

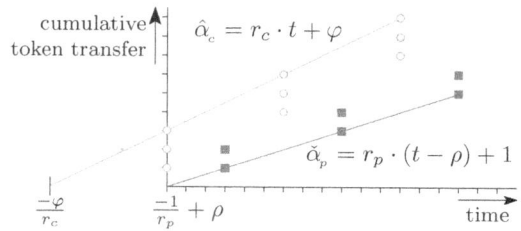

Figure 7: Linear bounds on a schedule for the actor shown in Figure 6a with $\varphi = 3$, $\pi = 2$ and $\rho = 3$

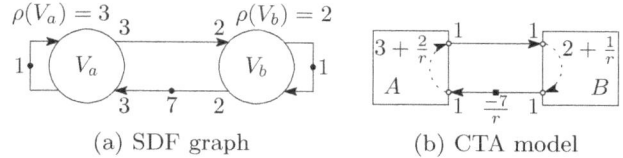

(a) SDF graph   (b) CTA model

Figure 8: SDF to CTA example

rate is equal to $3 \cdot \frac{2}{7} = \frac{6}{7}$ tokens/time unit. Furthermore, all the rates in the dataflow are equal and are called r. With Algorithm 1 we can calculate that $r = \frac{4}{5}$ is the maximum transfer rate that ensures consistency. The calculated maximum transfer rate using the abstraction to the CTA model is thus slightly less accurate than the calculated transfer rate of the SDF model, which is a result of using conservative linear bounds.

5.2 Periodic sources and sinks

Periodic sources are elements in an application that deliver data at a fixed transfer rate, they can not be delayed. Similarly, periodic sinks are elements that require data with a fixed transfer rate and can not be delayed too. Normal components in the CTA model are characterized with maximum transfer rates in contrast to what periodic sources and sinks require. If a periodic source or sink is composed with other components, the rate of the ports connected to this source or sink must adapt their transfer to this fixed rate to ensure that the components can keep up with the source or sink. To enforce this fixed rate, extra constraints need to be added for periodic sources and sinks.

Sources and sinks can be expressed in the CTA model by modeling it as a normal component with a maximum transfer rate for each port equal to its fixed transfer rate. This fixed transfer rate can then be enforced in the consistency algorithm, as defined in Algorithm 1, by adding an extra constraint that states that for each port p of the source or sink, λ_p is equal to $\frac{1}{r_s}$ with r_s the fixed transfer rate of the source or sink.

5.3 Buffer sizing

The CTA model can be used to calculate the required sizes of buffers in an application. In this section we show how this can be done if the CTA model is used as an abstraction for an SDF graph.

A buffer with d locations can be modeled in an SDF graph with two oppositely directed edges. One edge modeling the flow of empty locations and one modeling the flow of filled locations. A token corresponds with a location so the sum of the number of tokens on the two edges always needs to be less or equal to d tokens, to take the size of the buffer into account. The two edges in the middle of Figure 8a model for example a buffer with 7, initially empty, locations.

Typically, real-time stream processing applications have a throughput constraint. For example because they need to process values from a periodic source. The throughput which the application can meet depends, among other things, on the sizes of the buffers. Therefore, correct sizes of the buffers need to be calculated to ensure that the throughput constraint can be met.

As we have seen in Section 5.1, the variable delay δ of a connection that corresponds to an edge in an SDF graph is equal to $-d$ with d the number of tokens on the edge. If the size of the buffer is not fixed, this size d is also variable. We can use the CTA model of an SDF graph to find sufficient values for d such that the throughput constraint can be met. Finding the smallest buffer sizes for which the throughput constraint can be met is equivalent to finding the maximum possible variable delays given the constraints.

For simplicity we assume a fully connected SDF graph which means that the corresponding CTA model also is fully connected. This means that one source or sink in the model immediately leads to fixed transfer rates of all the ports in the CTA model. This allows us to define an algorithm which calculates the values for the variable delay for which the transfer rates indeed can be met.

Because all the ports of the CTA model are connected, we can assume that there is one port which defines the throughput constraint. We call this port p_τ with the throughput constraint $\frac{1}{\tau}$ which can be enforced by enforcing that $\bar{\lambda}(p_\tau)$ is equal to τ. Next to that we introduce a set of connections C_v which contains all the connections for which we need to compute the variable delay. Because the numbers of tokens on the edges corresponding to these connections can only be positive we have a constraint on the variable delay on these edges: $\delta(c) \leq 0$.

Algorithm 2 : Buffer sizing

Maximize $\sum_{c \in C_v} \delta(c)$

Subject to

$$\forall c_{ij} \in C : \bar{\lambda}(j) = \frac{1}{\gamma(c_{ij})} \cdot \bar{\lambda}(i) \quad (4)$$

$$\forall c_{ij} \in C : s(j) \geq s(i) + \varepsilon(c_{ij}) + \delta(c_{ij}) \cdot \bar{\lambda}(i) \quad (5)$$

$$\forall p \in P : \bar{\lambda}(p) \geq \frac{1}{\hat{r}(p)} \quad (6)$$

$$\forall c \in C_v : \delta(c) \leq 0 \quad (7)$$

$$\bar{\lambda}(p_\tau) = \tau \quad (8)$$

Sufficient variable delays can now be computed with Algorithm 2. Algorithm 2 can be solved with an LP solver because the given constraints can be simplified using the fact that all the $\bar{\lambda}(p)$ variables are in fact constants. Because $\bar{\lambda}(p)$ is a constant, Equation 5 also forms a linear constraint.

The algorithm finds assignments to the variable delays on connections such that the throughput constraint of the corresponding application can be met. With these variable delays, sufficient numbers of tokens can be computed. The variable delay δ_c of a connection c is equal to $-d$ with d the number of tokens on the corresponding edge in the dataflow graph. The number of tokens on an edge is thus equal to $-\delta_c$ with c the connection corresponding to the edge.

However, tokens in SDF graphs are integers while the so-

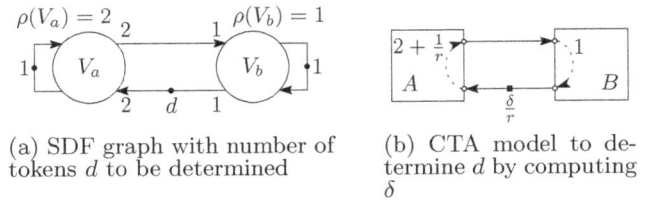

(a) SDF graph with number of tokens d to be determined

(b) CTA model to determine d by computing δ

Figure 9: Buffer sizing example for an SDF graph with a conservative CTA model

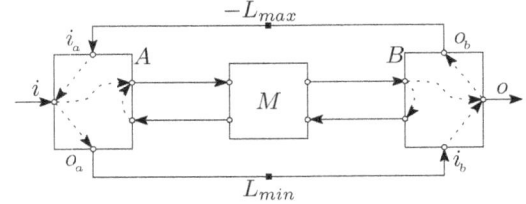

Figure 10: A CTA model with latency constrained connections

lution of an LP algorithm is in general a set of real values. To solve this issue we can make use of the monotonicity property of SDF graphs [15]. This property tells us that increasing the number of tokens on an edge cannot lead to worse temporal results. We therefore know that the throughput constraint of the application can still be met even if we increase the token sizes. We therefore choose the number of tokens on an edge corresponding to a connection c equal to $\lceil -\delta_c \rceil$.

Example 2:

For the SDF graph shown in Figure 9a we want to compute the number of tokens d such that a throughput requirement of $r = \frac{1}{2}$ tokens/time unit can be met. We first generate the conservative CTA model shown in Figure 9b with the method presented in Section 5.1. We now use Algorithm 2 on this CTA model to compute δ such that $\lambda = \frac{1}{r} = 2$ can be achieved. The algorithm tells us that $\delta = -2.5$ is the largest value that can achieve a transfer rate of $\frac{1}{2}$. Thus with $d = \lceil 2.5 \rceil = 3$ the dataflow graph should be able to meet its throughput constraint. An MCM [9] algorithm on the equivalent HSDF graph indeed tells us that this is the case.

5.4 Latency constraints

In the CTA model it is also possible to take latency constraints into account. Two components that have latency constraints, should provide ports on which the latency constraint can be set. These ports should internally be correctly connected to the other ports of the component to enforce that these ports also adhere to the latency constraints. Adding a latency constraint can then be done by adding a connection between two such latency constraint ports of the components.

Figure 10 shows how this can be done in the CTA model. In the model, the ports i_a, o_a, i_b and o_b are added to specify a maximum and a minimum latency constraint. The connection (o_b, i_a) specifies a maximum latency constraint of L_{max} time units between port o and port i and the connection (o_a, i_b) specifies a minimum latency constraint of L_{min} time units between o and i.

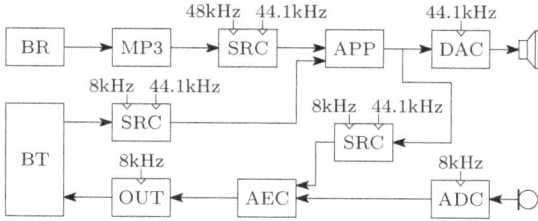

Figure 11: Block diagram of an Audio Echo Cancellation application

For the maximum latency constraint, internal connections (i_a, i) and (o, o_b) are added such that together with (o_b, i_a) a delay constraint is created on ports i and o. The start time constraint of ports enforces that data arrives at port i, maximally L_{max} time units before it arrives at o.

The minimal latency constraint, imposed by the path through the connections (i, o_a), (o_a, i_b) and (i_b, o), specifies a minimal delay between the ports i and o. The start time constraint on ports ensures that data arrives at least L_{min} time units later at port o than it arrives at port i.

The other connections between components A and B now need to have delays such that the maximum and minimum latency constraints can be met. These connections need to allow delays that adhere to the start time constraints imposed by (o_b, i_a) and (o_a, i_b).

5.5 Case-Study

In this section we use the CTA model to analyze the temporal behavior of a car-radio application. The application is taken from the case-study of [17] in which it is analyzed using SDF graphs. We show that with the CTA model the application and its constraints can be modeled more accurately than with the SDF graphs. The application can also be analyzed, and thus designed, incrementally.

Figure 11 shows the block diagram of this application. A phone call can be handled using a Bluetooth (BT) device simultaneously with playing music at a lower volume. To prevent the howling effect and to cancel the sound from the speaker, audio echo cancellation is used. This ensures that only the speech of the user is sent via the BT device. The latency between the microphone and BT may be at most 30 ms.

In this case-study we focus on the Audio Echo Cancellation (AEC) task and its adjacent tasks. The OUT and ADC task execute periodically at a frequency of exactly 8kHz. The adjacent Sample Rate Conversion (SRC) task transforms a 44.1kHz stream to a 8kHz stream. Rate consistency is ensured if the AEC task can achieve a transfer rate higher or equal to 8kHz.

Figure 12a contains an SDF graph of the AEC task together with its adjacent tasks. The self-edges of all actors are omitted for clarity. The AEC actor processes blocks of 80 samples to reduce the synchronization and scheduler overhead. The firing durations of the SRC, ADC and OUT actors are $\frac{1}{8}$ms such that they can fire at a rate of 8kHz. The firing duration of the AEC actor is defined in [17] as 9.091ms which means that its maximum transfer rate is $\frac{80}{9.091} > 8$. However, the AEC task contains a 48 taps filter which causes the first 48 samples to be used only for filling the taps. Therefore, AEC has an extra algorithmic delay of $\frac{48}{8} = 6ms$. An actor in the SDF graph can only model this

delay inaccurately, which would lead to the conclusion that the maximum transfer rate of AEC is less than 8kHz.

The SDF graph can be analyzed using a CTA model that can be found with the technique presented in Section 5.1. Because the CTA model decouples the delay from the transfer rate of a component, we can model the extra algorithmic delay more accurately. The CTA model in which the AEC task is modeled with the algoritmic delay is shown in Figure 12b. Each port in the CTA model has a transfer rate of 8kHz, except the port denoted by 44.1 which has a transfer rate of 44.1kHz. The delays of the connections inside SRC, ADC and OUT are all equal to $\frac{1}{8}$ms except for the connection denoted by c. The delay of this connection is slightly larger than $\frac{1}{8}$ms and we assume it to be equal to $\frac{2}{8}$ms. The connections inside AEC denoted by a have a delay equal to $9.091 + \frac{79}{8}$. The connections denoted by b include the algorithmic delay and have a delay equal to $15.091 + \frac{79}{8}$. We also modeled the maximum latency constraint between the microphone and BT with the connection denoted by -30.

The presented CTA model is consistent if the 158 initial tokens from [17] are used for d_0, d_1 and d_2. With these initial tokens, the delays on the corresponding three connections in the CTA model are equal to $\frac{-158}{8}$ with which all the delay constraints can be satisfied. The maximum delay between the microphone and BT is equal to $15.091 + \frac{81}{8}$ which is less than 30.

Hiding can be applied to the ports of the SRC component. This will result in the CTA model shown in Figure 12c. A new component AEC' is formed which now also does sample rate conversion on one of its inputs. The delay of the SRC is moved inside the AEC'. This results in the change of the delay of one internal connection compared to the delays of AEC. This connection is denoted by e and its delay is $15.091 + \frac{81}{8}$. There is no loss of accuracy when applying hiding because the end-to-end delays do not change.

6. RELATED WORK

A compositional analysis method for real-time systems is presented in [12]. It defines adaptive interfaces of components to enable the validation of system constraints and introduces properties like refinement and independent implementability. The methods presented in [4, 7] extend this analysis method with a uniform interface, based on arrival curves. This allows the composition of different types of modeling and analysis methods. However, the use of communication buffers with a finite capacity result in cyclic dependencies. Such cyclic dependencies result in an exponential worst-case computational complexity of the analysis algorithms while the presented analysis algorithms for the CTA model have a polynomial computational complexity. Furthermore, buffer sizing for cyclic task graphs is not addressed.

A formal algebra for the analysis of temporal properties is presented in [3]. It defines an algebra for composing components based on the description of their interface. These interfaces are characterized similarly as the interfaces of our components, with an arrival rate function for ports and a latency specification for tasks. It supports both incremental design and independent refinement of components but does not support cyclic dependencies between tasks.

To support hierarchical composition of actors in untimed SDF graphs, non-monolithic profiles are introduced in [13]. These profiles consist of SDF graphs extended with shared FIFOs.

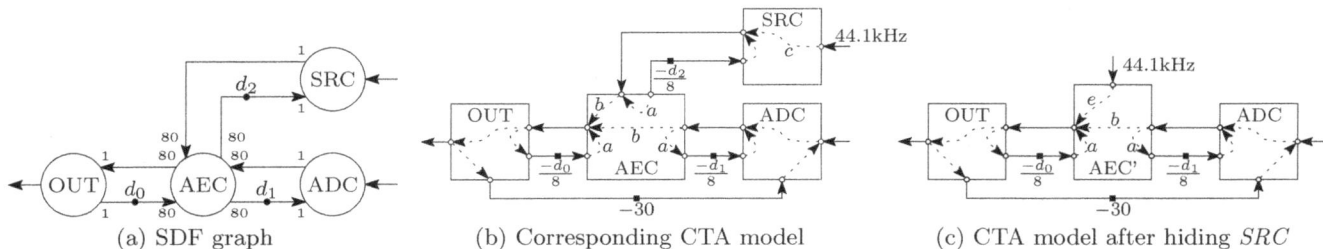

Figure 12: Modeling the AEC tasks together with its adjacent tasks

An analysis method which uses transfer rates of SDF actors to calculate schedules is introduced in [16]. This method is extended in [14] for Cyclo-Static Dataflow (CSDF) [1] graphs. The CTA model also uses transfer rates and can be seen as a generalization of these works because it supports compositionality. Furthermore, the inclusion of the effects of run-time scheduling in dataflow graphs has been presented in [15]. This run-time scheduling is restricted to the use of starvation free schedulers.

7. CONCLUSION

In this work we have introduced a compositional temporal analysis model in which components are characterized using ports with maximum transfer rates and connections with delays. This CTA model can be used to analyze applications with arbitrary cyclic dependencies, periodic sources and sinks and can take latency constraints into account. The analysis algorithms have a polynomial time-complexity.

We also provided an abstraction from an SDF graph to a conservative CTA model on which the analysis can be performed. With the CTA model more pessimistic results are usually obtained than when using SDF graphs. However, unlike the SDF model, the CTA model has compositional analysis properties.

We have also shown that the analysis with the CTA model suports independent implementability which helps to reduce the complexity when designing and developing stream processing applications. We furthermore presented a method for hiding the internal connections of a composition. This results in components which are only specified by their external ports with maximum transfer and connections between these ports with delays.

The practical applicability of the CTA model has been illustrated with an audio echo cancellation application.

8. REFERENCES

[1] G. Bilsen et al. Cyclo-Static Dataflow. *IEEE Transactions on Signal Processing*, 44(2):397–408, 1996.

[2] M. Geilen, S. Tripakis, and M. Wiggers. The Earlier the Better: A Theory of Timed Actor Interfaces. In *Int'l Conf. on Hybrid Systems: Computation and Control (HSCC'11)*, April 2011.

[3] T. Henzinger and S. Matic. An Interface Algebra for Real-Time Components. In *Proc. of the IEEE Real-Time and Embedded Technology and Applications Symposium*, pages 253–266. IEEE Computer Society, 2006.

[4] K. Lampka, S. Perathoner, and L. Thiele. Analytic real-time analysis and timed automata: a hybrid method for analyzing embedded real-time systems. In *Proc. of the ACM Int'l Conf. on Embedded software*, pages 107–116. ACM, 2009.

[5] E. Lee and D. Messerschmitt. Synchronous Data Flow. *Proc. of the IEEE*, 75(9):1235–1245, 1987.

[6] J. Ostroff. Abstraction and composition of discrete real-time systems. *Proc. of CASE*, 95:370–380, 1995.

[7] S. Perathoner, K. Lampka, and L. Thiele. Composing heterogeneous components for system-wide performance analysis. In *Proc. of Design, Automation and Test in Europe (DATE'11)*, 2011.

[8] J. Pino, E. Lee, and S. Bhattacharyya. A hierarchical multiprocessor scheduling system for DSP applications. In *asilomar*, page 122. Published by the IEEE Computer Society, 1995.

[9] R. Reiter. Scheduling parallel computations. *Journal of the ACM (JACM)*, 15(4):590–599, 1968.

[10] S. Sriram and S. Bhattacharyya. *Embedded Multiprocessors: Scheduling and Synchronization*. Signal Processing and Communications Series. Marcel Dekker, Inc., 2000.

[11] L. Thiele, S. Chakraborty, and M. Naedele. Real-time calculus for scheduling hard real-time systems. In *Proc. IEEE Int'l Symposium on Circuits and Systems*, volume 4, pages 101–104. IEEE, 2000.

[12] L. Thiele, E. Wandeler, and N. Stoimenov. Real-time interfaces for composing real-time systems. In *Proc. of the ACM/IEEE Int'l Conf. on Embedded Software*, pages 34–43. ACM, 2006.

[13] S. Tripakis, D. Bui, B. Rodiers, and E. Lee. Compositionality in synchronous data flow: Modular code generation from hierarchical sdf graphs. In *Proc. of the ACM/IEEE Int'l Conf. on Cyber-Physical Systems*, page 199. ACM, 2010.

[14] M. Wiggers, M. Bekooij, and G. Smit. Efficient Computation of Buffer Capacities for Cyclo-Static Dataflow Graphs. In *Proc. of the Design Automation Conference*, page 663. ACM, 2007.

[15] M. Wiggers, M. Bekooij, and G. Smit. Monotonicity and Run-Time Scheduling. In *Proc. of the ACM Int'l Conf. on Embedded Software*, pages 177–186. ACM, 2009.

[16] M. Wiggers et al. Efficient computation of buffer capacities for multi-rate real-time systems with back-pressure. pages 10–15, 2006.

[17] M. Wiggers et al. Efficient Computation of Buffer Capacities for Cyclo-Static Real-Time Systems with Back-Pressure. In *Proc. of the IEEE Real Time and Embedded Technology and Applications Symposium*, pages 281–292. IEEE Computer Society, 2007.

Invited Session: an Overview of the Career of Paul Caspi

Albert Benveniste
INRIA Rennes
albert.benveniste@inria.fr

Edward A. Lee
UC Berkeley
eal@eecs.berkeley.edu

Marc Pouzet
École Normale Supérieure,
Paris
marc.pouzet@ens.fr

Stavros Tripakis
UC Berkeley
stavros@eecs.berkeley.edu

Florence Maraninchi
Grenoble INP/Verimag
florence.maraninchi@imag.fr

ABSTRACT

This session is dedicated to Paul Caspi. It is made of five talks, each of them addressing one aspect of Paul Caspi's contributions to the development of safe embedded software and systems: synchronous languages and models, the implementation of synchronous languages, the relation between functional and synchronous languages, the relation between continuous and discrete models, and the definition of embedded software and systems master curricula. This session is only a selection of recent work; Paul Caspi also worked on dependability and fault-tolerance, code distribution, and formal verification with theorem provers.

Categories and Subject Descriptors

D.4.7 [**Operating Systems**]: Organization and Design—*Distributed systems; Real-time systems and embedded systems*; D.3.1 [**Programming languages**]: Formal Definitions and Theory—*Semantics*

General Terms

Design, Languages, Reliability, Theory, Verification

Keywords

Synchronous languages, formal models, semantics, implementation, real-time systems, control theory

1. BEYOND SYNCHRONY TO TIMED SYSTEMS

Edward A. Lee, UC Berkeley

The term "synchronous" means (1) occurring or existing at the same time or (2) moving or operating at the same rate. In engineering and computer science, the term has a number of meanings that are mostly consistent with these definitions. One of these meanings underlies the synchronous languages. Two key ideas govern these languages. First, the outputs of components in a program are (conceptually) simultaneous with their inputs (this is called the "synchrony hypothesis"). Second, components in a program execute (conceptually) simultaneously and instantaneously. Real executions do not literally occur simultaneously nor instanta-

neously, and outputs are not really simultaneous with the inputs, but a correct execution must behave as they were. This interpretation of the word "synchronous" is consistent with both definitions (1) and (2) above, since executions of components occur at the same time and operate at the same rate. This interpretation is also consistent with the use of the term "synchronous" in circuit design.

Synchronous programs execute a sequence of (conceptually) simultaneous and instantaneous computations. Each step in the sequence is called a "tick" of a conceptual clock that governs the execution. Distinctly lacking, however, is any notion of metric or measurable time in this clock. The ticks form a sequence, not a time line. In fact, a correct execution of a synchronous program (conformant with the semantics) can take as much time as it likes between ticks. The intervals need not even be constant or defined.

In this talk, I will review the principles of synchronous semantics and show how they can be extended to provide a rigorous foundation for timed systems that do have a metric notion of time. In particular, I will show how discrete-event (DE) and continuous-time models can be built on top of synchronous semantics. I will also introduce a hierarchical multiform time that allows time progress at different rates in different parts of the system, and I will show how the underlying synchronous semantics ensures determinacy and preserves causality.

2. SEMANTICS-PRESERVING IMPLEMENTATION OF SYNCHRONOUS MODELS

Stavros Tripakis, UC Berkeley

Synchronous programs have traditionally been implemented as single-task read-compute-write loops on "bare iron" architectures (i.e., without an RTOS). To ensure that this type of implementation preserves the synchronous semantics, it is sufficient to ensure that the WCET of the body of the loop is smaller than the minimum loop inter-activation interval. Modern cyber-physical systems require less traditional implementations, involving distribution and multitasking. In this talk we review some of Paul Caspi's seminal work on how to implement synchronous models in a semantics-preserving manner on a variety of execution platforms, including: distributed synchronous architectures such as the Time Triggered Architecture (TTA), distributed asynchronous execution platforms, as well as single-processor multitasking architectures with preemptive scheduling policies such as fixed-priority or EDF.

3. A FUNCTIONAL LOOK AT SYNCHRONOUS LANGUAGES

Marc Pouzet, ENS Paris

Synchronous data-flow languages have been invented to program the most critical real-time applications. Their expressive power would appear miserable for the everyday C programmer, even in 1985: no pointer nor dynamically allocated data-structures, no side effect, no thread/process/lock mechanism and even no recursion! But synchronous data-flow languages were providing the essential combination of deterministic parallelism and a compiler rejecting programs which cannot be proved to be deadlock-free and to run in bounded time and space.

In the early nineties, Paul Caspi observed the close relationships between synchronous and lazy functional languages, based on the Kahn's relationship between data-flow and stream functions. He showed that synchrony was related to Wadler's deforestation and the so-called *clock calculus*, to a type inference problem. This made it possible to define more expressive synchronous languages by incorporating features from functional languages as well as to widen their scope to program a large class of reactive applications. This gave rise to new synchronous languages (e.g., Lucid Synchrone, ReactiveML), new program constructs and it radically changed the way synchronous compilers, both academic and industrial, are implemented now.

4. SOME TRIALS BY PAUL CASPI IN EXPLORING MODELING BEYOND THE USUAL FRAMEWORKS

Albert Benveniste, INRIA

As a few people know, Paul Caspi started his career as a control scientist, working at ADERSA, a research SME. Of course, this particular profile was a cause of his co-invention of Lustre. But it was, for sure, also the cause for Paul to look around the traditional avenues of computer science frameworks, throughout his entire life. I will try to discuss some of the trials Paul Caspi made in investigating alternative avenues to understand robustness of reactive programs, how to accomodate artifacts of a distributed computing platform, and more.

5. TEACHING EMBEDDED SOFTWARE AND SYSTEMS

Florence Maraninchi, Grenoble INP

In this short talk, we review some of Paul Caspi's work on the definition of teaching curricula on embedded software and systems, at the master level. The originality of his proposal lies in the close association of: control engineering, real-time operating systems, semantics of dedicated programming languages, modeling and formal validation.

Programming Parallelism with Futures in Lustre

Albert Cohen
INRIA Paris-Rocquencourt
DI, École normale supérieure
45 rue d'Ulm, 75230 Paris
albert.cohen@inria.fr

Léonard Gérard
Univ. Paris-Sud
DI, École normale supérieure
45 rue d'Ulm, 75230 Paris
leonard.gerard@ens.fr

Marc Pouzet
Univ. Pierre et Marie Curie
DI, École normale supérieure
45 rue d'Ulm, 75230 Paris
marc.pouzet@ens.fr

ABSTRACT

Efficiently distributing synchronous programs is a challenging and long-standing subject. This paper introduces the use of *futures* in a LUSTRE-like language, giving the programmer control over the expression of parallelism. In the synchronous model where computations are considered instantaneous, futures increase expressiveness by decoupling the beginning from the end of a computation.

Through a number of examples, we show how to desynchronize long computations and implement parallel patterns such as fork-join, pipelining and data parallelism. The proposed extension preserves the main static properties of the base language, including static resource bounds and the absence of deadlock, livelock and races. Moreover, we prove that adding or removing futures preserves the underlying synchronous semantics.

Categories and Subject Descriptors

C 3 [**Real-time and embedded systems**]; D 3.2 [**Data-flow languages**]; D 3.4 [**Programming languages**]: Compilers, parallelism; F 1.2 [**Parallelism and concurrency**]

General Terms

Languages, Theory, Performance

Keywords

Synchronous languages; Block-diagrams; Semantics; Parallelism; Futures; Kahn process networks

1. INTRODUCTION

Synchronous languages are devoted to the design and implementation of embedded software. They are particularly successful for safety-critical real-time systems. They facilitate the parallel modular specification and formal verification of systems to the generation of target embedded code. The synchronous model is based on the hypothesis of a logical global time scale shared by all processes which compute and communicate wich each other instantaneously. This ideal model is then validated by computing the worst case execution time (WCET) of a single reaction. Nonetheless, global logical time may be difficult to preserve when the implementation is done on a parallel machine or performance is an issue. For example, when running a rare but long duration task concurrently with a frequent and faster task, the logical time step could naively be forced to be big enough for the longest task to fit in and short enough to keep up with the frequency of the small task. The classical solution is to decouple these tasks, running the long one accross several steps. This is usually stated as the problem of long duration tasks in the litterature [10].

Several approaches have been considered in the past, always using distribution as a means to decouple the tasks, be it explicit language constructs to call external distributed functions or automatic/guided repartition techniques. The current practice of distribution is mostly manual [1] with no warranty that it preserves the functional behavior of the model. We believe that decoupling should be explicitly controlled by the programmer, *within* the synchronous language itself as a programming construct. The distribution will then be done according to this decoupling. The natural expression of decoupling is given by the notion of *future* introduced in Act1 and MultiLisp [16] and present in modern languages like C++11, Java, F#.

A future a is the promise of the result of a computation. Whereas a call to $f(x)$ couples the computation of $f(x)$ and the return of the result y, the asynchronous call $\mathtt{async}\,f(x)$ returns instantaneously a future a. Possibly latter on, when the actual result is needed, $!a$ will block until $f(x)$ has finished and return the result y. With the help of futures, we claim that synchronous languages are fit, not only to design the control and computations, but also to *program* the decoupling and distribution.

Contribution of the Paper.

In this paper, we consider a LUSTRE-like language extended with futures and explicit asynchronous function calls. This extension is modular and conservative w.r.t. the base language, in the following sence: a sequence of input/output values of the annotated (asynchronous) program is equal to the one of the unannotated one. In other words, the annotations preserve the original synchronous semantics. The implementation handles futures as a support library. They are treated like any value of an abstract type, the get operation $!y$ is translated to the library one, and an asynchronous call $\mathtt{async}\,f(x)$ is a matter of wrapping it inside a concurrent task, managing inputs, and dealing with the filling of futures. The crucial memory boundedness of synchronous programs is preserved, as well as the ability to generate efficient sequential code for each separate process resulting from the distribution. The distributed program also stays free of deadlocks, livelocks and races.

To our knowledge, the use of futures in a synchronous language is unprecedented. We show via numerous examples how to desynchronize long-running computations, how to express pipelining, fork-join, and data-parallelism patterns. This way, we achieve much higher expressiveness than coordination languages with comparable static properties [12]. In particular, the language captures arbitrary data-dependent control flow and feedback. It also highlights the important reset operator, leveraging rarely exploited sources of data-parallelism in stateful functions.

Section 2 introduces our language proposal informally. Section 3 explores its expressiveness through numerous examples. Section 4 details its formal semantics. Section 5 discusses implementation and embedded design issues. Section 6 reviews related work, before we conclude in Section 7.

2. PRESENTATION

The language used in this paper is Heptagon, a synchronous data-flow language which extends LUSTRE with static parameters, automata, arrays, and an optimizing code generator [8]. A program defines infinite streams through sets of recursive equations. Usual data-types including arrays and records are implicitly lifted to streams. It follows closely the syntax of LUSTRE. This section recalls informally the main features of the language, then introduces the new elements to desynchronize programs and enable their parallel execution. Consider, for example:

```
node sum(x:int)=(y:int)      class Sum {
let                            int m_y;
    y = x + (0 fby y);         void reset() {m_y = 0;}
tel                            int step(int x) {
                                   int y = x + m_y;
```

A chronogram of sum:

```
                               m_y = y;
                               return y;
```

x	0	1	0	2	4	0	−2	−8	...
y	0	1	1	3	7	7	5	−3	...

```
                               }
                             }
```

The Heptagon code on the left declares a node sum that converts an integer input stream x to an output stream y. Each sample in y is declared to be the sum of x and the stream 0 fby y, which consists of a zero followed by the samples in y. This amounts to introducing an intialized register that delays the stream y by one cycle. The chronogram shows the beginning of y derived from a random x.

Synchronous stream programs can be compiled to scalar sequential code with internal state, such as the code on the right. Here, reset intitializes the internal state. Once reset is called, each call to step takes the next input sample, modifies the state, and produces the next output sample.

```
node period<< n :int | (n > 0) >> () = (c :bool)
var cpt , next_cpt :int;
let
    next_cpt = if (cpt = n) then 1 else (cpt + 1);
    cpt = 1 fby next_cpt;
    c = (cpt = 1);
tel
```

This second example declares period with no input, but a static parameter n required to be positive. It uses two local streams cpt and next_cpt. The equations are recursive and their relative order is not relevant. Usual constructs like

conditional expressions (if then else) and comparisons (=) are lifted to streams by applying them pointwise. The following chronogram shows the beginning of the streams defined by the equations in period<<3>>(), the application of period with static parameter 3:

next_cpt	2	3	1	2	3	1	2	3	...
cpt	1	2	3	1	2	3	1	2	...
c	*true*	*false*	*false*	*true*	*false*	*false*	*true*	*false*	...

Two additional operators allow finer control on streams. x when c is the sampling of x by the Boolean stream c; it is the stream made of the elements of x for which the matching element of c is *true*. merge c x1 x2 is the lazy combination of x1 and x2: it produces the stream made of elements of x1 when the matching element of c is *true* and x2 when c is *false*. whenot stands for when not. Consider the following diagram with x as input. Notice that y equates x.

	c	*true*	*false*	*false*	*true*	*false*	*false*	*true*	...
	x	0	1	2	3	4	5	6	...
x1 = x when c		0	.	.	3	.	.	6	...
x2 = x whenot c		.	1	2	.	4	5	.	...
y = merge c x1 x2		0	1	2	3	4	5	6	...

We say that x1 is on clock c, x2 on clock not c and x on the base clock. Clock c is made of ticks, which are logical instants associated with the truth values of the Boolean stream c. We also say that the elements of x1 are present on the ticks of its clock c, and absent at any other logical instant. Note that clocks are inferred by a static analysis called clock calculus. They give activation conditions and so are used to build the control flow of the generated program [5].

2.1 A Motivating Example

The following example models a classical use case for these operators. [11] The node slow implements an expensive operation (reduced here to a mere addition to simplify the exposition). The output is required at a higher rate than slow allows for. Between these precise values, interpolation is done using a fast function fast. Below, on the left side the source code with its chronogram, and on the right side the compilation of the node slow_fast into JAVA code. Note that ys is on clock big since it is the first argument of merge, thus slow and the register defining ys are activated only when big is true. v is on the base clock and so is updated at each tick. It contains the last value of y.

```
node fast                    class Slow_fast {
    (i :float) = (o :float)     Period period;
let                             Slow slow; Fast fast;
    o = i +. 1.                 float m_ys, m_v;
tel                             Slow_fast() { /*...*/ }
node slow                       float step () {
    (i :float) = (o :float)         float y, yf;
let                                 boolean big;
    o = i +. 3.14                   big = period.step();
tel                                 if (big) {
node slow_fast()=(y :float)             y = m_ys;
var big :bool;                          m_ys = slow.step(y);
    ys, yf, v :float;               } else {
let                                     yf = fast.step(m_v);
    big = period<<3>>();                y = yf;
    ys = 0. fby slow(y when big);   }
    yf = fast(v whenot big);        m_v = y;
    y = merge big (ys) (yf);        return y;
    v = 0. fby y;               }
tel                             public void reset () {
                                    period.reset();
                                    slow.reset();
                                    fast.reset();
                                    m_ys = m_v = 0.f;
                                }
                            }
```

big	*true*	*false*	*false*	*true*	*false*	...
ys	0.0	.	.	3.14	.	...
yf	.	1.0	2.0	.	4.14	...
y	0.0	1.0	2.0	3.14	4.14	...
v	0.0	0.0	1.0	2.0	3.14	...

Considering dataflow dependences, y depends on the value of y at the previous tick and of ys three ticks before. This should allow slow to last over three ticks of fast without slowing down the duration of an instant. Unfortunately, with the traditional compilation of LUSTRE into single-loop code, the generated code prevents ticks from overlapping, and the compilation of delayed streams like ys require the memory to be updated before the end of the tick. We have framed in the JAVA code the update of the memory storing the result of slow.

The diagram below details the consequence of this compilation strategy. It represents the computation of slow_fast progressing over physical time from left to right. The dashed vertical lines represent the frontiers separating ticks. Computation is depicted by the bubbles and arrows are data-dependences. Ticks are logical time, but in real-time systems this logical time is usually fixed to a constant physical duration, which here will need to be of the width of slow instead of fast.

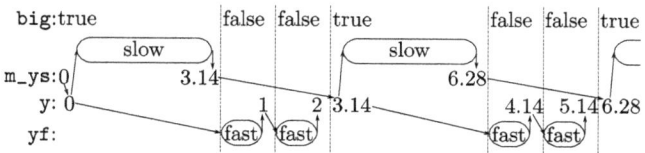

2.2 Decoupling With Futures

We introduce two additional constructs, async and (!). async may be seen as a wrapper or a polymorphic higher-order operator of type: $\forall t, t'.(t \to t') \to t \to (\text{future } t')$, while (!) is simply $\forall t.(\text{future } t) \to t$. Moreover, a constant future holding a constant value i may be created with async i. Let us present our proposal on this example:

```
node a_slow_fast() = (y :float)
var big :bool; yf, v :float; ys :future float;
let
  big = period<<3>>();
  ys = (async 0.0) fby (async slow(y when big));
  yf = fast (v whenot big);
  y = merge big_step (!ys) (yf);
  v = 0.0 fby y;
tel
```

The programmer wants slow to compute asynchronously, so he adds async to the call to slow. The fby operator needs to be initialized with a value of the same type as the result of async slow, i.e., a future float. async 0.0 is a construct returning a future holding the constant 0.0. ys is consequently declared as a variable of type future float. The ! operator is used to retrieve the actual value of ys when it is actually needed; here it is needed three ticks later to define y. In the diagram below, the gray box represents the wrapper in which slow executes concurrently. a_i are the futures returned instantly by the wrapper each time an input is given. y depends on these futures and on the fact that their corresponding computation is finished. This last dependence is not represented on diagrams for clarity:

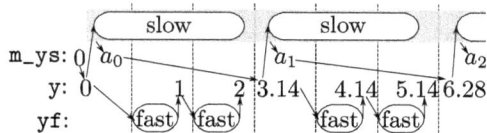

Changes to the compilation result are very few: the variable slow is of type Async_Slow, m_ys of type Future<Float>,

the equation y = m_ys is changed into y = m_ys.get() according to the added call to (!) and m_ys is initialized to StaticFuture(0.f). The futures are provided by a library. The real changes in the compilation are found in the wrapper sketched below. It exhibits a step and a reset function as any node, but at the creation, it also spawns a worker thread. This thread is meant to execute concurrently the steps of an instance of the node Slow. Decoupling is achieved by using a queue q storing the inputs together with the corresponding future and instance of Slow. The decoupling is bounded by a static parameter N (default to 1), thanks to q being a blocking and bounded FIFO of size N. Note that the reset method creates a new instance of Slow instead of resetting it. This ease the code and presentation since otherwise caution is needed to prevent from resetting an instance still computing. It also follows the semantics presented in section 4. Static allocation of both futures and instances will be discussed in section 5.1.

```
class Async_Slow { //Sketch of the real code
  Slow instance; BoundedQueue q;
  Async_Slow(int N) { //Default N=1
    q = new BoundedQueue(N);
    new Thread(){ public void run() {
      while(true) { //Pseudocode with tuple
        (n, f, x) = q.pop();
        f.set(n.step(x));
    }}}.start(); //Spawn worker thread
  }
  Future<Float> step(float x) {
    Future<Float> f = new Future<Float>();
    q.push(instance, f, x);
    return f;
  }
  void reset() { instance = new Slow().reset(); }
}
```

3. PROGRAMMING PARALLELISM

Beyond the desynchronization of the classical slow_fast example, futures capture a full range of concurrency patterns. This section explores this expressiveness on examples.

3.1 Jitter Smoothing With Delays

One of the elementary but crucial use of desynchronization is to smooth time-jittering computations. By adding a delay between the input and the output, one may achieve a more regular output. A decoupling of n ticks relies on two things, *data dependence:* the delay before the result is asked should at least be of n, *back pressure:* the input buffer needs to be at least of size $n - 1$.

```
node smooth2<<node f(int)=(int)>> (x :int) = (y :int)
let
  y = !(async 0 fby<<2>> async<<1>> f(x));
tel
```

Here, f is a node given as static parameter, it is called with a decoupling of two ticks. The 1 given as static parameter to async is the size N of the input queue. The 2 given to fby gives a delay of 2. In the diagram below, ticks are of fixed duration. Buffering of the inputs is represented in the top part of the gray box. Notice the arrows between successive activations of f which depict the dependence created by its internal state.

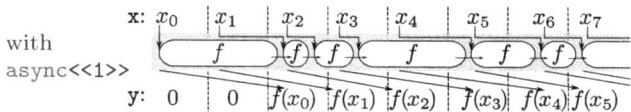

With a buffer of size 0, decoupling is limited to one tick, and to keep the throughput, ticks have to be of variable duration:

with `async<<0>>`

x:	x_0		x_1	x_2	x_3		x_4	x_5	x_6

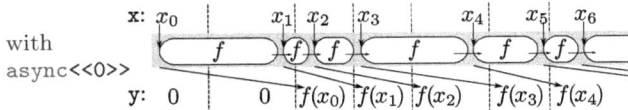

| y: | 0 | | 0 | $f(x_0)$ | $f(x_1)$ | $f(x_2)$ | $f(x_3)$ | $f(x_4)$ |

3.2 Partial Desynchronization

Synchronous programs often sample the result of a computation. This loosen partially the dependence on this computation. Running it asynchronously gives partial decoupling:

```
node partial_desync() = (y:int; c:bool)
var ay0, ay1 : future int
let
  ay0 = (async<<2>> sum(1)) when c;
  ay1 = (async<<2>> sum(2)) when c;
  c = false fby (false fby (true fby c));
  y = !ay0 + !ay1;
tel
```

sum(1)	1	2	3	4	5	6	7	8	9	...
sum(2)	2	4	6	8	10	12	14	16	18	...
c	*false*	*false*	*true*	*false*	*false*	*true*	*false*	*false*	*true*	...
y	.	.	9	.	.	18	.	.	27	...

Only one of every three results of each `sum` is used. For simplicity, `sum` is here a simple integrator, but it could exhibit a jittering behavior which would be smoothed out by this partial desynchronization:

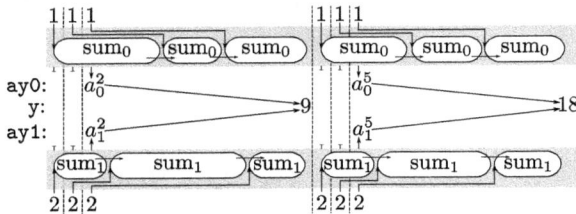

3.3 Temporal Fork-Join

In stream programs, an array is often represented as the (scalar) stream of the array's elements. The following example shows the stream of arrays `x` and the associated scalar stream `lx` resulting from the flattening of the arrays in `x`.

x	$[x_0, x_1]$		.	$[x_2, x_3]$		.	$[x_4, x_5]$		.	...
lx	x_0	x_1	x_2	x_3	x_4	x_5	...			

Note that `lx` is clocked at twice the rate than `x`. The temporal fork-join applies a node to a chunk of stream elements in parallel rather than to the elements of an array. Heptagon is not yet expressive enough to give a parametric version of the temporal fork-join, but here is the version of size 2:

```
node temporal_fj_2<<node f(int) = (int)>>
  (lx :int) = (ly :int)
var turn :bool; ay0, ay1, ay :future int;
let
  turn = true fby (false fby turn);
  ay0 = async f(lx when turn);
  ay1 = async f(lx whenot turn);
  ay = merge turn (ay0) (ay1);
  ly = !(async 0 fby<<2>> ay);
tel
```

`turn` alternates between *true* and *false*. Depending on `turn`, one of the two asynchronous instances of `f` is activated, `ay` is the joined output of theses instances. If we called (!) directly on `ay`, the instances of `f` would run sequentially, so a delay of 2 is added. Let us use this generic node with `sum` and the stream alternating the constants 1 and 3:

```
lx = 1 fby (3 fby lx);
ly = temporal_fj_2<<sum>>(lx);
```

lx	1	3	1	3	1	3	1	3	1	3	...
turn	*true*	*false*	*true*	*false*	*true*	*false*	*true*	*false*	*true*	*false*	...
ly	0	0	1	3	2	6	3	9	4	12	...

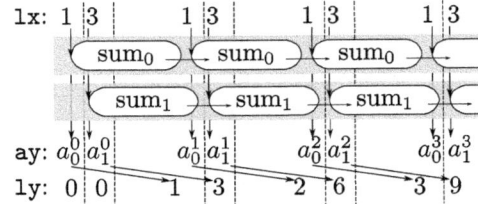

For clarity, the (!) operator is not represented, but `ly` does wait for sum_0 to finish before getting its result; this delays the computation of the third, fifth and seventh values of `ly`.

Notice `ay` is the result of the `merge` operator applied to futures. Without futures, this stream manipulation would depend on the actual results of the computations, eliminating all parallelism. Alternatively, it is possible to retime the computations to such that the streams of actual values are merged, while preserving parallelism:

```
node retimed_tfj2<<node f(int) = (int)>>
  (lx :int) = (ly :int)
var turn :bool; ay0, ay1 :int;
let
  turn = true fby (false fby turn);
  ay0 = !(async 0 fby async f(lx when turn));
  ay1 = !(async 0 fby async f(lx whenot turn));
  ly = merge turn (ay0) (ay1);
tel
```

This transformation involves distributing the delay inside the `merge` branches, which is quite difficult because it depends on the understanding that `turn` defines a periodic alternation. If `turn` was more complex or statically unknown, no retiming would be possible. The ability to merge streams of futures is thus a clear progress.

3.4 Pipelining

It is possible to fully pipeline a three-node composition such as `h(g(f(x)))` assuming the result is requested with a minimal delay of 2. The easiest way to enforce this delay is to define `0 fby<<2>> h(g(f(x)))`. Since pipelined execution is a matter of chaining asynchronous computations, we define a generic combinator `pipeline_task<<f>>(ax)` which waits for the future `ax` to be ready before executing `f` on it. Here is the implementation of this combinator and its application to our three-node composition:

```
node pipeline_task<<node f(int) = (int)>>
  (i :future int) = (o :int)
let
  o = f (!i);
tel

node hgf(x :int) = (y :int)
var ax0, ax1, ax2 :future int;
let
  ax0 = async f (x);
  ax1 = async<<1>> pipeline_task<<g>> (ax0);
  ax2 = async<<2>> pipeline_task<<h>> (ax1);
  y = !(async 0 fby<<2>> ax2);
tel
```

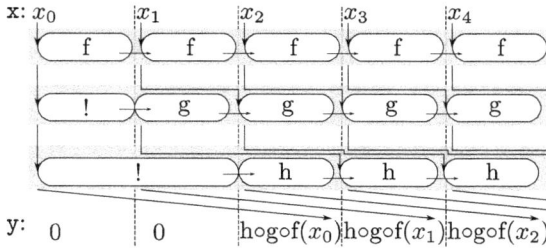

Note that the input of a pipeline stage needs to be buffered for as long as its depth in the pipeline, that is why the async of g has a buffer of 1 and the one of h 2. Being able to give a future as input to an asynchronous task seems interesting, but it makes memory handling much harder (see 5.1). A simpler and more explicit version is to bufferize with a `fby` between each stage. The `fby` adds dummy values to the flow. It would be possible with clocks to prevent it, but for simplicity reasons we keep them here:

```
node retimed_hgf(x :int) = (y :int)
var ax0, ax1, ax2 :future int;
let
  ax0 = async f (x);
  ax1 = async g (!(async 0 fby ax0));
  ax2 = async h (!(async 0 fby ax1));
  y = !ax2;
tel
```

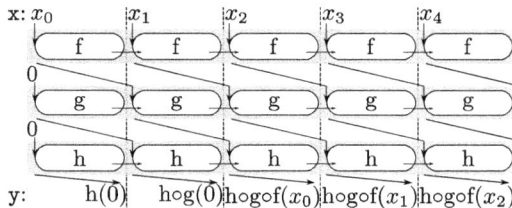

3.5 Stateless Data-Parallelism

In a dataflow language like ours, data-parallelism is the possibility to compute several successive values of a flow at the same time. For example with the code $y = f(x)$, computing $y_0 = f_0(x_0)$ and $y_1 = f_1(x_1)$ at the same time. When f is stateful, it is impossible since f_1 needs the state of f resulting from the computation of $f_0(x_0)$. But it is not a problem when f is a pure function.

The example below asks for a stateless function f as parameter (using the keyword `fun`). At each tick i, async `f(x)` being stateless, a new task may be created to compute $f(x_i)$. To keep resources bounded, the number of concurrent tasks created by a given async is by default one and may be specified as second static parameter of async. Here we allocate two tasks, each with an input buffer of 0:

```
node data_parallel_2<<fun f(int) = (int)>>
  (x :int) = (y :int)
let
  y = !(async 0 fby async<<0,2>> f(x));
tel
```

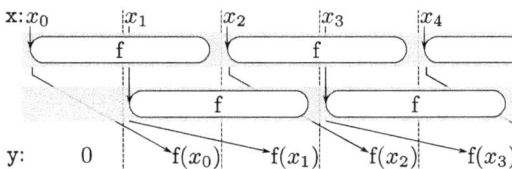

3.6 Data-Parallelism From Resetting

Consider `lx` a scalar stream resulting from the flattening of a stream of arrays of size n. It is often the case that we would like to apply a node f on each element of the array and to reset it at every beginning of the flattened array. To do so we define a Boolean stream r which is *true* every n ticks, and we reset the application of f every r. Computing in parallel on each element of a chunk as was done in the temporal fork-join example is impossible since f is stateful, but computing f on m successive chunks at the same time is possible:

```
node array_dp<<node f(int) = (int); n, m :int>>
  (lx :int) = (ly :int)
var new :bool;
let
  r = period<<n>>();
  reset
    ay = async<<n-1, m>> f(lx);
  every r;
  ly = ! (async 0 fby<<n*(m-1)>> ay);
tel
```

Data-parallel execution requires that each set of computations on a chunk should not prevent the next one to begin. This is ensured by setting an input buffer of size n-1 for each set of computations on a chunk. In the same way, the results of the first computations should not be requested before another chunk is fed in to the m-th task. This requires a delay of n*(m-1) on the output. To illustrate this generic node, we can apply it to `sum` with arrays of size 2 flattened into chunks, and with 2 tasks:

```
lx = 1 + (0 fby lx);
y = array_dp<<sum, 2, 2>>(lx);
```

Which gives the following chronogram and diagram:

x	1	2	3	4	5	6	7	8	9	10	...
r	*true*	*false*	*true*	*false*	*true*	*false*	*true*	*false*	*true*	*false*	...
y	0	0	1	3	3	7	5	11	7	15	...

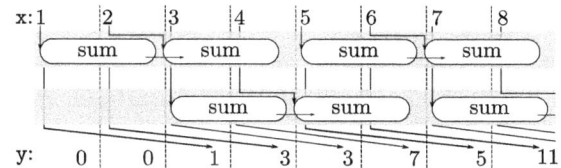

Stateless parallelism may be seen as a case of stateful parallelism reset at every tick. In the rest of the paper we only consider stateful parallelism. The wrapper with two static arguments async<<N,T>> has to spawn T threads and allocate an input queue for each. At each reset, the sequential dependence is cut and it may use another worker thread. We use a simple round-robin scheme to choose it:

```
class Async_F { //Sketch of the real code
  F instance; BoundedQueue[] q; int i; int T;
  Async_F(int N, int T) { //Default N=1 and T=1
    q = new BoundedQueue[T];
    this.T = T; i = 0;
    for (int j=0; j<T; j++) {
      q[j] = new BoundedQueue(N);
      new Thread(){ public void run() {
        while(true) { //Pseudocode with tuple
          (n,f,x) = q[j].pop();
          f.set(n.step(x));
      }}}.start(); //Spawn worker threads
    }
  }
  Future<Integer> step(int x) {
    Future<Integer> f = new Future<Integer>();
    q[i].push(instance, f, x);
    return f;
```

```
    }
    void reset() {
        instance = new F().reset();
        i = (i + 1) % T;
    }
}
```

3.7 Reordering Futures for Performances

Futures are strictly more expressive than FIFOs, in that they allow to retrieve the result of some computation at any time and in any order. In the case of a stream of futures coming from a stateful asynchronous computation without reset, trying to get the result of a future a_2, created after a_1, is useless since the result of a_1 needs to be computed for the computation of a_2 to begin. It may however be interesting, if the stream of futures is a combination of different sources, or if it comes from a function with `reset`. This is what we illustrate with our last example.

Consider a scalar stream representing a square matrix given line by line, element by element. Consider it is computed linewise with the node `line` reset every beginning of line, like with `array_dp`. In order to feed this matrix columnwise to a consumer node `cc`, the matrix needs to be transposed. Transposing the matrix of futures, then getting the values and feeding `cc` with them is much better than getting the values of the matrix, then transposing them and feeding them to `cc`. Indeed, thanks to the reset-induced data-parallelism, the first element of each line will be ready before the second element of each line, etc. This allows the column-width computation to beginning while the second element of the matrix is not even computed.

```
node transpose_adp<<n :int>>(x :int) = (c :bool)
var ay, ayt :future int; r :bool;
let
    r = period<<n>>();
    reset
        ay = async<<n-1, n>> line(x);
    every r;
    ayt = atranspose<<n>>(ay);
    c = cc(!ayt);
tel
```

We write `atranspose` for the matrix of futures transposition, instead of writing the code which is cluttering. It returns the transposition with a delay of the size of one matrix, `t = atranspose<<3>>(a)` returns:

a	a_1	a_2	a_3	a_4	a_5	a_6	a_7	a_8	a_9	a_{10}	a_{11}	a_{12}	a_{13}	a_{14}	a_{15}	a_{16}	a_{17}	s_{18}
t	0	0	0	0	0	0	0	0	a_1	a_4	a_7	a_2	a_5	a_8	a_3	a_6	a_9

The diagram below correspond to calling this node with `lx = 1 + (0 fby lx); y = transpose_adp<<3>>(lx);` The parenthesized values are the ones which would be computed if `line` and `cc` were identity functions: the result of `transpose_adp<<n>>(x)` would be equal to the transposition of x considered as a n^n scalar stream of flattened matrices. Transposing on the futures allows the computation of `cc` on 4 to be done before `line` finishes computing 2 and 3, etc.

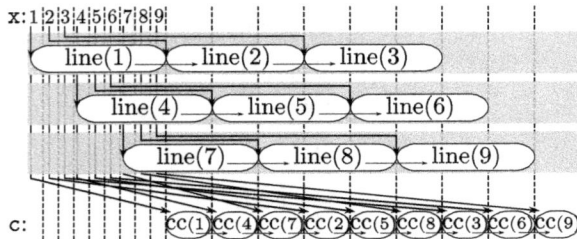

4. SEMANTICS

Our language Heptagon is compiled source to source into a data-flow core language [5], allowing the formal semantics to be provided on a smaller language. The semantics builds on the construction and presentation of Delaval et al. [7].

A program P declares some definitions d and a main set of equations D. Definitions are either stateless (**fun**) or stateful (**node**) function declarations. A function inputs a variable x and defines an expression e with the help of some local equations. An expression e may be the usual immediate value i, variable x, pair (e, e), first (resp. second) element of a variable holding a pair `fst(x)` (resp. `snd(x)`), initialized synchronous register i `fby` x, sampling x `when` x, combination `merge` x x x, and the conditionally reset application of a function $f(x)$ `every` x.

We added to this classical core the conditionally reset asynchronous function application `async` $f(x)$ `every` x, the get operator $!\,x$, and the immediate future `async` i.

$$P ::= d; D \qquad d ::= d; d \mid f(x) = e \text{ with } D$$
$$D ::= D \text{ and } D \mid x = e$$
$$i ::= \text{async } i \mid \text{true} \mid \text{false} \mid 0 \mid \ldots$$
$$e ::= i \mid x \mid (x, x) \mid \text{fst}(x) \mid \text{snd}(x) \mid i \text{ fby } x$$
$$\mid x \text{ when } x \mid \text{merge } x\, x\, x \mid f(x) \text{ every } x$$
$$\mid \text{async } f(x) \text{ every } x \mid !\,x$$

4.1 Standard Synchronous Semantics

Before dealing with futures and the asynchronous part of the semantics, let us present the baseline synchronous semantics of the core language.

A synchronous program *reacts* to some input performing so-called synchronous reactions. Formally, a synchronous program reacts by rewriting itself into another program, while emitting a reaction environment R_o containing all the values of the streams it defines. The semantics does not express the schedule of equations inside a reaction: all variables are seen as being defined simultaneously. To this matter, the predicate for some equations D at the same time emits R_o and reacts in the environment $R = R_i, R_o$, which already contains R_o and is augmented with the inputs in R_i. A is the asynchronous environment. The reaction environment R is a function from variables to extended values w which are either values v or absence of value *abs*. The second predicate defines that an expression rewrites itself while emitting an extended value.

$$R ::= x \mapsto w \qquad\qquad w ::= v \mid abs \mid (w, w)$$
$$v ::= i \mid (v, v) \qquad\qquad abs ::= \perp \mid (abs, abs)$$
$$A; R \vdash D \xrightarrow{R_o} D' \qquad A; R \vdash e \xrightarrow{w} e'$$

The rules are in Figure 1, they follow the classical [15] with a usual presentation [7]. By looking together at the TAUTOLOGY and DEF rules, it is clear that the environment emitted matches R. The AND rule illustrate that equations are recursive, each one emitting part of the result but reading R in full. The synchronous behavior is given by the fact that is an *abs* value is emitted, the expression doesn't change and requires everything to be absent. The rule INSTANTIATE uses the "do until then" construct which is not in the syntax. The idea is that a node f, when called, is the first time instantiated by inlining its code *until* the node is to be reset, in which case the program is again set to be a call to

$$\frac{\text{IMMEDIATE}}{w = i \mid abs}{A; R \vdash i \xrightarrow{w} i} \qquad \frac{\text{TAUTOLOGY}}{R(x) = w}{A; R \vdash x \xrightarrow{w} x} \qquad \frac{\text{PAIR}}{R(x_1) = w_1 \qquad R(x_2) = w_2}{A; R \vdash (x_1, x_2) \xrightarrow{(w_1, w_2)} (x_1, x_2)}$$

$$\frac{\text{FIRST}}{R(x) = (w_1, w_2)}{A; R \vdash \mathtt{fst(x)} \xrightarrow{w_1} \mathtt{fst(x)}} \qquad \frac{\text{SECOND}}{R(x) = (w_1, w_2)}{A; R \vdash \mathtt{snd(x)} \xrightarrow{w_2} \mathtt{snd(x)}}$$

$$\frac{\text{WITH}}{A; R, R_1 \vdash D \xrightarrow{R_1} D' \qquad A; R, R_1 \vdash e \xrightarrow{w} e'}{A; R \vdash e \mathtt{\ with\ } D \xrightarrow{w} e' \mathtt{\ with\ } D'} \qquad \frac{\text{DEF}}{A; R \vdash e \xrightarrow{w} e'}{A; R \vdash x = e \xrightarrow{x \mapsto w} x = e'} \qquad \frac{\text{AND}}{A; R \vdash D_1 \xrightarrow{R_1} D_1' \qquad A; R \vdash D_2 \xrightarrow{R_2} D_2'}{A; R \vdash D_1 \mathtt{\ and\ } D_2 \xrightarrow{R_1, R_2} D_1' \mathtt{\ and\ } D_2'}$$

$$\frac{\text{FBY-ABS}}{R(x) = abs}{A; R \vdash v \mathtt{\ fby\ } x \xrightarrow{abs} v \mathtt{\ fby\ } x} \qquad \frac{\text{FBY}}{R(x) = v'}{A; R \vdash v \mathtt{\ fby\ } x \xrightarrow{v} v' \mathtt{\ fby\ } x} \qquad \frac{\text{WHEN-ABS}}{R(x_1) = R(x_2) = abs}{A; R \vdash x_1 \mathtt{\ when\ } x_2 \xrightarrow{abs} x_1 \mathtt{\ when\ } x_2}$$

$$\frac{\text{WHEN-T}}{R(x_1) = v_1 \qquad R(x_2) = true}{A; R \vdash x_1 \mathtt{\ when\ } x_2 \xrightarrow{v_1} x_1 \mathtt{\ when\ } x_2} \qquad \frac{\text{WHEN-F}}{R(x_1) = v_1 \qquad R(x_2) = false}{A; R \vdash x_1 \mathtt{\ when\ } x_2 \xrightarrow{abs} x_1 \mathtt{\ when\ } x_2} \qquad \frac{\text{MERGE-ABS}}{R(x_1) = R(x_2) = R(x_3) = abs}{A; R \vdash \mathtt{merge\ } x_1\ x_2\ x_3 \xrightarrow{abs} \mathtt{merge\ } x_1\ x_2\ x_3}$$

$$\frac{\text{MERGE-T}}{R(x_1) = true \qquad R(x_2) = v_2 \qquad R(x_3) = abs}{A; R \vdash \mathtt{merge\ } x_1\ x_2\ x_3 \xrightarrow{v_2} \mathtt{merge\ } x_1\ x_2\ x_3} \qquad \frac{\text{MERGE-F}}{R(x_1) = false \qquad R(x_2) = abs \qquad R(x_3) = v_3}{A; R \vdash \mathtt{merge\ } x_1\ x_2\ x_3 \xrightarrow{v_3} \mathtt{merge\ } x_1\ x_2\ x_3}$$

$$\frac{\text{INSTANTIATE-ABS}}{R(x_1) = R(x_2) = abs}{A; R \vdash f(x_1) \mathtt{\ every\ } x_2 \xrightarrow{abs} f(x_1) \mathtt{\ every\ } x_2} \qquad \frac{\text{INSTANTIATE}}{\mathrm{code}(f) = f(x) = e \mathtt{\ with\ } D \qquad A; R \vdash e \mathtt{\ with\ } (x = x_1 \mathtt{\ and\ } D) \xrightarrow{w} e'}{A; R \vdash f(x_1) \mathtt{\ every\ } x_2 \xrightarrow{w} \mathtt{do\ } e' \mathtt{\ until\ } x_2 \mathtt{\ then\ } f(x_1) \mathtt{\ every\ } x_2}$$

$$\frac{\text{DOUNTIL-F/ABS}}{R(x) = false \mid abs \qquad A; R \vdash D_1 \xrightarrow{R_1} D_1'}{A; R \vdash \mathtt{do\ } D_1 \mathtt{\ until\ } x \mathtt{\ then\ } D_2 \xrightarrow{R_1} \mathtt{do\ } D_1' \mathtt{\ until\ } x \mathtt{\ then\ } D_2} \qquad \frac{\text{DOUNTIL-T}}{R(x) = true \qquad A; R \vdash D_2 \xrightarrow{R_2} D_2'}{A; R \vdash \mathtt{do\ } D_1 \mathtt{\ until\ } x \mathtt{\ then\ } D_2 \xrightarrow{R_2} D_2'}$$

Figure 1: Synchronous semantics

f. $\mathrm{code}(f)$ is a simple lookup in the immutable definitions d of the program. The tricky part is that while inlining, the first reaction needs to take place, and this is why e' is set instead of the inlined code (e with $x = x_1$ and D). The same remark applies to the DOUNTIL rules, which model strong preemption; it replaces itself by D_2' which is the result of the reaction of D_2.

4.2 Asynchronous Tasks

We give to each asynchronous, concurrent task an unique identifier a. It basically represent the result of the new done in the reset method of async wrappers. As we have seen in the examples, a concurrent task buffers an input and returns a future holding the corresponding output within the same tick. The asynchronous part is the reaction of a which is done in parallel. To allow for this, the asynchronous environment A stores for each a the streams of its inputs (in), outputs (out) and task state ($state$). To keep track of what has been computed by a, it also stores a counter (cnt), which indexes the current position of a in its streams:

$$A ::= a \mapsto \{in; out; state; cnt\} \qquad out ::= n \mapsto w$$

$$in ::= n \mapsto w \quad cnt ::= n \quad state ::= n \mapsto f(x) = e \mathtt{\ with\ } D$$

The reaction of a task a is similar to the reaction of a synchronous program, the difference being that inputs are read in the input stream in, and the result is stored in the output stream out. This reaction is written $A \xrightarrow{a} A'$ and is a correct evolution of A, if the cnt counter of a is incremented, and if the input, output and state streams agree to define

the cnt reaction of a:

$$\frac{\begin{array}{c} A(a) = \{in; out; state; n\} \qquad state(n) = f(x) = e \mathtt{\ with\ } D \\ R = R_i, R_o \qquad R_i = x \mapsto in(n) \\ A; R \vdash D \xrightarrow{R_o} D' \quad A; R \vdash e \xrightarrow{w} e' \quad out(n) = w \\ A'(a) = \{in; out; state; n + 1\} \\ state(n + 1) = f(x) = e' \mathtt{\ with\ } D' \end{array}}{A \xrightarrow{a} A'}$$

As we saw in the examples, the reaction of a may need the reaction of other tasks to happen. It may even require multiple reactions of a given task. Let $\xrightarrow{a}^*$ denote the reflexive transitive closure of $\xrightarrow{a}$. We are finally able to define the transition $\leadsto^*$ which provides an abstraction of the interleaving of the asynchronous tasks, while ensuring proper evolution of A:

$$A \leadsto^* A' \overset{\text{def}}{=} \forall a, A \xrightarrow{a}^* A'$$

4.3 Execution of a Program

A program reacts to a sequence of inputs $S_i = R_i^0 R_i^1 \ldots$, generating a sequence of outputs $S_o = R_o^0 R_o^1 \ldots$, in a sequence of asynchronous environments $B = A^0 A^1 \ldots$.

$$S_i \vdash_\infty P : B; S_o$$

The execution of $P = d; D^0$ is defined, synchronous step by synchronous step, with for all $k \geq 0$:

$$\frac{R_i^k \vdash_k d; D^k : A^k; R_o^k \qquad A^k; R^k \vdash D^k \xrightarrow{R_o^k} D^{k+1} \qquad A^k \leadsto^* A^{k+1}}{R_i^{k+1} \vdash_k d; D^{k+1} : A^{k+1}; R_o^{k+1}}$$

We saw that in order to abstract the schedule of equations, the semantic rules construct and check the validity of R in one go. R is temporary and can be thrown away after the reaction. On the contrary, A is a continuously evolving environment, and a snapshot A^k is taken at each reaction. Similarly to R, a snapshot is constructed *and* checked during the reaction: inputs are queued up, asynchronous tasks advance and tasks with fresh code are attached, while all of this is already in the premise of the rules. This is fundamental to hide the interleaving between the main program and the asynchronous task. Note that, by the definition of $\rightsquigarrow^*$:

$$A^k.cnt \leq A^{k+1}.cnt \qquad A^k.state \subseteq A^{k+1}.state$$
$$A^k.in \subseteq A^{k+1}.in \qquad A^k.out \subseteq A^{k+1}.out$$

This permits to define the asynchronous environment A^∞ as the limit of the sequence. It is very important to note that A^∞ is thus scheduling-independent.

4.4 Extension of the Synchronous Semantics

A future is a *synchronous value* used through an indirection. It is basically is a reference holding a value guarded by a readiness condition. In the semantics, instead of using a generic reference representation, since any future is the result of a computation performed by an asynchronous task, we define a future as a special couple $\langle a, n \rangle$, with n the index of the value in the output stream of a. We add futures in the values of the semantics:

$$v ::= i \mid (v, v) \mid \langle a, n \rangle$$

To get the value of a future $\langle a, n \rangle$, we ensure that it is ready by asking a to have a current counter not less than n:

GET
$$\frac{R(x) = \langle a, n \rangle \quad A(a) = \{\_; out; \_; n'\} \quad out(n) = w \quad n' \geq n}{A; R \vdash \;!x \xrightarrow{w} \;!x}$$

The first time a node is called in an `async`, an asynchronous task a is dedicated to this computation. One has to make sure that a holds the right initial code in $state(0)$ and that the input queue at instant 0 is set with the correct input. The program is then rewritten into the simpler inputs$(,,)$ construct, which increments the input counter by one, ensuring that the input queue is filled in order. A task a operates a synchronous program and for each input, one output is set. Thus, the future emitted holds the input counter which also indicates the corresponding index in the output stream:

INSTANTIATE-ASYNC
$$\frac{\text{code}(f) = f(x) = e \text{ with } D \quad A(a) = \{in; \_; state; \_\}}{in(0) = R(x_1) \quad state(0) = e \text{ with } (x = x_1 \text{ and } D)}$$
$$A; R \vdash \text{async } f(x_1) \text{ every } x_2 \xrightarrow{\langle a, 0 \rangle}$$
$$\text{do inputs}(a, 1, x_1) \text{ until } x_2 \text{ then async } f(x_1) \text{ every } x_2$$

INPUTS
$$\frac{A(a) = \{in; \_; \_; \_\} \quad in(n) = R(x)}{A; R \vdash \text{inputs}(a, n, x) \xrightarrow{\langle a, n \rangle} \text{inputs}(a, n+1, x)}$$

Instantiation is not done until the input is present:

INSTANTIATE-ASYNC-ABS
$$\frac{R(x_1) = R(x_2) = abs}{A; R \vdash \text{async } f(x_1) \text{ every } x_2 \xrightarrow{abs} \text{async } f(x_1) \text{ every } x_2}$$

An immediate future is not the result of a computation, but for homogeneity, we simulate it with a stalled task:

IMMEDIATE-ASYNC
$$\frac{A(a) = \{\_; out; \_; 0\} \quad out(0) = i}{A; R \vdash \text{async } i \xrightarrow{\langle a, 0 \rangle} \text{async } i}$$

4.5 Semantics Preservation

We need to compare our code with a fully synchronous code. To this mean, we define the ra function, which removes the asynchronous features. We will call ra(P) the synchronized version of P, it is the identity except for:

$$\text{ra}(\text{async } f(x_1) \text{ every } x_2) = f(x_1) \text{ every } x_2$$
$$\text{ra}(!x) = x \qquad \text{ra}(\text{async } i) = i$$

The preservation theorem states that any value computed by the synchronized program is either the same in the original program, or replaced by a future holding that value. We express this property with the sync$_A$ function, mapping extended values to extended values without futures:

$$\text{sync}_A(\langle a, n \rangle) = A\langle a, n \rangle$$
$$\text{sync}_A(w, w) = (\text{sync}_A(w), \text{sync}_A(w)) \quad \text{sync}_A(abs) = abs$$
$$\text{sync}_A(v, v) = (\text{sync}_A(v), \text{sync}_A(v)) \qquad \text{sync}_A(i) = i$$

$A\langle a, n \rangle$ is a notation for the value associated to $\langle a, n \rangle$ in A, that is $A(a).out(n)$.

THEOREM 1 (PRESERVATION). *Under a stream of inputs without future, a program produces the same, or a future holding the same extended value as its synchronized version:*

$$\text{if} \qquad \forall R_i \in S_i, \forall x, R_i(x) \neq \langle a, n \rangle$$
$$\text{then} \qquad S_i \vdash P : A^\infty; S_o \iff S_i \vdash \text{ra}(P) : \emptyset; S'_o$$
$$\text{with property } p: \quad \forall k, \forall x, R'^k_o(x) = \text{sync}_{A^\infty}(R^k_o(x))$$

First, note that we use A^∞ as an asynchronous environment, thanks to the remark in section 4.3. Second, restricting the inputs as not being futures is a sound simplification as the main program inputs actual values.

The proof relies on the stronger property P:

$$A^k; R^k_i \vdash D^k \xrightarrow{R^k_o} D^{k+1} \quad \wedge \quad \emptyset; R^k_i \vdash \text{ra}_{A^k}(D^k) \xrightarrow{R'^k_o} D'$$
$$\implies \begin{cases} (1) \quad \forall x, R'^k_o(x) = \text{sync}_{A^k}(R^k_o(x)) \\ (2) \qquad \wedge \; D' = \text{ra}_{A^{k+1}}(D^{k+1}) \end{cases}$$

with

$$\text{ra}_A(w) = \text{sync}_A(w)$$
$$\text{ra}_A(\text{inputs}(a, n, x)) = \text{ra}_A((A(a).state(n))(x))$$

It states that synchronizing a program at any execution step k and performing a reaction leads to the same as performing a reaction and synchronizing the resulting program: synchronization commutes with reaction. Synchronizing the program at any step during its execution requires to extend ra on elements outside the syntax and makes ra dependent on the asynchronous environment. ra synchronizes futures by looking up their value, and instead of putting a value at the nth place in the input queue of a, it directly applies the code $state(n)$ of a to this input. Synchronizing a program is not possible if a future is not ready in A, or if a task a is not up to date with its input. So the property P does not hold with every schedule of the asynchronous tasks, but holds with an *eager scheduling*. The proof is done by induction over the constructs and is a bit verbose, but we look here at two symptomatic examples:

The simplest case is `x = async i; y = !x;` in which x holds a future $\langle a, 0 \rangle$, and the asynchronous environment A is so that $A\langle a, 0 \rangle = i$. y is equal to $A\langle a, 0 \rangle$ which is i.

Its synchronized version is x = i; y = x;. Both codes are rewritten without change, and so holds property P.

The case of x = async f(z); y = !x; rewrites itself into
x = do inputs($a, 1, $z) until false then ...; y = !x;
in which x holds a future $\langle a, 0 \rangle$, with $A^0(a).state(0)$ equal to the code of f, y asks for the result of this code applied on the input z. The synchronized version x = f(z); y = x; does immediately apply the code of f to z and writes the result in x and y (we have property P.(1)). It rewrites itself into x = do e with D until false then ...; y = x;. The next step, $A^1(a).state(1)$ is computed and is equal to e with D (we have property P.(2)). Next steps are similar.

An eager scheduling ensures that $A^1(a).state(1)$ is computed in time. Since S_o and A^∞ are independent of the interleaving, we can choose an eager scheduling, which gives the property P and the theorem follows.

4.6 Typing, Clocking and Causality

The preservation theorem 1 proves that the usual validity checks of data-flow synchronous programs—clocking and causality—can cope with the asynchronous constructs without modification. One simply ought to apply ra, which discard our extensions before running the checks.

Typing needs to deal with the paramteric type future t and with the introduced operators of section 2.2.

5. DISCUSSION

So far, real-time constraints and scheduling of tasks have not been dealt with. One would have to look for example at SynDEx [14] and the AAA methodology, to import these techniques into our context. Nonetheless, being able to program in a clean synchronous semantics the beginning and the end of concurrent tasks should be beneficial to the designer. Task priority, periodic schedule, and anything which is statically decided by the designer should be provided as static parameters of the async constructs. In our implementation, we experimented with the priority as a third argument and a processor identifier as a fourth one.

Scheduling of asynchronous tasks has to ensure any static constraints from the source: input queue size, thread number, etc. Note that there exists always an eager, dynamic schedule mimicking the sequential compilation of the synchronous semantics. The schedule may also be fixed and offline for static Kahn networks [17]. In a real-time system, the schedule may also be time-triggered, and the get operator can be handled as any inter-task dependence [14].

5.1 Static Resource Usage

In the presented semantics, A^∞ is unbounded in two ways: at each application of the rule INSTANTIATE-ASYNC, a fresh task is used, and the input and output streams, for each task, are entirely stored. In Section 3, we discussed the fact that in our implementation, the input queue size (q) and the number of tasks (p) are finite and set by the programmer as static arguments to the async construct. We saw that these resource constraints have an influence on the possible schedules, but do not change the semantics, indeed, the asynchronous version even with these bounds is still looser than the synchronous version.

The bound on the input queue prevents an asynchronous task to lag more than q ticks behind the task providing its input. So all inputs older than the last q ones may be dropped.

The number of tasks specified by async allows to statically allocate them at the beginning of the program. Indeed, an async does have only one current task and a task has finished if it is not the current one and has emptied its input queue. So, when a task is needed to become the new current one (rule INSTANTIATE-ASYNC), either a fresh one exists, or it waits for one to finish emptying its input queue.

Without further restriction, futures may escape their scope and require concurrent garbage-collection. Indeed, contrary to the input queue, it is not because a task is defining the nth output value that we are sure some older output value is no more needed. An output value is needed as long as a future holding it is in the program. To avoid garbage collection, we propose that a node may not return or take a future as input. Among our examples, the only violation of this rule is the version of the pipelining pattern, which was better rewritten with explicit delays. With this restriction, futures do not escape a node. At the end of the node's step, every futures it has used are dead, except for those stored in the registers of the node. Dealing with the futures is then a matter of a simple, constant time scan of a the node's bounded memory at the end of each step.

5.2 Safety of Asynchronous Constructs

If shared memory is used in the actual implementation, it is not directly accessible to the programmer, and the correctness of the futures library is sufficient to prevent races.

Under the assumption of a correct scheduling, the preservation theorem 1 ensures that if the synchronized version of a program is causal, the original program is deadlock-free. Finally, livelocks are impossible thanks to the fact that decoupling is bounded by the input queue sizes. Indeed, consider that a task is never given a chance to compute, since the decoupling with its caller is bounded, the caller also is stalled. Inductively it would imply the main program to be stalled. The bound on the decoupling enforce then that all tasks are stalled, which would be an incorrect schedule.

6. RELATED WORK

The distribution and parallelization of synchronous programs has been an active topic. The majority of these works are on Globally Asynchronous Locally Synchronous (GALS) approaches, targeting ESTEREL [4] or SIGNAL [21], and are discussed in a survey by Girault [10]. Model-based design has been applied to the distribution of a LUSTRE program into a real-time task graph [2]. The language PRELUDE [20], inspired by LUSTRE, is a real-time Architecture Description Language (ADL) to handle multi-rate but periodic systems. The generation of multi-threaded code from ESTEREL has been studied by Yuan et al. [25] but does not decouple computations across synchronous instants. CRP in ESTEREL [3, 4] introduces an exec construct to launch an external function with the result returned to the caller as a signal. The caller needs to handle the result whenever it arrives. The main purpose of exec is to trigger external tasks like robot actuation. At the opposite, OCREP [9] for LUSTRE considers the automatic distribution of the intermediate imperative language OC used by the LUSTRE compiler. The programmer does not control the desynchronization, she controls the distribution by indicating where variables should be located. Then OCREP automatically generate a distributed code with FIFOs trying, by using bi-simulation techniques, to link directly production to consumption. It is able [11] in the classical `slow_fast` example to determine the actual consumption and to remove the register `m_ys`. In the general case, it is impossible to do so, as it would require to predict whether and when a value of a stream is used. Moreover, the decoupling achieved by OCREP is, by design, bounded by one tick [11], and depends on choices and optimizations performed when generating OC.

Since futures have been used in a wide range of settings, they are themselves very diverse. The principal distinction opposes explicit vs. implicit futures. Implicit futures are futures without explicit get operator: they require language support but allow for elegant, implicit pipelining. It often comes with laziness support or continuation passing style. Recent works include F# concurrency [24] and many results from the Haskell community [22], the central library being `Control.Concurrent`. Alice ML implements an elegant concurrent lambda calculus with implicit futures [19]. Explicit futures are also coming in C11, C++11, etc.

The cyclo-static data flow model of computation [18, 6, 23] computations over a variety of shared and distributed memory targets. Our approach is more general since languages like LUSTRE do not have any periodic restrictions. On the other hand, cyclo-static approaches leverage the periodicity restrictions to allocate resources and partition computations automatically [13]. We see as an advantage for embedded system design that the programmer remains in control of parallelization and resource allocation. In addition, these decisions may still be automated on periodic subsets of a LUSTRE program.

7. CONCLUSION

We presented a novel approach to the distribution of synchronous programs, using futures in a semantics-preserving desynchronization. We showed that resources for parallel execution can be bounded statically, and that desynchronization does not lead to deadlock, livelock or races. We illustrated the expressiveness of our proposal on numerous examples, comparing with automatic techniques. We presented natural ways to exploit task and data parallelism, hiding the computation and communication latencies through explicit delays set by the designer. We also highlighted the importance of the reset operator to extract data parallelism from stateful tasks. We formally defined the semantics of our language and we validated the examples using a prototype compiler and runtime library.

Acknowledgments.

This work was partly supported by the INRIA large scale initiative Synchronics and by the European FP7 project PHARAON id. 288307. We are thankful to Stephen Edwards, Louis Mandel, Adrien Guatto and Guillaume Baudart for their valuable recommendations on the paper.

8. REFERENCES

[1] http://aadl.info.

[2] M. Alras, P. Caspi, A. Girault, and P. Raymond. Model-based design of embedded control systems by means of a synchronous intermediate model. In *Design and Test in Europe (DATE)*, May 2009.

[3] G. Berry, S. Ramesh, and R. K. Shyamasundar. Communicating reactive processes. In *Principles Of Programming Languages*, pages 85–98. ACM, 1993.

[4] G. Berry and E. Sentovich. An implementation of constructive synchronous programs in polis. *Formal Methods In System Design*, 17(2):135–161, Oct. 2000.

[5] D. Biernacki, J.-L. Colaco, G. Hamon, and M. Pouzet. Clock-directed modular code generation of synchronous data-flow languages. In *International Conference on Languages, Compilers, and Tools for Embedded Systems (LCTES)*, Tucson, Arizona, June 2008.

[6] G. Bilsen, M. Engels, L. R., and J. A. Peperstraete. Cyclo-static data flow. In *Acoustics, Speech, and Signal Processing (ICASSP'95)*, pages 3255–3258, Detroit, Michigan, May 1995.

[7] G. Delaval, A. Girault, and M. Pouzet. A type system for the automatic distribution of higher-order synchronous dataflow programs. In *International Conference on Languages, Compilers, and Tools for Embedded Systems (LCTES)*, Tucson, Arizona, June 2008.

[8] L. Gérard, A. Guatto, C. Pasteur, and M. Pouzet. A Modular Memory Optimization for Synchronous Data-Flow Languages. Application to Arrays in a Lustre Compiler. In *Languages, Compilers, Tools and Theory for Embedded Systems (LCTES'12)*, Beijing, 12-13 June 2012. Best paper award.

[9] A. Girault. *Sur la Répartition de Programmes Synchrones*. Phd thesis, INPG, Grenoble, France, January 1994.

[10] A. Girault. A survey of automatic distribution method for synchronous programs. In *International workshop on synchronous languages, applications and programs, SLAP*, volume 5, 2005.

[11] A. Girault, X. Nicollin, and M. Pouzet. Automatic rate desynchronization of embedded reactive programs. *Transactions on Embedded Computing Systems (TECS)*, 5(3):687–717, 2006.

[12] M. Gordon. *Compiler Techniques for Scalable Performance of Stream Programs on Multicore Architectures*. PhD thesis, MIT, 2010.

[13] M. Gordon, W. Thies, and S. Amarasinghe. Exploiting coarse-grained task, data, and pipeline parallelism in stream programs. In *Architectural Support for Programming Languages and Operating Systems*, San Jose, CA, Oct 2006.

[14] T. Grandpierre, C. Lavarenne, and Y. Sorel. Optimized rapid prototyping for real-time embedded heterogeneous multiprocessors. In *International Workshop on Hardware Software Co-Design, CODES'99*, Rome, Italy, May 1999.

[15] N. Halbwachs, P. Raymond, and C. Ratel. Generating efficient code from data-flow programs. In *Programming Language Implementation and Logic Programming*, volume 528 of *Lecture Notes in Computer Science*, pages 207–218, 1991.

[16] R. H. Halstead, Jr. Multilisp: a language for concurrent symbolic computation. *ACM Trans. Program. Lang. Syst.*, 7:501–538, 1985.

[17] R. L. Jeronimo Castrillon and G. Ascheid. Maps: Mapping concurrent dataflow applications to heterogeneous mpsocs. *IEEE Trans. on Industrial Informatics*, page 19, nov 2011.

[18] E. A. Lee and D. G. Messerschmitt. Static scheduling of synchronous data flow programs for digital signal processing. *IEEE Trans. Computers*, 36(1):24–25, 1987.

[19] J. Niehren, J. Schwinghammer, and G. Smolka. A concurrent lambda calculus with futures. *Theoretical Computer Science*, 364(3):338–356, Nov. 2006.

[20] C. Pagetti, J. Forget, F. Boniol, M. Cordovilla, and D. Lesens. Multi-task implementation of multi-periodic synchronous programs. *Discrete Event Dynamic Systems*, 21(3), 2011.

[21] D. Potop-Butucaru, B. Caillaud, and A. Benveniste. Concurrency in synchronous systems. *Formal Methods in System Design*, 28(2):111, 2006.

[22] D. Sabel and M. Schmidt-Schauß. A contextual semantics for concurrent haskell with futures. In *Principles and Practices of Declarative Programming*, pages 101–112. ACM, 2011.

[23] S. Stuijk, T. Basten, M. Geilen, and H. Corporaal. Multiprocessor resource allocation for throughput-constrained synchronous dataflow graphs. In *Design Automation Conference*, pages 777–782. IEEE, 2007.

[24] D. Syme, T. Petricek, and D. Lomov. *The F# Asynchronous Programming Model*, volume 6539 of *Lecture Notes in Computer Science*, pages 175–189. Springer Verlag, 2011.

[25] S. Yuan, L. H. Yoong, and P. S. Roop. Compiling esterel for multi-core execution. In *Euromicro Conference on Digital System Design*, pages 727–735, 2011.

Towards Network-on-Chip Agreement Protocols

Borislav Nikolić and Stefan M. Petters *
CISTER/INESC-TEC, ISEP, IPP
Porto, Portugal
borni@isep.ipp.pt, smp@isep.ipp.pt

ABSTRACT

Demands for functionality enhancements, cost reductions and power savings clearly suggest the introduction of multi- and many-core platforms in real-time embedded systems. However, when compared to uni-core platforms, the many-cores experience additional problems, namely the lack of scalable coherence mechanisms and the necessity to perform migrations. These problems have to be addressed before such systems can be considered for integration into the real-time embedded domain.

We have devised several agreement protocols which solve some of the aforementioned issues. The protocols allow the applications to plan and organise their future executions both temporally and spatially (i.e. *when* and *where* the next job will be executed). Decisions can be driven by several factors, e.g. load balancing, energy savings and thermal issues. All presented protocols are analytically described, with the particular emphasis on their respective real-time behaviours and worst-case performance. The underlying assumptions are based on the multi-kernel model and the message-passing paradigm, which constitutes the communication between the interacting instances.

Categories and Subject Descriptors

C.3 [**Special-purpose and application-based systems**]: Real-time and embedded systems

Keywords

Real-Time, Many-Core, Embedded Systems, Agreement Protocols, Worst-Case Execution-Time

---

*This work was partially supported by National Funds through FCT (Portuguese Foundation for Science and Technology) and by ERDF (European Regional Development Fund) through COMPETE (Operational Programme 'Thematic Factors of Competitiveness'), within REPOMUC project, ref. FCOMP–01-0124-FEDER-015050, by FCT and the EU ARTEMIS JU funding, within RECOMP project, ref. ARTEMIS/0202/2009, JU grant nr. 100202 and by FCT and the ESF (European Social Fund) through POPH (Portuguese Human Potential Operational Program), under PhD grant SFRH/BD/81087/2011.

1. INTRODUCTION

With the current improvements in technology, there is an ever increasing need for *embedded systems*. So far these devices often had limited capacities, performed only predefined set of functions and operated in the conditions with explicitly posed constraints, such as occupied space and/or consumed power. Additionally, many embedded systems perform time-critical jobs (e.g. automotive industry, avionics), where not only the correctness of the computation is important, but also the duration of the execution itself. These systems are called *real-time embedded systems*.

1.1 Single-core → Multi-core → Many-core

Current real-time embedded systems are mostly single-core devices. However, there are several reasons which require a reassessment of this concept. Firstly, there is an increasing demand for functionality enhancements (i.e. more complex processing requires more powerful devices). Secondly, significant cost reduction can be achieved by integrating several of those devices into one. Very similar trends apply for power conservation reasons. Finally, some applications, due to their distributed nature, clearly demand extensive communication between interacting modules and can also benefit from further integration (e.g. trading systems, air traffic control).

The platforms in the server and high performance computing areas were progressing from single-cores to multi-cores and finally many-cores. The same evolution is visible in general purpose computers, although with an offset in time. Embedded systems lag even more behind the aforementioned technologies but the same trend exists.

However, the application of many-core platforms in the real-time embedded domain is far from trivial and brings new overheads. Firstly, isolation has to be provided between different executing applications (previously located on separate, independent devices). For instance, failures or misbehaving of one shouldn't influence the execution of the other applications which share the same system. Secondly, the concept of mixed criticalities has to be introduced and proper isolation has to be assured between applications of different importance.

1.2 Message-passing $\underset{predictability}{\overset{scalability}{\gg}}$ Coherency

Finally, current cache coherency mechanisms used in multi-cores are not applicable to many-core platforms, even for general purpose computers, due to scalability issues [9]. Current cache policies even cause performance drops when the number of cores increases to more than a dozen. [15] claims that future commodity systems will drop the idea of having a completely coherent system.

Sharing paradigm also imposes additional problems which are common for both uni- and many-core platforms, namely unpredictability and pessimism. Including the cache effects into the real-

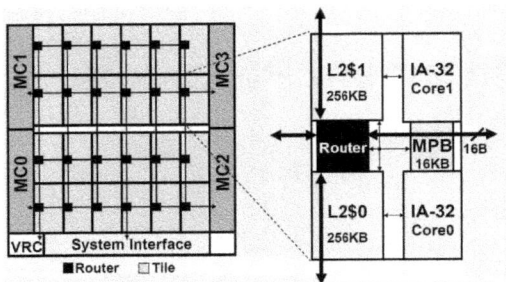

Figure 1: Intel's Single-Chip-Cloud (SCC)

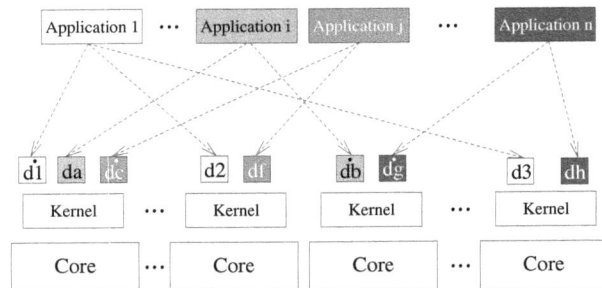

Figure 2: Architectural structure of the assumed model

time analysis presents a serious challenge even for single-cores as can be seen from the following works: [3] presents the idea how to incorporate the cache effects into the schedulability analysis by taking a probabilistic approach, while [18] governs code analysis so as to predict the cache misses. Performing the same in the many-core environment is even more complex and one solution to this outstanding problem is a methodology shift.

Although the message-passing paradigm was introduced many years ago, it was largely neglected due to the efficiency of the sharing paradigm when applied to the systems with small number of cores. [13] and [12] show that two approaches are dual and the dominance of one over another is highly dependant on the concrete purpose.

Current many-core devices, such as [20] and [10] (Figure 1) present experimental platforms which don't facilitate cache coherence mechanisms. The depicted system contains 24 tiles, each shared by two cores. The cores have private caches and communicate with the environment through hardware built-in support for message-passing called *Message-Passing Buffer* (MPB, see Figure 1).

Some operating systems, such as Barrelfish [2], advocate a *multi-kernel* approach in which every core runs a light-weight version of the OS. In such a system the kernel instances and respective applications running on top communicate with the corresponding entities located on other cores by utilising a message-passing paradigm, not only to maintain the correct system-wide state, but also to discuss temporal and spatial properties of future executions. The benefits of this approach are twofold; primarily the scalability is not an issue anymore, since it is well known from distributed and cloud computing areas that agreement protocols scale. Secondly, the message-passing model is predictable and therefore suitable for real-time analysis and, in our opinion, presents promising platform for further investigation. Secondary benefits that come with the design are the possibilities to perform load balancing, energy savings by deliberately shutting down some of the cores, thermal management, even wear out, etc.

The areas of networking, distributed and parallel computing study agreement protocols with the emphasis on either security [1], [14] or fault-tolerance [5], [7]. The performance of network-on-chip synchronisation is discussed in [21] and [6]. Present many-core scheduling algorithms [4], [11] assume instantaneous migrations with negligible overhead. However, no work was done in calculating and incorporating the communication and the migration costs into the schedulability analysis.

Based on the assumption of a non-coherent many-core platform utilising message passing as a primary primitive, our contribution is to present several agreement protocols that facilitate the task-level job migrations. The protocols provide mechanisms to derive such a decision but do not prescribe a specific policy for the migration for e.g. load balancing purposes. All protocols are analytically described and compared in terms of the amount of messages generated as well as their worst-case behaviour in successfully migrating a given job.

In the next section we give an in-detail description of the assumed model. Then, in Section 3 several agreement protocols are described with particular emphasis on their real-time characteristics. Section 4 focuses on the evaluation of the protocols. Finally, Section 5 concludes the paper with the summary of the findings, and the description of the future work.

2. MODEL

2.1 The Hardware

The platform of interest is one many-core device with network-on-chip as an interconnection network, such as [20], [10] or [19]. The system is non-coherent, which means that assuring and maintaining correct and coherent system-wide state is the responsibility of either the OS or the applications themselves. The transfer on the mesh network is packet-based, utilising wormhole routing technique [8] with the routes computed by dimensioned-ordered routing algorithm XY (the packets always travel in the X direction first) which is present in [10] and [19] platforms. Additionally we assume the classification of the bus traffic on *agreement protocol messages* (in subsequent text referred to as agreement messages) and *data messages* transporting the context of a task between cores. We assign different priorities to these two types of messages and allow preemptions on the bus between them, as is presented in [17]. Current many-core platforms, such as [10] have the facilities which can be instrumented to implement this concept (e.g. virtual channels and message classes). The purpose of message classification will be described later.

2.2 The Kernels

Every core in the system runs its own independent kernel instance. All the kernels are mutually connected and constitute the basic communication facility. The kernel exposes some of its functionalities to the applications so that they can communicate with the application instances on the other cores. The kernel instances perform local, on-core scheduling and give higher priority to protocol-related OS operations such as sending/receiving agreement/data messages, and computations related to the agreement protocol, than to the task execution which is preemptable at any point.

2.3 The Applications

The applications periodically or sporadically generate a sequence of jobs. The execution of a job has to complete on the core where it started, but the execution of the next job can commence on some other core (task-level migrations). Every application a can execute only on a subset of cores. On each of those cores, the execution code exists, constituting an entity called dispatcher d. During one protocol instance, the dispatchers of the same application, each located on a different core, communicate between themselves and agree on the location where the next job will be executed. The dispatcher that performs the execution at current time instance is called *master dispatcher* - $\overset{\bullet}{d}$ and at any given point in time an application has exactly one master. It is also responsible for initiating the protocol once a job execution on its core is completed. The other dispatchers are considered as *slave dispatchers* - $\overset{o}{d}$ and they only participate in the protocol execution, until they are elected master, at which point in time the former master becomes a slave dispatcher. The example in Figure 2 follows the aforementioned convention.

After a job execution is completed, a master initiates the protocol; i.e. it communicates with the slaves in order to select new master. The messages exchanged by the dispatchers during this stage are called agreement messages. They are light in size and have a high priority on the mesh. The new master is selected by some criteria (least utilised core, the core with the lowest temperature, the least used core, etc.). The actual policy is immaterial for the discussion in this paper, but might be centred around e.g. load balancing or likelihood of successful execution. If the newly selected master is also the current one, then no further activities are required and the protocol stops until the master executes the next job and starts the protocol again. In the other case, when the newly selected master is different from the current one, the migration occurs. It is performed in the following way:

The current master sends the execution context to the new master. The context is the state of a task used during the execution of the next job. Its size depends on the application and may range from minimal to rather large contexts (e.g. streaming applications). For that reason the messages carrying the context are classified as data messages, have lower priority on the mesh and therefore can be preempted by agreement messages as described in [17]. The preemption points are on the granularity of one packet - the size of the agreement message m_c. Therefore the agreement message can be blocked on the mesh by data message m_d^a, belonging to some application a, for at most one packet traversal time. Similarly, the OS instructions related to the agreements messages (sending/receiving of the agreement message l_s^a, l_r^a or protocol related computation l_c) are non-preemptable, serviced in fifo order and have higher priority than the OS instructions related to the data messages (sending/receiving of the data l_s^d, l_r^d) which are preemptable at any point.

The selection of the data for the context transfer can be the responsibility of either the kernels or the applications themselves. In the first case the local kernel extracts the context from the data section of the current master process and sends it to remote kernel which stores it into the data section of the next master process. In the latter case the programmers are responsible for classifying the variables on those which are shared among all the dispatchers and those which are purely local.

In this work, we assume no dispatcher failures, cross-applications independence, the protocol is always of higher priority than the task execution, which is preemptable at any point. In addition to previously described, we use the following variables:
- a_d - the number of dispatchers belonging to application a
- $a(d)$ - the application to which dispatcher d belongs
- $c(d)$ - the core on which dispatcher d is located
- $p(d)$ - the on-core protocol overhead of dispatcher d
- $\widehat{m_a}$ - the maximum number of the agreement messages exchanged by the dispatchers of the application a during one protocol execution
- r_s - the latency of the router to switch to new port
- r_t - the latency of the router to transfer the packet

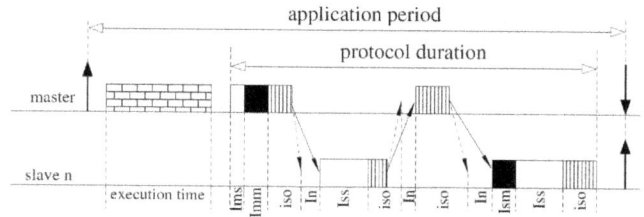

Figure 3: Master-slave protocol

Algorithm 1 MS(a) The execution algorithm of the protocol MS

Input: a

1: $\overset{\bullet}{d}.broadcast()$
2: **repeat**
3:    $wait()$
4: **until** $(received == a_d)$
5: $d = \overset{\bullet}{d}.calculate\_next()$
6: **if** $d! = \overset{\bullet}{d}$ **then**
7:    $\overset{\bullet}{d}.send\_context(d)$
8: **end if**

- w - mesh width
- $T(d)$ - the minimum inter-arrival time of the application to which dispatcher d belongs
- $C(d)$ - the execution time of one job of the application to which dispatcher d belongs
- $n_h(i)$ - the number of hops the message i takes when traversing from the source to the destination
- $\widehat{n_h(d)}$ - the maximum distance in hops between the dispatcher d and any other dispatcher of the same application

3. THE PROTOCOLS

3.1 Master-slave - MS

3.1.1 Protocol description

For easier comprehension, the protocol is illustrated with Algorithm 1. Firstly, the master dispatcher requests the statuses from all the slave dispatchers (the statuses can be system parameters such as current cpu utilisation, temperature, hardware characteristics, line 1). Every slave responds with its current status. Once the master receives all the replies (line 4) it selects the dispatcher which will execute the next job and therefore become the new master (line 5). Then, if the master is changing, the migration occurs, so the current execution context has to be transferred to the new master (lines 6-8). The aim is to calculate the worst-case protocol duration - *WCPD*.

The WCPD consists of several components, as depicted in Figure 3. It gives a graphical representation of one possible scenario, with the main objective to recognise and emphasize all the delay components. Note that in some other example the components might appear in different order, while some of them might even not exist. The first one is the execution of the protocol by the application of interest in the isolation (without any interference from the other applications) and we denote it by *iso*. Additionally, the master dispatcher can suffer an on-core interference caused by the other master and slave dispatchers while participating in their own protocols. These delays we denote by I_{mm} and I_{ms} respectively. Furthermore, the slave dispatchers can also suffer an on-core interference caused by the other on-core dispatchers and we recognise these interferences as I_{sm} and I_{ss}. Finally, the application of interest can suffer the interference from all the other applications within the network, noted down as I_n.

The total number of the agreement messages exchanged by the dispatchers of the application a can be calculated as the sum of the broadcast messages from the master to all the slaves and their respective responses:

$$\widehat{m_a} = 2(a_d - 1) \tag{1}$$

The master is involved in every communication step and therefore suffers the overhead of sending and receiving $a_d - 1$ messages and performs a single computation. The slaves communicate with the master (1 receive, 1 send) and perform 1 computation. It is important to emphasize that at this stage only the agreement messages are under analysis. Consequently, the protocol execution on the master core and on the slave cores causes the following overheads:

$$p(\overset{\bullet}{d}) = (a_d - 1)l_s^a + (a_d - 1)l_r^a + l_c \tag{2}$$

$$p(\overset{\circ}{d}) = l_s^a + l_r^a + l_c \tag{3}$$

Since all the slave dispatchers process their messages in parallel, it is sufficient to recognise only the one which causes the greatest delay, while safely assuming that all the others have already finished their processing before.

Given this, the protocol latency when run in isolation - *iso* can be described as the sum of several terms (Equation 4). The first and the second are the protocol overheads on the master and only one slave core along with the overheads of sending and receiving the context, recognised as *master delay* and *slave delay*. The traversal of the messages that two aforementioned dispatchers exchange (the status request from the master and the response from the slave) is described with the *protocol delay*. Since the master is sending out a number of requests in rapid succession, we need to conservatively assume that the slave we consider is receiving the message last and that the reply is equally received last, that is, these two messages can be blocked within the network by all the other $\widehat{m_a} - 2$ messages of the same protocol. That delay is described with the *interference delay*. In order to analyse the worst-case, in this and all the subsequent protocols it is assumed that the context transfer is needed (i.e. the migration always occurs). The overhead of performing said operation is represented with the *context transfer delay*. Additional safe assumption is that the slave of interest is located the furthest away from the master, when compared to all the other slaves belonging to that application. Therefore, the traversal of the messages that the slave of interest and the master exchange is described with the term $\overset{\frown}{n_h(\overset{\bullet}{d})}$.

$$
iso = \overbrace{p(\overset{\bullet}{d}) + l_s^d}^{\text{master delay}} + \overbrace{p(\overset{\circ}{d}) + l_r^d}^{\text{slave delay}} + \overbrace{2n_h(\overset{\bullet}{d}) \left\lceil \frac{m_c}{w} \right\rceil (r_s + r_t)}^{\text{protocol delay}} +
$$

$$
\underbrace{(\widehat{m_a} - 2)\left\lceil \frac{m_c}{w} \right\rceil (r_s + r_t)}_{\text{interference delay}} + \underbrace{n_h(\overset{\bullet}{d})\left\lceil \frac{m_d}{w} \right\rceil (r_s + r_t)}_{\text{context transfer delay}} \tag{4}
$$

Furthermore, a master and the slaves may suffer the on-core interference caused by the masters and the slaves of the other applications, so these values also contribute to the WCPD.

In order to calculate the interference a master dispatcher of interest $\overset{\bullet}{d}$ suffers from the other on-core master dispatcher $\overset{\bullet}{d'}$ within the time interval t, we firstly compute the maximum number of protocol executions a master dispatcher $\overset{\bullet}{d'}$ can perform during the interval t.

THEOREM 3.1. *The number of protocol executions of any application within the time interval t can be at most $1 + \left\lceil \frac{t - C(d)}{T(d)} \right\rceil$*

PROOF. The theorem is proven by contradiction. Let us assume that $2 + \left\lceil \frac{t - C(d)}{T(d)} \right\rceil$ protocol executions occurred within the time

interval t. There are $\left\lceil \frac{t - C(d)}{T(d)} \right\rceil$ protocol executions surrounded by the first and the last and we refer to them as to *inner executions*. All the inner executions contribute to t with their entire application period and therefore require time interval of at least $\left\lceil \frac{t - C(d)}{T(d)} \right\rceil \times T(d)$ where only these can execute. Additionally, let us assume that ϵ is infinitesimally low but finite value representing the shortest possible duration of the protocol and that the first protocol execution with the duration of ϵ was delayed as much as possible and hence completed just before the interval of the inner executions started. Finally, the last protocol execution could not start before its application execution time $C(d)$ expires.

$$\epsilon + \left\lceil \frac{t - C(d)}{T(d)} \right\rceil \times T(d) + C(d) \geq \epsilon + \left(\frac{t - C(d)}{T(d)} \right) T(d) + C(d) = \epsilon + t \leq t \quad \square$$

The calculated value (see Theorem 3.1) is then multiplied by the overhead of a single protocol execution. Additionally, due to the higher priority that the protocol-related OS operations have over data-related, the master dispatcher of interest can suffer the interference from the context transfer performed by $\overset{\bullet}{d'}$ only once (when it tries to send its own context). The final value is represented with Equation 5.

$$I_{im}(t) = \left(1 + \left\lceil \frac{t - C(\overset{\bullet}{d'})}{T(\overset{\bullet}{d'})} \right\rceil \right) p(\overset{\bullet}{d'}) + l_s^d \tag{5}$$

If we elevate the reasoning presented in Equation 5 from the single on-core master to all the on-core masters, the interference a master $\overset{\bullet}{d}$ suffers can be calculated as:

$$I_{mm}(t) = \sum_{\forall \overset{\bullet}{d'} \in c(d) \wedge \overset{\bullet}{d'} \neq d} I_{im}(t) =$$

$$\sum_{\forall \overset{\bullet}{d'} \in c(d) \wedge \overset{\bullet}{d'} \neq d} \left(\left(1 + \left\lceil \frac{t - C(\overset{\bullet}{d'})}{T(\overset{\bullet}{d'})} \right\rceil \right) p(\overset{\bullet}{d'}) + l_s^d \right) \tag{6}$$

The same logic applies for the interference caused by the on-core slaves $\overset{\circ}{d'}$ to $\overset{\bullet}{d}$, where I_{is} stands for the interference caused by an individual on-core slave:

$$I_{ms}(t) = \sum_{\forall \overset{\circ}{d'} \in c(\overset{\bullet}{d})} I_{is}(t) = \sum_{\forall \overset{\circ}{d'} \in c(\overset{\bullet}{d})} \left(\left(1 + \left\lceil \frac{t - C(\overset{\circ}{d'})}{T(\overset{\circ}{d'})} \right\rceil \right) p(\overset{\circ}{d'}) + l_r^d \right) \tag{7}$$

Similarly, for the slave dispatcher of interest $\overset{\circ}{d}$ we define the interference it suffers from the masters $\overset{\bullet}{d'}$ and the slaves $\overset{\circ}{d'}$ located on its core.

$$I_{sm}(t) = \sum_{\forall \overset{\bullet}{d'} \in c(\overset{\circ}{d})} \left(\left(1 + \left\lceil \frac{t - C(\overset{\bullet}{d'})}{T(\overset{\bullet}{d'})} \right\rceil \right) p(\overset{\bullet}{d'}) + l_s^d \right) \tag{8}$$

$$I_{ss}(t) = \sum_{\forall \overset{\circ}{d'} \in c(\overset{\circ}{d}) \wedge \overset{\circ}{d'} \neq \overset{\circ}{d}} \left(\left(1 + \left\lceil \frac{t - C(\overset{\circ}{d'})}{T(\overset{\circ}{d'})} \right\rceil \right) p(\overset{\circ}{d'}) + l_r^d \right) \tag{9}$$

Additionally, every existing application a' can cause the interference to the application of interest a within the network. We calculate the network interference delay in a very naïve and simplistic way - Equation 10, i.e. by assuming that every application can cause the interference.

$$I_n(t) = \overbrace{\sum_{a' \neq a} \left(1 + \left\lceil \frac{t - C(a')}{T(a')} \right\rceil \right) \widehat{m_{a'}} \left\lceil \frac{m_c}{w} \right\rceil (r_s + r_t)}^{\text{agreement messages}} + \tag{10}$$

$$\underbrace{\sum_{a' \neq a} \left(1 + \left\lceil \frac{t - C(a') - l_s^d - l_r^d}{T(a')} \right\rceil \right) \left\lceil \frac{m_d^{a'}}{w} \right\rceil (r_s + r_t)}_{\text{data messages (contexts)}}$$

For every existing application, different than the application of interest, we calculate the maximum number of protocol occurrences during the time interval t (Theorem 3.1) and multiply it by the number of the agreement messages that the dispatchers of that application produce within the time of a single protocol execution. This value represents the maximum number of agreement messages that can utilise the network in the given time and that can belong to all the applications a' different than the application of interest a. Further, we conservatively assume that every one of those messages may block the application of interest. Finally, we calculate the maximum number of context transfers that can happen in a given time interval (the proof is a slight modification of the Theorem 3.1 and is therefore omitted). The same reasoning used for the agreement messages applies here; we assume that the context transfer of every application a' different than the application of interest a may block the context transfer of a within the network and hence causes the interference.

Therefore, the total delay $WCPD$ for the master m and the slave s is represented as the sum of all the aforementioned components:

$$WCPD(m,s) = \overbrace{iso}^{\text{isolation}} + \overbrace{I_{mm}(\text{WCPD}) + I_{ms}(\text{WCPD})}^{\text{master core interference}} + \underbrace{I_{sm}(\text{WCPD}) + I_{ss}(\text{WCPD})}_{\text{slave core interference}} + \underbrace{I_n(\text{WCPD})}_{\text{network}} \quad (11)$$

Due to the space constraints, inefficiency of this protocol and general non-applicability to the real-time domain, which will be discussed in the subsequent section, the process of finding the critical slave s (one that induces the greatest latency) for which the calculation would be performed is of no importance. Additionally, the solutions to the Equations 6-9 require a concrete classification of the on-core dispatchers (i.e. the exact information about which will be assumed as masters and which as slaves), so as to produce the greatest interference. This step of finding that particular setup is also omitted. Still, this protocol is presented because, given its simplicity, it is useful for the introduction of basic analytic parameters and helps the reader to develop an intuition about the assumed model, which will be helpful when reasoning about subsequent, more complex protocols.

3.1.2 Protocol limitations

The decision made on the master core is based on the data received from every individual slave. However, in the moment the master makes a decision, there are no guarantees that the state of the system on all the slave cores is identical as in the moment of their individual observations. One extreme, yet possible scenario occurs when one slave reports very high likelihood of accommodating the next execution on its core (e.g. the core is low utilised). Additionally, many other dispatchers from the same core might have also reported low utilisation during their protocol executions. As a result many of the applications might elect that particular core for the next execution and hence overload it, i.e. the sum of the individual utilisations of the applications might exceed the capacity of the core. We recognise *the race condition* as the greatest flaw of this approach. The protocol performance will receive additional attention in Section 4.

3.2 List

3.2.1 Protocol description

One approach in solving the aforementioned problem would be to change the topology of the connections between the dispatchers of the same application. Forming a linked list of dispatchers, besides reducing the total number of the messages, presents a concept that also excludes parallel processing through atomicity and as such is not prone to race conditions. Every dispatcher communicates only with its predecessor and successor in the list. The behaviour

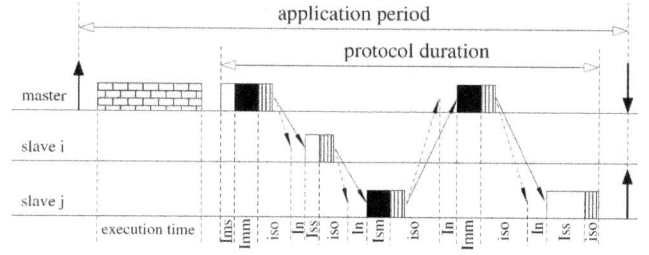

Figure 4: List protocol

Algorithm 2 LIST(a) The execution algorithm of the protocol LIST

Input: a
1: $a.scheduled = false$
2: $d = \overset{\bullet}{d}$
3: **repeat**
4:     **if** $(c(d).can\_schedule(a))$ **then**
5:         $a.scheduled = true$
6:         **if** $(d = \overset{\bullet}{d})$ **then**
7:             {master stays the same}
8:         **else**
9:             $d.request\_context(\overset{\bullet}{d})$
10:         **end if**
11:     **else**
12:         $d = d.next$
13:     **end if**
14: **until** $(a.scheduled = true)||(d = null)$

---

of the protocol is described with the Algorithm 2. When the protocol starts, firstly the master checks whether it can continue the execution and if so, stops the protocol (lines 4-7). In the other case, a master sends the message to the next dispatcher to try to schedule the application (line 12). If one of the slaves can do that, it recognizes itself as the new master and requests the context from the previous master dispatcher (lines 8-9). If during the whole traversal of the list none of the dispatchers can fit the execution on its core, the application is considered as not scheduled.

$$\widehat{m_a} = a_d \quad (12)$$

$$p(\overset{\bullet}{d}) = p(\overset{o}{d}) = l_c + l_s^a + l_r^a \quad (13)$$

The maximum number of the messages is equal to the total number of slave dispatchers $a_d - 1$ (in order to reach the tail of the list all of them have to be traversed) and 1 to request the context from the old master. The protocol overhead a master and all the slaves suffer is the same (1 send, 1 receive and 1 compute operation), however the master and only one of the slaves may additionally have to perform the transfer of the context. As stated in the description of the previous protocol, the worst-case analysis will assume that the migration occurs and therefore will incorporate that overhead into the calculation of the WCPD. Additional conservative assumption we exploit is that only the last dispatcher in the list will announce the possibility to schedule the application and hence the traversal of the entire list is required. For easier comprehension the WCPD is decomposed into several components, as depicted in Figure 4. Similarly to Figure 3, note that it illustrates only one possible scenario and that the ordering of the components is purely example specific.

$$iso = \overbrace{p(\overset{\bullet}{d}) + l_s^d}^{\text{master delay}} + \overbrace{\sum_{\forall \overset{o}{d} \in a} p(\overset{o}{d}) + l_r^d}^{\text{slaves delay}} + \overbrace{\sum_{i=1}^{\widehat{m_a}} n_h(i) \left\lceil \frac{m_c}{w} \right\rceil (r_s + r_t) +}^{\text{protocol delay}}$$
$$\underbrace{n_h(\overset{\bullet}{d}) \left\lceil \frac{m_d}{w} \right\rceil (r_s + r_t)}_{\text{context transfer delay}} \quad (14)$$

211

Algorithm 3 $MMD(\overset{\bullet}{d}, t)$ Maximum master delay over period t

Input: $\overset{\bullet}{d}, t$
Output: $delay$
1: $l_{mm} = l_{ms} = \varnothing$
2: **for all** $d \in c(\overset{\bullet}{d})$ **do**
3:     **if** $(size(l_{mm}) < \widehat{d_m} - 1)$ **then**
4:         ADD(l_{mm}, d)
5:     **else**
6:         **if** $(I_{im}(t) > min(l_{mm}))$ **then**
7:             MOVE$(l_{ms}, min(l_{mm}))$
8:             ADD(l_{mm}, d)
9:         **else**
10:             ADD(l_{ms}, d)
11:         **end if**
12:     **end if**
13: **end for**
14: **for all** $d \in c(\overset{\bullet}{d})$ **do**
15:     **if** $(d \in l_{mm})$ **then**
16:         $delay+ = I_{im}(t)$
17:     **else**
18:         $delay+ = I_{is}(t)$
19:     **end if**
20: **end for**
21: **RETURN** $delay$

Algorithm 4 $MSD(\overset{o}{d}, t)$ Maximum slave delay over period t

Input: $\overset{o}{d}, t$
Output: $delay$
1: $l_{mm} = l_{ms} = \varnothing$
2: **for all** $d \in c(\overset{o}{d})$ **do**
3:     **if** $(size(l_{sm}) < \widehat{d_m})$ **then**
4:         ADD(l_{sm}, d)
5:     **else**
6:         **if** $(I_{im}(t) > min(l_{sm}))$ **then**
7:             MOVE$(l_{ss}, min(l_{sm}))$
8:             ADD(l_{sm}, d)
9:         **else**
10:             ADD(l_{ss}, d)
11:     **end if**
12:     **end if**
13: **end for**
14: **for all** $d \in c(\overset{o}{d})$ **do**
15:     **if** $(d \in l_{sm})$ **then**
16:         $delay+ = I_{im}(t)$
17:     **else**
18:         $delay+ = I_{is}(t)$
19:     **end if**
20: **end for**
21: **RETURN** $delay$

The protocol overheads of the master and all the slaves contribute to the delay of the execution performed in isolation (see Equation 14). They are described with the terms *master delay* and *slaves delay* respectively and also include the on-core overheads of context transfer. Note that only one slave dispatcher (future master) receives the context. The traversal of the messages within the network is denoted by *protocol delay*. In this protocol the messages are sequentially sent and hence can not mutually interfere. Therefore the term *interference delay* described in the previous protocol does not exist here but at the same time all the messages contribute to the protocol delay with their entire traversal times. The last term accounts for the transmission of the context.

For the on-core interferences $I_{mm}, I_{sm}, I_{ms}, I_{ss}$ and for the network interference I_n the Equations 6-10 hold. Therefore, WCPD can be expressed by the Equation 15, where $\overset{\star}{d}$ presents the next master.

The **previous** and the **next master** can suffer the interference two times (see Figure 4); when performing the protocol routine and when sending/receiving the state. Note that these intervals are not of the same duration. The exact analysis, which requires the consideration of said intervals as well as the distance between them when calculating potential interferences, is cumbersome, computationally demanding and in our opinion unjustifiable approach. On the other hand, treating these intervals independently (i.e. not taking the distance into account) and assuming all the potential interferences that might occur in any of said intervals is very pessimistic and still computationally demanding. We obtain less pessimistic values and save the computation time by considering the entire WCPD as a single interval of interest during which both previous and next master may suffer the interference. The calculation performed for the current master is trivial, however in order to compute the worst-case delay of the future master, the slave which might suffer the greatest interference in the given period has to be recognised and used in further calculations.

$$WCPD(\overset{\bullet}{d}, \overset{\star}{d}) = \overbrace{iso}^{\text{isolation}} + \overbrace{I_{mm}(\text{WCPD}) + I_{ms}(\text{WCPD})}^{\text{master core interference}} + \overbrace{I_n(\text{WCPD})}^{\text{network}} +$$
$$\overbrace{\sum_{\forall \overset{o}{d} \in a \wedge \neq \overset{\star}{d}} \left(I_{sm}(t') + I_{ss}(t')\right)}^{\text{interference on slave cores / } \overset{\star}{d}} + \overbrace{I_{sm}(\text{WCPD}) + I_{ss}(\text{WCPD})}^{\text{next master core interference}} \quad (15)$$

All the **other slaves** can suffer the interference from all the other dispatchers residing on their respective cores only once - when they are performing their protocol routine (receive the message from the predecessor l_r^a, unsuccessfully try to schedule the application l_c, send the message to the successor in the list l_s^a). Therefore, for every slave the greatest possible interference from the on-core dispatchers (I_{sm}, I_{ss}) within that time interval t' has to be calculated. The relationship between the time t' and the interference suffered within that time is expressed with Equation 8 and Equation 9.

Note that some of the terms that constitute the WCPD are calculated by solving the Equations 6-10, which have a recursive notion and the calculation of the exact values requires an iterative approach. Also note that these Equations assume that for all the on-core, potentially blocking dispatchers it is already known whether they are masters or slaves, which is not true at the beginning of the calculation process. In order to solve this problem we firstly introduce two helper functions $MMD(\overset{\bullet}{d}, t)$ and $MSD(\overset{o}{d}, t)$ presented by Algorithm 3 and Algorithm 4 respectively.

Algorithm 3 calculates the maximum delay a master dispatcher can suffer from the other on-core dispatchers within the time interval t: $MMD(\overset{\bullet}{d}, t) = I_{mm}(t) + I_{ms}(t)$, and similarly Algorithm 4 calculates the maximum delay a slave dispatcher might suffer from the on-core dispatchers within the time interval t: $MSD(\overset{o}{d}, t) = I_{sm}(t) + I_{ss}(t)$. Every dispatcher residing on the core of interest can be either master or slave. The aim is to find the assignment (i.e. which dispatchers should be considered as masters and which as slaves) that will lead towards the greatest possible interference suffered by the master (for MMD) or the slave (for MSD) dispatcher of interest. Both algorithms exploit the strategy of finding the dispatchers that can induce the most protocol-related overhead within observed time and assume them as the masters, while considering all the others as the slaves. Note that the only difference is that MMD already assumes one preselected master - the master of interest, while that is not the case with the MSD.

Firstly, the lists of the on-core masters l_{mm} and the on-core slaves l_{ms} are cleared (line 1). Then, the iterations cover all dispatchers residing on that core. If the number of currently assumed master dispatchers is less than the maximum allowed number of the masters per core $\widehat{d_m}$, the dispatcher is declared as one and added to the list (lines 3, 4, 5). If the master list is full, but the dispatcher,

Algorithm 5 WCPD($\overset{\bullet}{d}$) The worst-case delay of the protocol List

Input: $\overset{\bullet}{d}$
1: $delay = 0$
2: **for all** $\overset{o}{d} \in a(d)$ **do**
3:    $t' = l_r^a + l_c + l_s^a$
4:    **repeat**
5:       $t' = MSD(\overset{o}{d}, t')$
6:    **until** balanced(t')
7: **end for**
8: **repeat**
9:    $MMD(\overset{\bullet}{d}, delay)$
10:    $wc\_slave\_delay = 0$
11:    $\overset{\star}{d} = null$
12:    **for all** $\overset{o}{d} \in a(d)$ **do**
13:       **if** $(MSD(\overset{o}{d}, delay) > wc\_slave\_delay)$ **then**
14:          $wc\_slave\_delay = MSD(\overset{o}{d})$
15:          $\overset{\star}{d} = \overset{o}{d}$
16:       **end if**
17:    **end for**
18:    $delay = WCPD(\overset{\bullet}{d}, \overset{\star}{d})$
19: **until** fix_point($delay$)
20: **RETURN** $delay$

Algorithm 6 HYBRID(a) The execution algorithm of the protocol HYBRID

Input: a
1: $\overset{\bullet}{d}.broadcast()$
2: **repeat**
3:    $wait()$
4: **until** ($received == a_d$)
5: $list = \overset{\bullet}{d}.calculate\_list()$
6: $a.scheduled = false$
7: $d = list.next()$
8: **repeat**
9:    **if** $(c(d).can\_schedule(a))$ **then**
10:       $a.scheduled = true$
11:    **else**
12:       $d = list.next()$
13:    **end if**
14: **until** ($a.scheduled$)
15: **if** $(d = \overset{\bullet}{d})$ **then**
16:    {master stays the same}
17: **else**
18:    $d.request\_context(\overset{\bullet}{d})$
19: **end if**

---

acting as a master, can incur the delay greater than the minimum of all the existing masters, it will automatically be assumed as one, causing the master with the minimum delay to be demoted to the slave group (lines 6, 7, 8). Otherwise, the dispatcher is added to the slave group (line 10). Therefore, the calculation of the total delay is a cumulative process and includes the summation of the master delay of all the dispatchers belonging to l_{mm} and the slave delay of the dispatchers belonging to l_{ms} (lines 14-20). The complexity of the algorithm is $O(\hat{d}_c \times \hat{d}_m \times log(\hat{d}_m))$, where $\hat{d}_c$ stands for the maximum number of the dispatchers per core (the number of iterations performed), while $\hat{d}_m \times log(\hat{d}_m)$ presents the computational complexity of keeping the master list sorted. Algorithm 4 behaves in very similar way, has the same complexity and does not require further discussion.

Finally, the Algorithm 5 performs the calculation of the WCPD. Firstly, for all the slaves the interference they suffer during their protocol routine $MSD(\overset{o}{d}, t') = I_{sm}(t') + I_{ss}(t')$ is calculated (lines 2-6). Then, the maximum interference a master may locally suffer within the observed time is computed (line 9). In order to find the future master, the maximum interference is calculated for all the slaves and their respective cores (lines 10-17). The aim of this computation is to find the critical slave (one suffering the greatest interference within the observed time) and recognise it as the next master dispatcher, while conservatively assuming that it is positioned at the end of the list. For all the other slaves the interference they suffer from the on-core dispatchers is already calculated (lines 2-6). Then, the total delay is augmented (line 18) and fed back into the calculation of the individual terms. The procedure repeats until the equation reaches the fix point (line 19). The computational complexity of the algorithm is $O(a_d \times C \times n)$, where C stands for the complexity of the algorithm MSD (calculated above), and n corresponds to the number of performed iterations before completion.

3.2.2 Protocol limitations

The execution stops at the moment when one of the traversed dispatchers announces the possibility to perform the execution. In most cases that dispatcher might not be the optimal option, e.g. some other core yet not traversed might have better characteristics. As implicitly stated, the greatest limitation of this protocol is that it always traverses the list in predefined, non-intelligent order and therefore is unable to easily perform any selective scheduling for load balancing, power management or any other purpose. If those issues are of no importance, then this concept presents one of the most suitable options, due to its low complexity. The performance of the protocol is additionally analysed in Section 4.

3.3 MS + LIST = HYBRID

3.3.1 Protocol description

In order to solve the aforementioned problems, a protocol named **HYBRID** is presented. It combines two already covered approaches with the primary objective of gaining the benefits of their respective positive sides.

The protocol is described with the Algorithm 6. The execution can be divided into two phases. The first one is similar to the MS protocol - the master broadcasts the request for the statuses of all the slave dispatchers and waits for corresponding responses (lines 1-4). Upon receiving all the messages, the master generates the list where all the dispatchers are ordered by the preference and likelihood of accommodating the next execution (line 5). Then, the second phase begins and it is similar to the execution of the List protocol. The dispatchers are being sequentially traversed according to their position in the generated list. The first one which announces the possibility to schedule the application stops the protocol (lines 7-14). We further apply the same conservative assumption used in the List protocol; the last dispatcher in the list is the only one that announces the possibility to schedule the application, and hence the list is entirely traversed.

$$\widehat{m_a} = \overbrace{2(a_d - 1)}^{\widehat{m_a}(ms)} + \overbrace{a_d}^{\widehat{m_a}(list)} \quad (16)$$

$$\overset{\bullet}{p(d)} = (a_d + 1)l_s^a + (a_d + 1)l_r^a + 2l_c \quad (17)$$

$$\overset{\triangle}{p(d)} = 2(l_r^a + l_c + l_s^a) \quad (18)$$

$$\overset{o}{p(d)} = l_r^a + l_c + l_s^a \quad (19)$$

The total number of the messages is equal to the sum of the messages exchanged during the execution of the MS protocol: $\widehat{m_a}(ms)$ and the List protocol: $\widehat{m_a}(list)$. The number of the messages a master and all the slaves exchange is also equal to the sum of the individual terms from both algorithms. Dispatcher $\overset{\triangle}{d}$ represents the one whose first phase (master-slave part of the protocol) executed with the greatest latency when compared to all the other dispatchers and we refer to it as to the critical slave. Due to the parallel nature of this process, for all the other slaves it can be assumed that their master-slave part finished before that of critical slave. Therefore, only the messages they exchange during the second phase (list part of the protocol) directly contribute to the delay, while the messages they exchange during the first phase contribute only indirectly (can interfere with the two messages the critical slave exchanges with the master, also in the first phase of the protocol).

The protocol execution when running in isolation is described with Equation 20. Firstly, the overhead of executing the protocol by the master, the critical slave and all the other slaves are recognised as *master delay*, *critical slave delay* and *all slaves / $\overset{\triangle}{d}$ delay*, respectively. Then, the latency of the two messages a master and the critical slave exchange during the first phase of the protocol is denoted by *MS delay*. Additionally, all the messages exchanged by the other dispatchers during this phase ($\widehat{m_a}(ms) - 2$) could potentially block the aforementioned two messages within the network and that delay is recognised as *interference delay*. In the second stage the messages are sequentially sent and processed so no further interferences can be caused by the messages of the same protocol. *LIST delay* stands for the latency of their traversal. Finally, the context transfer additionally augments the calculated value.

$$\begin{aligned} iso = & \overbrace{p(\overset{\bullet}{d})}^{\text{master delay}} + \overbrace{p(\overset{\triangle}{d})}^{\text{critical slave delay}} + \overbrace{\sum_{\forall \overset{o}{d} \in a \wedge \neq \overset{\triangle}{d}} p(\overset{o}{d})}^{\text{all slaves / } \overset{\triangle}{d} \text{ delay}} + \\ & \underbrace{2 n_h(\overset{\bullet}{d}) \left\lceil \frac{m_c}{w} \right\rceil (r_s + r_t)}_{\text{MS delay}} + \underbrace{(\widehat{m_a}(ms) - 2) \left\lceil \frac{m_c}{w} \right\rceil (r_s + r_t)}_{\text{interference delay}} + \\ & \underbrace{\sum_{i=1}^{\widehat{m_a}(list)} n_h(i) \left\lceil \frac{m_c}{w} \right\rceil (r_s + r_t)}_{\text{LIST delay}} + \underbrace{l_s^d + l_r^d + n_h(\overset{\bullet}{d}) \left\lceil \frac{m_d}{w} \right\rceil (r_s + r_t)}_{\text{context transfer delay}} \end{aligned}$$
(20)

By $\overset{\star}{d}$ we denote the future master. Although it is of no importance for the calculation of *iso*, it has a huge impact on the WCPD and has to be recognised. There are several additional factors which also contribute, namely the interferences a master and the slaves suffer from the other on-core master and slave dispatchers ($I_{mm}, I_{sm}, I_{ms}, I_{ss}$). Additionally, all the applications may block the messages of the application of interest within the network (I_n). For all of these terms the Equations 6-10 hold.

In order to calculate the interferences the **current master** $\overset{\bullet}{d}$ and the **next master** $\overset{\star}{d}$ may suffer we apply the same reasoning as for the List protocol; assume that the entire WCPD is an interval where the interferences might occur.

The **critical slave** $\overset{\triangle}{d}$ may suffer the interference at most twice (once during both phases of the protocol). Since the exact analysis is computationally demanding and the intervals are of the same length, we take an slightly modified approach: 1) calculate the interference during one interval and double it so as to assume two independent intervals of equal length, 2) calculate the interference during entire WCPD treating it as a single interval 3) take the minimum of those two, which represents a less pessimistic value.

All the **other slaves** may suffer the interference only once (during the second phase of the protocol), since the interference they suffer in the first phase of the protocol is already incorporated in the interference the critical slave suffers. The term t' has the same meaning as in the List protocol.

The solution to the Equation 21 requires an iterative approach. The calculation steps are described with the Algorithm 7. Firstly, for every slave the minimum interval t' and the interference suf-

---

Algorithm 7 WCPD($\overset{\bullet}{d}$) The worst-case delay of the protocol Hybrid

Input: $\overset{\bullet}{d}$
1: $delay = 0$
2: **for all** $\overset{o}{d} \in a(d)$ **do**
3:     $t' = l_r^a + l_c + l_s^a$
4:     **repeat**
5:        $t' = MSD(\overset{o}{d}, t')$
6:     **until** balanced(t')
7: **end for**
8: **repeat**
9:     $MMD(\overset{\bullet}{d}, delay)$
10:     $next\_master\_delay = 0$
11:     $\overset{\star}{d} = null$
12:     **for all** $\overset{o}{d} \in a(d)$ **do**
13:        **if** $(MSD(\overset{o}{d}, delay) > next\_master\_delay)$ **then**
14:           $next\_master\_delay = MSD(\overset{o}{d})$
15:           $\overset{\star}{d} = \overset{o}{d}$
16:        **end if**
17:     **end for**
18:     $crit\_sl\_delay = 0$
19:     $\overset{\triangle}{d} = null$
20:     **for all** $\overset{o}{d} \in a(d) \wedge \neq \overset{\star}{d}$ **do**
21:        **if** $(min\{2 \times MSD(\overset{o}{d}, t'), MSD(\overset{o}{d}, delay)\} > crit\_sl\_delay)$ **then**
22:           $crit\_sl\_delay = min\{2 \times MSD(\overset{o}{d}, t'), MSD(\overset{o}{d}, delay)\}$
23:           $\overset{\triangle}{d} = \overset{o}{d}$
24:        **end if**
25:     **end for**
26:     $delay = WCPD(\overset{\bullet}{d}, \overset{\star}{d}, \overset{\triangle}{d})$
27: **until** fix_point($delay$)
28: **RETURN** $delay$

---

fered during that time are calculated (lines 2-7). Then, the delay a master suffers during the observed time interval is computed (line 9). The next master is found such that it causes the maximum possible delay within observed time (lines 10-17). Then, the critical slave is recognised (lines 18-25). For all the other slaves the maximum interference is already computed (lines 2-7). Finally, the calculation of the WCPD is performed with the selected dispatchers and their respective roles (current master, next master and critical slave, line 26). Note that in order to elaborate the scenario which causes the greatest delay, it is required to assume that the next master and the critical slave are not the same dispatcher, although in the actual execution it may happen. The process repeats until WCPD reaches fix point (line 27). The computational complexity is twice of that for List protocol.

$$\begin{aligned} WCPD(\overset{\bullet}{d}, \overset{\triangle}{d}, \overset{\star}{d}) = & \overbrace{iso}^{\text{isolation}} + \overbrace{I_{mm}(\text{WCPD}) + I_{ms}(\text{WCPD})}^{\text{master core interference}} + \overbrace{I_n(\text{WCPD})}^{\text{network}} + \\ & \underbrace{min\{2(I_{sm}(t') + I_{ss}(t')), (I_{sm}(\text{WCPD}) + I_{ss}(\text{WCPD}))\}}_{\text{latest slave } \overset{\triangle}{d} \text{ core interference}} + \\ & \underbrace{I_{sm}(\text{WCPD}) + I_{ss}(\text{WCPD})}_{\text{next master } \overset{\star}{d} \text{ core interference}} + \underbrace{\sum_{\forall \overset{o}{d} \in a \wedge \neq \overset{\star}{d} \wedge \neq \overset{\triangle}{d}} (I_{sm}(t') + I_{ss}(t'))}_{\text{slave cores interference / } \{\overset{\triangle}{d}, \overset{\star}{d}\}} \end{aligned}$$
(21)

3.3.2 Protocol limitations

During the master-slave part of the protocol, all the dispatchers are queried for their current statuses, while during the list part they sequentially try to schedule the application. The strategy of the protocol is to firstly attempt to assign the execution to those dispatchers which reported the best possible environment for the accommodation of the next execution. Due to its optimistic nature, when compared to the other protocols, this one has higher probabilities of completing before the WCPD, but at the expense of greater number of messages. In fact, since the most suitable candidates are checked firstly, it is reasonable to expect that they will be able to accommodate the execution and therefore stop the protocol at early stages. Note that the race condition still exists but its effect is mitigated. The behaviour of the protocol is the focus of subsequent section.

4. EVALUATIONS

The experiments were performed on the extended version of the simulator *SPARTS* [16]. The 2D-mesh characteristics have been chosen to be equivalent to those available for SCC [10], while for OS operations we assume latencies valid for present micro-kernels (OS calls for accessing the local router to send/receive the message). The aim is to observe the relations between the predicted and the measured WCPD for different protocols under a given workload. Additionally, by varying the number of dispatchers we investigate how this protocol parameter and the amount of traffic influence aforementioned relations and affect the overall protocol behaviour. We allow the mapping of the dispatchers to the cores to be a random process, since dispatcher placement is not in the scope of this paper. We test three presented protocols, each of them with synchronous and asynchronous application releases. In the former case, the idea is to trigger and observe the state where all the applications in the system try to communicate at the same time (i.e. to generate significant network contention), while the latter models a more realistic scenario.

WCET of protocol-related OS operations ($l_s^a, l_r^a, l_c, l_s^d, l_r^d$)	100.000 cycles
Router switch time (r_s)	1 cycle
Router transfer time (r_t)	3 cycles
2D mesh width (w)	16 bytes
Agreement message size (m_c)	4 bytes
Data message size (m_d^a)	1024 bytes

4.1 Observing the pessimism

We simulate the execution of 200 applications on a 10×10 platform. The applications are represented with 5 dispatchers each, have the utilisation of 25% and constitute the workload with the overall system utilisation of 50%.

In Figure 5 the horizontal axis represents the measured WCPD, expressed as the fraction of the analytical (theoretical) WCPD. The vertical axis stands for the amount of the applications which fall into given category (certain ratio between observed and calculated WCPD), expressed as the percentage of the total application-set size.

Since the **MS protocol** always generates the constant amount of messages, it induces the least amount of pessimism. As a consequence, measured WCPD represents greater fraction of calculated WCPD than in other protocols.

As expected, the **List protocol** overestimates the number of messages (always assumes the traversal of the entire list while in real cases it does not occur often) and hence induces greater pessimism.

The **Hybrid protocol** consists of the messages of the both aforementioned approaches. Since the messages exchanged in the first phase of the protocol follow the logic explained for the MS protocol (are constant), and since they constitute 2/3 of the maximum number of messages, it is reasonable to expect that the pessimism induced by the Hybrid protocol will place it in between of two aforementioned approaches. However, the fact that the Hybrid approach sorts the dispatchers and traverses them according to desired criteria has a significant impact. As a consequence, the number of visited dispatchers is small and hence the protocol is efficient,

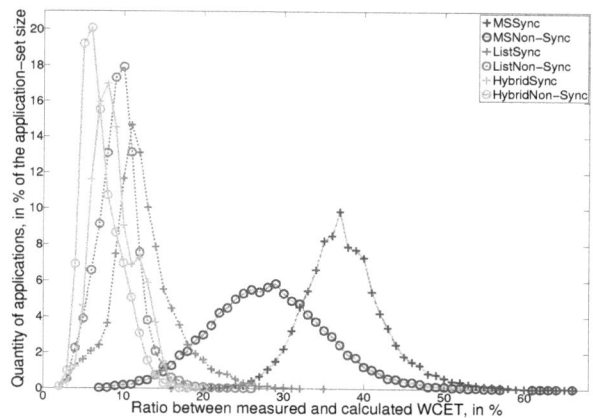

Figure 5: Distribution of pessimism

which results with low execution times and high pessimism. On the other hand, the List protocol pays the price of non-intelligent pre-determined traversing order, causing many long routes which eventually result with longer execution times and lower level of pessimism. Due to aforementioned facts, the amount of pessimism is greater in the Hybrid than in the List protocol.

As expected it holds for all the protocols that the **synchronous releases** create additional overhead as a result of the extensive amount of traffic generated in short periods of time and hence cause longer execution times and less pessimism.

4.2 Parameter variations

The aim is to observe how parameter changes influence the behaviour of the protocols. The simulation inputs are equal to ones used in the previous experiment, with the only difference that the number of the dispatchers that form an application is not constant and ranges from 2 to 15.

In Figure 6 and Figure 7 the horizontal axis represents the number of dispatchers per application. The vertical axis in Figure 6 stands for the measured WCPD, expressed as the percentage of the analytic WCPD, while in Figure 7 the absolute values of the aforementioned terms are presented.

The **MS protocol** with non-synchronised releases shows approximately constant level of pessimism on the whole domain. The increase of the pessimism in the beginning of the graph is explained with low saturated network and the overestimation of the network congestion. As the number of the dispatchers and hence messages increase, the pessimism slowly starts decreasing. Very similar reasoning applies for MS protocol with synchronised releases; fewer messages and simultaneous protocol executions cause low amount of pessimism. Until certain point, the network successfully copes with the increased amount of the dispatchers and the messages, hence causing the raise of the pessimism. Near the end of the graph, the traffic congestion becomes more significant and similar trend of slight pessimism decrease is noticeable.

As expected, both the **List protocol** runs (with and without synchronous releases) show the decrease of the pessimism when the number of the dispatchers increases. The explanation is that in many cases the dispatchers placed near the end of the list are not traversed, while the analysis always assumes the traversal of the entire list. Figure 7 demonstrates that on the most of the domain additional dispatchers cause a barely noticeable increase of the WCPD, confirming previous statement that the dispatchers positioned in the list far from the master are in most of the cases not used. However, after a certain point, the protocol starts to pay the price of predetermined, non-intelligent traversing, hence causing long routes as a re-

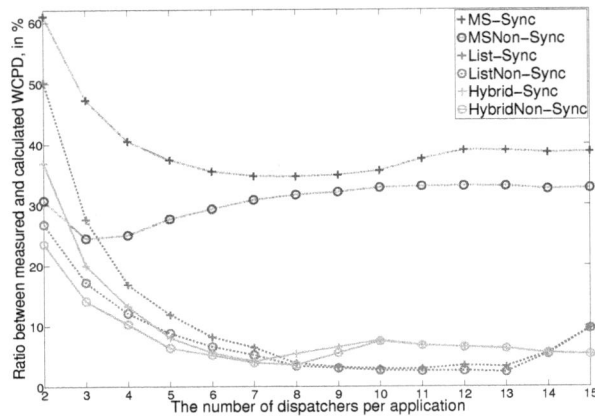

Figure 6: The impact of the number of the dispatchers on the protocol delay

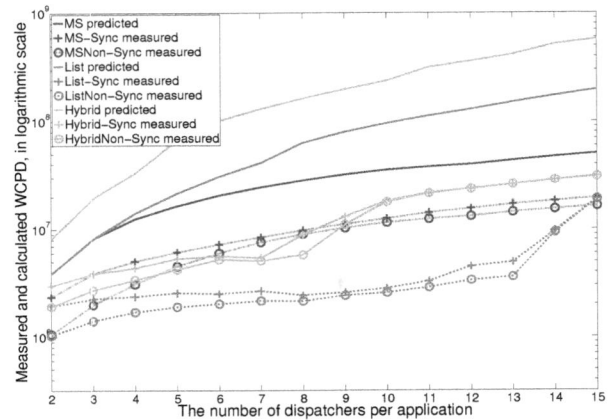

Figure 7: The impact of the number of the dispatchers on the protocol delay

sult of frequent visits to the dispatchers which can't accommodate the execution. Therefore, significant decrease of the pessimism near the end of the graph is visible, leading to a counter-intuitive conclusion that this protocol does not scale when the number of dispatchers is more than a dozen.

Finally, when compared to the List, the **Hybrid protocol** shows similar behaviour and due to the safe assumption of the entire list traversal causes steady decrease in the pessimism as the number of the dispatchers increases. However, after a certain point, the Hybrid protocol pays the price of the extensive communication, causes network congestion and shows steady but only temporary increase in WCPD in the middle of the graph. One surprising conclusion drawn from the Figure 7 is that there exists an interval (between 3 and 8 dispatchers) where the Hybrid protocol has a shorter WCPD than MS protocol, despite the fact that it always induces more messages. The explanation is that Hybrid efficiently selects the next master dispatcher, while MS protocol due to race conditions causes fragmentation and highly loaded cores, where on-core overhead of the communication becomes a predominant factor. Additional surprising fact is that the Hybrid protocol successfully copes with the network congestion by drastically minimising the duration of its second phase (i.e. efficiently finding the next master dispatcher, unlike the List protocol). As is visible in Figure 6 and Figure 7, the Hybrid protocol scales well, shows good average and worst-case performance in both relative and absolute values, but causes high pessimism which is a price paid for more complex analysis.

5. CONCLUSIONS AND FUTURE WORK

In this paper we presented the model for incorporation of many-core platforms into the real-time domain. It is based on the multi-kernel paradigm and utilises message-passing as a communication primitive. We devised several agreement protocols and analytically described their characteristics. Through simulations, we tested said protocols and compared the measured WCPD against analytical predictions, so as to evaluate the pessimism of the analysis. Finally, we gave a head-to-head comparison of all the protocols, where we compared corresponding WCPDs and elaborated on the individual potentials for scalability.

The future work can include further simulations of concrete applications and protocols, in order to observe the deviations between the WCPD and the average cases, but also for the comparison between the measured and theoretically predicted WCPD. The simulations can also be used to give head-to-head comparison of different protocols in terms of efficiency, e.g. when analysing generated traffic, power management or load balancing. The model and the respective protocol overheads can be integrated in the schedul-

ing analysis. Furthermore, new protocols can be devised with the characteristics which fit some particular requirements: strong guarantees, good average-case behaviour, limited communication, dispatcher failure, etc. Finally, the placement of the dispatchers belonging to one application (locality) is of great importance and tighter bounds could be derived with some assumptions which are addressing that issue.

6. REFERENCES

[1] Y. Amir, Y. Kim, C. Nita-Rotaru, and G. Tsudik. On the performance of group key agreement protocols. In *22th ICDCS*, 2002.

[2] A. Baumann, P. Barham, P.-E. Dagand, T. Harris, R. Isaacs, S. Peter, T. Roscoe, A. Schüpbach, and A. Singhania. The multikernel: A new os architecture for scalable multicore systems. In *SOSP*, 2009.

[3] G. Bernat, A. Colin, and S. M. Petters. WCET analysis of probabilistic hard real-time systems. In *24th RTSS*, pages 279–288, Austin, Texas, USA, Dec 3–5 2002.

[4] K. Bletsas and B. Andersson. Preemption-light multiprocessor scheduling of sporadic tasks with high utilisation bound. In *30th RTSS*, 2009.

[5] S. Chakravorty and L. Kale. A fault tolerance protocol with fast fault recovery. In *PDPS*, 2007.

[6] X. Chen and S. Chen. Dsbs: Distributed and scalable barrier synchronization in many-core network-on-chips. In *TrustCom*, 2011.

[7] J. Cowling, D. Myers, B. Liskov, R. Rodrigues, and L. Shrira. Hq replication: a hybrid quorum protocol for byzantine fault tolerance. In *7th OSDI*, 2006.

[8] W. Dally and C. Seitz. The torus routing chip. *Distr. Comput.*, 1986.

[9] N. Eisley, L.-S. Peh, and L. Shang. In-network cache coherence. *J. Comp. Arch. Lett.*, 2006.

[10] Intel. *Single-Chip-Cloud Computer*. http://techresearch.intel.com/ProjectDetails.aspx?Id=1.

[11] S. Kato, N. Yamasaki, and Y. Ishikawa. Semi-partitioned scheduling of sporadic task systems on multiprocessors. In *21st ECRTS*, 2009.

[12] H. C. Lauer and R. M. Needham. On the duality of operating system structures. *SIGOPS Oper. Syst. Rev.*, 1979.

[13] T. LeBlanc and E. Markatos. Shared memory vs. message passing in shared-memory multiprocessors. In *PDPS*, 1992.

[14] P. Lee, J. Lui, and D. Yau. Distributed collaborative key agreement protocols for dynamic peer groups. In *Int. Conf. Netw. Protocols*, 2002.

[15] T. G. Mattson, R. Van der Wijngaart, and M. Frumkin. Programming the intel 80-core network-on-a-chip terascale processor. In *Int. Conf. Supercomp.*, 2008.

[16] B. Nikolić, M. A. Awan, and S. M. Petters. SPARTS: Simulator for power aware and real-time systems. In *8th IEEE Int. Conf. Emb. Softw. & Syst.*, Changsha, China, Nov 2011. IEEE.

[17] Z. Shi and A. Burns. Real-time communication analysis for on-chip networks with wormhole switching. In *Int. Symp. Netw.-on-Chip*, 2008.

[18] F. Stappert and P. Altenbernd. Complete worst-case execution time analysis of straight-line hard real-time programs. *J. Syst. Arch.*, 46:339–355, Feb 2000.

[19] Tilera. *TILEPro64 Processor*. http://www.tilera.com/products/processors/TILEPRO64.

[20] S. Vangal, J. Howard, G. Ruhl, S. Dighe, H. Wilson, J. Tschanz, D. Finan, A. Singh, T. Jacob, S. Jain, V. Erraguntla, C. Roberts, Y. Hoskote, N. Borkar, and S. Borkar. An 80-tile sub-100-w teraflops processor in 65-nm cmos. *J. Solid-State Circ.*, 2008.

[21] O. Villa, G. Palermo, and C. Silvano. Efficiency and scalability of barrier synchronization on noc based many-core architectures. In *CASES*, 2008.

Input-Output Robustness for Discrete Systems *

Paulo Tabuada
University of California
Los Angeles
tabuada@ee.ucla.edu

Ayca Balkan
University of California
Los Angeles
abalkan@ucla.edu

Sina Y. Caliskan
University of California
Los Angeles
caliskan@ee.ucla.edu

Yasser Shoukry
University of California
Los Angeles
yshoukry@ee.ucla.edu

Rupak Majumdar
Max Planck Institute
for Software Systems
rupak@mpi-sws.org

ABSTRACT

Robustness is the property that a system only exhibits small deviations from the nominal behavior upon the occurrence of small disturbances. While the importance of robustness in engineering design is well accepted, it is less clear how to verify and design discrete systems for robustness. We present a theory of *input-output robustness* for discrete systems inspired by existing notions of *input-output stability (IO-stability)* in continuous control theory. We show that IO-stability captures two intuitive goals of robustness: bounded disturbances lead to bounded deviations from nominal behavior, and the effect of a sporadic disturbance disappears in finitely many steps. We show that existing notions of robustness for discrete systems do not have these two properties. For systems modeled as finite-state transducers, we show that IO-stability can be verified and the synthesis problem can be solved in polynomial time. We illustrate our theory using a reference broadcast synchronization protocol for wireless networks.

Categories and Subject Descriptors

D.2.4 [**Software Engineering**]: Software/program verification

General Terms

Design

Keywords

Robustness, stability, discrete systems, automata

---

*This work was partially supported by the NSF awards 0820061, 0953994, 1035916, and by the NSF Expeditions in Computing project ExCAPE: Expeditions in Computer Augmented Program Engineering.

1. MOTIVATION

A robust system is one that only modestly deviates from the nominal correct behavior upon the occurrence of small disturbances. Although it is accepted that engineered systems should be robust, it is less clear how to define robustness for discrete systems, such as finite-state transition systems.

In this paper, we present a theory of robustness for discrete systems. Our starting point is the research on robustness in continuous control theory, where one designs a controller for a "nominal" behavior assuming no disturbances and provides two guarantees: bounded disturbances have bounded consequences, and "nominal" behavior is eventually resumed after disturbances disappear. We adapt this view of robustness to the discrete setting by taking an input-output perspective of discrete systems. We define systems as transducers $f : \Sigma^* \to \Lambda^*$ mapping streams over an alphabet of inputs $\Sigma = \Sigma^c \times \Sigma^d$ to streams over an alphabet of outputs Λ. The alphabet Σ^c represents system inputs (also called *control* inputs) and the alphabet Σ^d represents *disturbances*. Typically, the designer designs the system assuming a nominal model of the environment, modeled by the stream $\perp^*$ for a special symbol $\perp \in \Sigma^d$. Disturbances represent deviations from the nominal model due to mismatches between the assumptions made about the environment at design time and the environment at run time. What goal should a robust design have? In keeping with robust continuous control, we postulate the following two natural requirements. First, every small disturbance should lead to a small deviation from the nominal behavior. Second, we require the effect of a sporadic disturbance to disappear over time. That is, if the environment deviates from the nominal for one step and subsequently follows the nominal environment, we require the effect of the deviation to disappear in finitely many steps. In this paper, we present a theory of robustness that captures both requirements.

To proceed, we must quantify "small" disturbances and "close" behaviors. In control theory, the elements in the sets Σ and Λ have well defined physical meaning —*e.g.*, voltages, currents, pressures, velocities— and thus these sets are equipped with norms that quantify the magnitude of their elements. In our setting, we endow Σ^* and Λ^* with quantitative information. We assume the existence of maps I and O taking strings in Σ^* and Λ^* respectively to *costs* in $\mathbb{N}_0$. Moreover, we require that $O(f(\sigma)) = 0$ for $\sigma \in \Sigma^*$ iff the behavior is correct.

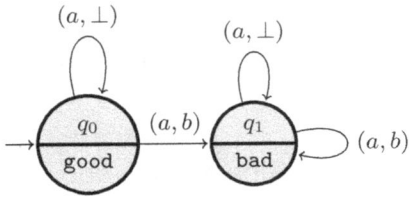

Figure 1: **Automaton satisfying inequality (1) but for which the effects of sporadic disturbances do not disappear.**

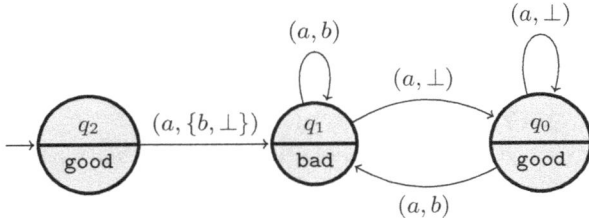

Figure 2: **Automaton where the effects of sporadic disturbances disappear in finite time, but where the system deviates from the nominal behavior even when there is no disturbance.**

The requirement that small disturbances lead to small deviations from nominal behavior is formulated as the inequality:

$$O(f(\sigma)) \leq \gamma I(\sigma) \qquad \forall \sigma \in \Sigma^*, \qquad (1)$$

requiring the consequences $O(f(\sigma))$ to be no greater than the disturbance magnitude $I(\sigma)$ amplified by a gain γ. This inequality, or a variation of it, appeared in the recent work of Tarraf et al. on robustness of systems with finite input and output alphabets [20] and in Bloem et al. [4]. The same inequality also appeared in studies of robustness in control theory as old as [22], see [23] for a historical account. While it captures the first requirement on robust designs, it ignores the second, and we show through an example why this is not totally satisfactory.

Consider the automaton in Figure 1. The alphabets are $\Sigma^c = \{a\}$, $\Sigma^d = \{\perp, b\}$, $\Lambda = \{\mathsf{good}, \mathsf{bad}\}$, and $O(\lambda) = 0$ for any string $\lambda \in \Lambda^*$ whose last symbol is good and $O(\lambda) = 100$ for any string whose last symbol is bad. For the input strings we have $I(\sigma^c, \sigma^d) = 0$ for any string such that σ^d consists of only $\perp$s and $I(\sigma^c, \sigma^d) = 10$ for any string such that σ^d contains at least one b. It is simple to see that the inequality $O(f(\sigma)) \leq 10 I(\sigma)$ holds, and thus the system is robust if we take inequality (1) as the definition of robustness. However, it is also clear that a sporadic disturbance described by the input string $b \perp^*$ will force the output to be bad for every time step after the first. Intuitively, we would expect that a robust system would return to normal behavior once a disturbance disappears. As this example shows,[1] the in-

equality (1) *does not* require such behavior and thus needs to be strengthened.

This leads us to our second requirement, the effect of a sporadic disturbance should disappear in finite time. This property appeared in the work of Doyen et al., see [9], as a different notion of robustness. Requiring the effects of sporadic disturbances to disappear in finite time does not guarantee that bounded disturbances lead to bounded consequences as the automaton in Figure 2 shows. The output alphabet and the output cost functions are the same as in the previous scenario. The alphabet Σ^d is now given by $\Sigma^d = \{\perp, b\}$ and $I(\sigma^c, \sigma^d)$ is 0 for any string σ^d containing only $\perp$'s and is 10 for any string σ^d containing at least one b. We then see that although the effect of the sporadic disturbance $b \perp^*$, disappears in one step, the system deviates from the nominal behavior even in the absence of the disturbances, e.g., when $\sigma^d = \perp$. It is easily seen that in this case it is not possible to find any γ that satisfies inequality (1) since $I(\sigma) = 0$ and $O(f(\sigma)) = 100$ for $\sigma = (a, \perp)$.

Interestingly, for linear control systems under the assumption of observability and controllability, the inequality (1) *does imply* that the effect of sporadic disturbances fades with time.[2] This observation explains why no additional requirement appears in the control literature dealing with robustness of linear control systems. The relevant notion of robustness that captures these two effects was introduced in Sontag's celebrated paper [19] addressing nonlinear control systems. Although the notion introduced by Sontag had a tremendous impact in control theory, it does not lend itself to the *quantitative* analysis, based on costs, that one typically expects when dealing with software systems. The reason is that for nonlinear control systems it is extremely difficult to obtain quantitative results and one settles for qualitative results ensuring the existence of certain bounds but not insisting on precise values for the constants appearing in these bounds. Therefore, instead of using the notion proposed by Sontag, we based our work on a recent notion proposed by Grüne [12] that is qualitatively equivalent to Sontag's notion but that allows for quantitative reasoning. Precisely, we say a transducer f is *input-output stable* (IOS) w.r.t. cost functions I and O if

$$O(f(\sigma)) \leq \max_{\sigma' \preceq \sigma} \{\gamma I(\sigma') - \eta(|\sigma| - |\sigma'|)\} \quad \forall \sigma \in \Sigma^*, \quad (2)$$

where $\preceq$ is the prefix ordering and γ and η are parameters. Here, γ describes how much the disturbance in the input is amplified at the output of the system and η quantifies the rate at which the system returns to its nominal behavior after a sporadic disturbance disappears. Our definition is inspired by Grüne's definition for nonlinear systems. A precise technical comparison is given in Section 6.

We show that (2) satisfies the two requirements for robust systems. Additionally, when the transducer f and costs I and O are modeled using finite-state automata, we can verify IOS (and find parameters γ and η) in polynomial time. In case a system is not IOS, we give a procedure to synthesize a controller enforcing IOS, again in polynomial time. We demonstrate our theory on a time synchronization protocol for wireless networks.

---

[1] This phenomenon also depends on the choice of the functions I and O. For control systems, the aforementioned phenomenon happens when I and O are both the infinity norm. When I and O are L_p norms ($p \neq \infty$), a persistent disturbance of small magnitude can lead to consequences of arbitrary magnitude if we wait sufficiently long. This is a different but equally undesired phenomenon.

[2] For control systems the relevant notion is to have the disturbance effects disappearing asymptotically rather than in finite time.

Finally, we demonstrate that our definition is compatible with IOS for control systems [12] by showing that if a control system is IOS then any transducer ε-approximate bisimilar to it is ε-practical IOS.

2. PROBLEM FORMULATION

2.1 Transducers and Cost Functions

An alphabet Σ is a finite set of letters. We write Σ^* for the set of words or strings over the alphabet Σ and ε for the empty word. The set of non-empty words over the alphabet Σ is denoted by Σ^+. Given a string $\sigma \in \Sigma^*$ we denote by $|\sigma|$ its length and by σ_{i-1} its ith element. We also use the notation $|S|$ to denote the cardinality of a set S. This should cause no confusion since sets are denoted by upper case letters while strings are denoted by lower case letters. For words $\sigma, \sigma' \in \Sigma^*$, we say σ' is a *prefix* of σ, written $\sigma' \preceq \sigma$, if there exists $\sigma'' \in \Sigma^*$ such that $\sigma'\sigma'' = \sigma$. In order to distinguish between elements of Σ and Σ^* we reserve the symbol s for letters and the symbol σ for words.

Let Σ and Λ be alphabets. A function $f : \Sigma^* \to \Lambda^*$ is called a *transducer* if for each $\sigma, \sigma' \in \Sigma^*$ such that $\sigma \preceq \sigma'$, we have $f(\sigma) \preceq f(\sigma')$.

In order to define robustness we assume an alphabet $\Sigma = \Sigma^c \times \Sigma^d$ where Σ^c is called the *control alphabet* and Σ^d is the *disturbance alphabet*. Every element $s \in \Sigma$ is thus a pair (s^c, s^d) where s^c is called a *control* input and s^d is a *disturbance* input. Furthermore, we assume Σ^d to contain a special element $\perp$ denoting the absence of disturbances.

We define the *nominal* behavior of a transducer $f : \Sigma^* \to \Lambda^*$ as the set of pairs of strings $(\sigma, f(\sigma)) \in \Sigma^* \times \Lambda^*$, where $\sigma^d \in \perp^*$, that is, there is no disturbance input.

In order to define robustness for transducers we associate cost functions to behaviors. Given an alphabet Σ, a *cost function* $c : \Sigma^* \to \mathbb{N}_0$ maps strings from Σ^* to the natural numbers. Given a cost function and a string σ, we define $c_\infty(\sigma) = \max_{\sigma' \preceq \sigma} c(\sigma')$. For a transducer $f : \Sigma^* \to \Lambda^*$, we denote the cost function on input strings Σ^* by I while the cost function on output strings Λ^* is denoted by O.

2.2 Input-Output Stability for Transducers

We can draw a formal analogy between a transducer and the response of a differential equation to a continuous-time input signal. This formal analogy leads to the following notion of Input-Output Stability inspired by Grüne's notion of stability in [12] and Sontag's notion of stability in [19].

Definition 1. [IOS] Let $f : \Sigma^* \to \Lambda^*$ be a transducer and let $I : \Sigma^* \to \mathbb{N}_0$ and $O : \Lambda^* \to \mathbb{N}_0$ be cost functions. Given parameters $\gamma, \eta \in \mathbb{N}$, we say the transducer f is (γ, η)-*input-output stable* (or (γ, η)-IOS) w.r.t. (I, O) if for each $\sigma \in \Sigma^*$ we have

$$O(f(\sigma)) \leq \max_{\sigma' \preceq \sigma} \{\gamma I(\sigma') - \eta(|\sigma| - |\sigma'|)\}. \quad (3)$$

The parameter γ is called the *robustness gain* and the parameter η is called the *rate of decay*. We say a transducer f is *input-output stable* (or IOS) w.r.t. (I, O) if there exist $\eta, \gamma \in \mathbb{N}$ such that f is (γ, η)-IOS w.r.t. (I, O).

For ease of exposition we require the robustness gain and the decay rate to be natural numbers. The extension to the rational case is conceptually simple and thus not pursued in this paper.

We show that our notion of IOS captures two important properties: bounded disturbances lead to bounded consequences, and that the effects of a sporadic disturbance disappear in finite time.

For the first property, note that for every $\sigma \in \Sigma^*$, we have

$$
\begin{aligned}
O_\infty(f(\sigma)) &= \max_{\sigma' \preceq \sigma} O(f(\sigma')) \\
&\leq \max_{\sigma' \preceq \sigma} \max_{\sigma'' \preceq \sigma'} \{\gamma I(\sigma'') - \eta(|\sigma'| - |\sigma''|)\} \\
&\leq \max_{\sigma' \preceq \sigma} \max_{\sigma'' \preceq \sigma'} \{\gamma I(\sigma'')\} = \gamma I_\infty(\sigma). \quad (4)
\end{aligned}
$$

Therefore, any bounded disturbance produces a bounded consequence. Moreover, the robustness gain γ measures how much the disturbance will be amplified by the transducer f.

Consider now a sporadic disturbance modeled as a string $s\sigma \in \Sigma^*$ such that $I(s\sigma') = 0$ for any prefix σ' of σ with $|\sigma'| > 0$. We regard the equality $I(s\sigma') = 0$ as the statement that the disturbance, as measured by I, disappears after s. We now note that it follows from (3) that for every σ' of length j we have:

$$O(f(s\sigma')) \leq \max\{0, \gamma I(s) - \eta j\}. \quad (5)$$

Therefore, after $\lceil \gamma I(s)/\eta \rceil$ steps the effect of the disturbance has disappeared. Note how the number of steps depends on the magnitude of the effect of the disturbance, as measured by $\gamma I(s)$, and also on the rate of decay η.

Notice that in our formulation, we place only mild assumptions on cost functions. In particular, we do not require the cost functions to be monotonic. If the cost is monotonic then a disturbance that occurs at a certain time will never be forgotten, thus enabling the output to deviate from the desired one for all future time. Alternatively, we can have a cost that is not monotonic and thus forgets the effect of a disturbance. Such costs are adequate in situations where it is acceptable that upon the occurrence of a disturbance the system can restart the computation of the correct output.

We also note that no relation between the input cost and the presence of disturbances in the input is required for our results to hold. While one typically expects that in the absence of disturbances the cost of the input strings should be zero, there are situations where this is not the case, and it may be natural to consider the presence of certain errors in the computation. For example, consider computing a mathematical expression involving real numbers on a microcontroller using fixed-point arithmetic. In this case, it is convenient to have the input cost on input strings without disturbances to be non-zero so that we allow the output string to have non-zero output cost even in the absence of external disturbances.

3. VERIFICATION AND SYNTHESIS

We study the following verification problems.

(γ, η)-**IOS Verification** Given transducer f, input and output cost functions I and O respectively, and parameters γ and η, is the transducer f (γ, η)-IOS for I and O?

IOS Verification Given transducer f and input and output cost functions I and O respectively, does there exist γ and η such that f is (γ, η)-IOS for I and O? (If so, find such γ and η.)

We also consider the *synthesis problem*. A *controller* is a map:

$$C : \Sigma^* \times \Sigma^c \to \Sigma^c \qquad (6)$$

transforming the history of past inputs $\sigma \in \Sigma^*$ and a given control input request s^c into the control input $C(\sigma, s^c)$ to be provided to the system. Composing a transducer f with a controller C results in a new transducer $f_C : \Sigma^* \to \Lambda^*$, called the *controlled system*, defined, intuitively, by filtering the input stream by C. Formally, define the *filtration* $\mathsf{filter}_C : \Sigma^* \to \Sigma^*$ of a stream by a controller C inductively as:

$$\mathsf{filter}_C(\varepsilon) = \varepsilon$$
$$\mathsf{filter}_C(\sigma \cdot (s^c, s^d)) = \mathsf{filter}_C(\sigma) \cdot (C(\sigma, s^c), s^d)$$

The composition f_C is then given by $f_C(\sigma) = f(\mathsf{filter}_C(\sigma))$. The synthesis problem is the following.

Synthesis Given transducer f, cost functions (I, O), and parameters (γ, η), does there exist a controller C such that f_C is (γ, η)-IOS w.r.t. (I, O)?

We will study the verification and synthesis questions for transducers and cost functions described by finite-state (weighted) automata.

Definition 2. An automaton $A = (Q, q_0, \Sigma, \delta, \Lambda, H)$ consists of:

- a finite set of states Q;
- an initial state $q_0 \in Q$;
- a set of inputs Σ;
- a transition function $\delta : Q \times \Sigma \to Q$;
- a set of outputs Λ;
- and an output function $H : Q \to \Lambda$.

A run r of A on an input string $\sigma \in \Sigma^*$ is a string $r \in Q^*$ such that $r_0 = q_0$ and $r_{i+1} = \delta(r_i, \sigma_i)$ for $i = 0, 1, \dots, |\sigma| - 1$. A run r of A on input $\sigma \in \Sigma^*$ defines an *output run* $\lambda \in \Lambda^*$ by $\lambda_i = H(r_i)$ for $i = 0, 1, \dots, |\sigma| - 1$.

We denote by δ^* the extension of δ to $Q \times \Sigma^*$ defined in the usual manner: $\delta^*(q, \varepsilon) = q$ and $\delta^*(q, \sigma s) = \delta(\delta^*(q, \sigma), s)$. The set of *predecessors* of a state $q \in Q$, denoted by $\mathrm{Pre}(q)$, is defined by $\mathrm{Pre}(q) = \{q' \in Q \mid \exists s \in \Sigma \ \ \delta(q', s) = q\}$.

An automaton A defines a transducer $\mathsf{xduce}(A) : \Sigma^* \to \Lambda^*$ as follows:

$$f(\sigma) = H(\delta^*(q_0, \sigma_0)) H(\delta^*(q_0, \sigma_0 \sigma_1)) \dots$$

In addition to transducers we also consider cost functions described by finite-state weighted automata. A weighted automaton A is an automaton $A = (Q, q_0, \Sigma, \delta, \mathbb{N}_0, H)$ whose set of outputs or *weights* is $\mathbb{N}_0$ and whose output map satisfies $H(q_0) = 0$. The *cost* of a string $\sigma \in \Sigma^*$ is given by $H(\delta^*(q_0, \sigma))$. A weighted automaton A *defines* the cost function I_A as follows: $I_A(\sigma) = H(\delta^*(q_0, \sigma))$. We define the size of an automaton as the number of bits required to encode an automaton when all weights are given in unary.

3.1 Solving the Verification Problems

In this section we show how to solve the verification problem for transducers, input cost, and output cost defined by finite-state automata. It will be convenient to combine the automaton A^f describing the transducer, the automaton A^I describing the input cost I, and the automaton A^O describing the output cost O into the automaton A obtained by synchronizing A^I on the same input of A^f and synchronizing A^O on the output of A^f. Formally, A is defined by:

- $Q = Q^I \times Q^f \times Q^O$ with $q_0 = (q_0^I, q_0^f, q_0^O)$;
- $\Sigma = \Sigma^f$;
- $\Lambda = \mathbb{N}_0 \times \mathbb{N}_0$ and $H(q^I, q^f, q^O) = (H^I(q^I), H^O(q^O))$;

and the transition function:

$$\delta((q^I, q^f, q^O), s) = \left(\delta^I(q^I, s), \delta^f(q^f, s), \delta^O(q^O, H^f \circ \delta^f(q^f, s)) \right).$$

In the following, we will abuse notation by using $H^I(q)$ and $H^O(q)$ to denote $H^I(q^I)$ and $H^O(q^O)$, respectively, for $q = (q^I, q^f, q^O)$. Without loss of generality we assume every state of A to be reachable from the initial state.

In addition to A we will also work with the set of all functions from Q to $M = \{0, 1, \dots, \overline{m}\}$, denoted by M^Q, and where $\overline{m} = \max_{q \in Q} \gamma H^I(q)$. The set M^Q is a lattice with order relation denoted by $\sqsubseteq$ and defined for any $f_1, f_2 \in M^Q$ by $f_1 \sqsubseteq f_2$ if $f_1(q) \leq f_2(q)$ for every $q \in Q$. The join of f_1 and f_2 is given by $\max\{f_1, f_2\}$ while the meet is given by $\min\{f_1, f_2\}$. We note that M^Q is a finite lattice and all the operators used in this paper satisfy the conditions of Tarski's theorem [21] so that the least fixed point of a monotonic operator exists and can be algorithmically found in $|Q| \cdot |M|$ steps.

3.1.1 (γ, η)-IOS Verification Problem

We formulate the solution of the (γ, η)-IOS verification problem as a fixed-point computation for the operator $F : M^Q \to M^Q$ defined by:

$$F(W)(q) = \max \left\{ \gamma H^I(q), W(q), \min_{q' \in \mathrm{Pre}(q)} W(q') - \eta \right\}. \quad (8)$$

THEOREM 1. *Let A^f be a finite-state automaton. Let A^I and A^O be finite-state weighted automata defining costs I and O, respectively. Given $\eta, \gamma \in \mathbb{N}$, the transducer $\mathsf{xduce}(A^f)$ is (γ, η)-IOS with respect to (I, O) iff the infimal fixed point of F, denoted by W^*, satisfies the following inequality for every $q \in Q$:*

$$H^O(q) \leq W^*(q). \quad (9)$$

PROOF. Let $f = \mathsf{xduce}(A^f)$. Any fixed point V of F satisfies:

$$V(q) = \max \left\{ \gamma H^I(q), V(q), \min_{q' \in \mathrm{Pre}(q)} V(q') - \eta \right\}$$

which implies:

$$V(q) \geq \max \left\{ \gamma H^I(q), \min_{q' \in \mathrm{Pre}(q)} V(q') - \eta \right\}.$$

Hence, the infimal fixed-point is characterized by the equality:

$$W^*(q) = \max \left\{ \gamma H^I(q), \min_{q' \in \mathrm{Pre}(q)} W^*(q') - \eta \right\}. \quad (10)$$

$$U(q) = \min_{\sigma \in \Sigma^* | \delta^*(q_0,\sigma)=q} \max \left\{ \max_{\sigma' \preceq \sigma''} \left\{ \gamma I(\sigma') - \eta (|\sigma''| - |\sigma'| + 1) \right\}, \gamma I(\sigma) \right\}$$

$$= \min_{\sigma'' \in \Sigma^* | \delta^*(q_0,\sigma'') \in \mathrm{Pre}(q)} \max \left\{ \max_{\sigma' \preceq \sigma''} \left\{ \gamma I(\sigma') - \eta (|\sigma''| - |\sigma'|) \right\} - \eta, \gamma H^I(q) \right\}$$

$$= \max \left\{ \min_{\sigma'' \in \Sigma^* | \delta^*(q_0,\sigma'') \in \mathrm{Pre}(q)} \max_{\sigma' \preceq \sigma''} \left\{ \gamma I(\sigma') - \eta (|\sigma''| - |\sigma'|) \right\} - \eta, \gamma H^I(q) \right\}$$

$$= \max \left\{ \min_{q' \in \mathrm{Pre}(q)} U(q') - \eta, \gamma H^I(q) \right\}. \tag{7}$$

Let now:

$$U(q) = \min_{\sigma \in \Sigma^* | \delta^*(q_0,\sigma)=q} \max_{\sigma' \preceq \sigma} \left\{ \gamma I(\sigma') - \eta (|\sigma| - |\sigma'|) \right\}.$$

We now show that U is the infimal fixed point of F by showing that U satisfies (10). Let σ'' be the prefix of σ of length $|\sigma| - 1$. Using σ'' we can write U as (7).

We can now use the fact that U is the infimal fixed point of F to finalize the proof. By definition of U, for any string $\sigma \in \Sigma^*$ such that $\delta^*(q_0,\sigma) = q$ we have:

$$U(q) \leq \max_{\sigma' \preceq \sigma} \left\{ \gamma I(\sigma') - \eta (|\sigma| - |\sigma'|) \right\}. \tag{11}$$

Hence, if the inequality $H^O(q) \leq W^*(q)$ holds we conclude that f is IOS by chaining $O(f(\sigma)) = H^O(q)$, $H^O(q) \leq W^*(q)$, $W^*(q) = U(q)$, and (11).

Conversely, if f is IOS then:

$$O(f(\sigma)) = H^O(q) \leq \max_{\sigma' \preceq \sigma} \left\{ \gamma I(\sigma') - \eta (|\sigma| - |\sigma'|) \right\}$$

for every $\sigma \in \Sigma^*$ such that $\delta^*(q_0,\sigma) = q$ and thus $H^O(q) \leq U(q) = W^*(q)$. $\square$

3.1.2 IOS Verification Problem

We now check, for a transducer and cost functions given by automata, if there exists a choice of γ and η for which the transducer is (γ, η)-IOS. In addition to answer this question algorithmically, we also provide a subset of all the possible choices of γ and η. This will be done through an operator $G : (M \times \{0, 1, \ldots, |Q|\})^Q \to (M \times \{0, 1, \ldots, |Q|\})^Q$ closely related to F. We use the notation $G(f,q) = (G_W(f,q), G_D(f,q))$ to define G as:

$$G_W(W)(q) = \max \left\{ H^I(q), W(q), \min_{q' \in \mathrm{Pre}(q)} W(q') \right\}$$

$$G_D(D)(q) = \begin{cases} D(q') + 1 & \text{if } \min_{q' \in \mathrm{Pre}(q)} W(q') > W(q) \\ D(q) & \text{otherwise.} \end{cases}$$

Note that we now work on the lattice $(M \times \{0, 1, \ldots, |Q|\})^Q$ with order given by $(W, D) \sqsubseteq (W', D')$ when for any $q \in Q$, we have one and only one of the following cases:

- $W(q) < W'(q)$,
- $W(q) = W'(q)$, $D(q) \leq D'(q)$.

It is easy to check that G is monotone with respect to this order.

THEOREM 2. *Let A^f be a finite-state automaton. Let A^I and A^O be finite-state weighted automata defining the costs I and O, respectively. There exist $\gamma, \eta \in \mathbb{N}$ so that $\mathsf{xduce}(A^f)$ is (γ, η)-IOS with respect to (I, O) iff the least fixed point*

of G, denoted by (W^*, D^*), satisfies the following inequality for every $q \in Q$:

$$W^*(q) = 0 \implies H^O(q) = 0. \tag{12}$$

Furthermore, when (12) holds, $\mathsf{xduce}(A^f)$ is (γ, η)-IOS for any γ satisfying:

$$H^O(q) > \gamma H^I(q) \implies H^O(q) < \gamma W^*(q), \qquad \forall q \in Q \tag{13}$$

and any η (dependent on the choice of γ) satisfying:

$$\eta \leq \left\lfloor \frac{\beta}{d} \right\rfloor, \tag{14}$$

where

$$d = \max_{q \in Q} D^*(q),$$

$$\beta = \min_{q \in Q \,|\, H^O(q) > \gamma H^I(q)} \gamma W^*(q) - H^O(q).$$

PROOF. Let $f = \mathsf{xduce}(A^f)$. We first show that if f is (γ, η)-IOS for some γ and η then (12) holds. By definition of IOS and since $\eta(|\sigma| - |\sigma'|) \geq 0$ we have:

$$O(f(\sigma)) \leq \max_{\sigma' \preceq \sigma} \left\{ \gamma I(\sigma') - \eta (|\sigma| - |\sigma'|) \right\}$$

$$\leq \max_{\sigma' \preceq \sigma} \left\{ \gamma I(\sigma') \right\} \tag{15}$$

for every $\sigma \in \Sigma^*$. Hence, we also have:

$$O(f(\sigma)) = H^O(q)$$

$$\leq \min_{\sigma \in \Sigma^* | \delta^*(q_0,\sigma)=q} \max_{\sigma' \preceq \sigma} \left\{ \gamma I(\sigma') \right\} = V^*(q)$$

where V^* is the infimal fixed point of F for $\eta = 0$. Note that $V^*(q) = 0$ implies $H^O(q) = 0$ since H^O is a non-negative function. Furthermore, $W^* = V^*/\gamma$ and thus:

$$W^*(q) = 0 \implies V^*(q) = 0 \implies H^O(q) = 0.$$

We now show that (12) implies IOS. We will do so by constructing γ and η and we will conclude from the construction that any choice of γ satisfying (13) and any choice of η satisfying (14) works.

We start by showing that under the stated assumptions there exists $\gamma > 0$ so that $O(f(\sigma)) < \max_{\sigma' \preceq \sigma} \{ \gamma I(\sigma') \}$. We first note that W^* equals the infimal fixed point of F for $\gamma = 1$ and $\eta = 0$. It then follows from the proof of Theorem 1 that W^* is given by:

$$W^*(q) = \min_{\sigma \in \Sigma^* | \delta^*(q_0,\sigma)=q} \max_{\sigma' \preceq \sigma} \{ I(\sigma') \}. \tag{16}$$

For any q we can find $\gamma_q > 0$ so that $H^O(q) < \gamma_q W^*(q)$. Note that when $W^*(q) = 0$ we have $H^O(q) = 0$, by assumption, so any γ_q works in this case but for simplicity we take

$\gamma_q = 0$. With $\gamma = \max_{q \in Q} \gamma_q$ we have:

$$O(f(\sigma)) = H^O(q) < \gamma W^*(q)$$
$$\leq \gamma \max_{\sigma' \preceq \sigma}\{I(\sigma')\} = \max_{\sigma' \preceq \sigma}\{\gamma I(\sigma')\}$$

for every $\sigma \in \Sigma^*$ such that $\delta^*(q_0, \sigma) = q$. If we define $\beta_q > 0$ by $-\beta_q = H^O(q) - \gamma W^*(q)$ for every $q \in Q$ for which $W^*(q) \neq 0$ and define $\beta > 0$ by $\beta = \min_{q \in Q} \beta_q$ we have $H^O(q) = \gamma W^*(q) - \beta_q \leq \gamma W^*(q) - \beta$. In order to express β in the form $\eta(|\sigma| - |\sigma'|)$ we note that the evaluation of the fixed point (W^*, D^*) at q tells us that the run of A on any $\sigma \in \Sigma^*$ such that $\delta^*(q_0, \sigma) = q$ visits a state q' such that $\gamma H^I(q') \geq W^*(q)$. Furthermore, if we denote by $q' = q_1 q_2 \ldots q_{D(q)} q_{D(q)+1} = q$ the states visited between q' and q we also know that $\gamma H^I(q_i) > \gamma H^I(q_{i+1})$ for $i = 1, \ldots, D(q)$. We now consider two cases. If $\gamma H^I(q) < H^O(q)$ then the inequality $H^O(q) < \gamma W^*(q)$ implies that $D^*(q) > 0$ since $W(q)$ had to be updated in order to increase to $W^*(q)$. Let $d = \max_{q \in Q} D^*(q)$ (note that d is no larger than the number of states in Q) and define η as $\eta = \lfloor \beta/d \rfloor$ to obtain:

$$
\begin{aligned}
O(f(\sigma)) = H^O(q) &\leq \gamma W^*(q) - \beta \\
&\leq \max_{\sigma' \preceq \sigma}\{\gamma I(\sigma') - \beta\} \\
&\leq \max_{\sigma' \preceq \sigma}\{\gamma I(\sigma') - \eta(|\sigma| - |\sigma'|)\}.
\end{aligned}
$$

The second case to be considered is $\gamma H^I(q) \geq H^O(q)$. In this case we directly have:

$$
\begin{aligned}
O(f(\sigma)) = H^O(q) &\leq \gamma H^I(q) \\
&= \gamma I(\sigma) \leq \max_{\sigma' \preceq \sigma}\{\gamma I(\sigma') - \eta(|\sigma| - |\sigma'|)\} \quad (17)
\end{aligned}
$$

where the last inequality follows by taking $\sigma' = \sigma$. We then conclude that any choice of γ and η satisfying (13) and (14), respectively, renders f IOS. $\square$

Notice that our characterization gives a natural dynamic programming formulation for verification.

3.2 Solving the Synthesis Problem

We now consider the synthesis problem for a transducer $f : \Sigma^* \to \Lambda^*$. Recall that the purpose of synthesizing a controller C is to render f_C (γ, η)-IOS for a desired choice of γ and η. Once again we follow the perspicacious work of Grüne et al. [13], where it is shown how control systems can be augmented with a monitor for the stability property introduced in [12].

Let A be the automaton introduced in Section 3.1 obtained by synchronizing A^I on the same input of A^f and synchronizing A^O on the output of A^f. We now extend this automaton to $A^{\gamma \eta}$ by enlarging the set of states to:

$$Q^{\gamma \eta} = Q \times M, \qquad q_0^{\gamma \eta} = (q_0, 0)$$

and extending the transition function to:

$$\delta^{\gamma \eta}((q, m), s) = \left(\delta(q, s), \max\left\{m - \eta, \gamma H^I \circ \delta(q, s)\right\}\right).$$

Automaton $A^{\gamma \eta}$ monitors IOS in the sense that if the input $\sigma \in \Sigma^*$ takes the initial state to $(q, m) \in Q \times M$ then:

$$m = \max_{\sigma' \preceq \sigma}\{\gamma I(\sigma') - \eta(|\sigma| - |\sigma'|)\}. \quad (18)$$

This is proved by induction on the length of the trace. As a direct consequence, we can monitor IOS by testing the inequality $H^O(q) \leq m$, as stated in the next result.

THEOREM 3. *Let A^f be a finite-state automaton. Let A^I and A^O be finite-state weighted automata defining the costs I and O, respectively. Given $\gamma, \eta \in \mathbb{N}$, the transducer* $\mathsf{xduce}(A^f)$ *is (γ, η)-IOS with respect to (I, O) iff every reachable state (q, m) of $A^{\gamma \eta}$ satisfies $H^O(q) \leq m$.*

Note that Theorem 3 provides an alternative algorithm to check (γ, η)-IOS: check that

$$S = \{(q, m) \in Q \times M \mid H^O(q) \leq m\}$$

is an invariant set of $A^{\gamma \eta}$. However, the fixed-point representation provided by the functional (8) is of independent interest, as well as key to Theorem 2.

Theorem 3 also suggests a synthesis algorithm for IOS: construct a controller rendering the set S invariant. This will require a modification of $A^{\gamma \eta}$ that we denote by $A^{\gamma \eta c}$, and define as follows. The new state set is:

$$Q^{\gamma \eta c} = \Sigma^c \times Q \times M = \Sigma^c \times Q^I \times Q^f \times Q^O \times M$$

and the new transition function is:

$$\delta\left((s^c, q^I, q^f, q^O, m), (s^{c''}, s^{d''})\right) = (s^{c'}, q^{I'}, q^{f'}, q^{O'}, m'),$$

with:

$$s^{c'} = s^{c''}, \qquad q^{I'} = \delta^I\left(q^I, \left(s^{c''}, s^{d''}\right)\right)$$

$$q^{f'} = \delta^f\left(q^f, (s^{c''}, s^{d''})\right), \qquad q^{O'} = \delta^O\left(q^O, H^f\left(q^{f'}\right)\right),$$

$$m' = \max\left\{m - \eta, \gamma H^I\left(q^{I'}\right)\right\}.$$

We can now apply the usual invariance controller synthesis algorithm (see, e.g., [17]) to $A^{\gamma \eta c}$ to construct a (memoryless) controller forcing S to be an invariant set. This observation immediately leads to the next result.

THEOREM 4. *Let A^f be a finite-state automaton, and let $f = \mathsf{xduce}(A^f)$. Let A^I and A^O be finite-state weighted automata defining the costs I and O, respectively. Given $\gamma, \eta \in \mathbb{N}$, there exists a controller C rendering f_C (γ, η)-IOS with respect to (I, O) iff there exists a controller rendering the set S invariant for $A^{\gamma \eta c}$.*

Since safety games can be solved in linear time [17], the complexity of synthesis is linear in the size of $A^{\gamma \eta c}$, i.e., it runs in $O(|A^I||A^f||A^O||M||\Sigma|)$ time.

4. EXAMPLE: ROBUSTNESS FOR THE RBS PROTOCOL

We consider the problem of time synchronization in wireless networks using the Reference Broadcast Synchronization (RBS) protocol [10]. To simplify the presentation we consider a network of three nodes: one master node and two slave nodes that we denote by node a and node b. Nodes transmit packets composed by a message identifier (small number of bits) and the message payload (large number of bits). We assume the packets to be encoded with an error correcting code that can always correct the message identifier but not necessarily the message payload when there are communication errors.

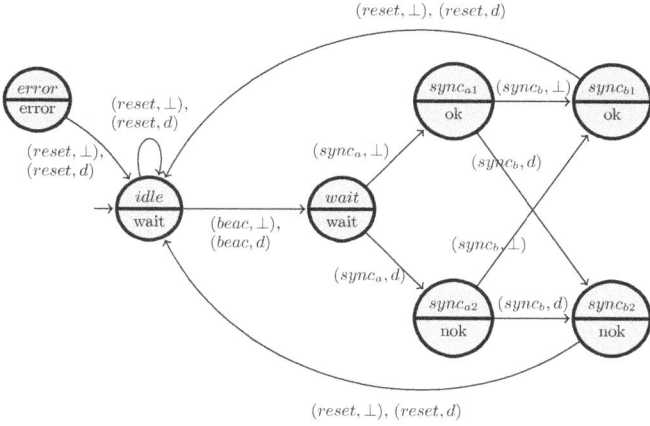

Figure 3: Automaton representation of the RBS time synchronization protocol. Not represented in the automaton are transitions to the error state. These depart from every state so as to make the automaton input-enabled.

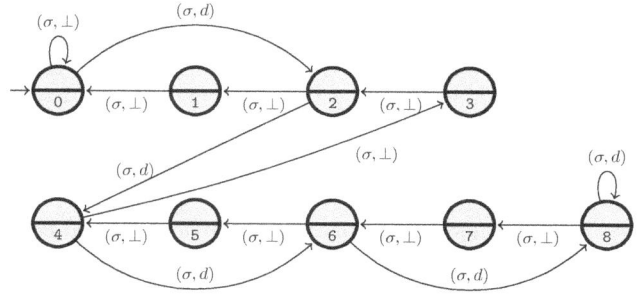

Figure 4: Input cost I^d penalizing disturbance inputs.

The RBS protocol starts with the master node broadcasting a beacon message $beac$ at time t_1. This packet contains no payload. Due to access, propagation, and queuing delays both slave nodes will receive the packet at global time t_2 which is represented in the local time of node a as t_{2a} and in the local time of node b as t_{2b}. Node a then sends a synchronization message $sync_a$ to node b containing t_{2a} as payload and then node b sends a synchronization message $sync_b$ to node a containing t_{2b} as payload. If there are no communication errors, node a can compute the offset of its clock with respect to the clock of node b as $t_{2a} - t_{2b}$ and similarly for node b.

Consider now the effect of communication errors modeled as a disturbance. Since the message $beac$ contains no payload it can always be correctly decoded even in the presence of communication errors. The $sync_a$ message, however, contains t_{2a} as payload and a communication error may cause the payload to be incorrectly decoded as $t_{2a} + d$ where d the decoding error. In the presence of communication errors the computed time offset becomes $t_{2a} - t_{2b} + d$ and similarly for node b. The protocol also includes a $reset$ message that can be sent at any time to re-start the synchronization process. Since the $reset$ message has no payload it is not affected by communication errors. A second source of errors in the protocol are out of order messages. In this scenario, the protocol goes to the $error$ state until a $reset$ message is received. Figure 3 shows an automaton representation for this protocol. For simplicity, all the incoming edges to the $error$ state, departing from every state, are not displayed. The input and output alphabets are given by:

$$\Sigma^c = \{beac, sync_a, sync_b, reset\}, \quad \Sigma^d = \{\perp, d\},$$

$$\Lambda = \{error, wait, ok, nok\}$$

the initial state is $idle$ and the output corresponding to any given state is depicted in the bottom part of the state.

In order to study the robustness properties of the RBS protocol we need to equip Σ^* and Λ^* with quantitative information through the input and output cost functions. The

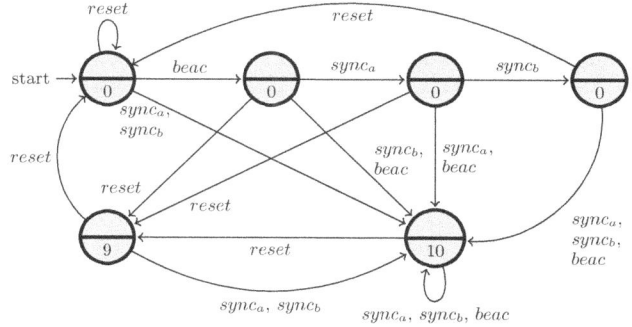

Figure 5: Input cost I^c penalizing control inputs.

input cost function is defined in two steps. First, we describe how disturbances are penalized by the cost function. We denote this cost function by I^d. It counts the number of d symbols that appear in σ^d up to a maximum of 4. Every time a d symbol appears, the input cost increases by 2 otherwise the input cost decreases by 1. The choice of the upper bound 4 is a consequence of the RBS protocol described by the automaton in Figure 3 where we can see that at most 4 disturbances can take place before returning to an $error$ or $idle$ state. A complete description is provided in Figure 4. In addition to I^d we also consider a cost function I^c penalizing the control inputs. This cost maps the sequences of strings of control inputs expected by the protocol to 0 and any other sequence to 9 or 10. We reserve 9 for the occur-

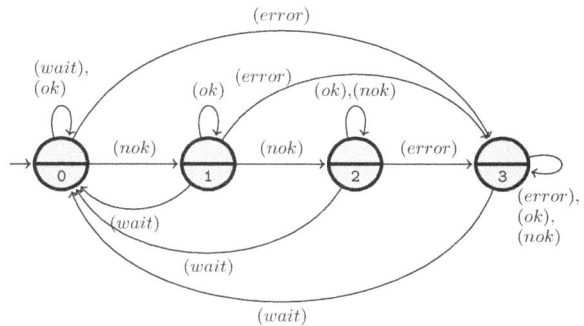

Figure 6: Output cost O.

rence of a *reset* message appearing in the middle of the protocol execution and use 10 for all other messages appearing out of order. We regard as more damaging a control input appearing out of order over a reset message out of order. A complete description of I^c is given in Figure 5. Finally, we define the input cost I by $I(\sigma) = \max\{I^c(\sigma), I^d(\sigma)\}$. Note that the values for I^c and I^d were chosen so that I ranges in the set $\{0, 1, 2, 3, 4, 5, 6, 7, 8, 9, 10\}$.

In order to completely specify the problem we also need to define the output cost O. The output cost counts the number of *nok* output symbols up to a maximum of 2 and penalizes the occurrence of the *error* output symbol with a 3 as depicted in Figure 6. The upper bound of 2 is a consequence of only having at most two consecutive *nok* output symbols. The choice of 2 and 3 reflects our belief that it is preferable to compute an incorrect estimate of the clock offsets than not being able to compute any estimate. Clearly, other choices of input and output cost functions are possible and they would lead to different conclusions.

Although the RBS protocol is guaranteed to work when there are no communication disturbances, we are interested in analyzing its behavior when such disturbances are present. By applying Theorem 1 with $\gamma = 2$ and $\eta = 1$ we conclude that the RBS protocol is $(2, 1)$-IOS. By using Theorem 2 we reach a stronger conclusion: IOS only holds for $\gamma > 0.5$. The range of allowable η changes according to the choice of γ. For example when $\gamma = 0.6$ and by applying Theorem 2 we find that $\eta < 0.0067$.

Moreover, for $\gamma \geq 1$, IOS holds for any value of $\eta > 0$. These values of γ and η give us very precise information about the robustness of the RBS protocol. We first note that if we consider only inputs strings $\sigma \in \Sigma^*$ satisfying $I(\sigma) \leq 8$ we are only considering disturbances due to communication errors. In that case IOS provides the guarantee $O(f(\sigma)) \leq 2$ and an analysis of the cost O shows that we never reach the *error* state, *i.e.*, the protocol is able to compute the clock offsets, albeit with an error. When $I(\sigma) > 8$ incorrect control inputs are being used and for this reason the protocol may enter the *error* state and not be able to compute an estimate of the clock offsets. Hence, smaller disturbances lead to smaller consequences. Recall that for an IOS transducer, the nominal behavior can be resumed in no more than $\lceil \gamma I(\sigma)/\eta \rceil$ steps once a disturbance disappears. In this present case, since IOS holds for arbitrarily large η the nominal behavior can be resumed in one time step. This can be readily verified by noticing that the reset input can be used for this purpose at any state of the system.

5. IOS AND REFINEMENT

Since IOS is a property of the input-output behavior of a system, and since refinement relations preserve input-output behaviors, we immediately have that if two automata A_1 and A_2 are bisimilar, then $\mathsf{xduce}(A_1)$ is (γ, η)-IOS w.r.t. (I, O) iff $\mathsf{xduce}(A_2)$ is (γ, η)-IOS w.r.t. (I, O). We generalize this observation to ε-approximate bisimulation relations [11, 18] using *practical IOS* of systems. We start with some notation. We denote by $\mathbb{R}$ the set of real numbers, by $\mathbb{R}_0^+$ the set of non-negative real numbers, and, for $n \in \mathbb{N}$, we denote by $\mathbb{R}^n$ the n-dimensional Euclidean space.

5.1 Practical IO-stability and Approximate Bisimulation

IOS is an "ideal" property of transducers. We define the notion of *practical IOS*, that requires that the output and inputs of a transducer satisfy the relation (3) up to a parameter ε. Let $f : \Sigma^* \to \Lambda^*$ be a transducer and let $I : \Sigma^* \to \mathbb{R}_0$ and $O : \Lambda^* \to \mathbb{R}_0$ be cost functions. Given parameters $\gamma, \eta \in \mathbb{R}$, we say the transducer f is $(\varepsilon, \gamma, \eta)$-*practical input-output stable* (or $(\varepsilon, \gamma, \eta)$-*practical IOS*) w.r.t. (I, O) if for each $\sigma \in \Sigma^*$ we have

$$O(f(\sigma)) \leq \max_{\sigma' \preceq \sigma} \left\{ \gamma I(\sigma') - \eta (|\sigma| - |\sigma'|) \right\} + \varepsilon. \quad (19)$$

In order to define approximate bisimulation we consider $\varepsilon \in \mathbb{R}_0^+$ and two automata $A_1 = (Q_1, q_{01}, \Sigma, \delta_1, \Lambda, H_1)$ and $A_2 = (Q_2, q_{02}, \Sigma, \delta_2, \Lambda, H_2)$ with the same sets of inputs and outputs. Let $I : \Sigma^* \to \mathbb{R}_0$ and $O : \Lambda^* \to \mathbb{R}_0$ be cost functions. A relation $R \subseteq Q_1 \times Q_2$ is said to be an ε-*approximate bisimulation* if $(q_1, q_2) \in R$ implies:

1. $|O(H_1(q_1)) - O(H_2(q_2))| \leq \varepsilon$;

2. for each $\sigma_1 \in \Sigma$ there is a $\sigma_2 \in \Sigma$ such that $|I(\sigma_1) - I(\sigma_2)| \leq \varepsilon$ and $(\delta_1(q_1, \sigma_1), \delta_2(q_2, \sigma_2)) \in R$; and

3. for each $\sigma_2 \in \Sigma$ there is a $\sigma_1 \in \Sigma$ such that $|I(\sigma_1) - I(\sigma_2)| \leq \varepsilon$ and $(\delta_1(q_1, \sigma_1), \delta_2(q_2, \sigma_2)) \in R$.

The automaton A_1 is ε-approximate bisimilar to A_2 if there is an ε-approximate bisimulation relation R such that $R(q_{01}, q_{02})$.

We now consider ε-bisimilar automata A_1 and A_2 and assume $\mathsf{xduce}(A_2)$ to be (γ, η)-IOS. Since A_1 is ε-bisimilar to A_2, the behavior of A_1 determined by any string $\sigma_1 \in \Sigma^*$ can be ε-bisimulated by the behavior of A_2 determined by a string $\sigma_2 \in \Sigma^*$. Making use of this fact we have the following sequence of inequalities where the first and third are a consequence of ε-bisimulation while the second is simply the definition of *IOS*.

$$
\begin{aligned}
O(\mathsf{xduce}(A_1)(\sigma_1)) & \leq O(\mathsf{xduce}(A_2)(\sigma_2)) + \varepsilon \\
& \leq \max_{\sigma_2' \preceq \sigma_2} \left\{ \gamma I(\sigma_2') - \eta (|\sigma_2| - |\sigma_2'|) \right\} \\
& \quad + \varepsilon \\
& \leq \max_{\sigma_1' \preceq \sigma_1} \left\{ \gamma I(\sigma_1') + \gamma\varepsilon - \eta (|\sigma_1| - |\sigma_1'|) \right\} \\
& \quad + \varepsilon \\
& \leq \max_{\sigma_1' \preceq \sigma_1} \left\{ \gamma I(\sigma_1') - \eta (|\sigma_1| - |\sigma_1'|) \right\} \\
& \quad + (\gamma + 1)\varepsilon.
\end{aligned}
$$

The next result summarizes the previous discussion.

THEOREM 5. *Let A_1 be ε-approximate bisimilar to A_2. If A_1 is (γ, η)-IOS then A_2 is $((\gamma + 1)\varepsilon, \gamma, \eta)$-practical IOS.*

5.2 Relationship with Control Systems

Finally, we relate our notion of IOS with related notions for continuous time control systems. We assume the reader is familiar with standard control-theoretic notation, see e.g., [15]. We start with a notion of input-output stability for control systems (IODS) introduced in [12].

We consider nonlinear control systems of the form:

$$\dot{x} = f(x(t), u(t)), \quad x(0) = x_0 \quad (20)$$

where we assume that $f : \mathbb{R}^n \times \mathbb{R}^m \to \mathbb{R}^n$ and the input function $u : \mathbb{R} \to \mathbb{R}^m$ have enough regularity properties to ensure existence and uniqueness of solutions. The trajectories of (20) with initial value x_0 at time $t = 0$ are denoted by $\varphi(t, x, u)$.

Let $|\cdot|$ denote the Euclidean norm, $|\cdot|_\infty$ the L_∞ norm for functions in $\mathcal{U}$, and for $t > 0$ and any measurable function $g : \mathbb{R} \to \mathbb{R}_0^+$, let $\operatorname{ess\,sup}_{\tau \in [0,t]} g(\tau)$ denote the essential supremum of g on $[0, t]$. The following definition is inspired by a similar definition in [12].

Definition 3. [IODS] The system (20) is called (γ, η)-*IO-dynamically stable* (IODS), if the inequality

$$|\varphi(t, x, u)| \leq \operatorname{ess\,sup}_{\tau \in [0,t]} \max\{0, \gamma |u(\tau)| - \eta(t - \tau)\}$$

holds for all $t \geq 0$, $x \in \mathbb{R}^n$, and all $u \in \mathcal{U}$.

The notion of IODS introduced in Definition 3 is a special case of Input-to-State Dynamical Stability (ISDS) introduced by Grüne in [12] as a quantitative version of the notion of Input-to-State Stability introduced by Sontag in [19]. This can be seen by defining the functions σ, γ, and μ in Definition 2.1 of [12] as:

$$\sigma \equiv \lambda r. \gamma \, r, \quad \gamma \equiv \lambda r. \gamma \, r, \quad \mu \equiv \lambda(r, s). \max\{0, r - \eta \, s\},$$

respectively. We also eliminated the distinction between overshoot gain and robustness gain in [12].

We now wish to relate IODS for a control system with the notion of practical IOS defined for discrete systems. First, we notice that the control system (20) defines an automaton $A_{dyn} = (\mathbb{R}^n, x_0, \mathcal{U}, \delta, \mathbb{R}^n, \lambda x. x)$, where $\delta(x, u) = x'$ if $\varphi(t, x, u) = x'$ for some $t \in \mathbb{R}_0^+$.[3] The results of [11, 18] show that under certain assumptions on the dynamics of (20), we can define a finite automaton that is ε-bisimilar to the automaton A_{dyn} obtained from the control system (20). Using Theorem 5, we obtain the following.

THEOREM 6. *Let A_{dyn} be the automaton defined by (20) assumed to be (γ, η)-IODS and let A be an automaton that is ε-approximate bisimilar to A_{dyn}. Then A is $((\gamma + 1)\varepsilon, \gamma, \eta)$-practical IOS w.r.t. the cost functions $I(u) = |u|$ and $O(x) = |x|$.*

6. RELATED WORK

The notion of IO-stability discussed in this paper captures two very natural properties and it is natural to find different formalizations of related properties. For example, in fault-tolerant computation, one studies programs p that are F-tolerant for a class of faults F and a given specification S [3]. This definition requires the existence of a predicate T such that: 1) $S \Rightarrow T$; 2) T is invariant under program p and faults from F; 3) in the absence of faults, a computation that starts by satisfying T will eventually satisfy S. This notion can be captured in our setting by taking S to be the correct behaviors defined by $O_\infty(f(\sigma)) = 0$, by taking F to be the class of faults defined by $I(\sigma) \leq c$ for some $c \in \mathbb{N}$, and by taking T to be the set of streams satisfying $O_\infty(f(\sigma)) \leq \gamma c$.

By definition of S and T, we clearly have $S \Rightarrow T$. Inequality (4) implies that T is invariant under the computations of f and faults, and inequality (5) implies that the system will eventually return to S. IOS not only captures the notion of fault-tolerance in [3], it *quantifies* it by providing a different set T for each disturbance bound c and a bound on the number of steps required to return to S as a function of c. Similarly, one can regard IOS as a quantitative version of the notion of self-stabilization introduced by Dijkstra in [8].

Closer to our work are the results reported in [20, 4, 9] that, as mentioned in the introduction, capture one but not all of the properties of IOS. Chaudhuri et al. [7] and Majumdar and Saha [16] have considered continuity properties of software implementations, checking that a deviation in a program's inputs cause a proportional deviation in its outputs. However, the notion of dissipation over time have not been considered in this setting.

As mentioned before, our notion of IOS is a simplification of the notion of ISDS introduced by Grüne in [12]. Although we believe these simplifications to be justified by polynomial-time verification algorithms (see Section 3), it remains to investigate if there are examples that require the full power of ISDS. The algorithms in Section 3.2 are inspired by the approach taken in the paper [13] to compute Lyapunov functions through viability theory. Although [13] only considered the verification problem, the extension to synthesis is conceptually clear. The algorithm for verification of IOS in Section 3.1 is inspired by the work of Alur et al. on verification and synthesis for ranking specifications [2]. Also related is the work reported in [14] where dynamic programing is used to characterize the stability properties of control systems. Although some of our algorithms have a dynamic programming flavor, the algorithms in [14] are not computationally efficient as they require solving a dynamic program for each different value of $I(\sigma)$.

Our use of finite-state automata as a means to define cost functions that depend on the evolution of states is inspired by similar representations in [1, 2, 6, 5]. The finite-state condition is usually needed for effective algorithms, and can be seen as abstractions of more general cost models.

7. CONCLUSION

We have provided a definition of robustness for discrete systems that satisfies two conditions: bounded disturbances have bounded consequences, and sporadic disturbances dissipate over time. We believe IOS forms a natural basis for developing a theory of robust behaviors. For example, one can prove "small gain" like theorems for the composition of systems.

Although many extensions of the proposed ideas are possible, we are particularly interested in providing a similar theory of robustness for infinite strings and liveness properties. Finally, while we study IOS in a discrete setting, the natural next step is to combine with IOS for continuous control systems [12]. This will allow reasoning about robustness of cyber-physical systems, in which discrete components interact with physical systems.

---

[3]Strictly speaking, the automata in Definition 2 are defined over finite state spaces. However, if we are not concerned with effective constructions, we can define automata over possibly infinite set of states (by dropping the finiteness requirement in the definition.

8. REFERENCES

[1] R. Alur and G. Weiss. RTComposer: a framework for real-time components with scheduling interfaces. In *EMSOFT 08: Embedded Software*, pages 159–168. ACM, 2008.

[2] Rajeev Alur, Aditya Kanade, and Gera Weiss. Ranking automata and games for prioritized requirements. In *Proceedings of the 20th international conference on Computer Aided Verification*, CAV '08, pages 240–253, Berlin, Heidelberg, 2008. Springer-Verlag.

[3] A. Arora and S.S. Kulkarni. Detectors and correctors: a theory of fault-tolerance components. In *Distributed Computing Systems, 1998. Proceedings. 18th International Conference on*, pages 436 –443, may 1998.

[4] R. Bloem, K. Greimel, T.A. Henzinger, and B. Jobstmann. Synthesizing robust systems. In *Formal Methods in Computer-Aided Design, 2009. FMCAD 2009*, pages 85 –92, nov. 2009.

[5] Krishnendu Chatterjee, Laurent Doyen, and Thomas A. Henzinger. Expressiveness and closure properties for quantitative languages. *Logical Methods in Computer Science*, 6(3), 2010.

[6] Krishnendu Chatterjee, Laurent Doyen, and Thomas A. Henzinger. Quantitative languages. *ACM Trans. Comput. Log.*, 11(4), 2010.

[7] S. Chaudhuri, S. Gulwani, and R. Lublinerman. Continuity analysis of programs. In *POPL: Principles of Programming Languages*, pages 57–70. ACM, 2010.

[8] E. W. Dijkstra. Self-stabilizing systems in spite of distributed control. *Communications of the ACM*, 17:643–644, 1974.

[9] L. Doyen, T.A. Henzinger, A. Legay, and D. Nickovic. Robustness of sequential circuits. In *Application of Concurrency to System Design (ACSD), 2010 10th International Conference on*, pages 77 –84, june 2010.

[10] J. Elson, L. Girod, and D. Estrin. Fine-grained network time synchronization using reference broadcasts. In *Proceedings of the 5th symposium on Operating systems design and implementation*, OSDI '02, pages 147–163. ACM, 2002.

[11] A. Girard. Approximately bisimilar finite abstractions of stable linear systems. *in Proceedings of 10th Internation Conference on Hybrid Systems: Computation and Control*, 4416:231–244, 2007.

[12] L. Grüne. Input-to-state dynamical stability and its lyapunov function characterization. *Automatic Control, IEEE Transactions on*, 47(9):1499 – 1504, sep 2002.

[13] L. Grüne and P. Saint-Pierre. An invariance kernel representation of ISDS Lyapunov functions. *Systems & Control Letters*, 55(9):736–745, 2006.

[14] S. Huang, M.R. James, D. Nesic, and P.M. Dower. Analysis of input-to-state stability for discrete time nonlinear systems via dynamic programming. *Automatica*, 41(12):2055–2065, 2005.

[15] H. K. Khalil. *Nonlinear systems*. Prentice-Hall, Inc., New Jersey, 2nd edition, 1996.

[16] R. Majumdar and I. Saha. Symbolic robustness analysis. In *IEEE Real-Time Systems Symposium*, pages 355–363. IEEE Computer Society, 2009.

[17] O. Maler, A. Pnueli, and J. Sifakis. On the synthesis of discrete controllers for timed systems. In E.W. Mayr and C. Puech, editors, *STACS 95: Theoretical Aspects of Computer Science*, Lecture Notes in Computer Science 900, pages 229–242. Springer-Verlag, 1995.

[18] G. Pola, A. Girard, and P. Tabuada. Approximately bisimilar symbolic models for nonlinear control systems. *Automatica*, 44(10):2508–2516, 2008.

[19] E.D. Sontag. Smooth stabilization implies coprime factorization. *Automatic Control, IEEE Transactions on*, 34(4):435 –443, apr 1989.

[20] Danielle C. Tarraf, Alexandre Megretski, and Munther A. Dahleh. A framework for robust stability of systems over finite alphabets. *IEEE Transactions on Automatic Control*, 53(5):1133–1146, 2008.

[21] A. Tarski. A lattice-theoretical fixpoint theorem and its applications. *Pacific Journal of Mathematics*, 5(2):285–309, 1955.

[22] G. Zames. Functional analysis applied to nonlinear feedback systems. *IEEE Transactions on Circuit Theory*, 10:392–404, 1963.

[23] G. Zames. Input-output feedback stability and robustness, 1959–85. *IEEE Control Systems Magazine*, 16(3):61–66, 1996.

On Model Based Synthesis of Embedded Control Software

Vadim Alimguzhin[*]   Federico Mari   Igor Melatti   Ivano Salvo   Enrico Tronci
Computer Science Department, Sapienza University of Rome
via Salaria, 113 – 00198 Rome, Italy
{alimguzhin, mari, melatti, salvo, tronci}@di.uniroma1.it

ABSTRACT

Many *Embedded Systems* are indeed *Software Based Control Systems* (SBCSs), that is control systems whose controller consists of control software running on a microcontroller device. This motivates investigation on *Formal Model Based Design* approaches for control software. Given the formal model of a plant as a *Discrete Time Linear Hybrid System* and the implementation specifications (that is, number of bits in the *Analog-to-Digital* (AD) conversion) correct-by-construction control software can be automatically generated from System Level Formal Specifications of the closed loop system (that is, *safety* and *liveness* requirements), by computing a suitable finite abstraction of the plant.

With respect to given implementation specifications, the automatically generated code implements a time optimal control strategy (in terms of set-up time), has a *Worst Case Execution Time* linear in the number of AD bits b, but unfortunately, its size grows exponentially with respect to b. In many embedded systems, there are severe restrictions on the computational resources (such as memory or computational power) available to microcontroller devices.

This paper addresses model based synthesis of control software by trading system level non-functional requirements (such us optimal set-up time, ripple) with software non-functional requirements (its footprint). Our experimental results show the effectiveness of our approach: for the inverted pendulum benchmark, by using a quantization schema with 12 bits, the size of the small controller is less than 6% of the size of the time optimal one.

Categories and Subject Descriptors

D.2.2 [**Software**]: Design Tools and Techniques—*Computer Aided Software Engineering*; D.2.4 [**Software**]: Software/Program Verification—*Model Checking, Formal Methods*

Keywords

Design and implementation of embedded software, Model- and component-based software design and analysis

---

[*]Vadim Alimguzhin is also with the Department of Computer Science and Robotics Ufa State Aviation Technical University 12 Karl Marx Street, Ufa, 450000, Russian Federation

1. INTRODUCTION

Many *Embedded Systems* are indeed *Software Based Control Systems* (SBCSs). An SBCS consists of two main subsystems, the *controller* and the *plant*, that form a *closed loop system*. Typically, the plant is a physical system consisting, for example, of mechanical or electrical devices whereas the controller consists of *control software* running on a microcontroller. Software generation from models and formal specifications forms the core of *Model Based Design* of embedded software [16]. This approach is particularly interesting for SBCSs since in such a case *System Level Formal Specifications* are much easier to define than the control software behavior itself. The typical control loop skeleton for an SBCS is the following. Measure x of the system state from plant *sensors* go through an *analog-to-digital* (AD) conversion, yielding a *quantized* value $\hat{x}$. A function *ctrlRegion* checks if $\hat{x}$ belongs to the region in which the control software works correctly. If this is not the case a *Fault Detection, Isolation and Recovery* (FDIR) procedure is triggered, otherwise a function *ctrlLaw* computes a command $\hat{u}$ to be sent to plant *actuators* after a *digital-to-analog* (DA) conversion. Basically, the control software design problem for SBCSs consists in designing software implementing functions *ctrlLaw* and *ctrlRegion* in such a way that the closed loop system meets given *safety* and *liveness* specifications.

For SBCSs, system level specifications are typically given with respect to the desired behavior of the closed loop system. The control software is designed using a *separation-of-concerns* approach. That is, *Control Engineering* techniques (e.g., see [8]) are used to design, from the closed loop system level specifications, *functional specifications* (*control law*) for the control software whereas *Software Engineering* techniques are used to design control software implementing the given functional specifications. Such a separation-of-concerns approach has several drawbacks.

First, usually control engineering techniques do not yield a formally verified specification for the control law when quantization is taken into account. This is particularly the case when the plant has to be modelled as a *Hybrid System*, that is a system with continuous as well as discrete state changes [1, 14, 4]. As a result, even if the control software meets its functional specifications there is no formal guarantee that system level specifications are met since quantization effects are not formally accounted for.

Second, issues concerning computational resources, such as control software *Worst Case Execution Time* (WCET), can only be considered very late in the SBCS design activity, namely once the software has been designed. As a result, the control software may have a WCET greater than the sampling time. This invalidates the schedulability analysis (typically carried out before the control software is completed) and may trigger redesign of the software or even of its functional specifications (in order to simplify its design).

Last, but not least, the classical separation-of-concerns approach does not effectively support design space exploration for the control software. In fact, although in general there will be many functional specifications for the control software that will allow meeting the given system level specifications, the software engineer only gets one to play with. This overconstrains a priori the design space for the control software implementation preventing, for example, effective performance trading (e.g., between number of bits in AD conversion, WCET, RAM usage, CPU power consumption, etc.).

1.1 Motivations

The previous considerations motivate research on Software Engineering methods and tools focusing on control software synthesis rather than on control law as in Control Engineering. The objective is that from the plant model (as a hybrid system), from formal specifications for the closed loop system behavior and from *Implementation Specifications* (that is, the number of bits used in the quantization process) such methods and tools can generate correct-by-construction control software satisfying the given specifications.

A *Discrete Time Linear Hybrid System* (DTLHS) is a discrete time hybrid system whose dynamics is modeled as a *linear predicate* over a set of continuous as well as discrete variables that describe system state, system inputs and disturbances. System level safety as well as liveness specifications are modeled as sets of states defined, in turn, as predicates. By adapting the proofs in [15] for the reachability problem in dense time hybrid systems, it has been shown that the control synthesis problem is undecidable for DTLHSs [22]. Despite that, non complete or semi-algorithms usually succeed in finding controllers for meaningful hybrid systems.

The tool *QKS* [20] automatically synthesises control software starting from a plant model given as a DTLHS, the number of bits for AD conversion, and System Level Formal Specifications of the closed loop system. The generated code, however, may be very large, since it grows exponentially with the number of bits of the quantization schema [21]. On the other hand, controllers synthesised by considering a finer quantization schema usually have a better behaviour with respect to many other non-functional requirements, such as *ripple* and *set-up time*. Typically, a microcontroller device in an Embedded System has limited resources in terms of computational power and/or memory. Current state-of-the-art microcontrollers have up to 512Kb of memory, and other design constraints (mainly costs) may impose to use even less powerful devices. As we will see in Sect. 4, by considering a quantization schema with 12 bits on the inverted pendulum system, *QKS* generates a controller which has a size greater than 8Mbytes.

This paper addresses model based synthesis of control software by trading system level non-functional requirements with software non-functional requirements. Namely, we aim at reducing the code footprint, possibly at the cost of having a suboptimal set-up time and ripple.

1.2 Our Main Contributions

Fig. 1 shows the model based control software synthesis flow that we consider in this paper. A specification consists of a plant model, given as a DTLHS, System Level Formal Specifications that describe functional requirements of the closed loop system, and Implementation Specifications that describe non functional requirements of the control software, such as the number of bits used in the quantization process, the required WCET, etc. In order to generate the control software, the tool *QKS* takes the following steps. First (step 1), a suitable finite discrete abstraction (*control abstraction* [20]) $\hat{\mathcal{H}}$ of the DTLHS plant model $\mathcal{H}$ is computed; $\hat{\mathcal{H}}$ depends on the quantization schema and it is the plant as it can be seen from

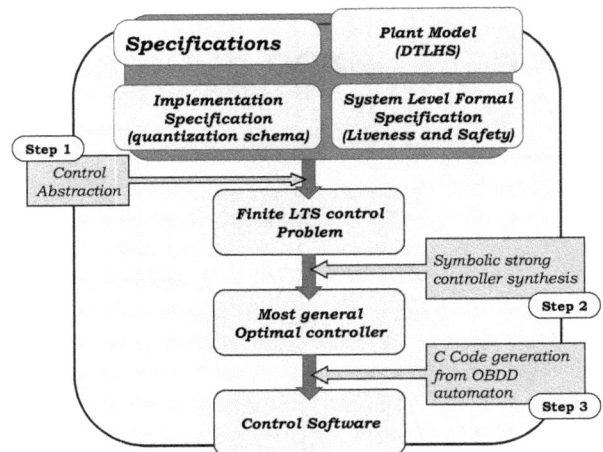

Figure 1: Control Software Synthesis Flow.

the control software after AD conversion. Then (step 2), given an abstraction $\hat{G}$ of the goal states G, it computes a controller $\hat{K}$ that starting from any initial abstract state, drives $\hat{\mathcal{H}}$ to $\hat{G}$ regardless of possible nondeterminism. Control abstraction properties ensure that $\hat{K}$ is indeed a (quantized representation of a) controller for the original plant $\mathcal{H}$. Finally (step 3), the finite automaton $\hat{K}$ is translated into control software (C code). Besides meeting functional specifications, the generated control software meets some non functional requirements: it implements a (near) time-optimal control strategy, and it has a WCET guaranteed to be linear in the number of bits of the quantization schema.

To find the quantized controller $\hat{K}$, *QKS* implements the symbolic synthesis algorithm in [9], based on *Ordered Bynary Decision Diagrams* (OBDDs) manipulation. This algorithm finds a time-optimal solution, i.e. the controller $\hat{K}$ drives the system $\hat{\mathcal{H}}$ to $\hat{G}$ always along shortest paths. The finer the control abstraction is (i.e. when the quantization schema is more precise), the better is the control strategy found. Unfortunately, such time optimal control strategies may lead to very large controllers in terms of the size of the generated C control software.

Driven by the intuition that by enabling the very same action on large regions of the state space we may decrease the control software size, we design a controller synthesis algorithm (Alg. 2 in Sect. 3.1) that gives up optimality and looks for maximal regions that can be controlled by performing the same action. We formally prove its correctness and completeness (Theor. 1 and 2 in Sect. 3.2).

Experimental results in Sect. 4 show that such a heuristic effectively mitigates the exponential growth of the controller size without having a significant impact on non-functional system level requirements such as set-up time and ripple. We accomplish this result without changing the WCET of the synthesized control software. For the inverted pendulum benchmark, by using a quantization schema with 12 bits, the size of our controller is less than 6% of the size of the time optimal controller.

1.3 Related Work

Control Engineering has been studying control law design (e.g., optimal control, robust control, etc.), for more than half a century (e.g., see [8]). Also *Quantized Feedback Control* has been widely studied in control engineering (e.g. see [13]). However such research does not address hybrid systems and, as explained above, focuses on control law design rather than on control software synthesis. Traditionally, control engineering approaches model *quantization errors* as statistical *noise*. As a result, correctness of the control law holds in a probabilistic sense. Here instead, we model quantization errors as nondeterministic (*malicious*) *disturbances*. This guarantees system level correctness of the generated control software (not just that of the control law) with respect to *any* possible sequence of quantization errors.

Formal verification of *Linear Hybrid Automata* (LHA) [1] has been investigated in [14, 12, 29, 27]. Quantization can be seen as a sort of abstraction. In a hybrid systems formal verification context, abstractions has been widely studied (e.g., see [2, 3]), to ease the verification task. On the other hand, in control software synthesis, quantization is a design requirement since it models a hardware component (AD converter) which is part of the specification of the control software synthesis problem. As a result, clever abstractions considered in a verification setting cannot be directly used in our synthesis setting where quantization is given.

The abstraction–based approach to controller synthesis has also been broadly investigated. Based on a notion of suitable finite state abstraction (e.g. see [24]) control software synthesis for continuous time linear systems (no switching) has been implemented in the tool PESSOA [23]. On the same wavelength, [30] generates a control strategy from a finite abstraction of a *Piecewise Affine Discrete Time Hybrid System* (PWA-DTHS). Also the Hybrid Toolbox [6] considers PWA-DTHSs. Such tools output a feedback control law that is then passed to Matlab in order to generate control software. Finite horizon control of PWA-DTHSs has been studied using a MILP based approach (e.g. see [7]). Explicit finite horizon control synthesis algorithms for discrete time (possibly non-linear) hybrid systems have been studied in [11]. All such approaches do not account for state feedback quantization since they all assume *exact* (i.e. real valued) state measures. Optimal switching logic, i.e. synthesis of optimal controllers with respect to some cost function has also been widely investigated (e.g. see [17]). In this paper, we focus on non-functional sofware requirements rather than non-functional system-level requirements.

Summing up, to the best of our knowledge, no previously published result is available about model based synthesis of small footprint control software from a plant model, system level specifications and implementation specifications.

2. CONTROL SOFTWARE SYNTHESIS

To make this paper self-contained, first we briefly summarize previous work on automatic generation of control software for *Discrete Time Linear Hybrid Systems* (DTLHSs) from System Level Formal Specifications. We focus on basic definitions and mathematical tools that will be useful later.

We model the controlled system (i.e. the plant) as a DTLHS (Sect. 2.3), that is a discrete time hybrid system whose dynamics is modeled as a *linear predicate* (Sect. 2.1) over a set of continuous as well as discrete variables. The semantics of a DTLHS is given in terms of a *Labeled Transition Systems* (LTSs, Sect. 2.2).

Given a plant $\mathcal{H}$ modeled as a DTLHS, a set of *goal states* G (*liveness specifications*) and an *initial region* I, both represented as linear predicates, we are interested in finding a *restriction K of the behaviour* of $\mathcal{H}$ such that in the *closed loop system* all paths starting in I lead to G after a finite number of steps. Moreover, we are interested in controllers that take their decisions by looking at *quantized states*, i.e. the values that the control software reads after an AD conversion. This is the *quantized control problem* (Sect. 2.3.1).

The quantized controller is computed by solving an *LTS control problem* (Sect. 2.2.1), by using a symbolic approach based on *Ordered Binary Decision Diagrams* (OBDDs) (Sect. 2.4.1). Finally, we briefly describe how C control software is automatically generated from the OBDD controller representation (Sect. 2.4.2).

2.1 Predicates

We denote with $[n]$ an initial segment $\{1, \ldots, n\}$ of the natural numbers. We denote with $X = [x_1, \ldots, x_n]$ a finite sequence of distinct variables, that we may regard, when convenient, as a set. Each variable x ranges on a known (bounded or unbounded) interval $\mathcal{D}_x$ either of the reals or of the integers (discrete variables). Boolean variables are discrete variables ranging on the set $\mathbb{B} = \{0, 1\}$. We denote with $\mathcal{D}_X$ the set $\prod_{x \in X} \mathcal{D}_x$. To clarify that a variable x is *continuous* (resp. discrete, boolean) we may write x^r (resp. x^d, x^b). Analogously X^r (X^d, X^b) denotes the sequence of real (integer, boolean) variables in X. Unless otherwise stated, we suppose $\mathcal{D}_{X^r} = \mathbb{R}^{|X^r|}$ and $\mathcal{D}_{X^d} = \mathbb{Z}^{|X^d|}$. Finally, if x is a boolean variable we write $\bar{x}$ for $(1 - x)$.

A *linear expression* $L(X)$ over a list of variables X is a linear combination of variables in X with rational coefficients. A *linear constraint* over X (or simply a *constraint*) is an expression of the form $L(X) \leq b$, where b is a rational constant. In the following, we also write $L(X) \geq b$ for $-L(X) \leq -b$, $L(X) = b$ for $(L(X) \leq b) \wedge (L(X) \geq b)$, and $a \leq x \leq b$ for $x \geq a \wedge x \leq b$.

Predicates are inductively defined as follows. A constraint $C(X)$ over a list of variables X is a predicate over X. If $A(X)$ and $B(X)$ are predicates over X, then $(A(X) \wedge B(X))$ and $(A(X) \vee B(X))$ are predicates over X. Parentheses may be omitted, assuming usual associativity and precedence rules of logical operators. A *conjunctive predicate* is a conjunction of constraints.

A *valuation* over a list of variables X is a function v that maps each variable $x \in X$ to a value $v(x) \in \mathcal{D}_x$. Given a valuation v, we denote with $X^* \in \mathcal{D}_X$ the sequence of values $[v(x_1), \ldots, v(x_n)]$. We also call valuation the sequence of values X^*. A *satisfying assignment* to a predicate $P(X)$ is a valuation X^* such that $P(X^*)$ holds. If a satisfying assignment to a predicate P over X exists, we say that P is *feasible*. Abusing notation, we may denote with P the set of satisfying assignments to the predicate $P(X)$.

Two predicates P and Q over X are *equivalent*, denoted by $P \equiv Q$, if they have the same set of satisfying assignments. Two predicates $P(X)$ and $Q(Z)$ are *equisatisfiable*, notation $P \simeq Q$ if P is satisfiable if and only if Q is satisfiable. A variable $x \in X$ is said to be *bounded* in P if there exist $a, b \in \mathcal{D}_x$ such that $P(X)$ implies $a \leq x \leq b$. A predicate is bounded if all its variables are bounded.

Given a constraint $C(X)$ and a fresh boolean variable (*guard*) $y \notin X$, the *guarded constraint* $y \rightarrow C(X)$ (if y then $C(X)$) denotes the predicate $(y = 0) \vee C(X)$. Similarly, we use $\bar{y} \rightarrow C(X)$ (if not y then $C(X)$) to denote the predicate $(y = 1) \vee C(X)$. A *guarded predicate* is a conjunction of either constraints or guarded constraints. It is possible to show that, if a guarded predicate P is bounded, then P can be transformed into an equisatisfiable conjunctive predicate.

2.2 Labeled Transition Systems

A *Labeled Transition System* (LTS) is a tuple $\mathcal{S} = (S, A, T)$ where S is a (possibly infinite) set of states, A is a (possibly infinite) set of *actions*, and $T : S \times A \times S \rightarrow \mathbb{B}$ is the *transition relation* of $\mathcal{S}$. Let $s \in S$ and $a \in A$. We denote with $\mathrm{Adm}(\mathcal{S}, s)$ the set of actions admissible in s, that is $\mathrm{Adm}(\mathcal{S}, s) = \{a \in A \mid \exists s' : T(s, a, s')\}$ and with $\mathrm{Img}(\mathcal{S}, s, a)$ the set of next states from s via a, that is $\mathrm{Img}(\mathcal{S}, s, a) = \{s' \in S \mid T(s, a, s')\}$. A *run* or *path* for an LTS $\mathcal{S}$ is a sequence $\pi = s_0, a_0, s_1, a_1, s_2, a_2, \ldots$ of states s_t and actions a_t such that $\forall t \geq 0 \ T(s_t, a_t, s_{t+1})$. The length $|\pi|$ of a finite run π is the number of actions in π. We denote with $\pi^{(S)}(t)$ the $(t + 1)$-th state element of π, and with $\pi^{(A)}(t)$ the $(t + 1)$-th action element of π. That is $\pi^{(S)}(t) = s_t$, and $\pi^{(A)}(t) = a_t$.

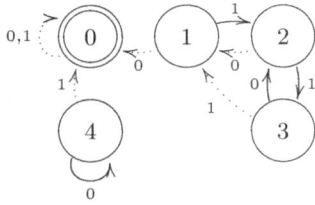

Figure 2: The LTS $\mathcal{S}$ in Example 1.

2.2.1 LTS Control Problem

A *controller* for an LTS $\mathcal{S}$ is used to restrict the dynamics of $\mathcal{S}$ so that all states in the initial region will eventually reach the goal region. We formalize such a concept by defining the LTS control problem and its solutions. In what follows, let $\mathcal{S} = (S, A, T)$ be an LTS, $I, G \subseteq S$ be, respectively, the *initial* and *goal* regions.

DEFINITION 1. *A controller for $\mathcal{S}$ is a function $K : S \times A \to \mathbb{B}$ such that $\forall s \in S$, $\forall a \in A$, if $K(s, a)$ then $\exists s'\ T(s, a, s')$. If $K(s, a)$ holds, we say that the action a is* enabled *by K in s.*

The set of states for which at least one action is enabled is denoted by $\mathrm{dom}(K)$. *Formally,* $\mathrm{dom}(K) = \{s \in S \mid \exists a\ K(s, a)\}$.

We call a controller K a control law *if K enables at most one action in each state. Formally, K is a control law if, for all $s \in \mathrm{dom}(K)$, $K(s, a)$ and $K(s, b)$ implies $a = b$.*

The closed loop system *is the LTS $\mathcal{S}^{(K)} = (S, A, T^{(K)})$, where $T^{(K)}(s, a, s') = T(s, a, s') \wedge K(s, a)$.*

We call a path π *fullpath* [5] if either it is infinite or its last state $\pi^{(S)}(|\pi|)$ has no successors (i.e. $\mathrm{Adm}(\mathcal{S}, \pi^{(S)}(|\pi|)) = \varnothing$). We denote with $\mathrm{Path}(s, a)$ the set of fullpaths starting in state s with action a, i.e. the set of fullpaths π such that $\pi^{(S)}(0) = s$ and $\pi^{(A)}(0) = a$. Given a path π in $\mathcal{S}$, we define $j(\mathcal{S}, \pi, G)$ as follows. If there exists $n > 0$ s.t. $\pi^{(S)}(n) \in G$, then $j(\mathcal{S}, \pi, G) = \min\{n \mid n > 0 \wedge \pi^{(S)}(n) \in G\}$. Otherwise, $j(\mathcal{S}, \pi, G) = +\infty$. We require $n > 0$ since our systems are nonterminating and each controllable state (including a goal state) must have a path of positive length to a goal state. Taking $\sup \varnothing = +\infty$, the *worst case distance* of a state s from the goal region G is $J(\mathcal{S}, G, s) = \sup\{j(\mathcal{S}, \pi, G) \mid \pi \in \mathrm{Path}(s, a), a \in \mathrm{Adm}(\mathcal{S}, s)\}$.

DEFINITION 2. *An LTS control problem is a triple $\mathcal{P} = (\mathcal{S}, I, G)$. A* strong solution *(or simply a solution) to $\mathcal{P}$ is a controller K for $\mathcal{S}$, such that $I \subseteq \mathrm{dom}(K)$ and for all $s \in \mathrm{dom}(K)$, $J(\mathcal{S}^{(K)}, G, s)$ is finite.*

An optimal *solution to $\mathcal{P}$ is a solution K^* to $\mathcal{P}$ such that for all solutions K to $\mathcal{P}$, for all $s \in S$, we have $J(\mathcal{S}^{(K^*)}, G, s) \leq J(\mathcal{S}^{(K)}, G, s)$.*

The most general optimal (mgo) *solution to $\mathcal{P}$ is an optimal solution $\bar{K}$ to $\mathcal{P}$ such that for all optimal solutions K to $\mathcal{P}$, for all $s \in S$, for all $a \in A$ we have $K(s, a) \to \bar{K}(s, a)$. This definition is well posed (i.e., the mgo solution is unique) and $\bar{K}$ does not depend on I.*

EXAMPLE 1. *Let $\mathcal{S} = (S, A, T)$ be the LTS in Fig. 2, where $S = \{0, 1, 2, 3, 4\}$, $A = \{0, 1\}$ and the transition relation T is defined by all arrows in the picture. Let $I = S$ and let $G = \{0\}$. The controller K that enables all dotted arrows in the picture, is an mgo for the control problem $(\mathcal{S}, I, G)$. The controller $K' = K \setminus \{(0, 1)\}$ that enables only the action 0 in the state 0, would be still an optimal solution, but not the most general. The controller $K'' = K \cup \{(3, 0)\}$ that enables also the action 0 in state 3 would be still a solution (more general than K), but no more optimal. As a matter of fact, in this case $J(\mathcal{S}^{(K'')}, G, 3) = 3$, whereas $J(\mathcal{S}^{(K)}, G, 3) = 2$.*

2.3 Discrete Time Linear Hybrid Systems

Many embedded control systems can be modeled as *Discrete Time Linear Hybrid Sytems* (DTLHSs) since they provide an uniform model both for the plant and for the control software.

DEFINITION 3. *A* Discrete Time Linear Hybrid System *is a tuple $\mathcal{H} = (X, U, Y, N)$ where:*

$X = X^r \cup X^d$ *is a finite sequence of real (X^r) and discrete (X^d) present state variables. The sequence X' of next state variables is obtained by decorating with $'$ all variables in X.*

$U = U^r \cup U^d$ *is a finite sequence of input variables.*

$Y = Y^r \cup Y^d$ *is a finite sequence of auxiliary variables, that are typically used to model modes or "local" variables.*

$N(X, U, Y, X')$ *is a conjunctive predicate over $X \cup U \cup Y \cup X'$ defining the transition relation (next state) of the system.*

A DTLHS is bounded if the predicate N is bounded.

Since any bounded guarded predicate is equisatisfiable to a conjunctive predicate (see Sect. 2.1), for the sake of readability we use bounded guarded predicates to describe the transition relation of bounded DTLHSs. To this aim, we also clarify which variables are boolean, and thus may be used as guards in guarded constraints.

The semantics of DTLHSs is given in terms of LTSs as follows.

DEFINITION 4. *Let $\mathcal{H} = (X, U, Y, N)$ be a DTLHS. The dynamics of $\mathcal{H}$ is defined by the Labeled Transition System $LTS(\mathcal{H}) = (\mathcal{D}_X, \mathcal{D}_U, \tilde{N})$ where: $\tilde{N} : \mathcal{D}_X \times \mathcal{D}_U \times \mathcal{D}_X \to \mathbb{B}$ is a function s.t. $\tilde{N}(x, u, x') \equiv \exists y \in \mathcal{D}_Y\ N(x, u, y, x')$. A state x for $\mathcal{H}$ is a state x for $LTS(\mathcal{H})$ and a run (or path) for $\mathcal{H}$ is a run for $LTS(\mathcal{H})$.*

EXAMPLE 2. *Let T be a positive constant (sampling time). We define the DTLHS $\mathcal{H} = (\{x\}, \{u\}, \varnothing, N)$ where x is a continuous variable, u is a boolean variable, and $N(x, u, x') \equiv [\bar{u} \to x' = x + (\frac{5}{4} - x)T] \wedge [u \to x' = x + (x - \frac{3}{2})T]$. Since $N(\frac{5}{4}, 0, \frac{5}{4})$ holds, the infinite path $\pi_0 = \frac{5}{4}, 0, \frac{5}{4}, 0 \ldots$ is a run in $LTS(\mathcal{H}) = (\mathbb{R}, \{0, 1\}, N)$.*

2.3.1 DTLHS Control Problem

A DTLHS control problem $(\mathcal{H}, I, G)$ is defined as the LTS control problem $(LTS(\mathcal{H}), I, G)$. To manage real valued variables, in classical control theory the concept of *quantization* is introduced (e.g., see [13]). Quantization is the process of approximating a continuous interval by a set of integer values. In the following we formally define a quantized feedback control problem for DTLHSs.

A *quantization function* γ for a real interval $I = [a, b]$ is a nondecreasing function $\gamma : I \mapsto \mathbb{Z}$ such that $\gamma(I)$ is a bounded integer interval. We extend quantizations to integer intervals, by stipulating that in such a case the quantization function is the identity function.

DEFINITION 5. *Let $\mathcal{H} = (X, U, Y, N)$ be a DTLHS, and let $W = X \cup U \cup Y$. A quantization Q for $\mathcal{H}$ is a pair (A, Γ), where:*

A is a predicate over W that explicitly bounds each variable in W. For each $w \in W$, we denote with A_w its admissible region and with $A_W = \prod_{w \in W} A_w$.

Γ is a set of maps $\Gamma = \{\gamma_w \mid w \in W$ and γ_w is a quantization function for $A_w\}$.

Let $W = [w_1, \ldots w_k]$ and $v = [v_1, \ldots v_k] \in A_W$. We write $\Gamma(v)$ for the tuple $[\gamma_{w_1}(v_1), \ldots \gamma_{w_k}(v_k)]$.

A control problem admits a *quantized* solution if control decisions can be made by just looking at quantized values. This enables a software implementation for a controller.

DEFINITION 6. *Let $\mathcal{H} = (X, U, Y, N)$ be a DTLHS, $Q = (A, \Gamma)$ be a quantization for $\mathcal{H}$ and $\mathcal{P} = (\mathcal{H}, I, G)$ be a DTLHS control problem. A Q Quantized Feedback Control (QFC) solution to $\mathcal{P}$ is a solution $K(x, u)$ to $\mathcal{P}$ such that $K(x, u) = \hat{K}(\Gamma(x), \Gamma(u))$ where $\hat{K} : \Gamma(A_X) \times \Gamma(A_U) \to \mathbb{B}$.*

EXAMPLE 3. *Let $\mathcal{H}$ be the DTLHS in Ex. 2. Let $\mathcal{P} = (\mathcal{H}, I, G)$ be a control problem, where $I \equiv -2 \le x \le 2.5$, and $G \equiv \varepsilon \le x \le \varepsilon$, for some $\varepsilon \in \mathbb{R}$. If the sampling time T is small enough with respect to ε (for example $T < \frac{\varepsilon}{10}$), the controller: $K(x, u) = (-2 \le x \le 0 \wedge \overline{u}) \vee (0 \le x \le \frac{11}{8} \wedge u) \vee (\frac{11}{8} \le x \le 2.5 \wedge \overline{u})$ is a solution to $(\mathcal{H}, I, G)$. Observe that any controller K' such that $K'(\frac{5}{4}, 0)$ holds is not a solution, because in such a case $\mathcal{H}^{(K)}$ may loop forever along the path π_0 of Ex. 2.*

Let us consider the quantization (A, Γ) where $A = I$ and $\Gamma = \{\gamma_x\}$ and $\gamma_x(x) = \lfloor x \rfloor$. The set $\Gamma(A_x)$ of quantized states is the integer interval $[-2, 2]$. No solution can exist, because in state 1 either enabling action 1 or 0 allows infinite loops to be potentially executed in the closed loop system. The controller K above can be obtained as a quantized controller decreasing the quantization step, for example by taking $\tilde{\Gamma} = \{\tilde{\gamma}_x\}$ where $\tilde{\gamma}_x(x) = \lfloor 8x \rfloor$.

2.4 Control Software Generation

Quantized controllers can be computed by solving LTS control problems: the *QKS* control software synthesis procedure consists of building a suitable finite state abstraction (*control abstraction*) $\hat{\mathcal{H}}$ induced by the quantization of a plant modeled as a DTLHS $\mathcal{H}$, computing an abstraction $\hat{I}$ (resp. $\hat{G}$) of the initial (resp. goal) region I (resp. G) so that any solution to the LTS control problem $(\hat{\mathcal{H}}, \hat{I}, \hat{G})$ is a finite representation of a solution to $(\mathcal{H}, I, G)$. In [20], we give a constructive sufficient condition ensuring that the controller computed for $\hat{\mathcal{H}}$ is indeed a quantized controller for $\mathcal{H}$.

2.4.1 Symbolic Controller Synthesis

Control abstractions for bounded DTLHSs are finite LTSs. For example, a typical quantization is the *uniform quantization* which consists in dividing the domain of each state variable x into 2^{b_x} equal intervals, where b_x is the number of bits used by AD conversion. Therefore, the abstraction of a DTLHS induced by a uniform quantization has 2^B states, where $B = \sum_{x \in X} b_x$. By coding states and actions as sequences of bits, a finite LTS can be represented as an OBDD representing set of states and the transition relation by using their characteristic functions.

The *QKS* control synthesis procedure implements the function *mgoCtr* in Alg. 1, which adapts the algorithm presented in [9]. Starting from goal states, the most general optimal controller is found incrementally adding at each step to the set of states $D(s)$ controlled so far, the *strong preimage* of $D(s)$, i.e. the set of states for which there exists at least an action a that drives the system to $D(s)$, regardless of possible nondeterminism.

Algorithm 1 Symbolic Most General Optimal Controller Synthesis

---

Input: An LTS control problem $(\mathcal{S}, I, G)$, $\mathcal{S} = (S, A, T)$.
function $mgoCtr(\mathcal{S}, I, G)$

1. $K(s, a) \leftarrow 0, D(s) \leftarrow G(s), \tilde{D}(s) \leftarrow 0$
2. **while** $D(s) \ne \tilde{D}(s)$ **do**
3. $F(s, a) \leftarrow \exists s' \, T(s, a, s') \wedge \forall s' \, [T(s, a, s') \Rightarrow D(s')]$
4. $K(s, a) \leftarrow K(s, a) \vee (F(s, a) \wedge \nexists a \, K(s, a))$
5. $\tilde{D}(s) \leftarrow D(s), D(s) \leftarrow D(s) \vee \exists a \, K(s, a)$
6. **return** $\langle \forall s \, [I(s) \Rightarrow \exists a \, K(s, a)], \exists a \, K(s, a), K(s, a) \rangle$

2.4.2 C Code Generation

The output of the function *mgoCtr* is an OBDD K representing an mgo as a relation $K(x, u)$. Let k be the number of bits used to represent the set of actions. We are interested in a *control law* $F = [f_1, \ldots, f_k]$ such that $K(x, F(x))$ holds for all x [28]. We first compute k OBDDs $f_1, \ldots f_k$ representing F. For any f_i, by replacing each OBDD node with an if-then-else block and each OBDD edge with a goto statement, we obtain a C function f_i that implements the boolean function represented by f_i.

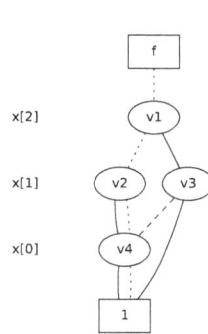

Figure 3: OBDD for F.

```
int ctrlLaw(unsigned char *x){
    int act=0;
    L_v1: if (x[2]==1) goto L_v3;
            else { act  = !act;
                    goto L_v2;}
    L_v2: if (x[1]==1) goto L_v4;
            else { act  = !act;
                    goto L_v4;}
    L_v3: if (x[1]==1) return act;
            else goto L_v4;
    L_v4: if (x[0]==1) return act;
            else { act  = !act;
                    return act;}
}
```

Figure 4: C control software.

Therefore, the size of f_i is proportional to the number of nodes in f_i. Its WCET is proportional to the *height* of f_i, since any computation of f_i corresponds to going through a path of f_i. As a consequence, the WCET of the control software turns out to be *linear* in the number of bits of the quantization schema. The C function ctrLaw is obtained by translating the k OBDDs representing F, whereas ctrReg is obtained by translating the OBDD representing the characteristic function of dom(K). The actual code implementing control software is slightly more complicated to account for node sharing among OBDDs $f_1, \ldots, f_k$. Full details about the control software generation can be found in [21].

EXAMPLE 4. *Let $\mathcal{P} = (\mathcal{S}, I, G)$ be the control problem in Ex. 1. The five states of $\mathcal{S}$ can be represented by three boolean variables (x_0, x_1, x_2). Taking as input $\mathcal{P}$, mgoCtr computes the mgo K given in Ex. 1. The control law F is the OBDD depicted in Fig. 3. In Fig. 4, it is shown a snapshot of the control software generated for F.*

3. SMALL CONTROLLERS SYNTHESIS

Within the framework defined in the previous section, when finer (i.e. with more bits) quantization schemas are considered, better controllers are found, in terms of set-up time and ripple (see Sect. 4). On the other hand, the exponential growth of control software size is one of the main obstacles to overcome in order to make model based control software synthesis viable on large problems. As explained in Sect. 2.4.2, the size of the control software is proportional to the size of the OBDD computed by the function *mgoCtr* in Sect. 2.4.1. To reduce the number of nodes of such an OBDD, we devise a heuristic aimed at increasing OBDD node sharing by looking for control laws that are constant on large regions of the state space.

While optimal controllers implement smart control strategies that in each state try to find the best action to drive the system to the goal region, the function *smallCtr* in Sect. 3.1 looks for more "regular" controllers that enable the same action in as large as possible regions of the state space.

Finally, note that changing the control synthesis algorithm does not change the WCET of the generated control software since it only depends on the number of quantization bits (Sect. 2.4.2).

3.1 Control Synthesis Algorithm

Our controller synthesis algorithm is shown in Alg. 2. To obtain a succinct controller, the function *smallCtr* modifies the *mgoCtr* preimage computation of set of states D by *finding maximal regions* of states from which the system reaches D in *one or more steps* by repeatedly performing the *same action*. This involves finding at each step a family of fixpoints: for each action a, $E(s, a)$ is the maximal set of states from which D is reachable by repeatedly performing the action a only.

The function $smallCtr(\mathcal{S}, I, G)$ computes a solution K to the control problem $(\mathcal{S}, I, G)$ (Theor. 1), such that $dom(K)$ is *maximal* with respect to any other solution (Theor. 2).

In Alg. 2 $K(s, a)$ denotes the OBDD that represents the controller computed so far, $D(s)$ the OBDD that represents its domain, and $\tilde{D}(s)$ the domain of the controller computed at the previous iteration. The computation starts by initializing $K(s, a)$ and its domain $D(s)$ to the empty OBDD, that corresponds to the always undefined function and the empty set (line 1).

At each iteration of the outer loop (lines 2–11), a target set of states $O(s)$ is considered (line 3): $O(s)$ consists of goal states $G(s)$ and the set $D(s)$ of already controlled states. The inner loop (lines 4–7) computes, for each action a, the maximal set of states $E(s, a)$ that can reach the target set $O(s)$ by repeatedly performing the action a only. For any action a_0, $E(s, a_0)$ is the mgo of the control problem $(\mathcal{S}', I, O)$, where the LTS $\mathcal{S}' = (S, \{a_0\}, T')$ is obtained by restricting the dynamics of $\mathcal{S}$ to the action a_0.

After that, K is updated by adding to it state-action pairs in $E(s, a)$. Instead of simply computing $K(s, a) \leftarrow K(s, a) \lor E(s, a)$, to keep the controller smaller, function $smallCtr$ avoids to add to K possible intersections between any pair of sets $E(s, a)$ and $E(s, b)$ for $a \neq b$ (line 9). As a consequence, the resulting controller K is a control law, i.e. it enables just one action in a given state s.

The order in which the loop in lines 8–9 enumerates the set of actions gives priority to actions that are considered before. Let $a_0, a_1, \ldots, a_n$ be the sequence of actions as enumerated by the **for** loop. If there exists at least one action a such that $E(s, a)$ holds, then we will have that $K(s, a_k)$ holds only for a certain a_k such that $k = \min\{i \mid E(s, a_i)\}$. In many control problems, this is useful as it allow one to give priority to some actions, e.g. in order to prefer "low power" actions.

The computation ends when no new state is added to the controllable region, i.e. when $D(s)$, is the same as $\tilde{D}(s)$.

Algorithm 2 Symbolic Small Controller Synthesis

Input: LTS control problem $(\mathcal{S}, I, G)$, with LTS $\mathcal{S} = (S, A, T)$
function $smallCtr(\mathcal{S}, I, G)$
1. $K(s, a) \leftarrow 0, D(s) \leftarrow 0$
2. **repeat**
3. $O(s) \leftarrow D(s) \lor G(s), E(s, a) \leftarrow 0$
4.   **repeat**
5. $F(s, a) \leftarrow \exists s' T(s, a, s') \land [T(s, a, s') \Rightarrow E(s', a) \lor O(s')]$
6. $\tilde{E}(s, a) \leftarrow E(s, a), E(s, a) \leftarrow E(s, a) \lor F(s, a)$
7.   **until** $E(s, a) = \tilde{E}(s, a)$
8.   **for all** $\tilde{a} \in A$ **do**
9. $K(s, a) \leftarrow K(s, a) \lor (E(s, a) \land a = \tilde{a} \land \nexists b\, K(s, b))$
10. $\tilde{D}(s) \leftarrow D(s), D(s) \leftarrow D(s) \lor \exists a K(s, a)$
11. **until** $D(s) = \tilde{D}(s)$
12. **return** $\langle \forall s\, [I(s) \Rightarrow \exists a K(s, a)], \exists a K(s, a), K(s, a) \rangle$

EXAMPLE 5. *Let $\mathcal{P}$ be the control problem described in Ex. 1. The first iteration of Alg. 2 computes the predicate $E(s, a)$ that holds on the set $\{(0, 0), (0, 1), (1, 0), (2, 0), (3, 0), (4, 1)\}$, that is $E(s, a) = E(s, 0) \lor E(s, 1)$, where the set of pairs that satisfies $E(s, 0)$ is $\{(0, 0), (1, 0), (2, 0), (3, 0)\}$ and the set of pairs that satisfies $E(s, 1)$ is $\{(0, 1), (4, 1)\}$. Depending on the order in which the **for** loop in lines 8–9 enumerates the set of actions, in the state 0 the resulting controller K^* enables the action 0 ($K^*(s, a) = E(s, 0) \cup (E(s, 1) \setminus \{(0, 1)\})$) or the action 1 ($K^*(s, a) = E(s, 1) \cup (E(s, 0) \setminus \{(0, 0)\})$). Observe that, in any case, K^* is not optimal. An optimal controller would enable the transition $T(3, 1, 1)$ rather than $T(3, 0, 2)$ (see Ex. 1).*

The OBDD representing the control law F such that $K^*(x, F(x))$

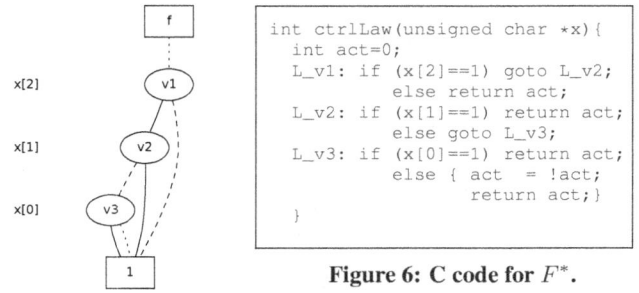

Figure 5: OBDD for F^*.

```
int ctrlLaw(unsigned char *x){
    int act=0;
  L_v1: if (x[2]==1) goto L_v2;
        else return act;
  L_v2: if (x[1]==1) return act;
        else goto L_v3;
  L_v3: if (x[0]==1) return act;
        else { act = !act;
               return act;}
}
```

Figure 6: C code for F^*.

holds, is depicted in Fig. 5. It has 3 nodes, instead of the 4 nodes required for the OBDD representation of the control law (Fig. 3) obtained from the controller K given in Ex. 1. Accordingly, the corresponding C code in Fig. 6 has 3 if-then-else blocks, instead of the 4 in the C code of Fig. 4.

REMARK 1. *Let $\pi = s_0, a_0, s_1, a_1, \ldots, a_{n-1}, s_n$ be a path. An action switch in π occurs whenever $a_i \neq a_{i+1}$. Controllers generated by Alg. 2 implement control strategies with a very low number of switches. In many systems this is a desirable property. A "switching optimal" control strategy cannot be, however, implemented by a memoryless state-feedback control law. As an example, take again the control problem $\mathcal{P}$ described in Ex. 1. The controller defined by $E(s, a)$ in Ex. 5 contains all switch optimal paths. However, to minimize the number of switches along the paths going through state 0, a controller should enable action 0 when coming from state 1, action 1 when coming from 4, and repeat the last action (0 or 1) when the system is executing the self-loops in state 0. In other words, only a feedback controller with memory can implement this control strategy.*

3.2 Synthesis Algorithm Correctness and Completeness

In the following, we establish the correctness of Alg. 2, by showing that the controller computed by $smallCtr$ is indeed a solution to the control problem given as input (Theor. 1), and its completeness, in the sense that the domain of the computed controller is *maximal* with respect to the domain of any other solution (Theor. 2).

THEOREM 1. *Let $\mathcal{S} = (S, A, T)$ be an LTS, and $I, G \subseteq S$ be two sets of states. If smallCtr(S, I, G) returns the tuple $\langle$TRUE, D, $K\rangle$, then K is a solution to the control problem $(\mathcal{S}, I, G)$.*

PROOF. If $smallCtr$(S, I, G) returns the tuple $\langle$TRUE, D, $K\rangle$, clearly $I \subseteq dom(K)$ (see Alg. 2, line12). We have to show that, for all $s \in dom(K)$, $J(\mathcal{S}^{(K)}, G, s)$ is finite.

First of all, we show that at the end of the inner **repeat** loop of $smallCtr$ (lines 4–7), if $E(s, a)$ holds, then we have that $J(\mathcal{S}^{(E)}, O, s)$ is finite. We proceed by induction on the number of iteration of the inner **repeat** loop. Denoting with $F_i(s, a)$ the predicate $F(s, a)$ computed in line 5 during the i-th iteration, we will show that if $F_n(s, a)$ holds, then $J(\mathcal{S}^{(E)}, O, s) = n$. If $F_1(s, a)$ holds, then for all s' such that $T(s, a, s')$, s' belongs to O, and hence $J(\mathcal{S}^{(E)}, O, s) = 1$. Along the same lines, if $F_{n+1}(s, a)$ holds, then $J(\mathcal{S}^{(E)}, F_n, s) = 1$, and by applying induction hypothesis, $J(\mathcal{S}^{(E)}, O, s) = n + 1$. As for termination, we have that if $\tilde{E}(s, a) \neq E(s, a)$ then at least one new state has been included in $E(s, a)$. Thus the function $|S| - |dom(E)|$ is strictly positive and strictly decreasing at each iteration.

The outer **repeat** loop behaves in a similar way. Denoting with $E_i(s, a)$ the predicate $E(s, a)$ computed in line 3 during the i-th iteration, if $s \in dom(K)$, then $E_i(s, a)$ holds for some i and some

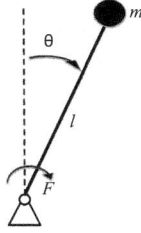

Figure 7: Inverted Pendulum with Stationary Pivot Point.

a. We prove the statement of the theorem by induction on i. If $i = 1$, we have that $O(s) = G(s)$ and that $J(\mathcal{S}^{(E_1)}, O, s)$ is finite, and hence trivially $J(\mathcal{S}^{(K)}, G, s)$ is finite. If $i > 1$, then we have that $J(\mathcal{S}^{(E_i)}, \text{dom}(E_{i-1}), s)$ is finite. Since, by inductive hypothesis, also $J(\mathcal{S}^{(E_{i-1})}, O, s)$ is finite, we have that $J(\mathcal{S}^{(K)}, G, s) \leq J(\mathcal{S}^{(E_i)}, \text{dom}(E_{i-1}), s) + J(\mathcal{S}^{(E_{i-1})}, O, s)$ is finite. $\square$

THEOREM 2. *Let $\mathcal{S} = (S, A, T)$ be an LTS, and $I, G \subseteq S$ be two sets of states. If smallCtr(S, I, G) returns the tuple $\langle \text{TRUE}, D, K \rangle$, then $D = \text{dom}(K)$ is the maximal controllable region, i.e. for any other solution K^* to the control problem $(\mathcal{S}, I, G)$ we have $\text{dom}(K^*) \subseteq \text{dom}(K)$.*

PROOF. Let $\text{dom}_n(K) = \{s \mid J(\mathcal{S}^{(K)}, s, G) = n\}$. We will show by induction that, for all n, $\text{dom}_n(K^*) \subseteq \text{dom}(K)$.

$(n = 1)$ Let $s \in \text{dom}_1(K^*)$. Then $\text{Adm}(\mathcal{S}, s) \neq \varnothing$ and there exists at least one action $a \in \text{Adm}(\mathcal{S}, s)$ such that $K^*(s, a)$ holds. Thus, for all s' such that $T(s, a, s')$ we have that $s' \in G$. But this means that $F(s, a)$ holds (Alg. 2, line 5) and therefore $K(s, a)$ holds. Hence $s \in \text{dom}(K)$.

$(n > 1)$ Let $s \in \text{dom}_n(K^*)$. Then $\text{Adm}(\mathcal{S}, s) \neq \varnothing$ and there exists at least an action $a \in \text{Adm}(\mathcal{S}, s)$ such that $K^*(s, a)$ holds. Thus, for all s' such that $T(s, a, s')$ we have that $s' \in \text{dom}_{n-1}(K^*)$. By inductive hypothesis, $\text{dom}_{n-1}(K^*) \subseteq \text{dom}(K)$. Therefore, for all s' such that $T(s, a, s')$ we have that $s' \in \text{dom}(K)$. Let us suppose that $s \notin \text{dom}(K)$. But this implies that $\text{Img}(\mathcal{S}, s, a) \not\subseteq \text{dom}(K)$, otherwise Alg. 2 would not terminated before adding s to $E(s, a)$ at some iteration. This leads to a contradiction, because $\text{Img}(\mathcal{S}, s, a) \subseteq \text{dom}_{n-1}(K^*) \subseteq \text{dom}(K)$. $\square$

4. EXPERIMENTAL RESULTS

In this section we present our experiments that aim at evaluating the effectiveness of our control software synthesis technique. We mainly evaluate the control software size reduction and the impact on other non-functional control software requirements such as set-up time (optimality) and ripple.

We implemented *smallCtr* in the C programming language using the CUDD [10] package for OBDD based computations. The resulting tool, QKS^{sc}, extends the tool *QKS* by adding the possibility of synthesising control software (step 2 in Fig. 1) by using *smallCtr* instead of the mgo controller synthesis *mgoCtr*.

In Sect. 4.1 and 4.2 we will present the DTLHS models of the inverted pendulum and the multi-input buck DC-DC converter, on which our experiments focus. In Sect. 4.3 we give the details of the experimental setting, and finally, in Sect. 4.4, we discuss experimental results.

4.1 The Inverted Pendulum as a DTLHS

The inverted pendulum [19] (see Fig. 7) is modeled by taking the angle θ and the angular velocity $\dot{\theta}$ as state variables. The input of the system is the torquing force $u \cdot F$, that can influence the velocity in both directions. Here, the variable u models the direction and the constant F models the intensity of the force. Differently from [19],

we consider the problem of finding a discrete controller, whose decisions may be only "apply the force clockwise" ($u = 1$), "apply the force counterclockwise" ($u = -1$)", or "do nothing" ($u = 0$). The behaviour of the system depends on the pendulum mass m, the length of the pendulum l, and the gravitational acceleration g. Given such parameters, the motion of the system is described by the differential equation $\ddot{\theta} = \frac{g}{l} \sin \theta + \frac{1}{ml^2} uF$. In order to obtain a state space representation, we consider the following normalized system, where x_1 is the angle θ and x_2 is the angular speed $\dot{\theta}$:

$$\begin{cases} \dot{x}_1 = x_2 \\ \dot{x}_2 = \frac{g}{l} \sin x_1 + \frac{1}{ml^2} uF \end{cases} \quad (1)$$

The discrete time model obtained from the equations in (1) by introducing a constant T that models the sampling time is:

$$(x_1' = x_1 + Tx_2) \wedge (x_2' = x_2 + T\frac{g}{l} \sin x_1 + T\frac{1}{ml^2} uF)$$

that is not linear, as it contains the function $\sin x_1$. A linear model can be found by under- and over-approximating the non linear function $\sin x$. In our experiments (Sect. 4), we will consider the linear model obtained as follows.

First of all, in order to exploit sinus periodicity, we consider the equation $x_1 = 2\pi y_k + y_\alpha$, where y_k represents the period in which x_1 lies and $y_\alpha \in [-\pi, \pi]^1$ represents the actual x_1 inside a given period. Then, we partition the interval $[-\pi, \pi]$ in four intervals: $I_1 = \left[-\pi, -\frac{\pi}{2}\right]$, $I_2 = \left[-\frac{\pi}{2}, 0\right]$, $I_3 = \left[0, \frac{\pi}{2}\right]$, $I_4 = \left[\frac{\pi}{2}, \pi\right]$. In each interval I_i ($i \in [4]$), we consider two linear functions $f_i^+(x)$ and $f_i^-(x)$, such that for all $x \in I_i$, we have that $f_i^-(x) \leq \sin x \leq f_i^+(x)$. As an example, $f_1^+(y_\alpha) = -0.637y_\alpha - 2$ and $f_1^-(y_\alpha) = -0.707y_\alpha - 2.373$.

Let us consider the set of fresh continuous variables $Y^r = \{y_\alpha, y_{\sin}\}$ and the set of fresh discrete variables $Y^d = \{y_k, y_q, y_1, y_2, y_3, y_4\}$, with $y_1, \ldots, y_4$ being boolean variables. The DTLHS model $\mathcal{I}_F$ for the inverted pendulum is the tuple (X, U, Y, N), where $X = \{x_1, x_2\}$ is the set of continuous state variables, $U = \{u\}$ is the set of input variables, $Y = Y^r \cup Y^d$ is the set of auxiliary variables, and the transition relation $N(X, U, Y, X')$ is the following predicate:

$$(x_1' = x_1 + 2\pi y_q + Tx_2) \wedge (x_2' = x_2 + T\frac{g}{l} y_{\sin} + T\frac{1}{ml^2} uF)$$
$$\wedge \bigwedge_{i \in [4]} y_i \to f_i^-(y_\alpha) \leq y_{\sin} \leq f_i^+(y_\alpha)$$
$$\wedge \bigwedge_{i \in [4]} y_i \to y_\alpha \in I_i \wedge \sum_{i \in [4]} y_i \geq 1$$
$$\wedge x_1 = 2\pi y_k + y_\alpha \wedge -\pi \leq x_1' \leq \pi$$

Overapproximations of the system behaviour increase system non-determinism. Since $\mathcal{I}_F$ dynamics overapproximates the dynamics of the non-linear model, the controllers that we synthesize are inherently *robust*, that is they meet the given closed loop requirements *notwithstanding* nondeterministic small *disturbances* such as variations in the plant parameters. Tighter overapproximations of non-linear functions makes finding a controller easier, whereas coarser overapproximations makes controllers more robust.

The typical goal for the inverted pendulum is to turn the pendulum steady to the upright position, starting from any possible initial position, within a given speed interval.

4.2 Multi-input Buck DC-DC Converter

The *multi-input* buck DC-DC converter [25] in Fig. 8 is a mixed-mode analog circuit converting the DC input voltage (V_i in Fig. 8) to a desired DC output voltage (v_O in Fig. 8). As an example, buck

---

[1]In this section we write π for a rational approximation of it.

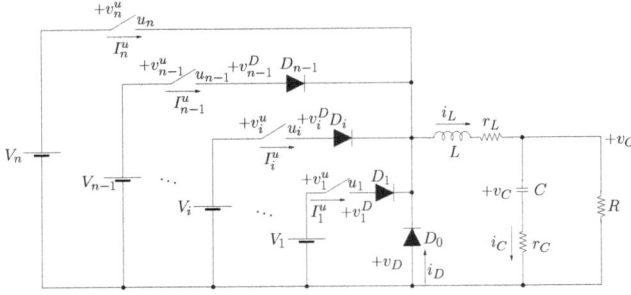

Figure 8: Multi-input Buck DC-DC Converter.

DC-DC converters are used off-chip to scale down the typical laptop battery voltage (12-24) to the just few volts needed by the laptop processor (e.g. [26]) as well as on-chip to support *Dynamic Voltage and Frequency Scaling* (DVFS) in multicore processors (e.g. [18]). The typical software based approach (e.g. see [26]) is to control the switches $u_1, \ldots, u_n$ in Fig. 8 (typically implemented with a MOSFET) with a microcontroller.

In such a converter there are n power supplies with voltage values $V_1, \ldots, V_n$, n switches with voltage values $v_1^u, \ldots, v_n^u$ and current values $I_1^u, \ldots, I_n^u$, and n input diodes $D_0, \ldots, D_{n-1}$ with voltage values $v_0^D, \ldots, v_{n-1}^D$ and current $i_0^D, \ldots, i_{n-1}^D$ (in the following, we will write v_D for v_0^D and i_D for i_0^D).

The circuit state variables are i_L and v_C. However we can also use the pair i_L, v_O as state variables in the DTLHS model since there is a linear relationship between i_L, v_C and v_O, namely: $v_O = \frac{r_C R}{r_C + R} i_L + \frac{R}{r_C + R} v_C$. We model the n-input buck DC-DC converter with the DTLHS $\mathcal{B}_n = (X, U, Y, N)$, with $X = [i_L, v_O]$, $U = [u_1, \ldots, u_n]$, $Y = [v_D, v_1^D, \ldots, v_{n-1}^D, i_D, I_1^u, \ldots, I_n^u, v_1^u, \ldots, v_n^u]$. From a simple circuit analysis we have the following equations:

$$\dot{i}_L = a_{1,1} i_L + a_{1,2} v_O + a_{1,3} v_D$$

$$\dot{v}_O = a_{2,1} i_L + a_{2,2} v_O + a_{2,3} v_D$$

where the coefficients $a_{i,j}$ depend on the circuit parameters R, r_L, r_C, L and C in the following way: $a_{1,1} = -\frac{r_L}{L}$, $a_{1,2} = -\frac{1}{L}$, $a_{1,3} = -\frac{1}{L}$, $a_{2,1} = \frac{R}{r_C + R}[-\frac{r_C r_L}{L} + \frac{1}{C}]$, $a_{2,2} = \frac{-1}{r_C + R}[\frac{r_C R}{L} + \frac{1}{C}]$, $a_{2,3} = -\frac{1}{L}\frac{r_C R}{r_C + R}$. Using a discrete time model with sampling time T (writing x' for $x(t+1)$) we have:

$$i_L' = (1 + T a_{1,1}) i_L + T a_{1,2} v_O + T a_{1,3} v_D$$

$$v_O' = T a_{2,1} i_L + (1 + T a_{2,2}) v_O + T a_{2,3} v_D.$$

The algebraic constraints stemming from the constitutive equations of the switching elements are the following:

$$q_0 \to (v_D = R_{on} i_D) \quad \bar{q}_0 \to (v_D = R_{off} i_D) \quad v_D = v_n^u - V_n$$

$$q_0 \to (i_D \geq 0) \quad \bar{q}_0 \to (v_D \leq 0) \quad i_L = i_D + \sum_{i=1}^n I_i^u$$

$$\bigwedge_{i \in [n]} q_i \to (v_i^D = R_{on} I_i^u) \quad \bigwedge_{i \in [n]} \bar{q}_i \to (v_i^D = R_{off} I_i^u)$$

$$\bigwedge_{i \in [n]} q_i \to (I_i^u \geq 0) \quad \bigwedge_{i \in [n]} \bar{q}_i \to (v_i^D \leq 0)$$

$$\bigwedge_{j \in [n-1]} u_j \to (v_j^u = R_{on} I_j^u) \quad \bigwedge_{j \in [n-1]} \bar{u}_j \to (v_j^u = R_{off} I_j^u)$$

$$\bigwedge_{i \in [n]} v_D = v_i^u + v_i^D - V_i$$

4.3 Experimental Settings

All experiments have been carried out on an Intel(R) Xeon(R) CPU @ 2.27GHz, with 23GiB of RAM, Kernel: Linux 2.6.32-5-686-bigmem, distribution Debian GNU/Linux 6.0.3 (squeeze).

As in [19], we set pendulum parameters l and m in such a way that $\frac{g}{l} = 1$ (i.e. $l = g$) and $\frac{1}{ml^2} = 1$ (i.e. $m = \frac{1}{l^2}$). As for the

quantization, we set $A_{x_1} = [-1.1\pi, 1.1\pi]$ and $A_{x_2} = [-4, 4]$, and we define $A_{\mathcal{I}_F} = A_{x_1} \times A_{x_2} \times A_u$. The goal region is defined by the predicate $G_{\mathcal{I}_F}(X) \equiv (-\rho \leq x_1 \leq \rho) \wedge (-\rho \leq x_2 \leq \rho)$, where $\rho \in \{0.05, 0.1\}$, and the initial region is defined by the predicate $I_{\mathcal{I}_F}(X) \equiv (-\pi \leq x_1 \leq \pi) \wedge (-4 \leq x_2 \leq 4)$.

In the multi-input buck DC-DC converter with n inputs $\mathcal{B}_n$, we set constant parameters as follows: $L = 2 \cdot 10^{-4}$ H, $r_L = 0.1$ Ω, $r_C = 0.1$ Ω, $R = 5$ Ω, $C = 5 \cdot 10^{-5}$ F, $R_{on} = 0$ Ω, $R_{off} = 10^4$ Ω, and $V_i = 10i$ V for $i \in [n]$. As for the quantization, we set $A_{i_L} = [-4, 4]$ and $A_{v_O} = [-1, 7]$, and we define $A_{\mathcal{B}_n} = A_{i_L} \times A_{v_O} \times A_{u_1} \times \ldots \times A_{u_n}$. The goal region is defined by the predicate $G_{\mathcal{B}_n}(X) \equiv (-2 \leq i_L \leq 2) \wedge (5 - \rho \leq v_O \leq 5 + \rho)$, where $\rho = 0.01$, and the initial region is defined by the predicate $I_{\mathcal{B}_n}(X) \equiv (-2 \leq i_L \leq 2) \wedge (0 \leq v_O \leq 6.5)$.

In both examples, we use uniform quantization functions dividing the domain of each state variable x into 2^b equal intervals, where b is the number of bits used by AD conversion. The resulting quantizations are $\mathcal{Q}_{\mathcal{I}_F, b} = (A_{\mathcal{I}_F}, \Gamma_b)$ and $\mathcal{Q}_{\mathcal{B}_n, b} = (A_{\mathcal{B}_n}, \Gamma_b)$. Since in both examples have two quantized variables, each one with b bits, the number of quantized (abstract) states is exactly 2^{2b}.

We run *QKS* and *QKS*[sc] on the inverted pendulum model $\mathcal{I}_F$ for different values of F (force intensity), and on the multi-input buck DC-DC model $\mathcal{B}_n$, for different values of parameter n (number of the switches). For the inverted pendulum, we use sampling time $T = 0.1$ seconds when the quantization schema has less than 10 bits and $T = 0.01$ seconds otherwise. For the multi-input buck, we set $T = 10^{-6}$ seconds. For both systems, we run experiments with different quantization schema.

For all of these experiments, *QKS* and *QKS*[sc] output a control software in C language. In the following, we will denote with K^{mgo} the output of *QKS*, and with K^{sc} the output of *QKS*[sc] on the same control problem.

4.4 Experiments Discussion

We compare the controller K^{mgo} and K^{sc} by evaluating their size, as well as other non-functional requirements such as the set-up time and the ripple of the closed loop system. Tables 1 and 2 summarize our experimental results.

In both tables, column $|K^{mgo}|$ (resp. $|K^{sc}|$) shows the size (in Kbytes) of the .o file obtained by compiling the output of *QKS* (resp. *QKS*[sc]) with gcc. Column $\frac{|K^{sc}|}{|K^{mgo}|}$ shows the ratio between the size of the two controllers and it illustrates how much one gains in terms of code size by using function *smallCtr* instead of *mgoCtr*.

Column Path[mgo] (resp. Path[sc]) shows the average length of (worst case) paths to the goal region in the closed loop abstract systems $\hat{\mathcal{H}}^{(K^{mgo})}$ (resp. $\hat{\mathcal{H}}^{(K^{sc})}$). This number, multiplied by the sampling time, provides a pessimistic estimation of the average set-up time of the closed loop system. Column $\frac{\text{Path}^{sc}}{\text{Path}^{mgo}}$ shows the ratio between the values in the two previous columns, and it provides an estimation of the price one has to pay (in terms of optimality) by using a small controller instead of the mgo controller.

The last three columns show the computation time of function *smallCtr* (column CPU[sc], in seconds), the ratio with respect to *mgoCtr* (column $\frac{\text{CPU}^{sc}}{\text{CPU}^{mgo}}$), and *smallCtr* memory usage (column Mem, in Kbytes). The function *smallCtr* is obviously slower than *mgoCtr*, because of non-optimality: it performs more loops, and it deals with more complex computations. Keep in mind, however, that the controller synthesis off-line computation is not a critical parameter in the control software synthesis flow.

As we can see in Tab. 1 and Tab. 2 the size of the controller K^{sc} tends to become smaller and smaller with respect to the size of the correspondent controller K^{mgo} as the complexity of the plant model grows. This is a general trend, both with respect to the number of

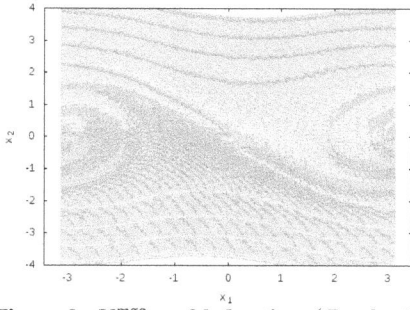

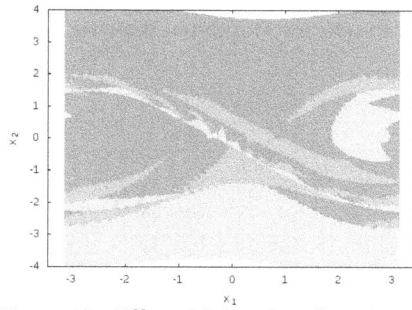

Figure 9: K^{mgo} **enabled actions** $(\mathcal{I}_{0.5}, b = 9)$ **Figure 10:** K^{sc} **enabled actions** $(\mathcal{I}_{0.5}, b = 9)$ **Figure 11: Simulation of** $\mathcal{I}_{0.5}^{K^{\mathrm{sc}}}, \mathcal{I}_{0.5}^{K^{\mathrm{mgo}}} (b = 9)$

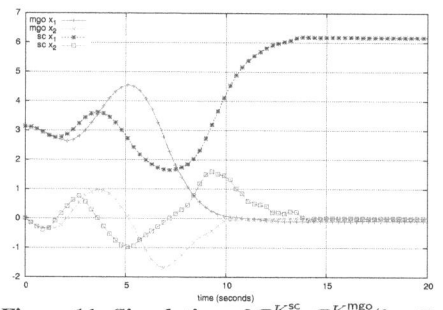

switches of the multi-input buck, and with respect to the number of bits of the quantization schema (in both examples). In particular, in the 12 bits controllers for the inverted pendulum, the size of K^{sc} is just about 5% of the size of K^{mgo}.

The average worst case length of paths to the goal in the closed loop system $\hat{\mathcal{H}}^{(K^{\mathrm{sc}})}$ tends to approach the one in $\hat{\mathcal{H}}^{(K^{\mathrm{mgo}})}$ as the complexity of the system grows. $\hat{\mathcal{H}}^{(K^{\mathrm{sc}})}$ simulations show an even better behaviour since most of the time, the set–up time of $\hat{\mathcal{H}}^{(K^{\mathrm{sc}})}$ is about the one of $\hat{\mathcal{H}}^{(K^{\mathrm{mgo}})}$.

For example, Fig. 11 shows a simulation of the closed loop systems $\mathcal{I}_{0.5}^{K^{\mathrm{sc}}}$ and $\mathcal{I}_{0.5}^{K^{\mathrm{mgo}}}$. It considers a quantization schema of 9 bits with trajectories starting from $x_1 = \pi, x_2 = 0$. In order to show pendulum phases, x_1 is not normalized in $[-\pi, \pi]$, thus also $x_1 = 2\pi$ is in the goal. As we can see, the small controller needs slightly more time (just about a second) to reach the goal. This behaviour can be explained by observing that the average worst case path length is a very pessimistic measure. Thus, in practice, both controllers stabilize the system much faster than one can expect by looking at Path^{mgo} and Path^{sc}. Similarly, the performarce of the small controller with respect to the optimal one is much better than one can expect by considering the ratio $\frac{\text{Path}^{\mathrm{sc}}}{\text{Path}^{\mathrm{mgo}}}$. Interestingly, however, $\mathcal{I}_{0.5}^{K^{\mathrm{mgo}}}$ follows a smarter trajectory, with one less swing.

Fig. 12 (resp. Fig. 13) shows the ripple of x_1 in the inverted pendulum closed loop system $\mathcal{I}_{0.5}^{K^{\mathrm{mgo}}}$ (resp. $\mathcal{I}_{0.5}^{K^{\mathrm{sc}}}$), by focusing on the part of the simulation in Fig. 11 which is (almost always) inside the goal. As we can see, the small controller yields a worst ripple (0.0002 vs 0.0001), which may be however neglected in practice.

To visualize the very different nature of these controllers, Fig. 9 (resp. Fig. 10) shows actions that are enabled by K^{mgo} (resp. K^{sc}) in all states of the admissible region of the inverted pendulum control problem $\mathcal{I}_{0.5}$, by considering a quantization schema of 9 bits. In these pictures, different colors mean different actions. We observe that in Fig. 9 we need 7 colors, because in a given state K^{mgo} may enable any nonempty subset of the set of actions. As expected, the control strategy of K^{sc} is much more regular and thus simpler than the one of K^{mgo}, since it enables the same action in relatively large regions of the state space. Some symmetries of Fig. 9 are broken in Fig. 10 because when more actions could be choosen, *smallCtr* gives always priority to one of them (Alg. 2, lines 8–9).

5. CONCLUSIONS

We presented a novel automatic methodology to synthesize control software for Discrete Time Linear Hybrid Systems, aimed at generating small size control software. We proved our methodology to be very effective by showing that we synthesize controllers up to 20 times smaller than time optimal ones. Small controllers keep other software non-functional requirements, such as WCET, at the cost of being suboptimal with respect to system level non-functional requirements (i.e. set-up time and ripple). Such ineffi-

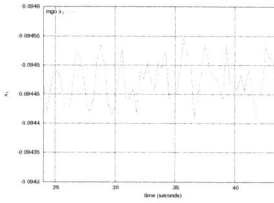

Figure 12: Ripple for K^{mgo} ($b = 9$)   **Figure 13: Ripple for** K^{sc} ($b = 9$)

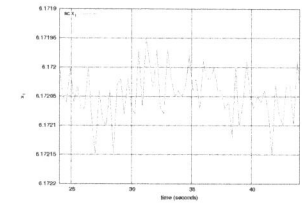

ciency may be fully justified since it allows a designer to consider much cheaper microcontroller devices.

Future work may consist of further exploiting small controller regularities in order to improve on other software as well as system level non-functional requirements. A more ambitious goal may consist of designing a tool that automatically tries to find control software that meets non-functional requirements given as input (such as memory, ripple, set-up time).

Acknowledgments

We thank our anonymous referees for their helpful comments. This work has been partially supported by the MIUR project TRAMP (DM24283) and by the EC FP7 projects ULISSE (GA218815) and SmartHG (317761).

6. REFERENCES

[1] R. Alur, C. Courcoubetis, N. Halbwachs, T. A. Henzinger, P. H. Ho, X. Nicollin, A. Olivero, J. Sifakis, and S. Yovine. The algorithmic analysis of hybrid systems. *Theoretical Computer Science*, 138(1):3–34, 1995.

[2] R. Alur, T.A. Henzinger, G. Lafferriere, and G.J. Pappas. Discrete abstractions of hybrid systems. *Proceedings of the IEEE*, 88(7):971–984, 2000.

[3] Rajeev Alur, Thao Dang, and Franjo Ivančić. Predicate abstraction for reachability analysis of hybrid systems. *ACM Trans. on Embedded Computing Sys.*, 5(1):152–199, 2006.

[4] Rajeev Alur, Thomas A. Henzinger, and Pei-Hsin Ho. Automatic symbolic verification of embedded systems. *IEEE Trans. Softw. Eng.*, 22(3):181–201, 1996.

[5] Paul C. Attie, Anish Arora, and E. Allen Emerson. Synthesis of fault-tolerant concurrent programs. *ACM Trans. on Program. Lang. Syst.*, 26(1):125–185, 2004.

[6] A. Bemporad. Hybrid Toolbox - User's Guide, 2004. http://www.ing.unitn.it/~bemporad/hybrid/toolbox.

[7] Alberto Bemporad and Nicolò Giorgetti. A sat-based hybrid solver for optimal control of hybrid systems. In *HSCC*, LNCS 2993, pages 126–141, 2004.

[8] William L. Brogan. *Modern control theory (3rd ed.)*. Prentice-Hall, Inc., Upper Saddle River, NJ, USA, 1991.

Table 1: Results for Multiinput Buck DC-DC Converter

b	n	$\lvert K^{mgo}\rvert$	$\lvert K^{sc}\rvert$	$\frac{\lvert K^{sc}\rvert}{\lvert K^{mgo}\rvert}$	Path^{mgo}	Path^{sc}	$\frac{\text{Path}^{sc}}{\text{Path}^{mgo}}$	CPU^{sc}	$\frac{\text{CPU}^{sc}}{\text{CPU}^{mgo}}$	Mem
9	1	36	30	83.9%	179.40	517.67	2.89	11.01	2.64	3.95e+04
9	2	62	34	56.0%	142.19	386.70	2.72	9.15	1.59	3.71e+04
9	3	110	41	37.3%	131.55	353.77	2.69	15.01	1.58	5.66e+04
9	4	157	42	27.3%	127.53	324.24	2.54	19.98	1.37	6.57e+04
10	1	91	56	61.4%	136.85	262.83	1.92	20.43	1.62	6.41e+04
10	2	149	61	41.0%	110.78	231.37	2.09	23.14	1.36	6.71e+04
10	3	244	65	26.9%	103.40	216.11	2.09	34.06	1.21	9.17e+04
10	4	341	70	20.6%	100.43	209.47	2.09	53.70	1.18	1.23e+05

Table 2: Results for the Inverted Pendulum

b	F	T	$\lvert K^{mgo}\rvert$	$\lvert K^{sc}\rvert$	$\frac{\lvert K^{sc}\rvert}{\lvert K^{mgo}\rvert}$	Path^{mgo}	Path^{sc}	$\frac{\text{Path}^{sc}}{\text{Path}^{mgo}}$	CPU^{sc}	$\frac{\text{CPU}^{sc}}{\text{CPU}^{mgo}}$	Mem
8	0.5	0.1	163	44	27.4%	132.96	234.35	1.76	16.25	2.16	4.15e+04
9	0.5	0.1	352	92	26.3%	69.64	147.74	2.12	33.59	2.12	8.47e+04
10	0.5	0.1	752	206	27.5%	59.16	133.70	2.26	123.94	2.57	2.27e+05
11	0.5	0.01	2467	213	8.6%	1315.69	1898.50	1.44	798.03	2.38	1.40e+05
12	0.5	0.01	8329	439	5.3%	674.39	1280.32	1.90	2769.08	1.07	8.82e+05
8	2.0	0.1	96	31	32.8%	24.30	58.00	2.39	3.41	1.87	4.13e+04
9	2.0	0.1	185	81	44.1%	22.29	40.13	1.80	9.64	1.94	8.39e+04
10	2.0	0.1	383	194	50.6%	21.91	43.24	1.97	49.26	2.13	2.25e+05
11	2.0	0.01	2204	128	5.8%	230.25	437.18	1.90	198.95	2.87	1.46e+05
12	2.0	0.01	5892	300	5.1%	207.31	390.48	1.88	561.18	0.45	9.63e+05

[9] Alessandro Cimatti, Marco Roveri, and Paolo Traverso. Strong planning in non-deterministic domains via model checking. In *AIPS*, pages 36–43, 1998.

[10] CUDD Web Page: http://vlsi.colorado.edu/~fabio/, 2004.

[11] G. Della Penna, D. Magazzeni, A. Tofani, B. Intrigila, I. Melatti, and E. Tronci. *Automated Generation of Optimal Controllers through Model Checking Techniques*, volume 15 of *LNEE*. Springer, 2008.

[12] Goran Frehse. Phaver: algorithmic verification of hybrid systems past hytech. *Int. J. Softw. Tools Technol. Transf.*, 10(3):263–279, 2008.

[13] Minyue Fu and Lihua Xie. The sector bound approach to quantized feedback control. *IEEE Trans. on Automatic Control*, 50(11):1698–1711, 2005.

[14] T.A. Henzinger, P.-H. Ho, and H. Wong-Toi. Hytech: A model checker for hybrid systems. *STTT*, 1(1):110–122, 1997.

[15] Thomas A. Henzinger, Peter W. Kopke, Anuj Puri, and Pravin Varaiya. What's decidable about hybrid automata? *J. of Computer and System Sciences*, 57(1):94–124, 1998.

[16] Thomas A. Henzinger and Joseph Sifakis. The embedded systems design challenge. In *FM*, LNCS 4085, pages 1–15, 2006.

[17] Susmit Jha, Sanjit A. Seshia, and Ashish Tiwari. Synthesis of optimal switching logic for hybrid systems. In *EMSOFT*, pages 107–116. ACM, 2011.

[18] W. Kim, M. S. Gupta, G.-Y. Wei, and D. M. Brooks. Enabling on-chip switching regulators for multi-core processors using current staggering. In *ASGI*, 2007.

[19] G. Kreisselmeier and T. Birkhölzer. Numerical nonlinear regulator design. *IEEE Trans. on on Automatic Control*, 39(1):33–46, 1994.

[20] Federico Mari, Igor Melatti, Ivano Salvo, and Enrico Tronci. Synthesis of quantized feedback control software for discrete time linear hybrid systems. In *CAV*, LNCS 6174, pages 180–195, 2010.

[21] Federico Mari, Igor Melatti, Ivano Salvo, and Enrico Tronci. From boolean relations to control software. In *ICSEA*, 2011.

[22] Federico Mari, Igor Melatti, Ivano Salvo, and Enrico Tronci. Undecidability of quantized state feedback control for discrete time linear hybrid systems. In *ICTAC12*, LNCS 7521, pages 243–258, 2012.

[23] Manuel Mazo, Anna Davitian, and Paulo Tabuada. Pessoa: A tool for embedded controller synthesis. In *CAV*, LNCS 6174, pages 566–569, 2010.

[24] Giordano Pola, Antoine Girard, and Paulo Tabuada. Approximately bisimilar symbolic models for nonlinear control systems. *Automatica*, 44(10):2508–2516, 2008.

[25] M. Rodriguez, P. Fernandez-Miaja, A. Rodriguez, and J. Sebastian. A multiple-input digitally controlled buck converter for envelope tracking applications in radiofrequency power amplifiers. *IEEE Trans on Pow El*, 25(2):369–381, 2010.

[26] Wing-Chi So, C.K. Tse, and Yim-Shu Lee. Development of a fuzzy logic controller for dc/dc converters: design, computer simulation, and experimental evaluation. *IEEE Trans. on Power Electronics*, 11(1):24–32, 1996.

[27] Claire Tomlin, John Lygeros, and Shankar Sastry. Computing controllers for nonlinear hybrid systems. In *HSCC*, LNCS 1569, pages 238–255, 1999.

[28] Enrico Tronci. Automatic synthesis of controllers from formal specifications. In *ICFEM*, pages 134–143. IEEE, 1998.

[29] H. Wong-Toi. The synthesis of controllers for linear hybrid automata. In *CDC*, pages 4607–4612 vol. 5. IEEE, 1997.

[30] B. Yordanov, J. Tumova, I. Cerna, J. Barnat, and C. Belta. Temporal logic control of discrete-time piecewise affine systems. *To Appear in IEEE Transactions On Automatic Control*, 2012.

A New Data Flow Analysis Model for TDM

Alok Lele
Mapscape, Eindhoven,
Netherlands
alok.lele@gmail.com

Orlando Moreira
ST-Ericsson B.V., Eindhoven,
Netherlands
orlando.moreira
@stericsson.com

Pieter J.L. Cuijpers
Eindhoven University of
Technology, Eindhoven,
Netherlands
p.j.l.cuijpers@tue.nl

ABSTRACT

This paper proposes a new data flow model for analyzing the worst-case temporal behavior of resource arbitration through Time Division Multiplexing (TDM).

TDM arbitration allows resource sharing amongst the tasks of concurrent applications, where each application may have its own end-to-end hard real time requirements, such as minimum throughput and maximum latency. Current data flow modeling techniques for the temporal analysis of TDM arbitration over-estimate the worst-case temporal behavior of tasks. This causes unnecessary over-reservation of resources to the application, leading to under-utilization of system resources and unnecessary rejection of additional applications.

We propose a conservative data flow model that accurately estimates the worst-case temporal behavior of TDM arbitration. Unlike existing models, we do not make restrictive assumptions on the characteristics of TDM, nor on the amount of resources reserved. This enables optimized resource allocation for TDM arbitration. We present a new model that closely mimics the worst-case temporal behavior of TDM arbitration. We formally prove that this model is conservative with respect to the worst-case behavior of TDM arbitration, and we prove that it is strictly more accurate than the state-of-the-art. Quantitatively, we show that our new model leads to a 20% improvement of resource allocation, in a case study of a wireless LAN radio downlink.

Categories and Subject Descriptors

C.4 [**Performance of Systems**]: Modeling techniques; Performance attributes

Keywords

real-time, temporal analysis, data flow

1. INTRODUCTION

An increasing number of embedded applications is being implemented on heterogeneous Multi Processor Systems on Chip (MPSoCs). These applications often need to satisfy hard real-time requirements such as guaranteed minimum throughput and maximum latency. For cost efficiency reasons, multiple applications share resources on a MPSoC. For instance, multi-radio modems have to process multiple streams of input independently with each stream having its own latency and throughput requirements [23, 1].

To establish hard real-time guarantees for each application on an MPSoC independently, we need to schedule their execution such that execution of one application will not influence the worst-case timing behavior of others.

One way to achieve separation of timing behavior is by allocating a separate budget to each task in an application. A *budget scheduler* guarantees a minimum amount of service for every scheduled task during a given time interval. In this way, the influence of the processing needs of one application on another is minimized.

Time division multiplexing (TDM) is a periodic type of budget scheduling, achieving independent execution of applications by dividing a fixed time frame (the replenishment period) into various slots, each assigned to a single task of an application. Within one replenishment period, an application can execute this task only in the time slot assigned to it, referred to as the slice or budget.

A TDM Scheduler is straightforward to implement with negligible run-time overhead, since it allows only time triggered context switches. This makes this kind of arbitration very popular in, for example, memory management and network routing. The time driven context switching between tasks enables the real-time analysis of the temporal behavior of a single task independently of all other tasks [19, 4, 24]. In order to reduce run-time overhead, there is usually no synchronization between TDM Schedulers of different resources. In particular, the precise phasing of the slices is not controlled and drift may occur. When calculating the execution times of interdependent tasks on different resources, the phasing is therefore usually assumed to be unknown.

A popular method for the temporal analysis of MPSoC applications, especially in the field of wireless telephony [23], is the use of *dataflow graphs* [20]. In this formalism, one starts by depicting task dependencies as a graph, where nodes (usually called actors) model tasks, and edges model channels [4, 16]. Starting from an application graph that only shows the division of an application into tasks, real-time analysis is made possible by graph transformation. The actors are replaced by subgraphs which contain timing information regarding the execution of each task in a scheduler [25]. Typically, the execution of a task in a TDM scheduler is modeled in dataflow by a graph transformation in which each actor is replaced by a so-called *latency-rate* response model [25]. This response model is based on the observation that a task with worst-case execution time τ will need to wait at most $P - S$ time units before it can start executing, where P denotes the period of the TDM scheduler and S denotes the size of the slice that is reserved for the task under study. Furthermore, if n iterations arrive at a task at the same time, they will need at most $\frac{n \cdot \tau}{S}$ periods to finish after their execution has started.

1.1 Problem statement

A problem with the latency-rate model for TDM scheduling is that it provides rather pessimistic estimates for the worst-case temporal behavior of tasks. This, in turn, causes pessimistic allocation of resources to guarantee the throughput and latency requirements of an application, and pessimism in resource allocation may lead to under-utilization of the system resources and unnecessary rejection of applications that could have been accommodated in the system.

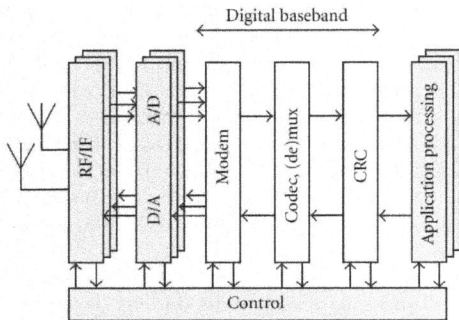

Figure 1: **Architecture for software defined radio**

As an example, consider the downlink of a Wireless LAN, as it runs in the software defined radio architecture depicted in figure 1. This application consists of a pipeline of tasks, with a required end-to-end latency of 9000 ns. The source produces new data tokens with a frequency of 250 kHz, subsequently defining the same as the end-to-end throughput requirement. Apart from the source, the tasks in this application are a demodulator, a decoder, and a cyclic redundancy checksum (CRC), as depicted in figure 2. The application is mapped onto a multiprocessor system comprising an ARM processor, an EVP (a vector processor developed by ST-Ericsson and delivered as a component in its baseband chips), and a Software Codec or SWC (a programmable core for baseband encoding and decoding operations). The demodulator task is mapped to the EVP and requires 920 ns, the decoder runs on the SWC and needs 920 ns, and the CRC needs 500 ns on an ARM processor.

If we decide to share the EVP processor using a TDM scheduler with a period of 2000 ns and a slice of 44% assigned to the demodulator, use a dedicated SWC for the decoder, and share the ARM processor using a TDM scheduler with a period of 2000 ns and a slice of 16% assigned to the CRC, we obtain finishing times as shown in figure 3 (for more details,

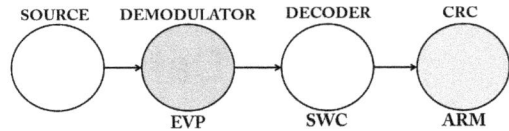

Figure 2: **Tasks in a WLAN downlink**

see section 5). In this figure, a downward arrow depicts the instant at which a task is enabled (sometimes referred to as a the arrival time of a job), the beginning of a block depicts the start of processing of an iteration (a job) of the task, and the end of a block depicts the finishing time of the iteration. For this picture, we have chosen the location of the slices in the TDM schedules such that the finishing times are worst case. The figure shows both the worst-case finishing times for the actual WLAN (the upper three lines) and the latency-rate estimate (the lower three lines). It is easy to see that the latency-rate estimates are overly pessimistic.

Studying this scenario further, we find that the allocation of 44% of the EVP as estimated by the latency-rate response model is sub-optimal given the required end-to-end latency of 9000 ns and throughput of 250 kHz. It would be sufficient to allocate only 24% of the EVP for demodulation to satisfy the same end-to-end requirement. This over-allocation of 20% of the EVP is due to the inherent pessimism in the latency-rate response model. We also find that allocating 13% of the ARM cycles to the CRC would be sufficient to satisfy the application requirements, leading to additional savings of 3% ARM cycles. By using a more refined response model, it should be possible to avoid this over-allocation.

1.2 Our contribution

In this paper, we show how the over-allocation of resources for TDM arbitration can be avoided in the temporal analysis of data flow. We exploit the fact that the finishing times of consecutive iterations of tasks scheduled using TDM display a cyclic pattern, as long as τ and S are rational numbers. More precisely, since for rational choices of τ and S there exist q and r such that $r \cdot S = q \cdot \tau$, we know that q consecutive iterations will need exactly r periods to finish. We construct a dataflow model that treats each of the q iterations in this cycle separately, thus accurately specifying the worst-case behavior per iteration, rather than generalizing over all iterations as was done in [4, 16, 25].

We formally prove that our new model is conservative with respect to the exact temporal behavior of TDM, and that it strictly improves the bounds provided by the latency-rate model. In fact, no further improvement can be made on the model as long as the precise phasing of the TDM arbiter is not under control [14]. Furthermore, we show that our model results in significant quantitative improvement regarding resource allocation, for our WLAN example.

1.3 Related work

A specialized dataflow model [21] already improves on the latency-rate model, under the condition that the slice size is an integer multiple of the execution time, i.e. $S = q \cdot \tau$. However, in many applications (such as the WLAN downlink), this assumption is unreasonable, since the period P (with $P \geq S$) has to be kept small to guarantee a low latency for all applications that share that resource. In practice,

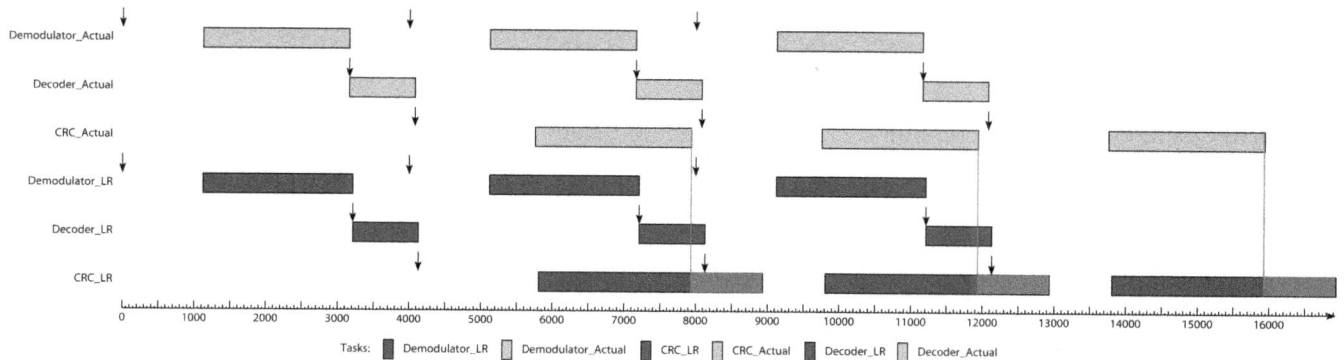

Figure 3: Execution of a WLAN downlink

many iterations need more than one slice to finish execution of a task. The model we introduce in this paper shows a tight approximation of resource requirements, regardless of the choice of execution time, period, and slice size of a task, thus enabling improved resource utilization for any periods P. In case $S = q \cdot \tau$, the timing behavior of our model can be shown to coincide with that of [21].

Outside of the dataflow framework, the allocation of resources using TDM has gained a lot of attention as well. In particular, we would like to point out the work performed in the field of real-time calculus [24] in which the influence of TDM is modeled and analyzed using service curves, rather than using start and finishtimes of iterations. Moreover, the work performed in the area of holistic scheduling [11] is relevant, where algorithms are developed to minimize the slices assigned to tasks and the over-all scheduling periods. Indeed, those papers give a good impression on how to solve the allocation of tasks under TDM scheduling. However, the modeling techniques that are used in these papers are not easily transferred to the dataflow formalism. For dataflow, generic design-space exploration algorithms are in place [16], hence our desire to have better models for TDM in dataflow as well.

Our approach is reminiscent of earlier observations made in the field of schedulability analysis, where the schedulability of TDM-scheduled tasks was first analyzed using the *bounded delay resource model* of [15] (governed for TDM scheduling by a supply bound function that has an initial waiting time of $P - S$ and a slope of $\frac{\tau}{S}P$) and later improved using the *periodic resource model* of [19, 2] (governed by a more complex supply bound function that takes the behavior of individual iterations into account). This work, however, is concerned with the scheduling of independent tasks that each have their own deadline, while the dataflow formalism focusses on the analysis of interdependent tasks with only an end-to-end real-time requirement. One should notice that the over-all effect of improving the worst-case bounds for individual tasks is even greater in the latter case, since multiple tasks are part of the end-to-end real-time requirement, and the estimate for each of these tasks is improved.

1.4 Structure of the paper

The remainder of this paper is structured as follows. Section 2 presents the preliminary concepts of dataflow and timing analysis of embedded (streaming or iterative) applications. The addressed problem, and previous attempts to solve it, are explained in Section 3. Our newly proposed model is formally characterized and analyzed in Section 4. Experimental results that illustrate the quantitative benefit of our new model are presented in Section 5. Finally, we draw our conclusions in Section 6.

2. PRELIMINARIES ON DATAFLOW

In this section, we present the basic concepts of the analysis of real-time systems using dataflow. For simplicity, we restrict ourselves to Single-Rate Data Flow (SRDF) graphs. This makes our model applicable to other variants of dataflow as well, since single-rate dataflow graphs are a subset of synchronous dataflow [13], cyclostatic dataflow [6], parameterized dataflow [5], and dynamic variants like [7]. Furthermore, dataflow variants such as synchronous dataflow and cyclostatic dataflow can be converted into SRDF [5], [10].

Below, we formalize the syntax and semantics of SRDF graphs, and we discuss how the example given in the introduction can be refined to reflect the influence of scheduling mechanisms. As an example of such a refinement, we consider the latency-rate model, which was used in [25] as a conservative estimate for the behavior of tasks scheduled using TDM. In the next section, we discuss the relation between the latency-rate model and TDM scheduling in more detail, and point out the limitations of this model.

2.1 Single Rate Dataflow Graphs

A variety of dataflow formalisms can be used to model, analyze, and map signal processing streaming applications. The single rate dataflow (SRDF) model, also referred to as 'homogeneous synchronous data-flow' [13], is one of the simplest dataflow models that can be effectively used to express the temporal behavior of concurrent tasks [18].

A timed SRDF graph is denoted by tuple $G = (V, E, \delta, \theta)$. The finite set V of vertices, or *actors*, represents the set of deterministic computational functions, or *tasks*, that need to be carried out by an application. The directed edges $E = \{(v, w) | v, w \in V\}$ represent first-in-first-out communication channels between tasks. Data is transported in discrete containers, or *tokens*, also known as *task iterations*. There is an initial placement of tokens on edges, represented by the function $\delta : E \rightarrow \mathbb{N}$. Every firing (activation) of an actor consumes (removes) a token from every incoming edge and produces (places) a token on every outgoing edge. In this paper, the firing of actors is considered to be self-timed, i.e. an actor fires *if and as soon as* there is at least one token on every incoming edge of that actor. The time between consumption and production of tokens is defined as the execution time $\theta(v)$ of actor $v \in V$, represented by the function $\theta : V \to \mathbb{R}$.

An SRDF graph that has no cycles with zero delay sum is *deadlock-free* [20, 3], and we can give mathematical semantics to it using *dating functions* [3]. I.e. for each edge of the graph there is a function that, for each n'th token appearing on that edge, returns the time at which the token appeared on that edge. For input edges this is usually called the arrival time of an iteration of a taks, and for output edges it is called the finishing time. Thus an SRDF graph $G = (V, E, \delta, \theta)$ leads to a set of monotone functions $D_{(v,w)} : \mathbb{N} \to \mathbb{R}^{\geq 0}$ with $(v, w) \in E$, such that $D_{(v,w)}(n) = 0$ for $n \leq \delta(v, w)$, and for all $n > \delta(v, w)$ we have:

$$D_{(v,w)}(n) = \max_{(u,v) \in E} D_{(u,v)}(n - \delta(v, w)) + \theta(v)$$

Dually, we can also *count* the number of tokens that have appeared on an edge of the graph until a given time. This leads to a set of monotone functions $C_{(v,w)} : \mathbb{R}^{\geq 0} \to \mathbb{N}$ such that $C_{(v,w)}(t) = \delta(v, w)$ for $t < \theta(v)$, and for $t \geq \theta(v)$ we have:

$$C_{(v,w)}(t) = \min_{(u,v) \in E} C_{(u,v)}(t - \theta(v)) + \delta(v, w)$$

These two views on the semantics of SRDF represent two dual approaches that exist in the real-time systems community. In classic books like [8], explanations in terms of start and finish times predominate, while recent work on real-time calculus [22] applies the 'counting' approach (although counters there are typically functions that return for each time t an amount $C(t) \in \mathbb{R}^{\geq 0}$ of work that has been done, rather than representing the 'full' completion of an instance). In [3], the relation between the approaches is summarized as:

$$\begin{aligned} D_{(v,w)}(n) &= \inf\{t \mid C_{(v,w)}(t) \geq n\} \\ C_{(v,w)}(t) &= \sup\{n \mid D_{(v,w)}(n) \leq t\} \end{aligned}$$

In this paper, we apply the dating view on SRDF semantics to describe the relation between arrival times $a(n) \in \mathbb{R}^{\geq 0}$ and finishing times $f(n) \in \mathbb{R}^{\geq 0}$ of iteration n for a given scheduler, because the cyclic behavior we intend to exploit is more easily defined from iterations than from a global notion of time. We mention the relation with the counting view here for the sake of completeness, and to enable the future use of our models in other areas. For example, it would be interesting to see how the equations we derive are related to the equations used in real-time calculus [24].

2.2 Timing Refinement of Dataflow Graphs

Recall the example of a WLAN downlink application, given in the introduction. Figure 2 shows an application graph, in which the actors are a source (modeling the incoming stream of data), a de-modulator, a decoder, and a cyclic redundancy checksum (CRC). The data processing for this application consists of a single pipeline, so the only actor with multiple outputs and inputs is the source. The periodic source is modeled using two actors, instead of just one actor with a self edge, to avoid interfering with the analysis of the application graph for determining its maximum latency [16] (see section 5). The initial placement of tokens puts a single token between the two parts of the source, $\delta(\text{source2}, \text{source1}) = 1$, and the timing function is set to

$\theta(\text{source2}) = 4000$ ns and $\theta(\text{source1}) = 0$ ns, thus defining that one new data packet arrives every 4000 ns. The timing of the other actors is set to 0 for the time being, as the actual timing of these depends on the deployment and scheduling of resources for these tasks.

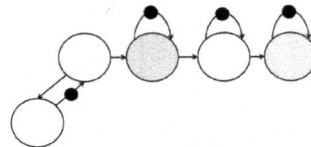

Figure 4: Deployment with dedicated resources

In order to model the scheduling of resources, each actor in the application graph is replaced by a *response model*. The simplest deployment, giving each actor a dedicated resource, results in replacing each actor by the *dedicated resource* response model (see Figure 4). In this model, each actor obtains a self-loop that carries a single token (modeling that only one iteration can be processed at a time). The execution time of each actor is given by the implementation of its task in the chosen processor type.

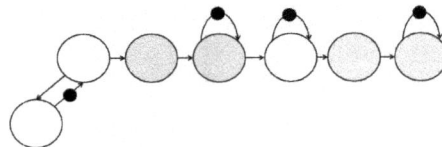

Figure 5: Deployment with the latency-rate model

In a more complex deployment, we may find that a resource is shared by several tasks belonging to other applications. If the assignment of the resource to tasks is periodic, its behavior can often be described using the *latency rate* response model, in which an initial latency-actor (representing the time that a task waits for competing tasks to finish) is followed by a rate-actor with a one-token self-edge (representing the use of resource as in the dedicated resource response model). In figure 5, we depict the WLAN model once more, but this time we used the latency-rate response model for the deployment of the demodulator and the CRC.

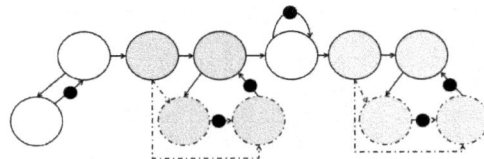

Figure 6: Deployment with our new response model

In this paper, we aim at an even more precise model for deployment using TDM, an impression of which is depicted in figure 6. The *latency rate* model defines a linear over-approximated bound on the (periodic) non-linear worst-case temporal behavior of TDM arbitration. The idea is to replace the *latency rate* model by a model with additional actors that captures the non-linear behavior of TDM arbitration. The number actors in our model depends on the execution time of the task and the size of the allotted slice.

3. THE LATENCY-RATE MODEL

3.1 Formalizing the exact TDM behavior

As explained in the introduction, time division multiplexing (TDM) is a periodic type of budget scheduler that achieves independent execution of applications by dividing a fixed time frame – the *replenishment period* – into various slots, where each slot is assigned to a single task. Figure 7 shows an example of such a division of slots over a time period.

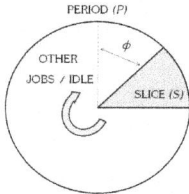

Figure 7: Division of slots over a TDM period

Formally, the behavior of TDM arbitration can be described from the point of view of a single task j, by considering the following parameters:

- P represents the replenishment period of the TDM scheduler;

- $S_j \leq P$ represents the time slice allotted to task j;

- $\phi_j \leq P - S_j$ represents the start time of the slice relative to the start time of the scheduler;

- τ_j represents the total execution time of task j;

- Dating function $a_j : \mathbb{N} \to \mathbb{R}^{\geq 0}$, where $a_j(n)$ is the time at which the n'th iteration for task j arrived;

- Dating function $f_j : \mathbb{N} \to \mathbb{R}^{\geq 0}$, where $f_j(n)$ is the time at which the n'th iteration for task j finished;

In this paper, task j is usually clear from the context, and we write $S, \phi, \tau, a(n)$ and $f(n)$, respectively.

In order to define the relation between the dating functions for arrival and finish, we first define a function $F_{P,S,\phi,\tau} : \mathbb{R}^{\geq 0} \to \mathbb{R}^{\geq 0}$ that returns, for a given period P, slice S, phase ϕ, and execution time τ, the finishing time $F_{P,S,\phi,\tau}(t)$ for a single iteration arriving at time t. This time depends on when the iteration arrives exactly with respect to the position of the TDM wheel, and on the division of the execution time τ over consecutive periods. We denote the modulo function by $x \% y \triangleq x - \lfloor \frac{x}{y} \rfloor y$ and use it to calculate the relative position of times in the TDM wheel. For example, $(\phi - t)\% P$ denotes the time to the next start of the alloted slice. In the best case, when the iteration arrives exactly at the start of the slice (i.e. when $(t - \phi)\% P = 0$), we know that at least $\lceil \frac{\tau}{S} - 1 \rceil$ full periods are needed to execute the task, plus a remainder of $\tau - \lceil \frac{\tau}{S} - 1 \rceil S$. If the iteration arrives outside the slice, the time to the next slice needs to be added, and if the iteration arrives within the slice but too late to finish the 'remainder', a full $P - S$ needs to be added.

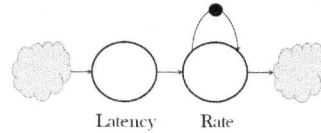

Figure 8: Latency-rate response model

Thus, three cases are distinguished:

$$
F_{P,S,\phi,\tau}(t) = \begin{cases}
t + \tau + \lceil \frac{\tau}{S} - 1 \rceil (P - S) + (\phi - t)\% P \\
\quad ; \text{for } (\phi - t)\% P \leq (P - S) \\
t + \tau + \lceil \frac{\tau}{S} \rceil (P - S) \\
\quad ; \text{for } (\phi + S - t)\% P < \tau - \lceil \frac{\tau}{S} - 1 \rceil S \\
t + \tau + \lceil \frac{\tau}{S} - 1 \rceil (P - S) \\
\quad ; \text{elsewhere}
\end{cases}
$$

An important property of TDM scheduling is that if a second iteration arrives while the first is being processed, the finishing time is the same as when a burst of iterations arrives. Formally, this translates to the following additivity property of F:

$$
F^i_{P,S,\phi,\tau}(t) = F_{P,S,\phi,i\tau}(t) \tag{1}
$$

Given the function F, the relation between arrival and finishing times of iterations for a task is obtained by realizing that a new iteration can only be started after it arrives and after the previous one has finished. Using the above additivity property we thus derive:

$$
\begin{aligned}
f_j(0) &= 0 \\
f_j(n+1) &= F_{P,S_j,\phi_j,\tau_j}(\max(f_j(n), a_j(n+1))) \\
&\quad \{\text{monotonicity and induction}\} \\
&= \max_{k \leq n}(F^{k+1}_{P,S_j,\phi_j,\tau_j}(a_j(n+1-k))) \\
&\quad \{\text{additivity}\} \\
&= \max_{k \leq n}(F_{P,S_j,\phi_j,(k+1)\cdot\tau_j}(a_j(n+1-k)))
\end{aligned}
$$

Now that we have a formalization of the input-output relation between dating functions for TDM arbitration, we can formalize our requirement on dataflow response models and how they should over-approximate this behavior.

3.2 Over-approximation using latency-rate

In dataflow analysis, TDM behavior is usually approximated using the latency-rate response model. To ensure that response time analysis results in an upper bound of the actual behavior, the response model must be *conservative*.

DEFINITION 1. *A response model of a scheduler is conservative with respect to an exact model of that scheduler if an over-approximation of the input results in an over-approximation of the output. Formally: for any given arrival functions $a, \hat{a} : \mathbb{N} \to \mathbb{R}^{\geq 0}$ of the exact and the response model, respectively, we find that the associated finishing functions $f, \hat{f} : \mathbb{N} \to \mathbb{R}^{\geq 0}$ satisfy*

$$
(\forall_n \ \hat{a}(n) \geq a(n)) \Rightarrow \left(\forall_n \ \hat{f}(n) \geq f(n)\right).
$$

The behavior of the latency rate model (see figure 8), with execution times L for the Latency actor R for the Rate actor R, is characterized by the following equations:

$$
\begin{aligned}
\hat{f}_{\text{LR}}(0) &= 0 \\
\hat{f}_{\text{LR}}(n+1) &= \max(\hat{a}(n+1) + L, \hat{f}_{\text{LR}}(n)) + R \\
&= \max_{k \leq n}(\hat{a}(n+1-k) + L + (k+1) \cdot R)
\end{aligned}
$$

Take $L = P - S$ and $R = \tau \frac{P}{S}$, and assume $\hat{a}(n) \geq a(n)$ for all n. Furthermore, observe that the condition $(\phi - t)\%P \leq P - S$ guarantees that the value of $F_{P,S,\phi,\tau}(t)$ is bounded by $t + \tau + \left\lceil \frac{\tau}{S} \right\rceil (P - S)$. Hence we derive for all $k \leq n$ that:

$$\hat{a}(n + 1 - k) + L + (k + 1) \cdot R$$
$$= \hat{a}(n + 1 - k) + (P - S) + (k + 1) \cdot \tau \cdot \frac{P}{S}$$
$$\geq a(n + 1 - k) + (P - S) + (k + 1) \cdot \tau \cdot \frac{P}{S}$$
$$= a(n + 1 - k) + (k + 1) \cdot \tau + (\frac{(k+1) \cdot \tau}{S} + 1)(P - S)$$
$$\geq a(n + 1 - k) + (k + 1) \cdot \tau + \left\lceil \frac{(k+1) \cdot \tau}{S} \right\rceil (P - S)$$
$$\geq F_{P,S,\phi,(k+1) \cdot \tau}(a(n + 1 - k))$$

From this we conclude that $\hat{f}_{\mathrm{LR}}(n) \geq f(n)$ for all n, and the latency-rate response model is conservative with respect to the exact TDM model for a task j.

However, as we have seen in the introduction, the error that is introduced by this over-estimation can be quite large. Intuitively, the latency-rate response model gives a linear approximation of the worst-case behavior, which in case of a burst does not depend on the behavior of previous iterations. If the previous iteration in a burst finished just after the allotted slice started, then the next iteration in the queue can in principle start immediately while the latency rate model still assumes a delay. In the next section, we will show how a more detailed model of the behavior of TDM can resolve this.

4. AN IMPROVED RESPONSE MODEL

4.1 Analysis of consecutive iterations

In this section we present a dataflow model for TDM that approaches the exact model as closely as possible, assuming that the actual phasing ϕ of the TDM scheduler is unknown and that S and τ are rational numbers, rather than reals. The crucial observation for our approach is that, if S and τ are rational numbers, it possible to pick $q, r \in \mathbb{N}$ such that $q \cdot \tau = r \cdot S$. This gives us a kind of hyper-period, in which q consecutive iterations will need exactly r periods to finish execution, provided one starts within the allotted slice. One additional consecutive iteration will take us into the allotted slice, so that we can derive two further properties of F that form the core of our improvement. The first tells us that F is periodic, while the second tells us that if we start a burst of q iterations precisely at the beginning of a slice, then the burst ends exactly at the end of the slice.

$$F_{P,S,\phi,\tau}^{q+1}(t) = F_{P,S,\phi,\tau}(t) + r \cdot P \tag{2}$$

$$F_{P,S,\phi,\tau}^{q}(\phi) - \phi = r \cdot P - (P - S) \tag{3}$$

Recall that the problem with the latency-rate response model is that it disregards information about the processing of previous iterations in case of a burst. Assuming that our processing is periodic in the above sense, we can build a model that remembers the processing of the previous q iterations in the cycle, and use this information to improve our response model.

Our new dataflow model details the timing of $q + 1$ consecutive iterations in the cycle. Each of these iterations becomes a vertex in the SRDF graph component $G_j = (V, E, \delta, \theta)$ which will replace the node of the TDM-scheduled task j in the original application graph. Adding the initial

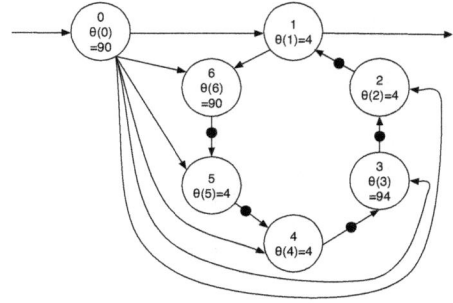

Figure 9: Example of the new TDM response model. Assume $\tau = 4$, $P = 100$, $\phi = 90$, $S = 10$, $q = 5$ and $r = 2$.

latency, the graph will have $q + 2$ vertices in total, so the set V of actors of the model is given by:

$$V = \{i \mid 0 \leq i \leq q + 1\},$$

where actor 0 denotes the initial 'latency' or 'black-out' of TDM, and the other nodes form a cycle:

$$E = \{(i + 1, i) \mid 1 \leq i \leq q\} \cup \{(1, q + 1)\}$$
$$\cup \{(0, i) \mid 1 \leq i \leq q + 1\}$$

Each edge of the cycle obtains an initial token, except the edges from 0 and the edge from 1 to $q + 1$:

$$\delta(i, j) = \begin{cases} 0 & ; \text{for } i = 0 \\ 0 & ; \text{for } i = 1 \wedge j = q + 1 \\ 1 & ; \text{elsewhere} \end{cases}$$

Each actor in the cycle gets an execution time that corresponds to the response of a job arrival at that point in the cycle, taking into account that actor 0, like in the latency-rate model, has an execution time of $P - S$ to compensate for the phasing. Note that $\theta(q + 1)$ also takes a value of $P - S$ since the last iteration in a hyper-period ends exactly at the end of the slice.

$$\theta(i) = \begin{cases} P - S & ; \text{for } i \in \{0, q + 1\} \\ F_{P,S,\phi,\tau}(\phi) - \phi & ; \text{for } i = 1 \\ F_{P,S,\phi,\tau}^{i}(\phi) - F_{P,S,\phi,\tau}^{i-1}(\phi) & ; \text{for } 1 < i < q + 1 \end{cases}$$

As an example, assume a task with $\tau = 4$ mapped to a TDM scheduler with $P = 100$, $\phi = 90$, and $S = 10$. We solve $q \cdot \tau = r \cdot S$ to find $q = 5$ and $r = 4$. The resulting response model therefore has $q + 2 = 7$ nodes, and is depicted in figure 9. Note, that the graph gets additional input and output edges, connected respectively to actor 0 and 1, that are associated with the arrival times $\hat{a}(n)$ and the finishing times $\hat{f}_{\mathrm{new}}(n)$ of iterations.

4.2 Proof of conservativity

In order to show that our new response model for TDM is conservative with respect to the exact model for TDM, we first determine the relation between arrival and finishing times for it. According to the dating function semantics of dataflow graphs we find a dating function for each edge in the graph, plus the arrival and finishing times which are associated with an incoming and outgoing edge into actor 0 and from actor 1 respectively. Taking $0 \leq i \leq q + 1$ and $1 \leq j < q$ we find:

$$D_{(0,i)}(0) = 0$$
$$D_{(1,q+1)}(0) = 0$$
$$D_{(i+1,i)}(0) = 0$$
$$D_{(i+1,i)}(1) = 0$$
$$D_{(0,i)}(n+1) = \hat{a}(n+1) + \theta(0)$$
$$D_{(1,q+1)}(n+1) = \max\left(\begin{array}{c} D_{(0,1)}(n) \\ D_{(2,1)}(n) \end{array}\right) + \theta(1)$$
$$D_{(q+1,q)}(n+2) = \max\left(\begin{array}{c} D_{(0,q+1)}(n+1) \\ D_{(1,q+1)}(n+1) \end{array}\right) + \theta(q+1)$$
$$D_{(j+1,j)}(n+2) = \max\left(\begin{array}{c} D_{(0,j+1)}(n+1) \\ D_{(j+2,j+1)}(n+1) \end{array}\right) + \theta(j+1)$$
$$\hat{f}_{\text{new}}(n) = D_{1,q+1}(n)$$

Eliminating variables and solving the ensuing recursion with the definition of θ and equations (1), (2) and (3) gives us:

$$\hat{f}_{\text{new}}(0) = 0$$
$$\hat{f}_{\text{new}}(n+1) = \max_{i \leq \min(q,n)} \left(\begin{array}{c} \hat{a}(n+1-i) + \sum_{j=0}^{i+1}\theta(j) \\ \hat{f}_{\text{new}}(n+1-q) + \sum_{j=1}^{q+1}\theta(j) \\ ; \text{if } n+1 > q \end{array}\right)$$
$$= \max_{i \leq \min(q,n)} \left(\begin{array}{c} \hat{a}(n+1-i) + \sum_{j=0}^{i+1}\theta(j) \\ \hat{f}_{\text{new}}(n+1-q) + rP \\ ; \text{if } n+1 > q \end{array}\right)$$
$$= \max_{i \leq n} \left(\hat{a}(n+1-i) + P - S + F_{P,S,\phi,\tau}^{i+1}(\phi) - \phi\right)$$

Finally, we need one more property of F to account for the fact that the worst-case black-out before processing is $P - S$:

$$P - S + F_{P,S,\phi,\tau}^{i+1}(\phi) - \phi \geq F_{P,S,\phi,\tau}^{i+1}(t) - t \qquad (4)$$

Using this inequality we can derive by induction that:

$$\hat{f}_{\text{new}}(0) = f(0)$$
$$\hat{f}_{\text{new}}(n+1) = \max_{i \leq n}\left(\hat{a}(n+1-i) + P - S + F_{P,S,\phi,\tau}^{i+1}(\phi) - \phi\right)$$
$$\geq \max_{i \leq n}\left(a(n+1-i) + P - S + F_{P,S,\phi,\tau}^{i+1}(\phi) - \phi\right)$$
$$\geq \max_{i \leq n}\left(F_{P,S,\phi,\tau}^{i+1}(a(n+1-i))\right)$$
$$= f(n+1)$$

Hence, if $\hat{a}(n) \geq a(n)$ for all n, we also find $\hat{f}_{\text{new}}(n) \geq f(n)$ for all n, and we conclude that our new response model is conservative with respect to the exact model.

In a similar vein, we can prove that a) the latency-rate model is conservative with respect to our new response model, and b) our model provides exactly the same timing behavior as the model used in [21] when $S = q \cdot \tau$ (see [14]). Next, we will show that our model is *strictly* better than the latency-rate model by calculating the difference between the two.

4.3 Comparison with the latency rate model

Given an estimated arrival $\hat{a}(n)$ of job iterations, we are interested in the difference $\hat{f}_{\text{LR}}(n) - \hat{f}_{\text{new}}(n)$ between the predicted finished times of the latency-rate model and our new model.

Since we have $\hat{f}_{\text{LR}}(0) = \hat{f}_{\text{new}}(0) = 0$, the difference is initially 0, but for larger values we find:

$$\hat{f}_{\text{LR}}(n+1) - \hat{f}_{\text{new}}(n+1)$$
$$= \max_{k \leq n}(\hat{a}(n+1-k) + L + (k+1) \cdot R)$$
$$- \max_{i \leq n}\left(\hat{a}(n+1-i) + P - S + F_{P,S,\phi,\tau}^{i+1}(\phi) - \phi\right)$$
$$= \min_{i \leq n}\max_{k \leq n}(\hat{a}(n+1-k) + L + (k+1) \cdot R)$$
$$- \left(\hat{a}(n+1-i) + P - S + F_{P,S,\phi,\tau}^{i+1}(\phi) - \phi\right)$$
$$\geq \min_{i \leq n}\max_{k=i}(\hat{a}(n+1-k) + L + (k+1) \cdot R)$$
$$- \left(\hat{a}(n+1-i) + P - S + F_{P,S,\phi,\tau}^{i+1}(\phi) - \phi\right)$$
$$= \min_{i \leq n}\left((i+1) \cdot R - F_{P,S,\phi,(i+1)\tau}(\phi) - \phi\right)$$
$$= \min_{i \leq n}\left((i+1)\tau\frac{P}{S} - (i+1)\tau - \lceil\frac{(i+1)\tau}{S} - 1\rceil(P-S)\right)$$
$$= \min_{i \leq n}\left(\frac{(i+1)\tau}{S} - \lceil\frac{(i+1)\tau}{S}\rceil + 1\right)(P-S)$$
$$\geq \min_{i < q}\left(\frac{(i+1)\tau}{S} - \lceil\frac{(i+1)\tau}{S}\rceil + 1\right)(P-S)$$

Where the last inequality (which is in fact an equality if $n \geq q$) once more uses the periodicity induced by the relation $q\tau = rS$. This value is strictly larger than 0 (assuming $P \neq S$), meaning that the estimates of the new response model are strictly better than those of the latency rate model.

On the other hand, we may also derive that

$$\hat{f}_{\text{LR}}(n+1) - \hat{f}_{\text{new}}(n+1)$$
$$= \max_{k \leq n}(\hat{a}(n+1-k) + L + (k+1) \cdot R)$$
$$- \max_{i \leq n}\left(\hat{a}(n+1-i) + P - S + F_{P,S,\phi,\tau}^{i+1}(\phi) - \phi\right)$$
$$= \max_{k \leq n}\min_{i \leq n}(\hat{a}(n+1-k) + L + (k+1) \cdot R)$$
$$- \left(\hat{a}(n+1-i) + P - S + F_{P,S,\phi,\tau}^{i+1}(\phi) - \phi\right)$$
$$\leq \max_{k \leq n}\min_{i=k}(\hat{a}(n+1-k) + L + (k+1) \cdot R)$$
$$- \left(\hat{a}(n+1-i) + P - S + F_{P,S,\phi,\tau}^{i+1}(\phi) - \phi\right)$$
$$= \max_{k \leq n}\left((k+1) \cdot R - F_{P,S,\phi,(k+1)\tau}(\phi) - \phi\right)$$
$$= \max_{k \leq n}\left((k+1)\tau\frac{P}{S} - (k+1)\tau - \lceil\frac{(k+1)\tau}{S} - 1\rceil(P-S)\right)$$
$$= \max_{k \leq n}\left(\frac{(k+1)\tau}{S} - \lceil\frac{(k+1)\tau}{S}\rceil + 1\right)(P-S)$$
$$\leq P - S$$

So the difference between the new response model and the latency rate model will never be more than $P - S$.

Now that we know the relation between our new response model and the latency-rate model, it is time to quantify the benefits of our model using an illustrative case-study.

5. EXPERIMENTS AND RESULTS

In this section, we take a closer look at the wireless LAN downlink, which was already presented in the introduction. We compare the resource allocation determined using the latency-rate response model to the resource allocation determined using our proposed TDM response model, for the given real-time requirement of a 9000 ns latency and a 250kHz throughput.

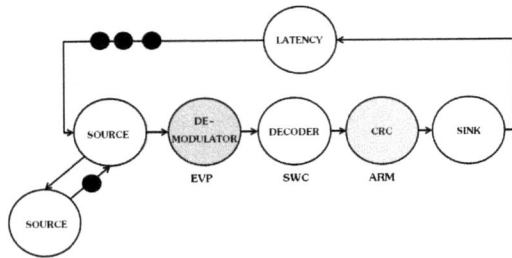

Figure 10: Adapted WLAN graph for MCM analysis

For this analysis, each actor in our WLAN graph is replaced by a response model, to obtain a temporal analysis graph. Furthermore, we use the minimum-cycle mean (MCM) analysis technique [16] on the resulting temporal analysis graphs to verify that the resource allocation guarantees the throughput and latency requirements.

The MCM analysis involves the addition of a sink actor and a latency feedback path in the application graph (see figure 10) and its refinements (see figure 6). The latency feedback path (constituted by the LATENCY actor and its incoming and outgoing edges) is added according to the method described in [16] to model a maximum latency requirement: given a required throughput T and a required latency L, the initial placement of k tokens on the edge and the execution time of the latency actor are chosen such that a violation of the maximum latency between SOURCE and SINK will be detected by the MCM analysis algorithm as an infraction of the throughput requirement caused by a critical cycle that includes the latency-feedback path. The execution time of the latency actor must be set to $\frac{k}{T} - L$ [16].

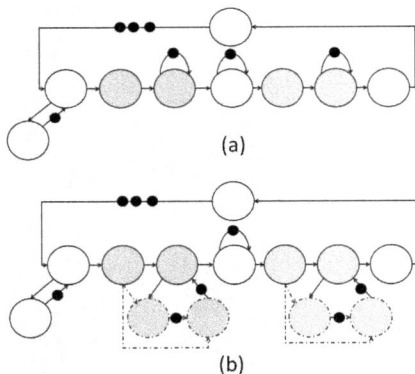

Figure 11: Adapted temporal analysis model using (a) the latency-rate model (b) the new model

Subsequently, the MCM analysis is repeated for different slice sizes in a design space exploration that ultimately leads to the results displayed in table 1. This table summarizes the resource allocation estimated using the latency-rate response model viz-a-viz the results for our new TDM response model, for both the EVP and the ARM processor. We observe that,

especially for the EVP, the resource allocation estimated using the TDM response model is significantly lower than the estimation via the latency-rate model. This shows that our new TDM response model can indeed be used to improve resource allocation.

5.1 Modeling bursty input behavior

Consider the WLAN downlink example (Figure 3), but consider, instead of the periodic arrival of inputs, an input burst such that before the current input is processed by the demodulator task, the next input has already arrived. In other words, the allocated slice is never wasted idling, it is always utilized for processing some input. Also consider that the arrival of the first input in the burst is just after the allocated slice for the demodulator has ended. This means that there is a $P - S$ initial waiting time before the first input starts to be processed. Figure 12 shows the duration of the start to completion of the execution per iteration during actual execution viz. the execution defined by the LR-model and our proposed model. The vertical red lines in figure 12 show the actual finish time per iteration. The difference between the actual finish time and the finish time defined by a given models shows the over-approximation made by that particular model. We observe that the finish times per iteration defined by our model exactly coincide with the actual execution, while the Latency Rate model finish times are over-approximated. We conclude that in case of bursty arrival of input tokens, our model defines a tight conservative bound on the worst-case temporal behavior of TDM arbitration, while the Latency-Rate model defines an over-approximated bound for the same behavior.

6. DISCUSSION AND CONCLUSIONS

We have proposed a new dataflow response model for the analysis of the real-time behavior of tasks on a multiprocessor, scheduled using TDM arbitration. Starting from an exact formalization of the behavior of TDM arbitration, we have proven that our new response model gives a conservative estimate of that behavior. Furthermore, the model gives strictly better estimates than the traditional latency-rate model. Using the new model in MCM analysis, we have shown a 20% decrease in the allocation of resources for a simplified wireless LAN downlink application, compared to the analysis using the latency-rate model.

We have generalized the model presented in [21], and lifted the restriction that the slice size S should be a multiple of the worst-case execution time τ of a TDM scheduled task, by realizing that, for rational choices of τ and S, we can find integers q and r such that $q \cdot \tau = r \cdot S$, meaning that q consecutive iterations take exactly r periods to complete.

An advantage of dataflow modeling, and of our TDM model, is that it can be applied in a heterogenous deployment setting. In fact, the running example of this paper uses a simple heterogenous deployment, where one of the processors is dedicated to a single task while others run a TDM scheduler. More complex settings are easily conceivable, and are analyzable without changing the real-time analysis method, as long as the desired scheduling strategy can be captured as a response model. This makes dataflow very suitable for design-space exploration in heterogenous systems.

Our model can be used to represent resource provision for multi-rate [13] and cyclo-static [6] actors. In data flow

Task	Processor	Exec. time	Period	Latency-Rate Model				New model		
				Slice	Allocation	$l = P - S$	$r = \frac{\tau \cdot P}{S}$	Slice	Allocation	q
Demod.	EVP	920	2000	880	44 %	1120	2091	480	24 %	12
Decoder	SWC	920								
CRC	ARM	500	2000	320	16 %	1680	3125	260	13 %	11

Table 1: WLAN downlink setup

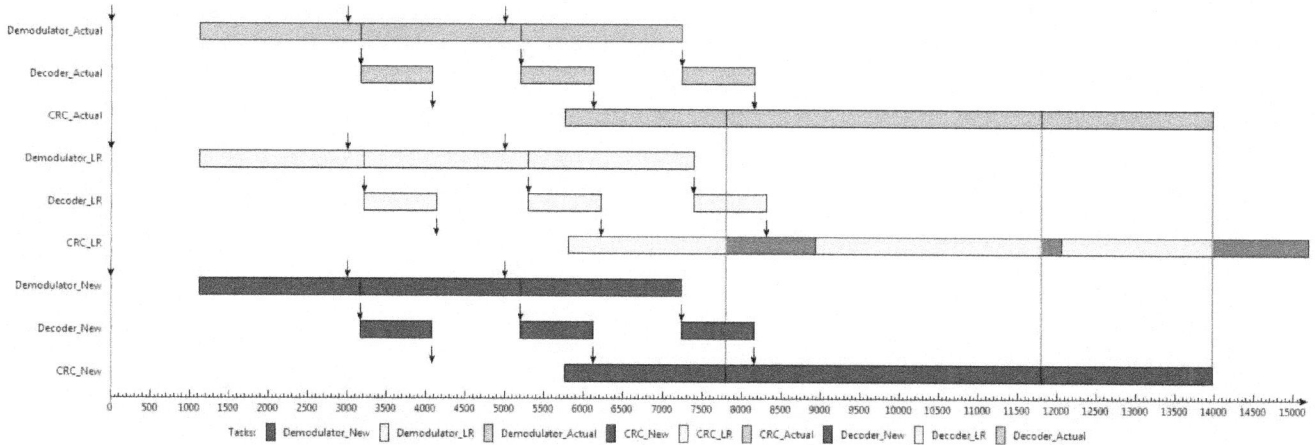

Figure 12: Execution of demodulator for a bursty input

analysis, the arrival time of a job is the time when the firing condition of a task is met. Our model does not restrict this condition from requiring different amounts of tokens per incoming edge. The model can thus handle both multi-rate and cyclo-static consumption rates. Similarly, our model can handle different production rates per outgoing edge. These just become the production rates of the output actor in the model. However, typically, cyclo-static data flow actors are allowed to have different execution times at each iteration. Since our model assumes a fixed execution time for all iterations, it cannot handle varying execution times (although it can provide conservative analysis by taking the worst case execution time).

Figure 13 shows how the execution of a multi-rate actor can be represented using our model. The consumption rules defined on the incoming edges of actor A are modeled as the consumption rules for actor W in our model. Similarly the production rules defined for the outgoing edges of A are modeled as the production rules for the outgoing edges of actor X1 in our model. The internals of the model are still single-rate (there is a 1:1 production/consumption for all internal edges)s.

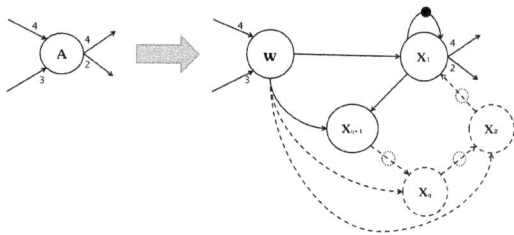

Figure 13: Multi-rate actor using our model

A disadvantage of our model is that it can be very large. Given that $q \cdot \tau = r \cdot S$, the number of nodes in the TDM response model will be $q + 2$. For inconvenient choices of τ and S, the smallest value of q that satisfies the equation can be very large. An increase of the number of nodes and edges in the model implies an increase in the complexity of the temporal analysis, which typically involves the computation of the maximum cycle mean of the graph. According to [9] the theoretical complexity of the analysis is $O(|V| \cdot |E|)$, but in tests there are weakly polynomial algorithms with much better performance. On the bright side, [9] also contains extensive experimental analyses where, for a test set of circuit graphs and random graphs containing over 1 million nodes and 3 million edges, the analysis time is still below 3 seconds. In radio applications [17], typical graphs have less than one hundred nodes, so there is room for very large q factors. Finally, if analysis time does become a problem, one may over-approximate by taking a larger worst-case execution time for τ, i.e. by finding acceptable values of q,r and $\tau' \geq \tau$ such that $q \cdot \tau' = r \cdot S$. The analysis will still be conservative for τ, so this approach gives us a trade-off between model-size and accuracy of the analysis. This is only interesting in the case where our model for the overestimated value of τ still gives tighter estimates that the LR model for the original value of τ. A study on how and when to apply this technique is a topic for future work.

Our current model assumes that a task can be perfectly interrupted by the TDM scheduler at any point in time. In real processor architectures, however, an interrupt can only be serviced at specific points in time, due, for instances, to the need to flush and restart pipelines when context-switching, or due to multi-cycle instructions. Investigating how long worst-case interrupt times may affect the analysis of the TDM scheduler is left for future work.

We are currently looking at modeling extensions of TDM,

for example, TDM with static-order schedules (or cyclo-static actors with varying execution times per phase) within each slice. We will also study how to adapt our technique to model other budget schedulers.

Acknowledgements

We would like to thank Martijn van den Heuvel and Reinder Bril for their initial involvement in this project and their feedback on early drafts of this paper, Mike Holenderski for the GRASP tool [12], which we used to produce figures 3 and 12, and Kaushal Butala for testing our exact temporal model for TDM.

7. REFERENCES

[1] A. Ahtinen et al. Multi-radio Scheduling and Resource Sharing on a Software Defined Radio Computing Platform. In *SDR Forum Conference*, 2008.

[2] L. Almeida and P. Pedreiras. Scheduling within temporal partitions: response-time analysis and server design. In *Proceedings of ACM EMSOFT*, 2004.

[3] F. Baccelli et al. *Synchronization and Linearity*. John Wiley and Sons, 1992.

[4] M. Bekooij et al. Dataflow analysis for real-time embedded multiprocessor system design. *Dynamic and Robust Streaming in and between Connected Consumer Electronic Devices*, 2005.

[5] B. Bhattacharya and S. S. Bhattacharyya. Parameterized dataflow modeling for dsp systems. *IEEE Trans. on Signal Processing*, 2001.

[6] G. Bilsen et al. Cyclo-static dataflow. *IEEE Trans. on Signal Processing*, 1996.

[7] J. T. Buck. *Scheduling Dynamic Dataflow Graphs with Bounded Memory Using the Token Flow Model*. PhD thesis, University of California at Berkeley, 1993.

[8] G. Buttazzo. *Hard Real-Time Computing Systems: Predictable Scheduling Algorithms and Applications*. Springer Science+Business Media, Inc., 2005.

[9] A. Dasdan. Experimental analysis of the fastest optimum cycle ratio and mean algorithms. *ACM Trans. Des. Autom. Electron. Syst.*, 9, Oct. 2004.

[10] M. Geilen. Reduction techniques for synchronous dataflow graphs. In *Proceedings of DAC*, 2009.

[11] A. Hamann and R. Ernst. TDMA time slot and turn optimization with evolutionary search techniques. In *Proceedings of DATE conference*, pages 312–317, 2005.

[12] M. Holenderski et al. Grasp: Tracing, visualizing and measuring the behavior of real-time systems. In *International Workshop WATERS*, july 2010.

[13] E. Lee and D. Messerschmitt. Synchronous data flow. *Proceedings IEEE*, 75(9):1235–1245, Sep 1987.

[14] A. Lele. Data-flow based temporal analysis for TDM arbitration. Master's thesis, Technische Universiteit Eindhoven, 2011.

[15] A. K. Mok, A. X. Feng, and D. Chen. Resource partition for real-time systems. In *Proceedings of IEEE RTAS*. IEEE Computer Society, 2001.

[16] O. Moreira and M. Bekooij. Self-timed scheduling analysis for real-time applications. *EURASIP Journal on Advances in Signal Processing*, 2007.

[17] O. Moreira, F. Valente, and M. Bekooij. Scheduling multiple independent hard-real-time jobs on a heterogeneous multiprocessor. In *Proceedings of EMSOFT*, 2007.

[18] O. Moreira et al. Buffer sizing for rate-optimal single-rate dataflow scheduling revisited. *IEEE Transactions on Computers*, 2010.

[19] I. Shin and I. Lee. Periodic resource model for compositional real-time guarantees. In *IEEE RTSS*, Dec 2003.

[20] S. Sriram and S. S. Bhattacharyya. *Embedded Multiprocessors: Scheduling and Synchronization*. Marcel Dekker, Inc., 2000.

[21] J. Staschulat and M. Bekooij. Dataflow models for shared memory access latency analysis. In *Proceedings of EMSOFT*, 2009.

[22] L. Thiele, S. Chakraborty, and M. Naedele. Real-time calculus for scheduling hard real-time systems. In *Proc. IEEE ISCAS*, 2000.

[23] K. van Berkel et al. A Multi-Radio SDR Technology Demonstrator. In *SDR Forum Conference*, 2009.

[24] E. Wandeler and L. Thiele. Optimal TDMA time slot and cycle length allocation for hard real-time systems. In *Proceedings of ASP-DAC*. IEEE, 2006.

[25] M. Wiggers, M. Bekooij, and G. Smit. Modelling run-time arbitration by latency-rate servers in dataflow graphs. In *Proceedings of SCOPES*, 2007.

Mixed Critical System Design and Analysis

Rolf Ernst (organizer)
TU Braunschweig
Braunschweig, Germany
r.ernst@tu-bs.de

Alan Burns
University of York
York, United Kingdom
alan.burns@york.ac.uk

Lothar Thiele
ETH Zürich
Zürich, Switzerland
thiele@ethz.ch

Jimmy Le Rhun
Thales R&T
Paris, France
jimmy.lerhun@thalesgroup.com

ABSTRACT

With increasing use of embedded systems in safety critical systems, architectures and design processes for safety have become a primary objective in systems design. Most such systems are also time critical leading to safety and time critical systems. Safety standards impose strong requirements on such systems challenging system performance and cost. Very often, however, only part of the functions is safety and time critical calling for a design approach that both meets the safety requirements and provides efficiency and flexibility for less critical functions. These conflicting requirements have given rise to the new research area of mixed critical system design with enormous practical relevance.

The tutorial addresses key aspects of mixed critical system design. The tutorial starts with a short introduction to the topic summarizing requirements and challenges of mixed critical system design. The first lecture by Alan Burns gives an overview of scheduling issues in mixed critical systems and explains first solutions. The second lecture by Lothar Thiele ad-dresses the lack of multicore timing predictability which challenges mixed critical systems integration and proposes a solution based on reducing timing variation. The third lecture by Rolf Ernst and Jimmy Le Rhun explains integration solutions based on switched networks and presents a scalable manycore architecture for mixed critical systems integration.

Categories and Subject Descriptors

B.8.1 [Performance and Reliability]: Reliability, Testing, and Fault-Tolerance; B.8.2 [Performance and Reliability]: Performance Analysis and Design Aids

Keywords

Performance, Reliability, Design, Verification, Mixed Critical Systems

1. Mixed Critical Systems Design – Overview
Rolf Ernst, TU Braunschweig, Germany

2. Mixed Critical System Scheduling
Alan Burns, Univ. of York, UK

3. Increasing Predictability in Multicore Systems
Lothar Thiele, ETH Zürich, Switzerland

4. Switched Network Systems Integration for Manycore Architectures
Rolf Ernst, TU Braunschweig, Germany, and Jimmy Le Rhun, Thales R&T, France

Speakers Bios

Alan Burns is Professor of Real-Time Systems at the University of York, UK. He has pub-lished over 450 papers in the area of real-time systems and is an expert in scheduling theory. In 2009 he was elected a Fellow of the Royal Academy of Engineering and in 2012 he was elected a Fellow of the IEEE for contributions to fixed-priority scheduling for embedded real-time systems.

Jimmy Le Rhun is research engineer at Thales Research & Technology France, within the Embedded System Lab. He was recently in charge of middleware design for embedded multi-core processors on FPGA, and of the integration of a hardware operating system for heteroge-neous reconfigurable multicore platform. He is currently involved in the definition and inte-gration of a safety-critical manycore platform on FPGA.

Lothar Thiele joined ETH Zurich, Switzerland, in 1994. His research interests include models, methods and software tools for the design of embedded systems, embedded software and bioinspired optimization techniques.

Runtime Verification of Real-time Embedded Systems

Borzoo Bonakdarpour
School of Computer Science
University of Waterloo
200 University Ave West
Waterloo, Ontario, Canada, N2L 3G1
borzoo@cs.uwaterloo.ca

Sebastian Fischmeister
Department of Electrical and Computer
Engineering
University of Waterloo
200 University Ave West
Waterloo, Ontario, Canada, N2L 3G1
sfischme@uwaterloo.ca

ABSTRACT

Time-triggered runtime verification aims at tackling two defects associated with runtime overhead: *unboundedness* and *unpredictability*. In this approach, a monitor runs in parallel with the program under inspection and periodically samples the program state to evaluate a set of properties. The fact that the monitoring tasks place only at predictable time ticks makes the approach predictable and especially suitable for embedded systems.

In this tutorial, we will discuss the main challenges in implementing time-triggered runtime verification (TTRV) and our solutions. In particular, we will present our work on optimal program state reconstruction, where the problem is known to be NP-complete. This includes our techniques using modern SMT- and ILP-solvers and efficient heuristics. We will also describe our work on time-triggered self-monitoring programs, where a program under inspection is instrumented, so that it monitors its own state within fixed time intervals. We also describe our GPU-based monitoring technique. Such a technique accelerates monitoring tasks and effectively separates monitoring from functional concerns at hardware level. The tutorial will also present our tool chains as well as case studies on monitoring embedded systems using our tools.

Categories and Subject Descriptors

D.2.5 [**Software Engineering**]: Testing and Debugging—*Monitors*; D.4.7 [**Operating Systems**]: Organization and Design—*Real-time and embedded systems*

General Terms

Algorithms, Performance, Verification

Keywords

Embedded systems, Overhead predictability and containment, Real-time systems, Runtime monitoring.

1. BACKGROUND

Borzoo Bonakdarpour is a Research Assistant Professor with the School of Computer Science at the University of Waterloo, Canada. He obtained his Ph.D. from the Department of Computer Science and Engineering at Michigan

State University in 2009. His Ph.D. dissertation, "Automated Revision of Distributed and Real-Time Programs", studies a wide range of model repair problems in closed and open systems and was nominated for the 2010 ACM Doctoral Dissertation Award. He was a post-doctoral researcher at the Verimag Laboratory, France, working on model-based software development. His other research interests include runtime verification, compositional verification and synthesis of embedded systems, and distributed algorithms. He is the main developer of the tool SYCRAFT which is capable of synthesizing fault-tolerant distributed programs of size 10^{80} reachable states and beyond.

Sebastian Fischmeister is an Assistant Professor in the Department of Electrical and Computer Engineering at the University of Waterloo, Canada. He received his MASc in Computer Science at the Vienna University of Technology, Austria, and his Ph.D. degree at the University of Salzburg, Austria. He was awarded the APART stipend in 2005 and worked as a research associate at the University of Pennsylvania, USA, until 2008. He performs systems research at the intersection of software technology, distributed systems, and formal methods. His preferred application areas are distributed real-time embedded systems in the domain of automotive systems, avionics, and medical devices.

2. OVERVIEW OF TUTORIAL

In computing systems, *correctness* refers to the assertion that a system satisfies its specification. *Verification* is a technique for checking such an assertion and *runtime verification* refers to a lightweight technique where a *monitor* checks at run time whether the execution of a system under inspection satisfies or violates a given correctness property. Deploying runtime verification involves instrumenting the program under inspection, so that upon occurrence of events (e.g., value changes of a variable) that may change the truthfulness of a property, the monitor will be called to re-evaluate the property. We call this method *event-triggered* runtime verification, because each change prompts a re-evaluation. Event-triggered runtime verification suffers from two drawbacks: (1) *unpredictable* overhead, and (2) possible *bursts* of events at run time.

The above defects are not desirable in the context of real-time embedded systems, where predictability and timing constraints play a central role. This tutorial focuses on describing our solutions to two challenging problems:

- **Time-aware instrumentation [4, 5].** Instrumentation is a technique to extract information or trigger events in programs under inspection. Instrumentation is a vital step for enabling system monitoring; i.e. the system is augmented with instructions that invokes a monitor when certain events occur. Instrumentation of software programs while preserving logical correctness is an established field. However, current approaches are inadequate for real-time embedded applications. The key idea behind the time-aware instrumentation of a system is to transform the execution-time distribution of the system so as to maximize the coverage of the trace while always staying within the time budget.

- **Time-triggered monitoring [1–3, 6, 7].** In time-triggered runtime verification, a monitor runs in parallel with the program and samples the program state periodically to evaluate a set of system properties. The main challenge in time-triggered runtime verification is to guarantee accurate program state reconstruction at sampling time. Providing such guarantee results in solving an optimization problem where the objective is to find the minimum number of critical events that need to be buffered for a given sampling period. Consequently, the time-triggered monitor can successfully reconstruct the state of the program between two successive samples.

  A potential drawback of time-triggered monitoring is it requires certain synchronization features at operating system level and may suffer from various concurrency and synchronization dependencies. One approach to tackle this problem is instrument the program under inspection, so that it *self-samples* its state in a periodic fashion without requiring assistance from an external monitor or internal timer. We call this technique time-triggered *self-monitoring* [2]. Two optimization problems in this context are: (1) minimizing the number of self-sampling instructions in a program, and (2) minimizing the accumulated deviation of sampling instructions from the desired sampling period.

- **Monitoring in isolation.** One approach to reduce the overhead of runtime monitoring is to utilize the recent advances in the many-core architectures. That is, the monitor works along with the program in parallel and evaluates a set of properties. Using the recent advances in the GPU technology, our parallel monitoring technology effectively exploits the many-core platform available in the GPU. In addition to parallel processing, our approach benefits from a true separation of the monitoring and functional concerns, as it isolates the monitor in the GPU.

This tutorial will discuss in detail our techniques developed in the past few years to tackle the above problems. Our focus will be on time-sensitive systems, where violation of timing constraints are undesired. Our goal is to describe the challenges in instrumenting, measuring, and monitoring such systems and present our solutions developed in the past few years to deal with these challenges.

3. FORMAT OF THE TUTORIAL

This half-day tutorial will consist of the following three main parts:, each will be dedicated slightly less than one hour:

1. First, we will present challenge problems and corresponding solutions on instrumenting real-time systems,

so that timing constraints of the system are respected [4, 5].

2. The second part of the tutorial will focus on *time-triggered* runtime monitoring, where a monitor is invoked at equal time intervals, allowing designers to schedule regular and monitoring tasks hand-in-hand. We will present in detail our techniques for minimizing the overhead of time-triggered monitoring [1,3,6,7]. We will also discuss our recent results on exploiting the advances in the GPU technology to accelerate and isolate the execution of runtime monitors. The tutorial will also describe our work on programs that self-monitor themselves in a time-triggered fashion [2]. This part will take the majority of the tutorial. We will dedicate 2 hours to this part to explain time-triggered RV, self-monitoring, and GPU-based RV.

3. The last part of the tutorial will be dedicated to present our tool chains for deploying time-triggered runtime verification. Our tools implement and realize our algorithms and theoretical results. We will also present the results of experiments on efficiency and effectiveness of our tools on benchmark suits as well as real-world applications.

Finally, we will briefly discuss open problems and future work. We believe that our work on instrumentation and runtime verification of real-time systems has paved the path for numerous future research directions. Interesting open problems that will be discussed include (1) monitoring distributed real-time systems, (2) composability of time-triggered monitors, (3) runtime verification of component-based systems, and (4) applicability to broader classes of systems.

4. REFERENCES

[1] B. Bonakdarpour, S. Navabpour, and S. Fischmeister. Sampling-based runtime verification. In *Formal Methods (FM)*, pages 88–102, 2011.

[2] B. Bonakdarpour, J. J. Thomas, and S. Fischmeister. Time-triggered program self-monitoring. In *IEEE International Conference on Embedded and Real-Time Computing Systems and Applications (RTCSA)*, 2012. To appear.

[3] S. Fischmeister and Y. Ba. Sampling-based Program Execution Monitoring. In *ACM International conference on Languages, compilers, and tools for embedded systems (LCTES)*, pages 133–142, 2010.

[4] S. Fischmeister and P. Lam. On Time-Aware Instrumentation of Programs. In *Proceedings of the 15th IEEE Real-Time and Embedded Technology and Applications Symposium (RTAS)*, pages 305–314, San Fransisco, United States, Apr. 2009.

[5] S. Fischmeister and P. Lam. Time-aware Instrumentation of Embedded Software. *IEEE Transactions on Industrial Informatics*, 2010.

[6] S. Navabpour, B. Bonakdarpour, and S. Fischmeister. Path-aware time-triggered runtime verification. In *Runtime Verification (RV)*, 2012. To appear.

[7] S. Navabpour, C. W. Wu, B. Bonakdarpour, and S. Fischmeister. Efficient techniques for near-optimal instrumentation in time-triggered runtime verification. In *Runtime Verification (RV)*, pages 208–222, 2011.

Author Index